INVENTORY OF PRIMARY AND ARCHIVAL SOURCES:

Guelph And Wellington County To 1940

Elizabeth Bloomfield
with Jane Turner, Patricia Abbott and Joe Gabriel

GUELPH REGIONAL PROJECT
UNIVERSITY OF GUELPH
1989

Copies may be ordered from:

Media Production and Distribution
University of Guelph
Guelph, Ontario, Canada, N1G 2W1

This book has been published in a numbered edition of 400 copies,
of which this is ..9.0.

ISBN 0-88955-172-3

Canadian Cataloguing in Publication Data
Main entry under title:

Inventory of primary and archival sources : Guelph
and Wellington County to 1940

Includes indexes.
ISBN 0-88955-172-3

1. Wellington (Ont. : County) - Archival resources
- Union lists. 2. Guelph (Ont.) - Archival
resources - Union lists. 3. Wellington (Ont. :
County) - History - Archival resources - Union lists.
4. Guelph (Ont.) - History - Archival resources -
Union lists. I. Bloomfield, Elizabeth. II. Guelph
Regional Project.

Z1392.W395I5 1989   016.9713'42   C89-094363-X

ACKNOWLEDGEMENTS

The staff of the Guelph Regional Project's research unit deserve most of the credit in the preparation of this **Inventory**. It was a real pleasure to work with them. Jane Turner was with the project longest, coping imaginatively and cheerfully with a wide variety of tasks over more than a year. Joe Gabriel and Patricia Abbott contributed valuably to record research and description, data entry and editing during the first eight of the sixteen months that the **Inventory** was in the making.

On the initiative of Professor Gilbert Stelter, the Guelph Regional Project received a Research Excellence grant from the University of Guelph that met most of the research costs. The College of Arts also provided a publication subsidy to assist with printing the **Inventory**. The Department of History found a room for the research assistants and Mary Ellen Pyear helped with the personnel and payroll formalities.

Several other members of the University and the larger community showed a helpful concern for the technical aspects of the first **Bibliography** phase of the project, when the integrated methodology was being developed. We appreciate the support particularly of Ralph Daehn of the University of Guelph Library, Linda Kearns of the Guelph Public Library, and Peter McCaskell of the Department of Geography and Computing Services.

We are grateful to the many archivists, librarians or other custodians who helped us in the seventy or so repositories where we researched and described records. In Wellington County these included: Bonnie Callen of the Wellington County Archives; Nancy Sadek, Gloria Troyer and others of the University of Guelph Library's Archival and Special Collections; Linda Kearns of the Guelph Public Library; Wendy Hallman of the Guelph Civic Museum; Rowena Lewis of the Wellington County Board of Education; Bill McKinnie and staff of the GCVI Archives; Patrick Murray of the Wellington County Separate School Board; Ken McCrea and Jeff Gilbert of the Guelph Land Registry; Arvind Damley of the Arthur Land Registry; Judith Nasby of the Macdonald Stewart Art Centre; Mary Anne Neville of John McCrae House; Joan Moore of the Mount Forest Public Library; Kim Gordon, Helen Cunningham and other members of the Ennotville Library; Joyce Pharaoh of the Homewood Sanitarium Archives; Tim McClemont in relation to the St Joseph's Hospital Archives; Jean Forsyth of the Children's Aid Society in Guelph; and the clerks and other staff of all the municipal offices in Guelph and Wellington County.

We were assisted by the staff of several church archives: Jean Dryden and staff at the United Church Archives; Kim Moir at the Presbyterian Church Archives; Father Edward Dowling at the Jesuit Fathers of Upper Canada Archives; Ken Foyster at the Diocese of Hamilton Archives; the Rev. Dr. Peter Darch and Heather Darch of St Andrew's Presbyterian Church in Guelph; Terri Major of the Canadian Baptist Archives; and Carl Spadoni of McMaster University's Archives and Research Collections that holds Anglican church records for the Diocese of Niagara. Gilbert and James Stelter listed the extant records of the Dublin Street and Norfolk Street United churches in Guelph.

TABLE OF CONTENTS

GUIDE TO ARCHIVES AND REPOSITORIES 551

INDEXES

Guelph Regional Project

Academic Committee

Gilbert Stelter *(History)* Chair

Elizabeth Bloomfield *(History)*
Gerald Bloomfield *(Geography)*
Edward Cowan *(History and Scottish Studies)*
Terrence Crowley *(History)*
Fredric Dahms *(Geography and Settlement Studies)*
Ian Easterbrook *(Media Production)*
Kris Inwood *(Economics)*
Chandler Kirwin *(Fine Art)*
Richard Reid *(History)*
James Snell *(History)*
Ronald Sunter *(History and Scottish Studies)*
Elizabeth Waterston *(English)*

GRP Research Unit

Elizabeth Bloomfield *(Co-ordinator)*

Jane Turner
Patricia Abbott
Joe Gabriel

Outside Guelph-Wellington, we appreciated the help of the following people: Leon Warmski and others of the Public Service Unit at the Archives of Ontario; Gabrielle Blais and Sheila Watson at the National Archives of Canada; staff of the Baldwin Room at the Metropolitan Reference Library and the Thomas Fisher Rare Books Room at the University of Toronto Library; Wendy Law and Wendy Jackson of the Ontario Hydro Archives; Nancy Saunders Maitland of the Mutual Life Archives in Waterloo; Susan Saunders Bellingham, Head of Special Collections of the University of Waterloo Library; Susan Hoffman of the Kitchener Public Library; Barbara Holloway of the Registrar-General's Office; Susan Bennett at the Ontario Agricultural Museum Archives; Elizabeth McNaughton at Doon Heritage Crossroads; and Joan de Kat of the Brant County Museum. At the University of Western Ontario, Ed Phelps of the Regional History Collection in the D.B. Weldon Library advised on fire insurance plans and various other sources and George Emery of the Department of History discussed the Landon Project. Peter Baskerville of the University of Victoria provided details of the Vancouver Island Project's methodology. Joan Winearls of the University of Toronto Map Library generously advised on pre-1867 printed and manuscript maps and plans.

For the added touch given to this volume by the illustrations, we are indebted to staff of various repositories who allowed us to copy and reproduce art works, photographs, maps or plans. Illustrations were provided or permission granted by the Wellington County Archives, Guelph Public Library, Macdonald Stewart Art Centre, University of Guelph Library's Archival and Special Collections, National Archives of Canada, Ontario Ministry of Agriculture and Food, Guelph Civic Museum, Archives of Ontario, and Metropolitan Toronto Reference Library. People who helped with the illustrations were Bonnie Callen, Linda Kearns, Judith Nasby, Marilyn Armstrong-Reynolds, Mary Sutherland, Lorne Bruce, Gilbert Stelter and Gerald Bloomfield, as well as staff of Lumichrom of Guelph and of Photographic Services at the University of Guelph. Jane Turner wrote most of the captions. Marie Puddister laid out the preliminary pages and the indexes. Mary Ann Robinson of Print Publications helped with plans for the publication of the volume and Ian Easterbrook of Media Distribution is handling sales.

From the beginning, the production of the Guelph Regional Project's research tools has been a very large undertaking. I am deeply grateful for the moral support and practical help of my family. Gerald Bloomfield devoted many hours to intelligent discussion of the procedures developed for the project. In the University's perennial space crisis, he allowed his office and superior IBM computer to be used for the master databases for up to one hundred hours per week over a two-year period. While nursing the databases through their periodic bouts of colic and teething troubles as well as designing editing routines and report formats, I was immeasurably helped by the understanding and relief from household chores provided by all members of my family. In addition, Victoria Bloomfield generously gave several days to editing the final indexes.

Elizabeth Bloomfield
August 27, 1989

INTRODUCTION

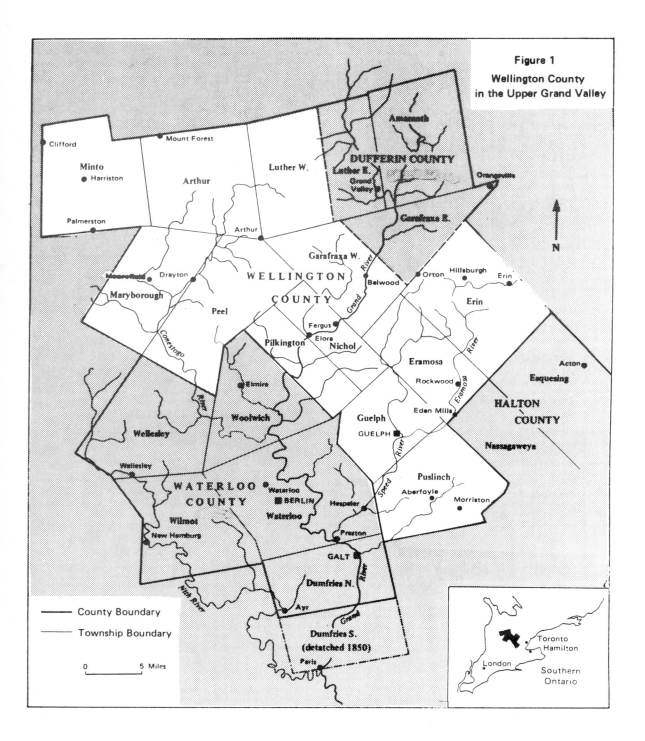

Figure 1

Wellington County
in the Upper Grand Valley

Clifford
Mount Forest
Minto
Harriston
Arthur
Palmerston
Luther W.
Amaranth
DUFFERIN COUNTY
Luther E.
Grand Valley
Orangeville
Arthur
Garafraxa E.
Garafraxa W.
Grand River
Maryborough
Drayton
Moorefield
WELLINGTON
COUNTY
Belwood
Orton
Hillsburgh
Erin
Peel
Erin
Conestogo
Pilkington
Fergus
Elora
Nichol
Eramosa
Rockwood
Acton
Esquesing
Elmira
Eramosa River
Woolwich
Eden Mills
Guelph
GUELPH
HALTON
COUNTY
Wellesley
Wellesley
Nassagaweya
WATERLOO
COUNTY
Waterloo
BERLIN
Hespeler
Puslinch
Aberfoyle
Morriston
Wilmot
Waterloo
New Hamburg
Preston
GALT
Dumfries N.
Speed River
Nith River
Ayr
Grand
River
Dumfries S.
(detatched 1850)
Paris

— County Boundary
— Township Boundary

0   5 Miles

Toronto
Hamilton
London
Southern
Ontario

CREATING AND USING THE INVENTORY

This volume is companion to the **Bibliography** of secondary sources published in 1988 by the Guelph Regional Project.[1] Both research tools have been compiled using computer methods and both may also be accessed in machine-readable format. They have been created as part of the project's plan to provide an information base for interdisciplinary historical research on the Upper Grand Valley Region, beginning with Guelph and Wellington County. The **Inventory** is designed as a guide to the primary source materials of all kinds that have informational value for the history of Guelph-Wellington to 1940.

Wellington County is an area of about 657,000 acres (266,000 hectares) in the watershed of the upper tributaries of the Grand River system in midwestern Ontario (Figure 1). The population of the county area grew from about 25,000 in 1851 to 64,640 in 1881, declined to a low of 54,160 in 1921 before recovering to 59,450 in 1941 and then increasing substantially to 140,000 in 1986. For the past one hundred and sixty years, the main administrative and commercial focus of the county has been the town and city of Guelph, which exercised such functions over a more considerable area before the separate formation of Waterloo County to the west in 1854 and Dufferin County to the northeast in 1881. Wellington County was settled by people of English, Scottish and Irish extraction in roughly equal proportions, with other smaller but distinctive groups such as black refugees from slavery and Germans and Mennonites along the borders with neighbouring Waterloo County. The area became quite notable for improved crop and livestock farming practices in the middle decades of the nineteenth century and Guelph was chosen as the site of the Ontario Agricultural College and Experimental Farm in 1874. The county area is broadly representative of much of southern Ontario rather than remarkably distinctive.[2]

---

[1] Elizabeth Bloomfield and Gilbert A. Stelter, **Guelph and Wellington County: A bibliography of settlement and development since 1800** (Guelph: University of Guelph, 1988). As convenient abbreviations, the terms **Bibliography** and **Inventory** are used in this introductory essay to refer, respectively, to the set of references of published and secondary sources (the **Bibliography**) and records of primary and archival sources (the **Inventory**) produced by the Guelph Regional Project.

[2] For a discussion of this theme and a survey of writing about Guelph and Wellington County, see Gilbert A. Stelter, 'Studying the region,' in Bloomfield and Stelter, **Guelph and Wellington County** (1988), 1-13. The representativeness of Wellington County is a central theme in Elizabeth Waterston and Douglas Hoffman, eds., **On middle ground: landscape and life in Wellington County, 1841-1891** (Guelph, 1974).

The **Bibliography** and **Inventory** have some distinctive qualities and the process of creating them has been innovative in several ways. In essence, we have combined references to bibliographic and archival records in one large machine-readable database to facilitate historical research. Our methodology has been designed to identify and describe material of all kinds -- archival record groups and series, books, booklets, brochures, theses, reports, articles in journals, chapters in books, as well as individual manuscripts, letters, maps and plans, photographs, and even art works -- and to combine them in a single database with one MARC-compatible record structure. Thus all records relating to a specific subject may be searched for and retrieved by an integrated strategy on the computer. Canadian bibliographic databases are scarce in the humanities and social sciences, and archives seldom use computer methods for physical or intellectual control of their records. It is especially rare for all the types of records in which we are interested to be combined in one database.

Other notable features of the Guelph Regional Project's research tools include:

*   A computerized methodology which has included testing the advantages of INMAGIC software in data entry and editing, indexing, search and retrieval and its ability to format machine-readable records and indexes into camera-ready text.

*   Particular thoroughness and consistency in compilation, references having been personally inspected, abstracted and indexed by the research team before inclusion in the database.

*   Indexing of all records according to six types of index terms-- places or geographical locations, corporate creators, personal creators, personal subjects, corporate subjects (such as businesses, churches, schools or associations), and topical subject headings for which a special thesaurus was designed for local and regional history.

*   Details of specific locations of all records so that the **Bibliography** and **Inventory** serve as 'union lists' of sources on this region.

*   Accessibility to University and community users in machine-readable and print formats.

In creating what is probably the most detailed and comprehensive guide to the history of any Ontario county or region, we are providing a solid information base for a wide range of users. We expect that the contents of the **Bibliography** and the **Inventory** and of the integrated database will benefit not only teachers and students at secondary and post-secondary levels, but also local historians, genealogists, archivists, librarians, municipal and museum staff, and heritage groups. Researchers, teachers and students are already finding new directions for their work in local and regional history in the **Bibliography**; these will be greatly enhanced with the publication of the **Inventory**. The methods used to create these research tools will also interest information specialists and scholars outside the immediate local region.

INVENTORIES OF PRIMARY AND ARCHIVAL SOURCES

As we moved from the compilation of the **Bibliography** of published materials to the creation of the **Inventory** of primary and archival sources, we left the relatively ordered librarian's world and entered what archivists themselves have called a 'jungle'. Frank Burke has remarked that librarianship is 'an exercise in bringing order out of chaos; of identification; classification, and placement in the universal scheme of things; and in the facilitation of retrieval.' By contrast, he declared, the archivist's world is chaotic:

.... with its tangle of traditions, generally accepted practices, local variations, idiosyncratic aberrations, and institutional improvisations. There is no central authority to impose dogma; the confusion in the public's mind between archivists and anarchists is not merely linguistic; and the tenets of the profession appear to include an absence of agreement, a paucity of procedures and a reaction against rules.[3]

For the past decade or so, the archivists' world has been in turmoil as they have wrestled with methods of establishing intellectual and physical control over historical records. In a time of substantial growth both in the number of archival repositories and in the number and variety of users, archivists are having to adapt to machine-readable methods of record control and also to the demands of larger groups of users for better systems of subject access.[4] New definitions and procedures have been formulated by archivists in the Canada and the United States, notably by the National Information Systems Task Force (NISTF) of the Society of American Archivists, and the Working Group on Archival Descriptive Standards of the Bureau of Canadian Archivists.[5]

---

[3] Frank G. Burke, 'Archival automation and the administrator,' in Lawrence J. McCrank, ed. **Automating the Archives** (White Plains, NY: American Society for Information Science, 1981) 3.

[4] Steven L. Hensen, **Archives, personal papers and manuscripts: a cataloguing manual for archival repositories, historical societies and manuscript libraries** (Washington: Library of Congress, 1983); H. Thomas Hickerson, **Archives and manuscripts: an introduction to automated access** (Chicago: Society of American Archivists, 1981); Richard M. Kesner, **Automation for archivists and records managers: planning and implementation strategies** (Chicago: American Library Association, 1984); Lawrence J. McCrank, ed. **Automating the archives: issues and problems in computer applications** (New York: Knowledge Industry Publications for American Society for Information Science, 1981).

[5] See Richard Lytle, 'An analysis of the National Information Systems Task Force,' **American Archivist** 47 (1984): 357-365 and **Toward descriptive standards: report and recommendations of the Canadian Working Group on Archival Descriptive Standards.** Ottawa: Bureau of Canadian Archivists, 1985.

4

There have long been tensions between archivists, as keepers of the records, and users such as historians who wish to extract information from the records on various subjects. Archivists have resisted the inferences in the writings of some historians that archives exist mainly to serve the interests of historical research. Historians are apt to feel impatient and frustrated that their research in archives is slowed by the absence of the subject indexes they are accustomed to using in library and bibliographic environments. As Terry Eastwood has pointed out, the basic difficulties derive from the nature of archives:

> Whether they are public or private, corporate or personal, archives arise as the result of corporate or personal business activity of some sort. As such, archives are part of transactions rather than about them. This characteristic distinguishes archives from books and other published materials, which are the organized product of intellectual activity and hence usually about some defineable subject or subjects... Hence, archives document particular and often discrete transactions each of which is part of a larger pattern of activity. The notion...of parts of a whole, is the organic conception of archives [that] finds expression in the cardinal archival principle of provenance, which dictates that archives are grouped according to their origins and not intermingled with those of other records creators. Provenance or **respect des fonds** is primarily a principle of the arrangement of archives... Of course, this does not mean that archives do not bear information which may be mined by those in search of subject matter... The problem...is how to preserve and reveal the patterns into which archives fit, that is, see the whole and its constituents in general terms, and still give access to discrete documents to those who seek it.[6]

Archivists in major national and provincial repositories have maintained that users should be able to infer the content or subject matter of records from the archivist's arrangement of the records in their original order, combined with careful documentation of their context and description of their physical composition. In practice, the basic problem is compounded by several factors. The original order of records may be hard to detect as the creators may have been untidy and haphazard or it may have been disturbed and altered by earlier custodians. Archivists themselves may separate what were originally parts of a whole on the basis of physical form, placing visual materials such as maps and photographs in separate special collections.

In local and regional repositories, the purely archival component may be small or even non-existent, in the sense of records and papers generated by the corporate agency that runs the archives. The holdings of these repositories often comprise a quantity of diverse materials that can be described as primary sources but may include a miscellany of even published

---

[6] Terry Eastwood, 'Improving the retrieval of information in archives,' in Peter A. Baskerville and Chad M. Gaffield, eds., **Archives, automation and access: proceedings of an interdisciplinary conference** (University of Victoria, 1986).

materials of local historical interest. 'Artificial collections' may be prominent in these local and regional archives -- sets of materials on some subject, person or place that have been gathered by a private collector, amateur historian, genealogist or historical society or grouped by a previous librarian. One may find that the records of the same government unit, voluntary organization, business, church or the papers of a family have been split between two or more collections in two or more repositories. Or the miscellaneous papers and ephemera of two families of quite different backgrounds and locations that became linked by marriage in the mid-twentieth century may have come into the public domain on the death of the last survivor. Some of the materials in local archives are photocopies or transcriptions. How do the principles of provenance and original order apply in these circumstances? What does one do with materials of dubious and anonymous origins?

Although we are aware of the contentious issues, it has seemed that the needs of users justified our objective of a research tool to help them to find material on specific themes that might be scattered among several or many repositories. This **Inventory** differs from the kinds of guides and finding aids generally produced by archivists in several ways. In particular, we do not have to be responsible for the physical control of the records we describe, though we certainly recognize the importance of physical arrangement to the archivist. Our computer-assisted methodology allows us to specify the original creator, the physical composition, and any accession or cataloguing details used by the repository that holds the material **and** to describe the information content in an abstract and various types of subject index terms. Presenting all this information in the bibliographic format that was used in our first research tool, the **Bibliography**, makes research easier for students and community users accustomed to that.

The Guelph Regional Project had several models of printed guides to primary and archival sources for Ontario regions or cities. The **Toronto Area Archivists Group** (TAAG) has co-ordinated procedures and published guides to archival resources for four Ontario regions. These guides list record series for municipalities, educational and religious institutions as well as for voluntary associations, from the Arthritis Association to the Zonta Club.[7] Current and recent record series predominate and the main emphasis is placed on locally held records, though brief appendices list additional archives that are located outside the region. A locator index lists the 3- or 4-letter abbreviations assigned to all repositories. The TAAG guides constitute models for the scope of the records that should be considered for inclusion in a regional project, and for the format of a published inventory.

Historical Records of the City of Hamilton, 1847-1973, compiled by Carolyn Gray (McMaster University, 1986) describes the records generated by a major city government. In addition to naming the record groups and series and specifying the time span and physical extent of each, this guide is notable for

---

[7] Archival guides in this series, each about 100 pages in length, have so far been published for Peterborough County (1978), Peel Region (1979), Northeastern Ontario (1980), and the Kingston-Frontenac area (1988).

outlining the principal responsibilities and administrative histories of each civic department and official. These descriptive notes provide excellent context for the prospective researcher, not only for Hamilton but also as a guide to the kinds of departments and records that should exist for any Ontario city. They also provide some guide to subject access. The volume's format is a very good example of a published inventory.

The objectives of the Guelph Regional Project involved us in additional complexities, beyond the scope of either the TAAG guides or the Hamilton record inventory. The most challenging of these was the goal of using computer methods to produce both a searchable database and a coherent printed volume. The computer methods, moreover, had to be compatible with those used in compiling the **Bibliography** of published and secondary materials. We set ourselves the further tasks of, first, annotating the records and papers relevant to Guelph-Wellington in abstracts and, secondly, defining subject terms that would assist users to gain subject access through the printed indexes or by machine searching of the database.

In planning the more complex features of the **Inventory of Primary and Archival Sources**, we have been informed by the experience of other regional projects with somewhat similar objectives and methods. Precedents for research projects on the history of Ontario regions that were designed to use both primary and secondary sources include, notably, the Landon Project based at the University of Western Ontario from 1973 to 1978. The project consisted of a multidisciplinary research team who prepared 12 working papers appraising various types of records for regional history. These included land records, municipal records, education records, court records, government-supported welfare institutions, Roman Catholic records, voluntary associations, news-papers, government publications, non-written sources and secondary sources.[8]

A more immediate model for the Guelph Regional Project's **Inventory** has been the **Vancouver Island Project (VIP)**. Based at the University of Victoria under the direction of historians Peter Baskerville and Chad Gaffield from 1982 to 1986, the VIP prepared a machine-readable annotated inventory of the records of all local public repositories of Vancouver Island. The project described the records of five cities, eight district municipalities, four towns, twelve villages, thirteen school districts, six regional districts, 75 improvement districts as well as 50 other repositories such as local museums and historical societies. The VIP had a more rigorously methodological purpose than the Guelph Regional Project, dealt with a narrower range of types of records, is not producing a hard-copy version and is not engaging in research based on its record inventory.

---

[8] For a description of the scope of the project, see R.S Alcorn, 'The ideal historical data base: a strategy for Southwestern Ontario,' in **The Landon Project: interdisciplinary studies in the evolution of southwestern Ontario, second annual report, 1977-8** (London, 1978). The Landon Project's files are held in the Regional History Collection of the D.B. Weldon Library, University of Western Ontario. A smaller project is the study of Essex County reported in John Clarke and David L. Brown, 'Focii of human activity, Essex County, 1825-52: archival sources and research strategies,' **Archivaria** 12 (1981): 31-57.

According to its principal investigators, the VIP was designed to help users gain subject access to the archival records while still respecting the primacy accorded by archivists to provenance and original order. Distinctive features were its innovative methodology that took account of the current initiatives of archivists in the United States and Canada. Its record form and procedures blended library and archival practice and combined archival description and qualitative assessment.[9] The Vancouver Island Project has encapsulated recent issues in the automation of archives as well as debates among archivists and historians on the priority that should be given to subject access. Aspects of the debate were reported in the proceedings of a 1985 conference organized at the University of Victoria by the VIP and are reflected in recent issues of **Archivaria**.[10]

In designing the Guelph Regional Project's Inventory of archival records and primary source materials, we were informed by recent discussions and innovations among archivists, historians and social scientists. We also had to take account of current archival and library practices, including those of the archives, libraries and museums which now hold materials on the Region.

Published and other secondary materials for local history are held mainly by the Guelph Public Library, the Wellington County Archives and the University of Guelph Library, while primary source materials are more widely dispersed. The Guelph Public Library has long held a local history collection, which has been expanded and systematically organized with a computerized inventory by its present archivist-librarian[11]. The Wellington County Archives is a rapidly expanding repository for historical records, including print materials, that is associated with the County Museum in the renovated Wellington County House of Industry. The Guelph Civic Museum, which holds a good deal of original primary material, has also become properly established with professional staff during the past decade. The University of Guelph Library was early in using computer methods for cataloguing and circulation, pioneering the CODOC system for government documents for example,[12] and

[9] Peter Baskerville and Chad Gaffield, 'The Vancouver Island Project: historical research and archival practice,' **Archivaria** 17 (1983-4): 173-187; Gaffield and Baskerville, 'The automated archivist: interdisciplinarity and the process of historical research,' **Social Science History** 9, 2 (1985): 167-184; Vancouver Island Project, **Field definitions and data entry guide for archival material: a working document** (Victoria, 1985).

[10] Peter A. Baskerville and Chad M. Gaffield, eds. **Archives, automation and access: proceedings of an interdisciplinary conference at the University of Victoria** (Victoria: Vancouver Island Project, 1986).

[11] Linda J. Kearns, 'John Galt meets VICTOR 9000,' **Canadian Library Journal** 43, 2 (1986): 97-103.

[12] Caroline Knowles and Ellen M. Pearson, 'The Documentation Centre of the University of Guelph Library,' **Government Publications Review** 1 (1974): 241-250; Virginia Gillham, 'CODOC as a consortium tool,' **Government**

offering ready user access through, first, the GEAC Library System and now the development of the CD-ROM catalogue terminals. References to the rare books and archival materials in Library's Macdonald-Stewart Room are also entered on the online cataloguing system.

Existing systems of cataloguing and describing archival materials relating to Guelph and Wellington County varied as to whether they are strictly based on traditional archival practice or had modified this according to library cataloguing systems; whether they used computer methods at all; and how users were granted access to the system, including the availability and scope of finding aids. All the local repositories used different systems, each system being generally appropriate to the purpose and principal users of the library, museum or archives. Only two (Guelph Public Library's Local History Collection and the Archival and Special Collections of the University of Guelph Library) used computer-based methods.

No comprehensive guide to primary sources on Guelph-Wellington was available, such as the Toronto Area Archivists' Group guides for four Ontario counties, though Taylor's **Family Research in Waterloo and Wellington Counties**[13] formed a useful basis. Local librarians and archivists might generally know of significant resources held by other repositories, but users had to search hopefully through the various sorts of indexes and finding aids of all the collections before concluding that a particular study was not feasible. Potentially valuable resources outside the immediate region remained largely unknown. Local archivists, librarians and museum staff and representatives of the historical and genealogical societies,[14] individually and associated in the Wellington County Local History Council, have welcomed and supported our efforts to produce an integrated guide to the published and primary source materials on the region.

PROCESS OF COMPILING THE INVENTORY

The flow diagram (Figure 2) illustrates the successive stages in the process of creating the Guelph Regional Project's research tools. In reality, the process of compiling them was less orderly than the diagram might suggest. The predictable delays and setbacks in developing any complex and innovative methodology were compounded by various hardware and software problems. There were many more 'backward loops' in the process than are shown in the diagram, as we discovered new collections of materials or revised record

---

Publications Review 9 (1982): 45-53.

[13] Ryan Taylor, **Family research in Waterloo and Wellington Counties** (Kitchener: Waterloo-Wellington Chapter, Ontario Genealogical Society, 1986).

[14] There are two historical societies -- the Guelph Historical Society which has published an annual volume, **Historic Guelph**, since 1977, and the Wellington County Historical Research Society, which began publishing an annual volume, **Wellington County**, in 1988. The Waterloo-Wellington Branch of the Ontario Genealogical Society pursues an active programme of research and publication.

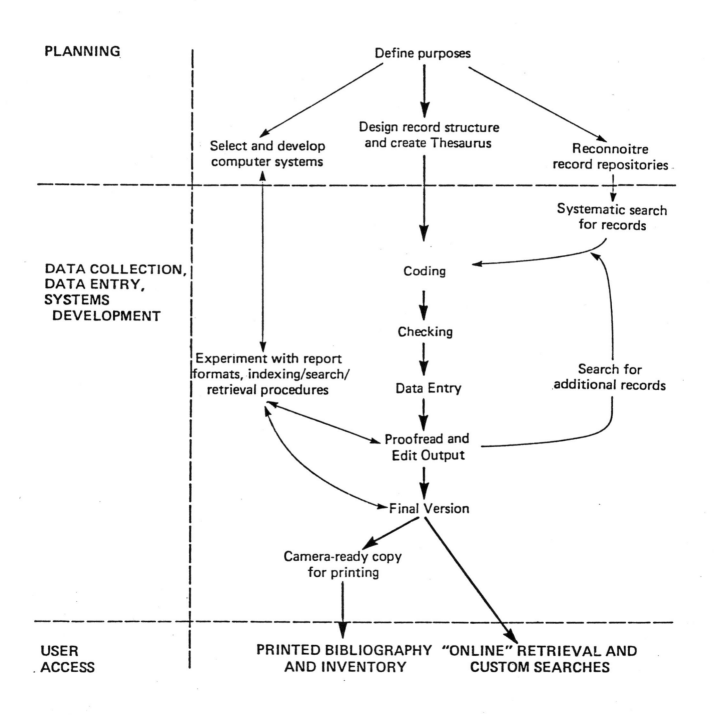

Figure 2
GUELPH REGIONAL PROJECT:
Process of Creating Bibliography and Inventory

structures, search strategies and report formats. In the computer aspects of creating the **Inventory**, we have been able to benefit from our earlier experience with the **Bibliography**, so the stages in the process have conformed quite closely to the stages summarized in the diagram. The new challenges in compiling the **Inventory** have been the greater numbers and complex nature of primary source materials and their dispersion among many more repositories.

1   **Planning**

Planning for both **Bibliography** and **Inventory** occurred during the first three months of the project in mid-1988. For the next seven months all energies were devoted to compiling the **Bibliography**. During the summer of 1988, the first phase of searching and describing primary source materials for **Inventory** overlapped the preparation of the camera-ready text of the **Bibliography**. For the next nine months to June 1989, a reduced staff searched and described additional primary records and entered and intensively edited them in the database. The entire process from the first conceptualization of research tools for regional history to print publication of the **Bibliography** of published materials and the **Inventory** of primary and archival sources lasted a total of 27 months from June 1987 to August 1989.[15]

Plans for the Guelph Regional Project's research tools involved critical choices, including the extent to which computer methods should be used and the feasibility of producing the research tools in both print and machine-readable formats. Obvious advantages were seen in using computer methods for bibliographic and archival description projects. One was the efficient storage provided in a database management system for full details of each record, with the capability of future maintenance and updating. Another was the potential for indexing, search and retrieval of all types of records by any indexed field or combination of fields, including precise place, period, person or corporate entity as well as general theme or specific subject. A third was the expectation that record descriptions could be programmed and formatted into camera-ready text for print publication, without the need for further rounds of typing and proof-reading. Another potential advantage could be the ability to interface with other machine-readable archives and to download records from machine-readable cataloguing systems in library and archival repositories.

Based on an assessment of the Project's needs and resources for the current year and a comparison of various archival and library models, we devised a sophisticated and innovative methodology. This combined the superior capabilities of INMAGIC software in indexing, search and retrieval with an ability to format machine-readable records into camera-ready text and indexes for print publication. The methodology assumed a dedicated micro-

[15] For a more detailed account, including a chronology of the tasks, see Elizabeth Bloomfield, 'Building a better bibliography: computer-aided research tools,' **Canadian Library Journal** 46 (August 1989): 239-247.

computer (with at least a 30-megabyte hard disk), INMAGIC software[16] and one MARC-compatible record structure designed to handle both bibliographic and archival records.

During the later planning phase, hardware was selected and the record structure and coding forms designed. The project co-ordinator visited the main library and archival repositories known to hold materials on the region in order to explain the purposes of the project and to set up procedures which would disrupt their routines as little as possible. A preliminary thesaurus was compiled and tested and principles of selection and procedures were codified in several working papers.

2   Research staff, record repositories and selection criteria

Project staff were appointed to begin their work in the fourth month of the whole project. For the **Inventory**, the same two assistants who had been principally responsible for describing the bibliographic records in the first phase, were able to continue full-time throughout the long, hot summer of 1988 researching the archival and other primary sources. Both with Masters degrees or higher qualifications, Jane Turner and Joe Gabriel spent five months systematically visiting archives and other repositories believed to contain the largest quantities of local materials. These were the Wellington County Archives, the Wellington County Board of Education, the Guelph Public Library, the Guelph Civic Museum, Guelph City Hall, the University of Guelph Library's Archival and Special Collections, most municipal offices in Wellington County, the Guelph and Arthur land registry offices, and the United Church Archives in Toronto. They also visited all the municipal offices in Wellington County. This phase was revealing for the different systems -- at times, the absence of system -- used to control primary records, as well as for the physical conditions in which records are held. The environments in which our team described primary source materials included former jail cells, the place where dynamite had been stored, and a municipal sewerage plant! Protective clothing and masks were needed in several locations where the dust was overpowering.

One of these two assistants, Jane Turner, was able to continue part-time for a further eight months, helping the co-ordinator with descriptions of records in the remaining archives and with intensive editing. Archives and

---

[16] INMAGIC is a database management software program, first introduced in 1980, which has been designed for the storage, manipulation and retrieval of bibliographic information. It is claimed by its creators to be 'particularly powerful and efficient in organizing and rapidly searching text records of varying length,' and has been adopted by libraries, archives, law firms, and research institutes in various fields. We chose INMAGIC (version 7.0) for its combination of qualities and for the scope it gave to add our own modifications, based on appraisals such as Ralph M. Daehn, 'Methods and software for building bibliographic databases,' **Canadian Library Journal** 42 (1985): 147-152. A new version, INMAGIC 7.1, released in spring 1988, has various enhancements which have helped considerably in the creation of the **Inventory**. For a more detailed description and critique, see Bloomfield, 'Building a better bibliography,' 244-45.

repositories visited in this second phase were mainly those located outside the region or those with smaller and more specialized sets of records. In all, over 75 archives or other repositories were visited; the 69 with records cited in this **Inventory** are listed at the end of this introduction, with the 3-digit codes used in the records. More detailed descriptions of most may be found in the section entitled Guide to Archives and Record Repositories. Nineteen of these repositories were located in Guelph, twenty more elsewhere in Wellington County, 24 in other parts of Ontario, one in Montreal, one in Philadelphia, one in London, England and three in Scotland.

Repositories with at least 100 records included in this **Inventory** were, in order:

Wellington County Archives
Archives of Ontario, Toronto
University of Guelph Library: Archival and Special Collections
Guelph Land Registry Office
Wellington County Board of Education
Guelph Public Library
United Church Archives, Toronto
Guelph Civic Museum
National Archives of Canada, Ottawa
Arthur Land Registry Office
Presbyterian Church Archives, Toronto

We were interested in all kinds of archival and primary source materials that have informational value for historical research in the widest sense. Thus we looked for visual and graphic records such as maps, plans, architectural drawings, photographs and art works. Indeed, such visual records comprise over one fifth of all the records in this **Inventory**. We have not, however, included records of artifacts held in museums or privately.

Our search for primary sources was most intense in Guelph-Wellington and fairly thorough throughout the rest of Ontario. Within Wellington County, we attempted to trace and describe all primary source materials, relating to the history of Guelph-Wellington and dating from before 1940, that are held in libraries or archives or retained by the creating body and accessible to researchers. We did not try to include materials held privately by families, businesses or collectors, that cannot be consulted by students or other interested users. Some such materials have been placed in public collections as a result of our project. We hope that the publication of this **Inventory** may influence other owners of primary records and manuscripts to give the originals or copies to local libraries and archives.

In Ontario beyond the county boundaries, we made efforts to locate records relevant to Guelph-Wellington that are held as part of archives or libraries of larger scope. We followed leads provided in citations of primary sources by those who have undertaken research and written on the region and in the **Union list of manuscripts in Canadian repositories** and guides to archives in Ontario. We also consulted all inventories, finding aids and indexes in major repositories such as the Archives of Ontario and National Archives of Canada as well as church and corporate archives with interests in the region.

Outside Ontario, we did not try systematically to search for all records or manuscripts relevant to the history of Guelph and Wellington. However, a few such records have been included because of the special interests of project associates. Gilbert Stelter, for example, has described some manuscripts held by the National Library of Scotland and the Scottish Record Office that relate to the life and literary work of Guelph's founder, John Galt (#2350-#2352, #2354-#2355). Stelter also summarized the scope of the evidence in the British Colonial Office records of the role of the Canada Company in establishing the Guelph settlement (#999). Michael Vance, a graduate student in the Department of History who was researching other topics in the Strathclyde Regional Archives in Scotland, found a letter describing a visit to Guelph in 1889 (#2426). To complement the **Inventory**'s records of art works in the Macdonald Stewart Art Centre of Guelph, Judith Nasby has described the paintings by Guelph-born David Kennedy that are held by the Historical Society of Philadelphia (#3515, #3517-#3519, #3521-#3523, #3525-#3527, #3539-#3531).

The **Inventory** comprises records, papers and other primary source materials dating from before 1940. This matches the temporal span of the **Bibliography** which includes all the published or secondary items we could find that described or analyzed the processes of settlement and development in all or part of Wellington County to 1940. Any cutoff point will seem arbitrary or regrettable to some users. The rationale for 1940 was that this date seemed to mark a period of transition at the end of the first full century of settlement throughout the county and the development of a mature regional economy based on farming, commerce and manufacturing. After the depression of the 1930s and World War II, Guelph and the southern part of the region have undergone rapid population and economic growth. The integration of much of the region into the hinterlands of larger metropolitan and regional cities such as Kitchener-Waterloo, Hamilton and Toronto has weakened the local sense of identity. The expansion of the colleges into the University of Guelph in the 1960s has brought more cosmopolitan influences to the region, as well as larger numbers of people concerned to conserve the regional heritage.

It seemed to us that the pre-1940 period had some integrity and that any attempt to include post-1940 materials would have involved a huge increase in the number of records and a greater risk of bias and incompleteness. Thus we have no records for the University of Guelph (as distinct from the three founding colleges), for the Planning Department of the City of Guelph, for the Guelph Spring Festival, for the Local Architectural Conservancy Advisory Council (LACAC) or the wealth of service and sports clubs and social service agencies that have been formed since 1940. However, the record structure and methodology have been designed so that later records and other primary source materials could readily be added to the database. Moreover, for record series extending from before 1940 to the present, we entered the actual date span of accessible materials. We also included compilations and collections of primary materials actually assembled after 1940 if the component materials dated mainly from before 1940.

Though we have tried to locate all primary source materials relating to Guelph and Wellington County and dating from before 1940, there must be some that are not inventoried in this volume. We hope that users of the the **Inventory**, or of the **Bibliography**, will bring such items to our attention so that they may be added to the Guelph Regional Project's database.

3 Record structure, data entry and editing

Separate coding forms were designed for the bibliographic and archival records, but both are based on the single data structure planned to accommodate all types of primary and secondary source materials. The **Inventory** coding form had 24 fields to allow for all possible bibliographic elements, the abstract of scope and content, and index terms. During the **Bibliography** phase as well as in the first two months of the intensive research for the **Inventory**, we tested and modified the preliminary procedures in order to achieve the consistency and standardization essential for machine-readable record systems.

Whenever possible, the fields of the data structure were intended to be **MARC-compatible**, to match the MAchine-Readable Cataloguing systems that have been developed for libraries and archives.[17] Where we could use them, MARC labels are indicated in brackets after each field name in the list that follows. In some cases, we had to use additional fields that do not have a MARC equivalent. Our database had to include many types of documents that are not usually catalogued by librarians. Furthermore, our intention to format the records into camera-ready copy for a print publication complete with various indexes made it necessary for us to use some additional fields such as document type, and chronological and geographic subject headings. In addition, each record was assigned an overall summary classification (its CLAS code) to determine its order in the printed **Inventory**.

The **data structure** for all records comprises fields for the following elements, illustrated also in Figure 3. MARC codes, where we could use them, are specified in brackets:
* unique retrieval number (001)
* document type
* creator, personal (100)
* creator, corporate(110)
* title of record group/series/document/map/other type of item with date (or date span) of creation (245)
* published title of volume or newspaper (245)
* place of publication
* publisher
* year of publication
* details of collation including physical size (300)
* medium (340)
* condition
* alternate physical form (530)
* abstract or scope and content note in natural language (520)

[17] Max Evans and Lisa Weber, **MARC for archives and manuscripts: a compendium of practice** (Madison: State Historical Society of Wisconsin, 1984); Nancy Sahli, **MARC for archives and manuscripts: the AMC format** (Chicago: Society of American Archivists, 1985).

* library locations (535)
* restrictions on access (538)
* existence of finding aid and catalogue/accession codes (555)
* start and end dates of time span

Four kinds of **subject headings** were also assigned:
* personal (600)
* corporate (610)
* topical according to the controlled vocabulary of a thesaurus (650)
* geographic

Subject headings should be used consistently by bibliographers and indexers so that users are provided with a clear and comprehensive guide to the scope of material. For the **Bibliography** we compiled a **thesaurus** of topical subject terms, to control the terminology used when the natural language of documents, indexers and users is transposed into a stricter language suited for documentation handling and information retrieval. The GRP Thesaurus is based on the National Library of Canada's **Canadian Subject Headings** as well as consideration of subject headings used by the regional history collections of local libraries. For the **Inventory** we used the same thesaurus, expanded to include also the types of records and documents encountered.[18]

We also tried to standardize personal, corporate and geographic subject headings as well as authors' names, by compiling authority lists at the end of the first four months of research for the **Bibliography** and conforming to these with the **Inventory** as well.

INMAGIC software permits multiple subfields for such fields as creator, and for personal, corporate, topical and geographic subject headings, as well as locations. For example, if a document includes mention of many persons, organizations, places or subjects, these may all be specified as index terms. The user of INMAGIC decides in advance whether the various fields of the record structure are to have **keyword**, **term**, **term-and-keyword**, or **no** indexing. These choices affect the kind of machine searching and retrieval one may undertake once the database is created. With a Term Index, one can search efficiently among the search relations **Equal to**, **Greater than**, **Less than**, **Starts with**, **From..to**. A Keyword Index contains every word (except particles) in a field designated to be indexed, and can be searched quickly using the Search

[18] In designing the Guelph Regional Project Thesaurus for the **Bibliography**, we also consulted the following: Charles Abrams, **The language of cities: a glossary of terms** (New York: Viking Press, 1971); W.T. Durr and Paul M. Rosenberg, **The urban information thesaurus: a vocabulary for social documentation** (Westport, CT: Greenwood Press for Baltimore Region Institutional Studies Center, 1977); **Canadian Urban Thesaurus** (Ottawa: Ministry of State for Urban Affairs, 1979). In expanding the GRP Thesaurus for the **Inventory** to include terms for the types of records, we also drew upon the thesaurus printout of terms used by the Vancouver Island Project, for which we thank Peter Baskerville. See Elizabeth Bloomfield, 'The Guelph Regional Project Thesaurus for regional history,' (Working Paper #6, November 1987, with updates).

Relations **Contains word, Contains stem**. Some fields should have **both** Term and Keyword indexes to give the greatest flexibility in search and retrieval. For each field to be indexed in INMAGIC, one also chooses a **Sort** code, determining how information is treated when searched and sorted (letter-by-letter or word-by-word, punctuation significant or not, etc). **Emphasis** codes determine how multiple field entries (subfields) are to be treated when searched or sorted, whether all subfield entries or only the first are fully indexed.

The design of INMAGIC and our need to generate camera-ready copy from the database constrained the record structure in several other ways. First, INMAGIC was limited in the order and sort code, that we designed for printing out the final sequence of records, to the first 60 characters of each record. The 60 characters had to include the combination of CLAS code, corporate or personal creator, title and date. This meant that we had to state the names of the names of corporate agencies and the titles of documents and record series as brief as possible. Secondly, INMAGIC's order key works only for a maximum of 250 records, so we had to have no more than that number in any sequence of records with the same CLAS code. These constraints led us to adopt some standardized abbreviations for recurring titles and terms (evident especially in the municipal, school board and church records) and to subdivide some large sequences of records. The effect of both these is seen most clearly in the section on Church Records.

INMAGIC's usual **data entry** procedures were modified in several ways. We used the recommended batch-entry and batch-adding procedures, initially entering records into a database indexable only by retrieval key. We also entered a fair proportion of the records using DataStar software on an old Superbrain computer, and then converted batches of these records into INMAGIC format before adding them to the master database. Our main reason for doing so was to sidestep some problems of apparent incompatibility between INMAGIC software and the model of XT-compatible microcomputer we had chosen. But the DataStar routines, designed for us by Ralph Daehn of the University of Guelph Library, also provided some safeguards against error in entering the vital retrieval key data and permitted some efficiencies in repeating data fields common to several successive records. We were fortunate to have the same capable and experienced assistant, Patricia Abbott, for much of this data entry work through the project.

Batches of records, whether entered directly in INMAGIC or converted from DataStar format, were subjected to several stages of proofreading, editing and correcting. In later stages of editing, we frequently used the INMAGIC capabilities of **List**ing index terms and **Sort**ing by any field to check for consistency, possible duplicates or omissions, and the appropriateness of the sequence in which references would appear in the printed **Inventory**.

The task of producing text and indexes for the printed **Inventory** from the INMAGIC database was another challenge, although the earlier experience with the **Bibliography** was helpful. Concurrently with the data entry and editing phase, we experimented with INMAGIC **report formats**. While we knew that the machine-readable database would continue to have value for direct searches and for future updates, our first goal was to produce printed volumes.

Thus we had to be able to generate **camera-ready text** of the individual entries, grouped by type, and also to create **indexes** of creators (corporate and personal), places, subject headings, personal subjects and corporate subjects.

Though we had expected that we could use INMAGIC to format the final text and indexes, we found that we had to use other software as well. While INMAGIC could be used to generate a numbered list of references containing the required bibliographic elements, WordPerfect software was needed to produce conventionally acceptable text, complete with headings and page numbers and ready for final proportional laser printing. INMAGIC did allow us to create basic creator, place, subject, personal and corporate indexes matched with the sequential numbers of relevant entries. But SAS procedures on the mainframe computer were needed to sort the numbers in ascending order and convert them from columns to strings. WordPerfect and Ventura 'desktop publishing' software were used to format the indexes for final printing.

Figure 3 illustrates how several elements of the basic record structure of a record have been linked together or concatenated into an individual entry for the printed volume. The elements we used are: personal or corporate creator(s), title of record with span of dates (bolded), collation details, availability in microform, location or repository code(s), details of finding aids, cataloguing and accession numbers, and notes on any restrictions. The abstract, describing the scope and content of the record, follows in a small paragraph.

In its alternating rhythms of researching, coding, checking, data entry, proofreading and editing, the main work of compiling the **Inventory** database was largely complete by late May 1989. The tasks of generating text and indexes and copy-editing and finetuning them into camera-ready format for print publication took another three months.

GUIDE TO USERS OF THE PRINTED INVENTORY

The Guelph Regional Project's research tools have been designed to facilitate user access through both the printed **Bibliography** and **Inventory** and by search and retrieval of records held in the machine-readable database. Machine search, using Boolean logic to find records with various combinations of defined keywords and index terms, can provide users with much more specific and flexible subject access. Searching for references through the indexes of the printed volumes is a linear process that must be repeated for every term. By comparison, searching the database for any combination of subject heading, person, corporate body, place, date span and keyword in title or abstract is multi-dimensional. INMAGIC databases are specially suited to instant information retrieval, a capability already proven during the project in custom searches to serve varied research interests. Within a minute or two, one can search a database of over 3750 records for all the references to Scots in Nichol Township and Fergus that date from before 1850. Or all references to sports in Guelph before 1900, or business enterprises recorded as in operation by 1870. A few more minutes and the results of the machine search can be printed out in alternative sequences -- all maps and plans dating from before 1867 in chronological order or in geographical order. But general use of this capability awaits the installation of dedicated microcomputers or CD-

Figure 3 SAMPLE RECORD IN DATABASE AND AS PRINTED REFERENCE

Record Structure

```
REC/1     AW-01267
CLAS/1    CPCL
DOC/1     I
CORP/1    Fergus (St Andrew's) Pres
TI/1      Letter of protest, 1845
COLL/1    1 document
CON/1     G
AB/1      A copy of the original letter in which certain trustees, elders,
          deacons and a 'vast majority' of the congregation protest recent
          doctrinal statements of the Church of Scotland. The letter
          concludes by stating that 'while leaving for the present the
          Church and other property belonging to the congregation of St
          Andrew's Church, Fergus, we protest that we do not thereby
          compromise our right at any future period to assert an interest in
          these premises and that we are most unjustly and unwarrantably
          interfered with'. The letter is signed by 'G. Smellie, Minister'
          and forty leaders and members of the church. Burr Collection at
          Wellington County Archives; Adam Fergusson Papers at Archives of
          Ontario.
LOC/1     WCA
LOC/2     AO
FIND/1    AO: MU 1016; WCA: MU 13
SUP/1     Smellie, George, Rev.
SUP/2     Fergusson, Adam Johnston
SUP/3     Ferrier, A.D.
SUP/4     Allan, Charles
SUC/1     St Andrew's Presbyterian Church, Fergus
SUT/1     Correspondence
SUT/2     Churches, Presbyterian
SUT/3     Buildings, Church
SUT/4     Petitions
SUT/5     Religious dissension
SUG/1     Fergus
DAT/1     1845
DAT/2     1845
```

Format in Printed Inventory

Fergus (St Andrew's) Pres. **Letter of protest, 1845.** 1 document. Loc: WCA, AO. AO: MU 1016; WCA: MU 13.

A copy of the original letter in which certain trustees, elders, deacons and a 'vast majority' of the congregation protest recent doctrinal statements of the Church of Scotland. The letter concludes by stating 'while leaving for the present the Church and other property belonging to the congregation of St Andrew's Church, Fergus, we protest that we do not thereby compromise our right at any future period to assert an interest in these premises and that we are most unjustly and unwarrantably interfered with'. The letter is signed by 'G. Smellie, Minister' and forty leaders and members of the church. Burr Collection at the Wellington County Archives; Adam Fergusson Papers at the Archives of Ontario.

ROM readers in the University and other local libraries, we hope by the beginning of 1990.

The records in the printed **Inventory** are presented in CLAS code order, according to the type of provenance that brought the records into being (in contrast to the thematic subject order of references in the printed **Bibliography**). Thus the records are grouped in the following major sections, which are sometimes subdivided, and then the records are listed in alphabetical order by name of corporate or personal creator:

* Government records, with judicial, municipal, school, library and higher government records are distinguished first; within these major groups, individual records may be grouped by municipal units

* Business records

* Church records, arranged first by denomination, then alphabetically by abbreviated name of congregation

* Records of voluntary associations, arranged first by type of society, from farmers' and agricultural associations through to women's and youth welfare societies

* Records of special local institutions by type such as educational, medical, religious

* Family and personal papers

* Gazetteers and directories: national and provincial, county, and city

* Newspapers

* Land records

* Maps and plans, grouped by type and, in the case of registered plans, by municipality

* Architectural drawings

* Photographs

* Art works

* Compilations and special collections

The various index terms provide additional access points or means of retrieving records according to their alternative and more subtle characteristics and subject areas. There are six indexes in the printed **Inventory** in which terms or subject headings of various kinds are matched with the relevant numbers of the printed references. Figure 3 illustrates the CORP and AUT fields and the SUG, SUT, SUP, and SUC index terms referred to below.

1 and 2   Creator Indexes

Entries in the **corporate creator** or **personal creator** index, compiled from the CORP and AUT fields, allow users to find works by any one of the over 600 corporate creators or 475 personal creators represented in the **Inventory**. Corporate names in the CORP field may have had to be abbreviated for the INMAGIC order key to work properly. We tried to avoid abbreviations so that references in the database would be self-contained. When necessary, as few words as possible were abrreviated and always consistently. Abbreviations of coporate creators were used with various types of municipal status, school sections and names of denominations. See the list of Abbreviations at the end of this introductory essay. One minor effect of the INMAGIC-based methodology is the ordering of numbers in the names of corporate creators (or in corporate subject headings). Thus School Section 1 is followed by S.S.#10, S.S.#11, S.S. #12, before S.S. #2, S.S. #3 and so on.

3   Place Index

A place index of some 260 geographic locations, compared with 174 in the **Bibliography**, was compiled from the SUG field in the record structure. Places located within our region receive primary emphasis in the index and were not followed by 'Ontario' or 'Ont.' Places outside the region may have been included when apparently significant, as sources of migrants for example. hire are in England or Scotland, while those preceded by County are in Ireland. In ambiguous cases, foreign place names have the country name added to the locality name.

4   Subject Heading Index

Compiled from subject headings in the SUT field according to the Guelph Regional Project's Thesaurus, the subject heading index has a controlled vocabulary, of which about 460 terms were used in this volume. This index is particularly useful for gaining additional points of access to the resources of the **Inventory**. The primary organization of the printed volume is according to the type of record and type of creator (it is thus quite different from the mainly thematic organization of the printed **Bibliography**). It is only by using the subject heading index that researchers can locate the records of potential value for such themes and topics as agricultural education, building materials, children, climate, fairs, health care, hotels, and inns, the brewing industry, livestock, the militia, missionaries, mortgages, prices, public utilities, relief of poverty, separate schools, Scottish settlers, sports of various kinds, or street railways.

For example, the record describing a set of family and personal papers would be printed in the Family and Personal Papers section of the volume. But the papers might well contain useful information about many other specific places, topics, people, organizations or activities. A set of papers about the Connon or Clarke family, for example, might contain references to Elora itself and perhaps other places, to the family business, the church to which the family belonged, the local government unit to which one or more family members might have been elected, the voluntary associations in which family members were members or held office, the construction and improvement of the family house or other buildings, and other people to whom the primary family was realted by kin, marriage, business or other form of association. We have included in its machine-readable record all the appropriate index entries for the specific persons, corporate entities and places, and the relevant topical subject headings according to the thesaurus.

5 Corporate Subject Index

Compiled from entries in the SUC field of the record structure, the corporate subject index lists about 1,250 businesses, churches, schools, clubs or municipal governments. As with the personal index, most corporate entries have only one reference, but 55 have more than ten each. Most frequently cited are churches, schools and colleges, as is evident in the following list of corporate bodies with most citations: St Andrew's Presbyterian Church, Guelph (75), the Ontario Agricultural College (69), Knox Presbyterian Church, Guelph (50), the Guelph Collegiate and Vocational Institute (49), the Canada Company (40), Chalmers Presbyterian Church, Guelph (31), St George's Anglican Church, Guelph (30), the Macdonald Institute (27), the Church of Our Lady Catholic Church, Guelph (26) and the Grand Trunk Railway (26).

But the range and variety of these corporate entities is illuminating. So is our finding that there was only a 26 per cent overlap between the corporate subjects in the **Inventory** with those in the **Bibliography**. Clearly there are primary source materials on some schools, churches, businesses and municipalities that have not yet been tapped by historical researchers and writers. In the entire database, including both bibliographic and primary records, we captured references to about 1900 different corporate bodies.

6 Personal Subject Index

The personal subject index, compiled from the SUP field, lists some 1,400 individuals who have been identified as subjects of the records listed in the **Inventory**. This compares with the 1700 personal subjects identified in the **Bibliography**. It was interesting to discover that only 28 per cent of the persons indexed in the **Inventory** had been also indexed in the **Bibliography**, so that altogether we have caught about 2,700 persons in our personal subject net. As with the **Bibliography**, most of these persons are mentioned only once. Ten were cited at least 20 times each, and another 22 were cited at least ten times each. Those with at least 20 references in the **Inventory** are: George Sleeman (35), David Allan (32), Nathaniel Higinbotham (32), J.W. Lyon (27), Charles Clarke (25), Charles Allan (21), Adam Johnston Fergusson (21), John Galt (21), William Tytler (21), and the Rev. Robert Torrance (20).

As with the author index, we tried to standardize the form of personal names, but we did so cautiously. For example, only when Mr McDuff, J. McDuff and James McDuff were positively known to be the same person, did we standardize all citations to the form that appeared most commonly in the historical records or was least ambiguous. When we could not be certain, we left the alternative versions. The personal subject indexes of the **Bibliography** and **Inventory** constitute a base from which a 'dictionary of local biography' might be compiled, such as that published for Hamilton[19].

---

[19] T. Melville Bailey, ed. **Dictionary of Hamilton Biography** (Hamilton, 1981).

Users should consult the **Inventory** in conjunction with the **Bibliography**. Some browsing through both volumes for all the ramifications of a subject area would be productive; the two should be seen as complementary sources. The contents of the **Bibliography** should not be overlooked, as some of the printed materials listed there are contemporary with the events and conditions they describe. The introductory essays in the **Inventory** should give some sense of the context for each type of record. But the student or other researcher on most subjects will need to interlink references to many different types of records in various parts of the printed **Inventory**. A study of the history of Guelph churches, for example, would need to draw upon not only the church records themselves. The researcher should also consider a series of directories to provide a context of time and space; maps, plans, photographs and architectural drawings for visual evidence; and possibly family and personal papers relating to significant individuals and families in particular congregations.

In drawing up a short list of the records to search for, the user should note details of the location (or repository) code, the physical form and extent of the records, and any restrictions on their use. Specific cataloguing, accession or other information provided with the record will be vital in helping the archivist to locate the material. In many cases, archives and other repositories require prior appointment or impose restrictions on access. The user is referred to the GUIDE TO ARCHIVES AND REPOSITORIES (pp. 551-570) for details of these.

ABBREVIATIONS

General

C	City
Co	County
FA	Finding Aid
Loc	Location (repository)
mf	microform
mr	machine-readable
ms	manuscript
PV	Police Village
S.S.	School Section
T	Town
Tp	Township
V	Village

Abbreviations for corporate creator names in Church Records

Ang	Anglican
Cong	Congregational
EUB	Evangelical United Brethren
Meth	Methodist
MEpi	Methodist Episcopal
MNew	Methodist New Connexion
MWes	Wesleyan Methodist
MPri	Primitive Methodist
Pres	Presbyterian
UC	United Church

Repository Locations: see also the more detailed descriptions in the Guide to Archives and Repositories, after the annotated records and before the Indexes.

AGO	Art Gallery of Ontario, Toronto
ALR	Arthur Land Registry Office, North Wellington
AO	Archives of Ontario, Toronto
ATO	Arthur Township Office
BCM	Brant County Museum, Brantford
CAS	Children's Aid Society, Guelph
CBA	Canadian Baptist Archives, McMaster University, Hamilton
CNRL	Canadian Rail History Society, Montreal
DHA	Diocese of Hamilton Archives, Hamilton
DHC	Doon Heritage Crossroads, Kitchener
DVO	Drayton Village Office
EL	Ennotville Library
EMO	Elora Municipal Office
ETO	Erin Township Office
EVO	Erin Village Office
GAB	Guelph Armouries
GCC	Guelph Correctional Centre
GCH	Guelph City Hall
GCI	Guelph Collegiate & Vocational Institute Archives

GCM	Guelph Civic Museum
GDU	Guelph Dublin Street United Church
GLR	Guelph Land Registry Office
GNU	Guelph Norfolk United Church
GPL	Guelph Public Library
GSA	Guelph St Andrew's Presbyterian Church
GTO	Guelph Township Office
HSA	Homewood Sanitarium Archives, Guelph
HSP	Historical Society of Philadelphia
HTH	Harriston Town Hall
JA	Jesuit Archives, Regis College, Toronto
JMH	John McCrae House, Guelph
KPL	Kitchener Public Library
MBH	Maryborough Township Hall
MFH	Mount Forest Town Hall
MFL	Mount Forest Public Library
MLA	Mutual Life Archives, Waterloo
MNR	Ministry of Natural Resources, Toronto
MSC	Macdonald Stewart Art Centre, Guelph
MTH	Minto Township Hall
MTL	Metro Toronto Central Reference Library
MUL	McMaster (Mills) University Library/Archives, Hamilton
NAC	National Archives of Canada, Ottawa
NLC	National Library of Canada, Ottawa
NLS	National Library of Scotland
OAM	Ontario Agricultural Museum, Milton
OHA	Ontario Hydro Archives, Toronto
OMA	Ontario Ministry of Agriculture and Food, Guelph
PCA	Presbyterian Church Archives, Toronto
PKH	Pilkington Township Hall
PMF	Peel and Maryborough Mutual Fire Insurance Company
PRO	Public Record Office, Kew, London, England
PTO	Peel Township Office
PUS	Puslinch Township Office
RGO	Registrar-General of Ontario, Toronto
ROM	Royal Ontario Museum: Sigmund Samuel Library, Toronto
SJA	St Joseph's Hospital Archives, Guelph
SRA	Strathclyde Regional Archives, Glasgow, Scotland
SRO	Scottish Record Office, Edinburgh, Scotland
UCA	United Church Archives, Toronto
UGA	University of Guelph Library: Archival and Special Collections
UGL	University of Guelph Library
UTA	University of Toronto Archives/Rare Books
UTL	University of Toronto Library
UWL	University of Waterloo Library: Doris Lewis Room
UWO	University of Western Ontario, London: Regional History Collection
WBE	Wellington County Board of Education
WCA	Wellington County Archives
WCL	Wellington County Library
WSB	Wellington County Separate School Board

ANNOTATED INVENTORY

Government records

COURT AND JUDICIAL RECORDS

Some of the earliest official records created in the local communities of what became Ontario were related to the administration of justice.[1] From the 1790s, some attempt was made to provide decentralized court facilities to meet the colonists' needs. In the new judicial system created then, a central superior Court of King's Bench was established for the province. In the districts, the magistrates (or justices of the peace) met four times a year in the Courts of General Quarter Sessions of the Peace. Minor matters of criminal jurisdiction, such as assault, misdemeanour and petty larceny, were broght before them. In addition to their responsibility for district administration until 1841, the magistrates could also set up Courts of Requests (equivalent to the later Division Courts) to try minor cases in smaller localities. On the civil side, District Courts were set up in 1794 to decide cases of moderate importance not involving title to land; each District Court had a judge appointed by the Lieutenant Governor.

From 1841, (also the year when Wellington District was effectively constituted) administrative functions were transferred from the Court of General Quarter Sessions to the new District Councils which were replaced by a greater number of County Councils from 1850. After 1841, the Chairman of Sessions or presiding magistrate was no longer elected by his fellow magistrates. The senior District Judge, who had to be a member of the provincial Bar, became Chairman of Sessions ex officio. The District Courts, renamed County Courts in 1850, steadily gained enlarged powers and responsibilities of civil, and later, criminal jurisdiction. From 1853 they got equity jurisdiction in certain matters, and from 1864 they heard bankruptcy cases when sitting as Insolvency Courts. From 1874, the County Court Judges were allowed criminal jurisdiction in cases where the accused elected for trial without jury; they also became responsible for the general administration of justice in each county.

In the twentieth century, County Court Judges have been given even larger responsibilities including the administration of the Children's Protection Act, the Children of Unmarried Parents' Act, the Adoption Act and the Change of Name Act, as well as jurisdiction in property rights cases, elections and voting matters, disputes between debtors and creditors, arbitrations and municipal matters; they also preside over Citizenship Courts.

Within each District or County, the Division Courts have had a long history. From 1841 they could have trial by jury, from 1850 judgements had

---

[1] The following account is based on Frederick H. Armstrong, **Handbook of Upper Canadian Chronology** (Toronto: Dundurn, 1985): 115-136; C.J. Shepard, 'Court records as archival records,' **Archivaria** 18 (1984): 124-134; C.J. Shepard, **Preliminary inventory of court records (RG 22) in the Archives of Ontario** (1983).

to be registered in the County Court, and from 1868 Division Courts had to keep their own records. In 1970 they were renamed Small Claims Courts. For the settlement and registration of the estates of deceased persons, a provincial Court of Probate and district Surrogate Courts were established in the 1790s. After 1858, the senior County Court judge was ex officio the Surrogate Court judge.

Court records have long been appreciated as major sources for social, family and local history and for genealogy; they are now being valued also by social, economic and labour historians. But, although the local courts and lawyers must have produced a great quantity of records over the past 150 years, only quite small fragments have apparently survived for Wellington County.[2] The records that have been traced are grouped, first, those relating to Wellington District prior to c1850, then those relating to Wellington County, and finally the jury selection records at the municipal level have been distinguished.

A good many of the records grouped in this section are items only and some are semi-official. The record series with the longest time span are the minutes of the Clerk of the Peace from 1873 to 1948, dockets of criminal cases from 1860 to 1900 and writs from 1858 to 1918, all held by the Wellington County Archives. Quite good records survive for only one of the twelve Division Courts of Wellington County, the 6th Divisional Court (Elora), with one series only for the 10th Divisional Court (Harriston). The Archives of Ontario has good holdings of Surrogate Court estate files from 1840 to 1955, as well as other Surrogate Court records for Wellington County.

It may be noted that private legal papers relating to Wellington County are also scarce, which makes Judge Anson Spotton's handbook of legal cases in the 1920s (#8, held by the National Archives) all the more interesting. Some legal firm records, concerned with probate, mortgages and commercial contracts, are listed under Legal and Financial Businesses in a later section. Despite the longevity of legal firms and the public prominence of many local lawyers in this period, very few of their private papers have survived.[3]

---

[2] For a comparative discussion of the survival of court records, see Louis A. Knafla, '"Be it remembered": court records and research in the Canadian provinces,' **Archivaria** 18 (1984): 105-123. It would be very hard to reconstruct the organization of the judicial system from the surviving records for Wellington District/County. There is no evidence of the Circuit Courts, for example, for which Wellington County was part of the Oxford Circuit for criminal cases and part of the Home Circuit for civil cases.

[3] The scarcity of lawyers' records can be explained partly by the principle of solicitor-client privilege. See Doug Whyte, 'The acquisition of lawyers' private papers,' **Archivaria** 18 (1984): 142-153; James M. Whalen, 'The application of solicitor-client privilege to government records,' **Archivaria** 18 (1984): 135-141. For a discussion of sources for the history of Wellington County lawyers, see also Elizabeth Bloomfield, 'Lawyers as members of urban business elites, 1860-1920,' chapter in **Lawyers and business in Canada** (Toronto: University of Toronto Press for The Osgoode Society, forthcoming, 1990).

WELLINGTON DISTRICT

1. Wellington District. **Appointment of justices of peace, 1846.** 1 document. Loc:
    UGA. XR2 MS A048.
    A listing of justices of the peace appointed in 1846 including several
    residents of the area later called Wellington County. These included Adam
    Johnston Fergusson, A.D. Fordyce, Joseph Parkinson and Charles Julius Mickle.

2. Wellington District. **Appointment of magistrate, 1840.** 1 document. Loc: GPL.
    List of document contents.
    A record of the appointment of Adam Johnston Fergusson as Judge of the
    Surrogate Court of the District of Wellington. Held with the Byerly Collection.

3. Wellington District. **Bailiff's account book, 1846-1856.** 1 ledger. Loc: WCA.
    A record of funds exchanged between individuals involved in court cases.

4. Wellington District. **Court of General Quarter Sessions of the Peace. Filings,
    1843.** 1 box. Loc: AO. FA: RG 22, Series 51.
    This series consists only of five information and complaint cases, all in
    1843. Held with Ontario Court Records.

5. Wellington District. **First Small Claims Court. Court book, November 1849-
    December 1850.** 1 ledger. Loc: WCA.
    A record of individuals involved in court cases, the size of claims contested,
    and the judgement of the cases.

6. Wellington District/ Wellington Co. **Surrogate Court. Estate files, 1840-1944.**
    193 feet. Loc: AO. FA: RG 22, Series 318.
    Files consist of the original documentation filed with the court in order to
    obtain a grant of probate, administration or guardianship. To 1858, the
    documents are filed alphabetically by name. After 1858, they are organized
    chronologically by estate file number. Estate files are available on
    Genealogical Society microfilm to 1900. For the period from 1840 to 1858,
    alphabetical files are on microfilm MS 638; for 1858-1900, numeric files are on
    Genealogical Society microfilm; after 1900, estate files are available in the
    original. Held with Ontario Court Records.

7. Wellington District/ Wellington Co. **Surrogate Court. Registers, 1840-1859.** 7
    inches. Loc: AO. FA: RG 22, Series 317.
    Copies of all grants of probate, administration and guardianship issued by the
    court. Prior to late 1858, the format consisted of copies of the wills, the
    registrar's certification and affidavits of witnesses. Register 'A' covers
    1840-1847 and is indexed; register 'B' is from 1847 to 1853; and register 'C'
    covers from 1854 to 1859. Registers are available on Genealogical Society
    microfilm. Held with Ontario Court Records.

WELLINGTON COUNTY

8. Spotton, Anson, Judge. **Notebook of legal cases, 1922-1927.** 5 cm. Loc: NAC. MG
    30, E 245.
    Anson Spotton practiced law in Harriston from 1900 to 1914; from 1915 to 1921
    he was junior County Judge for Wellington and from 1922 to 1928 Surrogate County

Judge. The notebook lists cases tried by Judge Spotton between 1922 and 1927 with summaries of charges, testimonies and verdicts. The notebook also contains a judicial enquiry into relief irregularities in Guelph in 1925.

9.   Wellington Co. **Chancery Court. Decrees, 1873-1893.** 12 file folders. Loc: WCA. List of file folder headings.
     A record of chancery court decrees about failures to pay financial debts.

10. Wellington Co. **Clerk of the Peace. Account book, 1913-1924.** 1 ledger. Loc: WCA.
     A record of receipts and payments of the clerk of the peace.

11. Wellington Co. **Clerk of the Peace and Crown Attorney. Daily journal, 1914-1919.** 1 volume. Loc: WCA.
     A record of the proceedings and financial transactions of court cases. The volume includes a series of brief records of the Homewood Sanitarium from 1915 to 1919.

12. Wellington Co. **Clerk of the Peace. Court fines register, 1914-1922.** 1 ledger. Loc: WCA.
     A register including names of person fined, amounts paids and reason for fine.

13. Wellington Co. **Clerk of the Peace. Court records, 1865-1866.** 1 file folder. Loc: AO. MU 2014.
     Records for the December 1865 and March 1866 quarters and for Guelph in 1865, including lists of convictions by Justices of the Peace. Thomas Saunders was Clerk of the Peace. Part of Marston Collection.

14. Wellington Co. **Clerk of the Peace. Minutes, 1873-1948.** 2 volumes. Loc: WCA.

15. Wellington Co. **Correspondence about certificates of judgements, 1881-1884.** 4 file folders. Loc: WCA.
     Letters from lawyers to the sheriff of Wellington County requesting information about any executions against specified lands.

16. Wellington Co. **County and Divisional Courts. Sittings, 1894.** 1 file folder. Loc: AO. MU 2387.
     A printed calendar of all court sittings scheduled for the year by order of H.W. Peterson, Clerk of the Peace. The County Court met every month in Guelph, bimonthly in each of Fergus, Elora, Drayton, Arthur and Mount Forest, quarterly in Aberfoyle, Rockwood and Erin, while Divisional Court 10 met bimonthly, but alternately, in Harriston and Palmerston. Part of the Reynolds Collection.

17. Wellington Co. **County Jail. Correspondence, 1880-1899.** 12 file folders. Loc: WCA.
     Correspondence of the county jail that includes several letters regarding transfer of lunatics to the Hamilton Asylum.

18. Wellington Co. **County Jail. Registers and lists, 1840-1973.** 10 volumes. Loc: AO. FA: RG20, F-13.
     Records include the jail register, 1840-1863; register of confined debtors, 1845-1852; miscellaneous prisoners' lists, 1859-1863; jail registers, 1876-1973;

and inspection book, 1873-1921. Part of the major record group for the Ontario Ministry of Correctional Services.

19. Wellington Co. **Court and Jail. Reports and correspondence, 1911-1968.** 10 file folders. Loc: WCA.
    A record of financial reports and correspondence concerning the administration of justice and the jail. One of the files indicates that the Guelph Jail was condemned in 1911.

20. Wellington Co. **Court expenses, 1857-1891.** 36 file folders. Loc: WCA.
    A record of expenses including baliff's correspondence regarding dockets 1884-1885, and receipts and invoices 1880-1889.

21. Wellington Co. **Court judgements, certificates, bonds, orders, decrees, 1863-1918.** 11 file folders. Loc: WCA.

22. Wellington Co. **Court receipt book, 1860-1874.** 1 ledger. Loc: WCA.
    A record of individuals involved in court cases and amounts of funds received as result of court decisions.

23. Wellington Co. **Divisional Court (10th). Cash book, 1927-1951.** 1 ledger. Loc: HTH.
    A record of the date of cases, individuals involved, and amounts paid in proceedings of the 10th Division Court at Harriston.

24. Wellington Co. **Divisional Court (10th). Procedure book, 1894-1903.** 1 ledger. Loc: WCA.
    Records for 1894-1899 microfilmed with Wellington County Tax Roll 1868-1942 and Tax Land Sales Book, 1884-1946. Records for 1899-1903 microfilmed with records of Suburban Roads Commission 1918-1947 and Committee of Management of House of Industry, 1931-1949.

25. Wellington Co. **Divisional Court (6th). Cash books, 1891-1946.** 2 ledgers. Loc: WCA.
    A record of funds and the amount received from individuals involved in court cases heard in the Divisional Court in Elora.

26. Wellington Co. **Divisional Court (6th). Committee reports for selection of jurors, 1879-1971.** 1 ledger. Loc: WCA.
    Filed with Elora municipal records.

27. Wellington Co. **Divisional Court (6th). Court records, 1856-1875.** 1 file folder. Loc: UGA. XR1 MS A115019.
    A series of court records, including transcripts for a court case dealing with a child support dispute in the 1870s, several summonses, a record of convictions for 1865 and a number of specific court judgement statements. Held with the Connon Collection.

28. Wellington Co. **Divisional Court (6th). Foreign procedure book, 1891-1937.** 1 ledger. Loc: WCA.
    A record of summons received in Wellington County from individuals residing outside Elora. Filed with Elora municipal records.

29. Wellington Co. **Divisional Court (6th). Judges' list for sittings, 1916-1929.**
    1 ledger. Loc: WCA.
    Filed with Elora municipal records.

30. Wellington Co. **Divisional Court (6th). Lawyers' account books, 1880-1899;**
    1905-1906. 2 ledgers. Loc: WCA.
    A record of estate accounts. Filed with Elora municipal records.

31. Wellington Co. **Divisional Court (6th). Letter book, 1891-1903.** 1 ledger. Loc:
    WCA.
    Filed with Elora municipal records.

32. Wellington Co. **Divisional Court (6th). Order book of executions, 1872-1939.** 2
    volumes. Loc: WCA.
    A record of plaintiffs and defendants involved in court cases. Filed with
    Elora municipal records.

33. Wellington Co. **Divisional Court (6th). Procedure books, 1883-1914.** 2 volumes.
    Loc: WCA.
    A record of individuals involved in court cases that notes the claim of the
    plaintiff and the decision of the court. Filed with Elora municipal records.

34. Wellington Co. **Divisional Court (6th). Receipt book, 1915-1932.** 2 ledgers.
    Loc: WCA.
    Filed with Elora municipal records.

35. Wellington Co. **Dockets, 1860-1900.** 11 boxes, alphabetical by name. Loc: WCA.
    Records of criminal cases that include court proceedings and written witness
    accounts. Case dockets list defendant, residence and year.

36. Wellington Co. **High Court. Subpoena to John McAteer, November 1909.** 1
    document. Loc: GCM.
    A notice sent to McAteer commanding him to appear before the High Court of
    Justice, Guelph, regarding properties he owned in the city. The subpoena informs
    McAteer the issue is related to 'the matter of School Sites Act 9, Edward 7th,
    Chapter 93 and the Guelph Board of Education and Teehan'. The dispute was over
    properties McAteer owned on Waterloo and Galt Streets in Guelph.

37. Wellington Co. **Insolvency register, 1875-1878.** 1 ledger. Loc: GCM.
    A listing of the name of insolvent, residence, place of business, trade or
    profession, timing of assignment of writ, and a statement of assets and
    liabilities. The ledger has references to several areas in Wellington County
    including Guelph, Fergus, Drayton, Mount Forest, Elora, Harriston, Clifford and
    Erin. The record is held in a box entitled, 'Account books'.

38. Wellington Co. **Justices of the Peace. Return, 1872.** Loc: AO. FA: MU 455.
    Part of Byerly Papers.

39. Wellington Co. **Lawyers' correspondence regarding dockets, 1879-1883.** 5 boxes.
    Loc: WCA.

40. Wellington Co. **Record of convictions, 1898-1919**. 1 ledger. Loc: WCA.
    A record of name of prosecutor, name of defendant, nature of charge, date of conviction, name of convicting justice, amount of penalty, when paid, to whom paid, and general observations.

41. Wellington Co. **Record of sale of goods and land, 1856; 1859-1892**. 7 file folders. Loc: WCA.
    A record of sale of land that includes legal documents and letters.

42. Wellington Co. **Schedule of accounts, 1932-1948**. 2 ledgers. Loc: WCA.
    A record of accounts that notes name of claimant, name of office, amount of claim, amount allowed, and date paid.

43. Wellington Co. **Selection of Grand Jurors. Lists, 1840-1858; 1889; 1891-1892; 1894; 1910-1919; 1946-1947**. 18 volumes, 8 file folders. Loc: WCA.
    A record of grand jurors that lists name, number of lot, concession or street and employment of individual.

44. Wellington Co. **Sheriff. Account books, 1855-1874**. 1 ledger. Loc: WCA.
    Receipts and expenditures by the sheriff that notes the dates of various transactions. The record includes the records of the Court of Chancery 1861-1874, accounts 1861-1874, and pay list for court officials for the years 1863-1874.

45. Wellington Co. **Surrogate Court. Filings, 1860-1871**. 2.5 inches. Loc: AO. FA: RG 22, Series 319.
    Documents for which there is no entry in the registers (Series 317) and which appear to have never been formally registered with the court. There are files for Joseph Greasley, 1860; Hugh Stewart, 1861; Thomas Learmont, 1863; Silas Edwards, 1864; John Wood, 1865; James Haggett, 1866; D.W. Dayfoot, 1868; Sarah Thorp, 1868; Daniel Campbell, 1869; John Graham, 1869; Edward Lynch, 1869; William Smith, 1869; David Jones, 1870; Agnes Bolls, 1871; and Henry Grindle, 1871. Held with Ontario Court Records.

46. Wellington Co. **Surrogate Court. Letter of guardianship, 1874**. 1 document. Loc: WCA. MU42.
    A legal document appointing Mary Brown of Fergus guardian of Lawrence Munro, child of a recently deceased Fergus physician, Dr John Munro.

47. Wellington Co. **Writs, 1858-1918**. 2 boxes. Loc: WCA.
    A record of writs that notes the plaintiff, defendant and amount owed.

JURY SELECTION RECORDS

48. Arthur Tp. **Jury Selection. Minute book, 1879-1972**. 1 volume. Loc: ATO.
    A record of procedures for the selection of jurors, including notes of the number of jurors selected.

49. Eramosa Tp. **Jury Selection. Documents, 1895-1972**. 1 suitcase. Loc: ETO.
    A large number of rolls for jury selection in Eramosa Township. The rolls note the name, place of residence and occupation of jurors. The rolls are labelled 'for the roll of Jurors to serve in his Majesty's High Court of Justice'. The

collection also includes some oaths of service records for jurors selected.

50. Eramosa Tp. **Jury Selection. Minute books, 1879-1972.** 2 volumes. Loc: WCA, ETO. Records of the proceedings, including oaths of individuals who held the position of selector of jurors. The ledger for the years 1879-1912 is held by the WCA, that for 1913-1972 at the Eramosa Township Office.

51. Erin Tp. **Jury Selection. Lists, 1933-1961.** 1 ledger. Loc: WCA.

52. Garafraxa W Tp. **Jury Selection. Minute book, 1889-1947.** 1 ledger. Loc: WCA. The back of the ledger records the construction of drainage ditches from 1901 to 1906.

53. Guelph. **Jury Selection. Minute book, 1921-1972.** 1 volume. Loc: GCH. Proceedings of the selection includes names of the selectors and, in several instances, names of the jurors. The records are held in the Clerk's office vault.

54. Guelph Tp. **Jury Selection. List, 1853; minute book, 1879-1916.** 1 file folder; 1 volume. Loc: WCA. The 1853 list includes jurors' names, addresses and occupations. Most are listed as 'yeoman'. A note in the minute book states that a committee was established under the Jurors Act of 1879.

55. Maryborough Tp. **Jury Selection. Lists, 1907-1972.** 1 ledger. Loc: WCA. A record of the name of the last person selected for jury duty and the names of the officials who selected the jury.

56. Puslinch Tp. **Jury Selection. Lists, 1874-1875.** 1 file folder. Loc: WCA. The 1874 list is also held on microfilm.

Management in action: the Wellington County Council, 1896.
An extensive account of the council's activities is provided in a
complete set of council minutes from 1850 to 1968.
(Wellington County Museum and Archives)

MUNICIPAL RECORDS

Municipal records can provide rich material for research in many fields including history, geography, sociology, political science, planning, public administration and heritage conservation. They are particularly relevant to the new focus of social history on the experiences, perceptions and attitudes of ordinary people. All too often, however, such records have been inadequately preserved, despite legislation that compels municipal officers to draft and implement records retention policies. Scott James estimated in 1980 that only one per cent of North American municipalities had records management or archives programs.[1]

Wellington District was first defined for judicial and administrative purposes in 1838 and proclaimed in 1840 when the district courthouse and jail were built at Guelph. The territory of Wellington District included almost all of what later became Wellington, Waterloo and Grey Counties; and before 1849 much of the same area was also defined as the County of Waterloo for land registration, electoral and militia purposes. At first, there was an autocratic system of district government, the Justices of the Peace meeting four times a year to try legal cases and supervise local administration. In 1841, the first District Councils Act brought in an elected council to replace the Justices and in 1846 the central government gave up its powers of appointing officials of the council.[2]

Districts were generally replaced by counties as units of local government in 1850, and Wellington District was abolished and replaced by the County of Waterloo, though the county seat remained in Guelph. In 1852, this large county was subdivided into the counties of Waterloo (administered from Berlin), Grey (administered from Owen Sound) and Wellington (administered from Guelph). Until the early 1880s, when the new County of Dufferin was formed around the county town of Orangeville, Wellington County also included Amaranth Township, what became East Garafraxa and East Luther Townships and the village of Orangeville.[3]

---

[1] R. Scott James, 'Administration of municipal records: the Toronto experience,' **Government Publications Review** 8 (1981): 321. See also Peter A. Baskerville and Chad M. Gaffield, 'The crisis in urban documentation: "the shame of the cities" revisited,' **Urban History Review** 13 (1984): 1-8; H.G. Jones, **Local government records: an introduction to their management, preservation and use** (Nashville, TN: American Association for State and Local History, 1980).

[2] Frederick H. Armstrong, **Handbook of Upper Canadian Chronology** (Toronto: Dundurn, 1985), 195-6.

[3] Thomas A. Hillman, 'A statutory chronology of southwestern Ontario,' **Canadian Papers in Rural History** 6 (1988): 343-353.

Table 1

KEY EARLY DATES FOR TOWNSHIPS IN WELLINGTON COUNTY

Township	Indian Alienation	First Survey	First[1] Settler	Municipal Organization	Area[2] (acres)
Amaranth[3]	1818	1823	1827	1854	63,884
Arthur	1836	1819	1841	1850	68,823
Eramosa	1818	1819	1819	1827	45,127
Erin	1818	1819	1820	1824	70,400
Garafraxa[4]	1818	1821	1823	1842	92,632
Guelph	1793	1828	1827	1850	42,338
Luther[5]	1818	1837	1850	1860	89,000
Maryborough[6]	1825	1849	1849	1854	56,775
Minto[7]	1836	1853	1853	1857	72,587
Nichol	1793	1819	1823	1832	28,512
Peel	1793	1843	1846	1850	74,647
Pilkington[8]	1793	1808	1819	1852	30,033
Puslinch	1793	1828	1829	1836	59,800

Sources: Compiled from **Historical Atlas of Wellington County** (1906); F.H. Armstrong, **Handbook of Upper Canadian chronology** (1967, 1985), 141-8 (after Wightman); T.A. Hillman, 'A statutory chronology of southwestern Ontario, 1792-1981,' **Canadian Papers in Rural History Volume VI** (1988), 350-3; and **Inventory** contents.

Notes:
1. First legal settler.
2. **Historical atlas** (1906).
3. United with Garafraxa to 1854; detached from Wellington to form part of new County of Dufferin in 1881.
4. Divided in 1869 into two townships, West Garafraxa and East Garafraxa, the latter separating from Wellington County in 1881 to form part of Dufferin County. No municipal records earlier than 1869.
5. United with Arthur to 1860; divided in December 1880 into two townships of West Luther and East Luther, the latter being joined with Dufferin County in 1883.
6. United with Peel to 1854.
7. United with Arthur to 1857.
8. Separated from Woolwich Township (Waterloo County) in 1852.

Several townships exercised limited powers of self-government under the district system, Erin and Eramosa from the 1820s, Nichol and Puslinch from the 1830s and Garafraxa from 1842. But formal incorporation of these and other townships (Arthur, Guelph and Peel) dates only from the Municipal Corporations Act of 1850. As Table 1 shows, some townships were united with others for periods of time after 1850 before their populations had grown enough to warrant separate municipal status.

Table 2

URBAN MUNICIPALITIES OF WELLINGTON COUNTY

Place	Village	Town	City	Population 1881	Population 1941
Guelph		1851	1879	9,890	27,386
Elora	1858			1,387	1,247
Fergus	1858	1952		1,733	2,832
Orangeville	1863	1873		2,847	2,718[1]
Mount Forest	1864	1879		2,170	1,892
Arthur	1871			1,257	937
Harriston	1872			1,772	1,305
Clifford	1873			722	464
Drayton	1873			587	504
Palmerston	1874			1,828	1,418
Erin	1880			c500	499

Note: [1] Orangeville became county town for the new Dufferin County in 1881.

Eleven urban centres in Wellington County have been incorporated as cities, towns and villages (see Table 2). Under the legislation, a community was supposed to have a population of at least 1,000 to be incorporated as a village, 3,000 for town status and 15,000 for cityhood. In practice, these requirements were not enforced very strictly so that Wellington has three of the fifty Ontario villages that never reached a population of 750, let alone 1,000.

Each incorporated municipality -- township, city, town or village -- was defined as 'a Body Corporate' with all the powers and responsibilities for that grade of place. In all cases, councils elected by ratepayers on a property franchise had the power to levy taxes on assessed property and to borrow money (subject to certain limits) to pay for local improvements and services. Only cities were independent of the county council.[4]

Some small settlements attained the status of police village rather than formal incorporation as a separate municipality. Police villages are unincorporated and subordinate to the townships in which they are located, but have limited powers to 'abate nuisances' and provide some fire protection. Seven communities in Wellington County became police villages -- Moorefield (1898), Hillsburgh (1899), Belwood (1900), Orton (1901), Rockwood (1903),

---

[4] For an account of the incorporation of urban municipalities, which places Wellington County in the larger context of Ontario, see Elizabeth Bloomfield and Gerald Bloomfield, **Urban Growth and Local Services: the Development of Ontario Municipalities to 1981** (Guelph, 1983).

Morriston (1916) and Eden Mills (1929).[5] In addition, the archival records suggest that Aberfoyle in Puslinch Township was a police village, at least from 1876 to 1893.

Clerks of all municipalities -- counties, cities, towns, villages, townships -- have long been required to maintain the official records such as bylaws, minutes of council proceedings, cash books, annual financial statements, assessment rolls[6] and voters' lists. They may also hold special reports, correspondence, maps and plans, and the records of special boards and commissions, such as health, planning, parks, police and utilities. The extent to which these records have survived varies from place to place. Early in our survey, we appraised the completeness of what we had found and renewed our efforts to locate the specific materials that were missing. Some gaps that remain can be explained by fires in the municipal offices. Possibly other inactive records may have been stored offsite and then forgotten.

With the establishment of the Wellington County Museum and Archives in former County House of Industry and Refuge in the 1970s, the Archives became the designated repository for the older municipal records of the Wellington County Council itself and of the county's 21 component townships, towns and villages. At first, some municipalities decided to retain their inactive records but since the renovation of the Museum and Archives in 1986 the pace of transfer has quickened. Almost all of the records extant for the period before 1940 have now been transferred from the township and village offices to the Archives.

The City of Guelph has retained its surviving records in City Hall, but is now acting to ensure that microform copies of bylaws, minutes, and assessment rolls are placed in the Guelph Public Library and University of Guelph Library archival collections.[7]

In the 1960s the Genealogical Society of Salt Lake City microfilmed some types of local municipal records as part of a much larger microfilming project. Microfilm copies of the council minutes and assessment and collectors' rolls, usually for the period before 1900, were usually deposited in the Archives of Ontario. Copies of some of these microfilms are also held by local repositories.

---

[5] Hillman, 'A statutory chronology' has details of the erections of police villages (p. 353).

[6] Historical researchers in the past 20 years have made quite frequent use of assessment rolls in combination with the manuscript census and directories. The value and limitations of this source are described in G.O. Levine, 'Criticizing the assessment: views of the property evaluation process in Montreal 1870-1920 and their implications for historical geography,' **Canadian Geographer** 28 (1984): 276-284.

[7] We hope that the surviving records for the City of Guelph, when all traced, can be fully described following the excellent model of Carolyn Gray, **Historical records of the City of Hamilton, 1847-1973** (1986).

WELLINGTON DISTRICT

57. Wellington District. **Clerk-Treasurer. Cash book, 1840-1856.** mf. Loc: WCA, AO. AO: MS 132.
A record of cash transactions including collection of taxes, and the supply of goods and services.

58. Wellington District. **Clerk-Treasurer. Cash books, 1843-1850.** 1 ledger. Loc: WCA.
A record of the expenditures and receipts of the district, which lists individuals who paid or received funds, noting the date when transactions were made.

59. Wellington District. **Clerk-Treasurer. Correspondence, 1842-1851.** 17 file folders. Loc: WCA. List of file folder headings.
A record of correspondence of the district clerk on various municipal matters, including a record of salaries paid to teachers in 1848-1849, and a loan to erect a building to receive diseased emigrants in 1847.

60. Wellington District. **Clerk-Treasurer. Letter book, 11 May 1842 to 19 January 1849.** 1 reel. mf. Loc: WCA, AO. AO: MS 115.
The letter book covers the 2nd to the 24th session and shows that Richard Fowler Budd was District Clerk and A.D. Fordyce Warden.

61. Wellington District. **Council. Bylaws, 1842-1849.** 1 reel. mf. Loc: WCA.

62. Wellington District. **Council. Minutes, 1842-1856 (1842 indexed).** 3 volumes. Loc: WCA.

63. Wellington District. **Land register, 1839-1846.** mf. Loc: WCA, AO. AO: MS 132.
A record of grants of wild lands which lists individuals who received land, number of lots, and when payments were made for purchases.

64. Wellington District. **Marriages. Register, volume 7, 1843-1845.** 1 volume. Loc: WCA.
Official district register reproduced by the Archives of Ontario. The register lists name, residence, date and witnesses of the marriage. May be referenced under Gore District.

65. Wellington District. **Promissory notes, 1848; 1867.** 4 documents. Loc: GCM.

66. Wellington District. **Roads Department. Account of new roads, debentures, tolls, expenditures, 1841-1858.** 2 volumes. mf. Loc: WCA.
Transactions and bylaws for the building of new roads, including applications by various individuals. The 1841 roads ledger was later used to record information about residents of the House of Industry in 1887.

67. Wellington District. **School district boundaries, 1842.** 1 file folder. Loc: AO. FA: RG 2, F-1.
Legal definitions in terms of concessions, lots, divisions and blocks of each school section. Seven districts were defined in Guelph Township, four in

Garafraxa Township, nine in Erin Township, five in Eramosa Township, five in Nichol Township and nine in Woolwich Township (which included the Pilkington Block). Held with the records of the Ontario Ministry of Education.

68. Wellington District. **School population returns, 1842-1843.** 2 p. Loc: AO. FA: RG-2, F-2, Envelope #12.

A report by Richard Fowler Budd, Wellington District Clerk, to the provincial secretary, revising an earlier estimate of only 2,902 children aged between five and sixteen years to a total of 4,320. The higher figure was derived from the results of the 1842 census. Budd urgently requested that the apportionment of the school grant to Wellington District be increased proportionately. Held with the Ontario Department of Education records.

WATERLOO COUNTY

69. Waterloo Co. **7th Session. Journal of proceedings, December 1851.** 19 pp. Loc: UWL. F 10523.

Contains report of the committee to consider the petition of the Nichol Township Council for aid to destitute emigrants from the Highlands and Islands of Scotland who had arrived in Fergus. The County Council, meeting at Guelph, also approved a $2,000 loan to the Guelph and Arthur Road Company to build a gravelled road through Nichol Township.

70. Waterloo Co. **Letter to A.D. Ferrier forwarding resolution of Committee on Roads and Bridges, 1856.** Loc: AO. MU 4840 #2.

A letter from the Clerk of Waterloo County concerning road and bridge connections between Woolwich Township and Peel Township.

WELLINGTON COUNTY

71. Wellington Co. **Cemetery Commission. Minutes, 1932-1934; 1950-1964.** 1 box. Loc: WCA. List of file folder headings.

The minutes include a list of county cemeteries and a statement of condition.

72. Wellington Co. **Clerk-Treasurer. Committee reports, 1931-1966.** 5 boxes. Loc: WCA.

Reports of county committees of roads, schools, legislation, property, finance, assessment, hospitals and the Home for the Aged.

73. Wellington Co. **Clerk-Treasurer. Correspondence, 1850-1880; 1903; 1934-1948.** 27 file folders. Loc: WCA. List of file folder headings.

Correspondence regarding financial matters, including property taxes, road and bridges committee, and schools. The file also includes a report for 1888.

74. Wellington Co. **Clerk-Treasurer. Correspondence with City of Guelph, 1878-1944; account books of transactions, 1879-1911; 1946-1968.** 3 volumes and 3 file folders. Loc: WCA.

Correspondence includes financial statements of Guelph Township in 1878.

75. Wellington Co. **Clerk-Treasurer. Debenture register, 1857-1897.** 2 ledgers. Loc: WCA.

A record of county debentures that lists amount of money invested and use to be made of the investment.

76. Wellington Co. **Clerk-Treasurer. General accounts, 1923-1940.** 1 ledger. Loc: WCA.
A record of the finances of Wellington County which includes references to expenses incurred by or granted to specific departments and individuals.

77. Wellington Co. **Clerk-Treasurer. Legal agreements, 1866-1922.** 38 file folders. Loc: WCA.
Records of legal agreements between the county and various individuals and companies. The records include several agreements regarding inmates of the House of Industry.

78. Wellington Co. **Clerk-Treasurer. Municipal returns and statistics, 1938-1966.** 29 file folders. Loc: WCA. List of file folder headings.
A summary of the assessed value and equalized assessment rates for all the municipalities in the county, and municipal financial statistics for the years 1957 to 1960.

79. Wellington Co. **Clerk-Treasurer. Passbook for account at Ontario Bank, 1869-1872.** 1 item. Loc: WCA.

80. Wellington Co. **Clerk-Treasurer. Petitions and reports, 1872.** 300 file folders. Loc: WCA. List of file folder headings.

81. Wellington Co. **Council. Bylaws, 1852-1895.** 1 reel. mf. Loc: WCA.

82. Wellington Co. **Council. Consolidated bylaws and records, 1888; 1905; 1922.** 3 volumes. Loc: WCA.
Summaries of bylaws with lists of Wellington County officials for various years.

83. Wellington Co. **Council. Minutes, 1850-1968.** 118 volumes. Loc: WCA.
The organization of the minutes varies with some years being bound separately and later bound volumes including a number of years.

84. Wellington Co. **Council. Records and bylaws, 1842-1888.** 334 p. Loc: GPL.
A reprint of records and bylaws from the District Council's first meeting in 1842 to end of June 1888. Printed by John J. Kelso Ltd.

85. Wellington Co. **Council. Records and bylaws, 1842-1922.** 424 p. Loc: GPL.
A complete list of the records and bylaws of the County Council for each year. Printed by the Guelph Herald Ltd.

86. Wellington Co. **Council. Standing rules and regulations, 1869.** 8 p. Loc: GPL.
A reprint of the county council's rules on meetings, bylaws, committees. Printed by the Mercury.

87. Wellington Co. **Court House. Contract for a new addition, February 25, 1873.** mf. Loc: WCA, AO. AO: MS 132.
A contract between John Mair, Warden of the County, and Thomas Dobbie, contractor of the project, which also notes Stephen Boult was the architect.

88. Wellington Co. **Court House. Specifications for the court house and jail renovations, 1878; 1911; 1928; 1930.** 1 file folder. Loc: WCA.
Written reports that state exact specifications of renovations to be made. J.H. Hacking and W.A. Mahoney are listed as the architects of the 1878 and 1911 additions.

89. Wellington Co. **Electoral. Election proclamations, 1854; 1860-1861; 1866.** 2 file folders. Loc: WCA.
A record of five election proclamation posters which note when elections would take place in Wellington County. The posters refer to Wellington County as being part of the Electoral Division of Brock.

90. Wellington Co. **Electoral. Federal election expenses, nomination petitions and correspondence, 1857-1859; 1861; 1863; 1878-1879; 1890-1891.** 19 file folders. Loc: WCA. List of file folder headings.

91. Wellington Co. **House of Industry. Admission records, 1877-1971.** 1 ledger. Loc: WCA. Restricted.
A record of admission of residents of the institution which notes when specific individuals entered, lists their age and gender, municipality sent from, occupation of males who entered, and county officials who admitted residents. The records become less detailed by the 1880s with less information regarding how long each person remained at the institution.

92. Wellington Co. **House of Industry. Burial register, 1877-1971.** 1 ledger. Loc: WCA. Restricted.
A record of burial that includes name, date of death, cause of death, age, place interred and remarks.

93. Wellington Co. **House of Industry. Committee of Management minutes, 1931-1947.** mf. Loc: WCA.
Microfilmed with 10th Division Court Procedure Book, 1899-1903 and records of Suburban Roads Commission, 1918-1947.

94. Wellington Co. **House of Industry. Reports, minutes and correspondence, 1872-1957 (sporadic).** 8 file folders. Loc: WCA.

95. Wellington Co. **House of Industry. Reports of expenses, equipment, and building projects, 1931-1971.** 4 ledgers. Loc: WCA.
A record of various aspects of the institution including expenses, fees paid by inmates 1940-1971, tender for a new addition in 1956 and a ledger of cash accounts from 1939 to 1941.

96. Wellington Co. **House of Industry. Visitors' register, 1878-1931; 1970-1983.** 4 volumes. Loc: WCA.
A list of visitors and their addresses, with an occasional remark noted such as 'religious services'.

97. Wellington Co. **Marriages. Registers, 1858-1869.** 3 volumes, 1 reel. Loc: AO, WCA. FA: AO: RG 8, Series 1-6-B.
Legislation in 1857 to provide for the registration of all marriages performed

by clergymen led to the creation of county marriage registers. Wellington County marriages are recorded in Series 1-6-B, Volumes 78-80, also on microfilm as MS 248, Reel 17. Generation Press of Agincourt has produced a computerized index and printout to Wellington County marriages that includes details for person (bride or groom), father's name, name of spouse, year of marriage and reference (volume and page).

98. Wellington Co. **Ministers' Book. Register of oaths of allegiance, 1847-1864.** 1 ledger. Loc: WCA. MU46.
   Oaths of allegiance to the crown of ministers and leaders of the congregation, as required by the 1847 Act. Each oath is signed by the County Registrar, H.W. Peterson, Sr.

99. Wellington Co. **Old Age Pensions Board. Minutes, 1941-1948.** 1 volume. Loc: WCA.
   A record of recommendations of the pension board for various individuals for old age pension or mother's allowance.

100. Wellington Co. **Property Assessment. Non-resident land assessment registers, 1868-1943.** 17 ledgers. Loc: WCA.
   A record of tax arrears, interest charged and date paid, with an occasional record of name. There is a separate ledger for each municipality.

101. Wellington Co. **Property Assessment. Register of lands in arrears of taxes, 1870-1882; 1908-1948.** 1 ledger, 8 file folders. Loc: WCA.
   Records of tax arrears that note name, concession lot, acres and tax amounts due.

102. Wellington Co. **Property Assessment. Tax roll, 1868-1942.** mf. Loc: WCA.
   A record of the amount of tax paid which lists amounts according to municipality and lot or street number.

103. Wellington Co. **Property Assessment. Tax sales register, 1884-1949.** 1 ledger. Loc: WCA.
   A record of taxes paid for land sold in the county that notes location of lots, acreage of land, and date of sale. Also available on microfilm with the Tax Roll, 1868-1942.

104. Wellington Co. **Property Assessment. Valuation reports, 1881; 1887; 1891; 1942.** 3 ledgers, 1 file folder. Loc: WCA.
   A record of lots, buildings, improvements and value of property. The 1942 reports gives details of the place of residence and assessment of specific individuals in various localities.

105. Wellington Co. **Roads Department. Contracts 1920-1939; tenders, 1930-1939.** 16 file folders. Loc: WCA.

106. Wellington Co. **Roads Department. Correspondence, 1927-1935.** 15 file folders. Loc: WCA.

107. Wellington Co. **Roads Department. General account ledger, 1928-1939.** 1 ledger. Loc: WCA.
   A record of the costs of road construction and maintenance.

Austere charity: the Wellington County House of Industry and Refuge, c1880.
The 'Poor House' was opened in 1877 and administered by the County Council.
Monthly reports of its operation are found in the council minutes.
(Wellington County Museum and Archives)

108. Wellington Co. **Roads Department. Specification reports, 1926-1939.** 14 file folders. Loc: WCA.

109. Wellington Co. **Roads Department. Tolls book, 1864-1868.** mf. Loc: AO. MS 132, Reel 2.

    The preamble refers to Bylaw 119 of 8 December, 1865 which named the various main roads of Wellington County, numbered the toll gates on each and specified the toll-keepers and the monthly payments they had to make to the county. The record is combined on a microfilm reel with Wellington District records relating mainly to the 1840s.

110. Wellington Co. **School Fund. Legislative grants, 1858-1874.** 1 ledger. Loc: WCA. MU46.

    A list of school sections and amount of legislative and municipal grants for Erin, Eramosa, Guelph and Puslinch Townships. In 1871, Nichol, Pilkington and Garafraxa East Townships start to be included occasionally.

111. Wellington Co. **School Fund. Legislative grants to Wellington North, 1870-1872.** 3 items. Loc: AO. FA: RG-2, G-4, Box 1, Envelope #7.

    Statements by A.D. Fordyce, Superintendent of Schools, regarding government grants to school section boards in North Wellington. Amaranth Township had seventeen school sections (and two united sections); Arthur had eleven (and four united); Luther, ten (and two united); Pilkington, five (and two united); East Garafraxa, seven (and one united); West Garafraxa, nine; Maryborough, twenty (and one united); Peel, sixteen (and five united); Minto, ten (and three united); and Nichol, six. Held with records of Ontario Department of Education.

112. Wellington Co. **Suburban Roads Commission. Minutes and accounts, 1918-1947.** 2 volumes. Loc: WCA.

    Also microfilmed with 10th Division Court Procedure Book, 1899-1903 and minutes of House of Industry Committee of Management, 1931-1947.

GUELPH TOWN/CITY

113. Guelph/ Wellington Co. **Arbitration. Minutes, 1879.** 1 volume. Loc: GCH.

    Minutes of arbitration between the County of Wellington and the City of Guelph occasioned by the municipal separation of Guelph, as a city, from the county. The arbitration adjusted debts, liabilities, and claims between the two municipalities according to law.

114. Guelph. **Board of Conciliation. Dispute between Guelph Radial Railway Company and its workers, September 1919.** 1 document. Loc: GCH.

    A brief outline of the activities of the board to settle a dispute between Guelph Radial Railway Company and its workers that were part of the Amalgamated Association of Street and Electric Railway Employees of America. The document outlines representatives of both sides of the dispute but does not discuss the basis of the controversy.

115. Guelph. **Board of Health. Annual report of Medical Health Officer, 1909; 1911.** 1 document. Loc: GCH.

    A record of the incidence of diseases diagnosed during the year including smallpox, tuberculosis, diphtheria, scarlatina, and typhoid fever. The officer recommended that milk vendors should be required to purchase licenses and that records should be kept regarding standards of meat sold. The record is held in the Clerk's office vault.

116. Guelph. **Board of Health. Annual reports, 1909; 1911. 3 documents. Loc: GCH.**
A record of the board's activities which included brief discussions of issues such as the mortality rate, the 'milk question', high infant mortality, infectious diseases, health bylaws, and recommendations for specialized infectious hospital treatment centres.

117. Guelph. **Board of Health. Minutes, 1895-1967. 4 volumes. Loc: GCH.**
A record of regular meetings of the board that up to the 1920s are concerned with contagious diseases, water closets, sewage, inspection of slaughter houses, dairies, bakeries, garbage collection and the need for an isolation or quarantine hospital. The records are held in the Clerk's office vault.

118. Guelph. **Board of Parks Management. Financial statements, 1910-1913. 4** documents. Loc: GCH.
Four separate typewritten reports.

119. Guelph. **Board of Parks Management. Minutes, 1908-1918; 1948-1966. 4 volumes.** Loc: GCH.
The minutes for 1908-1909 are in the same volume as the minutes of the Parks and Shades Committee for 1897-1907 and the Markets and Public Buildings and the Parks and Shades Committee for 1903-1909.

120. Guelph. **Board of Water Commissioners. Bylaws, plans and deeds, 1891; 1900; 1909-1910; 1915-1916; 1919-1920. 3 file cabinet drawers. Loc: GCH.**
Cabinet drawer entitled, 'Waterworks Bylaws and Deeds'. The records describe the city's plans to expropriate land in order to extend a pipeline to Puslinch Township to preserve the purity of its water supply. The records are held in the Clerk's office.

121. Guelph. **Board of Water Commissioners. Bylaws, rules and regulations, 1918. 1** booklet. Loc: GCH.
A printed record of bylaws, an extract from the Ontario Public Utilities Act, and schedule of water rates. The report is held in the Clerk's office vault.

122. Guelph. **Board of Water Commissioners. Minutes and reports, 1878-1884; 1896-1902.** 2 volumes. Loc: GCH.

123. Guelph. **Board of Water Commissioners. Orders, specifications and agreements, 1908-1910; 1915-1916; 1920-1924. 1 file cabinet drawer. Loc: GCH.**
A record of plans, contracts and specifications to build water conduits, pumps, boilers, and agreements to expropriate lands. The records are held in a file cabinet drawer entitled, 'Waterworks, Orders of Railway Board, and Specification Agreements', in the Clerk's office.

124. Guelph. **Board of Water Commissioners. Report and financial statement, 1878-1880. 1 booklet. Loc: GCH.**
A brief history of the development of the water works begun in 1878, tenders

for the engine house, pumping engines, boilers and pipes, pipe laying and fire hydrant locations, service pipe locations, and a detailed financial statement that includes a monthly report of labourers' names and wages. The report is held in the Clerk's office vault.

125. Guelph. **Board of Water Commissioners. Reports, 1899; 1904-1905; 1909; 1914-1916.** 1 file cabinet drawer. Loc: GCH.

A record of various reports that includes an examination of the water supply for the fire department, the municipal fire preventive appliances in the city, provincial Board of Health inquiry about using water from the Torrance Creek, provincial Board of Health's bacteriological reports of the water supply indicating that purification would be necessary for safety, a proposed sewage system for St Patrick's Ward, and annual reports of the Guelph Water Commissioners from 1908 to 1913. The records are held in the Clerk's office.

126. Guelph. **Board of Water Commissioners. Water supply system at Exhibition Park specifications, 1919.** 2 documents. Loc: GCH.

A description of a plan to build a water supply system at the park for the superintendent's residence. The record includes an assessment and brochure from the National Equipment Company of Toronto outlining the procedures and costs of installing the system. The records are held in the Clerk's office vault.

127. Guelph. **Board of Works. Financial and project reports, 1908; 1910.** 3 documents. Loc: GCH.

A record of public works projects which notes where work was done and the costs incurred by the city. Projects included road paving, storm drains, sidewalks, storm sewers, and sewage disposal works. The records include a separate document noting financial statements incurred for building sewers in 1909. The records are held in the Clerk's office vault.

128. Guelph. **Board of Works. Minutes, 1879-1893; 1905-1914; 1918-1956; 1962-1965.** 2 volumes to 1893; 10 volumes from 1905. Loc: GCH.

Minutes for 1879-1883 are in the same volume as the minutes of the Road and Bridge Committee (1869-1879), while minutes for 1884-1893 are in the same volume at the Railway Committee minutes (1869-1884). The records are held in the Clerk's office vault.

129. Guelph. **Census report, April 1, 1861.** 1 ledger. Loc: GCH, GPL.

A manuscript record of name, age and religion of individuals in the east, south, west and north wards. At the end of each ward section the report lists totals for male and female population, place of birth, religion, boys and girls attending school, male and female illiterates over 20 years of age, deaths, widowers, widows, horses, cows, pigs, value of livestock, number of graveyards, number of stores and industries, number of dwelling houses made of frame, stone, brick and log, and number of coloured persons. The original report, compiled by W.S.G. Knowles, is held in the Clerk's office vault, and there is a typescript copy at the Guelph Public Library.

130. Guelph. **Council. Bylaw for the better government of the town, Bylaw No. 164, 9 July, 1867.** Loc: GCH.

A general bylaw to repeal and replace several bylaws previously enacted by the town, consisting of 88 clauses ranging over a wide variety of subjects regarding public morals or conduct or the operations of the town. An index is appended to the bylaw.

131. Guelph. **Council. Bylaws, 1851-1983.** 50 file cabinet drawers. Loc: GCH.
     The original bylaws, which are manuscript, typewritten, or sometimes apparently clipped from newspapers, are held in small filing cabinet drawers in the Clerk's office. In addition to the bylaws themselves, indentures, lists of ratepayers and assessments, debentures, details of public expenditure and projects, and acts of the provincial Legislature are often included. Several plans in the earlier decades have survey plans appended. The bylaws have also been microfilmed in 31 reels covering the years 1851 to 1970 and 1976 to 1983.

132. Guelph. **Council. Committee reports, 1910-1925; 1928-1946.** 21 volumes. Loc: GCH.
     A collection of committee reports in typewritten form held in the Clerk's office vault.

133. Guelph. **Council. Condolence letter, 1857.** 1 document. Loc: GCM.
     A letter expressing the sympathy of Guelph Council to the Sunley family on the death of Mayor George Sunley in March, 1857.

134. Guelph. **Council. Consolidated bylaws, 1924.** 323 p. Loc: WCA, GPL.
     A printed, cumulative summary of all Guelph bylaws in force in 1924.

135. Guelph. **Council. Minutes, 1851-1986.** 15 volumes. Loc: AO, WCA, GPL, GCH. AO: GS 3174-3176.
     The original minutes are held at Guelph City Hall. The minutes for 1851-1899 were microfilmed by Genealogical Society of Salt Lake City and are held by the Archives of Ontario, the Wellington County Archives and the Guelph Public Library.

136. Guelph. **Council. Rules of procedures, Bylaw No. 241, 15 December, 1873.** 1 item. Loc: GCH.
     A published version of the bylaw, printed by the Herald Book and Job Printing House in Guelph, to regulate the proceedings of the town council, define the powers of committees and regulate the payment of monies.

137. Guelph. **Electoral. Voters' lists, 1877-1880; 1882-1883; 1899; 1906; 1911; 1917-1934; 1937-1940; 1942-1963.** 64 volumes. Loc: GCH, UGA, GCM, AO. UGA: XR1 MS A195.
     Lists for 1879-1880, 1883 and 1911 are held by AO; 1899 by UGA; 1906 by GCM; other years are in GCH Clerk's office vault.

138. Guelph. **Finance Committee. Minutes, 1869-1890; 1895-1922; 1926-1963.** 11 volumes. Loc: GCH.

139. Guelph. **Finance Committee. Special report, 1929.** 1 document. Loc: GCH.
     Proceedings of a special meeting of the Finance Committee recommending changes to the antiquated system of municipal bookkeeping and tax assessment and the bookkeeper's duties. The records are held in the Clerk's office vault.

140. Guelph. **Fire, Light and Water Committee. Minutes and reports. 1903-1923.** 4 volumes. Loc: GCH.

The records are held in the Clerk's office vault.

141. Guelph. **Guelph Union Cemetery Committee. Auditor's report, 1908.** 1 document. Loc: GCH.

142. Guelph. **Guelph Union Cemetery Committee. Financial statements, 1910-1912.** 3 documents. Loc: GCH.

143. Guelph. **Investigations. Aldermen, 1907.** 1 document. Loc: GCH.

A brief discussion of allegations that two aldermen received gravel from city supplies and billed the Board of Works for labour needed to transfer supplies. The report recommends that the judge of the county be asked to conduct an investigation of aldermen Kennedy and Barber who were alleged to have improperly utilized municipal funds. The document is in the ledger of the Guelph City Council minutes from 1886 to 1964 and is held in the Clerk's office vault.

144. Guelph. **Investigations. Aldermen, 1909.** 2 documents. Loc: GCH.

A record of questions asked of several aldermen and witnesses to determine if certain municipal officials were bribed to support the passage of a bylaw extending the hours of pool halls on Saturday nights. Judge Chadwick concluded in an accompanying handwritten report that there was no evidence to find aldermen guilty of bribery. The inquiry was responding to allegations that 'H.N. Norrish had paid certain monies toward a fund to carry a certain bylaw and that a fund of 100 dollars had been raised and used for the purpose of bribing aldermen of the city'. Judge Chadwick found that Norrish had said he paid money to such a fund but concludes that such statements 'were without foundation'.

145. Guelph. **Investigations. Finance Committee, 1928.** 1 file. Loc: GCH.

A report and recommendations of the investigation into the Assessor's and Tax Collector's Department. The investigators were attempting to improve the efficiency of the department. The report was submitted May 4, 1928. The records are held in the Clerk's office vault.

146. Guelph. **Investigations. Fire Department, 1912.** 1 file. Loc: GCH.

A request for an investigation into the Fire Department of the City of Guelph by the Fire and Light Committee, April 30, May 1, 3, 4, 1912, that was unanimously requested by officers and men of the Fire Department. The men threatened that if the resignation of Chief Finch was not asked for, the entire company would immediately resign. The records are held in the Clerk's office vault.

147. Guelph. **Investigations. Police Department, 1913.** 1 file. Loc: GCH.

Proceedings of an investigation into the conduct of the chief of police that include charges of drunkenness, theft, driving his personal vehicle 'at an immoderate rate', receiving 'kickbacks', and making arrests and alleging criminal activities without due process of law. The records are held in the Clerk's office vault.

148. Guelph. **Investigations. Relief Department, February 10-12, 16-19, 1925.** 1 volume. Loc: GCH.

A record of the court proceedings of an investigation by Judge Spotton of the conduct of the City Relief Officer, James Cassidy, for failing to keep financial records, destroying records, granting relief to fictitious persons and retaining money and groceries for himself, and profiteering through the sale of a house to Moses Tudge, whose family received relief on two occasions. Alderman W.P. Evan's involvement was also implicated in the charges. The judge recommended that a new system of bookkeeping be instituted in order to minimize 'crookedness'. He concludes that 'in the end, the only real safeguard is the honesty and good sense of the official'.

149. Guelph. **Judicial. Appeal to Supreme Court of Canada, 1918**. 1 file. Loc: GCH.
A Guelph City appeal against an award of damages to Harry Mahoney, respondent and mayor, for personal injuries suffered in a 1916 explosion that demolished a dam on the Speed River in an attempt to prevent flooding at the Huskisson Street Bridge. Mahoney sought 4,000 dollars in damages. The record is held in the Clerk's office vault.

150. Guelph. **License Committee. Reports, 1869-1883**. 1 volume. Loc: GCH.
Reports on the granting of business licenses.

151. Guelph. **Light and Heat Commission. Reports, 1906-1912; financial statements, 1906-1916**. 8 documents. Loc: GCH.
A record of activities of various departments, including gas, electric, and community services, as well as a financial statement for each year.

152. Guelph. **Market House Committee. Minutes, 1860-1902**. 1 volume. Loc: GCH.
The 1860-1869 minutes are preserved in the same volume as the minutes of the Road and Bridge Committee (1860-1869). From 1877 to 1902, the Market House committee was also responsible for the Drill Shed and Public Buildings. The records are held in the Clerk's office vault.

153. Guelph. **Markets, Public Buildings, Parks and Shades Committee. Minutes, 1903-1923**. 3 volumes (parts) Loc: GCH.
The committee was also responsible for markets and public buildings and the winter fair from 1903 to 1909; the minutes for 1897-1909 are in the same volume as the minutes of the Board of Parks Management, 1908-1909.

154. Guelph. **Mortgage agreements, 1850; 1853; 1858; 1861; 1864; 1867; 1869; 1873-1875; 1877-1879; 1881-1885; 1887-1906; 1909-1927; 1929-1930; 1934-1935; 1942; 1944**. 47 documents. Loc: GCH.
A record of land transactions between individuals and companies which includes the sale and leasing of land. The records are held in the Clerk's office vault.

155. Guelph. **Mortgages, deeds and contracts, 1832-1954 (sporadic)**. 7 file cabinet drawers. Loc: GCH.
The records over various years are filed in drawers labelled, 'Items: 1-132'. The contracts are primarily concerned with construction, roads and drains, and include an agreement in 1887 for the Guelph Junction Railway Company to lease lands from the Canadian Pacific Railway Company. The records are held in the Clerk's office.

156. Guelph. **Parks and Shades Committee. Minutes and reports, 1878-1903.** 2 volumes. Loc: GCH.

The volume for 1878-1897 also includes minutes of the Drill Shed Committee (1869), the Central Exhibition Committee (1871 and 1876), and Parks and Exhibition Committee (1878). The minutes for 1897-1903 are in the same volume as the records of the Markets and Public Buildings and Parks and Shades (1903-1909) and the Board of Parks Management (1908-1909).

157. Guelph. **Petition in support of prohibiting the sale of alcohol, c1897.** 1 document. Loc: GCM.

A listing of several hundred Guelph residents who supported the prohibition of the sale of 'spirituous, fermented or other manufactured liquors'. The document is not dated but refers to a Liquor License Act passed in 1897. The record lists individuals and their place of residence in the city and was presented to Guelph City Council.

158. Guelph. **Plan of Guelph water supply showing location of springs and proposed conduit, c1880.** Loc: AO. D-3.

159. Guelph. **Police Commission. Financial statements, 1907-1912.** 4 documents. Loc: GCH.

A record of four handwritten reports listing the costs of operating the police force.

160. Guelph. **Printing Committee. Reports, 1869-1879.** 1 volume. Loc: GCH.

In the same volume as the reports of Special Committees, 1886-1907.

161. Guelph. **Property Assessment. Assessment rolls, 1852-1853; 1855-1902; 1904-1913; 1928-1939.** 92 ledgers. Loc: GCH.

These original records are held in the Clerk's office barrel vault.

162. Guelph. **Property Assessment. Assessment rolls, 1852-1898.** 17 reels. mf. Loc: UGL, AO, WCA, GPL.

A record of tax assessments, dividing the town by ward and division, including names and occupations, description and value of real property, personal and statistical information and the date by which notice of assessment was given. The Archives of Ontario and Guelph Public Library hold the full set of microfilms; the University of Guelph holds only 1852-1861, 1870-1871, and 1880-1881; the Wellington County Archives has 1852 and 1862-1865. Microfilmed by the Genealogical Society of Salt Lake City.

163. Guelph. **Property Assessment. Collectors' rolls, 1885-1888; 1891-1905; 1908-1909; 1911-1920.** 28 ledgers. Loc: GCH.

The records are held in the Clerk's office barrel vault.

164. Guelph. **Property Assessment. Court of Revision minutes, 1932-1956.** 1 volume. Loc: GCH.

Minutes and proceedings of appeals of taxation assessment rates previously approved. The volume records the names of those granted an appeal, their addresses, and rate upon appeal. The records are held in the Clerk's office vault.

165. Guelph. **Property Assessment. Individuals' tax assessments, 1899-1925 (sporadic).**
12 documents. Loc: GCM.
Twelve tax assessments of residents of Guelph.

166. Guelph. **Property Assessment. Separate school supporters, 1933-1949.** 2 ledgers.
Loc: GCH.
A record of individuals who supported Catholic schools which notes the name,
place of residence and amount paid. The records are held in the Clerk's office
barrel vault.

167. Guelph. **Railway and Manufacturers Committee. Reports, 1903-1923.** 2 volumes.
Loc: GCH.
Reports on railway matters including stations and the Guelph Junction Railway
and invitations to manufacturing businesses to locate in Guelph.

168. Guelph. **Railway Committee. Minutes, 1869-1893.** 1 volume. Loc: GCH.
In the same volume as the minutes of the Works Committee, 1884-1893. Held in
the Clerk's office vault.

169. Guelph. **Railway Committee. Reports, 1883-1902.** 2 volumes. Loc: GCH.
Reports on railway matters including stations and the Guelph Junction Railway
and invitations to manufacturing businesses to locate in Guelph.

170. Guelph. **Relief Committee. Minutes, 1939-1959.** 1 volume. Loc: GCH.
Short accounts of meetings that offer little specific information about
persons and types of relief payments. The records are held in the Clerk's office
vault.

171. Guelph. **Road and Bridge Committee. Minutes, 1860-1879.** 2 volumes. Loc: GCH.
Minutes for 1860-1869 are in the same volume as minutes of the Market House
Committee; minutes for 1869-1879 are in the same volume as the minutes of the
Board of Works from 1879 to 1883. The records are held in the Clerk's office
vault.

172. Guelph. **Sewerage and Public Works Committee. Minutes and reports, 1903-1910;
1914-1918.** 2 volumes. Loc: GCH.
The records are held in the Clerk's office vault.

173. Guelph. **Special and Standing Committees. Reports, 1869-1910.** 6 volumes. Loc:
GCH.

174. Guelph. **Special Committee. Reports, 1910-1964.** 3 volumes. Loc: GCH.

175. Guelph. **Treasurer. Auditors' reports, 1897-1941.** 74 volumes, 4 documents. Loc:
GCH.
The annual auditors' reports include financial statements for the city of
Guelph, the Board of Light and Heat Commissioners, the Waterworks Department,
the General Hospital, the Elliott Home, Guelph Junction Railway, public schools,
Guelph Collegiate Institute, Guelph Board of Education, Guelph Public Library,
Guelph Cemetery Commission, and summaries of the 'sinking fund investments'. The
record includes four individual documents of the auditor's reports for the years
1906; 1912-1914. The records are held in the Clerk's office vault.

176. Guelph. **Treasurer. Cash book, 1879.** 1 ledger. Loc: GCH.

Cash book and ledger with notations regarding expenditures for municipal and county buildings, a select list of bylaws with costs attached c1848-1879, a list of assessment totals for the municipality from 1851 to 1877, and private notes from a Court of Arbitration meeting of July 30, 1879. The record is held in the Clerk's office vault.

177. Guelph. **Treasurer. Financial statements, 1892; 1908-1912.** 3 booklets, 22 documents. Loc: GCH.

A record of receipts and expenditures for the city of Guelph, including Free Library, public schools, Collegiate Institute, and the police commissioners for the year 1892. The record includes 22 individual documents listing the receipts and expenditures from 1908 to 1912. The records are held in the Clerk's office vault.

178. Guelph. **Waterworks Office. Receipts, 1910; 1925.** 2 documents. Loc: GCM.

Two receipts to individuals for water service.

ARTHUR TOWNSHIP

179. Arthur Tp. **Board of Health. Minutes, 1932-1948.** 1 volume. Loc: ATO.

The Board of Health usually met three times each year. There are only brief entries for each meeting.

180. Arthur Tp. **Council. Bylaws, 1909-1940.** 1 volume. Loc: ATO.

A record of bylaws relating to financial agreements between Arthur Township and Arthur Village.

181. Arthur Tp. **Council. Minutes, 1850-1862; 1864-1921.** 2 reels. mf. Loc: WCA.

182. Arthur Tp. **Council. Minutes, 1850-1899.** 2 reels. mf. Loc: AO. GS 3080-3081.

Microfilmed by the Genealogical Society of Salt Lake City.

183. Arthur Tp. **Council. Minutes, 1850-1921; 1931-1978.** 12 volumes. Loc: ATO.

184. Arthur Tp. **Electoral. Voters' list, 1880.** 1 ledger. Loc: WCA.

A list of voters eligible for provincial and municipal elections, noting names, place of residence, and whether an owner or tenant.

185. Arthur Tp. **Financial. Cash books, 1856-1864.** 1 ledger. Loc: ATO.

A record of municipal expenditures and accounts with companies and individuals.

186. Arthur Tp. **Financial. Cash books, 1930-1948.** 2 ledgers. Loc: ATO.

A record of municipal expenditures which includes references to hydroelectricity accounts, families and individuals receiving relief in the 1930s. The ledger indicates the type of relief granted to families and individuals.

187. Arthur Tp. **Property Assessment. Assessment rolls, 1930-1937; 1940.** 8 ledgers. Loc: ATO.

188. Arthur Tp. **Property Assessment. Collectors' rolls, 1932-1938; 1940-1941.** 10 ledgers. Loc: ATO.

ERAMOSA TOWNSHIP

189. Eramosa Tp. **Board of Health. Minute books, 1884-1898; 1913-1948.** 2 volumes. Loc: WCA.
A record of the activities of the board with notes of incidence of diseases reported in the township.

190. Eramosa Tp. **Cemeteries. Plan of Everton Cemetery.** 1 file folder. Loc: WCA.
A record of the location of the plots of specific interments in the cemetery.

191. Eramosa Tp. **Census and assessment records, 1825-1828; 1832-1833; 1837-1840.** mf. Loc: AO. MS 700.
A series of extracts from the Gore District municipal records. The census and assessment data are separate for 1825 and 1840, combined for all other years.

192. Eramosa Tp. **Clerk-Treasurer. Letter books, 1883-1909.** 2 volumes. Loc: WCA.
A record of correspondence of municipal officials implementing the decisions of the township council.

193. Eramosa Tp. **Council. Bylaws, 1850-1875; 1900-1908.** 2 volumes. Loc: WCA.
A record of bylaws with years 1850 to 1875 in original and microfilm copy, and the years 1900 to 1908 available on microfilm. Bylaws and minutes of the township council are also available in printed form for the years 1858, 1867 and 1900.

194. Eramosa Tp. **Council. Correspondence, 1866; 1880.** 4 file folders. Loc: WCA.
A letter regarding sale of land, two undated envelopes, and three declarations of office for overseer, fence viewer and pound keeper.

195. Eramosa Tp. **Council. Journal of proceedings, 1854.** 27 p. Loc: WCA.
A record of the council proceedings that include minutes, bylaws and accounts for 1854.

196. Eramosa Tp. **Council. Minutes, 1836-1940.** mf. Loc: WCA.
A record of minutes, handwritten for the years 1836 to 1872 and 1891 to 1936, and printed for the period 1863 to 1867, and 1867 to 1940.

197. Eramosa Tp. **Council. Minutes, bylaws and financial statements, 1883-1884; 1886-1890; 1895-1899; 1932; 1935-1938.** 17 volumes. Loc: GPL, ETO.
Annual printed summaries of Eramosa Township minutes, bylaws, and financial statements. The Guelph Public Library has the records for 1883-1884 and 1886-1890, while the Eramosa Township Office has the records for 1895-1899, 1932 and 1935-1938.

198. Eramosa Tp. **Electoral. Poll book, 1865-1874.** 3 volumes. Loc: WCA.
A record of the municipal poll book which lists candidates and individuals who voted for them. The source also indicates individuals who held the position of returning officer.

199. Eramosa Tp. **Electoral. Voters' list, 1910.** Loc: AO.

200. Eramosa Tp. **Financial. Accounts, 1867-1926.** 1 ledger. Loc: WCA.
A record of funds granted various services including poor relief, schools, road and bridge work, and salaries of employees.

201. Eramosa Tp. **Financial. Cash books, 1894-1936.** 2 ledgers. Loc: ETO.
The date spans of the two ledgers overlap.

202. Eramosa Tp. **Financial. Receipts, 1835; 1875.** 3 file folders. Loc: WCA.
Receipts for payment of taxes, books, and surveying.

203. Eramosa Tp. **Property Assessment. Assessment rolls, 1851-1899.** 4 reels. mf.
Loc: AO. GS 3109-3112.
Microfilmed by the Genealogical Society of Salt Lake City.

204. Eramosa Tp. **Property Assessment. Assessment rolls, 1851-1946; 1947; 1953.** 97
volumes. Loc: WCA.

205. Eramosa Tp. **Property Assessment. Collectors' rolls, 1886-1904; 1906-1921;
1923-1953.** 63 volumes. Loc: WCA.

206. Eramosa Tp. **Property Assessment. Non-resident assessment register, 1869-1933.**
1 ledger. Loc: WCA.
A record of taxes paid by non-residents land owners.

207. Eramosa Tp. **Rockwood Board of Health. Minutes, 1899-1912.** 1 volume. Loc: ETO.
A record of regular meetings of the board in which William Sunter and Noah
Sunley participated. The volume contains several letters in 1903 and 1904
regarding James Keough's Slaughter House in Rockwood.

208. Eramosa Tp. **Rockwood PV. Account books, 1930-1936.** 1 ledger. Loc: WCA.
A record of the accounts and expenditures of Rockwood Police Village.

ERIN TOWNSHIP

209. Erin Tp. **Board of Health. Minutes, 1909-1947.** 1 volume. Loc: WCA.
A record of meetings held twice annually.

210. Erin Tp. **Census and assessment records, 1824-1834; 1837-1840.** mf. Loc: AO. MS
700.
A series of extracts from the Gore District municipal records. The census and
assessment data are combined for most years but separate for 1825 and 1840. The
1833 details are with those for Garafraxa Township.

211. Erin Tp. **Clerk-Treasurer. Account books, 1887-1905.** 2 ledgers. Loc: WCA.
The ledger from 1900 to 1905 is a day book of expenditures of the Police
Village of Hillsburgh.

Purchasing winter firewood at the Guelph City Hall and Market, c1880.
The Bell organ factory is visible in the left background.
(Guelph Public Library, Alf Hales Collection)

212. Erin Tp. **Clerk-Treasurer. Correspondence, 1890-1973.** 1 box. Loc: WCA.
A collection of correspondence regarding utilities, taxes, ditches, fences and general municipal financial issues.

213. Erin Tp. **Council. Annual reports with financial statements, 1866; 1895; 1898-1899; 1902; 1904; 1919; 1921-1927; 1930; 1933.** 20 volumes. Loc: WCA.
Printed annual reports of council sessions, bylaws and financial statements of receipts and expenditures.

214. Erin Tp. **Council. Auditors' reports, 1874-1877; 1880-1910; 1938-1941.** 1 box. Loc: WCA.

215. Erin Tp. **Council. Bylaws, 1874-1932.** 24 file folders. Loc: WCA.
A collection of handwritten bylaw documents.

216. Erin Tp. **Council. Declarations of office and qualifications of office, 1890-1910; 1918-1966.** 7 file folders. Loc: WCA.
Declarations of oaths of municipal council officers.

217. Erin Tp. **Council. Journal of proceedings, 1866; 1903.** 2 volumes. Loc: WCA.
A published record of council activities which includes financial statements.

218. Erin Tp. **Council. Minutes, 1855-1878; 1889-1949.** 7 volumes. mf. Loc: WCA.

219. Erin Tp. **Electoral. Legislative franchise assessment rolls, 1922-1926.** 3 ledgers. Loc: WCA.
Each page is entitled, 'persons assessed for legislative franchise only'.

220. Erin Tp. **Electoral. Nomination records for municipal council, 1915-1939.** 1 ledger. Loc: WCA.
Included in the ledger are newspaper clippings of bylaws from 1911 to 1923.

221. Erin Tp. **Electoral. Voters' lists, 1910; 1920; 1924; 1931.** 4 booklets. Loc: WCA, AO.
A record of eligible voters which lists lot and concession number, name and occupation of specific township residents. AO has only the 1910 list.

222. Erin Tp. **Financial. Cash books, 1854-1875; 1898-1950.** 8 ledgers. Loc: WCA.
A record of individual and company accounts with the township.

223. Erin Tp. **Financial. Receipts and expenditures, 1903.** 1 ledger. Loc: WCA.
A detailed, printed financial statement.

224. Erin Tp. **Financial statements, 1892; 1896-1899; 1903-1904; 1919-1920; 1923-1924; 1927; 1929; 1932.** 16 volumes. Loc: WCA.

225. Erin Tp. **Property Assessment. Assessment rolls, 1870; 1875; 1877; 1879; 1881; 1883-1884; 1895; 1900; 1904; 1908-1909; 1911-1918; 1920-1959.** 52 ledgers. Loc: WCA.
The volumes from 1870 to 1900 are in very poor condition. The records from 1881 to 1900 are also on microfilm.

226. Erin Tp. **Property Assessment. Collectors' rolls, 1871; 1907-1935; 1937. 30** ledgers, 1 reel. mf. Loc: WCA.
    The 1871 records are on microfilm.

227. Erin Tp. **Property Assessment. Statute labour register, 1919-1925. 1 ledger.** Loc: WCA.

228. Erin Tp. **Skating Rink Board. Minutes, 1934-1956. 1 volume. Loc: WCA.**

WEST GARAFRAXA TOWNSHIP

229. Garafraxa E Tp. **Property Assessment. Assessment rolls, 1861. 1 ledger. Loc:** WCA.

230. Garafraxa Tp. **Census and assessment records, 1833-1834; 1837. mf. Loc: AO. MS** 700.
    A series of extracts from the Gore District municipal records. The 1833 details are combined with those for Erin Township.

231. Garafraxa W Tp. **Board of Health. Minutes, 1885-1947. 1 volume. Loc: WCA.**
    A record of meetings held approximately four times a year that, in the early years, discussed cases of diphtheria, typhoid, smallpox, unsafe slaughter houses and school water closets.

232. Garafraxa W Tp. **Clerk-Treasurer. Correspondence and financial statements, 1871;** **1884; 1887; 1920; 1922; 1924; 1931; 1933; 1935-1957; 1962-1968. 14 file** folders. Loc: WCA.
    Records of finances and land and road agreements, appointment of a police constable, and the installation of street lights. The files include a brief letter written in 1884 outlining the terms of the Land Improvement Fund by the central government in the 1850s.

233. Garafraxa W Tp. **Council. Bylaws, 1861; 1880; 1883; 1887; 1889; 1896; 1905;** **1907; 1911-1912; 1914-1923; 1926; 1928-1929; 1935-1952; 1954-1963. 52 file** folders. Loc: WCA.
    A record of bylaws which includes an index ledger for the years 1936 to 1970.

234. Garafraxa W Tp. **Council. Minutes, 1867-1899. 1 reel. mf. Loc: AO. GS 3144.**
    Microfilmed by the Genealogical Society of Salt Lake City.

235. Garafraxa W Tp. **Council. Minutes, 1869-1965. 9 volumes. Loc: WCA.**
    The minutes are held in manuscript form for the entire period and in microfilm only for the years 1869-1899.

236. Garafraxa W Tp. **Electoral. Nominations for council, 1889-1912. 1 file folder.** Loc: WCA.
    A record of the nomination of reeves, deputy reeves, and councillors which also notes who was elected in various years.

237. Garafraxa W Tp. **Electoral. Voters' list; 1910. Loc: AO.**

238. Garafraxa W Tp. **Financial. Account books, 1869-1881; 1896-1901; 1916-1956.** 3 ledgers. Loc: WCA.
    A record of receipts and expenditures.

239. Garafraxa W Tp. **Financial. Bank passbooks, 1934-1948.** 7 items. Loc: WCA.
    A record of banking transactions of the township at the Imperial Bank of Canada in Fergus.

240. Garafraxa W Tp. **Financial. Cash books, 1907-1940.** 3 ledgers. Loc: WCA.

241. Garafraxa W Tp. **Financial. Debentures, 1917.** 1 file folder. Loc: WCA.
    A record of township debentures and amount of interest to be paid when debenture matures.

242. Garafraxa W Tp. **Financial. Insurance policies, 1927-1941.** 1 ledger. Loc: WCA.
    A record of accident and fire insurance policies held by the township.

243. Garafraxa W Tp. **Financial. Tax arrears, 1868; 1918-1957.** 1 box. Loc: WCA.

244. Garafraxa W Tp. **Local Improvements. Ditches and water courses award record, 1908-1944.** 1 ledger. Loc: WCA.
    A record of an agreement between the owner of land and the engineer to construct drainage ditches.

245. Garafraxa W Tp. **Local Improvements. Drainage ditch awards, 1885-1960.** 1 box. Loc: WCA.
    A record of correspondence and plans between individuals and township officials regarding construction of ditches.

246. Garafraxa W Tp. **Local Improvements. Wire fence grants, 1907-1927.** 1 ledger. Loc: WCA.
    A record of names, number of rods, and amount of grant to construct wire fences.

247. Garafraxa W Tp. **Property Assessment. Collectors' rolls, 1912-1949; 1952-1973.** 36 volumes. Loc: WCA.
    The collectors' rolls from 1952 to 1973 are combined with the assessment rolls for the same years and are held in 10 large ledgers.

GUELPH TOWNSHIP

248. Guelph Tp. **Agreement with Hydro Electric Power Commission. Correspondence, petitions and plans, 1916-1941.** 3 file folders. Loc: WCA.
    Proposed agreement for power supply and petition for light and power signed by eleven residents in 1916. Also letter and plan of land in Lot D, Division F, Concession BF, purchased by the commission in 1941.

249. Guelph Tp. **Board of Health. Minutes, 1884-1895; 1916-1948.** 2 volumes. Loc: WCA.
    Captain Walter Clark was Sanitary Inspector during most of the period from 1884 to 1895. The minute book for 1916 to 1948 has various items of correspondence, reports and returns attached.

250. Guelph Tp. **Census and assessment records, 1828-1834; 1837-1840**. mf. Loc: AO. MS 700.

   A series of extracts from the Gore District municipal records in which the census and assessment data are sometimes combined in one table and sometimes presented separately. The 1829 record also includes the Town of Guelph.

251. Guelph Tp. **Council. Bylaws, 1850-1914**. 5 volumes. Loc: WCA.

252. Guelph Tp. **Council. Bylaws and correspondence relating to Toronto and Guelph Railway, 1851-1870**. 2 volumes. Loc: WCA.

   The township subscribed a ten thousand pound bonus to the railway in 1851 and passed three further bylaws on the subject between 1852 and 1854. Only twenty-four pages of the bylaw volume have been used and only twenty-seven pages of the letterbook. The letterbook also contains details of tax arrears between 1856 and 1870.

253. Guelph Tp. **Council. Correspondence, 1851-1888**. 1 ledger; 4 file folders. Loc: WCA.

   A record of correspondence of the warden, reeve and clerk.

254. Guelph Tp. **Council. Minutes, 1850-1885**. 2 reels. mf. Loc: AO, WCA. AO:GS 3206.

   Microfilmed by Genealogical Society of Salt Lake City.

255. Guelph Tp. **Council. Minutes, 1850-1975**. 14 volumes. Loc: GTO, WCA.

   The minutes for the years 1850 to 1949 are at WCA; those for later years at the Guelph Township Office.

256. Guelph Tp. **Council. Notebook used for taking minutes, 1915-1920**. 1 volume. Loc: WCA.

   Short notes taken at various municipal meetings that include items to discuss and newspaper clippings about council issues.

257. Guelph Tp. **Electoral. Voters' lists, 1876; 1899; 1910; 1917; 1925; 1932**. 4 brochures, 1 file folder. Loc: GPL, UGA, AO, WCA. UGA: XR1 MS A195.

   The 1876 list is held at the GPL, the 1899 list at the UGA, the 1910 list at the AO, and the rest are at the WCA.

258. Guelph Tp. **Financial. Cash books, 1907-1970**. 6 ledgers. Loc: WCA.

   A record of cash receipts and payments of the township, with some years having more detailed entries.

259. Guelph Tp. **Financial. Invoices, 1886-1888**. 1 file folder. Loc: WCA.

   Ten invoices from various area companies.

260. Guelph Tp. **Financial. Passbooks, 1872-1877; 1911-1944**. 9 books. Loc: WCA.

   A selection of passbooks that record township accounts with the Royal Bank of Canada, and Wellington County accounts with the Ontario Bank of Guelph and the Traders Bank of Canada.

261. Guelph Tp. **Financial. Relief accounts, 1933-1940**. 4 ledgers, 1 file folder. Loc: WCA.

A record of food, fuel, and clothing given to residents of the township which also indicates companies and individuals who made donations. The record at times indicates the number of people in families receiving relief, and also lists amounts spent in some months on relief. The records note the relative amount of relief paid by the township and the provincial government.

262. Guelph Tp. **Financial. Tax arrears, 1911-1935.** 1 ledger. Loc: WCA.
A record of name, property and amount owed.

263. Guelph Tp. **Guelph Union Cemetery. Minutes, correspondence and financial report, 1856.** 19 p. Loc: WCA.

264. Guelph Tp. **Housing Commission. Minutes, 1919-1921.** 1 volume. Loc: WCA.
As in other municipalities at the time, the commission was set up to assist in housing veterans returning from World War I. The records show that only one application was processed, that of James Innes McIntosh of Crawford Street, College Heights.

265. Guelph Tp. **Local Improvements. Ditch awards, 1895-1921.** 2 ledgers. Loc: WCA.

266. Guelph Tp. **Plans. Sketch of Caraher's Bridge, c1900.** 1 plan. Loc: WCA.

267. Guelph Tp. **Property Assessment. Assessment and collectors' rolls, 1852; 1854; 1859-1866.** 1 reel. mf. Loc: AO, WCA. AO: GS 3205.
Microfilmed by the Genealogical Society of Salt Lake City.

268. Guelph Tp. **Property Assessment. Assessment rolls, 1927; 1929-1936.** 9 ledgers. Loc: GTO.

269. Guelph Tp. **Property Assessment. Collectors' rolls, 1851-1853; 1895-1900; 1928-1966.** 35 ledgers. Loc: GTO, WCA.
Tax records for the period 1851 to 1853 are held at the Wellington County Archives and include a section noting residents with tax payments in arrears. The ledgers for the years 1895-1900 and 1928-1936 are now held at the WCA and later records by the Guelph Township Office. Beginning in 1949 the assessment and collectors' rolls are held together in the same ledger each year.

270. Guelph Tp. **Property Assessment. Non-residents collectors' roll, 1855-1868.** 1 reel. mf. Loc: WCA, AO. AO: MS 132.
A record of tax arrears on land belonging to non-residents.

271. Guelph Tp. **Property Assessment. Statute labour list, 1849.** 1 file folder. Loc: WCA.
A record of householder's name, amount of assessment, number of days and name of person making claim. The brochure is entitled, 'List of persons liable for to perform Statute Labour in the Township of Guelph' and contains approximately 620 names including David Allan and George Elliott.

272. Guelph Tp. **Property Assessment. Statute labour petition, 1853.** Loc: AO. FA: MU 454.
A copy of Anne Keough's petition to be relieved from statute labour on lot belonging to Andrew Daly. Part of Byerly Papers.

273. Guelph Tp. **Reply by Adam Johnston Fergusson to petition regarding tavern licenses, 1851.** Loc: AO. FA: MU 454.
   Fergusson acknowledges the petition and promises to present it to the House of Assembly. Part of Byerly Papers.

WEST LUTHER TOWNSHIP

274. Luther W Tp. **Council. Minutes, 1869-1880; 1908-1985.** 10 volumes. Loc: WCA.
   A record of council meetings which includes periodic financial statements and notes details of some bylaws passed by council.

275. Luther W Tp. **Council. Minutes, 1869-1886.** 1 reel. mf. Loc: AO. GS 3214.
   Microfilmed by the Genealogical Society of Salt Lake City.

276. Luther W Tp. **Electoral. Voters' lists, 1910; 1924.** 1 ledger. Loc: WCA, AO.
   The AO has the 1910 list, WCA the 1924 list.

277. Luther W Tp. **Financial. Auditors' report, 1937.** 1 document. Loc: WCA.
   The handwritten document is held in the school accounts ledger.

278. Luther W Tp. **Financial. Cash books, 1889-1980.** 8 ledgers. Loc: WCA.

279. Luther W Tp. **Financial. Tax arrears, 1927-1935.** 1 document. Loc: WCA.

280. Luther W Tp. **Local Improvements. Drain cash book, 1889-1897; 1904-1936.** 2 ledgers. Loc: WCA.

281. Luther W Tp. **Property Assessment. Assessment rolls, 1915; 1920; 1922; 1924-1983.** 62 ledgers. Loc: WCA.

282. Luther W Tp. **Property Assessment. Collectors' rolls, 1902-1903; 1914-1954.** 66 ledgers. Loc: WCA.

283. Luther W Tp. **School accounts, 1889; 1895.** 1 ledger. Loc: WCA.
   A record of municipal grants to S.S.#1.

MARYBOROUGH TOWNSHIP

284. Maryborough Tp. **Clerk-Treasurer. Correspondence, 1868-1878; 1880; 1882-1942.** 23 file folders. Loc: WCA.
   A record of correspondence, contracts, roads, leases, four inspectors' reports of taverns in 1869, and a list of fence viewer awards for various years.

285. Maryborough Tp. **Council. Bylaws, 1885-1925; 1952-1970.** 5 volumes. Loc: MBH.

286. Maryborough Tp. **Council. Minutes, 1851-1935.** 10 volumes. Loc: MBH, WCA, AO.
   A record of regular council meetings that include copies of bylaws in an appendix at the end of each ledger. The minutes from 1851 to 1869 are held at WCA and AO as a microfilm copy made by the Genealogical Society of Salt Lake City.

63

287. Maryborough Tp. **Electoral. Election nominations, 1892-1918.** 1 ledger. Loc: WCA.
A record of nominations of municipal officers. The ledger also contains copies of correspondence on various matters.

288. Maryborough Tp. **Electoral. Voters' lists, 1879-1883; 1885; 1887-1911; 1917; 1925.** 1 box. Loc: WCA, AO.
AO has only the 1910 list.

289. Maryborough Tp. **Financial. Annual reports of receipts, expenditures, assets and liabilities, 1858; 1859; 1862; 1869-1871; 1878-1879; 1883; 1885; 1887; 1892; 1899; 1901; 1905; 1906; 1909-1911; 1913-1915; 1932-1933; 1935; 1936-1963; 1966.** 2 boxes. Loc: WCA.
A record of township council financial statements with reports in the years 1858 to 1885 in handwritten form, and records from 1887 to 1966 in a series of separately bound annual reports.

290. Maryborough Tp. **Financial. Cash books, 1879; 1890-1904; 1919-1924.** 5 ledgers, 1 file folder. Loc: WCA, MBH.
Cash books for the period 1894 to 1900 are held by the MBH.

291. Maryborough Tp. **Financial. Debenture ledger, 1899-1963.** 1 ledger. Loc: MBH.
A record of debentures issued by the Township of Maryborough. Each entry lists the amounts of debentures, bylaw number the transaction was issued under and when accounts were due on transactions. The majority of the entries are for the years after 1930.

292. Maryborough Tp. **Financial. Postal expenses, 1896-1904.** 1 ledger. Loc: WCA.
A record of monthly postal expenses.

293. Maryborough Tp. **Financial. Statements of treasurers' accounts, 1859; 1862; 1866; 1869; 1870-1871; 1873-1874; 1877-1878; 1883; 1887; 1892; 1897; 1901.** 1 box. Loc: WCA.
A series of handwritten treasurers' and auditors' reports for various years from 1859 to 1901.

294. Maryborough Tp. **Land records, 1878-1879; 1886; 1893; 1900; 1912.** 8 documents. Loc: MBH.
A record of seven land record agreements for land in Moorefield which includes a conveyance, mortgage and six deeds.

295. Maryborough Tp. **Local Improvements. Ditch agreements, 1886-1959 (sporadic).** 2 file folders. Loc: MBH. Agreements with owners for ditches.
A record of agreements between owners and council to construct a ditch.

296. Maryborough Tp. **Local Improvements. Ditches and drains, financial accounts, awards, agreements, and correspondence, 1883-1957.** 2 ledgers, 34 file folders. Loc: WCA. List of file folder headings.
A record of municipal accounts and transactions regarding the construction and maintenance of township ditches which includes references to ditch awards, agreements, reports, petitions, plans and contracts.

297. Maryborough Tp. **Moorefield PV. Council nominations, 1922-1966.** 1 volume. Loc: MBH.

 A record of yearly nominations for various municipal offices.

298. Maryborough Tp. **Moorefield PV. Minutes, 1919-1958.** 1 volume. Loc: MBH.

 A record of motions carried, members attending meetings and financial expenditures of the council. The meetings were held usually at least once every two months, with only brief entries for each council sitting. The volume is labelled, 'Police Village of Moorefield'.

299. Maryborough Tp. **Petitions, 1893; 1897; 1907.** 5 documents. Loc: MBH.

 A record of correspondence to township council with three documents relating to objections to the dismissal of a township engineer and two applications for a ditch award.

300. Maryborough Tp. **Property Asessment. Assessment rolls, 1879-1884; 1886-1891; 1895; 1897.** 1 reel. mf. Loc: AO. GS 3221.

 Microfilmed by Genealogical Society of Salt Lake City.

301. Maryborough Tp. **Property Assessment. Assessment rolls, 1879-1974.** 95 ledgers. Loc: WCA.

302. Maryborough Tp. **Property Assessment. Collectors' rolls, 1883-1884; 1911-1970.** Loc: WCA.

 The records are held on microfilm for the years 1883, 1884, and from 1911 to 1940, and in manuscript form for the years 1883, and 1911 to 1970.

303. Maryborough Tp. **Property Assessment. Statute labour ledger, 1919-1924.** 1 ledger. Loc: WCA.

304. Maryborough Tp. **Property Assessment. Tax receipts of John Dixon, 1894-1912; 1915-1934.** 1 envelope. Loc: WCA. MU43.

 A record of annual taxes paid by John Dixon who lived in Maryborough Township.

MINTO TOWNSHIP

305. Minto Tp. **Board of Health. Minutes, 1909-1944.** 2 volumes. Loc: MTH.

 A record of meetings that were monthly in the early years. By 1925, the board was meeting only several times per year.

306. Minto Tp. **Council. Bylaws, 1867-1924.** 3 volumes. Loc: MTH.

307. Minto Tp. **Council. Minutes, 1868-1877; 1891-1900.** 1 reel. mf. Loc: AO. GS 3235.

 Microfilmed by the Genealogical Society of Salt Lake City.

308. Minto Tp. **Council. Minutes, 1868-1877; 1891-1940.** 6 volumes. Loc: MTH.

309. Minto Tp. **Electoral. Voters' lists, 1893; 1910; 1924; 1965.** 3 books. Loc: WCA, AO.

 AO has only the 1910 list.

310. Minto Tp. **Financial. Cash book, 1889-1912.** 1 ledger. Loc: MTH.
     A record of money paid to individuals for providing municipal services.

311. Minto Tp. **Financial. Journal of accounts, 1916-1944.** 1 ledger. Loc: WCA.
     A record of annual receipts from taxes and debentures.

312. Minto Tp. **Local Improvements. Ditch awards, 1885-1916; 1919-1951.** 2 ledgers.
     Loc: MTH, WCA.
     A few entries indicating which individuals were granted ditch awards and
     where awards were filed. The ledger recording awards from 1885 to 1916 is held
     at the Wellington County Archives.

313. Minto Tp. **Property Assessment. Assessment rolls, 1861; 1868-1871; 1873-1875;
     1880-1886; 1888-1892; 1894-1899.** 3 reels, 84 volumes. mf. Loc: WCA, AO. GS
     3232-3234.
     Microfilmed by Genealogical Society of Salt Lake City. AO is reported to hold
     an original roll for 1861 as well as a set of microfilms. WCA hold both
     originals and microfilms for other years.

314. Minto Tp. **Property Assessment. Collectors' rolls, 1874-1898; 1900-1920;
     1940-1959.** Held individually by year. Loc: WCA.

NICHOL TOWNSHIP

315. Nichol Tp. **Census and assessment records, 1832-1834; 1837-1840.** mf. Loc: AO.
     MS 700.
     A series of extracts from the Gore District municipal records.

316. Nichol Tp. **Council. Bylaws, 1850-1954.** 4 boxes. Loc: WCA.

317. Nichol Tp. **Council. Minutes, 1832-1849.** 1 file folder. Loc: GPL.
     A handwritten copy by Hugh Douglass taken from the original minute book. The
     original minutes are noted to have been held by Mrs K. Marston of Elora.

318. Nichol Tp. **Council. Minutes, 1833-1964.** 5 reels. 3 boxes. Loc: AO, WCA. AO:
     MS 126; GS 3097.
     The Archives of Ontario holds microfilmed minutes in two series, 1833-1857
     and 1858-1899, the second having been filmed by the Genealogical Society of Salt
     Lake City. The early records show that James Elmslie was the first township
     clerk and that meetings were held in the homes of councillors. Minutes of the
     meetings after the Municipal Act came into force in January, 1850 are more
     systematic and detailed. Some pages at the end of the early ledger were
     apparently used by the new Elora Village Council in 1865. The Wellington County
     Archives holds original and microfilmed minutes for the period 1854-1965.

319. Nichol Tp. **Council. Municipal papers, 1851; 1864-1866.** 5 items. Loc: UGA. XR1
     MS A115018.
     A record of an oath of a police constable taken in 1851, auditors' statement
     in 1864, a notice calling for the holding of the Nichol Township Court of
     Revision in 1865, and a record of plans for nominating municipal officials in
     1866. The records are held with the Connon Collection in a folder entitled

'Nichol Township, 1851–1874'.

320. Nichol Tp. **Electoral. Voters' lists, 1867–1873; 1875–1877; 1879; 1882; 1886; 1891–1893; 1898–1899; 1903; 1910; 1912; 1915; 1921–22; 1924–1930; 1938.** 2 boxes. Loc: WCA, AO.
A record of eligible voters that notes those allowed to vote in both municipal and provincial elections, as well as listing individuals who could vote only at the municipal level. AO holds only the 1910 list.

321. Nichol Tp. **Financial. Auditors' statements, 1909; 1914–1930; 1938; 1945–1946.** 1 file folder. Loc: WCA.

322. Nichol Tp. **Financial. Receipts and expenditures, 1850–1903.** 41 file folders. Loc: WCA.

323. Nichol Tp. **Financial. Transactions, 1851; 1855–1860.** 6 file folders. Loc: WCA.
A collection of miscellaneous financial records with brief references to land debentures in 1851, township receipts in 1856 and from 1859 to 1860, orders to pay teachers in 1860, and receipts of the clergy reserve fund in 1859.

324. Nichol Tp. **Granting of tavern licenses, 1864.** 1 document. Loc: UGA. XR1 MS A115003.
A brief discussion of procedures relating to the granting of tavern licenses in Nichol Township. Held with the Connon Collection.

325. Nichol Tp. **Property Assessment. Assessment journals, 1900–1913.** 3 ledgers. Loc: WCA.
Assessment journals kept by A. Moir that notes name, address, age, occupation, property assessment, religion, births, deaths and dogs. Each year also includes a postage account and the names of children between the ages of 8 and 14.

326. Nichol Tp. **Property Assessment. Assessment rolls, 1841–1842; 1850; 1855; 1860–1900; 1902; 1913; 1915–1939.** Loc: WCA.

327. Nichol Tp. **Property Assessment. Assessment rolls, 1841–1842; 1850; 1863–1876; 1884–1894; 1896.** 3 reels. mf. Loc: AO. GS 3257–3258.
The 1841–2 and 1850 records are on MS 56 (reel 1) while the later years were microfilmed by Genealogical Society of Salt Lake City in 2 reels of the GS series.

328. Nichol Tp. **Property Assessment. Collectors' roll, 1841–1842; 1850–1851.** 1 reel; 1 item. Loc: UGA, AO. UGA: XR1 MS A115018.
AO has the 1841–2 and 1850 rolls on MS 56 (reel 1) while the 1851 roll is held with the Connon Collection at UGA.

329. Nichol Tp. **Property Assessment. Separate school supporters, 1874.** 1 item. Loc: UGA. XR1 MS A115018.
A list of supporters in Nichol Township which includes a note of the lot and concession number of each school supporter. Held with the Connon Collection in a folder entitled 'Nichol Township, 1851–1874'.

PEEL TOWNSHIP

330. Peel Tp. **Board of Health. Minute book, 1910-1944.** 1 volume. Loc: WCA.
A record of public health measures and financial transactions.

331. Peel Tp. **Council. Bylaws, 1854-1977.** 7 volumes. Loc: PTO, WCA.
The Wellington County Archives holds the bylaws from 1854 to 1948 on microfilm.

332. Peel Tp. **Council. Minutes, 1872-1899.** 1 reel. mf. Loc: AO. GS 3271.
Microfilmed by the Genealogical Society of Salt Lake City.

333. Peel Tp. **Council. Minutes, 1872-1974.** 11 volumes. Loc: PTO, WCA.
A record of council meetings usually held in Goldstone but at times council also convened in Yatton and Parker. The Wellington County Archives holds the minutes from 1872 to 1961 on microfilm.

334. Peel Tp. **Electoral. Voters' lists, 1884; 1893; 1895; 1898; 1903; 1906; 1910.** Loc: WCA, AO.
AO has only the 1910 list.

335. Peel Tp. **Financial. Auditors' reports, 1887; 1891; 1893-1896; 1926; 1935.** 7 items. Loc: WCA, PTO.
The Peel Township Office has only the 1935 report.

336. Peel Tp. **Financial. Non-resident tax book, 1895-1938.** 1 ledger. Loc: PTO.

337. Peel Tp. **Financial. Receipts and expenditures, assets and liabilities, 1892; 1894; 1905.** 3 items. Loc: WCA.
Three annual statements, two being bound and the 1894 record a single loose-leaf poster.

338. Peel Tp. **Financial. Treasurer's accounts, 1864.** 1 file folder. Loc: AO. MU 2014.
Includes school accounts. Part of the Marston Collection.

339. Peel Tp. **Local Improvements. Ditch awards correspondence, 1883; 1909; 1935-1936.** 1 volume. Loc: PTO.
A small collection of letters from contractors and attorneys about tenders and disputes regarding ditch awards.

340. Peel Tp. **Property Assessment. Assessment rolls, 1895; 1901; 1917; 1923-1935.** 29 ledgers. Loc: WCA, AO. GS 3271.
The 1895 roll was also microfilmed by the Genealogical Society of Salt Lake City, with a copy in the Archives of Ontario.

341. Peel Tp. **Property Assessment. Collectors' rolls, 1932.** 1 ledger. Loc: WCA.

PILKINGTON TOWNSHIP

342. Pilkington Tp. **Board of Health. Minute book, 1884-1945.** 1 volume. Loc: WCA.
The body met only on an irregular basis during most years.

Waiting for a call: taxis beside the Guelph City Hall and Market
in the CN Station forecourt, c1923. The Provincial Winter Fair building
may be seen to the right of City Hall.
(Guelph Public Library, Hammill Collection)

343. Pilkington Tp. **Clerk-Treasurer. Correspondence, 1892; 1895; 1905; 1925.** 4 file folders. Loc: WCA.

   A record of correspondence regarding Ontario Hydro, gravel and school area awards.

344. Pilkington Tp. **Council. Bylaws, 1867-1972.** 3 volumes. 2 mf. Loc: WCA.

   The handwritten ledgers are held for the years 1867-1897, 1953, and 1959-1972.

345. Pilkington Tp. **Council. Minutes, 1852-1881.** 1 reel. mf. Loc: AO. GS 3281.

   Microfilmed by the Genealogical Society of Salt Lake City.

346. Pilkington Tp. **Council. Minutes, 1852-1957.** 6 volumes. Loc: WCA.

   The records are held in handwritten form for the entire period and printed minutes are also held for the years 1928 to 1959. The printed minutes include a record of bylaws, annual financial statements, auditors' reports, and notes of the activities of the township council. The record includes a single document which details receipts and expenditures of the township in 1895.

347. Pilkington Tp. **Electoral. Voters' lists, 1870; 1871; 1910; 1924; 1928-1930; 1933-1940; 1942-1950; 1962-1963; 1967; 1970; 1976.** 27 volumes. Loc: WCA, AO.

   Voters' lists for 1870 and 1871 are in manuscript form. AO has only the 1910 list.

348. Pilkington Tp. **Financial. Cash books, 1898-1913; 1916-1931; 1938-1942.** 4 ledgers. Loc: PKH.

349. Pilkington Tp. **Land records. Deeds, 1868; 1871; 1893; 1895; 1906.** 5 file folders. Loc: WCA.

   A record of the transfer of lands between individuals.

350. Pilkington Tp. **Local Improvements. Ditch awards, 1893-1895; 1898-1900; 1904-1906; 1909-1910; 1912-1913; 1917; 1922-1923; 1925; 1927; 1940.** 26 file folders. Loc: WCA.

   A record of transactions involved in the construction of ditches which outlines plans for specific projects.

351. Pilkington Tp. **Local Improvements. Fence viewer awards, 1877; 1930.** 2 file folders. Loc: WCA.

   A record of the decisions of fence viewers in disputes caused by the building of fences between properties.

352. Pilkington Tp. **Property Assessment. Assessment notebook, 1873-1875.** 1 ledger. Loc: WCA.

   An assessor's notebook that records assessment information and date assessment was done. The book is inscribed in the front with 'H. Halls book, Pilkington, Feb. 18th 1873'.

353. Pilkington Tp. **Property Assessment. Assessment rolls, 1852-1853; 1855; 1858.** 2 reels. mf. Loc: WCA, AO.

   The 1858 assessment roll is reprinted by the Ontario Genealogical Society in brochure and microfilm. The 1852, 1853, and 1855 are microfilm reproductions of the originals. The Archives of Ontario also has a microfilm for 1858, filmed by the Genealogical Society of Salt Lake City.

354. Pilkington Tp. **Property Assessment. Collectors' rolls, 1851-1853; 1919; 1926.** 2 file folders; 1 reel. Loc: WCA, AO.
AO has the 1851-3 rolls on MS 56 (reel 1); the later rolls are at WCA.

PUSLINCH TOWNSHIP

355. Puslinch Tp. **Aberfoyle PV. Account book, 1876-1893.** 1 ledger. Loc: WCA.
A monthly record of receipts and expenditures.

356. Puslinch Tp. **Board of Health. Minutes, 1884-1946.** 1 volume. Loc: PUS.
A record of quarterly meetings.

357. Puslinch Tp. **Census and assessment records, 1833-1835; 1837-1844.** mf. Loc: AO. MS 700.
A series of extracts from the Gore District municipal records. The census and assessment data are combined for some years and separate for others.

358. Puslinch Tp. **Council. Bylaws, 1850-1939.** 5 volumes. Loc: PUS.

359. Puslinch Tp. **Council. Minutes, 1849-1899.** 2 reels. mf. Loc: AO, WCA. AO: GS 3290-3291.
The years 1849-1856 also include township bylaws. Microfilmed by Genealogical Society of Salt Lake City.

360. Puslinch Tp. **Council. Minutes, 1849-1968.** 14 volumes. Loc: PUS.

361. Puslinch Tp. **Council. Pathmaster journal, 1874-1902.** 1 ledger. Loc: WCA.
A record of signatures of those who pledged to serve the township in the office of pathmaster.

362. Puslinch Tp. **Electoral. Voters' lists, 1878-1880; 1910; 1922; 1924; 1957; 1960-1963.** 8 volumes. Loc: WCA, AO.
AO has only the 1910 list. Voters' lists for 1879-1880, 1922, 1924, 1962-1963 as originals and on microfilm at WCA.

363. Puslinch Tp. **Financial. Account book, 1870-1903.** 1 ledger. Loc: WCA.
A monthly record of money regarding municipal grants, fines, sheep fund, roads, salaries, schools, drains, loans, printing and bridges.

364. Puslinch Tp. **Financial. Cash books, 1850-1895; 1898-1915; 1941-1951.** 5 ledgers. Loc: WCA, PUS.
The Puslinch Township Office holds the ledger for 1850-1895; the later records are at the WCA.

365. Puslinch Tp. **Local Improvements. Ditch awards register, 1910-1916.** 1 ledger. Loc: PUS.
Only a few entries of ditch awards in the township.

366. Puslinch Tp. **Local Improvements. Drainage bylaws and assessments, 1916-1921.**
1 ledger. Loc: PUS.
     A record of drainage works done in the township which lists owners of drains,
where they lived and the cost of construction of specific drainage projects.

367. Puslinch Tp. **Pathmaster list, 1857-1860.** 1 ledger. Loc: WCA.
     Held in the Wellington County Historical Research Society Collection. A
handwritten copy of original that lists names of individuals and number of days.
Each page is titled 'Return of Pathmasters'.

368. Puslinch Tp. **Petitions, 1865-1866; 1924.** 4 documents. Loc: WCA.
     Held in the Wellington County Historical Research Society Collection. A
collection of petitions of several ratepayers of Puslinch Township to the
municipal council about several matters, including better road service.

369. Puslinch Tp. **Property Assessment. Assessment rolls, 1869-1906; 1908; 1911-1913;
1918; 1938-1955.** 52 volumes, 2 boxes. Loc: WCA, PUS.
     The years 1869-1899 are also held on microfilm at the Wellington County
Archives. The Puslinch Township Office holds volumes from 1938 to 1955.

370. Puslinch Tp. **Property Assessment. Assessment rolls, 1875-1877; 1879-1899.** 2
reels. mf. Loc: AO. GS 3288-3289.
     Microfilmed by the Genealogical Society of Salt Lake City.

371. Puslinch Tp. **Property Assessment. Collectors' rolls, 1881-1912; 1914-1917.** 36
volumes. Loc: WCA.

ARTHUR VILLAGE

372. Arthur V. **Council. Bylaws, 1933-1979.** mf. Loc: WCA.

373. Arthur V. **Council. Minutes, 1872-1877; 1949-1982.** 2 reels. mf. Loc: WCA.

374. Arthur V. **Electoral. Voters' lists, 1880-1881; 1892-1893; 1910; 1922; 1925;
1950.** 1 file folder. Loc: WCA, AO.
     AO has only the 1910 list.

375. Arthur V. **Property Assessment. Assessment rolls, 1895-1896; 1904-1935.** 3
reels. mf. Loc: WCA.

376. Arthur V. **Property Assessment. Collectors' rolls, 1909-1936; 1938.** 3 reels.
mf. Loc: WCA.

CLIFFORD VILLAGE

377. Clifford V. **Council. Bylaws, 1908-1924.** 1 mf. mf. Loc: WCA.

378. Clifford V. **Council. Minutes, 1933-1971.** 2 reels. mf. Loc: WCA.

379. Clifford V. **Electoral. Voters' list, 1910.** Loc: AO.

DRAYTON VILLAGE

380. Drayton V. **Board of Health. Minute book, 1896-1946.** Loc: WCA.

381. Drayton V. **Cemetery. Cash book, 1929-1987.** 1 ledger. Loc: DVO.
A record of individuals purchasing graves and the amount paid.

382. Drayton V. **Clerk-Treasurer. Correspondence, 1928; 1930.** 1 file folder. Loc: WCA.
Four letters written to the clerk regarding various issues relevant to Drayton. One letter includes a blueprint of a proposed highway from Stratford to Orangeville.

383. Drayton V. **Council. Bylaws, with index, 1875-1987.** 1 volume, 1 file drawer. Loc: DVO.

384. Drayton V. **Council. Minutes, 1875-1900.** 1 reel. mf. Loc: AO. GS 3097.
Microfilmed by the Genealogical Society of Salt Lake City.

385. Drayton V. **Council. Minutes, 1875-1985.** 8 volumes. Loc: DVO, WCA.
Microfilmed minutes for the period from 1875 to 1956 are held by the Wellington County Archives.

386. Drayton V. **Electoral. Voters' lists, 1882; 1884; 1904; 1909-1919; 1921; 1923; 1925-1928; 1940; 1943-1945; 1947-1950; 1952.** 22 volumes. Loc: DVO, WCA, AO.
WCA has the 1882, 1884, 1904, 1909 and 1952 list in a file folder, AO has only the 1910 list, while the rest are held in the municipal offices.

387. Drayton V. **Financial. Auditors' reports, 1911-1919; 1921; 1925-1926; 1929; 1940-1946.** 20 volumes. Loc: DVO.

388. Drayton V. **Financial. Cash book, 1896-1971.** 1 ledger. Loc: DVO.
A record of municipal receipts and expenditures with a majority of entries relating to the operation of the Victoria Cemetery in Drayton.

389. Drayton V. **Financial. Cash books, 1880-1900; 1898-1920; 1920-1940.** 3 books. Loc: WCA.

390. Drayton V. **Financial. Debentures, 1901-1905.** 1 ledger. Loc: DVO.
A record of debentures issued by the Village of Drayton. The majority of the entries contain records for the period after 1940.

391. Drayton V. **Financial. Treasurers' reports, 1912; 1917-1918; 1921-1925; 1927-1929; 1943.** 11 volumes. Loc: DVO.

392. Drayton V. **Police Magistrate. Correspondence, 1916-1926.** 1 file folder. Loc: WCA.

393. Drayton V. **Police Magistrate. Deposition and complaint forms, 1913; 1916; 1919; 1922; 1924; 1928.** 1 file folder. Loc: WCA.
Legal records of individuals charged for various offences including references to marital disputes.

394. Drayton V. **Police Magistrate. Record of convictions, 1902-1924.** 12 p. Loc: WCA.

 A record of convictions that lists prosecutor, defendant, nature of charge, date of conviction, amount of penalty, when paid, and reason if not paid. Many convictions are liquor related.

395. Drayton V. **Property Assessment. Assessment rolls, 1904-1945.** 41 ledgers. mf. Loc: WCA.

396. Drayton V. **Property Assessment. Collectors' rolls, 1904-1906; 1909-1911; 1913-1918; 1920-1958.** 61 ledgers. Loc: WCA.

ELORA VILLAGE

397. Elora V. **Cemetery. Registers, 1864-1965.** mf. Loc: WCA.

 A record of lots sold in the Elora cemetery which includes an index of individuals at the beginning of the record.

398. Elora V. **Clerk-Treasurer. Correspondence, 1900-1906; 1911-1957.** 1 ledger, 19 file folders. Loc: WCA.

 A record of correspondence including matters relating to council minutes, assessment appeals, bylaws, railways, the fire department, taxes, court appeals and revisions, and oaths of members of the court of revision.

399. Elora V. **Council. Bylaws, 1858-1940.** 3 volumes, 20 file folders. Loc: EMO, WCA.

 The file folders contain a sporadic collection of bylaws from 1900 to 1940. The ledgers end at 1927. The Wellington County Archives hold records from 1858 to 1927 on microfilm.

400. Elora V. **Council. Minutes, 1858-1950.** 10 volumes. Loc: EMO, WCA.

 Microfilmed records for the period 1898-1950 are held by the Wellington County Archives, while the originals for the period 1858-1931 are in the Elora municicpal offices.

401. Elora V. **Electoral. Poll book subdivision 2, 1923.** 1 book. Loc: WCA.

 A record of those who voted that notes name, description of property, freeholder, tenant, farmer's son or income voter, residence of voter and occupation.

402. Elora V. **Electoral. Voters' lists, 1860; 1910; 1920; 1926; 1936; 1938; 1939; 1942; 1946; 1947; 1954-1961; 1963; 1966; 1970; 1972.** 32 p., 1 file folder, 1 box. Loc: WCA, UGA, GPL, AO. UGA: XR1 MS A029.

 The UGA holds the list for 1860, AO the 1910 list and the GPL the list for 1926. All the rest are at the WCA.

403. Elora V. **Financial. Accounts and statements, 1915-1922; 1925; 1947-1948.** 1 box. Loc: WCA.

 The financial accounts include a detailed statement of the receipts and expenditures of Elora from 1916 to 1922.

404. Elora V. **Financial. Auditor's report, 1866.** 1 document. Loc: UGA. XR1 MS A115005.

    A handwritten report of the municipal finance of Elora. Held with the Connon Collection.

405. Elora V. **Financial. Bank passbooks, 1910; 1926-1930; 1939-1955.** 13 items. Loc: WCA.

406. Elora V. **Financial. Cash book for taxes paid, 1909-1916.** 1 ledger. Loc: WCA.

    A listing of taxes paid by various individuals noting the amount and date of payment.

407. Elora V. **Financial. Financial statement, 1906.** 1 item. Loc: UGA. XR1 MS A332.

    A listing of receipts and expenditures. Held with the Connon Collection.

408. Elora V. **Financial. Land records, 1860-1910.** 1 box. Loc: WCA.

    A record of land sales debentures and conveyances in Elora.

409. Elora V. **Financial. Municipal cash books, 1869-1957.** 12 ledgers. Loc: WCA.

    A record of cash receipts and cash payments with years 1933-1934 giving debit only, and 1933-1935 listing credits only. A number of cash books overlap in the years covered in the same periods.

410. Elora V. **Financial. Record of supplies, light and general expenses, 1918-1920.** 1 ledger. Loc: WCA.

    A record of funds paid to individuals and companies for municipal services and utilities.

411. Elora V. **Financial. Register of debentures, 1906-1963.** 1 ledger. Loc: WCA.

    A record of municipal funds spent for supply of services which includes projects such as the enlargement of the Elora High School, waterworks systems, and heating systems for area schools.

412. Elora V. **Petition by ratepayers and businessmen, 1865.** 1 file folder. Loc: UGA. XR1 MS A115009.

    A petition by Elora ratepayers and businessmen to have July 24, 1865 declared a holiday. The document is signed by several Elora residents. Held with the Connon Collection.

413. Elora V. **Property Assessment. Assessment rolls, 1853; 1867; 1890-1908; 1936-1952.** 35 volumes. Loc: WCA, AO.

    AO has only the 1853 roll on MS 156 (reel 1). The collectors' rolls and assessment rolls were combined into a single source in the years 1943-1959.

414. Elora V. **Property Assessment. Collectors' rolls, 1890-1959.** 62 volumes. Loc: WCA.

    The collectors' rolls and assessment rolls were combined into a single source in the years 1943-1959.

ERIN VILLAGE

415. Erin V. **Board of Health. Minutes, 1898-1911; 1930-1944.** 1 volume. Loc: WCA.
The meetings were held three times per year during the early years, but in later years only occasionally.

416. Erin V. **Cemetery. Lot purchases, 1886-1926.** 1 ledger. Loc: EVO.
A record of name of purchaser, number of lot and number of square feet.

417. Erin V. **Certificates of sale of land for taxes, 1937-1940.** 3 ledgers. Loc: WCA.

418. Erin V. **Electoral. Voters' list, 1910.** Loc: AO.

419. Erin V. **Erin Cemetery. Trustees' minutes, 1883-1890.** 1 volume. Loc: EVO.
A record of minutes which also contains financial statements.

420. Erin V. **Financial. Cash books, 1893-1944.** 3 ledgers. Loc: WCA.

421. Erin V. **Property Assessment. Assessment rolls, 1897-1898; 1909-1952.** 11 ledgers. Loc: WCA.

422. Erin V. **Property Assessment. Collectors' rolls, 1895-1896; 1905-1908; 1914-1946.** 7 ledgers. Loc: WCA.

FERGUS

423. Fergus V. **Agreement with Hydro Electric Power Commission of Fergus, 1913-1914.** 2 volumes. Loc: WCA.
A record of a formal agreement to supply hydro electric power in 1913 and also a record of the cost incurred in the 'reconstruction of the municipal system' for hydro in Fergus.

424. Fergus V. **Belsyde Cemetery. Account book, 1920-1940.** 1 ledger. Loc: WCA.
A record of individuals having accounts with the cemetery which indicates the amount paid by specific clients.

425. Fergus V. **Centennial celebrations, 1833-1933.** 1 brochure. Loc: WCA. Detailed list of contents.
A pamphlet announcing centennial celebrations that contains a brief historical sketch of the village. Part of the Templin-Dow Collection.

426. Fergus V. **Construction agreement, 1866.** 1 document. Loc: WCA.
An unsigned agreement between Fergus and Wellington County to construct a drill shed.

427. Fergus V. **Council. Letter regarding contributions to Quebec Fire Relief Fund, 1866-1869.** 10 p. Loc: NAC. MG 29, C 10.
Letter from Joseph Cauchon, Mayor of Quebec, to A.D. Ferrier, regarding contributions to the relief fund. Also included is a list of subscriptions received to February, 1869.

428. Fergus V. **Council. Minutes, 1858-1863; 1867-1944.** 15 volumes. Loc: AO, WCA.
The 1858-1899 records were microfilmed by the Genealogical Society of Salt Lake City, with copies in the Archives of Ontario (GS 3136-3137).

429. Fergus V. **Electoral. Legislative franchise assessment rolls, 1930; 1932; 1938-1944.** 5 ledgers. Loc: WCA.
A record of name, age, if British subject, occupation, address and whether married, widowed, bachelor or spinster.

430. Fergus V. **Electoral. Voters' lists, 1879; 1910; 1922-1923.** 3 volumes. Loc: WCA, AO.
A copy of the 1879 list only is held with the Adam Fergusson Papers at the Archives of Ontario (MU 5016); AO also has a copy of the 1910 list.

431. Fergus V. **Financial. Auditors' reports, 1931-1936.** 6 volumes. Loc: WCA.
Carbon copies of municipal finances audited by Peters, Morrison and Brown, chartered accountants in Toronto.

432. Fergus V. **Financial. Cash books, 1910-1922.** 2 ledgers. Loc: WCA.

433. Fergus V. **Financial. Tax arrears day book, 1930-1934.** 1 ledger. Loc: WCA.
A record of name and amount owed.

434. Fergus V. **Financial. Tax collection day book, 1936-1940.** 1 ledger. Loc: WCA.
A record of name, amount of taxes and interest paid.

435. Fergus V. **Petition by electors to prohibit sale of alcohol, 1912.** 15 p. Loc: AO. MU 1016.
Petition signed by approximately two hundred and seventy electors to prohibit sale of liquor in Fergus, under the Liquor Licensing Act of 1897. Held with Adam Fergusson Papers.

436. Fergus V. **Property Assessment. Assessment rolls, 1902-1904; 1906-1923; 1925-1945.** 48 ledgers. Loc: WCA.
The assessment rolls and collectors' rolls are combined from 1932 to 1945.

437. Fergus V. **Property Assessment. Collectors' rolls, 1899-1901; 1903-1932.** 33 ledgers. Loc: WCA.

438. Fergus V. **Public Utilities Commission. Auditors' reports, 1934; 1938-1946.** 11 volumes. Loc: WCA.
Printed records of receipts and expenditures of the Public Utilities Commission in Fergus.

439. Fergus V. **Public Utilities, Hydro Department. Account book of construction of new services, 1935-1936.** 1 ledger. Loc: WCA.
An account of costs incurred in developing new hydro services in Fergus.

440. Fergus V. **Public Utilities, Hydro Department. Account books, 1921-1958.** 2 ledgers. Loc: WCA.
A record of clients receiving services from Fergus Hydro.

441. Fergus V. **Registered debentures and dogs, 1896-1899; 1903-1914; 1922-1950.** 2 ledgers. Loc: WCA.

    A record of purchase of debentures that notes date, name, amount, and yearly interest. The registration of dogs that is recorded for the years 1903 to 1914 in the first ledger, notes number of dogs, species, description, owner, number of tag and license fee.

442. Fergus V. **Relief Committee. Minutes, 1938-1939.** 1 volume. Loc: WCA.

    A record of activities of the committee which lists individuals receiving aid and those who were to be 'cut off relief'. One entry dated February 1, 1939 indicated relief recipients who were 'able-bodied and in good condition would be expected to give their services voluntarily at least three days per week to Corporation work', and that those who did not comply would not continue receiving aid.

HARRISTON TOWN

443. Harriston T. **Council. Bylaws, 1879-1889.** 1 volume. Loc: MTH.

    The bylaws are held at the Minto Township municipal office.

444. Harriston T. **Electoral. Voters' lists, 1910; 1924.** Loc: WCA, AO.

    AO has only the 1910 list.

445. Harriston T. **Property Assessment. Assessment rolls, 1897-1931.** 2 ledgers. Loc: HTH.

MOUNT FOREST TOWN

446. Mount Forest T. **Council. Bylaws, 1880-1972.** 1 box, 2 ledgers. Loc: WCA.

    Bylaws are held for sporadic years from 1880 to 1929 in a box in the cellar vault. The ledger in the clerk's office contains all bylaws from 1916 to 1972.

447. Mount Forest T. **Council. Committee reports, 1938.** 1 envelope. Loc: MFH.

    A record of various committees including Relief, Finance, Property and Board of Works and Parks.

448. Mount Forest T. **Council. Correspondence, 1937.** 1 envelope. Loc: MFH.

    A record of correspondence on various municipal issues.

449. Mount Forest T. **Council. Minutes, 1865-1899.** 3 reels. mf. Loc: AO. GS 3250-3252.

    Microfilmed by the Genealogical Society of Salt Lake City.

450. Mount Forest T. **Council. Minutes, 1865-1932; 1935-1944.** 11 volumes. Loc: WCA.

    A record of monthly meetings.

451. Mount Forest T. **Electoral. Voters' lists, 1910; 1921; 1924.** Loc: WCA, AO.

    AO has only the 1910 list.

452. Mount Forest T. **Financial. Bank passbook, 1931-1937.** 1 item. Loc: MFH.

    A record of banking transactions of the municipality with the Bank of Montreal in Mount Forest.

453. Mount Forest T. **Financial. Cash book, 1899-1908.** 1 ledger. Loc: MFH.

454. Mount Forest T. **Financial. Debentures, 1898-1946 (sporadic).** 3 ledgers. Loc: MFH.

455. Mount Forest T. **Financial. Tax arrears, 1915-1932.** 1 ledger. Loc: MFH.
      A record of individuals owing taxes which notes where they lived and the amount owed.

456. Mount Forest T. **Financial. Treasurer's accounts, 1938.** 1 envelope. Loc: MFH.

457. Mount Forest T. **Local Improvements. Petitions under Bylaw 274, 1897-1928.** 1 ledger. Loc: WCA.
      A record of petitions for sidewalks.

458. Mount Forest T. **Marriages. Register, 1921-1952.** 1 ledger. Loc: MFH.
      A record of date of issue of license and name and address of bride, bridegroom and clergy.

459. Mount Forest T. **Property Assessment. Assessment rolls, 1865-1878; 1880-1898.** 3 reels. mf. Loc: AO. GS 3247-3249.
      Microfilmed by Genealogical Society of Salt Lake City.

460. Mount Forest T. **Property Assessment. Assessment rolls, 1865-1898; 1900-1934.** 88 ledgers. Loc: WCA.

461. Mount Forest T. **Property Assessment. Collectors' and assessment rolls, 1937-1938.** 3 ledgers. Loc: MFH.
      The collectors' and assessment rolls are held in the same ledgers for 1937 and 1938.

462. Mount Forest T. **Property Assessment. Collectors' rolls, 1865-1870; 1872; 1877; 1880-1909; 1911-1934.** 99 ledgers. Loc: WCA.

ORANGEVILLE TOWN

463. Orangeville T. **Council. Minutes, 1864-1904.** 3 reels. mf. Loc: AO. GS 3584-3586.
      Microfilmed by the Genealogical Society of Salt Lake City.

464. Orangeville T. **Property Assessment. Assessment rolls, 1865-1899.** 3 reels. mf. Loc: AO. GS 3577-3579.
      Microfilmed by the Genealogical Society of Salt Lake City.

465. Orangeville T. **Property Assessment. Collectors' rolls, 1869-1899.** 3 reels. mf. Loc: AO. GS 3590-3592.
      Microfilmed by the Genealogical Society of Salt Lake City.

PALMERSTON VILLAGE

466. Palmerston V. **Council. Bylaws, 1875-1903.** 2 reels. mf. Loc: WCA.

467. Palmerston V. **Council. Minutes, 1891-1964.** 4 reels. mf. Loc: WCA.

468. Palmerston V. **Electoral. Voters' lists, 1884; 1900; 1910; 1924; 1938.** Loc: WCA, AO.
    AO has only the 1910 list.

469. Palmerston V. **Financial. Cancelled cheques, 1908-1910; 1916-1917.** 2 files. Loc: WCA.

470. Palmerston V. **Financial. Cash books, 1898-1926.** 4 ledgers. Loc: WCA.

471. Palmerston V. **Property Assessment. Assessment rolls, 1907-1957.** 50 ledgers. Loc: WCA.

472. Palmerston V. **Property Assessment. Collectors' rolls, 1900-1957.** 60 ledgers. Loc: WCA.

The rigours of domestic science at Macdonald Consolidated School, c1904:
a girls' cooking class with teacher Miss Margaret Park. This is part of a collection of photographs of the school (#3447).
(Macdonald Stewart Art Centre)

SCHOOL RECORDS

It is most discreditable to this fair province, that in the majority of school sections, unless some problem of expenditure has to be discussed, it is almost impossible to get a well-attended school meeting. Instances are known of where the deepest, bitterest feelings of a whole neighbourhood have been aroused, by the proposal of the trustee to purchase maps to the value of five or ten dollars. The mere mention of a picket-fence in front of the school once put a whole section into convulsions. A suggestion to increase the teacher's salary will certainly prove the theme of many denunciations against the 'Board' at all the threshing bees for miles around.[1]

The rather mundane school history of Wellington County is lent a touch of distinction by the fact that David Boyle taught here for sixteen years, at the Middlebrook School in rural Pilkington Township from 1865 to 1871 and then at the Elora Public School until 1881.[2] Not only was he a remarkably gifted teacher who introduced 'surprises in every lesson' but he left accounts of his experiences in scrapbooks and a satirical novel of the life of a rural teacher.[3] These help to put flesh on the dry bones of the official records and to illumine the prevailing value systems of those who administered the local schools.

In Wellington County, as elsewhere in Ontario a wealth of material may be found in the school records, both those of the local section, township or county level of trustees and the central records of the successive provincial agencies and departments of education. For the past twenty years historians have found new meaning in surviving school records, not only for the history of schooling but also for understanding family and household structure, class, childhood experience, local government, tensions between municipal and

---

[1]. The ups and downs of No.7, Rexville, being a full, true and correct account of what happened in the said school section during a period of twelve months, more or less, and of some things that were enacted beyond its limits, with a few judicious remarks on religious instruction in public schools, the morality of fresh air, teacher's "recommends" and bogus certificates by an old maid (who was "plucked") published anonymously by David Boyle c1885; microfiche #14019 in Canada: The Printed Record (Insitute of Historical Microrereproductions),p.24.

[2] Gerald Killan, **David Boyle: from artisan to archaeologist** (Toronto: University of Toronto Press, 1983).

[3] Boyle's papers, including the scrapbooks covering schools and education in Guelph and Wellington County between 1859 and 1881, are held in the Baldwin Room of the Metro Toronto Central Reference Library (#2304).

provincial levels of government, and the professionalization of teaching.[4]

We know very little about the provision of schooling in Wellington County before the mid-1840s. **Common schools** could qualify for government grants from 1815, but many localities seem to have been poorly served. Guelph residents petitioned the Governor, Sir John Colborne in about 1830, chiefly complaining of the inadequate management of education.[5] Only the few district towns were eligible for some provincial funding to support **grammar schools** that offered a more academic education for middle-class students.

Legislation of the 1840s shaped the common schools in several enduring ways that were reinforced by later acts. First, it created two highly centralized and powerful bodies both dominated by Egerton Ryerson: the **Council of Public Instruction** which formulated policy, and the **Department of Public Instruction** which carried it out. This led to a strongly centralized pattern of educational policy-making and administration that is reflected in the immense volume of provincial government records in this department (see #940-#964 in the section of Higher Government records).

Next, the legislation made municipalities responsible for the detailed administration of local education and established a pattern of funding derived from local property assessments to match the provincial grants. In rural areas, the basic unit of school administration was made the **school section**, a portion of a township in which qualified voters met each January to elect trustees who had to maintain the school building, hire the teacher and ensure that school taxes were raised in the section. In incorporated cities, towns and villages, under the 1840s legislation, there was a single board of trustees with similar responsibilities for larger numbers of pupils and teachers.

The county council had to levy a school assessment on the county as a whole to match its share of the government grant and had to appoint either a superintendent with county-wide authority or individual township superintendents. The local **superintendent** allocated the township school fund among the various school sections based on average attendance. He visited all the schools in his territory to see that the teachers were obeying the regulations and reported annually to the Chief Superintendent in Toronto. **County Boards of Public Instruction**, consisting of the local superintendents and the grammar school trustees for each county, examined common school teachers and gave them certificates.

The 1840s acts also made provision for **separate schools** to serve any minority group that held a different religious faith from that of the majority in a township or other municipality. Under an act of 1853, separate schools shared equally with common schools in the provincial school grants.

---

[4] The new approach is notably exemplified in Susan E. Houston and Alison Prentice, **Schooling and scholars in nineteenth-century Ontario** (Toronto: University of Toronto Press, 1988).

[5] National Archives, RG 1, E 16, vol. 5, no. 17 (#935).

Grammar schools in the early nineteenth century were limited to the district towns, but new legislation in 1841 led to a rapid increase of this more academic type of school in most towns. The numbers of grammar schools grew from 14 in 1840 to 65 by 1855 and 86 in 1861. At first the grammar schools were managed locally by trustees but from the mid-1850s the Department of Public Instruction regulated their curricula, certified their teachers and sent inspectors to enforce the regulations. County councils could raise taxes to support the grammar schools but were not required to do so until 1865. In some towns and cities, **central schools** were established in the 1850s and 1860s, taking in children from feeder primary schools and offering higher levels of the basic curriculum as well as elements of the traditional grammar schools.

The Common and Grammar School Improvement Act of 1871 made several significant changes. Elementary-level schools were renamed **public schools** and were to be free; the legislation also provided for compulsory school attendance though enforcement proved difficult until 1919. New subjects such as the mechanical arts, agriculture and bookkeeping were added to the old common school curriculum. Two types of secondary schools were created in 1871: **high schools** to provide a general education including commercial subjects, and the **collegiate institutes** offering a classical education to prepare selected students for University. To provide partial secondary schooling in rural areas, **continuation classes** were added to some rural schools from 1894; the curriculum was the same as for the first two years of high school but the teachers did not have to be fully trained to the standard usually required for high school teaching. From 1908 these classes could be organized into continuation schools.

The 1871 Act also shifted responsibility from the local superintendent to the **county inspector**, who though appointed by the county council answered to the Minister of Education. In 1877, fewer than one in five of all teachers had received any professional training, the rest holding 'third class' certificates. County Boards of Examiners were then required to establish a **model school** and ensure that all 'third class' teachers attended for a term. From 1908, all teachers were required to attend **normal school** so the model schools were closed and normal schools were opened in Hamilton, North Bay, Peterborough and Stratford to supplement those already operating in Toronto, Ottawa and London.

In the early twentieth century, manual training, domestic science and agriculture were introduced into public schools (and later some high schools) with the help of funds from the philanthropist Sir William Macdonald. Macdonald also funded an experimental prototype of a **consolidated school** to which pupils were transported from a larger rural area that would normally have had at least four one-room school-houses each administered by a school section board of trustees. Located adjacent to the Macdonald Institute in Guelph Township, the school gave the domestic science students there the opportunity to put their theory into practice what they learned with sample groups of children. As an experiment in the consolidation of rural schools, the Macdonald School's example was not followed until the 1960s. The Industrial Education Act in 1911 authorized municipalities to establish day and evening **industrial and technical schools**, but few were properly launched before federal money was made available for the purpose in 1919.

At least some records -- minutes, cash books and attendance registers-- have been traced for 157 school authorities in the twelve townships and ten urban centres of the county. Most records of public elementary schools are in the care of the Wellington County Board of Education which was created in 1969 to absorb all the governing bodies for public education in the county and thus inherited extant records from the various units. The Board also holds some records of the Wellington County School Board that had responsibilities for examinations, inspection and salaries of teachers, and the adminsitration of the county model school. Some school records were retained in the municipal offices of the various townships, towns and villages and have been acquired by the Wellington County Archives in the 1980s. A few items have come into public repositories from private papers and collections.

Comparatively few of the records for public education date from before the 1890s, good examples being the full set of the Guelph Board of Education minutes from 1856, minutes for Eramosa Township S.S.#4 from 1847, Eramosa Township S.S.#2 from 1854, Erin Township S.S.#3 from 1858, Arthur Township S.S.#4 from 1857, Guelph Township S.S.#2 from 1858, Maryborough Township S.S.#15 from 1865 and Minto Township S.S.#14 from 1872. Continuation classes and schools are reflected in the records of some school sections from the early twentieth century. The Guelph Central School was established by the 1860s but primary records from before the 1930s have not been found.

Records of the Elora Grammar School survive from 1854, through its renaming as the Elora High School in 1872, until 1939. The Guelph Collegiate and Vocational Institute Archives holds records as well as other items relating to the history of its predecessor schools -- the Wellington District Grammar School of 1842, the Guelph Grammar School of 1854, the Guelph High School of 1879, the Guelph Collegiate Institute of 1887, renamed the Guelph Collegiate and Vocational Institute in 1923. Most of the primary material in the GCVI Archives dates from the 1880s and later. In the absence of early original records, the copies and compilations of school board minutes and inspectors' reports made by Hugh Douglass in the mid-twentieth century are all the more valuable (#3596, #3598, in the Guelph Public Library).

Only a little primary material has been found relating to separate schools in Guelph and Wellington County. The Wellington County Roman Catholic Separate School Board holds the minutes of its predecessor, the Guelph Separate School Board, for the years 1879-1905 and 1914-1959 as well as cash books for much the same period and a few items of correspondence from before 1940. Records from the separate school sections in the county have not come to light locally. The best evidence for the County's separate schools probably lies in the records of the Ontario Department of Education in the Archives of Ontario (#948, #960-#961)[6].

----

[6] See also Franklin A. Walker, **Catholic education and politics in Upper Canada: a study of the documentation relative to the origin of Catholic elementary schools in the Ontario school system** (Toronto: Federation of Catholic Education Associations of Ontario, 1955); and **Catholic education and politics in Ontario: a documentary study** (Toronto: Thomas Nelson, 1964).

WELLINGTON COUNTY

473. Wellington Co. **Grammar School Board. Annual reports, attendance records, 1854-1857; 1859-1867.** 1 file folder. Loc: GCI.
A photocopy of the original financial statements, lists of textbooks used, salaries of headmasters and assistant headmasters and references to the attendance of students. The records are apparently copies of originals in the Archives of Ontario.

474. Wellington Co. **High School Board. Student entrance examination results, 1900-1949.** 1 ledger. Loc: WBE.
A record of examinations for several municipalities in various years.

475. Wellington Co. **Model School. Grade reports, 1887-1907.** 1 ledger. Loc: WBE.
A record of the grades of students in various subjects in the county Model School. The record is held in the same file cabinets as the registers of the Elora Public School.

476. Wellington Co. **School Board. Examination questions, 1925-1926; 1929.** 1 envelope. Loc: WCA. MU77.
A series of county school exams in several subject areas including arithmetic, geography, literature and history.

477. Wellington Co. **School Board. Examiners, 1871-1893.** 1 ledger. Loc: WBE.
A record of dates of exams directed by the board of examiners.

478. Wellington Co. **School Board. Staff records, 1921-1929.** 1 ledger. Loc: WBE.
A record of teachers, secretaries, clerks, treasurers and attendance officers for several townships in the county.

479. Wellington Co. **School Board. Student records, 1922-1929.** 2 volumes. Loc: WBE.
A record of students' name, age, school, address and marks at various schools in the county.

480. Wellington Co. **School Board. Teachers' salaries, 1890-1933.** 1 file folder. Loc: WBE.
A record of teacher, year and salary for various schools in the county.

ARTHUR TOWNSHIP

481. Arthur Tp. **S.S.#1 Board. Minutes, 1916-1936.** 1 ledger. Loc: WBE.

482. Arthur Tp. **S.S.#10. Registers, 1902-1904; 1906; 1910-1913; 1916; 1920-1921; 1923-1927; 1929-1954; 1961.** 27 ledgers. Loc: WBE.

483. Arthur Tp. **S.S.#11. Registers, 1934-1961.** 7 ledgers. Loc: WBE.

484. Arthur Tp. **S.S.#15. Registers, 1930-1961.** 8 ledgers. Loc: WBE.

485. Arthur Tp. **S.S.#2. Registers, 1930-1961.** 9 ledgers. Loc: WBE.

486. Arthur Tp. S.S.#4 Board. Minutes, 1857-1894. 1 volume. Loc: WCA.
A record of annual and other special meetings held by the school trustees. The minutes are held with the Meyler Collection at the Wellington County Archives.

487. Arthur Tp. S.S.#4. Cash book, 1862-1921. 1 ledger. Loc: WCA.
A record of receipts and expenditures with several entries each month. The ledger is held with the Meyler Collection at the Wellington County Archives.

488. Arthur Tp. S.S.#4. Registers, 1935-1961. 7 ledgers. Loc: WBE.

489. Arthur Tp. S.S.#5. Registers, 1912-1913; 1915-1916; 1918-1928; 1930-1939; 1944-1961. 23 ledgers. Loc: WBE.

490. Arthur Tp. S.S.#6. Registers, 1935-1961. 7 ledgers. Loc: WBE.

491. Arthur Tp. S.S.#7. Registers, 1929-1961. 10 ledgers. Loc: WBE.

492. Arthur Tp/ Luther W Tp. Union S.S.#12 Board. Minutes, 1910-1950. 1 volume. Loc: WBE.
A record of the minutes of the board which met on an irregular basis during the year.

ARTHUR VILLAGE

493. Arthur V. High School Board. Contracts, 1915-1918. 5 p. Loc: WBE.
A record of a contract between the trustees of the school and an individual to do janitorial work.

494. Arthur V. Public School. Registers, 1921; 1928; 1931-1944. 5 ledgers. Loc: WBE.

495. Arthur V. School Board. Minutes, 1937-1953. 1 volume. Loc: WBE.

DRAYTON VILLAGE

496. Drayton V. Public School. Census records, 1931-1948. 2 ledgers. Loc: DVO.

497. Drayton V. Public School. Census register, 1893-1928. 2 ledgers. Loc: WCA.
A record of student name, age, parent or guardian, and place of residence.

498. Drayton V. School Board. Account book, 1893-1909. 1 ledger. Loc: WCA. Book indexed by name.

499. Drayton V. School Board. Cash books, 1903-1927; 1928-1940; 1950-1962. 3 ledgers. Loc: WCA.
A record of receipts and payments of the Drayton School Board. The ledger also records teachers salaries.

500. Drayton V. School Board. Minutes, 1905-1911. 1 volume. Loc: WCA.

ELORA VILLAGE

501. Elora V. **County Grammar School. Cash and account book, 1864-1880.** 1 ledger. Loc: WCA.
A record of expenditures.

502. Elora V. **County Grammar School. Minutes, 1854-1856; 1863-1879.** 2 volumes. Loc: WCA.
A record of meetings that notes various committee reports, teachers, students, educational prizes, accounts and trustees.

503. Elora V. **High School Board. Cash book, 1931-1951.** 1 ledger. Loc: WBE.

504. Elora V. **High School Board. Catalogue of library, apparatus and maps, 1895-1908; 1910-1914; 1919-1924; 1940-1944.** 5 ledgers. Loc: WBE.
A record of titles, publisher and cost of books purchased for the library.

505. Elora V. **High School Board. Correspondence, 1874-1888.** 10 file folders. Loc: WCA.
Correspondence regarding tenders, admission requirements, education grants, course of instruction, appointment of trustees and provincial grants.

506. Elora V. **High School Board. Insurance policies, 1877-1884.** 1 file folder. Loc: WCA.
Insurance policies for fire and liability.

507. Elora V. **High School Board. Minutes, 1879-1905.** 418 p. Loc: WCA.
A record of monthly meetings that notes education committee reports, teachers, students and attendance.

508. Elora V. **High School Board. Monthly inspectors' reports, 1874-1883.** 1 file folder. Loc: WCA.
A record of inspectors' reports that note number of students on roll, average attendance, and state general assessments of accommodation, equipment and organization.

509. Elora V. **High School Board. Personnel, 1873-1881.** 1 file folder. Loc: WCA.
Letters of resignation from headmasters and trustees, and requests for salary changes.

510. Elora V. **High School Board. Receipts and invoices, 1878-1890.** 3 file folders. Loc: WCA.

511. Elora V. **High School Board. Reports of examinations, 1878-1883.** 1 file folder. Loc: WCA.
A record of marks received by students in various subjects and names and sometimes ages of students writing exams.

512. Elora V. **High School Board. Staff and students' complaints, 1875-1889.** 1 file folder. Loc: WCA.
Written complaints regarding disobedience and suspensions of students, and

one letter requesting the dismissal of the headmaster because of conduct that was not in the 'moral interests' of the community.

513. Elora V. **High School Board. Teachers' applications, 1879-1882.** 1 file folder. Loc: WCA.
     Letters of application for the position of headmaster.

514. Elora V. **High School Board. Teachers' contracts, 1872-1882.** 1 file folder. Loc: WCA.
     Letters of resignation or acceptance that note date of appointment and salary to be granted.

515. Elora V. **High School Board. Treasurer's book, 1880-1905.** 85 p. Loc: WCA.
     A record of expenditures.

516. Elora V. **High School. Examination marks books, 1898-1940.** 2 ledgers. Loc: WBE.
     A record of students' names and marks scored on various exams. The ledgers also include newspaper clippings of results of term examinations and oratorial contests.

517. Elora V. **High School. Registers, 1888-1893; 1901-1959.** 1 file cabinet drawer. Loc: WBE.

518. Elora V. **High School. Reports, correspondence, attendance records, 1926-1938.** 13 ledgers. Loc: WBE.
     A record of attendance, grades of students, exam questions for various subjects, financial accounts, and references to salaries of teachers in some years. The records are indexed at the beginning of ledgers in several years.

519. Elora V. **Public School. Admission register, 1885-1948.** 1 ledger. Loc: WBE.

520. Elora V. **Public School. Census books, 1925-1926; 1933-1934; 1936; 1938-1949.** 15 books. Loc: WCA.
     A record of name and age of children (5-18 years), parent or guardian, public or separate school supporter, and residence.

521. Elora V. **Public School. Examination records, 1872; 1908.** 3 documents. Loc: WCA. MU51.
     A record of the marks of three students including a grade report for a student attending Elora Public School in 1872.

522. Elora V. **Public School. Registers, 1882-1906; 1908-1969.** 3 file cabinet drawers. Loc: WBE.

523. Elora V. **Public School. School certificates, 1912.** 2 documents. Loc: UGA. XR1 MS A193019.
     Two certificates certifying Katherine Archibald's completion of Lower School at the Elora Public School. Held with the Marston-Archibald Collection.

524. Elora V. **School Board. Cash books, 1858-1930.** 3 ledgers. Loc: WCA.
     A record of receipts and expenditures which notes balance of financial accounts each year.

525. Elora V. **School Board. Minutes, 1891-1936**. 3 volumes. Loc: WCA.

ERAMOSA TOWNSHIP

526. Eramosa Tp. **Continuation School. Cash book, 1921-1934**. 1 ledger. Loc: WBE.
The arrangement of the records suggests that the Continuation School may have been administered by the S.S.#9 Board.

527. Eramosa Tp. **Continuation School. Minutes, 1921-1927; 1932-1946**. 2 volumes. Loc: WBE.
The arrangement of the records suggests that the Continuation School may have been administered by the S.S.#9 Board.

528. Eramosa Tp. **Rockwood Continuation School. Registers, 1921-1947**. 46 ledgers. Loc: WBE.

529. Eramosa Tp. **Rockwood Public School. Day book, 1936-1937**. 1 item. Loc: WBE.
A teacher's plan of daily instruction.

530. Eramosa Tp. **S.S.#1 Board. Minutes, 1905-1942; Cash book, 1905-1942**. 1 volume. Loc: WBE.
The minute book is held in the same ledger as the cash book. The meetings of the school board were held only once each year. There are brief entries outlining activities.

531. Eramosa Tp. **S.S.#1. Registers, 1917; 1919; 1921-1926; 1928-1962**. 21 ledgers. Loc: WBE.

532. Eramosa Tp. **S.S.#10 Board. Cash book, 1906-1945**. 1 ledger. Loc: WBE.

533. Eramosa Tp. **S.S.#10 Board. Minutes, 1906-1945**. 2 volumes. Loc: WBE.
A record of minutes with several meetings held each year.

534. Eramosa Tp. **S.S.#10. Registers, 1934-1965**. 8 ledgers. Loc: WBE.

535. Eramosa Tp. **S.S.#2 Board. Minutes, 1854-1869; Cash book, 1901-1917**. 1 volume. Loc: WBE.
A brief record of annual meetings and financial receipts and expenditures. The cash book is held in the same ledger as the minute book.

536. Eramosa Tp. **S.S.#2. Registers, 1918; 1920-1969**. 24 ledgers. Loc: WBE.

537. Eramosa Tp. **S.S.#3 Board. Minutes, 1890-1945; Cash books, 1887-1945**. 3 volumes. Loc: WBE.
The minutes for the years 1939-1945 are held in the same ledger as the cash books for the years 1924 to 1945. The minute books demonstrate that meetings were held only once each year with brief entries of activities.

538. Eramosa Tp. **S.S.#3. Registers, 1906; 1920-1922; 1924-1965**. 22 ledgers. Loc: WBE.

539. Eramosa Tp. S.S.#4-1/2 Board. Minutes, 1920-1945; Cash book, 1920-1945. 1 volume. Loc: WBE.

540. Eramosa Tp. S.S.#4-1/2. Registers, 1912-1965. 28 ledgers. Loc: WBE.

541. Eramosa Tp. S.S.#4 Board. Cash book, 1910-1945. 1 ledger. Loc: WBE.

542. Eramosa Tp. S.S.#4 Board. Minutes, 1909-1945. 1 volume. Loc: WBE.

543. Eramosa Tp. S.S.#4. Registers, 1860; 1897; 1899; 1902; 1905-1906; 1910; 1912; 1915-1923; 1925-1959. 28 ledgers, 1 file folder. Loc: WBE.

544. Eramosa Tp. S.S.#5 Board. Minutes, 1935-1945; Cash book, 1936-1945. 1 volume. Loc: WBE.
    The minutes are held in the same ledger as the cash book records.

545. Eramosa Tp. S.S.#5. Registers, 1921-1962. 18 ledgers. Loc: WBE.

546. Eramosa Tp. S.S.#6 Board. Cash books, 1897-1945. 1 ledger. Loc: WBE.

547. Eramosa Tp. S.S.#6 Board. Minutes, 1897-1945. 1 volume. Loc: WBE.
    A brief record of several meetings each year.

548. Eramosa Tp. S.S.#6. Registers, 1913; 1915-1916; 1918-1923; 1926-1965. 23 ledgers. Loc: WBE.

549. Eramosa Tp. S.S.#7 Board. Minutes, 1892-1922; Cash books, 1922-1945. 4 volumes. Loc: WBE.

550. Eramosa Tp. S.S.#7. Registers, 1911; 1913-1914; 1916; 1918; 1921; 1923-1924; 1926-1928; 1930-1965. 19 ledgers. Loc: WBE.

551. Eramosa Tp. S.S.#8 Board. Cash books, 1860-1945. 4 ledgers. Loc: WBE.
    Until 1871 the school was united with Eramosa Tp, S.S.#4.

552. Eramosa Tp. S.S.#8 Board. Minutes, 1847-1945. 2 volumes. Loc: WBE.
    Until 1871 the school was united with Eramosa Township S.S.#4.

553. Eramosa Tp. S.S.#8. Registers, 1890; 1893-1895; 1897; 1901; 1903; 1911-1914; 1916-1965. 34 ledgers. Loc: WBE.

554. Eramosa Tp. S.S.#9 Board. Cash books, 1872-1946. 3 ledgers. Loc: WBE.

555. Eramosa Tp. S.S.#9 Board. Minutes, 1872-1932. 2 volumes. Loc: WBE.
    A record of monthly meetings.

556. Eramosa Tp. S.S.#9. Registers, 1900; 1902-1964. 90 ledgers. Loc: WBE.

ERIN TOWNSHIP

557. Erin Tp. Continuation School. Student grade reports, 1925-1945. 1 ledger. Loc: WBE.

A record of students' grades which also notes where they lived, lists the ages of students, and at times indicates the occupation of the parents.

558. Erin Tp. **Public School. Census books, 1921; 1938-1939.** 3 ledgers. Loc: WCA.

559. Erin Tp. **Public Schools. Assessment registers, 1919-1922; 1932-1937.** 2 ledgers. Loc: WCA.
A record of school support payments by individuals for school sections 1 to 14.

560. Erin Tp. **S.S.#1 Board. Cash book, 1939-1946.** 1 ledger. Loc: WBE.

561. Erin Tp. **S.S.#1. Registers, 1930-1964.** 7 ledgers. Loc: WBE.

562. Erin Tp. **S.S.#10 Board. Cash book, 1898-1940.** 1 ledger. Loc: WBE.

563. Erin Tp. **S.S.#10 Board. Minutes, 1899-1944.** 1 volume. Loc: WBE.

564. Erin Tp. **S.S.#10. Home and School Association minutes, 1939-1943.** 4 ledgers. Loc: WBE.

565. Erin Tp. **S.S.#10. Registers, 1911-1912; 1914-1918; 1921-1924; 1926-1929; 1934-1948; 1955-1969.** 22 ledgers. Loc: WBE.

566. Erin Tp. **S.S.#11 Board. Cash book, 1903-1947.** 2 ledgers. Loc: WBE.

567. Erin Tp. **S.S.#11 Board. Minutes, 1939-1947.** 1 volume. Loc: WBE.

568. Erin Tp. **S.S.#11 Board. Recording equipment catalogue, 1913-1929.** 2 ledgers. Loc: WBE.
The catalogue is for recording equipment in either public or separate schools.

569. Erin Tp. **S.S.#11. Registers, 1892; 1901; 1907; 1915; 1917-1921; 1923-1959.** 26 ledgers. Loc: WBE.

570. Erin Tp. **S.S.#12 Board. Minutes, 1935-1945; Cash book, 1929-1946.** 1 volume. Loc: WBE.

571. Erin Tp. **S.S.#12. Registers, 1934-1952; 1954-1961.** 8 ledgers. Loc: WBE.

572. Erin Tp. **S.S.#13 Board. Minutes, 1918-1946.** 1 volume. Loc: WBE.

573. Erin Tp. **S.S.#13. Registers, 1912; 1915-1916; 1920-1927; 1929-1965.** 26 ledgers. Loc: WBE.

574. Erin Tp. **S.S.#14 Board. Minutes, 1876-1909; 1911; 1914-1947; Cash books, 1859-1898.** 2 ledgers. Loc: WBE.
The cash books are kept in the same ledgers as the minutes.

575. Erin Tp. **S.S.#14 Board. Teachers' contracts, 1862; 1864-1871.** 1 ledger. Loc: WBE.
A record of agreements for the hiring of teachers, which are held in the same

ledgers as the cash book of the school section.

576. Erin Tp. S.S.#14. Registers, 1909; 1915-1919; 1921-1922; 1924-1964. 24 ledgers. Loc: WBE.

577. Erin Tp. S.S.#16 Board. Cash book, 1901-1941. 1 ledger. Loc: WCA.

578. Erin Tp. S.S.#16 Board. Minutes and cash book, 1900-1946. 1 volume. Loc: WCA.
    The school is also listed as Brisbane Public School. The volume includes a cash book from 1901 to 1936.

579. Erin Tp. S.S.#16. Registers, 1901-1964. 43 ledgers. Loc: WBE.

580. Erin Tp. S.S.#2 Board. Minutes, 1882-1883; Cash book, 1882-1885. 1 volume. Loc: WBE.

581. Erin Tp. S.S.#2 Board. Minutes, 1936-1948. 1 ledger. Loc: WBE.

582. Erin Tp. S.S.#2. Registers, 1900-1901; 1905; 1909-1911; 1913-1914; 1916-1920; 1922-1964. 32 ledgers. Loc: WBE.

583. Erin Tp. S.S.#3 Board. Minutes, 1858-1947; Cash books, 1858-1946. 3 ledgers. Loc: WBE.
    The cash books are kept in the same ledgers as the minutes.

584. Erin Tp. S.S.#3 Board. Teachers' contracts, tax assessments, 1857-1876. 21 ledgers. Loc: WBE.
    A record of teachers' contracts and taxes paid by area residents in support of the school section. The records are held in the same ledgers as the early records of minute books and cash books.

585. Erin Tp. S.S.#3. Certificates of promotion, 1889-1891; 1893. 4 documents. Loc: WCA. MU34.

586. Erin Tp. S.S.#3. Registers, 1920-1961. 8 ledgers. Loc: WBE.

587. Erin Tp. S.S.#4 Board. Cash book, 1898-1939. 1 ledger. Loc: WBE.

588. Erin Tp. S.S.#4. Registers, 1934-1948; 1959-1964. 3 ledgers. Loc: WBE.

589. Erin Tp. S.S.#5. Registers, 1883-1885; 1898; 1902-1903; 1905-1908; 1910-1928; 1930-1961. 37 ledgers. Loc: WBE.

590. Erin Tp. S.S.#6 Board. Cash book, 1937-1945. 1 ledger. Loc: WBE.

591. Erin Tp. S.S.#6. Lower school examination certificates, 1933; 1935. 4 documents. Loc: WCA. MU42.

592. Erin Tp. S.S.#6. Registers, 1879-1880; 1917; 1930-1959. 9 ledgers. Loc: WBE.
    The first page of the ledger contains a printed course of study for the public schools of Ontario prescribed by regulations of the Education Department of Ontario, 1877.

593. **Erin Tp. S.S.#7 Board. Cash book, 1936-1946.** 1 ledger. Loc: WBE.

594. **Erin Tp. S.S.#7. Registers, 1934-1954; 1959-1964.** 7 ledgers. Loc: WBE.

595. **Erin Tp. S.S.#8 Board. Cash book, 1936-1946.** 1 ledger. Loc: WCA.

596. **Erin Tp. S.S.#8. Registers, 1903-1965.** 36 ledgers. Loc: WBE.

597. **Erin Tp. S.S.#9. Registers, 1934-1959.** 8 ledgers. Loc: WBE.

598. **Erin Tp. School Board. Cash book, 1920-1935.** 1 ledger. Loc: WBE.

599. **Erin Tp. School Board. Minutes, 1909-1935.** 1 volume. Loc: WBE.

ERIN VILLAGE

600. **Erin V. Public School. Census book, 1910-1941.** 1 ledger. Loc: WCA.
     A list of name and age of child, name of parent or guardian and place
     of residence. The students were all listed as residents of Erin Village.

FERGUS VILLAGE

601. **Fergus V. High School. Alumni, 1928.** 1 envelope. Loc: WCA.
     A book with names and amounts of money subscribed to the club and a
     register of those who attended the reunion. Part of the Templin-Dow Collection.

602. **Fergus V. High School. Commencement, 1921-1922.** 2 documents. Loc: WCA. MU33.
     A photocopy of original commencement celebrations which lists staff and
     school board members and graduating students.

603. **Fergus V. High School. Entrance examination certificates, 1896; 1905; 1907.** 3
     documents. Loc: WCA. MU51.
     A record of notices indicating three students who were eligible to enter the
     Fergus High School.

604. **Fergus V. High School. Program for opening of new building, 1928.** 1 document.
     Loc: WCA, AO. WCA: MU33.
     A photocopy of an original document announcing the opening of a new Fergus
     High School. The document lists members of the staff and school board and
     outlines plans of the ceremony commemorating the opening of the new school. The
     Templin Collection at the Archives of Ontario also includes a file on schools
     which contains two copies of the original brochure.

605. **Fergus V. Old Lot School House Association. Reunion, 1901.** 1 envelope. Loc:
     WCA.
     A letter announcing and a newspaper clipping describing the event that was
     held in memory of the teacher, James McQueen. Part of the Templin-Dow
     Collection.

606. **Fergus V. Public School. Census books, 1929; 1932-1940; 1945-1946.** 14 ledgers.
     Loc: WCA.

A record of name and age of student and name and address of parent or guardian.

607. Fergus V. **Public School. Registers, 1879-1973.** 5 file cabinet drawers. Loc: WBE.

608. Fergus V. **Public School. Visitors' book, 1872-1876.** 1 ledger. Loc: WCA.
A listing of the names and addresses of visitors, as well as periodic comments regarding school operations. The ledger does not identify the specific names of schools. The book is held with the Pollock Collection.

609. Fergus V. **School Board. Minutes, 1921-1946.** 2 volumes. Loc: WBE.

WEST GARAFRAXA TOWNSHIP

610. Garafraxa W Tp. **Public School. Census books, 1913-1915; 1924; 1926-1942; 1945-1946; 1948-1949.** 25 volumes. Loc: WCA.

611. Garafraxa W Tp. **S.S.#1 Board. Minutes, 1872-1903; Cash book, 1872-1926.** 1 volume. Loc: WBE.
The cash book is held in the same ledger as the minute book.

612. Garafraxa W Tp. **S.S.#1. Registers, 1964-1966.** 1 ledger. Loc: WBE.
The register is held in the same ledger as the one for S.S.#11.

613. Garafraxa W Tp. **S.S.#10 Board. Minutes, 1916-1917; 1920-1944.** 1 volume. Loc: WBE.

614. Garafraxa W Tp. **S.S.#10. Registers, 1916; 1919-1922; 1924-1965.** 22 ledgers. Loc: WBE.

615. Garafraxa W Tp. **S.S.#11. Registers, 1964-1966.** 4 ledgers. Loc: WBE.
One of the ledgers also includes registers for both S.S.#11 and S.S.#1.

616. Garafraxa W Tp. **S.S.#2 Board. Minutes, 1916-1919; Cash book, 1931-1947.** 1 volume. Loc: WBE.
The cash book is held in the same ledger as the minute book. The record includes two deeds for land granted to the school section in the years 1874 and 1918.

617. Garafraxa W Tp. **S.S.#2. Registers, 1899; 1902-1906; 1909-1912; 1914; 1916; 1919-1924; 1927; 1934-1945; 1954-1959; 1964-1968.** 23 ledgers. Loc: WBE.

618. Garafraxa W Tp. **S.S.#2. Registers, 1930-1934.** 1 ledger. Loc: WCA. MU77.
The ledger includes several loose leaf pages which present a history of the school section.

619. Garafraxa W Tp. **S.S.#3 Board. Cash books, 1873-1952.** 3 ledgers. Loc: WBE, WCA.
Cash books for the years 1873-1897 and 1936-1952 are held in fair condition by the Wellington County Board of Education; cash books for 1898-1935 are in poor condition and held by the Wellington County Archives.

620. Garafraxa W Tp. S.S.#3 Board. Minutes, 1854-1869; 1874-1955. 4 volumes. Loc: WBE.

621. Garafraxa W Tp. S.S.#3. Registers, 1892; 1894; 1898-1899; 1902; 1904; 1907; 1909-1919; 1921-1926; 1928; 1964-1966. 26 ledgers. Loc: WBE.

622. Garafraxa W Tp. S.S.#4. Registers, 1903; 1905; 1907-1910; 1912; 1930-1958. 16 ledgers. Loc: WBE.

623. Garafraxa W Tp. S.S.#6. Registers, 1927; 1945-1947; 1954-1959; 1964-1966. 4 ledgers. Loc: WBE.

624. Garafraxa W Tp. S.S.#7 Board. Cash book, 1898-1937. 1 ledger. Loc: WBE.

625. Garafraxa W Tp. S.S.#7 Board. Minutes, 1895-1948. 2 volumes. Loc: WBE.

626. Garafraxa W Tp. S.S.#7. Registers, 1964-1966. Loc: WBE.
Contained in the same ledger as the register for S.S.#1.

627. Garafraxa W Tp. S.S.#8 Board. Minutes and cash book, 1856-1891. 1 volume. Loc: WCA. MU13.
The minutes indicate that in 1869, because of the division of the township, Garafraxa Township S.S.#3 became Garafraxa West Township S.S.#8.

628. Garafraxa W Tp. S.S.#9 Board. Cash book, 1923-1924; 1926-1936. 1 ledger. Loc: WBE.

629. Garafraxa W Tp. S.S.#9 Board. Minutes, 1881-1943; 1948. 1 volume. Loc: WBE.

630. Garafraxa W Tp. S.S.#9. Registers, 1949-1953; 1960-1961. 2 ledgers. Loc: WBE.

631. Garafraxa W Tp. School Board. Requisitions, 1931-1932; School assessments, 1913-1914; 1923. 1 file folder. Loc: WCA.
A record of estimated costs of operating of schools, as well as an outline of assessment costs for S.S.#1, S.S.#7, and S.S.#9.

GUELPH TOWN/CITY

632. Guelph. Alexandra School. Registers, 1930-1939; 1941-1949. 17 ledgers. Loc: WBE.

633. Guelph. Alexandra School. Student notebook, 1925. 1 item. Loc: GCM.
A spelling notebook of Mary Marsh who attended Alexandra School.

634. Guelph. Board of Education. Advisory industrial committee, 1912-1929. 2 ledgers. Loc: WBE.

635. Guelph. Board of Education. Advisory vocational committee, 1930-1941. 1 ledger. Loc: WBE.

636. Guelph. Board of Education. Cash books, 1857-1859; 1892-1952. 26 ledgers. Loc: WBE.

637. Guelph. **Board of Education. Cash journal, 1871-1891.** 1 ledger. Loc: WBE.

638. Guelph. **Board of Education. Committee reports, 1922-1932.** 8 booklets. Loc: WBE.

    A report of the school management committee, property committee and finance committee.

639. Guelph. **Board of Education. High School entrance exams, 1932-1947.** 2 ledgers. Loc: WBE.

    A record of name, age, address and school of those who passed high school entrance examinations.

640. Guelph. **Board of Education. Honour pupil cards, 1872; 1893; 1896-1899; 1901; 1923-1924.** 1 envelope. Loc: GCM.

    A certificate award to honour pupils.

641. Guelph. **Board of Education. Honour pupil certificates, 1886; 1888; 1892; 1905; 1913-1917; 1919; 1923.** 16 documents. Loc: GCM.

    A certificate for good attendance and conduct.

642. Guelph. **Board of Education. Inspector's annual report, 1901.** 1 volume. Loc: GCM.

    A printed report of William Tytler's assessment of Guelph schools that mentions teachers, salaries, attendance, school buildings, examinations, writing, manual training, finances, teachers' association and inspector's duties. It includes a brief report on the Guelph Collegiate Institute.

643. Guelph. **Board of Education. Inspectors' annual reports, 1877-1918.** 36 printed booklets. Loc: WBE.

    Printed reports of public schools by the inspector that includes statistics of the school population, accounts of changes in legislation, descriptions of curriculum and school accommodation, religious exercises, examinations, teachers and finances. Reports on specific public schools are sometimes included and on the Guelph Collegiate Institute for 1885, 1887 and 1897-1916. The Rev. Robert Torrance was secretary and Public School Inspector to 1891, followed by W. Tytler. Members of the Board of Education and its various committees are listed. Copies of reports for 1880, 1881, 1883, 1884, 1889, 1890 and 1916 are missing from this series.

644. Guelph. **Board of Education. Minutes, 1856-1962.** 12 volumes. Loc: WBE.

    The first volume contains minutes of the Board of Common School Trustees for January-March, 1856 when it joined with the Board of Grammar School Trustees to form the Joint Board of Grammar and Common School Trustees. In April, 1871 the board was renamed the Joint Board of Trustees of the Guelph High School and Public School Trustees of Guelph or the United Boards of High and Public School Trustees. In April, 1874 the board was renamed the Guelph Board of Education. The minutes are handwritten to 1955.

645. Guelph. **Board of Education. Public schools ledger, 1871-1891.** 1 ledger. Loc: WBE.

    Financial records of the board's accounts with suppliers, contractors and staff.

646. Guelph. **Board of Education. Rules and regulations, 1876.** 15 p. Loc: WBE.

A printed summary of regulations for the government of the public schools of Guelph as revised and adopted in November 1876 that includes an address to parents and guardians, regulations relating to teachers, pupils and duties of the caretaker. Bound with the regulations of 1865 and 1881 and with inspectors' reports, 1877 to 1918.

647. Guelph. **Board of Education. Rules and regulations, 1881.** 10 p. Loc: WBE.

A printed summary of rules of proceedings of the Guelph Board of Education, as revised in 1881 that includes rules of order at meetings, duties of committees (finance, school property, school management, sites and buildings, visiting), duties of secretary, local inspector, treasurer, chairman and caretakers of ward schools. George Murton was chairman and Robert Torrance was secretary. Bound with Regulations of 1865 and 1876 and with Inspectors' Reports, 1877 to 1918.

648. Guelph. **Board of Education. Rules and regulations, 1881; 1919; 1934.** 3 booklets. Loc: WBE.

649. Guelph. **Board of Education. Rules and regulations relating to administrators and committee members, 1930.** 1 brochure. Loc: GPL.

Rules to govern behaviour of administrators and committee members of the Board of Education. The brochure is held in the Brimmell Collection.

650. Guelph. **Board of Education. Rules and regulations relating to teachers, students and school inspectors, 1930.** 92 p. Loc: GPL.

A collection of the rules and regulations of the Guelph Board of Education that outlines the duties of teachers, students and school inspectors. The book outlines the history of the establishment of Guelph schools.

651. Guelph. **Board of Education. Rules and regulations relating to pupils, 1912.** 1 brochure. Loc: GPL.

Rules to govern behaviour and discipline of students. The brochure is held in the Brimmell Collection.

652. Guelph. **Board of Education. School management committee, 1935-1940.** 1 ledger. Loc: WBE.

653. Guelph. **Board of Education. Sites and buildings committee, 1894-1899; 1900-1913.** 3 ledgers. Loc: WBE.

654. Guelph C.I. **Diploma, 1907.** 1 item. Loc: GCI.

A commercial diploma for a student who graduated in stenography and penmanship.

655. Guelph C.I. **Examination papers, c1870-c1892.** 1 file folder. Loc: GCM.

A collection of graded essays and exams in history, arithmetic, English, grammar, geography, algebra, French and geometry. Most of the papers are signed by E.E. Bailey. There is a list of contents included in the file. Filed with the Allan Gray Collection.

Another professional activity day of the Elora Model School teachers
held at the Elora Gorge, 1893. Photographed by John Connon of Elora.
(Wellington County Museum and Archives)

656. Guelph C.I. **Geography Department. Examination questions, 1904-1905.** 1 file folder. Loc: GCI.

657. Guelph C.I. **History Department. Examination questions, 1904-1905.** 1 file folder. Loc: GCI.
    Three photocopied exam papers.

658. Guelph C.I. **Household science notebook, 1912.** 2 items. Loc: UGA. XR1 MS A061.
    A collection of recipes and notes on yeasts and molds. The notebooks are inscribed with the name of Edna Hartley.

659. Guelph C.I. **Literary Society. Minutes, 1893-1895.** 1 volume. Loc: GCI.
    A record of meetings that include debates, essays and musical recitals. Several debate topics include: civilization at the present day is a hindrance to the production of any great literary work; single tax is preferable to present way of levying taxes; and, free trade as they have it in England would be beneficial to Canada. Both men and women participated and many G.C.I. teachers were active in the society.

660. Guelph C.I. **Staff timetable, 1886.** 1 file folder. Loc: GCI.
    The table records the schedule of classes for Tytler, Davison, Campbell, Nicol and Young.

661. Guelph C.I. **Student records, 1913; 1918.** 2 items. Loc: GCI.
    A record of an honour roll student for the year 1913 and a commercial diploma of a student for 1918.

662. Guelph C.V.I. **Commencement. Programs, 1896-1987.** 5 boxes. Loc: GCI, GPL, WCA, GCM.
    A record of commencement programs which lists the staff, students and the various awards, medals and prizes presented each school year. Copies of 1896 and 1897 programs held in Douglass Collection at GPL, 1902 and 1904 programs also at GPL, 1896 program at WCA, and 1905 program at GCM.

663. Guelph C.V.I. **Commerce Department. Examination questions, 1936; 1940.** 1 file folder. Good. Loc: GCI.

664. Guelph C.V.I. **Course calendars, 1924-1989.** 2 boxes. Loc: GCI.
    A record of the types of courses offered.

665. Guelph C.V.I. **Departmental examination results, 1927-1968.** 3 ledgers. Loc: GCI.
    A record of annual examination results which are labelled either lower, middle or upper school exams.

666. Guelph C.V.I. **Examination mark books, 1892-1945.** 12 ledgers. Loc: GCI.
    A record of students' names, marks achieved in tests and final examination results.

667. Guelph C.V.I. **Examination questions and results, 1885; 1904-1905; 1937.** 1 box. Loc: GCI.
    A record of admission examination results from 1885 and also copies of exams

given at the school in 1904 and 1905. The collection includes newspaper clippings highlighting student grades during the spring of 1937 school term.

668. Guelph C.V.I. **Financial. Cash books, 1888-1952.** 22 ledgers. Loc: WBE, GCI.
The ledgers vary in terms of arrangement with early records covering the accounts of the collegiate and vocational together. However, in later years, collegiate and vocational accounts are divided into separate ledgers. GCI also has cash books for 1910-1929.

669. Guelph C.V.I. **Girls' Athletic Association. Cash book, 1932-1957.** 1 ledger. Loc: GCI.

670. Guelph C.V.I. **History. Centennial celebrations, 1854-1954.** 1 box. Loc: GCI.
A collection of memoirs of early teachers and students, 1954 newspaper clippings, souvenirs of centennial celebrations, and a list of graduates who fought in World War I and II. The collection contains several old photographs of the old school building.

671. Guelph C.V.I. **History. Publications, student essays, newspaper clippings, photographs, 1842-1988.** 1 box. Loc: GCI.
A collection of several essays describing the development of history, location and building of the District of Wellington Grammar School on Waterloo Road, 1842; Guelph Grammar School on Paisley Street, 1854; Guelph High School, 1879; Guelph Collegiate Institute, 1887; and Guelph Collegiate Vocational Institute, 1923. William Tytler was principal from 1875 to 1892, James Davison from 1892 to 1923, and John F. Ross from 1923 to 1945.

672. Guelph C.V.I. **Library records, 1893-1903; 1926-1950.** 4 ledgers. Loc: GCI.
A record of books utilized as well as periodic references to the cost of maintaining the library.

673. Guelph C.V.I. **Music Department. Examination questions, courses of study, musical arrangements, photographs, 1907; 1927; 1929; 1930; 1934.** 1 box. Loc: GCI.
The collection contains several photographs of the school band.

674. Guelph C.V.I. **Newspaper clippings of Guelph history, 1827-1970.** 1 box. Loc: GCI.
A series of historical sketches of the history of Guelph printed in the newspaper, Guelph Mercury.

675. Guelph C.V.I. **Photographs, clippings, 1888; 1942.** 2 file folders. Loc: GCI.
An original photograph of Captain Clark's Daughters of the Empire taken in 1888. The files also contain a pamphlet describing the history of the corps.

676. Guelph C.V.I. **Photographs, sports teams, students, 1875-1986.** 1 box. Loc: GCI.
A number of photographs of students and sports teams in various years including an early photograph in the 1870s, probably of the students of the Guelph Grammar School.

677. Guelph C.V.I. **Principals' reports, 1935-1963.** 1 box. Loc: GCI.
A record of student enrolment in various programs and in later years a note of

the salaries of teachers.

678. Guelph C.V.I. **Principals' reports, correspondence, newspaper clippings, 1847-1940.** 1 box. Loc: GCI.

A record of principals focusing on William Tytler and including letters he had written in 1888 and 1891 favouring the hiring of specific teachers at G.C.I. The record also includes a sketch of the earlier Wellington District Grammar School and its headmaster in the 1840s, Arthur Cole Verner. The collection presents brief historical sketches of prominent area educationalists, including William Tytler and John F. Ross, and a single ledger catalogue of books utilized at G.C.I. from 1896 to 1903.

679. Guelph C.V.I. **Principals' statement of teaching staff, 1924-1971.** 1 box. Loc: GCI.

A record of reports of teachers to be given to the Provincial Inspector each year. The record notes the qualifications, experience, date of appointment and subjects taught by specific teachers.

680. Guelph C.V.I. **Registers, 1911-1927; 1931.** 2 ledgers. Loc: GCI.

681. Guelph C.V.I. **Registers, 1949-1953; 1956-1964; 1966-1968.** 464 ledgers. Loc: WBE.

682. Guelph C.V.I. **Yearbooks, 1926-1987.** 245 volumes. Loc: GCI.

683. Guelph. **Central School. Registers, 1930-1969.** 151 ledgers. Loc: WBE.

684. Guelph. **High School Board. Cash book, 1871-1887.** 1 ledger. Loc: WBE.

685. Guelph. **Joint School Board. Rules and regulations, 1865.** 8 p. Loc: WBE.

A printed summary of regulations governing the proceedings of the Joint Board of Guelph County Grammar School and Common School Trustees of Guelph. Henry W. Peterson was chairman and Robert Torrance secretary. Bound with regulations of 1876 and 1881 and with inspectors' reports, 1877 to 1918.

686. Guelph. **King Edward School. Registers, 1930-1954.** 21 ledgers. Loc: WBE.

687. Guelph. **Public School Cadet Corps. Certificates, 1925-1927.** 3 documents. Loc: GCM.

A record of the corps competing in rifle matches of the Canadian Rifle League.

688. Guelph. **Public School Cadet Corps. Membership roll, 1911.** 1 ledger. Loc: GCM.

A record of name, address, date of joining and date of promotion.

689. Guelph. **Public School. Census registers, c1939; 1942-1949.** 86 registers. Loc: GCH.

Most registers list the total number of children by age for public and separate school supporters and are signed by the assessor. Some are not dated.

690. Guelph. **Public Schools. Registers, 1891-1927.** 7 file cabinet drawers. Loc: WBE.

The registers are bundled by year for all Guelph schools. Most individual registers are unidentified as to name of school.

691. Guelph. **St George's School. Registers, 1892-1922; 1924-1934; 1939-1942; 1945-1954; 1960-1969.** 165 ledgers. Loc: WBE.

692. Guelph. **St John's School. Registers, 1930-1954.** 11 ledgers. Loc: WBE.

693. Guelph. **Torrance School. Registers, 1930-1939.** 19 ledgers. Loc: WBE.

694. Guelph. **Tytler School. Registers, 1930-1954.** 52 ledgers. Loc: WBE.

695. Guelph. **Victoria School. Registers, 1930-1953.** 7 ledgers. Loc: WBE.
In several registers, the title, John McCrae, is added in brackets.

696. Guelph. **Victory School. Registers, 1930-1954.** 72 ledgers. Loc: WBE.

GUELPH TOWNSHIP

697. Guelph Tp. **Collector's roll for school assessment, 1864.** 1 ledger. Loc: WCA.
Lists of local taxpayers grouped in six school sections.

698. Guelph Tp. **Macdonald Consolidated School Board. Cash books, 1929-1942.** 3 ledgers. Loc: WBE.

699. Guelph Tp. **Macdonald Consolidated School Board. Minutes, 1904-1941.** 3 volumes. Loc: WCA.
A detailed record of the monthly meetings of trustees of the first consolidated rural school in Ontario.

700. Guelph Tp. **Macdonald Consolidated School. Examination questions and answers, 1927-1962.** 9 ledgers. Loc: WBE.

701. Guelph Tp. **Macdonald Consolidated School Home and School Association. Constitution, 1925.** 1 item. Loc: WBE.

702. Guelph Tp. **Macdonald Consolidated School Home and School Association. Minutes, 1921-1935; 1937-1948.** 3 ledgers. Loc: WBE.

703. Guelph Tp. **Macdonald Consolidated School Parents' and Teachers' Association. Minutes, 1915-1922.** 1 volume. Loc: WBE.

704. Guelph Tp. **Macdonald Consolidated School. Registers, 1905-1909; 1911-1969.** 150 ledgers. Loc: WBE.
The school is referred to at times as S.S.#6-1/2 and 7 of Guelph Township. The records include separate registers for S.S.#7 beginning in the 1920s. The school's location is referred to as 'Guelph' in the 1949-1956 ledgers.

705. Guelph Tp. **Plans. Septic tank for Guelph Consolidated School, c1920.** 1 plan. Loc: WCA.

706. Guelph Tp. **S.S.#1 Board. Cash books, 1863-1941.** 2 ledgers. Loc: WCA, WBE.
The cash book for the years 1863 to 1935 is held by the WCA, that for the

period 1936 to 1941 by WBE.

707. **Guelph Tp. S.S.#1 Board. Minutes, 1872-1909; 1925-1941.** 3 ledgers. Loc: WBE, WCA.
     The minute book for 1872-1909, held at WCA, is in poor condition. The book for 1925-1940, at the WBE, is fair. Only six pages of the 1940-1941 book, held at WCA, have been used.

708. **Guelph Tp. S.S.#1. Registers, 1902-1904; 1949-1954; 1956-1959.** 5 ledgers. Loc: WBE.

709. **Guelph Tp. S.S.#2 Board. Cash books, 1858-1919; 1924-1934.** 2 volumes. Loc: WCA.
     Cash books for the period 1858 to 1919 are combined with the minute book for the same period. The cash books for 1924 to 1934 are combined with minutes for 1930 to 1941.

710. **Guelph Tp. S.S.#2 Board. Minutes, 1858-1919; 1930-1941.** 2 volumes. Loc: WCA.
     Combined with cash book in one volume for period 1858 to 1919. The minute book for 1930 to 1941 also contains the cash book for 1924 to 1934.

711. **Guelph Tp. S.S.#2. Registers, 1906; 1930-1964.** 10 ledgers. Loc: WBE.

712. **Guelph Tp. S.S.#3 Board. Cash book, 1936-1941.** 1 ledger. Loc: WBE.

713. **Guelph Tp. S.S.#3 Board. Minutes, 1883-1908; Cash book, 1883-1908.** 1 volume. Loc: WBE.

714. **Guelph Tp. S.S.#3. Registers, 1879-1882; 1921; 1923-1924; 1926-1964.** 18 ledgers. Loc: WBE.

715. **Guelph Tp. S.S.#4-1/2 Board. Cash book, 1894-1930; 1934-1941.** 1 volume. Loc: WCA.
     Combined in one large volume with minutes for the period 1894 to 1930.

716. **Guelph Tp. S.S.#4-1/2 Board. Minutes, 1894-1930; 1935-1942.** 2 volumes. Loc: WCA.
     Minutes for the period 1894 to 1930 are combined in one large volume with the accounts for the same period and with reports of trustees' meetings and the auditors' annual reports. Only twenty pages of the 1935 to 1942 minute book have been used.

717. **Guelph Tp. S.S.#4-1/2. Registers, 1909; 1920; 1945-1963.** 7 ledgers. Loc: WBE.

718. **Guelph Tp. S.S.#4 Board. Cash books, 1878-1941.** 3 ledgers. Loc: WBE, WCA.
     The cash book for 1878-1927 is in the same volume as the minutes for those years and is held at WBE. The cash book for 1929-1937 is combined with the minutes for 1928-1941 in a volume held by WCA. The WBE has a separate cash book for 1938-1941.

719. **Guelph Tp. S.S.#4 Board. Minutes, 1878-1941.** 2 ledgers. Loc: WBE, WCA.
     The minute book for 1878-1928, held by WBE, also contains the accounts. The

minute book for 1928-1941, held by WCA, also has the accounts for 1928-1937.

720. Guelph Tp. S.S.#4. Registers, 1900-1904; 1930-1962. 14 ledgers. Loc: WBE.

721. Guelph Tp. S.S.#5 Board. Minutes, 1931-1941. 1 volume. Loc: WCA.

722. Guelph Tp. S.S.#5. Deed and contract, 1897; 1901. 1 envelope. Loc: WCA. MU19.
A contract to hire James Grant as teacher for 1897 and a deed to purchase land for the school from John Laidlaw in 1901.

723. Guelph Tp. S.S.#5. Plan of residences of individuals in Concession 4, Division D, 1850. Loc: AO. FA; MU 454.
Part of Byerly Papers.

724. Guelph Tp. S.S.#5. Registers, 1895; 1902; 1906; 1909; 1911-1923; 1926; 1928; 1929-1964. 29 ledgers. Loc: WBE, GCM.
The register for 1909 only is held by GCM.

725. Guelph Tp. S.S.#6 Board. Cash book, 1931-1941. 1 ledger. Loc: WBE.

726. Guelph Tp. S.S.#6 Board. Minutes, 1910-1941. 1 volume. Loc: WCA.

727. Guelph Tp. S.S.#6. Registers, 1901; 1904-1905; 1922-1923; 1927-1928; 1934-1964. 19 ledgers. Loc: WBE.

728. Guelph Tp. S.S.#6. Support fees, 1857. 1 document. Loc: WCA.
A record of the names of school supporters noting the amount of money due and whether or not fees were paid by specific residents. Part of the Pollock Collection.

729. Guelph Tp. S.S.#7 Board. Minutes, 1895-1922. 1 volume. Loc: WCA.
This school section appears to have overlapped with the territory of the Macdonald Consolidated School, but separate minute books were maintained for S.S.#7 and for the Macdonald Consolidated School. Various professors at the O.A.C. served as trustees for S.S.#7, notably Professor C.A. Zavitz as secretary. Several documents that outline the history of the Macdonald Consolidated School and comment on the rural school consolidation movement are folded into the minute book.

730. Guelph Tp. School Board. Cash book, 1942-1946. 2 ledgers. Loc: WBE.

731. Guelph Tp. School Board. Minutes, 1933-1959. 2 ledgers. Loc: WBE.
These minutes provide information on area school fairs and picnics.

732. Guelph Tp/ Nichol Tp/ Pilkington Tp. Union S.S.#3 Board. Minutes, 1910-1941; Cash books, 1910-1941. 1 volume. Loc: WBE.

WEST LUTHER TOWNSHIP

733. Luther W Tp. S.S.#11 Board. Cash books, 1899-1950. 1 ledger. Loc: WBE.

734. **Luther W Tp. S.S.#11 Board. Minutes, 1898-1950.** 1 volume. Loc: WBE.
A record of minutes of board meetings held several times each year.

735. **Luther W Tp. S.S.#11. Registers, 1945-1949.** 1 ledger. Loc: WBE.

736. **Luther W Tp. S.S.#14. Registers, 1919; 1921; 1925-1927; 1930-1964.** 8 ledgers.
Loc: WBE.

737. **Luther W Tp. S.S.#18. Registers, 1923; 1930-1966.** 11 ledgers. Loc: WBE.

738. **Luther W Tp. S.S.#3. Registers, 1930-1965.** 10 ledgers. Loc: WBE.

739. **Luther W Tp. S.S.#4. Registers, 1930-1969.** 11 ledgers. Loc: WBE.

740. **Luther W Tp. S.S.#5 Board. Cash book, 1903-1945.** 1 ledger. Loc: WBE.

741. **Luther W Tp. S.S.#5. Registers, 1930-1965.** 9 ledgers. Loc: WBE.

742. **Luther W Tp. S.S.#6. Registers, 1930-1965.** 10 ledgers. Loc: WBE.

743. **Luther W Tp. S.S.#7 Board. Cash book, 1897-1944.** 1 ledger. Loc: WBE.

744. **Luther W Tp. S.S.#8. Registers, 1930-1969.** 9 ledgers. Loc: WBE.

745. Luther W Tp/ Garafraxa W Tp. **Union S.S.#1 Board. Registers, 1934-1965.** 7
ledgers. Loc: WBE.

746. Luther W Tp/ Arthur Tp. **Union S.S.#12. Registers, 1919-1928; 1930-1966.** 21
ledgers. Loc: WBE.

747. Luther W Tp/ Luther E Tp. **Union S.S.#2 Board. Cash book, 1908-1964.** 1 ledger.
Loc: WBE.

748. Luther W Tp/ Luther E Tp. **Union S.S.#2. Registers, 1959-1964.** 1 ledger. Loc:
WBE.

749. Luther W Tp/ Arthur Tp. **Union S.S.#7. Registers, 1930-1969.** 9 ledgers. Loc:
WBE.

MARYBOROUGH TOWNSHIP

750. Maryborough Tp. **Public School. Census, 1899-1903; 1943.** 3 registers in 1 file
folder. Loc: WCA.
A record of name and age of child, parent or guardian, and name of school.
There were 19 school sections in the township.

751. Maryborough Tp. **S.S.#10 Board. Minutes, 1869-1887; 1923-1960; Cash books,
1869-1887; 1923-1944.** 2 ledgers. Loc: WBE.
The cash book is held in the same ledger as the minute book.

752. Maryborough Tp. **S.S.#10. Registers, 1934-1962.** 6 ledgers. Loc: WBE.

753. Maryborough Tp. S.S.#11 Board. **Minutes, 1890-1909; 1926-1962.** 4 ledgers. Loc: WBE.

754. Maryborough Tp. S.S.#11. **Registers, 1921; 1924-1925; 1927; 1929-1944; 1954-1964; 1966-1969.** 12 ledgers. Loc: WBE.
A catalogue for recording the equipment of the school is held with the registers.

755. Maryborough Tp. S.S.#12 Board. **Minutes, 1880-1953; Cash books, 1880-1903.** 2 ledgers. Loc: WBE.

756. Maryborough Tp. S.S.#12. **Registers, 1890-1891; 1893; 1895-1899; 1902; 1912; 1914; 1916; 1920-1923; 1925-1939.** 12 registers in 1 file folder. Loc: WCA.

757. Maryborough Tp. S.S.#12. **Visitors' book, 1916-1932.** 1 ledger. Loc: WBE.

758. Maryborough Tp. S.S.#13 Board. **Cash book, 1921-1943.** 1 ledger. Loc: MBH.

759. Maryborough Tp. S.S.#13 Board. **Minutes, 1920-1957.** 1 volume. Loc: MBH.
A record of annual meetings and of periodic sittings held a few times each year. The minutes list motions carried and the election of auditors and trustees. The minutes are held in the same ledger as the cash book records of the school section.

760. Maryborough Tp. S.S.#13. **Register, 1916.** 1 ledger. Loc: WCA. MU74.

761. Maryborough Tp. S.S.#14. **Registers, 1896; 1901-1912; 1915-1919; 1922-1926; 1928-1949; 1953-1962.** 32 ledgers. Loc: WBE.

762. Maryborough Tp. S.S.#15 Board. **Cash books, 1865-1883; 1891-1947.** 2 ledgers. Loc: WBE.

763. Maryborough Tp. S.S.#15 Board. **Minutes, 1865-1883; 1893-1907; 1910-1956.** 6 ledgers. Loc: WBE.
For the period from 1910 to 1956, one ledger records annual meetings from 1910 to 1952, and 3 volumes record various meetings held throughout each year from 1927 to 1956.

764. Maryborough Tp. S.S.#15 Board. **Teachers' contracts and inspectors' reports, 1887-1890; 1902; 1904.** 1 file folder. Loc: WBE.

765. Maryborough Tp. S.S.#15. **Registers, 1909; 1911-1912; 1917; 1919-1926; 1930-1962.** 20 ledgers. Loc: WBE.
The records include a listing of the marks of students in the 1909 ledger.

766. Maryborough Tp. S.S.#15. **Visitors' book, 1890-1938.** 1 ledger. Loc: WBE.

767. Maryborough Tp. S.S.#17 Board. **Minutes, 1905-1954.** 1 volume. Loc: WBE.

768. Maryborough Tp. S.S.#17. **Registers, 1915-1917; 1921-1922; 1930-1934; 1939-1949; 1954-1961.** 10 ledgers. Loc: WBE.

769. Maryborough Tp. **S.S.#19 Board. Minutes, 1876-1938; Cash books, 1876-1933.** 2 ledgers. Loc: WBE.
The cash books are held in the same ledgers as the minute books.

770. Maryborough Tp. **S.S.#2 Board. Cash books, 1883-1935.** 2 ledgers. Loc: WBE.

771. Maryborough Tp. **S.S.#2 Board. Minutes, 1869-1876; 1903-1935; 1939-1953; Cash books, 1869-1876.** ledgers. Loc: WBE.
The first ledger also includes financial accounts.

772. Maryborough Tp. **S.S.#2. Registers, 1897; 1899-1910; 1916-1918; 1922; 1926-1942; 1945-1957.** 30 ledgers. Loc: WBE.

773. Maryborough Tp. **S.S.#4. Registers, 1898-1903; 1905-1912; 1916-1920; 1922-1923; 1925; 1934-1960.** 30 ledgers. Loc: WBE.

774. Maryborough Tp. **S.S.#5. Registers, 1896; 1899; 1901; 1903-1909; 1911-1912; 1917-1918; 1928-1960.** 26 ledgers. Loc: WBE.

775. Maryborough Tp. **S.S.#7 Board. Minutes, 1880-1944; Cash books, 1880-1944.** 2 ledgers. Loc: WBE.

776. Maryborough Tp. **S.S.#7 Board. Minutes, 1899-1927.** 1 volume. Loc: WBE.

777. Maryborough Tp. **S.S.#7. Registers, 1895-1899; 1904; 1913; 1915; 1918-1919; 1921-1923; 1930-1962.** 20 ledgers. Loc: WBE.

778. Maryborough Tp. **S.S.#9 Board. Minutes, 1936-1960.** 1 volume. Loc: WBE.

779. Maryborough Tp. **S.S.#9. Registers, 1879-1880; 1882-1885; 1896; 1904-1905; 1909; 1911-1914; 1917-1929; 1930-1958.** 89 ledgers. Loc: WBE.
A catalogue for recording the equipment of the school is held with the registers.

780. Maryborough Tp. **S.S.#9. Student notebook, 1927.** 1 item. Loc: WCA. MU33.
The notebook of Eleanor McLean of Moorefield that includes entries for science, mathematics and history.

781. Maryborough Tp. **School Board. School assessment and register, 1924-1927.** 1 ledger. Loc: WCA.
A record of name and amount of assessment.

782. Maryborough Tp/ Peel Tp. **Union S.S.#8, Riverside. Registers, 1892; 1897-1898; 1900-1903; 1907-1910; 1913-1914; 1916-1919; 1921-1929.** 26 ledgers. Loc: WBE.

MINTO TOWNSHIP

783. Minto Tp. **S.S.#1 Board. Cash book, 1866-1903.** 1 ledger. Loc: WCA.

784. Minto Tp. **S.S.#1 Board. Cash books, 1896-1935; 1940-1946.** 1 ledger. Loc: WBE.

785. **Minto Tp. S.S.#1 Board. Minutes, 1933-1945; 1949-1962.** 1 ledger. Loc: WBE.
     The minutes include financial accounts.

786. **Minto Tp. S.S.#1. Registers, 1930-1965.** 10 ledgers. Loc: WBE.
     A number of the registers refer to Minto Township as 'little Ireland'.

787. **Minto Tp. S.S.#11 Board. Minutes, 1913-1945; Cash book, 1913-1945.** 1 volume.
     Loc: WBE.
     The cash book is held in the same ledger as the minutes.

788. **Minto Tp. S.S.#12 Board. Minutes, 1927-1945.** 1 volume. Loc: WBE.

789. **Minto Tp. S.S.#12. Registers, 1913; 1917-1920; 1922-1965.** 22 ledgers. Loc:
     WBE.

790. **Minto Tp. S.S.#13 Board. Cash book, 1903-1945.** 1 ledger. Loc: WBE.

791. **Minto Tp. S.S.#13 Board. Minutes, 1926-1929.** 1 volume. Loc: WBE.

792. **Minto Tp. S.S.#13. Registers, 1879-1887; 1909; 1911-1923; 1926-1965.** 32
     ledgers. Loc: WBE.

793. **Minto Tp. S.S.#14 Board. Minutes, 1872-1909; 1937-1945; Cash books, 1872-1909.**
     2 volumes. Loc: WBE.
     The minutes from 1872-1909 are included in the cash book for the same period.

794. **Minto Tp. S.S.#14. Registers, 1917; 1921; 1923; 1930-1965.** 13 ledgers. Loc:
     WBE.

795. **Minto Tp. S.S.#15 Board. Minutes, 1934-1945.** 1 volume. Loc: WBE.

796. **Minto Tp. S.S.#15. Registers, 1919-1965.** 21 ledgers. Loc: WBE.
     The school section was called Minto and Wallace Townships S.S.#15 prior to
     1930, and after that date was called Minto Township, S.S.#15.

797. **Minto Tp. S.S.#17 Board. Minutes, 1904-1944.** 1 volume. Loc: WBE.

798. **Minto Tp. S.S.#18 Board. Minutes, 1920-1931; Cash book, 1926-1945.** 1 volume.
     Loc: WBE.

799. **Minto Tp. S.S.#18. Registers, 1921-1965.** 18 ledgers. Loc: WBE.

800. **Minto Tp. S.S.#2 Board. Cash book, 1926-1944.** 1 ledger. Loc: WBE.

801. **Minto Tp. S.S.#2. Registers, 1918-1919; 1921-1926; 1928-1965.** 23 ledgers. Loc:
     WBE. The record includes equipment inventories for S.S.#2 and S.S.#14

802. **Minto Tp. S.S.#3 Board. Cash and minute book, 1861-1897.** 1 volume. Loc: WBE.
     The minute book is held in the back half of the cash book.

803. **Minto Tp. S.S.#3 Board. Cash books, 1898-1945.** 2 ledgers. Loc: WBE.

804. Minto Tp. S.S.#3 Board. Minutes, 1897-1943. 1 volume. Loc: WBE.

805. Minto Tp. S.S.#3. Registers, 1907-1922; 1924-1927; 1930-1965. 29 ledgers. Loc: WBE.

806. Minto Tp. S.S.#6 Board. Cash books, 1884-1945. 3 ledgers. Loc: WBE.
    The cash book records do not always appear in chronological order, especially in the years 1884-1899.

807. Minto Tp. S.S.#6 Board. Minutes, 1868-1933; 1936-1945; Cash books, 1868-1933. 4 volumes. Loc: WBE.
    The first two volumes of minutes, which cover the period 1868 to 1933, also include the cash books.

808. Minto Tp. S.S.#6. Registers, 1895-1896; 1898-1911; 1913; 1916-1922; 1924-1964. 51 ledgers. Loc: WBE.
    The records include 11 ledgers which list school equipment in various school sections in the late 1940s.

809. Minto Tp. S.S.#6. Visitors' book, 1874-1887. 1 ledger. Loc: WBE.

810. Minto Tp. S.S.#7 Board. Minutes, 1906-1945; Cash book, 1906-1945. 1 volume. Loc: WBE.
    The cash book is held in the same volume as the minute book.

811. Minto Tp. S.S.#7. Registers, 1893; 1896-1898; 1904; 1907; 1909; 1912; 1920; 1922-1927; 1929-1964. 26 ledgers. Loc: WBE.

812. Minto Tp. S.S.#8 Board. Minutes, 1898-1945; Cash book, 1897-1945. 21 volumes. Loc: WBE.
    The cash book and minutes for the years 1897-1929 are in the same volume, which is in very poor condition; the cash books and minutes for the years 1929-1945 are in the same volume.

813. Minto Tp. S.S.#8. Registers, 1907; 1909; 1918-1925; 1927-1929; 1934-1965. 23 ledgers. Loc: WBE.

814. Minto Tp. S.S.#9. Registers, 1892-1893; 1895-1896; 1899; 1903-1914; 1916; 1919-1922; 1927-1965. 37 ledgers. Loc: WBE.

815. Minto Tp/ Clifford V. Union Continuation School. Registers, 1913; 1916-1950. 66 ledgers. Loc: WBE.

816. Minto Tp/ Clifford V. Union Continuation School. Student examination records, 1927-1938. 1 ledger. Loc: WBE.

817. Minto Tp/ Clifford V. Union S.S.#10 Board. Cash books, 1905-1951. 2 ledgers. Loc: WBE.

818. Minto Tp/ Clifford V. Union S.S.#10 Board. Minutes, 1917-1956. 3 volumes. Loc: WBE.
    The volumes refer to the school section as Union S.S.#10.

819. Minto Tp/ Clifford V. **Union S.S.#10. Registers, 1930-1965.** 37 ledgers. Loc: WBE.

The school section was called Clifford S.S.#10 until 1938, then Clifford Public School until the 1960s when it was referred to as Clifford Central School.

820. Minto Tp/ Arthur Tp. **Union S.S.#16 Board. Cash book, 1900-1944.** 1 ledger. Loc: WBE.

821. Minto Tp/ Arthur Tp. **Union S.S.#16. Registers, 1901-1902; 1904-1905; 1907; 1916; 1921; 1927; 1930-1965.** 19 ledgers. Loc: WBE.

The records include two early twentieth century registers which are not fully dated. The school section was originally called Arthur Township, S.S.#16 but by 1905 is labelled on registers as Arthur and Minto Townships, S.S.#16.

822. Minto Tp/ Arthur Tp. **Union S.S.#17 Board. Minutes, 1903-1905; 1915-1946; Cash books, 1905-1946.** 3 volumes. Loc: WBE.

The cash book also includes the minutes of the school section, but they are in very poor condition for the years 1903, 1904 and 1905. The 1903 minutes indicate the school section was formed in 1900.

823. Minto Tp/ Arthur Tp. **Union S.S.#17. Registers, 1905; 1907-1909; 1912-1926; 1928-1964.** 32 ledgers. Loc: WBE.

MOUNT FOREST TOWN

824. Mount Forest T. **High School. Examination results, 1931.** 2 documents. Loc: WCA. MU23.

A record of the marks of students in British history and algebra.

825. Mount Forest T. **High School. Programs, 1931-1933.** 3 documents. Loc: WCA. MU23.

A list of programs of annual concerts and lists of the names of students graduating, teachers and members of the board of education.

NICHOL TOWNSHIP

826. Nichol Tp. **Ponsonby Private School. Register, 1898.** 1 ledger. Loc: WBE.

827. Nichol Tp. **Public School. Census registers, 1924; 1927.** 1 file folder. Loc: WCA.

A record of children attending schools which notes the ages and place of residence of students and lists school section attended. The record includes 4 census books of township schools with two being undated.

828. Nichol Tp. **S.S.#2 Board. Minutes, 1903-1962.** 1 volume. Loc: WBE.

829. Nichol Tp. **S.S.#2. Cash book, 1862-1950.** 1 ledger. Loc: WCA.

A record of monthly receipts and expenditures

830. Nichol Tp. **S.S.#2. Registers, 1915; 1917; 1920-1923; 1925-1928; 1930-1963.** 31 ledgers. Loc: WBE.

831. Nichol Tp. **S.S.#3 Board. Minutes, 1878-1925; Cash books, 1878-1923.** 2 ledgers. Loc: WBE.
 The cash books are held in the same ledgers as the minute books.

832. Nichol Tp. **S.S.#3. Registers, 1930-1964.** 17 ledgers. Loc: WBE.

833. Nichol Tp. **S.S.#4 Board. Minutes, 1863-1866; 1868-1908; 1920-1945; Cash books, 1860-1945.** 3 ledgers. Loc: WBE.
 The minute book is held in the same ledger as the cash book. The minute book includes the annual reports of the school trustees.

834. Nichol Tp. **S.S.#4. Notebooks, 1867; 1880.** 3 volumes. Loc: WCA.
 Penmanship notebooks of Elsbet and Mary Dow. One notebook is marked 'S.S.#4, Nichol'. Part of the Templin-Dow Collection.

835. Nichol Tp. **S.S.#4. Registers, 1904-1905; 1908; 1930-1964.** 14 ledgers. Loc: WBE, AO, WCA.
 The Archives of Ontario (FA: MU 2956) hold the registers for the years 1904 and 1905, as part of the Templin Family Collection. The Wellington County Archives holds the 1908 register which forms part of the Templin-Dow Collection.

836. Nichol Tp. **S.S.#6. Registers, 1930-1962.** 7 ledgers. Loc: WBE.

837. Nichol Tp. **S.S. Union #8. Correspondence and report of court hearing, 1896-1897..** 1 file folder. Loc: UGA, WCA. UGA: XR1 MS A007; WCA: MU 101.
 Two letters and a newspaper article regarding a legal suit of the school trustees of S.S.#4 and S.S.#5 Pilkington Township and S.S.#3 Nichol Township against the school trustees of the proposed Union S.S.#8 of Nichol and Pilkington Townships. The file also includes letters of Alexander Moir to James Dow concerning the school union. The file at the Wellington County Archives also includes a photograph of the school.

838. Nichol Tp. **Salem School. Registers, 1930-1949.** 1 file cabinet drawer. Loc: WBE.

839. Nichol Tp. **School Board. School assessment schedules, 1894-1896; 1898; 1910-1916.** 1 file folder. Loc: WCA.
 A record of the financial transactions of township school sections.

840. Nichol Tp. **School. Registers, 1923-1924.** 1 ledger. Loc: WCA. MU77.
 School section is not stated.

841. Nichol Tp/ Garafraxa W Tp. **Union S.S.#3 Board. Minutes, 1926-1944; Cash book, 1926-1944.** 1 volume. Loc: WBE.

842. Nichol Tp/ Pilkington Tp. **Union S.S.#5 Board. Cash book, 1921-1944.** 2 ledgers. Loc: WBE.

843. Nichol Tp/ Pilkington Tp. **Union S.S.#5. Registers, 1879-1889; 1914; 1916-1919; 1921; 1923-1954; 1959-1964.** 62 ledgers. Loc: WBE.

844. Nichol Tp/ Pilkington Tp. **Union S.S.#8. Registers, 1897; 1900-1904; 1907; 1909; 1911-1912; 1914-1919; 1921-1930; 1934; 1939**. 27 ledgers. Loc: WBE.

PEEL TOWNSHIP

845. Peel Tp. **Public School. Census book, 1893-1898.** 1 ledger. Loc: WCA.
A record of the name and age of students, a list of their guardians, and a note of the lot and concession number where they lived.

846. Peel Tp. **S.S.#1. Registers, 1916-1950; 1930-1964.** 34 ledgers. Loc: WBE.
The records include a ledger listing costs incurred in purchasing school supplies for the years 1916-1964.

847. Peel Tp. **S.S.#10. Registers, 1892; 1894; 1901-1916; 1920; 1925; 1927-1961.** 30 ledgers. Loc: WBE.

848. Peel Tp. **S.S.#11. Registers, 1902; 1908; 1910; 1917; 1921-1924; 1926-1961.** 21 ledgers. Loc: WBE.

849. Peel Tp. **S.S.#13 Board. Minutes, 1929-1964; Cash books, 1927-1946.** 1 volume. Loc: WBE.
The cash book is held in the same ledger as the minute book.

850. Peel Tp. **S.S.#13. Registers, 1921; 1929-1969.** 6 ledgers. Loc: WBE.
A number of the ledgers record student grades for various school years.

851. Peel Tp. **S.S.#14. Registers, 1930-1962.** 9 ledgers. Loc: WBE.

852. Peel Tp. **S.S.#15. Registers, 1934-1944; 1949-1961.** 4 ledgers. Loc: WBE.

853. Peel Tp. **S.S.#16. Registers, 1896-1898; 1900; 1905-1906; 1909-1911; 1913-1916; 1920-1926; 1928-1956.** 30 ledgers. Loc: WBE.

854. Peel Tp. **S.S.#17 Board. Minutes, 1917-1964.** 1 volume. Loc: WBE.

855. Peel Tp. **S.S.#17. Registers, 1954-1959.** 1 ledger. Loc: WBE.

856. Peel Tp. **S.S.#18 Board. Minutes, 1916-1925.** 1 ledger. Loc: WBE.

857. Peel Tp. **S.S.#18. Registers, 1918-1962.** 29 ledgers. Loc: WBE.

858. Peel Tp. **S.S.#2. Certificate of promotion, 1887.** 1 envelope. Loc: WCA.

859. Peel Tp. **S.S.#3. Registers, 1929-1961.** 7 ledgers. Loc: WBE.

860. Peel Tp. **S.S.#5. Registers, 1917-1920; 1926-1959.** 16 ledgers. Loc: WBE.

861. Peel Tp. **S.S.#7 Board. Minutes, 1919-1933.** 1 volume. Loc: WBE.

862. Peel Tp. **S.S.#8. Registers, 1896; 1930-1961.** 10 ledgers. Loc: WBE.

863. Peel Tp. **S.S.#9. Registers, 1930, 1959.** 8 ledgers. Loc: WBE.

864. Peel Tp/ Pilkington Tp/ Nichol Tp. **Union S.S.#7. Registers, 1904-1918; 1921; 1924; 1927; 1929-1964.** 47 ledgers. Loc: WBE.
The union school section is labelled S.S.#7, Peel Township, after 1929.

865. Peel Tp/ Maryborough Tp. **Union S.S.#8 Board. Minutes, 1931-1961; Cash book, 1932-1944.** 1 volume. Loc: WBE.
The cash book is held in the same ledger as the minute book.

866. Peel Tp/ Garafraxa W Tp. **Union S.S.#9. Registers, 1894-1896; 1898-1901; 1904-1905; 1907-1909; 1913-1918.** 20 ledgers. Loc: WBE.

PILKINGTON TOWNSHIP

867. Pilkington Tp. **S.S.#1 Board. Minutes, 1884-1963; Cash books, 1884-1946.** 2 ledgers. Loc: WBE.
The financial accounts are included with the minutes.

868. Pilkington Tp. **S.S.#1. Registers, 1890-1892; 1896; 1898-1916; 1918-1965.** 44 ledgers. Loc: WBE.

869. Pilkington Tp. **S.S.#2. Registers, 1901; 1903; 1905-1906; 1908; 1911-1914; 1918-1921; 1923; 1925-1965.** 28 ledgers. Loc: WBE.

870. Pilkington Tp. **S.S.#4 Board. Cash book, 1913-1945.** 1 ledger. Loc: WBE.

871. Pilkington Tp. **S.S.#4 Board. Minutes, 1932-1960.** 1 ledger. Loc: WBE.

872. Pilkington Tp. **S.S.#4. Registers, 1893; 1898-1899; 1900-1908; 1914; 1917-1918; 1920-1921; 1923-1927; 1929-1964.** 33 ledgers. Loc: WBE.

873. Pilkington Tp. **S.S.#5. Registers, 1907-1910; 1912; 1916-1917; 1919-1921; 1925-1963.** 33 ledgers. Loc: WBE.

874. Pilkington Tp. **S.S.#6. Registers, 1927-1958; 1930-1934; 1939-1964.** 17 ledgers. Loc: WBE.

875. Pilkington Tp. **S.S.#7 Board. Assessment, 1891-1892.** 1 file folder. Loc: WCA.
A record of correspondence pertaining to the increase in acreage and assessment of the school section.

876. Pilkington Tp/ Woolwich Tp. **Union S.S.#2 Board. Minutes, 1903-1955; Cash books, 1903-1955.** 3 ledgers. Loc: WBE.
The minutes are held in the same ledgers as the cash books for the years 1903 to 1931 and from 1944 to 1955.

PUSLINCH TOWNSHIP

877. Puslinch Township, S.S.#1. **Miscellaneous records, 1854-1928.** 1 file. Loc: WCA. MU 104.
The file, relating to the Arkell school, includes land records dating from 1854 to 1907, vouchers from the education inspector's office concerning grants,

and a 1928 report by a sanitary inspector of the Ontario Department of Health.

878. Puslinch Tp. S.S.#1. **Registers, 1898; 1913-1958.** 26 ledgers. Loc: WBE.

879. Puslinch Tp. S.S.#2. **Registers, 1879; 1883-1885; 1894; 1897; 1900; 1902-1905; 1908; 1910-1912.** 13 ledgers. Loc: WBE.

880. Puslinch Tp. S.S.#3. **Rough plan of extent, 1851.** Loc: AO. FA; MU 454.
Part of Byerly Papers.

881. Puslinch Tp. S.S.#6 Board. **Cash book, 1862-1910.** 1 ledger. Loc: WBE.

882. Puslinch Tp. S.S.#6. **Certificate of promotion, 1891.** 1 document. Loc: WCA.
MU23.
A record of promotion of Jennie MacPherson at Crieff Public School.

883. Puslinch Tp. S.S.#6. **Photo of class and teachers, 1906; 1911.** 2 photos. Loc:
WBE.

SEPARATE SCHOOLS

884. Guelph Separate School Board. **Boys' Separate School. Building specifications,
1914.** 1 document. Loc: WSB.
A record of alterations and additions to the school.

885. Guelph Separate School Board. **Bylaws, 1896.** 1 brochure. Loc: WSB.
A printed copy of board bylaws that refers to the information of three
standing committees: finance and assessment, school management and school
property. J.E. McElderry was the chair of the board.

886. Guelph Separate School Board. **Correspondence, 1856-1903 (sporadic).** 5
documents. Loc: WSB.
A record of six brief letters dealing with payment of salaries of teachers,
types of textbooks used in schools and regrets of a teacher for being
transferred to Hamilton from her position teaching in a Guelph school.

887. Guelph Separate School Board. **Financial. Cash books, 1879-1921; 1932-1951.** 6
ledgers. Loc: WSB.

888. Guelph Separate School Board. **Honour pupil cards, 1904.** 1 envelope. Loc: GCM.
A certificate awarded to honour pupils.

889. Guelph Separate School Board. **Minutes, 1879-1905; 1914-1959.** 7 volumes. Loc:
WSB.
A record of monthly meetings.

890. Guelph Separate School Board. **Student notebooks, c1895-1906.** 6 items. Loc:
GCM.
Student notebooks of four McAteer children who attended Catholic schools in
Guelph. The father of the children, John McAteer, owned the American Hotel in
Guelph which he operated during the late nineteenth and early twentieth century.

891. Loretto Academy. **Award of merit, 1906.** 1 document. Loc: GCM.
A certificate presented to Genevieve McAteer.

892. Loretto Academy. **Report to Department of Education, n.d..** Loc: AO. FA: RG-2, G-4, Box 1, Envelope #1.
A brief statistical report which notes that the Catholic girls' school was established in 1856, had three hundred and ninety students and five departments of study, and that annual fees for tuition and board were one thousand dollars. Held with Miscellaneous School Records of the Ontario Department of Education.

A study in contrasts: the simplicity of a hay cart passing by the ornate exterior of the **Guelph Carnegie Library, c1908**. Andrew Carnegie granted $24,000 to the Building Fund for its construction in 1905. Records relating to the construction of the building include #920, #3406 (plans) and #3435 (photographs). Taken by Guelph photographer John Woodruff. (National Archives of Canada)

Absent scholars: a view of the Guelph Carnegie Library reading room soon after its opening. At this time the stacks were closed and users had to ask the librarian for each book. (Guelph Public Library)

PUBLIC LIBRARIES

The library is not merely a collection of books; it is a combination of social and civilizing forces ennobling the community in which it is situated. It is a home missionary society whose tentacles reach all classes. It is not a charity but a necessity.[1]

Until the early 1880s, and much later in rural Ontario, library services were provided mainly by the voluntary associations known as farmers' and mechanics' institutes, whose role is discussed in a later section of this volume. In almost all cases, nineteenth-century libraries led a tenuous existence, chronically under-funded and without proper premises or staff.[2]

From the 1880s, municipal councils began to assume responsibility for libraries. The Free Libraries Act of 1882 provided for the establishment and maintenance of free public libraries in incorporated cities, towns and villages.[3] Existing mechanics' institutes and other library associations might transfer their property and operations to the municipal council, to be supported by a tax on local property assessment of up to half a mill on the dollar. The free public library was then to be administered by a Board of Management with members appointed by the council and the school board. But adoption of the Free Libraries Act had to be approved by a majority of the local property-owners voting on this by-law. Municipalities were slow to adopt the Act, even after an amendment of 1883 allowed a public library board which had taken over the local mechanics' institute to continue to receive the legislative grant paid to an institute. In January 1883, Guelph (closely followed by Toronto) was the first municipality in Ontario to adopt the Free Libraries Act. But only six other centres followed by 1889 and another four by 1894.

The Public Libraries Act of 1895 was intended to speed the transition to municipal responsibility for libraries.[4] A municipal council could now take over a mechanics' institute as a free public library without a specific vote by

[1] T.W. Leavitt, 'Annual report of the Inspector of Libraries,' **Ontario Sessional Papers 12, 1909,** 152.

[2] For a general survey of the development of local library services throughout Ontario, see Elizabeth and Gerald Bloomfield, **Urban growth and local services: the development of Ontario municipalities to 1981** (Department of Geography, University of Guelph, 1983) chapter 8.

[3] **Statutes of Ontario** 45 Vic. c. 22, 1882.

[4] **Statutes of Ontario** 58 Vic. c. 45, 1895. The legislative and administrative history of the transition from Mechanics' Institutes to free public libraries is discussed in Lorne Bruce, 'Public libraries in Ontario, 1882-1920,' **Ontario History** 77 (1985): 123-149.

the electors. However, in such cases the council could not levy a special library rate and had to undertake to pay out of general revenues an annual sum equivalent to the provincial grant. Townships were permitted to establish free libraries from 1896 and police villages from 1909. But mechanics' institute libraries, renamed 'public association libraries' in 1895, still provided two-thirds of Ontario communities with their library service in 1900. These voluntary associations continued to depend on members' dues matched by the legislative grants.

Few Ontario libraries in 1900 occupied buildings designed for the purpose. But in the next two decades, more than 110 Ontario communities gained permanent and appropriate structures which were 'monuments to Mr Andrew Carnegie's liberality.'[5] The purpose of the grant, according to the Carnegie Corporation, was to foster the concept of a 'free public library as an institution of social service, education and recreation under local ownership and control.'[6] In order to qualify for a Carnegie grant, a municipality had to guarantee to raise from local taxes an annual amount for library maintenance equivalent to one-tenth of the capital grant. Local initiative was an important factor in those communities that applied early, and 'free library' status helped to guarantee the tax support. Local communities were not always unanimously in favour of applying for a Carnegie grant. In several industrial towns and cities including Guelph, the Trades and Labor Council condemned any Carnegie aid as 'blood money', the price of workers killed in the riots at Carnegie's Homestead works. But such scruples were usually outweighed by the attraction of a debt-free building.

Wellington County obtained more than its share of Carnegie library buildings. Guelph was one of the first in Ontario, qualifying for a $20,000 grant in 1903 and erecting a building in 1905 (#3406). Carnegie library buildings were also erected in Palmerston (1903), Harriston (1908), Elora (1910), Fergus (1910) and Mount Forest (1913). Some municipalities were inclined to rather grandiose dreams of the building their Carnegie grant might buy. In reminding them of the basic purpose for which the grant was given, the Inspector of Public Libraries in 1910 praised the design of the Fergus Library as a very appropriate model.

Public library records usually consist of minutes of the board of management, correspondence, catalogues of books, accession records, membership registers and circulation statistics. Fairly complete records exist for the public libraries in Guelph, Mount Forest, Elora and Drayton. The organization of library services by mechanics' institutes in the nineteenth century is discussed briefly in the later section on Voluntary Associations.

---

[5] Carnegie Corporation of New York, **Carnegie grants for library buildings** (New York, 1943). See also **Urban growth and local services** (1983) chapter 8, and Margaret Beckman, Stephen Langmead and John Black, **The best gift: a record of the Carnegie libraries in Ontario** (Toronto: Dundurn Press, 1984).

[6] Carnegie Corporation of New York, **Carnegie grants for library buildings, 1890-1917** (1943).

893. Drayton Mechanics' Institute/ Drayton Public Library. **Board. Minutes, 1884-1966.** 3 volumes. Loc: WCA.

894. Drayton Public Library. **Annual reports, 1905-1939; 1946-1948.** 1 file folder. Loc: WCA.
    A series of annual reports which includes receipts, expenditures, number of books purchased, held and issued by the library, as well as a list of board members.

895. Drayton Public Library. **Cataloguing records, c1900; c1940.** 2 volumes. Loc: WCA.

896. Drayton Public Library. **Correspondence, inspector of public libraries, 1934-1949.** 1 file folder. Loc: WCA.

897. Drayton Public Library. **Dominion Bureau of Statistics library statistics, 1920; 1935; 1939; 1941; 1949.** 1 file folder. Loc: WCA.
    A questionnaire about the types of books held by the library. The later years record receipts and expenditures.

898. Drayton Public Library. **Financial. Bank passbooks, 1900-1954.** 1 file folder. Loc: WCA.

899. Drayton Public Library. **Financial. Cheque registers, 1910-1965; 1972-1977.** 1 file folder. Loc: WCA.
    A record of cheques paid by the library to various individuals.

900. Drayton Public Library. **Financial. Invoices for book purchases, 1904-1949.** 4 file folders. Loc: WCA.

901. Drayton Public Library. **Fire insurance policies, 1907-1979.** 1 file folder. Loc: WCA.

902. Drayton Public Library. **Legislative grants, 1934-1977.** 1 file folder. Loc: WCA.
    A record of amount of provincial grants to the library in various years. Also included is an annual financial statement for the library in 1959.

903. Drayton Public Library. **Membership registers, 1922-1937; 1938-1959.** 2 volumes. Loc: WCA.

904. Drayton Public Library. **Miscellaneous, 1898-1949.** 1 file folder. Loc: WCA.
    A group of documents that includes 2 applications for employment, 2 declarations of office to the library board, financial report of the building fund, and report on the feasibilty of a county co-operative library.

905. Drayton Public Library. **Record of circulation, 1934-1940.** 1 ledger. Loc: WCA.

906. Elora Mechanics' Institute/ Elora Public Library. **Board. Minutes, 1871-1877; 1921-1976.** 6 volumes. Loc: WCA.
    A record of meetings, financial transactions and the activities of the

library. The earliest minute book of the 1870s includes discussions of potential lectures at the Elora Mechanics' Institute, and lists the constitution of the institution.

907. Elora Mechanics' Institute/ Elora Public Library. **Stock catalogues, 1881; c1895; 1895-1930; 1931-1940.** 4 volumes. Loc: WCA.
   A written record of books purchased by the library that notes title, author and cost. The 1881 catalogue was printed and includes a brief history of the library, the 1871 constitution, and bylaws. The constitution states that the library's purpose was to diffuse useful knowledge, establish a reading room, evening classes, debating club, and offer public lectures.

908. Elora Public Library. **Accession register, 1931-1947.** 1 ledger. Loc: WCA.
   A record of books purchased that notes author, title, cost and library code.

909. Elora Public Library. **Book list, 1918.** 1 file folder. Loc: UGA. XR1 MS A116006.
   Details of books held by the Elora Public Library with a list of members of the library board in 1918. Held with the Connon Collection.

910. Elora Public Library. **Circulation record books, 1935-1940; 1941-1946.** 3 volumes. Loc: WCA.
   A record of books signed out from the library which notes the types of sources circulated in various years.

911. Elora Public Library. **Correspondence and annual reports, 1909-1920.** 1 file folder. Loc: UGA. XR1 MS A115012.
   Correspondence regarding library construction and administration, circulation reports dated 1911 and 1912 and annual reports from 1915 to 1918. The records also include a brief financial statement. Held with the Connon Collection.

912. Elora Public Library. **Financial. Account book, 1893-1931.** 1 ledger. Loc: WCA.
   A record of receipts and expenditures of the library.

913. Elora Public Library. **Financial. Receipt register for fines, 1896-1925.** 1 ledger. Loc: WCA.
   A record of name and amount owed in library fines.

914. Elora Public Library. **Membership applications, 1932.** 1 file folder. Loc: WCA.
   A record of rules and regulations signed by individuals applying to become members. The record contains four applications for membership.

915. Elora Public Library. **Roll and record books, 1915-1921.** 2 volumes. Loc: WCA.
   A record of members of the Elora Public Library that does not consistently date entries.

916. Guelph Free Public Library/ Guelph Public Library. **Accession catalogues, 1887-1903.** 2 ledgers. Loc: GPL.
   A record of date, numbers, title, author and class of books purchased by the library.

917. Guelph Free Public Library/ Guelph Public Library. **Accession records, 1883-1908.** 1 ledger. Loc: GPL.

A record of books acquired by the library that notes title, author, publisher and date.

918. Guelph Free Public Library/ Guelph Public Library. **Annual reports, 1896-1900; 1902-1960.** 2 boxes. Loc: GPL.

A record of receipts and expenditures, with notes of volumes purchased, volumes in the library, and the number of volumes of various subject materials. The reports also indicate the hours of the library, number of pupils enrolled in evening classes, and the total number of members. The records include a good deal of correspondence beginning in the 1930s outlining the status of library operations.

919. Guelph Free Public Library/ Guelph Public Library. **Board. Minutes, 1883-1951.** 5 volumes. Loc: GPL.

Minutes of the Board of Management created after the electors of Guelph adopted the bylaw to establish a free public library in January 1883. The Board included the mayor and three other representatives of the city council, three nominees of the Public School Board and two nominees of the Separate School. Board. The minutes provide evidence of the long service of some members such as the lawyer James Watt, who was on the board for about 45 years including a substantial period as chair. Watt was instrumental in obtaining a Carnegie grant of over $20,000 to erect a library building in 1903.

920. Guelph Free Public Library/ Guelph Public Library. **Building Fund. Financial statements, 1903-1909; Newspaper clippings of library history, 1850-1940.** 4 documents, 1 file folder. Loc: GPL.

A record of the financial transactions of the building of a new library which indicates Andrew Carnegie granted 24,000 dollars to the building fund. The record includes brief correspondence regarding the library projects, and notes the disbursements of the building fund account with references to several Guelph companies. The records indicate W. Frye Colwill was the architect of the building. The file includes several photocopies of Guelph newspapers describing the project, and the copy of a speech by Frederick Watt in the 1940s surveying the history of the Guelph Public Library from the 1850s to the 1940s.

921. Guelph Free Public Library/ Guelph Public Library. **Catalogue of books, 1894.** 131 p. mf. Loc: GPL.

A list of the library's rules and regulations, dated February 9, 1883, signed by the chairman D. McCrae, and the secretary, W. Tytler. Approximately 3,000 books and journals are listed in the following categories: biography, history, voyage and travel, general literature, poetry and drama, periodicals, theology and religion, science, industrial science and art, reference and illustrated. Authors include Wollstonecraft, Darwin, Locke, Smiles, Mill, George, Elliott, Parkman and Lampman.

922. Guelph Free Public Library/ Guelph Public Library. **Catalogues, 1884; 1891; 1894; 1906.** 4 volumes. Loc: GPL.

A printed record of authors and titles organized by categories of biography, fiction, history, voyage and travels, general literature, poetry and drama, periodicals, theology and religion, science, industrial science and art, reference and illustrated.

923. Guelph Free Public Library/ Guelph Public Library. **Cornerstone. Contents, 1903.**
1 box. Loc: GPL.
The contents include an 1850 constitution of the Guelph Farmers' and
Mechanics' Institute, an official report of the development of the library
written by James E. Day, seals of the City of Guelph, a sketch of the proposed
library building, Vernon's City of Guelph Directory 1903 to 1905, the Canadian
Almanac 1903, and City of Guelph Auditors' reports for 1900 to 1902.

924. Guelph Free Public Library/ Guelph Public Library. **Correspondence, 1914-1915;**
1922; 1930-1931; 1934-1935; 1939. 2 file folders. Loc: GPL.

925. Guelph Free Public Library/ Guelph Public Library. **Membership records,**
1887-1914. 2 ledgers. Loc: GPL.
A record of name, date and residence of readers, plus the name of a person
listed as 'voucher'. The list of readers include many women's names. The box
contains a 1911 membership card for Arthur Chapman.

926. Guelph Free Public Library/ Guelph Public Library. **Newspaper clippings of**
library history, 1850-1903. 1 file folder. Loc: GPL.
A number of clippings outlining the history of the library including a special
April 24, 1903 Guelph Mercury article describing the completion of the Carnegie
Library, noting Guelph residents prominent in its construction.

927. Guelph Public Library Board. **Indenture, 1902.** 1 document. Loc: GPL.
An agreement between the city council and the Guelph Public Library to
construct a reading room at the library.

928. Mount Forest Public Library. **Accession records, 1937-1945.** 1 ledger. Loc: MFL.

929. Mount Forest Public Library. **Financial. Cash books, 1909-1934; 1942-1966.** 2
ledgers. Loc: MFL.

930. Mount Forest Public Library. **Minutes, 1919-1949.** 2 volumes. Loc: MFL.
A record of meetings which were held usually once a month. The volumes include
periodic financial statements.

931. Palmerston Public Library. **Board. Minutes and cash books, 1902-1928; 1930-1970.**
1 volume, 2 file folders. Loc: WCA.

932. Speedside Public Library. **Financial. Records, 1904-1925.** 1 envelope. Loc: WCA.
MU54.
A record of annual reports, books utilized in the years 1904 to 1912, as well
as insurance policies and invoices of the library.

HIGHER GOVERNMENTS

The main focus in this **Inventory** is on locally generated records and papers. Thus a large proportion of all the records are those of municipal governments and school boards. But researchers should not overlook the large quantities of material created by higher levels of government and containing information that is useful or even vital for understanding processes at the local level. The records of higher government are generally retained permanently as a matter of public and legal record in the national and provincial archives.

Higher government records may be relevant to local and regional research in various ways. Some statistical information is collected from local areas and then synthesized and perhaps published only by central authorities such as provincial or federal government departments and agencies. Census data, whether on the original manuscript schedules or in published summaries, has been the responsibility of the Government of Canada since Confederation, as has the collection of other statistical information between censuses.[1]. At the provincial level, statistical and other information submitted by local municipalities was received by the Department of Agriculture, the Department of Education, the Provincial Secretary and other departments. The information was filed and sometimes compiled into statistical tables reported in departmental reports of various kinds. In some cases, such material may be the best available for certain research topics; it may also compensate for the disappearance of the original local records and it can provide helpful context because the data have been aggregated and presented comparatively.

Higher governments make the laws and frame the policies within which municipal governments, businesses, voluntary organizations, churches and individuals have to work. Thus some knowledge of the legislative and administrative context may be essential in understanding the particular local and regional details.[2] Relevant legislation may be found in the Statutes of Upper Canada 1792-1840, the Statutes of the Province of Canada 1841-1867, the Statutes of Canada 1867-present, and the Statutes of the Province of Ontario 1867-present. It is frequently necessary to check on the precise wording and application of legislation to a particular issue, problem and area.

---

[1] The most accessible general guide to the statistical records is:
Statistics Canada, **Historical catalogue of Statistics Canada publications 1918-1980** (Ottawa: 1982), Catalogue No. 11-512. General Canadian historical statistics (with an occasional reference to Ontario) are presented in:
Statistics Canada, **Historical statistics of Canada** (Ottawa: 1983, 2nd edition), Catalogue No. 11-516.

[2] For legislative details see: Debra Forman ed., **Legislators and legislatures of Ontario: a reference guide** (Toronto: Ministry of Government Services, 1984): Vol. 1 1792-1866; Vol. 2 1867-1929; Vol. 3 1930-1984.

A federal presence: The Guelph Public Building, St George's Square, c1930.
From the 1870s, the Dominion Government began constructing federal buildings
in major towns and cities. A two-storey structure was completed in 1878 to
accommodate the Post Office, Inland Revenue and Customs Departments.
The building was enlarged with a third story and clock tower in 1903-4.
Records relating to the construction and enlargement of the building are
#977 and #3361-#3363. (Guelph Public Library)

The private statutes that incorporated businesses, railways and utilities and gave municipalities special powers may be relevant to some research problems. The annual volumes and the **Revised Statutes** (compiled every 5-10 years) are the authoritative source. The volumes of **Regulations** should also be consulted for some detailed research.

Parliamentary and legislative papers should be noted as potential sources. The proceedings of the House of Commons, Senate and the Legislatures are described in the **Journals** (which generally list the daily proceedings and the voting). Annual reports of departments, commissions, special inquiries, budgets and accounts were reported in bound volumes known generally as **Sessional Papers**. The federal series ended in 1924 and the Ontario Sessional Papers ceased publication in 1954. The material previously bound in these annual volumes is now presented and collected as separate items. Departmental annual reports provide essential details, including statistics, for reconstructing elements of the past. The changing agriculture of Ontario can be documented from the annual reports; the diffusion of public libraries can be compiled from the Department of Education annual reports; the role of the post office as a measure of central place hierarchies can be developed from the federal Post Office Department annual reports.

This section of the **Inventory** describes some of the archival records of provincial and federal governments (and of the British Colonial Office) that were found to have some specific relevance to the history of Guelph and Wellington County. Most are held by the Archives of Ontario and the National Archives of Canada. But we have not systematically inventoried the regularly printed government publications that are outlined below.[3] Researchers should not overlook these as sources on a wide variety of local and regional subjects. For example, a survey of the Ontario government publications since 1867 showed that the following had specific details for localities and counties such as Wellington County:

1. Department of Agriculture:
    Annual reports, 1868-
    Agricultural and Experimental Union. Annual reports, 1867-1938 (to 1924
        also in Sessional Papers)
    Agricultural Societies/Canadian Association of Fairs and Exhibitions
    Bureau of Industries, 1882-1917 which published the Municipal Bulletin,
        1906-1916
    Institutes Branch: Reports of farmers' institutes, 1888-1915; Reports of
        women's institutes, 1906-1930

---

[3] Major guides to government publications include the following:
Olga B. Bishop, **Publications of the Provinces of Upper Canada and of Great Britain relating to Upper Canada 1791-1840** (Toronto: Ministry of Citizenship and Culture, 1984); Olga B. Bishop, **Publications of the Government of the Province of Canada 1841-1867** (Ottawa: National Library of Canada, 1963); Olga B. Bishop, **Publications of the Government of Ontario 1867-1900** (Toronto: Ministry of Government Services, 1976); Hazel I. MacTaggart, **Publications of the Government of Ontario 1901-1955** (Toronto: Queen's Printer, 1964).

Statistics and Publications Branch: agricultural statistics for Ontario from
  1918

2. Department of Education
    Regular series of reports
    Special historical surveys
    Public Libraries Branch

3. Department of Health

4. Department of Highways

5. Registrar of Insurance Companies and Friendly Societies

6. Registrar of Loan and Trust Corporations

7. Department of Lands and Forests,

8. Department of Municipal Affairs

9. Provincial Secretary, 1867 -
    Prisons and public charities
    Liquor License Branch, 1876-1915
    Registrar General (vital statistics)
    Superintendent of Neglected and Dependent Children

10. Department of Public Works
    Bureau of Labour, 1900-
    Trades and Labour Branch, 1916

11. Ontario Municipal Board
    Annual reports and data on the telephone system from 1911

The archival materials that have been inventoried in this section are arranged with the provincial government records first, followed by those of the federal government. Finally one summary record describes the scope of the British Colonial Office correspondence relating to the foundation of Guelph by the Canada Company.

933. Government of Canada. **Proclamation. Dissolving union of the United Counties of Wellington and Grey, 1853**. photocopy. Loc: GPL.

934. Government of Canada. **Proclamation. Uniting Wellington and Grey Counties, 1853**. photocopy. Loc: GPL.

935. Government of Upper Canada. **Petition. Inhabitants of Guelph asking for reform in Executive Council, n.d.**. 1 large parchment sheet. Loc: NAC. RG 1, E 16, vol. 5, no. 17.

Address to Sir John Colborne signed by about fifty inhabitants of Guelph, including Samuel Strickland, John McDonald and Thomas Husband. The main grievance is the inadequate provision of education, the petitioners noting that they had to appoint their own master and asking that management be transferred to the Presbyterian Kirk Session of Guelph. The petition also praised the roads built by the Canada Company in the immediate vicinity of Guelph.

DEPARTMENT OF AGRICULTURE

936. Canada West Department of Agriculture. **Questions to an emigrant farmer, c1853**. 2 documents. Loc: WCA.

Photocopies of two government questionnaires filled out by Robert Cromar and James McQueen stating particulars about their emigrant experience. Both forms are signed 'Charles Clarke, J.P.'. There are no dates on the form, but an archival note identifies the date as c1853. The original document is held in the National Archives of Canada.

937. Ontario Department of Agriculture. **Agricultural Representatives. Annual reports, 1907-1968**. 72 reels. mf. Loc: AO. FA: RG 16, MS 597.

Ontario's system of Agricultural Representatives had experimental beginnings in six counties in 1907, with salaries paid by the Department of Education and office and other expenses by the Department of Agriculture. By 1912, when full responsibility was assumed by Agriculture, there were representatives in twenty-seven counties and six districts. Early reports, such as those for Waterloo, are particularly revealing. Unfortunately annual reports survive for Wellington County only for the period from 1936 to 1938.

938. Ontario Department of Agriculture. **Foulbrood Act. Certificate of registration, 1925**. 1 document. Loc: GCM.

A record of certification that Fred Marsh of Guelph had complied with the provisions of the act.

939. Ontario Department of Agriculture. Home Economics Branch. **Correspondence with Women's Institutes, 1909-1910**. 1 box (21 file folders) Loc: AO. RG 16, Series 16-87, Box 3.

Letters from women all over rural Ontario to Mary Watson, principal of the Macdonald Institute, with requests for information and advice. In most cases, the women wanted help in preparing talks for Women's Institute meetings. Subjects ranged from new uses for apples or eggs to 'labour saving devices in the home', 'Christmas on the farm', 'Books we should read' or 'The duties of children in the home'. A few requests were annotated 'could not help', as in the case of a farmer's wife with seven children who wanted a few ideas on 'how to spend the winter evenings profitably'. The records illustrate the wider role of the Macdonald Institute throughout Ontario.

DEPARTMENT OF EDUCATION

940. Canada West Board of Public Instruction. **County Grammar Schools. Inspectors' reports, 1855-1871.** 5 volumes. Loc: AO. FA: RG-2, G-1-A.
   The Grammar Schools Amendment Act of 1853 provided for an increase in numbers of such schools and for the appointment of trustees by the county councils. The councils were to give the schools a solid tax base, which was further strengthened in 1865. Reports on the Elora Grammar School, Fergus Grammar School and Guelph Grammar School are included.

941. Canada West Board of Public Instruction. **District Superintendent and Councils. Annual reports, 1842-1849.** 5 boxes. Loc: AO. FA: RG-2, F-3-A.
   The brief reports are organized first chronologically, then alphabetically by name of district.

942. Canada West Board of Public Instruction. **District Superintendents. Annual reports, 1842-1849.** 5 boxes. Loc: AO. FA: RG 2, F-3-A.
   Reports for each district are filed alphabetically for each year.

943. Canada West Board of Public Instruction. **Grammar School Trustees. Returns and annual reports, 1854-1871.** 21 boxes. Loc: AO. FA: RG 2, G-1-B.
   The Grammar Schools Amendment Act of 1853 provided for an increase in numbers of such schools and for the appointment of trustees by the county councils. The act also gave the schools a solid tax base which was further strengthened in 1865. Trustees were required to submit annual reports and statistical returns to the chief superintendent by January 15 of each year. Reports for the Elora Grammar School (1854-1867) and the Fergus Grammar School (1865-1867) are in Box 6, while the reports for the Guelph Grammar School (1854-1867) are in Box 8.

944. Canada West Board of Public Instruction. **Letter discussing school visitation procedures, 1866.** 1 file folder. Loc: GCI.
   A letter from an assistant headmaster in Guelph discussing procedures for visiting schools. Photocopy of the original apparently held in the Archives of Ontario.

945. Canada West Board of Public Instruction. **Letters to A.D. Ferrier, 1850; 1852.** 2 documents. Loc: UGA. XRI MS A138006-7.
   Photocopies of letters to Ferrier. One letter requested names of superintendents of Wellington County common schools. The other is an extensive request from Egerton Ryerson to complete tax assessment forms. Part of the Goodwin-Haines Collection.

946. Canada West Board of Public Instruction. **Local Superintendents and Local Boards of Trustees. Annual reports, 1850-1870.** 42 boxes. Loc: AO. FA: RG 2, F-3-B.
   Local superintendents were usually clergymen or physicians who served part-time. The annual reports consisted partly of financial statistics and partly of details of the salaries, religion and qualifications of teachers, enrolment in each subject, textbooks, the construction of school buildings and their general condition. Reports are organized first in alphabetical order by

place, then by year, so that all the reports for Guelph are together. In Box 1, two geographical indices identify all the local superintendents in 1864 and 1870.

947. Canada West Board of Public Instruction. **Local Superintendents and Boards of Trustees. Annual reports, 1850-1870.** 42 boxes. Loc: AO. FA: RG-2, F-3-B.
   The reports consist of two parts. First, financial statistics. Second, records of the names, salaries, religion, experience and qualifications of teachers, enrolment in each subject, textbooks and school buildings (type and date of construction and general conditions). Box 1 also contains geographical indexes and lists of the superintendents in 1864 and 1870. The reports are arranged primarily alphabetically, by townships, cities and towns, with all years grouped together for a particular place.

948. Canada West Board of Public Instruction. **Roman Catholic Separate Schools. Trustees annual reports, 1852-1871; semi-annual attendance returns, 1854-1871.** 1 box. Loc: AO. FA: RG-2, F-3-F, Box 1.
   The reports and returns were submitted on forms printed by the Department of Education. Wellington County returns at the beginning of this period survive for the Townships of Nichol and Arthur (where there were three separate school sections). John Cadenhead reports that most of the Nichol school pupils resided in Pilkington Township which had not legalized separate schools, which led to 'great trouble and dispute'. For Guelph, Robert Torrance reported in 1854 on the circumstances of founding Roman Catholic schools in the town, noting that it was his 'impression that if teaching in common schools had been purely secular, no application would have been made for a separate school'. In the 1869-1871 period, attendance returns were filed for separate schools in Peel Township, R.C.S.S.#12; Mount Forest, Arthur, and Peel Townships, R.C.S.S.#13 (Macton); Pilkington Township, R.C.S.S.#6 (Freiburg); Fergus; and Peel Township, R.C.S.S.#6 (Creek Bank).

949. Canada West Board pf Public Instruction. **Annual report of the Normal, Model and Common Schools, 1852.** Quebec: John Lovell, 1853. 310 p. Loc: WCA.
   A detailed report of schools in Canada West including statistical details of attendance, accounts, textbooks, teachers, school visits, separate schools, other educational institutions, extracts from selected superintendents' reports, circulars from chief superintendents and selections from Schools Acts. John Cadenhead and John Kirkland are listed as superintendents for Wellington County. The volume is held in the Templin-Dow Collection.

950. Ontario Board of Public Instruction. **Announcement of meeting of teachers certificate applicants, 1867.** 1 envelope. Loc: WCA. MU13.
   An announcement of a meeting of teachers certificate applicants in the North Riding of Wellington County, signed by A. Dingwall Fordyce.

951. Ontario Department of Education. **Continuation School Inspectors. Annual reports, 1906-1944.** 5 volumes, 5 boxes. Loc: AO. FA: RG-2, G-3.
   Reports are organized alphabetically by place. The inspectors' notes which are more detailed, are closed until 1993.

952. Ontario Department of Education. **G.C.V.I. Inspectors' annual reports, 1885-1902; 1905; 1907-1908; 1910; 1912; 1915; 1917; 1919; 1922.** 1 box. Loc:

GCI.

The reports describe and assess accommodations, equipment, attendance, staff, organization and discipline and character of teaching in the different departments. Details given for staff in the early years include educational degrees, experience, date of appointment, salary and duties.

953. Ontario Department of Education. **G.C.V.I. Inspectors' annual reports, vocational evening classes, 1927-1930.** 1 file folder. Loc: GCI.

954. Ontario Department of Education. **Guelph Public Schools. Inspectors' annual report, 1885-1886.** 1 file folder. Loc: GCI.

A photocopy of originals held at the Archives of Ontario. The reports note number of pupils and teachers, cost per pupil, salaries and rate of taxation.

955. Ontario Department of Education. **High School Inspectors. Annual reports, 1872-1932.** 106 volumes, 19 feet. Loc: AO. FA: RG-2, G-2-A.

Reports include names and qualifications of teaching staff, quality of work and grade of accommodation and equipment, with suggestions for improvement. Arrangements chronologically by year then alphabetically by place. The inspectors' field notes for 1917-1953, which are more detailed and candid, are in Series G-2-B (17 boxes) but are closed until 2003 A.D.

956. Ontario Department of Education. **High Schools. Entrance examinations, 1901; 1903; 1908; 1934-1949.** 3 envelopes, 1 ledger. Loc: GCI, GCM.

Examinations from 1934 to 1949 are held at Guelph Collegiate Vocational Institute.

957. Ontario Department of Education. **Inspectors of Manual Training and Household Science. Annual reports, 1903-1940.** 27 volumes. Loc: AO. FA: RG-2, F-3-H.

Reports are arranged alphabetically by place within each year.

958. Ontario Department of Education. **Local school histories, c1894.** Loc: AO. FA: RG-2, E-2, Boxes 1-2.

References to schools and teachers in Wellington County may be found in Files #63, #65 and #66 of Box 1 and File #83 of Box 2. These materials were assembled by Dr Hodgins for his documentary History of Education in Ontario.

959. Ontario Department of Education. **Provincial Training School. Register, 1912-1914.** 1 ledger. Loc: WBE.

A record of teachers' names, a percentage mark under the title, Report on Student's Criticism, and a percentage mark under the title, Report on Lessons Taught.

960. Ontario Department of Education. **Roman Catholic Separate School Inspectors. Reports, 1882-1909.** 65 volumes. Loc: AO. FA: RG-2, F-3-F, Box 3.

Arranged chronologically and then alphabetically by cities, towns, villages and townships. There are reports on separate schools in Guelph, Fergus and Elora and the various Roman Catholic school sections in the townships for most years except 1902 and 1905. The records are very fragile so that it was impossible to explore them in more detail.

961. Ontario Department of Education. **Roman Catholic Separate Schools. Minutes of annual meetings of supporters, 1884; 1888-1891.** 1 box. Loc: AO. FA: RG 2, F-3-F, Box 2.

The records are arranged chronologically by year, then alphabetically by locality. Wellington County separate schools noted in the 1884 records are Elora, Arthur Township R.C.S.S.#6, Nichol Township R.C.S.S.#1 and Guelph. The Arthur School Section Board consisted of Patrick Reidy, Jeffery Feehan, Francis Dillon, James Morrisey and Denis McNamara. The Guelph Separate School Board included John Harris as chair, James Ryan, James Mays, John McElderry, Michael Burns, Michael J. Doran, Felix Devlin, Christian Kloepfer and James Keough as secretary.

962. Ontario Department of Education. **Summer school for teachers at the Ontario Agricultural College, 1910; 1912.** 2 booklets. Loc: GPL.

A description of courses to be taught to teachers at the Ontario Agricultural College. The booklet indicates that it was compulsory for teachers to take a course in agriculture.

963. Ontario Department of Education. **Teachers' examinations, 1859; 1861; 1871-1872.** 5 ledgers. Loc: WBE.

A record of exams on various subjects required for qualifying for a second-class provincial certificate as a public school teacher. One copy is signed by A.D. Fordyce, inspector of schools for North Wellington County.

964. Ontario Normal School of Domestic Science and Art. **Examination results, 1900-1903.** 1 ledger. Loc: UGA. XR1 MS A012.

A record of the grades in various subjects of specific students, and a timetable of the school for the year 1901-1902. The exam records refer to a few students who attended the school after it was transferred to Guelph in 1903.

LEGISLATIVE ASSEMBLY

965. Ontario Legislative Assembly. **Election register, 1920-1936.** 1 box. Loc: AO. RG 49, I-7-A-9, Box 13.

A page is devoted to each riding in Ontario. The arrangement is chronological depending on when the election was called, with the following information provided: name of riding, date of issue of writ, name of returning officer, date of proclamation, date of nomination, date of polling, return of writ, when member was gazetted, whether there was a protest, names of all candidates and their financial agents, number of polling places and votes cast, with remarks.

966. Ontario Legislative Assembly. **Index to railway legislation, 1867-1919.** 1 box. Loc: AO. FA: RG 49, I-7-A-9, Box 12.

Volume lists chapters and titles for each railway in alphabetical order.

967. Ontario Legislative Assembly. **Railway sessional papers, 1867-1911.** 13 boxes. Loc: AO. FA: RG 49, I-7-B-3.

Includes correspondence between various railways, municipalities and the government regarding the building of railway lines Hamilton, Guelph and North Shore (Box 2); Toronto, Grey and Bruce (Box 9); Georgian Bay and Wellington (Box 2); Wellington, Grey and Bruce (Box 7); Waterloo Wellington (Box 13); and People's Railway (Box 12).

968. Ontario Legislative Assembly. **Sessional papers, 1867-1984.** 356 boxes. Loc: AO. FA: RG 49, I-7-B-2.

Unprinted sessional papers tabled in the legislature and covering every conceivable facet of public administration (the user should consult the index in Series I-7-B-1). A good example of an unprinted sessional paper with considerable local information is Sessional Paper No. 69 of 1900: 'Return respecting municipal aid to manufacturing industries by way of bonus, loan or exemption', which includes details for Guelph, Harriston, Mount Forest, Palmerston, Elora and Fergus.

REGISTRAR-GENERAL

969. Ontario Registrar-General. **Vital Statistics. Birth registers, 1869-1940.** 92 ledgers. Loc: RGO. By permission of Registrar-General.

The statistics for Wellington County births are recorded by municipality in a section of the annual volumes. The registers record name, sex, name of father, maiden name of mother, occupation of father except for the years 1897 to 1905, when registered, name of accoucheur and signature of registrar. In 1930, the ledgers record municipality, address, age, ethnic origin and birthplace of parents, if the parents were married and the trade or profession of the father. They also indicate if the birth was single, twin or triplet, if the child was born alive and if the child was born prematurely.

970. Ontario Registrar-General. **Vital Statistics. Death registers, 1869-1940.** 70 volumes. Loc: RGO. By permission of Registrar-General.

The statistics for Wellington County deaths are recorded by municipality in a section of the annual volumes. The spines of the volumes list the names of the counties they contain and are arranged alphabetically each year until 1930 when only volume number and year are noted. In 1869, entries record the name and surname of the deceased, when died, sex, age, rank or profession, where born, certified cause of death, name of physician if any, signature and residence of informant, when registered, religious denomination, and signature of registrar. In 1890, marital status and length of illness began to be noted. In 1908, medical certificate of death was included that noted date last seen by physician, date and cause of death. In 1909, divorce began to be noted in the category of marital status. In 1920, trade or occupation, kind of industry and former occupation was noted. The medical certificate noted if an operation preceded death or if an autopsy was performed. In 1930, the ledgers became a bound collection of registered death certificates that, as well as the above information, noted immediate cause of death and morbid conditions giving rise to the immediate cause. The 1930 statistics are held in volumes 36 and 37, 1931 to 1935 in volume 35, 1936 in volumes 36 and 37, 1937 in volume 37, 1938 to 1939 in volume 36, and 1940 in volume 38.

971. Ontario Registrar-General. **Vital Statistics. Marriage registers, 1873-1940.** 67 ledgers. Loc: RGO. By permission of Registrar-General.

The statistics for Wellington County marriages are recorded by municipality in a section of the annual volumes. The spines of the volumes list the names of the counties they contain and are arranged alphabetically each year until 1912 when only volume number and year are noted. By 1887, the registers record, for both bride and bridegroom, name, age, residence, when married, place of birth, whether bachelor spinster or widower, rank or profession of bridegroom, name of parents, name and residence of witnesses, date and place of marriage, religious denomination and name of clergyman. In 1912, the ledgers became a bound collection of marriage certificates. The 1912 statistics are held in volume 22, 1913 in volume 18, 1914 in volume 22, 1915 in volume 17, 1916 in volume 23, 1917 in volume 20, 1918 in volume 19, 1919 in volume 21, 1920 in volume 27, 1921 in volume 23, 1922 in volume 22, 1923 in volume 23, 1924 in volume 21, 1925 in volume 21, 1926 in volume 47, 1927 in volume 23, 1928 in volume 24, 1929 in volume 25, 1930 in volume 23, 1931 in volume 22, 1932 in volume 20, 1933 in volume 20, 1934 in volume 23, 1935 in volume 24, 1936 in volume 25, 1937 in volume 27, 1938 in volume 27, 1939 in volume 31, and 1940 in volume 37.

PROVINCIAL SECRETARY

972. Ontario Provincial Secretary. **Annual report upon the prisons and reformatories of the Province of Ontario, 1932-present (sporadic).** 48 volumes. Loc: GCC.

The annual reports contain evidence of attitudes to inmates, prison reform, crime and morality. They also contain statistical charts comparing all Ontario institutions that note inmates' marital status, education, temperance, drug addiction, occupation, nationality, religion, length of sentence, ages at time of committal, number of crimes against person-property-public morals-public order, employment of prisoners in institutions, number of escaped prisoners, employees' salaries, and maintenance cost per inmate. Also included in many issues are reports from individual reformatories, including the Ontario Reformatory in Guelph. The individual reports comment on social issues such as the depression in the 1930s, reform, and assess demographic changes in prison population, the 'unfortunate beings' in the Criminal Insane Section, industrial labour, discipline and agitators, medical services, school, library, farm and dairy. A special report written by Dr J.D. Heaslip, Superintendent of the Ontario Reformatory in Guelph is included in the 1938 report, entitled, Educational Results as Shown by a Study of Reformatory Inmates. Heaslip argues that the central cause of criminality in 1938 was 'defective home conditions' including, among other things, 'pampering by the mother', and mental abnormalities. Starting in 1933 the Annual Report includes a report of city and county 'gaols' in Ontario, including Guelph. The old spelling of the word is used up to and including the 1943 report. From 1948 the annual reports were issued by the Department of Reform Institutions. The series lacks 1934, 1935, 1937, 1944-1952, 1956 and 1958.

973. Ontario Provincial Secretary. **Company records, 1867-.** Loc: AO. FA: RG 8, Series I-1-D; RG 55.

Company records prior to 1909 are interfiled with General Correspondence files (RG 8, Series I-1-D). Annual Returns (financial statements) for one year were usually filed in the succeeding year. Company records after 1909, and possibly also pre-1909 records of companies still active in 1909, are in RG 55, some only on microfilm, and must be ordered from the Record Centre. A partial index to companies, 1889 to 1906, is available on microfilm as MS-292.

974. Ontario Provincial Secretary. **Company Records. Letters patent, 1867-1971.** Loc: AO. FA: RG 55, RG 53, MS-508.

Includes company charters (1867-1971), supplementary letters patent (1929-1971), changes of name (1919-1971), and cancellations and surrenders of company charters (1908-1971). Some records for other time spans are in RG 53, as explained in Finding Aid. Indexes to company charters, changes of name, etc. to 1946 are on microfilm in MS-508. Company registration was a responsibility of the Provincial Secretary's Department to 1969 and was later transferred to the Ministry of Consumer and Commercial Relations.

975. Ontario Provincial Secretary. **Municipal financial statements and audit reports, 1873-1960**. 50 boxes for Wellington County. Loc: AO. RG 19, Series F-4.

Annual returns filed by the clerk of each township, village, town or city with the Provincial Secretary and later the Department of Municipal Affairs. Information provided on these printed forms includes population, assessed value, taxes levied, debentures, bonuses for railways or manufacturers, tax exemptions, and operation of public utilities for every municipality in Wellington County. The earliest date for most townships is 1879, but Nichol begins in 1873 and West Luther not until 1885. Information for most cities, towns and villages begins in 1884 but a little earlier for Elora and Fergus (1879) and Mount Forest (1878). In all cases, the records for Wellington County municipalities run to 1960. As there is no publicly accessible finding aid and the records are stored offsite, users should make prior appointments to examine these materials. The statements are grouped by municipality within broad groups of townships, villages, towns, cities, counties, and districts.

FEDERAL GOVERNMENT RECORDS

976. Canada Department of Labour. **Labour Gazette Reports on Employment. Guelph, 1910-1917.** Loc: NAC. RG 27; FA 27-14, v.1 #10, v.9.

These files include a special report on Guelpoh in 1914-15 and the monthly reports for Guelph, 1910-1917.

977. Canada Department of Public Works. **Chief Architect's Office. Specifications, drawings, 1846-1920.** 5.1 metres (vols. 3909-3963, 3965-3973) Loc: NAC. RG 11, FA 11-47.

Specifications and drawings for public buildings as well as harbour and river works. The finding aid notes the Guelph Public Building of 1876 (pages 168-171), and Guelph Military Building of 1906 (pages 389-428), as well as public buildings in Galt (1884) and Berlin (1883) and the military building in Galt (1914).

978. Canada Department of Public Works. **Registers and indexes, 1841-1950.** 115.3 metres, 31,905 index cards. Loc: NAC. RG 11, shelf lists.

The Board of Works, established in 1839 in Lower Canada and in 1841 for United Canada, was elevated to a Department of Public Works in 1859. Control of railways passed to the Department of Railways and Canals in 1879. There have been five successive phases of organizing public works records, 1841-1859, 1859-1867, 1867-1879, 1879-1919 and 1910-1950. A twenty-drawer card index was begun around 1910, of which five drawers relate to Ontario. However, not all entries in the card index have extant files to match. A test of Guelph entries showed that just half of them related to extant files.

979. Canada Post Office. **Divisional inspectors' reports, c1800-1951.** 280.8 metres. Loc: NAC. RG 3, FA3-1, 3-3, 3-5, 3-10, 3-11, 3-17.

Contains descriptions, maps and site plans of communities requesting new postal service, biographical data about persons recommended for or seeking postmasterships, and details of suggested name changes, site changes and closings of post offices. A computerized index by place names is available for volumes 1-136, covering 1870-1902.

980. Canada Post Office. **Elora Post Office. List of letters remaining in the Elora Post Office, 1864-1865.** 1 file folder. Loc: UGA. XR1 MS A115014.

Names of people with 'advertised letters' remaining in the post office are listed. Held with the Connon Collection.

981. Canada Post Office. **Luther Post Office. Correspondence and petition, 1877-1878.** 1 file folder. Loc: UGA. XR1 MS A005051.

Correspondence to individuals including Nathaniel Higinbotham and Charles Clarke requesting assistance in the appointment of a new postmaster who would have the confidence of both Tories and Reformers. Part of Allan-Higinbotham Collection.

982. Canada Post Office. **Mail. Rural delivery, 1905-1922.** 24 cm. Loc: NAC. RG 3, FA3-2.

Scrapbooks of circulars, reports of rural mail inspectors and sample forms.

983. Canada Post Office. **Mail. Service contracts, 1839-1970.** 23.75 metres. Loc: NAC. RG 3, FA3-43; mf: T-2046 to T-2059.

Registers and correspondence describing individual mail contracts, including details of name of route, name of contractor, number of trips per week, distances and rate of payment. The earlier registers have more details than later.

984. Canada Post Office. **Mail. Tender registers, 1851-1966.** 7.53 metres. Loc: NAC. RG 3, FA3-2.

Details are provided on individual mail service tenders including name of service, commencement of contract, duration, mode of conveyance, names of all persons submitting tenders and amounts of tender bids.

985. Canada Post Office. **Personnel, 1836-1945.** 9 metres. Loc: NAC. RG 3, FA3-8.

Records of appointments and vacancies, establishment of post offices, letterpress copies of names of employees, pay lists and retirees.

986. Canada Post Office. **Regional and local records, 1807-1953.** 3.5 metres. Loc: NAC. RG 3, FA3-2, 3-4, 3-8, 3-12.

Mainly details of receipt and dispatch of mail and scrapbooks. Also includes microfilm copy of Post Office impression books of stamps, seals and postal advertising of which the originals are in the National Postal Museum.

987. Canada Secretary of State. **Board of Trade Charters. Register, 1874-1974.** Loc: NAC. RG 68.

Charters of incorporation of local boards of trade under the federal Board of Trade Act (1874) are filed and indexed in the order they were received and processed by the Secretary of State. The certificates are cited by liber and folio numbers, indexed in general index volumes and may be examined on microfilm. The original charters include the details of names and occupation of charter members of each local board. Revivals of defunct boards and changes of name to chambers of commerce are also documented in this source.

988. Census of Canada. **Manuscript schedules, 1851.** 1 reel. mf. Loc: NAC, UGL, GPL, WCA. NAC. FA: C-11756.

Microfilms of the original manuscripts held by the National Archives are available through interlibrary loan. The University of Guelph Library holds a complete set for Ontario, while other local libraries have the microfilms for Wellington County. Schedules for parts of Wellington County in 1851 are missing, including the agricultural census for Amaranth, Arthur, Garafraxa, Luther, Maryborough, Minto, Nichol, Peel, Pilkington and Puslinch. No records have survived for Erin or Guelph Townships or for the Town of Guelph, and the personal schedules for Nichol and Puslinch are incomplete. Only for Eramosa Township are the records complete. The surviving census returns usually name the head of the household; indicate the number of persons in each household by age, sex and marital status; and may include details of place of birth, infirmities, religion, education and occupation. Agricultural and industrial data may include land occupied, implements, crops, livestock, taverns, shops, distilleries, mills, manufacturers and wages paid.

989. Census of Canada. **Manuscript schedules, 1861.** 3 reels. mf. Loc: NAC, UGL, GPL, WCA. NAC. FA: C-1082--C-1084.

Microfilms of the original manuscripts held by the National Archives are generally available. Almost all the returns for Wellington County survive, except for the agricultural census for Elora, Fergus and Guelph. The types of information are much the same as for 1851, but users are advised that the agricultural census returns are grouped at the end of the nominal census returns for the whole county.

990. Census of Canada. **Manuscript schedules, 1871.** 6 reels. mf. Loc: NAC, UGL, GPL, WCA. NAC. FA: C-9945, C-9950.

These schedules, which are the most comprehensive census records surviving from the nineteenth century, have been organized and filmed so that all nine schedules for each enumeration district are brought together as a unit. The nine schedules are as follows: (1) nominal return of the living; (2) nominal return of the deaths within the last twelve months; (3) return of public institutions, real estate, vehicles and implements; (4) return of cultivated land, of field products and of plants and fruits; (5) livestock, animal products, homemade fabrics and furs; (6) return of industrial establishments; (7) return of products of the forest; (8) return of shipping and fisheries; and (9) return of mineral products. Users of the 1871 census records should be aware that it is possible to relate the information in Schedules 3, 4, 5, 7, 8 and 9 directly to the nominal return Schedule 1. In these six schedules, page and line references to the nominal census returns are located in the first column of each page, entitled 'Reference to Schedule 1'. Machine-readable and print indexes to the nominal census returns of 1871 are being prepared by the Ontario Genealogical Society. A machine-readable version of the 1871 census schedules for industrial establishments has been created by a project based in the Department of Geography, University of Guelph.

991. Census of Canada. **Manuscript schedules, 1881.** 3 reels. mf. Loc: NAC, UGL, GPL, WCA. NAC. FA: C-13258, C-13260.

Though there were eight census schedules in 1881, only Schedule 1, the nominal return of the living, survived to the early 1950s and is available on microfilm. Because the microfilm is not of a consistent quality, not all images are decipherable.

992. Census of Canada. **Manuscript schedules, 1891.** 4 reels. mf. Loc: NAC, UGL, GPL, WCA. NAC. FA: T-6427, T-6376, T-6378.

Though there were nine census manuscript schedules in 1891, only a microfilm copy of Schedule 1 has survived. Because the microfilm made in the early 1950s was not of a consistent quality, not all images are decipherable.

993. Environment Canada. **Climatological station data catalogue, Ontario.** Downsview: 1981. Loc: UGL.

A summary of all climatological stations, active and inactive, in Ontario, with details of latitude, longitude, altitude, the period during which climate readings were recorded and the observing program. Stations noted in Wellington County are Clifford (1950-1972), Drayton (1883-1893), Elora (1882-), Fergus (1882-1894), Fergus Shand Dam (1939-), Guelph O.A.C. (1881-) and Mount Forest (1876-).

994. Railway Committee of Privy Council. **Railways. Reports of electric, street and suburban railways, 1893-1945.** 19 metres (vols. 1068-1152) Loc: NAC. RG 46, FA 11.

From 1875, street railway companies were required to submit annual reports that described construction, operations, details of passenger and freight traffic, accidents, property and routes. Some of this material was used in compiling the annual Railway Statistics printed in the Sessional Papers. Reports submitted to the Board of Railway Commissioners (1904-1938), and the Board of Transport Commissioners (1938-1967) are also filed with the earlier series. The finding aid notes returns for the Guelph Radial Railway and its municipal successor (1901-1939) in vols. 1086-1088.

995. Railway Committee of Privy Council. **Railways. Reports of steam railways, 1875-1938.** 43.1 metres (vols. 853-1067) Loc: NAC. RG 46, FA 10.

From 1875, railway companies were required to submit annual reports that described operations, principal officers, capitalization, data of passenger and freight traffic, equipment, profit and loss, construction progress, accidents, property and route. Some of this material was used by the Minister of Railways and Canals in the Railway Statistics printed in the Sessional Papers. Reports submitted to the Board of Railway Commissioners (1904-1938) and the Board of Transport Commissioners (1938-1967), are also filed with this series. The finding aid notes returns for the Georgian Bay and Wellington (1875-1882), Grand Trunk (1875-1922), Guelph Junction (1888-1909; many missing), Ontario and Quebec/CPR (1882-1906), Toronto, Grey and Bruce (1875-1906), and Wellington, Grey and Bruce (1875-1882).

996. Transport Canada. **Railways. Construction of main and branch lines, 1849-1938.** 34 volumes. Loc: NAC. RG 12.

Construction plans and reports for about two hundred and fifty railway projects that had to be approved by Transport Canada and its predecessors.

997. Transport Canada. **Railways. Index, 1866-1937.** 25 vols, 5 reels. Loc: NAC. RG 30 IF, FA 21.

Various indexes to numbered files of the Railway Branch of the former Department of Railways and Canals and the Central Registry files of Transport Canada, including an alphabetical index by railway company for Department of Railways and Canals files, 1901-1937 (vols. 978-979); a chronological index to Orders in Council for railways, 1893-1937 (vol. 980); a subject index to Canadian Government Railways for Department of Railway and Canal files, 1901-1937 (vol. 981); an alphabetical index by firm, person or location for Transport Canada central registry files containing correspondence created by the Department of Public Works and Railways and Canals, c1870-1885 (vols. 988-989); an alphabetical index by firm or person for Department of Railway and Canal files, 1901-1937 (vols. 990-997); an alphabetical index by location for the railway plans (vols. 998-1000); and an alphabetical index by railway company for the railway plans (vols. 1001-1002). Users should note that not all files referenced in the index are still intact, some having been incorporated into the Department's Central Registry file system. New computerized indexes and finding aids are being prepared by the Government Archives Division.

998. Transport Canada. **Railways. Legislation and charters, 1850-1937.** volume 1956. Loc: NAC. RG 12.

Records from old Department of Railways and Canals.

GREAT BRITAIN: COLONIAL OFFICE

999. Great Britain. Secretary of State for the Colonies. **Correspondence with Upper and Lower Canada, 1826-1831.** 11 volumes. Loc: PRO, NAC. PRO: No. 42.

This massive collection is a basic source for the imperial and colonial political contexts of regional development in Upper Canada, and is rich in material relating directly to the organization of the early settlement in the Guelph area. The manuscripts are organized into hundreds of bound volumes. Only those that concentrate on issues relating to the local region will be mentioned here. Volume 380, 1826, contains correspondence concerning the creation and chartering of the Canada Company. Included are a number of letters between John Galt and Wilmot Horton, British Under Secretary of State for the Colonies, outlining the evolution of the commercial scheme. Letters between Horton and his supervisor, Lord Bathurst, reveal their skepticism of Galt's proposals. Also included are several letters from Rev. John Strachan who attempted to scuttle the entire venture even before it began. Volumes 395-410, 1826-1831, deal specifically with the organization and operation of the Canada Company, and include correspondence, minutes of meetings and reports. The records clearly indicate the close relationship between imperial and provincial governments, and a commercially based colonization scheme. Volume 408 deals with Galt's activities in Guelph in 1827 and the increasingly tense relationship he had with provincial political officials. The issue of the LaGuayran settlers whom Galt received in Guelph in 1827 is covered in detail. Galt's act of charity in accepting the settlers led to a complicated jurisdictional dispute with both levels of government, and served to accentuate the difficulties he faced in attempting to colonize Guelph and the surrounding area. Part of the Colonial Office Papers. The National Archives of Canada holds a complete set of the records on microfilm.

139

Open for business: an unidentified general store, 1907.
Some brand names may be read, including 'Red Rose' tea and 'Chum' old
tobacco. The **Inventory** includes references to cash books and other records
of several such anonymous stores. (Wellington County Museum and Archives)

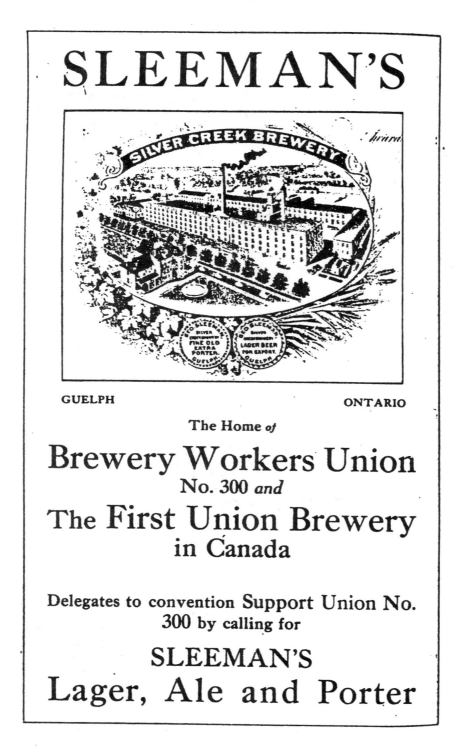

Sleeman's Beers, Strictly Union Made:
An advertisement that suggests a happy alliance between capital and labour, from the souvenir booklet of the 28th annual convention of the Trades and Labor Congress of Canada held in Guelph in 1912 (#2076).

BUSINESS RECORDS

Business archives are the primary evidence of the past at work.... Most people spend a major part of their life at work. The history of our working lives, therefore, is as important to the historian as our political, cultural or domestic past. Recent rapid technological changes have revolutionised the nature, methods and conditions of work, making positive action to preserve our records of the past vital.[1]

The efficient retention and organization of business records is essential for both the businesses themselves and for historical researchers concerned with economic and social change. The business historian is interested in records that will help 'to understand both the **record** of growth and change in a business (even its decline and death) and the **process** of change: to discover how and why a business grew as well as the factual record of its growth.'[2] Thus the business historian is interested in business entrepreneurs and managers, suppliers of capital and sources of credit, labour, raw materials, products, markets, technology and innovation.[3] Students of the rapidly expanding field of labour and working-class history also use business records to document such themes as the organization of work and production technologies, wages and working conditions, company labour policies of all kinds, the expectations and attitudes of workers and workers' efforts to maintain or assert control over their work.[4]

Such research can use all kinds of records generated by a business-- annual reports, share registers, minute books, correspondence and letter books for evidence of the persons involved and the decisions they made and committee reports, cash books and bank statements for details of day-to-day

---

[1] Survey leaflet of the Kent Business Archives Survey, reproduced in **Business Archives: Principles and Practice** 55 (1988): 57-9.

[2] Peter Mathias, 'What do we want? What do we need? A business historian speaks to business archivists,' **Business Archives** 42 (1976): 7-14.

[3] See, for example, Anthony Slaven, 'The uses of business records: research trends in British business history,' **Business Archives** 50 (1984): 17-36.

[4] Nancy Stunden, 'Labour, records, and archives: the struggle for a heritage,' **Archivaria** 4 (1977): 73-91; G.S. Kealey and Russell G. Hann, 'Documenting working-class history: North American traditions and new approaches,' **Archivaria** 4 (1977): 92-115; John C. Rumm, 'Working through the records: using business records to study workers and the management of labour,' **Archivaria** 27 (Winter 1988-89): 67-96. Rumm's article was part of a special theme issue on Canadian archival resources for labour history.

operations. Wage-books and other personnel and payroll records, house magazines, photographs and oral history can help to illuminate work environments, attitudes and processes. As business records tend to be bulky there may be some tension between archivist and historian over what records should be preserved.[5]

Records are more likely to be retained and made accessible to researchers when a business is old enough to have accumulated a considerable body of records and large enough to support its own archives. Next best are businesses that survived into the recent past, an era when the value of their records has been recognized and some resources provided to save them for a public repository.

Business history and business archives are relatively under-developed in Canada.[6] Yet, as Roger Hall has reminded us, 'Canada is a country which owes its existence more than most to the efforts of business firms.'[7] The Montreal Business History Project pioneered inventories of Canadian business records in its 1978 publication of a guide to the pre-1947 records held by selected Montreal businesses.[8] Imperial Oil in Toronto, Labatts in London and Seagrams in Waterloo have major collections of business papers. Ontario Hydro has a huge collection of documents (officially organized as an Archives since 1980) which supplements the very extensive annual reports published in the Ontario **Sessional Papers** (1906-   ).[9]

No business corporation in Guelph or Wellington County is old enough and large enough to support its own archives. Indeed, in contrast to several in neighbouring Waterloo County, very few businesses that were established on any scale before 1940 are still in operation. Most of the business records we have traced for this **Inventory** are mere fragments of the substantial paperwork their businesses must have generated. There are some exceptions, especially for financial businesses. One is the impressive bodies of records of the Guelph and Ontario Investment and Savings Society (#1104-#1111) and the associated Guelph Trust Company (#1115-#1119) that have been preserved in the archives of the Guelph Public Library. With minutes of annual meetings, annual financial reports, minutes of the board of directors, bylaws and transfer books

[5] K.G. Saur, **Business archives: studies on international practices** (International Council on Archives, Committee on Business Archives, 1983).

[6] Christopher L. Hives, 'History, business records and corporate archives in North America,' **Archivaria** 22 (Summer 1986): 40-57.

[7] Roger Hall, 'Minding our own business,' **Archivaria** 3 (1976-77): 73.

[8] Robert Sweeny, ed. **A guide to the history and records of selected Montreal businesses before 1947** (Montreal: Centre de recherche en histoire economique du Canada francais, 1978).

[9] Descriptions of the Ontario Hydro Archives and Labatt's Archives are contained in Christian Norman, 'Business archives and business history,' **The History and Social Science Teacher** 18, 2 (1982): 91-103.

spanning the period from 1876 to 1950, this material would repay intensive research. Records also survive for several fire insurance companies that operated at a very localized level, in contrast to the more centralized life insurance companies.[10] Records have been inventoried for the Guelph Township Mutual Fire Insurance Company (to 1942), the Puslinch Mutual Fire Insurance Company (to 1933) and for the Peel and Maryborough Mutual Fire Insurance that still operates in North Wellington and holds records spanning the century since 1887 (#-1158-#1159).

Among other significant sets of business records held locally are those of the Sleeman Brewing and Malting Company that operated the Silver Creek Brewery from the mid-1840s to 1906. These form part of the Sleeman Papers in the University Library's Archival and Special Collections (#1210-#1218). Records of the Guelph Railway Company (later known as the Guelph Radial Railway) which operated the Guelph electric street railway are divided among the University Library, the Guelph Public Library, the Guelph Civic Museum as well as the Ontario Hydro Archives (#1282-#1293).[11] Voluminous records of the John Thomson and Son Funeral Home of Fergus (#1065-#1067), in the Wellington County Archives, provide material for social as well as business history.

Major sets of business records relevant to Wellington County are held outside the region in the Mutual Life Assurance Company Archives in Waterloo (#1137-#1153) and the Ontario Hydro Archives in Toronto (#1289-#1293, #1317-#1320). Also relevant to the business history of this region are the immense collection of Canada Company records of land development and sales in the Archives of Ontario (#1233-#1237). Records of road and railway companies reveal the crucial importance of transportation and communications in the nineteenth century. Quite good records of the early road companies of the 1840s to the 1860s have been found, including minute books of the Guelph and Arthur Road Company (#1278), the Guelph and Elora Road Commission (#1279), and the Guelph, Elora and Peel Gravelled Road Company (#1281). The best railway records are of the companies that were merged into Canadian National in 1923 and are held in the National Archives of Canada. These include the records of the Galt and Guelph Railway (#1266-#1267), the Georgian Bay and Wellington (#1268), the Grand Trunk Railway (#1269-#1277), the Toronto and Guelph Railway (#1306-#1311) and the Wellington Grey and Bruce (#1315). The Buchanan Papers in the National Archives contain materials for these and other railways in the period to 1880. The papers and records of the railway engineers, Walter and Francis Shanly, should also be noted (#1299-#1300).

Most of the records in this section were generated by a great variety of quite small businesses such as blacksmiths, grocers, shoemakers, tailors, hotel-keepers, drugstores, dry goods merchants and general store keepers. Cash

[10] Darrell A. Norris, 'Flightless phoenix: fire risk and fire insurance in urban Canada, 1882-1886,' **Urban History Review** 16 (1987): 62-68.

[11] The records in the Ontario Hydro Archives were used in Steve Thorning, 'Streetcars in Guelph: the Guelph Radial Railway,' **Historic Guelph** 22 (1983): 4-40.

books and miscellaneous correspondence predominate. Although we have only fragmentary evidence of each enterprise, we can gain some collective impression of everyday business life. Useful sources that can provide context and some measure of the relative significance of particular businesses are the R.G. Dun credit advisory ledgers (#1100) maintained in manuscript from 1843 to 1881 and the Dun (later Dun and Bradstreet) printed reference books (#1101) begun in 1865.

The records are grouped in major types of business activity -- farming and agricultural, commercial, business education and entertainment, financial and legal, industrial, land subdivision and sales, medical practice, publishing, transportation (roads, railways and street railways) and utilities (electricity and telephone). We have found very little that might be described as labour records for Guelph and Wellington, though some of the photographs that illustrate this volume suggest the interest of more research in this field.

FARMS AND AGRICULTURE

1000. Cromar, Robert. **Diary, 1836-1849 (sporadic).** 1 folder. Loc: WCA. MU8.
    A diary of the journey of Robert Cromar in 1836 when he migrated from Aberdeen, Scotland to Upper Canada. The collection includes the financial transactions of Cromar with merchants and overall operation of his farm from 1838 to 1849. The Wellington County Archives has developed a genealogy file of the Cromar family indicating Robert Cromar was born in 1814 at Waterdown, Newsmills, Scotland. The file also notes he was a farmer in Pilkington Township from the 1850s until his death in 1892. The collection is a photocopy of the original diary and cash book records of Cromar.

1001. Day, Thomas. **Farm cash book, 1856-1881.** 1 ledger. Loc: WCA.
    The first page is marked 'Thomas Day, Eramosa', and 'Noah Sunley, Oustic'. Noah Sunley married Day's daughter, Ann Amelia, in 1879.

1002. Elliott, J.J. **Catalogue. Imported and homebred shorthorns from the Thornham herd.** 56 p. Loc: UGL.
    A catalogue of imported and homebred shorthorn cattle offered for auction by J.J. Elliott at the Winter Fair building, October 19, 1923. Each 'lot' states who bred the dame and sire, and lists other cattle statistics. Many of the cattle being auctioned were from Scotland or bred by Scottish breeders.

1003. Green Grove Stock Farm. **Program. Stock sale, June 5, 1930.** 1 item. Loc: WCA. MU51.
    A detailed listing of shorthorn cattle to be sold by George D. Fletcher at the Green Grove Farm in Erin Township.

1004. Holmwood, George. **Diary, 1888-1927.** 1 binder. Loc: WCA, UGA. WCA: MU 86, UGA: XRIM6 A314.
    A typed copy of the diary that contains brief daily entries regarding Holmwood's life and work on a farm situated on the northeast corner of Woodlawn Road and Highway 6. Entries list activities with stock, crops, prices and family activities.

1005. Jackson, W.R. **Cash book, 1891-1906.** 1 envelope. Loc: WCA. MU19.
    A photocopy of the ledger. An archival note states that the original is in the possession of Bill Thompson, Eramosa Township. The record suggests that the accounts are for a farm operation in Eramosa Township, concession 7, lot 14.

1006. Jeffrey, John. **Daybook, 1865-1913.** 21 ledgers. Loc: WCA. MU 89.
    A record of farm expenses and revenues. The farm was situated on Concession 8, Lot 16, Puslinch Township. The first ledger is from 1865 to 1884. Jeffrey emigrated from Stirlingshire, Scotland in 1838. Part of the Jeffrey Collection.

1007. Jeffrey, John. **Farm diaries, 1859-1911 (sporadic).** 18 volumes. Loc: WCA. MU 89.
    A record of farm and family life by Jeffrey who farmed on Concession 8, Lot 16, Puslinch Township. Part of the Jeffrey Collection. Diaries for 1861, 1873-4, 1878, 1889-90 and 1898-9 are missing.

Progress in Erin Township:
a new threshing machine on Will McMillan's farm, 1910. According to the 1906
Atlas of Wellington County, McMillan's farm was at Concession 5, Lot 14.
(Wellington County Museum and Archives)

1008. Leybourne, Peter. **Receipts, 1879-1897 (sporadic).** 1 envelope. Loc: WCA. MU51.
A series of business receipts of Peter Leybourne who appears to have lived in Belwood and had dealings with Fergus merchants. The Wellington County Archives has a genealogy file relating to the Leybourne family of Garafraxa West Township which indicates Peter Leybourne was a farmer in the township and was a native of Yorkshire, England.

1009. Louttit, William. **Property Assessment. Assessment notices, 1860-1897.** 1 file folder. Loc: AO. MU 2014.
Notices of assessment from Garafraxa Township which show that Louttit's property taxes rose from $10.60 to $34.78 per annum over the period. Part of the Marston Collection.

1010. Louttit, William. **Property Assessment. Tax receipts, 1851; 1859; 1898-1907; 1909-1911.** 1 file folder. Loc: WCA.
The receipts are issued by Garafraxa West Township to Louttit for property on Concession 5, lot 1/2 and 14. Part of the Pollock Collection.

1011. McDermott, James. **Personal papers, 1849-1895.** 1 file folder. Loc: WCA. MU 8; List of document contents.
Invoices of land, tax, insurance and business transactions of James McDermott, a farmer of Erin Township. The Wellington County Archives has developed a detailed finding aid noting the contents and dates of specific documents in the collection. Comprises the McDermott Collection.

1012. Moir, Forbes. **Farm diary, 1884-1914.** 1 envelope. Loc: WCA. MU 66.
A photocopy of the original diary that consists of daily entries about farming activities in Garafraxa West Township, the weather and travels.

1013. Morrison, George and McKenzie, George. **Farm lease, 1890.** 1 envelope. Loc: WCA. MU 19.
An agreement in which Morrison leased 100 acres in Nichol Township from McKenzie.

1014. Morriston Spring Seed Fair. **Broadside advertising fair, Village of Morriston, Wednesday April 1, 1866.** 1 item. Loc: UGA. XRI MS A116016.
Part of the Goodwin-Haines Collection.

1015. Pollock, George. **Invoices and receipts, 1900-1931.** 1 box. Loc: WCA. MU 19, 21; List of document contents.
A collection of invoices and receipts to George Pollock and Mrs Pollock from Elora and area businesses. The files include tax assessment records of the Pollock family for the years 1907, 1913, 1914, 1917 and from 1922 to 1925. Comprises the Pollock Collection.

1016. Potter, John. **Business correspondence, 1854-1855.** 4 file folders. Loc: WCA. MU 8; Detailed list of contents.
A collection of weekly correspondence from John McNaughton of Galt Mills to Potter discussing price and purchase of wheat. Also included is a letter from the Pilkington Township Agricultural Society requesting Potter to be a judge of grain at the Elora Seed Fair. Part of the Pollock Collection.

1017. L.R. Guild and Sons. **Poultry breeding stock sale advertisements, 1923.** 1 brochure. Loc: GCM.

    An advertisement of the Rockwood Company's annual sale.

1018. Ross, James. **Farm journal, October 1894-October 1895.** 1 file. Loc: WCA. MU 102.

    Ross, who farmed lots 18-20 of Concession 16, Nichol Township, describes farming activities, Fergus businesses, family events and the construction of his father's new stone barn and brick house, including details of costs and local contractors.

1019. Simpson, William. **Diary, 1875.** 1 volume. Loc: WCA. MU69.

    A record of daily activity on a farm.

1020. Stone, F.W. **Account book, 1854-1855.** 1 ledger. Loc: GCM.

    A listing of daily business transactions of Stone which lists his business contacts and the amount of money exchanged in specific transactions.

1021. Stone, F.W. **Correspondence, photographs, expense accounts, 1853-1960.** 1 box, 1 ledger. Loc: UGA. XR1 MS A049.

    A collection of account books of F.W. Stone's farming operations from 1853 to 1871, letters written between the Stone family in the 1860s and 1870s, biographical notes of the life of F.W. Stone, and photographs of the Stone family. The Stone Family Collection also includes the correspondence of descendants of F.W. Stone, the date of birth and death of family members, and a photograph of the original 1873 plan of the Ontario Agricultural College. Most of the account book records of F.W. Stone are held in microfilm form.

1022. Stone, F.W. **Legal documents, 1889-1955.** 1 file folder. Loc: UGA. XR1 MS A182.

    A collection of mortgages, deeds and related correspondence of the F.W. Stone property and a probate for Annie Louisa Macdonald. Part of the Stone Family Collection.

1023. Stone, F.W. **Letters, 1846; 1895.** 2 documents. Loc: GCM.

    Two letters written to Stone with one dated 1846 relating to business transactions with a nail works and iron warehouse in Hamilton. The second letter, written in 1895 and sent from the Canadian Bank of Commerce, asks for Stone's opinion regarding the financial standing of a cattleman in Fairhaven, Washington.

1024. Watson, Henry. **Accounts ledger, 1856-1859.** 1 ledger. Loc: WCA. MU84. List of dates and contents of ledger.

    A listing of expenses incurred by Wilson for building a new house and operating the family farm. The record is a photocopy of the original ledger. Part of the Watson Collection.

1025. Young, Thomas. **Farm diary, 1854-1866; 1870-1890.** 2 reels. mf. Loc: WCA.

    The diary of Thomas Young, a Scottish immigrant, which includes references to farm activities and crops cultivated, the weather, as well as school, travel and social experiences. The Wellington County Archives has a genealogy file on the Young family which indicates that Thomas Young was an Erin Township Clerk and operated a farm at Concession 9, Lot 25 in the township. The file also notes

Thomas Young came to Canada in 1851 from Glasgow, Scotland and was a teacher for a number of years and that he lived from 1834 to 1913.

COMMERCE

1026. Aberfoyle General Store. **Account book, 1868-1873; 1879-1935.** 2 ledgers. Loc: PUS.

The ledgers are from an unidentified store in the village that lists amount and cost of purchases of various customers.

1027. American Hotel. **Cash books, 1886-1902.** 2 ledgers. Loc: GCM.

A record of accounts for various boarders, bar and dinner purchases. One ledger is inscribed, John McAteer who was proprietor of the American Hotel. An archival note identifies one unmarked ledger as from the American Hotel in Guelph.

1028. American Hotel. **Guest registers, 1914-1916.** 2 ledgers. Loc: GCM.

A record of guests' names, room numbers and places of residence. The ledger includes many Guelph and Toronto advertisements.

1029. American Hotel. **Receipts and invoices, 1891-1920.** 2 boxes. Loc: GCM.

The invoices are from many different companies, including Sleeman and Sons Limited, Brewers and Maltsters. Two receipts are from Loretto Academy for tuition for Misses H. and G. McAteer.

1030. Andrich, A. **Account book, 1902-1903.** 1 ledger. Loc: WCA.

A record of the accounts of clients with A. Andrich, butcher in Elora, that lists products purchased by specific customers. Held with the Fischer Collection.

1031. Armstrong, Simon. **Financial. Cash book, 1868-1876.** 1 ledger. Loc: WCA. MU51.

A listing of the daily business transactions of Simon Armstrong a grocer in Moorefield in Maryborough Township.

1032. **Auction Notice. Harrison's Inn, Guelph, 1830.** Loc: WCA.

A list of items to be sold in a public auction at B. Harrison's Inn in Guelph in September, 1830. The notice is accompanied by an undated newspaper clipping which notes who found the source and includes a biography of Benjamin Harrison. Part of the Wellington County Historical Research Society Collection.

1033. Barber, R.H. **Calendar advertisement, 1904.** 1 file folder. Loc: GCM.

An advertisement for Barber who lists his services as 'Paper Hanger, House Painter, Sign Writer, Grainer, Decorator, Etc.'.

1034. Bogardus and Barton Druggists. **Invoices, 1912; 1922.** 2 documents. Loc: GCM.

Two invoices for goods sold by the Guelph company which was called Bogardus and Company in 1912, but by 1922 was called Bogardus and Barton.

1035. Boyer, Peter. **Cash book, 1910-1917.** 1 ledger. Loc: WCA. MU62.

A record of business transactions of Boyer who lived in Moorefield in Maryborough Township. The ledger appears to consist of accounts of a dry goods store.

1036. Buchanan, Isaac. **Correspondence, 1816-1883; Letterbooks, 1838-1868.** Loc: NAC. FA#26, vols 64-68.

    The very large collection includes business and political correspondence between Buchanan, a prominent Hamilton merchant, and various persons in Guelph and Wellington County. Among those noted are David Allan, Alfred Baker, W.R. Brock, William Clarke, John Davies, Andrew Geddes, John Gillespie, Thomas Gordon, George John Grange, Donald Guthrie, W. Kingsmill, James McMillan, E. Newton, G. Robins, Thomas Sandilands, Charles Sharpe, Rev. John Whyte, W. Wilkie and Rev. Samuel Young.

1037. Burt Brothers Department Store, Elora. **Correspondence, 1912-1929.** 2 file folders. Loc: WCA. MU 37; List of correspondence documents.

    A record of correspondence relating to orders. The letters include reference to the selling price of specific goods. The Wellington County Archives has developed a finding aid which indicates the date of correspondence and individuals engaging in specific letters. Part of the Ferguson Collection.

1038. Burt Brothers Department Store, Elora/ Carswell Brothers. **Insurance policies and receipts, 1910-1932.** 4 file folders. Loc: WCA. List of insurance company policies.

    A record of the insurance policies of the Burt Brothers who were merchants in Elora. The types of policies include casualty and fire insurance, with the majority of agreements being made with Toronto firms. Part of the Ferguson Collection.

1039. Burt Brothers Department Store, Elora. **Property Assessments. Tax records, 1913-1932.** 2 file folders. Loc: WCA. List of document headings.

    A record of tax assessments of the Burt Brothers who were merchants in Elora. The record also contains brief references to the Carswell Brothers of Elora including a tax assessment and a few pieces of business correspondence. Part of the Ferguson Collection.

1040. Campbell, Hugh. **Receipts, 1900.** 1 document. Loc: WCA. MU66.

    A receipt for a client's purchase of a coffin from Hugh Campbell who was an undertaker in Morriston.

1041. Connon, John. **Correspondence, agreements, patents, clippings, advertisements, notebooks, drawings and financial records, 1881-1900.** 13 file folders. Loc: AO. MU 752-753.

    Most of the files contain correspondence and clippings associated with Connon's photographic business and his invention of a cycloramic or 360-degree panoramic camera. One file folder contains correspondence in 1922-1923 with Dr C.K. Clarke, Medical Director of the Canadian National Committee for Mental Hygiene in Toronto, on the subject of Connon's research in Elora local history. There are files of correspondence with George Eastman of the Eastman-Kodak Company concerning Connon's grievance that he and his father had invented various photographic improvements which might have been adopted by Kodak without recognition or compensation. A letter of February 15, 1921 presents an historical summary of the Connon family.

1042. Connon, John. **Miscellaneous business records, 1845-1889 (sporadic)**. 3 ledgers, 1 file folder. Loc: UGA. XR1 MS A332.

The collection includes three unidentified merchant account books. One account book covers the years from 1853 to 1855 and has entries for Fergus and Elora businessmen. The other two ledgers appear to be owned by the same person and cover the years 1881 to 1884. These two ledgers also have historical notes on Elora which appear to be composed by John Connon. There are also a few individual receipts and invoices of Elora businesses dated from 1845 to 1889. Held with the Connon Collection.

1043. Connon, Thomas. **Account books, 1859-1864**. 1 box. Loc: UGA. XR1 MS A320.

A large number of accounting records and receipts of Connon who was a dry goods merchant in Elora in the 1850s and early 1860s. The account books include details of receipts and expenditures and prices of dry goods. The papers also contain invoices for goods purchased by partners Connon and Henderson from firms in Montreal and Hamilton. Held with the Connon Collection.

1044. Croft, Nathaniel. **Tailor's account book, 1862-1867**. 1 ledger. Loc: GCM.

A detailed listing of accounts of clients of Nathaniel Croft who appears to have been a tailor. The account book does not indicate Croft was a Guelph resident but clients listed were residents of the city. The ledger includes an alphabetical index by name of clients who had accounts with Croft. The record is held in a box labelled, Account Books.

1045. Davidson, Alexander. **Cash books, 1881-1895**. 4 ledgers. Loc: WCA.

The first journal is marked 'A. Davidson, Ennotville'. The later address is Elora. The third journal, from 1884-1900, is listed in the card index under C.A. Bignell, but internal evidence suggests it is a Davidson journal, and that he made boots and shoes and trunks.

1046. Davidson, James. **Unreserved auction sale, 1938**. 1 item, oversize. Loc: UGA. XR1 MS A040002.

A broadside, part of a larger collection, announcing the sale of farm stock, implements and household goods, ordered by William H. Bowley and auctioned by James A. Davidson. Held with the Guelph Historical Society Collection of maps of Guelph.

1047. E.R. Bollert Company. **Advertising bonus cards**. 1 envelope. Loc: GCM.

A series of undated cards for the company which was a mercantile venture in Guelph during the late nineteenth century. The firm notes 'This bonus card is issued by us as an advertising medium, and to stimulate a cash business'.

1048. Elora Dry Goods Store. **Receipts, invoices, correspondence, 1884-1898**. 1 box. Loc: WCA. MU 17, 75; Detailed list of contents.

A collection of receipts that the Elora Dry Goods Store received from various businesses in Montreal, Toronto, Hamilton, Guelph, Elora, Fergus, Berlin, Galt, London, Niagara Falls and Sarnia. The Collection includes several letters regarding invoice information. According to the archival finding aid, Frank Clark conducted this business from 1882 until 1919.

1049. Fergusson, Adam Johnston. **Receipts, correspondence, 1845-1849**. 3 documents. Loc: GCM.

The file includes invoices to Fergusson for goods purchased from C.H. Webster who was a druggist in Guelph in 1849. The file also contains a letter from the firm of Webster and Fordyce outlining details of malt whiskey they were selling to Fergusson in 1845.

1050. Fischer, Christian and Fischer, Frank. **Business records, 1877-1948**. 2 boxes. Loc: WCA. Detailed finding aid.

A record of the businesses of the Fischer family of Elora which included a funeral parlour, a dry goods store and a furniture store. The records contain account books for the businesses noting receipts and expenditures. The collection contains nine notebooks covering the period from 1900 to 1924 which record funerals. The Wellington County Archives has developed a detailed finding aid noting the dates and contents of specific documents. The finding aid notes that Christian Fischer operated a furniture business, a dry goods store and a furniture store from 1862 to 1919 and that his son, Frank, continued the family business until 1948. Part of the Fischer Collection.

1051. Frank Clark Grocery and Dry Goods Store. **Business records, 1891-1898**. 2 boxes. Loc: WCA. FA: MU 17,45.

A collection of invoices, statements and order forms from businesses in account with the store from 1891 to 1898. Frank Clark conducted his business in Elora from 1882 to 1919.

1052. G.B. Ryan and Company. **42 years in the glass of fashion, 1885-1927**. 32 p. Loc: GCM.

An illustrated brochure that describes the new building and services of the department store and offers a brief history of its development.

1053. G.B. Ryan and Company. **Advertisement, 1928**. 1 brochure. Loc: GCM.
An advertisement, with prices, promoting Easter fashions.

1054. Gordon, William. **Business advertisement, 1865**. 1 file folder. Loc: UGA. XR1 MS A322.

An advertisement by Gordon indicating he would pay cash for wool delivered to the store of John Henderson in Elora. Held with the Connon Collection.

1055. Guelph Corner Grocery Store. **Advertising circular, July 7, 1924**. 1 document. Loc: GCM.

A listing of prices of goods sold by Bard Whetstone at his store at the corner of Gladwin and Yorkshire Streets.

1056. Guelph Dry Goods Store. **Cash book, 1850-1854**. 1 ledger. Loc: GCM.

An itemized list of amount and cost of purchases made by various people. The ledger is three inches thick and the pages well preserved and legible, although no binding remains. The name of the store is unidentified; most clients are listed from Guelph.

1057. Halley, James L. **Business records, 1868**. 1 envelope. Loc: WCA. MU43. List of contents and dates of documents.

A record of receipts and correspondence of Halley who operated a general store in Ponsonby in Pilkington Township. The collection includes two invoices sent to Halley from Guelph Mills which was operated by David Allan. The Wellington

County Archives has developed a finding aid indicating the contents, date and names of individuals involved in specific transactions. This is held with the Van Norman Collection.

1058. Henderson, K.M. **One hundred years of funeral service in Palmerston, 1886-1986.** 7 p. Loc: WCA. MU 86.
  Recollections of early funerals and funeral directors in Palmerston that refers to embalming, hearses and caskets.

1059. Hoban, James. **Merchant's account book, 1872-1873.** 1 ledger. Loc: GCM.
  A listing of goods sold and prices charged by Hoban who was a general merchant in Guelph. The ledger indicates Hoban sold goods in Guelph, Elora, and the Townships of Puslinch and Nichol. The ledger is held in a box entitled, Account Books.

1060. Howe Skelton and Company. **Cash book, 1904-1907.** 1 ledger. Loc: WCA. MU 101.
  Records kept by a Palmerston drugstore.

1061. Hugh Walker and Son. **Stock book, 1862-1868.** 1 ledger. Loc: GPL. Description of ledger contents.
  A record of articles and cost of items purchased in several categories including crockery, glassware, groceries, sundries, liquors, shop furniture, and garden seeds. According to the library clipping file, Walker was a wholesale grocer who began his business in 1861 in a building near the CNR Station. The business flourished for 76 years until it was sold to National Grocers in 1937.

1062. Huxley, Samuel. **Cash book, 1874.** 1 ledger. Loc: WCA. MU59.
  Samuel Huxley's cash book that appears to record business of a dry goods store in Hillsburgh. Part of the Huxley Collection.

1063. Jeffrey, Jessie. **Daybook, 1892-1896.** 1 ledger. Loc: WCA. MU 89.
  A record of financial accounts for an unidentified dry goods store in Aberfoyle. Part of the Jeffrey Collection.

1064. John M. Bond and Company. **Invoices, 1870-1871; 1894; 1900; 1922.** 5 documents. Loc: GCM.
  Five receipts for hardware goods purchased by Alex MeikleJohn, a Harriston merchant, from John M. Bond and Company of Guelph. A receipt from 1870 indicates that John M. Bond and Company was the successor to H. Mulholland. The receipts include one reference to goods John M. Bond and Company sold to a Toronto client. The record also has a receipt of goods sold by the Bond Hardware Company to a Guelph resident in 1922.

1065. John Thomson and Son Funeral Home. **Burial registers, 1888-1898; 1903-1964; 1967-1978.** 8 ledgers. Loc: WCA. MU 100.
  Funeral accounts that list name of deceased, address, age, cause and date of death, physician, place of burial, location of grave, and itemized cost of funeral. The funeral business began operation in 1870 in the Village of Fergus.

1066. John Thomson and Son Funeral Home. **Cash books, 1880-1902; 1919-1927.** 3 ledgers. Loc: WCA. MU 100.
  A record of purchases or rentals made for funerals, including hearses, gloves,

ribbon, caskets, shrouds and headstones.

1067. John Thomson and Son Funeral Home. **Invoice, 1907.** 1 document. Loc: WCA. MU 42.
An invoice for funeral expenses for the John Mutch estate.

1068. Keith, John. **Account book, 1836-1855.** 1 volume. Loc: UGA.
A record of cost of carpentry work done for area residents including Alexander Watt, William Day and Sem Wissler. Keith emigrated from Aberdeenshire, Scotland in 1834 to the Bon Accord settlement near Elora.

1069. Larter Family and Wilson, Laura. **Business receipts, 1918-1919; 1921.** 7 documents. Loc: WCA. MU 25.
Held in the Wellington County Historical Research Society Collection. Seven business receipts for goods purchased by the Larter family and Laura Wilson from Fergus merchants.

1070. McCrea, Charles and McCrea, William. **Cash book, 1828.** 1 ledger. Loc: GCM.
An itemized list of purchases of various individuals including John Galt and Charles Prior. The ledger indicates that the McCreas ran a dry goods, grocery and liquor store. The cover is inscribed, '1828: Grocer's book in Guelph: owned by Robert Thompson, 1879'.

1071. McCready General Store, Harriston. **Financial records, 1857-1872.** 4 volumes. Loc: AO. MU 3684.
Day books (1857-1872) and ledgers (1864-1870) detailing goods supplied for cash or credit to customers who are sometimes identified by their occupations. Part of Harriston Collection.

1072. McCutcheon, William. **Cash book, 1877-1878.** 1 ledger. Loc: UGA. XR1 MS A003.
The ledger includes a photocopied business directory of 1885-1886 listing Wm. McCutcheon as a general merchant in Ospringe. The ledger outlines products sold and the cost of various products.

1073. McKinnon Cooperative Company. **Good news for the people, 1910.** 1 item. Loc: UGA. XR2 MS A044.
Poster advertising goods of the company, including apple parer, egg beater, sewing machines, irons, skates, lawn mower, bell and tool sets, reapers, mowers, fanning mills, ploughs and other agricultural implements and vehicles. The advertisement notes that the company did not employ agents or drummers and sold only through the Grange or other cooperative organizations.

1074. McKinnon, J. **Cash book, 1888-1895.** 1 ledger. Loc: WCA. MU75.
A record of purchases made by clients of McKinnon who was a general merchant in Everton.

1075. MeikleJohn, Alex and MeikleJohn, J. **Account book, 1876.** 1 ledger. Loc: UGA. XR1 MS A033.
A record of goods purchased in a hardware store in Harriston which notes the amount paid for various products. The ledger has been identified by University of Guelph archivists as the day book of A. and J. MeikleJohn.

1076. MeikleJohn, Alex. **Business papers, 1866-1912.** 4 ledgers, 1 file folder. Loc: WCA. MU 13, 45; List of document contents.

   Invoices, stocks, day books and correspondence of Alex MeikleJohn who was a hardware merchant in Harriston. The collection includes invoices from several Wellington County businesses that MeikleJohn dealt with in the period. The record also contains four ledgers listing sales of goods by MeikleJohn to customers in the years 1866 to 1869, 1871 to 1872 and 1877 to 1878. Also included are several photographs of family members. Comprises the MeikleJohn Collection.

1077. **Merchant's account book, 1871-1872.** 1 ledger. Loc: GCM.

   The account book of an unidentified general merchant with a number of references to Guelph residents. The ledger lists the date of business transactions, goods sold and the amount charged for various products. The ledger is held in a box entitled, Account Books.

1078. Mutch, James. **Account book, 1853-1868.** 1 ledger. Loc: WCA. MU 2.

   A record of the accounts of clients with James Mutch including residents of Elora, Salem and the Townships of Peel, Nichol and Pilkington.

1079. Pasmore, Walter J. **Cash books, correspondence and photographs, 1869-1930.** 2 boxes. Loc: UGA. XR1 MS A036.

   A record of investments, mortgages, several business letters and undated, untitled photographs. Walter J. Pasmore was a lumber merchant in Guelph after 1891.

1080. Petrie, A.B. **Spots and Stains. How to remove them.** 1 volume. Loc: GCM.

   An outline of methods utilized to clean clothes and households. The brochure is also an advertising item for Petrie who operated a drug store in Guelph. The document is undated but the Petrie family operated a drug store as early as the 1860s.

1081. Quinn, Charles A. **Diary and accounts, 1903.** 1 file folder. Loc: WCA. List of document headings.

   A photocopy of original daily diary entries describing weather conditions, travels and economic activities. The record also includes several receipts and expenditures of Charles A. Quinn, Fergus. Although the business is not labelled, there are several references to funds received for making ice. Part of the Ferguson Collection.

1082. Thompson, Arch. **Cash book, 1848-1854.** 1 ledger. Loc: WCA.
   Thompson's boots and shoes business was in Erin.

1083. Tyler, Mrs. **Millinery and dressmaking, 1845.** 4 p. Loc: UGL.

   An announcement of the opening of a dressmaking shop on the Market Square in Guelph, 1845. The brochure states that Mrs Tyler has had experience in London and New York. It is addressed to 'Mrs Stone, Guelph', and postmarked 'Guelph, August 19, 1845, U.C.'

1084. Ward-Price Ltd, Auctioneers. **Catalogue. Valuable objects of art being the contents of Riverslea, Guelph, Ontario, residence of the late Mrs Flora C. Hall for sale by public auction on the estate, Monday, September 23, 1946.** 64 p.

ill. Loc: UGA, GPL. UGA: XR1 MS A352.

A catalogue used to auction off the estate of the late Flora C. Hall. Included is a list of items auctioned off each day, during the six day dispersal, as well as photographs of some of the finer items.

1085. Wissler Collection. **Cash book and certificates, 1860-1871; 1877; 1879.** 1 ledger. Loc: WCA.

A merchant's business cash book that suggests it was a dry goods store. The book was found in a Salem shed by a Nichol Township road superintendent. Inserted into it are two pedigree certificates of shorthorn stock owned by J.E. Wilson of Salem, dated 1877 and 1879.

1086. Yeomans Family. **Business records, correspondence, photographs, 1865-1943.** 4 boxes. Loc: WCA. MU 79-81; List of document contents.

A collection of the drugstore business records, correspondence and photographs of the Yeomans family of Mount Forest. The business records include account books, prescription books, invoices, partnership agreements and apprenticeship contracts of the family. The collection also contains original newspapers including the, Mount Forest Confederate, and pamphlets of the Mount Forest Horticultural Society for the years 1876 and 1880. The Wellington County Archives has developed a detailed finding aid of the content, date and individuals mentioned in specific documents. Comprises the Yeomans Collection.

BUSINESS EDUCATION AND ENTERTAINMENT

1087. Griffin's Opera House. **Advertisement, c1920.** 1 document. Loc: GCM.

A list of 'photoplays' presented by the Opera House which was located opposite the Wellington Hotel on Wyndham Street and was a major centre of entertainment before the 1920s.

1088. Guelph Business College. **Business compendium, 1885.** Guelph: Guelph Business College, 1884. 48 p. Loc: GCM.

A course of study in the 'Practical Department' of the college after which the student would graduate from the college's 'miniature world of business to contend on that broad arena where fortune and fame await the competent'.

1089. Guelph Business College. **Catalogue, letterhead, 1885-1886.** 1 brochure; 1 envelope. Loc: GCM.

The second annual catalogue of the college whose motto was 'Integrity, Intelligence and Industry are the Fountain of True Success'. The principal, Malcolm MacCormack, writes that in the first year of the college's existence, in 1885, 'I had over 100 men and women in attendance who later became Book-keepers, Clerks, Shorthanders, Salesmen, Travellers, etc., or doing business successfully for themselves'. The catalogue includes a list of the college's first students who came from Guelph and area, Waterloo, Stratford, London, Niagara Falls, Peterborough, Montreal and New York City. Edward Higinbotham and George A. Sleeman were among the Guelph students.

1090. Guelph Business College. **Student notebook, c1900.** 1 item. Loc: UGA. XR1 MS A308.

A student notebook with a few entries that do not give a precise date. The front cover lists the student's name as Marian Kerr. The item is held with the

Hewat Family Collection.

1091. Mount Forest Business College. **Invoice book, n.d..** 1 ledger. Loc: WCA.
A record of credits, bills to pay and individuals involved with the college.
The ledger contains only two years of entries for the college. Part of the
Ferguson Collection.

1092. Rockwood Academy. **Cash book, 1875-1922.** 1 ledger. Loc: WCA. MU 59.
Part of Huxley Collection. Samuel Huxley's record of the purchase of grain,
stock and vegetables.

1093. Rockwood Academy. **Day book, 1875-1906.** 1 ledger. Loc: WCA. MU 59.
Part of Huxley Collection. Samuel Huxley's record of business transactions and
costs.

FINANCIAL AND LEGAL SERVICES

1094. Allan, David. **Financial. Cash book, 1900-1907.** 1 ledger. Loc: UGA. XR1 MS
A005.
The ledger appears to record rent collected by various individuals including
George Bard and David Allan. The ledger includes several letters addressed to
Colonel Higinbotham and several regarding the estate settlement of M.J.
Higinbotham. Part of Allan-Higinbotham Collection.

1095. Archibald, James. **Account book, 1924-1930.** 1 volume. Loc: UGA. XR1 MS A193003.
A record of monthly expenses for an unidentified business under headings of
subscriptions, jobs, advertising expenses, postage, miscellaneous and banks.
Other biographical information in the file indicates that Archibald was a banker
at Farran and Archibald Bank in Elora. Held with the Marston-Archibald
Collection.

1096. Archibald, James. **Correspondence, 1870-1901.** 23 file folders. Loc: UGA. XR1
MS A193003.
Letters written to Archibald from family, friends and business associates.
Many are from his lawyer brother, H. Archibald who lived in Portage la Prairie,
Manitoba, offering legal advice. Another brother, E.T. Archibald, operated a
flour mill in Dundar, Minnesota. Several letters are from the Farmers' Banking
House in Elora. James Archibald was a banker at Farran and Archibald in Elora.
Held with the Marston-Archibald Collection.

1097. Beattie's Banking House. **Land records, 1853-1943.** 1 box. Loc: WCA. List of
document contents.
A record of deeds and mortgage agreements between residents of Fergus and
Nichol Township which were held by the bank owned by the Beattie family. The
Wellington County Archives provides a detailed finding aid listing the type and
date of agreements with a note regarding individuals involved in specific
transactions. Held with the Beattie Collection.

1098. Canada Company. **Promissory notes for William Sunley, 1834.** 4 documents. Loc:
WCA. MU45A.

1099. Canada Life Assurance Company. **Insurance Policy. John Smith, Guelph, 1840-1899.** 3 documents. Loc: GCM.

A record of a policy held by John Smith with the Hamilton office of the Canada Life Assurance Company. The record includes a proposal by Smith for a policy with the Canada Life Assurance Company. The file also reproduces an obituary of Smith taken from the February 28, 1899 edition ot the Guelph Daily Mercury and Advertiser. Smith was the first mayor of the Town of Guelph and founded the Guelph Advertiser in the 1840s.

1100. Dun and Bradstreet/ R.G. Dun and Company. **Credit advisory ledgers, 1843-1881.** 8 reels, M-7753 to M-7760. mf. Loc: NAC. MG 28 III 106, FA 1653. Specific application required to use the collection.

The Mercantile Agency was founded in New York in 1841 as a credit advisory service to lenders. It was controlled by Robert G. Dun from 1859 to 1900 and became Dun and Bradstreet in the twentieth century. The information came from local correspondents and, later, travelling agents of the company. From the 1870s, the company had four branch offices in Canada. The manuscript originals are held by the Baker Library at the Harvard Business School. The ledgers were organized in geographical order by provinces and counties. Wellington County forms part of volume 24 and is also on microfilm reel M-7759 with Waterloo County and others. The manuscript ledgers contain anecdotal details about local businessmen in addition to estimates of their pecuniary strength and credit ratings. The ledgers should be distinguished from the printed quarterly reference books published by R.G. Dun and, later, Dun and Bradstreet from 1859. References to about four hundred businessmen in Guelph and Wellington County in this period may be found in volume 24, pages 199-245. These are prefaced by a manuscript index.

1101. Dun and Bradstreet/ R.G. Dun and Company. **Reference books, 1865-1978.** 323 reels. mf. Loc: AO. FA: MS 489. For research purposes only; permission to reproduce any material for publication must be obtained from Dun and Bradstreet Canada Ltd.

The reference books held by Dun and Bradstreet Canada Ltd, Toronto, were borrowed by the Archives of Ontario for microfilming in 1979. These volumes give credit ratings on businesses, trades, merchants and manufacturers throughout Canada. Dun and Bradstreet (or its predecessor companies, R.G. Dun and Co. or Dun, Wiman and Co.) rated businesses by 'pecuniary strength' and credit worthiness. Each volume is arranged internally by province, then alphabetically by city, town, village or hamlet. Dun and Bradstreet issued these volumes quarterly to its subscribing clients who were expected to return the previous volume on receipt of each new one. The volumes have been filmed in chronological order. Details for Wellington County localities are, therefore, distributed throughout the microfilm reels. Dun and Bradstreet Canada Ltd holds a complete set of the original printed volumes, but users are now directed to the Archives of Ontario. Selected volumes are occasionally found in local record collections. The Guelph Civic Museum, for example, has a reference book dating from 1876.

1102. Farmers' Bank of Newman Brothers. **Notarial register, 1880-1881.** 1 ledger. Loc: WCA.

A record of date of protest, name of maker, name of acceptor, amount due, where payable, time of mailing, fees and postage. Filed with Elora municipal records.

1103. Forsyth and Gethin. **Bank passbook, 1929-1950.** 1 ledger. Loc: GCM.
Banking transactions of Forsyth and Gethin with the Bank of Nova Scotia. No details are given as to the type of firm the partners operated or the geographic location of the business. The ledger is held in a box entitled, Account Books.

1104. Guelph and Ontario Investment and Savings Society. **Annual financial reports, 1885-1948.** 17 volumes. Loc: GPL. List of holdings, chronologically by year.
A record of the financial status of the company, listing assets and liabilities, profit and loss accounts and cash amount of loans applied for and granted. The reports offer a detailed financial statement on a consistent basis each year. The annual financial reports are held in the same ledgers as the minutes of the annual meetings and of the board of directors.

1105. Guelph and Ontario Investment and Savings Society. **Annual Meetings. Minutes, 1886-1907; 1911-1947.** 17 volumes. Loc: GPL. List of holdings, chronologically by year.
A record of the annual meeting usually held in February each year with procedures including the election of board directors, appointment of auditors and discussions of pertinent financial matters. The minutes are held in the same ledgers as the board of directors' minutes and the annual reports of the society.

1106. Guelph and Ontario Investment and Savings Society. **Annual report, 1890; 1920-1922.** 4 documents. Loc: GCM, WCA. MU 42.
A printed report of each annual meeting including financial statements. The 1922 report is held at the Wellington County Archives.

1107. Guelph and Ontario Investment and Savings Society. **Board of Directors. Minutes, 1876-1949.** 18 volumes. Loc: GPL. List of holdings, chronologically by year.
A record of the financial transactions of the firm which is very detailed in noting loans to Guelph and Wellington County residents. The board met several times each month. Most volumes are indexed by personal names, indicating the pages in the minutes where transactions with specific individuals and companies are listed. The board of directors' minutes are held in the same volume as the minutes of the annual meetings and the annual financial reports of the society.

1108. Guelph and Ontario Investment and Savings Society. **Bylaws, 1876-1947.** 1 ledger. Loc: GPL. Description of ledger contents.
A record of declaration of incorporation, prospectus, rules and bylaws. The society sought to 'encourage the accumulation of capital, and provide a safe permanent investment . . ., to assist in the acquisition and improvement of real estate . . ., and to purchase Dominion, Provincial and Municipal securities and debentures . . . .'

1109. Guelph and Ontario Investment and Savings Society. **Regulatory records, 1897-1920.** 4 file folders. Loc: AO. RG 31: Series 31-21.
Correspondence and returns filed with the Registrar of Loan Corporations and Inspector of Insurance. The records include a copy of the original charter as a building society in 1877 with names of the original shareholders. The society, whose president was Alex B. Petrie and managing director was J.E. McElderry through most of this period, first registered with the Provincial Registrar in

1897. It increased its capital stock from half a million to one million dollars in 1911 and to two million dollars in 1919. The files include documents relating to the incorporation and registration of the Guelph Trust Company (1917) which had the same president and managing director and was managed in association with the first society.

1110. Guelph and Ontario Investment and Savings Society/ Guelph Trust Company. **Scrapbook. Newspaper clippings about annual meetings and financial statements, 1937-1950.** 1 volume. Loc: GPL. Description of ledger contents.

A series of newspaper reports about annual meetings and financial statements taken from the Guelph Mercury, the Financial Post and the Hespeler Herald.

1111. Guelph and Ontario Investment and Savings Society. **Transfer books, 1876-1949.** 4 ledgers. Loc: GPL. Description of ledger contents.

A record of shares held by individuals in the capital stock of the society.

1112. Guelph Civic Museum. **Insurance policies, 1890-1926 (sporadic).** 8 documents. Loc: GCM.

A series of insurance policy documents for residents of Guelph and one person living in Erin Township.

1113. Guelph Township Mutual Fire Insurance Company. **Cash book, 1920-1934.** 1 ledger. Loc: WCA.

A record of individuals who held policies, noting the policy number and amount owed. Filed with Guelph Township municipal records.

1114. Guelph Township Mutual Fire Insurance Company. **Minutes, 1911-1942.** 1 volume. Loc: WCA.

The directors in 1911 were Robert Shortreed, John Laird, David McCrae, Frank Laidlaw, John McIntosh, J.P. Henderson and James Bowman. The minute book is held with the Guelph Township municipal records as Series 16.

1115. Guelph Trust Company. **Annual Meeting. Minutes, 1927-1935; 1937-1944.** 2 volumes. Loc: GPL. Description of ledger contents.

The records for the board of directors' meetings and annual reports are held in the same volumes. Each volume has an index.

1116. Guelph Trust Company. **Board of Directors. Annual report and financial statements, 1926-1943.** 2 volumes. Loc: GPL. Description of ledger contents.

The minutes of meetings of the board of directors and of annual meetings are held in the same volumes. Each volume has an index.

1117. Guelph Trust Company. **Board of Directors. Minutes, 1926-1945.** 2 volumes. Loc: GPL. Description of ledger contents.

The records for annual meetings and financial statements are also held in the same ledgers. Each ledger has an index.

1118. Guelph Trust Company. **Bylaws, 1917-1937.** 1 volume. Loc: GPL. Description of ledger contents.

A record of petition for incorporation, constitution, initial subscribers and bylaws. Bylaw No. 36 describes the employee's pension plan.

1119. Guelph Trust Company. **Regulatory records, 1917-1920.** 1 file folder. Loc: AO. RG 31: Series 31-21.

   Correspondence, final application for registration and returns filed with Registrar of Loan Corporations and Inspector of Insurance. The trust company was managed in association with the Guelph and Ontario Investment and Savings Society, having the same managing director, J.E. McElderry.

1120. Guthrie and Kerwin, Solicitors. **Account for settlement of M.J. Higinbotham estate, 1919.** 1 document. Loc: UGA. XR1 MS A005.

   Margaret Jane Higinbotham was the widow of Nathaniel Higinbotham. Part of Allan-Higinbotham Collection.

1121. Higinbotham and McLagan. **Correspondence, 1873-1885.** 1 file folder. Loc: UGA. XR1 MS A005033-5.

   Correspondence from McLagan in Victoria, B.C. to Nathaniel Higinbotham about their business partnership in land transactions. Part of Allan-Higinbotham Collection.

1122. Higinbotham and McLagan. **Financial statements, 1877-1879.** 4 documents. Loc: UGA. XR1 MS A005036.

   Balance sheets entitled 'Higinbotham and McLagan's Balance Sheet'. Assets listed include land purchased in Arthur, Luther, Proton, Amaranth, and stocks held at an oil refinery and at Canada Fire and Marine Insurance Company. A letterhead indicates the firm was entitled 'Higinbotham and McLagan – Estate, Loan, Insurance and General Brokers' and that the firm owned Wellington Oil Refinery and was an agent for Star and Montreal Line of steamers. Part of Allan-Higinbotham Collection.

1123. Higinbotham and McLagan. **Land records, 1876-1887.** 23 documents, 2 file folders. Loc: UGA. XR1 MS A005.

   A collection of deeds and mortgages recording land transactions in Guelph and area that includes property of John McLagan, Nathaniel Higinbotham, Alexander Dunbar, Noah and Ann Sunley, Robert and John Emslie and Rebecca Worsley. Two file folders contain correspondence and records of land transactions in Luther Township from 1878 to 1881. Part of Allan-Higinbotham Collection.

1124. Higinbotham, Harry. **Correspondence, 1927-1954.** 6 file folders. Loc: UGA. XR1 MS A005.

   Correspondence of business and family matters from Higinbotham who was Supervisor of Agencies in the London England office of Sun Life Assurance Company of Canada. Part of Allan-Higinbotham Collection.

1125. Higinbotham, Nathaniel. **Cancelled cheques, 1895-1927.** 2 file folders. Loc: UGA. XR1 MS A005081-2.

   A collection of cancelled cheques from the Guelph branches of the Central Bank of Canada and the Bank of Commerce. Part of Allan-Higinbotham Collection.

1126. Higinbotham, Nathaniel. **Cash books, 1893-1911.** 5 ledgers. Loc: UGA. XR1 MS A005019.

   A record of financial transactions including registration of land records. Part of Allan-Higinbotham Collection.

1127. Higinbotham, Nathaniel. **Correspondence regarding mortgages and insurance policies, 1887-1900.** 14 volumes. Loc: UGA. XR1 MS A005.

Correspondence regarding mortgages, insurance policies and other business matters. Part of Allan-Higinbotham Collection.

1128. Higinbotham, Nathaniel. **Correspondence with business associates, 1882-1890.** 3 file folders. Loc: UGA. XR1 MS A005031-2.

Correspondence of Higinbotham with various business associates. One set is from James Massie in Toronto about a barrel company and its patent of 1881 for the Patent Barrel Machine. The name of the company was Guelph Weight Patent Barrel and Veneer Manufacturing Company. A second file folder consists of correspondence from W.J. Martin, a Chatham lawyer, regarding Alexander Dunbar's indebtedness to Higinbotham. A third set concerns Cant, Laidlaw and Company, a woodworking machinery company in Galt. Part of Allan-Higinbotham Collection.

1129. Higinbotham, Nathaniel. **Daily journals, 1887-1890; 1894-1910.** 22 volumes. Loc: UGA. XR1 MS A005017.

A record of financial transactions and daily appointments. Part of Allan-Higinbotham Collection.

1130. Higinbotham, Nathaniel. **Insurance policies, 1879-1898.** 4 file folders. Loc: UGA. XR1 MS A005075-6.

Correspondence and insurance policies held by Higinbotham at various companies including London and Lancashire Life Assurance Company in Montreal, Colonial Life Assurance Company in Montreal, Unity Fire Insurance Company in London, Liverpool and London Fire and Life Insurance Company in Montreal, Scottish Imperial Insurance Company, Northern Assurance Company in London, Commercial Union Assurance Company in London, Star Life Assurance Society in London and Wellington Mutual Fire Insurance Company in Guelph. Part of Allan-Higinbotham Collection.

1131. Higinbotham, Nathaniel and Martin, E.R. **Land records, 1858-1861.** 1 file folder. Loc: UGA. XR1 MS A005074.

A record of purchase of land and a financial statement of renovation of building on Lot 108 in Guelph. Part of Allan-Higinbotham Collection.

1132. Higinbotham, Nathaniel. **Land records and correspondence, 1834-1909.** 21 file folders. Loc: UGA. XR1 MS A005.

Correspondence, mortgages and deeds in which Higinbotham was involved, often as mortgage grantor. Grantees include John Smith, Lena Soule Thomas, George Gibson, Elizabeth Worsley, George Stewart, Mary Henderson and Joseph Mays. Part of Allan-Higinbotham Collection.

1133. J.E. Carter Investment Broker. **Invoice, 1928.** 1 document. Loc: GCM.

A receipt for stocks sold for Roy Davidson. The invoice advertises Carter's motto as 'I link the seller to the buyer'.

1134. Lace, A. **Correspondence. Business letter requesting money, 1904.** 1 document. Loc: GCH.

A letter sent by A. Lace requesting payment of funds by another individual and noting that some business was lost because the money had not been paid. A. Lace appears to be a representative of J.W. Lyon. The record is held in the Clerk's office vault.

1135. Macdonald, A.H. **Legal ledger, 1877-1882**. 1 item. Loc: UGA. XR1 MS A324014.
Macdonald was a Guelph lawyer who also served on the City Council. Part of the Guelph Historical Society Collection.

1136. Munro, Fasken and Wilson. **Probate records, 1860-1910**. 1 file folder. Loc: WCA. MU 15; List of clients, alphabetical by name.
Wills processed by the Fergus law firm of Munro, Fasken and Wilson. The collection also includes documents of land agreements, sales and transfers. The Wellington County Archives has developed a detailed finding aid listing the type of legal document and its date of completion, and a note of individuals involved and their place of residence. Comprises the Meyler Collection.

1137. Mutual Life Assurance Company. **Agency Committee. Minutes, 1914-1972**. 2 files. Loc: MLA. 86.01.291-292. Specific permission required.
The committee, which included the president, managing-director, superintendent of agencies and company secretary, dealt with questions affecting the staff and work of the company's 85 agencies.

1138. Mutual Life Assurance Company. **Agency histories, 1871-1988**. 1 file. Loc: MLA. Specific permission required.
Historical summaries of the 85 Mutual Life insurance agencies throughout Canada. The Guelph Agency #40 was established by William Hart of Guelph and included Wellington, Grey, Bruce, Dufferin and Halton Counties until the mid-1880s, and Grey and Bruce until the early twentieth century. District Agents who served long periods at Guelph included J.W. Kilgour and George Chapman.

1139. Mutual Life Assurance Company. **Annual reports, 1870-1988**. 111 files in 6 boxes; 1 binder. Loc: MLA. 81.19.01. Specific permission required.
The first annual report mentions the original purposes of establishing the company, notably the success of the Waterloo County Mutual Fire Insurance Company in doing business on the 'mutual principle'. The names and places of residence of the shareholders are listed in the earliest reports. Robert Melvin of Guelph, for example, was a shareholder and director from the foundation of the company until his death in 1908.

1140. Mutual Life Assurance Company. **Biographical files, 1869-1950**. 1 file. Loc: MLA. Specific permission required.
Files of news clippings, obituaries and other ephemera about notable directors and officers, including Robert Melvin of Guelph who served on the board of directors from 1871 to 1908, being president for his final ten years.

1141. Mutual Life Assurance Company. **Board of Directors. Minutes, 1869-1986**. 19 vols. Loc: MLA. 84.08.01-07; 86.01.192-200; 89.07.92-94. Specific permission required.

1142. Mutual Life Assurance Company. **Bylaws, 1871-1938**. 4 files. Loc: MLA. 86.01.201-202, 293-294. Specific permission required.

1143. Mutual Life Assurance Company. **Debenture and bond ledgers, 1889-1920**. 2 vols. Loc: MLA. 81.13.19-20. Specific permission required.

Records of municipal and school board debentures from all over Ontario and, after 1900, Western Canada. Volume 2 contains a summary of debentures held in 1915.

1144. Mutual Life Assurance Company. **Executive Committee. Minutes, 1902-1917; 1962-1981.** 4 volumes. Loc: MLA. 84.08.16-17; 89.07.95-96. Specific permission required.

1145. Mutual Life Assurance Company. **Executive Officers Committee. Minutes, 1917-1968.** 5 files. Loc: MLA. 86.01.275-280. Specific permission required.

1146. Mutual Life Assurance Company. **Finance Committee. Minutes, 1932-1964.** 6 vols and 2 boxes. Loc: MLA. 84.08.18-23. Specific permission required.
Finance Committee minutes for later years, which are not open to the researcher, comprise 29 volumes in 10 boxes in 85.03.

1147. Mutual Life Assurance Company. **Investments. Mortgages, 1877-1911.** 1 vol. Loc: MLA. 81.13.21. Specific permission required.
Record includes details of mortgagor, amount, date, lot, concession, township, value of buildings and land, date discharged, with a place index at the beginning. For Wellington County, there are records of 178 mortgages, including individuals in all municipalities. For Guelph there are details of 13 mortgages, most notably on the Roman Catholic Church and schools ($142,300 in 1887) and St Joseph's Hospital ($32,000 in 1894 and $40,000 in 1901).

1148. Mutual Life Assurance Company. **List of policyholders, #1 to #632, March 1870.** 1 vol. Loc: MLA. 81.13.04. Specific permission required.
Details of policy number, date, person insured, beneficiary, place of residence, term of insurance, amount insured, and amount of premium. Among the first hundred policyholders are Guelph residents Robert Melvin, Jonathan Wilkinson, Malcolm McLean and Henry L. Drake.

1149. Mutual Life Assurance Company. **Loan ledger, 1873-1886.** 1 vol. Loc: MLA. 81.13.05. Specific permission required.
Records of about 950 loans, with details of policy number, name, place of residence, amount and date of loan, and schedule of annual payments on principal and interest. An early loan was to W. Wilkie of Guelph.

1150. Mutual Life Assurance Company. **Mortgages discharged and assigned, 1898-1983.** 24 vols, 7 boxes. Loc: MLA. 83.08.01-24. Specific permission required.
One-line entries with details of mortgage number, name, principal, interest and date discharged; this information would have to be used in conjunction with other records to know the locations of the persons and property mortgaged.

1151. Mutual Life Assurance Company. **Policy ledger, 1870-1882.** 2 vols. Loc: MLA. 81.13.02-03. Specific permission required.
Includes details of name, locality and county of residence, age, date of birth, amount of premium, and date payable.

1152. Mutual Life Assurance Company. **Progressive changes in the board of directors since the establishment of the company, 1869-1988.** 1 file. Loc: MLA. 89.04.01. Specific permission required.

A summary of all persons who served on the company's board of directors throughout its history. Robert Melvin of Guelph was a director from February 1871 until his death in October 1908, being president from 1897 to 1908.

1153. Mutual Life Assurance Company. **Record of investments, 1873-1886.** 1 vol. Loc: MLA. 81.13.17. Specific permission required.

Details include name, place of residence, date, schedule of payments due, with an index at the beginning of names and page numbers and a calendar of months in which payments were due. Two early Guelph investments were to James Glennie of Puslinch Township in relation to 200 acres of farmland and a Town of Guelph debenture in 1873.

1154. Newman Collection. **Separation agreements, 1859-1860.** 1 file folder. Loc: WCA.

Two separation agreements between John and Isabella Duncan in 1860 and William and Sophia Ellis in 1859.

1155. Newman, W.P. **Land records, 1850-1881 (sporadic).** 1 box. Loc: WCA. MU 35; Detailed list of contents.

A collection of land records of Walter Perkins Newman who was an Elora land conveyancer, insurance agent, accountant, municipal clerk and private banker with the Farmers' Bank. The records involve individuals from various municipalities, including Clifford, Drayton, Elora, Fergus, Minto Village, Salem and the Townships of Arthur, West Garafraxa, Luther, Maryborough, Minto, Nichol, Peel and Pilkington. Comprises the Newman Collection.

1156. Nichol Mutual Fire Insurance Company. **Annual reports, 1881; 1893.** 2 documents. Loc: WCA. List of document contents.

A record of financial assets, receipts and disbursements, claims paid to policy holders, and the report of the director of the company. The reports also list the officers and board of directors which indicate John Beattie was secretary in 1881, and by 1893 was president of the company. The reports note the company was active in Fergus, Mimosa, Salem, Ponsonby, Arthur and in the Townships of Nichol, Pilkington, West Garafraxa and Peel. The documents are held with the Beattie Collection.

1157. Northern Assurance Company. **Policy register, 1887-1913.** 1 ledger. Loc: WCA.

A record of insurance policies that note name, date, and amount insured, rate, premium, and a written description of objects insured. Filed with Elora municipal records.

1158. Peel and Maryborough Mutual Fire Insurance Company. **Bank passbook, 1919-1921.** 1 item. Loc: PMF.

A record of accounts held in the Drayton branch of the Bank of Hamilton.

1159. Peel and Maryborough Mutual Fire Insurance Company. **Board. Minutes, 1887-1981.** 10 volumes. Loc: PMF.

Minutes of the board of the company that was formed in 1887.

1160. Provincial Mutual and General Insurance Company, Guelph. **Insurance Policy. Susannah Alling, Guelph, 1851.** 1 document. Loc: GCM.

1161. Puslinch Mutual Fire Insurance Company. **Annual reports, 1909; 1915.** 2 documents. Loc: GCM, WCA. WCA: MU 13.

The annual report for 1909 is the company's fiftieth and lists agents, policy holders who received money from the company and includes financial statements. The Wellington County Archives holds the report for 1915.

1162. Puslinch Mutual Fire Insurance Company. **Consolidated bylaws, 1890.** 1 document. Loc: GCM.

A recording of terms and provisions for policy holders including references to clients using 'steam power for threshing purposes'. The brochure lists William Rae as president of the company and James Scott as secretary.

1163. Puslinch Mutual Fire Insurance Company. **Insurance policies, 1898; 1914; 1917.** 3 envelopes. Loc: GCM.

Three policies of clients of the company which outline the terms of each policy. The clients were all residents of Puslinch Township.

1164. Puslinch Mutual Fire Insurance Company. **Receipts, 1932-1933.** 4 documents. Loc: WCA. MU33.

A record of four receipts of transactions of specific individuals with the Puslinch Mutual Fire Insurance Company.

1165. Standard Bank of Canada, Harriston. **Bank cheques, 1893; 1901; 1904.** 7 envelopes. Loc: WCA.

Held in the Wellington County Historical Research Society Collection. A collection of seven cheques from the Standard Bank of Canada in Harriston.

1166. Wellington District Mutual Fire Insurance Company. **Annual meeting, 1842-1843.** 1 document. Loc: GCM.

A financial statement for the year 1842 that lists the president and secretary of the company. The record also lists members of the company for 1843 noting their place of residence. The document is the second annual report of the company.

1167. Wellington District Mutual Fire Insurance Company. **Policy. Dr Robert Alling, 1841-1844.** facsimile. Loc: UWO. CA9ONALL G21U1P54.

A 1919 facsimile of the policy signed by T. Sandilands, president of the company, insuring the doctor's log and plaster building on Priory Square, including the office, furniture and stable. The premium was 26 pounds on an insured value of 375 pounds.

1168. Wilson, Jack and Grant Law Firm. **Legal records, 1900-1959.** 29 boxes. Loc: WCA.

A record of land transfer documents, estate papers and legal correspondence generated by lawyers John Alexander Wilson from 1900 to 1945, Allan McNab Wilson from 1935 to 1949, John Douglas Wilson from 1937 to 1949 and David Hepburn Jack from 1949 to 1959.

1169. Wissler, Henry. **Land records, legal records and correspondence, 1848-1950.** 3 boxes. Loc: UGA. XR1 MS A050.

A collection of land transfers, mortgages, quit claims, correspondence, insurance policies and income tax records for clients of Henry Wissler who was an Elora lawyer c1870 to 1940. Records are arranged alphabetically by name of client. Corporate clients include the Elora Recreation Company from 1919 to 1950, the Elora Hockey Club from 1938 to 1939, and the Alma Methodist Church in 1876. Personal clients included many residents of Wellington County, Guelph and Elora. Wissler seems also to have been agent for the Waterloo Mutual Fire Insurance Company. Catalogued as the Henry Wissler Papers.

INDUSTRY

1170. Allan, David. **Diaries, 1845-1886.** 18 volumes, 4 ledgers. Loc: UGA. XR1 MS A005-004.

The small diaries, for the periods from 1845 to 1884, contain brief memos regarding business affairs and occasional roughly sketched outlines of unidentified machinery, culverts, lots and buildings. The diaries for 1882, and 1884 to 1886 record daily weather, family events and business affairs concerning Allan's Mill. Part of the Allan-Higinbotham Collection.

1171. Andrew Parker and Sons. **Invoice book, 1917-1919.** 1 ledger. Loc: WCA.

Andrew Parker and Sons made furniture in Elora. The invoices detail goods sold, the total cost of products and the person who purchased specific products. Held with the Fischer Collection.

1172. Beatty Brothers Limited. **Account book, 1909-1911.** 1 ledger. Loc: WCA. MU33.

A list of business transactions with clients throughout most of Canada. The record includes price lists and a list of machinery parts. The list also indicates that Beatty Brothers Limited had a plant in Winnipeg, Manitoba.

1173. Bell Organ Company. **Business file, 1864-1930.** 1 file folder. Loc: UGA. XR1 MS A140.

A series of photocopies of advertisements and articles from magazines in newspapers relating to the Bell Organ Company. The collection includes a photograph taken in 1900 of warehouses of the company in Guelph, Hamilton, Montreal, London England and Sydney Australia. The collection also includes an expense account book of salesmen of the company for 1892 to 1893.

1174. Bell Organ Company. **Posters, c1870-1887.** 1 poster. Loc: UGA, WCA. UGA: XR2 MS A040.

Undated advertising poster of the Bell Organ Company, probably prior to the company's incorporation in 1887 as it identifies W. Bell and Company Organs.

1175. Bell Organ Company. **Warranties, 1889; 1892; 1897.** 3 envelopes. Loc: GCM.

Three warranties for instruments made by the company. The instruments were guaranteed for either five or six years. The documents also list the places where the company had offices and factories. The record includes a trade card of the company.

1176. Chase, Caleb. **Advertisement, n.d..** 1 item. Loc: UGA.

The circular is entitled 'Caleb Chase, Manufacturer of mill picks, Guelph Ontario'. It lists prices of the cast steel picks and customers from Ottawa to Goderich, including the Guelph region. Several customers listed include W. Hortop, James Goldie and D. Allan.

Having a break from time and motion management: a Gilson Manufacturing Company picnic held at Waterloo Park, July 22, 1922. The Guelph company opened in 1907 with its motto, 'Once a Gilson customer, always a Gilson friend.' (Guelph Public Library)

1177. Cossitt's Agricultural Works. **Advertising circular, 1876.** 1 document. Loc: GCM.

     A circular sent to an agricultural implement dealer by Cossitt's Agricultural Implements Works of Guelph which outlines the terms of the 'Gang Plow' made by the company. The circular notes 'The price of the Gang Plow is $30.00 delivered at your nearest Railway Station'.

1178. Dalyte Electric Limited. **Invoices, correspondence, 1923; 1924; 1928.** 5 documents. Loc: GCM.

     The record includes an invoice of products sold by the company in 1928. The record also has correspondence related to the status of shares of the company and of arrangements to have life insurance policies for employees. The company agreed to pay part of the cost of insurance premiums for employees. The records indicate the company manufactured lamps and notes that J.E. Carter was president of the firm and J.S. Wheeler was secretary-treasurer.

1179. Dominion Linens. **Catalogue of linens, n.d..** 1 brochure. Loc: GCM.

     A catalogue of types and cost of linens to be purchased by the yard. The brochure is undated. It is held in a box entitled, Textiles and Costume.

1180. Dominion Linens. **The story of linenmaking in Canada, c1925.** 1 volume. Loc: GCM.

     An outline of flax spinning procedures practiced by Dominion Linens Company in Guelph. The brochure also notes Flax Spinners Limited was formed in 1918 as a subsidiary of Dominion Linens Limited. The brochure boasts of the great potential of the linen industry in Canada.

1181. Dooley, J.M. **Calender advertisement, 1909.** 1 file folder. Loc: GCM.

     An advertisement for Dooley, 'maker of Cream and Homemade Bread'.

1182. Drayton Brick Company. **Partnership agreement, 1902.** 1 file folder. Loc: WCA. MU 88.

     A record of partnership between James Pickle, Charles Stephenson, John Cowan and William Sturtridge. Part of the Wellington South Land Registry Office Record Collection.

1183. Elora Mill. **Grain account book, 1845-1846.** 1 ledger. Loc: WCA. MU 3.

1184. Everton Flour Mills. **Cash books, 1926-1930; 1942-1948.** 2 ledgers. Loc: WCA. MU 9.

     The only reference to the Everton Flour Mills is the achival note on the cover.

1185. Everton Flour Mills. **Receipts, 1927-1931.** 1 envelope. Loc: WCA. MU6.

     A collection of six receipts and invoices for the mill that notes W.H. Hortop was proprietor. Included is a 1931 letter from a Hamilton insurance company, Canadian Order of Chosen Friends, and a 1929 letter from a Rockwood farmer apologizing for his inability to pay his debts because of sick pigs and rotten turnips.

1186. Forbes, Robert. **Business records, 1839-1891.** 3 volumes. Loc: UWL. FA: GA 21.

     Robert Forbes was a native of Scotland who, by 1851, had a tannery, shoemaking business and sawmill in Puslinch Township and Hespeler. He and later generations of his family had business interests in Guelph. Accounts and brief diary entries are mingled in these records. One volume includes a cash book for 1839-1856 with a day book for 1856-1862. A second volume combines an accounts ledger for 1851-1857 with a day book for 1871 to 1881. A third volume combines accounts for 1843-1873 with a day book for 1882-1891. The day book entries include references to Guelph and Fergus, including the Guelph Fair.

1187. George Sleeman and Company. **Bank passbooks, 1864-1871.** 3 items. Loc: UGA. XR1 MS A334035.
A record of the bank accounts of George Sleeman held with the Ontario Bank and the Canadian Bank of Commerce. Part of the Sleeman Family Collection.

1188. Gilson Manufacturing Company. **Guelph, the Royal City, CFRB radio script, December 15, 1943.** 3 pp. Loc: GPL. Envelope 7.
A script for a regular show called 'Queer Quirks' produced by the Guelph firm, Gilson Manufacturing Company, that presents a brief thirteen minute anecdotal history of Guelph and concludes with a one minute advertisement that notes that at 'Gilson's of Guelph the spirit of John Galt goes marching on'. Part of the Douglass Collection.

1189. Gow Fergus Lime Kilns. **Day book, 1903; 1910-1914; 1931-1932; 1937-1941.** 4 ledgers. Loc: WCA. MU58.
A record of James Gow's business transactions.

1190. Gow, James. **Cash books, 1850-1852; 1854-1860.** 4 ledgers. Loc: GCM.
A record of transactions of a cobbler. One ledger is inscribed by Peter Gow, one has each page entitled Guelph, and one has entries for various individuals in Puslinch, Erin and Eramosa Townships. There is nothing to suggest that the four ledgers belong together except they all record purchases of leather and sales of boots and shoes.

1191. Guelph Lumber Company. **Account book, 1878-1880.** 1 ledger. Loc: AO. MU 595.
Financial records of a company apparently based in Guelph but operating sawmills in townships of the Parry Sound District. Only one third of the ledger has been used. Part of the Commercial Records Collection.

1192. Guelph Lumber Company. **Catalogue Number 22. Woodwork for the interior and exterior.** 68 p. ill. Loc: GPL.
A series of sketches of various styles of doors, window frames, and stairways manufactured and sold by the company, which includes a brief description of products with each illustration. The catalogue does not have a date of publication but was issued in the twentieth century.

1193. Guelph Mercury. **History of Stewart Lumber Company, 1854-1954.** 1 file folder, oversized. Loc: UGA. XR2 MS A064.
A special Guelph Mercury article providing an historical sketch of the company, written on December 4, 1954. The sketch includes biographies of company managers and traces the growth of the firm.

1194. Guelph Sewing Machine Company. **Directions for using the Osborne Sewing Machine, c1868-c1880.** 1 volume. Loc: GCM.

An undated pamphlet issued by the Guelph Sewing Machine Company demonstrating how to use the Osborne Sewing Machine.

1195. Harriston Stove Company. **Catalogue, 1905.** 1 brochure. Loc: OAM.

1196. Henry Wise Woodenware Company, Palmerston. **Catalogue, 1916.** Loc: DHC.

1197. J.W. Holling, Tobacco Manufacturer. **Stock book, 1880-1882.** 1 ledger. Loc: GCM.
A series of entries related to the manufacture and sale of cigars by Holling with notes regarding the value and weight of products. The ledger was compiled by the Guelph office of Canada Inland Revenue.

1198. Kloepfer Coal Company. **Cash books, 1907-1909; 1914-1915; 1917-1918; 1920-1922.** 4 volumes. Loc: GCM.
A record of amounts owed by various individuals and companies.

1199. Kloepfer Coal Company. **Order books, 1913-1918; 1922-1923.** 3 volumes. Loc: GCM.
A record of date, name, address and amount of coal ordered.

1200. Louden Machinery Company. **Advertising circulars, 1924.** 2 documents. Loc: GCM.
Two promotional letters indicating how factories could lower operating costs by using Louden 'Industrial Overhead Conveying Equipment'.

1201. McGregor, Robert. **Cash books, 1905-1915; 1936-1938.** 2 ledgers. Loc: WCA. MU 101.
Accounts for an unidentified blacksmith's operation that records number of horseshoes applied and carriages repaired. An archival note lists the owner of the business as Robert McGregor of Belwood in Garafraxa West Township.

1202. Mickle, Charles. **Cash books, 1874-1879.** 2 ledgers. Loc: AO. MU 2024-2030.
Records of Mickle's saw milling business based in Guelph but also operating in Bruce County. The files also contain details of Mickle's patent application for his invention of a steamboat propeller in 1871. Part of Charles Mickle Papers.

1203. Monkland Mills. **Advertisement, 1899.** 1 document. Loc: WCA. MU 17.
An advertising card of James Wilson who operated Monkland Mills in Fergus.

1204. Pole, Frederick H.G. **Business trade cards, c1880-1890.** 2 volumes. Loc: UGA. XR1 MS A149.
A number of trade cards of industries in Ontario with numerous references to manufacturing and mercantile firms in Guelph. The collection contains a number of trading cards of the Bell Organ Company and the Raymond Sewing Machine Company. The cards were collected by Frederick H.G. Pole, a resident of Rockwood, during his boyhood.

1205. Potter, John and Potter, David. **Business correspondence, 1865; 1868; 1872; 1894.** 3 file folders. Loc: WCA. MU 8; Detailed list of contents.
Correspondence to the Potters regarding payment for articles purchased from the Elora Foundry. Letters came from Mount Forest, Clifford, Minto Township, Nichol Township, Dundas, Peel Township, Douglas, Alma, Oshawa and Holland. The collection also includes five letters to David Potter from his family in Gallowflat, Scotland, addressed to Cambridge, New York and Dumfries, Galt. The

letters are dated 1822, 1824, 1827, 1831 and 1835. Held with the Potter Collection.

1206. Raymond Manufacturing Company. **Instruction booklet for the new improved Raymond sewing machines, n.d.**. 22 p. ill. Loc: GPL.
The booklet gives diagrams and instructions for sewing, seam binding, heming, quilting, ruffling, shirring and braiding.

1207. Raymond Sewing Machine Company. **Advertising cards and sewing machine warranty c1880-1890**. 4 documents. Loc: GCM.
Includes three advertising trade cards and a warranty for a sewing machine made by the company in 1890. The warranty offers a lifetime guarantee.

1208. Riverbank Cheese and Butter Company. **Board of Directors. Minutes, 1882-1905**. 1 volume. Loc: WCA. MU 16.
A record of the meetings of the directors and stockholders of the company. The minutes record the decision to erect a factory in Maryborough Township named Riverbank Factory.

1209. Shepard, A.B., Jr. **Account book, 1855-1859**. 1 ledger. Loc: GCM.
The front page of the ledger lists the name A.B. Shepard Junior, but is not labelled as a Guelph business. However, the ledger has several references to Guelph residents. The ledger lists the amount of lumber sold and the selling price of specific orders. The ledger is held in a box entitled, Account Books.

1210. Silver Creek Brewery. **Account books, 1861-1863; 1865; 1890**. 6 ledgers. Loc: UGA. XR1 MS A334.
A record of the financial transactions of the Sleeman family in operating their brewery. Part of the Sleeman Family Collection.

1211. Silver Creek Brewery. **Business correspondence, 1861-1905**. 2 file folders. Loc: UGA. XR1 MS A334.
The correspondence includes references to orders and the selling price of beer brewed by the Sleeman family in Guelph. The letters also include references to total sales by Silver Creek in various cities in 1894 and 1895. Part of the Sleeman Family Collection.

1212. Sleeman and Sons. **Indentures and legal documents, 1860-1903**. 2 file folders. Loc: UGA. XR1 MS A334.
A series of land transfer and business agreements of the firm of Sleeman and Sons with various individuals and companies in Guelph. The collection includes a petition sent to the provincial government in the 1870s listing four reasons why Guelph should be granted city status. The record also has a summons and copy of an inquiry into dealings between the Traders Bank of Canada and the firm of Sleeman and Sons. The inquiry discussed the financial involvement of Sleeman with the project to construct the Guelph Railway Company. Part of the Sleeman Family Collection.

1213. Sleeman Brewing and Malting Company. **Annual report, 1903**. 1 document. Loc: UGA. XR1 MS A334.
The report lists principal stockholders, directors, the total number and value of shares, and the total amount of capital of the company. Part of the Sleeman

Family Collection.

1214. Sleeman Brewing and Malting Company. **Brewing recipes, c1859-1900.** 2 file folders, 1 ledger. Loc: UGA. XR1 MS A334.

A series of undated recipes for making alcholic beverages which appear to have been developed by the Sleeman family. The file folders include a letter outlining a phrenological analysis of George Sleeman conducted in 1859. Part of the Sleeman Family Collection.

1215. Sleeman Brewing and Malting Company. **Business records, 1847-1906.** 7 file folders, 3 ledgers. Loc: UGA. XR1 MS A334.

A record of a large number of receipts and invoices for the business transactions of John Sleeman and his son, George. The collection includes two summons for John Sleeman to appear in court relating to business transactions and a number of cancelled cheques of George and Sarah Sleeman. The collection also contains a promisory note and trading cards of the Silver Creek Brewery and correspondence regarding investments of George Sleeman in the Wellington Mutual Fire Insurance Company and the Guelph Mining and Development Company. Part of the Sleeman Family Collection.

1216. Sleeman Brewing and Malting Company. **Patent records, 1897-1903.** 1 file folder. Loc: UGA. XR1 MS A334.

A record of transactions between George Sleeman and various companies in Canada and in Europe. Part of the Sleeman Family Collection.

1217. Sleeman, John. **Brewer's licences, 1860-1864.** 1 file folder. Loc: UGA. XR1 MS A334.

A record of licenses issued to John Sleeman indicating the fee charged for the document. The fee for licenses rose from ten dollars in 1860 to sixty dollars in 1864. Part of the Sleeman Family Collection.

1218. Sleeman, John. **Innkeeper's licenses, 1859.** 2 documents. Loc: UGA. XR1 MS A334.

A record of two licenses granted to John Sleeman to operate a tavern he called the 'Farmer's Arms'. It would seem that he operated a brewery in conjunction with the inn. Part of the Sleeman Family Collection.

1219. Standard Milling Company Limited. **Report on failure of Goldie Dam at Guelph, 1929.** 11 p. ill. Loc: GPL.

A brief explanation of the reasons for the failure of Goldie Dam and the subsequent damage that resulted in Guelph in 1929.

1220. Superior Barn Equipment Company. **Business records, 1911-1957.** 6 boxes. Loc: WCA. MU 11, 26-29; List of document contents.

A collection of price lists, promotional literature, invoices, ledgers, drafting designs and photographs of the Superior Barn Equipment Company of Fergus. The Wellington County Archives has developed a detailed finding aid noting the date and contents of specific business records of the company. Comprises the Superior Barn Collection.

1221. T.E. Bissell Company. **Advertisements, 1899; 1904; 1906-1908; 1911; 1918.** 1 file folder. Loc: OAM.

Photocopies of advertisements from several farm journals.

1222. T.E. Bissell Company. **Catalogue and price list, 1935.** 1 brochure. Loc: OAM.
In 1938 the company joined with J. Fleury's Sons in Aurora to become
Fleury-Bissell Limited.

1223. Taylor-Forbes Manufacturing Company. **Catalogues. Builders' and general
hardware, lawn mowers and specialities, 1913-1924.** 1 reel. mf. Loc: WCA.
A catalogue of the manufacturing company that was established in 1888.

1224. Taylor-Forbes Manufacturing Company. **Illustrated catalogues, 1909; 1922; 1925.**
3 volumes. Loc: GCM, AO.
Catalogues of radiators, boilers, lawnmowers and parts manufactured by the
company. The 1909 catalogue indicates that Taylor-Forbes Company was the
successor to the A.R. Woodyatt and Company and Guelph Malleable Works. The
1922 catalogue indicates the company was founded in 1888, incorporated in 1902,
and by 1922 had an authorized capital of one million dollars. AO also has a copy
of the 1909 catalogue.

1225. Taylor, John. **Cash book, 1872-1876.** 1 reel. mf. Loc: WCA.
John Taylor has beeen identified as a blacksmith of Clifford.

1226. Templin Manufacturing Company. **Advertising Catalogue. Seed and grain
separators, c1909.** 1 document. Loc: OAM.
A description of the features of 'Perfection seed and grain separators' made
by Templin Manufacturing Company of Fergus. The brochure indicates the
separators of the company were patented in 1909.

1227. Templin Manufacturing Company. **Correspondence. Farm implements sales, 1914.** 1
document. Loc: OAM.
A letter from the John Deere Plow Company in Toronto outlining the types of
goods the Templins should sell.

1228. Templin Manufacturing Company. **Day books, 1930-1939.** 5 ledgers. Loc: WCA.
MU32B; MU30.
A detailed record of financial accounts of the Templin Carriage Works which
was located in Fergus.

1229. Tolton Brothers Limited. **Miscellaneous papers, 1858-1908.** 1 file folder. Loc:
OAM.
A small number of photocopies of articles and advertisements relating to the
business of the Tolton brothers who manufactured farm implements in Guelph. The
file includes an article by David Tolton written in 1899 in the journal,
Farming, entitled, 'The History of the Root Cutter'. The Tolton advertisements
included the motto, 'not how cheap, but how good' in marketing goods made by the
company. Located in the vertical file.

1230. Williams, George. **Price lists, invoices, 1887-1922 (sporadic).** 4 documents.
Loc: GCM.
Includes a printed price list of goods sold by Williams, a Guelph baker and
confectioner, for the years from 1887 to 1888. The records also contain three
invoices for products sold by Williams.

LAND AND REAL ESTATE

1231. Allan, David. **Land records, 1855-1875.** 8 documents. Loc: UGA. XR1 MS A005.
    A record of deeds and mortgages held for Guelph land. Part of Allan-Higinbotham Collection.

1232. Allan, William. **Land records, 1831-1859.** 4 file folders. Loc: UGA. XR1 MS A005020/A005023-025.
    Copies of deeds of lots purchased in Guelph. Part of Allan-Higinbotham Collection.

1233. Canada Company. **Accounting section records, 1824-1952.** 23.65 m, 117 volumes. Loc: AO. FA.
    The Canada Company was incorporated by the British Parliament on July 27, 1824, with the aim of obtaining land in Upper Canada and promoting its sale to prospective settlers. In Canada during the 1820s the company's officers were John Galt and Dr William 'Tiger' Dunlop. The company received a total of 2.5 million acres, of which 1.1 million were in the Huron Tract, the rest in the Halton and Wilmot Blocks and Crown Reserves throughout the province. In 1952, the company terminated its activities. The Canada Company records in the Archives of Ontario comprise several major groups which are separately described in this inventory. The accounting records include ledgers, 1824-1926; journals, 1824-1952; bills receivable registers, 1834-1876; cash books, 1824-1952; letters of credit, 1832-1888; remittances, 1843-1852; accounts, 1827-1887; Bank of Upper Canada accounts 1838-1866; bills and accounts; tax records, 1882-1951.

1234. Canada Company. **Administrative records, 1824-1951.** 19.54 m. Loc: AO. FA.
    These records comprise Proceedings of the General Courts, Court of Directors Records, Minutes of Committees, Report (including the Diagrams of Upper Canada, described separately), Shareholders Records, Correspondence and Administration Records. Very little of this record group is specifically concerned with Guelph or Wellington County. One item is the Laguira (sic) Settlers Investigation of March 1829 in Series A-7-1, Box 3. This file contains the text of the petition by representatives of the LaGuayran settlers complaining that they had been unfairly treated by the Canada Company in Guelph after their arrival in 1827. The responses of each petitioner to thirty-seven detailed questions are also included with the text of a letter by other Guelph settlers expressing unbounded confidence in the Canada Company officials, John Galt, Dr Dunlop and Samuel Strickland. LaGuayran settlers for whom details are available in this source include the Butchart, Gillies, McTavish, McPhee, Robertson, McCrae, Reid, Halliday, Kennedy, McDonald, Peter Campbell, Wallace, Reid, McLeod, Rose and Stirton families. Settlers who expressed confidence in the Canada Company were James Corbet, Thomas Stewart, John Mount, William Dallimore, Uriah Lamport, David Gibbs, Charles Armstrong, John Mitchell, Benjamin Harrison and Andrew McVenn.

1235. Canada Company. **Correspondence and general business records, 1825-1887.** 514 p. Loc: NAC.
    While the Company played an important role in the founding of Guelph, no specific references to the town or district could be found in the finding aid.

1236. Canada Company. **Correspondence. Commissioners' letters and reports, 1826-1828.**
338 p. Loc: AO. FA: Series A-6-2.

Volume of transcribed correspondence, from November 1826 to December 1828, prefaced by a detailed index, that includes particular reports relating to the founding of Guelph. One is G.S. Tiffany's report on the inspection of the Halton Block (later Guelph Township) dated 5 February 1827. Another is John Galt's letter of 30 April 1827 describing the founding of Guelph that mentions the great water-power advantages with sites for seventeen mills on each side of the Speed River, with a further report on progress dated 31 May 1827, and Charles Prior's more detailed Report of the Operations at and Progress of Guelph, 1 October 1827 (pp. 176-190). Letters and instructions from the Canada Company directors convey their critical attitude to Galt's management, including discussions of the choice of town name, Galt's prodigal use of Canada Company capital and the quality of survey of the Guelph Block.

1237. Canada Company. **Vouchers and receipts, 1827-1828.** 1 volume of 47 items, 92 items unbound. Loc: MTL. Card index.

A collection of vouchers and receipts relating to transactions at the Canada Company office and store in Guelph. The 92 unbound items are dated between October 2, 1827 and May 26, 1828, most being requisitions from Thomas B. Husband to David Gilkison. Vouchers and receipts in the bound volume date from the months June to December 1828; some are requisitions for building materials for the Priory submitted by Samuel Strickland to Thomas B. Husband. Other names on these documents are John McDonald, George Tiffany, Donald McFarlane and Archibald McPhee.

1238. Clarke, Charles. **Circular advertising large brick store in Elora for rent, 1907.**
Loc: AO. FA; MU 455.

Part of Byerly Papers.

1239. Galt, John. **Correspondence, 1827-1829.** 49 cm, 1 reel. mf. Loc: NAC. MG 24, I 4, FA 175.

Four letters relate to Galt's experiences in Guelph. One, dated 30 April 1827, refers to the choice of the town site; two refer to the progress of the settlement (1 August 1827 and 5 October 1828); and one, dated 14 July 1829, criticizes the Canada Company and the conditions of his return to England.

1240. Galt, John. **Papers. Correspondence discussing the establishment of the Canada Company, 1823-1831.** 1 file folder, 3 cm. Xerox copies. Loc: AO. MU 7327 #5.

A collection of letters from John Galt to R.J. Wilmot Horton of the Colonial Office regarding the establishment of the Canada Company. The originals are in the Catton Manuscripts Collection at the Derby Central Library, England. The letters contain Galt's proposal to sell land in Upper Canada as a means of liquidating the Crown's debts to 'the Canadian sufferers' of damages during the War of 1812. As there is a break in the correspondence between February 1827 and July 1830, the letters contain no direct reference to the Guelph settlement. The collection includes a fifteen-page letter by R.J. Wilmot Horton dated 14 April 1831 that reviews Galt's proposals and activities in Upper Canada.

1241. Gilkison, David and Geddes, Andrew. **Broadside describing village lots for sale in Township of Nichol, District of Wellington, 1842.** 2 items. Loc: UGA. XRI MS A166003.

Part of the Goodwin-Haines Collection.

1242. Greenfield Cemetery. **Cemetery register, 1877-1985**. 3 file folders; 1 envelope. Loc: WCA. MU67.
    A record of lot purchases in the cemetery which is located in Arthur Township.

1243. Sleeman, George. **Puslinch Lake Resort. Business records, 1888**. 1 file folder. Loc: UGA. XR1 MS A334.
    A copy of a partnership agreement between George Sleeman and Mr Davidson to organize a resort. Davidson was a partner in the newspaper the Guelph Mercury. Part of the Sleeman Family Collection.

MEDICAL PRACTICE

1244. Groves, Abraham, Dr. **Correspondence and scrapbook, 1921-1933**. 1 file folder, 1 volume. Loc: WCA.
    The collection includes several letters about Groves' medical practice and his involvement in Fergus, programs for dinners held in his honour, and a scrapbook of newspaper clippings about his practice. Comprises the Groves Collection.

1245. Howitt, Henry, Dr. **Invoices and envelope, 1913**. 1 envelope. Loc: GCM.
    Three invoices from Howitt to John McAteer at the American Hotel for medical consultation for $4.00 a visit.

1246. Kerr, W.A., Dr. **Medical account books, 1903-1930**. 6 journals; 2 small account books. Loc: UGA. XR1 MS A298.
    Dr Kerr practised in Elora. Part of the Guelph Historical Society Collection.

1247. Orton, Henry, Dr. **Correspondence, 1832-1865**. Part of 1 box. Loc: UGA. XRI MS A136020-30.
    Correspondence to Orton's friends and British family describing his sea voyage to New York, his settlement, work, and family and community life in Guelph. Part of the Guelph Business Correspondence file in the Goodwin-Haines Collection.

1248. Orton, Henry, Dr. **Memoirs, c1830-1850**. 1 file folder, 39 p. typescript. Loc: GCM, MTL, AO, GPL. AO: MU 7149, #9.
    Born in the Nottingham district of England, Orton came to Guelph in 1834 and practised for many years in partnership with Dr William Clarke. Orton moved to New Hope (later renamed Hespeler) between 1854 and 1858 and revisited England from 1858 to 1861. On his return to Guelph, Orton practised in partnership with his son Henry, before retiring to Fergus. The memoirs provide a description of Orton's life in Guelph as a physician which includes references to his family life, medical experience and business partnerships as well as to general events in early Guelph. Orton had to send his wife to an insane asylum in Nottingham shortly after arriving in Guelph. Orton presents an unflattering view of his partnership with Dr Clarke and pessimistically appraises his own life, concluding that 'mine has been an unsuccessful career, a failure, an abortion, and I can't even say that I have had much enjoyment in it'. The copy in the Baldwin Room of MTL came from the University of Toronto Library, where it had been deposited by J.R. Howitt, the Guelph barrister. The Archives of Ontario holds a photocopy of the typescript.

1249. Skinner, H.C., Dr. **Invoice, 1924.** 1 envelope. Loc: GCM.
An invoice for dental work.

1250. Wallace, Norman, Dr. **The criminally insane at Guelph, 1928.** 13 p. Loc: UGA. XR1 MS A005.
An address presented at the Homewood about studies done at the Ontario Reformatory examining admissions, discharges, deportations, crimes and treatments. Part of Allan-Higinbotham Collection.

PUBLISHING

1251. Arthur Enterprise. **Day book, 1879.** 1 ledger. Loc: WCA. MU50.
A record of the receipts and expenditures of the newspaper.

1252. Elora Newspaper Job Printing and Bookbinding Company. **Legal agreement between Francis Frank and Charles Clarke, 1854.** 1 document. Loc: UGA. XR1 MS A193006.
An agreement for Clarke to edit the Elora Backwoodsman for one year. Held with Marston-Archibald Collection.

1253. Elora Newspaper Job Printing and Bookbinding Company. **Legal document, 1852.** 1 document. Loc: UGA.
An act to form an incorporated joint stock company for manufacturing, mining, mechanical or chemical purposes entitled, Elora Newspaper Job Printing and Bookbinding Company. It is signed by Charles Allan, Thomas Philip, Alex Watt, James Ross and Peter Paterson. Filed with the James Archibald Papers.

1254. Elora Newspaper Job Printing and Bookbinding Company. **Subscription list, 1852.** 1 document. Loc: UGA. XR1 MS A193.
Held with Marston-Archibald Collection.

1255. Elora Observer. **Advertisements, 1865-1907 (sporadic).** 1 file folder. Loc: UGA. XR1 MS A115020.
Manuscript documents of advertisements that were to be placed in the newspaper, The Elora Observer. Held with the Connon Collection.

1256. Elora Observer. **Correspondence, advertisements and clippings, 1865-1868.** 5 file folders. Loc: AO. MU 2014.
A varied collection of advertisements and notices submitted to the Elora Observer by individuals and organizations in the Elora district. The collection includes both manuscript and print formats. Examples include Thomas Connon's advertisement for a new picture gallery (1864), notice of vacancy for a teacher at Nichol S.S. #2, Dalby's Royal Mail announcing express stages from Elora to Fergus, Guelph, Rothsay and Drayton, as well as many church and club announcements, such as those of the North Wellington Agricultural Society, Chalmers Presbyterian Church and the Peel Circuit of Primitive Methodists which had preaching places in Peel and Maryborough Townships. Part of the Marston Collection.

1257. Guelph Mercury. **Guelph, the Royal City: the trial market city, 1926.** 20 p. Loc: GCM.
A detailed statistical survey of Guelph to promote advertising in the Mercury. The survey analyzes transportation, markets, annual food bills, homes, school

and stores. The brochure states that the Mercury covers ninety-eight percent of homes in Guelph.

1258. Lyon, James Walter. **Memoirs, 1848-1924**. 2 file folders. Loc: GCM.
An autobiographical account of the social, economic and travel activities, which also highlights Lyon's support for developing Niagara water power. The source includes several anecdotes of Lyon's life including training of book salesmen in his employ. Lyon notes the largest selling book he ever published was entitled the 'Practical Home Physician' which sold roughly three hundred thousand copies.

1259. **Newspaper subscription book, 1919-1920**. 1 volume. Loc: UGA. XR1 MS A193026.
A subscription book for many Ontario newspapers including the Guelph Mercury and the Guelph Herald. Each entry lists date, name and address of subscriber. There is no indication who owned the book. Held with the Marston-Archibald Collection.

1260. Templin, J.C. **Canadian press cards, 1907; 1914**. 1 envelope. Loc: WCA.
Two certificates of J.C. Templin verifying his membership in the Canadian Press Association. Part of the Templin-Dow Collection.

1261. World Publishing Company. **Advertising circulars, 1901**. 3 documents. Loc: GCM.
Three promotional letters distributed by the company of J.W. Lyon stressing the fact that it had recently published a book written about Queen Victoria of England. The circular warns 'Do not canvass for any book by American authors; they naturally cannot write in full sympathy with the British feeling, or do justice to our poor departed Queen'.

ROADS AND RAILWAYS

1262. Broadfoot, Mary. **History of the Guelph and Arthur Road, 1842-1856**. 4 p. Loc: UGA. XR1 MS A358.
A brief history, written c1950, of the Guelph and Arthur Road Company that was formed as a joint stock company in 1842, including members A.J. Fergusson, A.D. Ferrier, A.D. Fordyce and J. McCrae. The article quotes bylaws and council minutes to trace the road construction in 1848 and lists the toll gates for the road.

1263. Buchanan, Isaac. **Railway records, 1838-1880**. Loc: NAC. FA#26, vols 92-104.
Charters, prospectuses, minutes of shareholders' meetings, reports and returns, agreements, lawsuits, lists of shareholders and financial statements of railways in which Buchanan, the prominent Hamilton merchant, had interests. Railways that traversed the Wellington County area, and about which there are records, are Canadian Pacific Railway, Credit Valley Railway, Galt and Guelph Railway, Grand Trunk Railway, Preston and Berlin Railway, Toronto Grey and Bruce Railway and the Wellington, Grey and Bruce Railway.

1264. Fergus, Elora and Guelph Railway. **Bill of Incorporation. Galley proof, 1860**. Loc: AO.
Part of Byerly Papers.

Train time: The Guelph Junction Railway Station operated by the Canadian Pacific Railway, c1890. The station building was originally The Priory, the Canada Company store erected in 1827. (Guelph Civic Museum)

1265. Fleming, Sandford. **Correspondence, diaries, 1843-1914; journals of travels, 1845-1883**. 10.2 metres. Loc: NAC. MG 29, B 1, FA 75.

Sandford Fleming is known to have been concerned with the survey of several railway lines in the larger region around Wellington County. Users will have to search the actual records, however, as a 110-page finding aid yielded no clues to items relating to Guelph and Wellington County.

1266. Galt and Guelph Railway. **Minutes, 1853-1892; stock records, 1853; land records, 1851-1880**. 0.1 metre. Loc: NAC. RG 30; vols 326-331, 11988.

A wholly owned subsidiary of the Great Western, the Galt and Guelph was incorporated in November 1852. The 15.2 mile line was completed in 1857 and taken over, with all other Great Western properties, by the Grand Trunk in 1882, with which it formally amalgamated in 1893.

1267. Galt and Guelph Railway. **Miscellaneous records, 1853-1858**. 3 items. Loc: AO. FA; MU 454.

Notice to Reeve of Guelph Township in 1853 to call a public meeting to discuss a Guelph-Galt railway, letter from secretary of Galt and Guelph Railway in 1855 informing the Guelph Township Council that funds were not available to pay interest on bonds and financial statement of Galt and Guelph Railway for 1857-1858. Held with Byerly Papers.

1268. Georgian Bay and Wellington Railway. **List of deeds to property, 1882**. 0.1 metre. Loc: NAC. RG 30 IC, vol. 11989.

First incorporated as Wellington and Georgian Bay Railway in 1878 to build a line from Guelph, Listowel or Harriston to Owen Sound, and renamed in 1879. A 26.75 mile railway between Palmerston and Durham was opened in 1882. Amalgamated with two other railways to form Grand Trunk, Georgian Bay and Lake Erie Railway Company.

1269. Grand Trunk Railway. **Correspondence, cables, telegrams and diaries, 1877-1921**. 4.8 metres. Loc: NAC. RG 30 IA.

A variety of correspondence, letterbooks, diaries and registers. A file of regional interest is volume 2075, the Berlin GTR Agent's letterbook, 1909-1920.

1270. Grand Trunk Railway. **Legal agreements, 1853-1923**. 9.8 metres, 37 vols. Loc: NAC. RG 30 IA.

Includes agreements between Grand Trunk and other railways, companies, municipalities and provinces, as well as similar agreements entered into by railways that were subsequently absorbed by the Grand Trunk. Volumes 10189-10204 contain agreements, memoranda and reports covering all aspects of the operation of the Grand Trunk.

1271. Grand Trunk Railway. **Minutes, 1853-1923**. 3 metres. Loc: NAC. RG 30 IA, vols 1000-1055.

Includes minutes of the Canadian Board, 1853-1862 and the London Board, 1853-1923, as well as minutes of the meetings of stockholders and proprietors, 1853-1923, and of the Executive Committee, Finance Committee, Audit Board, Stores Committee and Rules and Regulations Committee.

1272. Grand Trunk Railway. **Operational records, 1855-1936**. 27.1 metres. Loc: NAC. RG 30 IA.

Operating records covering construction and expansion, repairs and improvements (including profiles), financial, staff, traffic and engineering records. The London Office records, 1853-1880, comprise 1.5 metres of cash books, journals, ledgers and balance sheets relating to operations in southwestern Ontario.

1273. Grand Trunk Railway. **Personnel records, 1862-1921.** 21.8 metres. Loc: NAC. RG 30 IA.

Permanent staff register, payrolls for the entire Grand Trunk system and for some specific branches, departments and offices.

1274. Grand Trunk Railway. **Property records, 1846-1925.** 1.9 metres. Loc: NAC. RG 30 IA.

Books of reference listing property and owners along the railway line, index to deeds, land books, land purchased, rent records, right-of-way register, schedule of insured property and trustees book with details of property purchases.

1275. Grand Trunk Railway. **Receipts. W.J. Hale, Goldstone, 1891; 1892.** 1 envelope. Loc: WCA. MU43.

Two receipts from the railway for goods, shipped by W.J. Hale of Goldstone, which lists the types of goods sent.

1276. Grand Trunk Railway. **Reports. Semi-annual and annual, 1883-1922.** 0.8 metres, 9 vols. Loc: NAC. RG 30 IA.

Reports were semi-annual to 1913 and annual from 1914 and include both handwritten originals and printed copies.

1277. Grand Trunk Railway. **Stock and bond records, 1853-1920.** 5 metres, 60 vols. Loc: NAC. RG 30 IA.

Includes list of shareholders, stock records (stock certificates, vouchers, records of dividends paid, stock transfer records and stock ledgers), and bond records.

1278. Guelph and Arthur Road Company. **Minutes, 1847-1864.** 1 volume. Loc: NAC. MG 24, F11.

Original manuscript minutes of meetings of directors and shareholders held at least quarterly. The minutes constitute a detailed record of the process by which early roads were built and managed, including negotiations with county and township councils, litigation with the contractor and the method of levying tolls. The book was presented by Mrs Robert Munro of Guelph in 1919 and was formerly with the Mitchell Papers.

1279. Guelph and Elora Road Commission. **Minutes and accounts, 1860-1864.** 6 file folders. Loc: UGA. XR1 MS A319.

The collection includes tenders, accounts and pay sheets from 1860 to 1862 and minutes from 1860 to 1864.

1280. Guelph and Wellington Road Company. **Act of Incorporation, 1859.** Loc: AO. FA: MU 454.

Part of Byerly Papers.

1281. Guelph, Elmira and Peel Gravelled Road Company. **Stock certificate, 1868.** 1 document. Loc: GCM.

A stock certificate for ten shares at twenty dollars each purchased by Nathaniel Higinbotham.

1282. Guelph Radial Railway. **Board of Directors. Minutes, April 1917–October 1918.** 1 vol. Loc: OHA. Bin 20-2-092, #17.

Minutes of the monthly board meetings including cash statements and stock reports. Minutes of one meeting in 1931 are also included.

1283. Guelph Radial Railway/ Guelph Railway Company. **Land. Transfer agreement between the City of Guelph, the Hydro Electric Power Commission of Ontario, and the Guelph Radial Railway Company, December 1919.** 1 document. Loc: GCH.

An agreement to transfer ownership of the Guelph Radial Railway Company and its land to the Hydro Electric Power Commission. The agreement notes the new owner of the company would continue operations until the railway line was completed. The document notes that the purchaser 'will construct and operate a line of railway from some point upon their proposed line between Guelph and Hespeler to Puslinch Lake'. The document also indicates the company would henceforth be called the 'Guelph Railway'. The record is held in the Clerk's office vault.

1284. Guelph Radial Railway. **Passenger fare account books, 1908–1916.** 1 ledger. Loc: GCM.

A detailed listing of numbers of passengers using the street railway and the amounts received in fares.

1285. Guelph Railway Company/ Guelph Radial Railway. **Account books, 1895–1932.** 18 volumes. Loc: GCM.

A record of monthly receipts and expenditures including passenger fares and general expenses. One ledger also includes amounts paid to various companies including the Traders Bank, Sleeman's Brewing and Malting Company, Guelph Cartage Company and the Canadian Pacific Railway. On page 54 of the 1903 to 1904 volume is a notice of incorporation of the company.

1286. Guelph Railway Company/ Guelph Radial Railway. **Correspondence, 1902–1904.** 1 volume. Loc: GCM.

Carbon copies of business correspondence.

1287. Guelph Railway Company/ Guelph Radial Railway. **Directors. Minutes, 1895–1917.** 2 volumes. Loc: GPL.

The first meeting after incorporation was held on May 15, 1895 with the folowing directors present: George Sleeman, George A. Sleeman, Charles E. Sleeman, William H. Sleeman and Sarah Sleeman. The minutes record monthly meetings, bylaws and, after 1905, monthly accounts.

1288. Guelph Railway Company/ Guelph Radial Railway. **Financial records, 1877–1911.** 1 file folder. Loc: UGA. XR1 MS A334043.

A record of financial statements, municipal legislation related to the company, and a discussion of George Sleeman's plan to transfer his shares of the railway to the City of Guelph. Part of the Sleeman Family Collection.

1289. Guelph Railway Company. **Stock subscription book, 1895.** 1 vol. Loc: OHA. Bin 20-2-100, #96.

A record of the subscription of $48,000 by George Sleeman and $1,000 each by seven other members of the Sleeman family.

1290. Hydro Electric Power Commission. **Guelph Radial Railway. Correspondence and memoranda, 1920-1939.** 1 file folder. Loc: OHA. GSI OR-519.

The file contains memoranda by Sir Adam Beck concerning the minor political crisis that erupted over Hydro's assumption of responsibility for operating the street railway system. There are various statistical reports on fares, payroll, state of track and equipment and the estimated cost of improvements, most dating from the early 1920s, as well as a report by Hydro agent who visited Guelph incognito in the mid-1920s to report on the efficiency of operations and the level of popular satisfaction with the service. The file also contains some memoranda relating to Hydro's transfer of the operation to the City of Guelph in 1939. Ontario Hydro Archives staff have prepared a useful brief history of the Guelph street railway system.

1291. Hydro Electric Power Commission. **Guelph Radial Railway. General correspondence, reports, right of ways etc, 1921-1943.** c50 linear inches. Loc: OHA. Bin 20-1-002/003/004 #s107-239.

A large quantity of material relating to the operation by HEPCO of the Guelph street railway system between 1921 and 1939 that is part of a larger record group concerned with radial railways.

1292. Hydro Electric Power Commission. **Guelph Radial Railway. Maps, plans, graphs, 1913-1925.** 1 file folder. blueprints. Loc: OHA. GSI OR-519.

Plan of street railway tracks distinguishing lines that were new, reconstructed old or proposed for reconstruction. Two maps of c1925 indicate proposed extensions and improvements. Two graphs show the operating performance of the system in terms of revenue, expenses and car miles between 1913 and 1921. The file also includes the operating accounts for 1921 and 1922.

1293. Hydro Electric Power Commission. **Guelph Radial Railway. Report of Chief Engineer to Chairman, 1919.** 1 file folder. Loc: OHA. GSI ORR-519-19.

An 11-page report of an investigation into the property, current condition, probable revenue and operating expenses of the street railway system, together with a pre-1914 operating statement and proposals for improvements and rationalization. The author predicted that the Guelph Radial Railway would lose $6,000 to $17,000 annually as long as it was operated by itself but that considerable savings could be effected if it were part of a HEPCO electric railway system linking Hamilton and Guelph.

1294. Hydro Electric Power Commission. **Hamilton, Elmira and Guelph Radial Railway. Proposals, 1914.** 1 file folder. Loc: OHA. GSI ORR-519.74.

A summary and map with copies of resolutions carried by municipalities relating to the proposed electric interurban railway. Municipalities included Puslinch Township and Guelph as well as most in Wentworth and Waterloo Counties.

1295. Mattaini, Charles. **Day book, 1906-1919.** 1 envelope. Loc: WCA. MU19.

Photocopy of a ledger recording general expenses, workers' names and wages for work done at various bridges in Guelph, Fergus, Rockwood, Garafraxa, Nichol Township, Arthur and Belwood. Many of the entries are in Italian.

1296. People's Railway Company. **Specifications. Report of route of the proposed People's Railway Company, c1912. 1 document. Loc: GCH.**
An outline of the plans to build the railway which was planned to pass from Waterloo County to Guelph and then run north through Pilkington and Nichol Townships to Fergus and on through Garafraxa and Peel Townships to the Village of Arthur. The document, which was sent to the Clerk of the City of Guelph, notes the types of equipment to be used, and indicates that future plans would be sent to the city. The document is not dated and is held in the Clerk's office vault.

1297. Richard Boyle Contractor. **Advertisement, c1900. 1 broadside. Loc: WCA. MU13.**
An advertisement for the Boyle Patent Bridge for which Boyle was awarded a gold medal by the Parisian Inventors' Academy, Paris, France. Many Wellington County residents are listed as references including J. Mutrie, M.P.P., John Beattie and John Rae. Boyle's business address is listed as Parker, which is in Peel Township.

1298. Shanly, Francis. **Guelph Water Works. Measurements, 1878. 1 file folder. Loc: AO. FA: MU 2678.**
A summary of the measurements of twelve-inch and six-inch pipe for the 1878 system. The routes of the water mains and the distributor pipes along Guelph streets are specified.

1299. Shanly, Francis. **Papers, 1852-1882. 43 feet, 133 boxes. Loc: AO. FA: MU 2644-2776.**
Francis Shanly (1820-1882) began a long engineering career when he joined his brother, Walter, in directing the survey and construction of the Toronto and Guelph Railway in 1852. Shanly was later engaged in many other railway projects, including the Galt and Guelph (1855-1857); the Wellington, Grey and Bruce (1862-1872); the Toronto, Grey and Bruce (1869-1975); the Credit Valley (1874-1880); and the Georgian Bay and Wellington (1875-1882). In 1875, Shanly was appointed City Engineer of Toronto and in 1880 Chief Engineer of the Intercolonial Railway. There are records on every phase of Shanly's engineering career, comprising correspondence, letterbooks, estimates, financial reports, specifications, bills for materials, notebooks, abstracts of earth works, instructions and notes to contractors, statements of farm and road crossings, maps, plans, longitudinal profiles, and cross sections. Records of work on the Toronto and Guelph Railway, which are particularly detailed, are described in a separate entry.

1300. Shanly, Francis. **Toronto and Guelph Railway. Engineering records, 1852-1856. 12 boxes, 2 oversized. Loc: AO. FA: MU 2690-2701.**
A very detailed set of records including correspondence, letterbooks, estimates, reports, payrolls, specifications, calculations of earthworks, notebooks, instructions and notices to contractors, statements of farm and road crossings, subscription lists, longitudinal profiles and cross sections along the entire length of the line. The notebooks trace the survey of the track between Toronto and Guelph and discuss the merits of four alternative routes, with sketch plans of the terrain on the left and notes on the right. A copy of

Walter Shanly's Report on Preliminary Surveys of the Toronto and Guelph Railway
(1852) is included, with its large map of the entire route between Toronto and
Sarnia. Local directors of the company were George Grange, Benjamin Thurtell
(Reeve of Guelph Township) and William Clarke (Reeve of Town of Guelph). MU
2701 contains architectural drawings for a 'second-class way station' and a freight
warehouse of the standard GTR design. There is also a copy of the 1853 plan of
town lots in Guelph. After 1856, the Toronto and Guelph Railway became known as
the Toronto and Sarnia Section, Grand Trunk Railway.

1301. Shanly, Walter. **Notebook, 1837-1852.** 1 volume. Loc: UGA. XRI MS A337.
    The notebook is inscribed 'Toronto and Guelph Railway, 1837' and notes mileage
to various urban centres, grade of land, distances surveyed, and bearings of
aspects of the land. It includes notes taken on Milton, Georgetown, Acton,
Brampton, Equesing, Great Lakes, Rockwood and Great Western Railway.

1302. Simpson, John. **Victoria Bridge over River Speed at Guelph. Tenders, estimates
    and specifications, 1874.** 1 file. Loc: NAC. MG 29, A 40, FA 882, File 4.
    John Simpson was an engineer who worked on contract for various railway
companies in the 1870s, 1880s and 1890s. Part of the Simpson Papers.

1303. Stratford and Huron Railway Company. **Railway Bonusing. Correspondence, 1878.**
    1 document. Loc: WCA. MU 12.
    A letter from a Mr Watson who represented the railway company, explaining that
Palmerston and Harriston would have to raise $75,000 to have the railway pass
through their area instead of Clifford. Watson writes the village council of
Harriston that: 'I know your difficulty and your willingness to give all that is
asked. I hope you will devise some way of getting over the difficulty'.

1304. **Toll gate tenders, 1864.** 1 file folder. Loc: UGA. XR1 MS A332.
    A few documents relating to fees to be paid for toll gates on roads in
Wellington County. Held with the Connon Collection.

1305. Toronto and Goderich Railroad. **Meeting announcement, 1847.** 1 document. Loc:
    GCM.
    A broadside announcing a meeting to be held in Thorpe's Hotel, Guelph, to
discuss the question of the railway's route through Guelph.

1306. Toronto and Guelph Railway. **Act of incorporation, 1852.** Loc: UWO.
    The file also includes the first annual report of the board of directors.

1307. Toronto and Guelph Railway. **Letter concerning amalgamation with Grand Trunk
    Railway, 1853.** Loc: AO. FA: MU 454.
    Letter from S. Thompson, secretary-treasurer of the railway company, informing
the Guelph Township Council of the impending amalgamation and of Casimir
Gzowski's stock offer. Part of Byerly Papers.

1308. Toronto and Guelph Railway. **Report of the special committee on the subject of
    the proposed railroad from Toronto to Guelph, 1851.** 12 p. mf. Loc: UGL.
    A report that promotes the benefits of railroads for the surrounding areas.
American examples are used to convince readers of the merits of a railroad
between Guelph and Toronto. Statistics are given on the growth of the 'Waterloo
District' in terms of population and agricultural output.

1309. Toronto and Guelph Railway. **Report on the preliminary surveys by W. Shanly, Chief Engineer, 1852.** 25 p. tables, maps. mf. Loc: UGL.

A report given to the Toronto and Guelph Railway by its chief engineer. The report includes a detailed comparison of the four proposed routes and how they rate in terms of terrain, grades, and river crossing. Precise cost comparisons are provided in tables examining grading, construction and overall total cost. The report concludes with the engineer's recommendations to the company directors for the construction of the railway, and many concerns that would require further examination.

1310. Toronto and Guelph Railway. **Second annual report of the board of directors, 1853.** 23 p. tables. mf. Loc: UGL.

An annual report, adopted at the annual general meeting on June 6, 1853, that was sent to the shareholders of the Toronto and Guelph Railway. The report includes financial statements and explanations of all transactions the board of directors undertook for the company from December 1851 to April 30, 1853.

1311. Toronto and Guelph Railway. **Stock and fiscal records, 1851-1855.** 0.3 metres. Loc: NAC. RG 30 ICI, vols 484-488.

First incorporated as the Toronto and Goderich Railway Company in 1848, the Toronto and Guelph was incorporated in 1851 to build a line from Toronto to Guelph and with a view to becoming part of the Grand Trunk Main Line. Amalgamated with five other companies under the name Grand Trunk Railway Company of Canada, 1 July 1853. Records include scrip book, transfer book, journal, ledger and cash books.

1312. Toronto and Lake Huron Railroad Company. **Subscription book, 1845.** 12 p. Loc: GPL.

The act of incorporation, an amendment to this act in 1845 and the names of Guelph stockholders who paid five pounds each. These included Robert Alling, William Clarke, William Orton, A.J. Fergusson, Arthur Palmer, William Day, J. Howitt, William Richardson, Edward Carroll, William Dyson, John Kerr, William Patterson, George Sunley, T. Sandilands, Jeremiah Richardson, T. Lacey, Charles Stewart and Thomas Saunders. The book was given to the Guelph Free Library 'as an interesting relic of the past' by Alfred A. Baker, Division Court Clerk, who noted that 13 of the 93 stockholders were still living in 1891.

1313. Toronto, Grey and Bruce Railway. **Agreement re working of the railway, 1880.** 33 p. Loc: CNRL.

The document is concerned with changing the gauge by the Grand Trunk Railway.

1314. Toronto Suburban Electric Railway. **Plans. Public Road, July 9, 1913.** 1 plan. Loc: WCA.

A plan of the route of the interurban railway showing a road crossing and diversion crossing of townline and the Townships of Guelph and Puslinch. The plan includes the area east of the Ontario Prison Farm along the Eramosa River and a lot owned by Thomas Arkell. The scale is 400 feet to one inch. The plan refers to the Toronto Suburban Railway running from Lambton Mills to Guelph. Held with Guelph Township records.

1315. Wellington, Grey and Bruce Railway Company. **Minutes, financial and right-of-way records, 1864-1938.** 0.4 metres, 4 vols. Loc: NAC. RG 30 IF.

Incorporated in 1864 to build a line from Guelph to Southampton with a branch to Owen Sound. Lines totalling 168.06 miles between Guelph and Southampton and from Palmerston to Kincardine were opened between 1870 and 1874. These lines were leased to the Great Western and passed with it to the Grand Trunk in 1893. These records, transferred from the CN Archives comprise minutes, 1867-1892; stock records, 1864-1938; right-of-way book, 1859-1866; cash book, 1867-1875; journals, 1869-1892; ledger, 1867-1875.

UTILITIES

1316. Bell Telephone Company. **Telephone directories, 1883; 1885-1899; 1907-1909; 1912-1914; 1919-1925; 1931-1979.** 25 reels. mf. Loc: GPL.

A listing of subscribers noting addresses of companies and of residences linked to the Bell Telephone system. The directories list occupation of subscribers in the early twentieth century. The entries are introduced alphabetically by name, city, town or village. By the early 1930s, directories include a classified telephone directory presenting an alphabetical listing of business firms and services.

1317. Hydro Electric Power Commission. **Municipal Correspondence. Wellington County municipalities, 1906-1945.** mf. Loc: OHA. FA.

Microfilmed correspondence between Wellington County municipalities and HEPCO on matters concerned with electricity supply and distribution. There are files for twelve urban municipalities or police villages in the county, for the years 1906 to 1945 unless otherwise stated: Arthur, Clifford, Drayton, Elora, Erin, Fergus, Guelph (only 1906-1925), Harriston, Moorefield, Mount Forest, Palmerston and Rockwood (only 1926-1945).

1318. Hydro Electric Power Commission. **Municipal Histories. Guelph, 1893-1966.** 1 file folder. Loc: OHA. GSI OR-510.011.

Miscellaneous items relating to the development and use of electrical power in Guelph, including references to the City's purchase of the Guelph Light and Power Company in 1903. At that time there was an electric generating plant at Allan's Bridge and a gas plant on Waterloo Street. There are many transcribed references to items in Electrical World and Electrical News between 1883 and 1910 and the file also contains a copy of Greta's Shutt's history of the Board of Light and Heat Commissioners.

1319. Hydro Electric Power Commission. **Municipal Histories. Wellington County municipalities, 1890-1935.** 8 file folders. Loc: OHA. GSI OR-510.001.

Collections of summary histories, press clippings and transcribed references to news items in the journals Electrical World and Electrical News on aspects of the electrification of Arthur, Drayton, Elora, Erin, Fergus, Harriston, Mount Forest and Palmerston. Each file contains minor items of correspondence between the municipality and HEPCO. The Mount Forest file contains a set of bylaws on municipal utilities.

1320. Hydro Electric Power Commission. **Operating instructions from Chief Operator to Guelph Operator-in-Charge, 1910-1936.** 3 folders. Loc: OHA. Bin 20-1-006.

Detailed administrative memoranda on procedures of operating the local transformer station, including safety considerations. The Chief Operator was based at Dundas and the local operator was T.R. Postle. Guelph was one of the first two places in Ontario to receive Niagara power over the HEPCO transmission lines in 1910 and these records are the only such administrative material to survive from any local transformer station.

1321. **Sixty-five year telephone history of Erin Township, 1911-1976.** 5 p. Loc: WCA. MU 86.

A description of the development of the telephone companies, including Consolidated Telephone Company Limited, which began in 1911 and Erin Municipal Telephone Company, which began in 1919. The article lists early directors, operators and linemen.

Sober thoughts of a primary Sunday School class
from the Guelph Congregational Church, c1905.
(Guelph Public Library, Shutt Collection)

CHURCH RECORDS

The large number of church records in this **Inventory** reflects the general importance of religion in Ontario society during the first century of settlement. In the words of John Webster Grant, we hold a 'substantially accurate' image of Ontario in the nineteenth century ago as consisting of:

> ...church-centred communities whose inhabitants wholeheartedly professed the traditional doctrines of Christianity, regularly said their prayers, and participated in a variety of communal religious activities with a fervour seldom approached today.[1]

Churches were a primary focus of identification for many people in the nineteenth century. The church provided opportunities for social interaction and recreation as well as for worship, and gave outlets for the organizing abilities of those with strong personalities. Women especially and also young people belonged to special organizations within the general sphere of the church. Sunday's sermons were reported verbatim in Monday's newspapers and doctrinal and theological issues mattered enough for churches to split up over them.

There are other reasons for the survival of official records about local religious organizations, some linked with other sections of this **Inventory**. Until 1869, churches and individual clergy had an obligation to maintain records of baptisms, marriages and burials performed.[2] After registration of vital statistics was taken over by the government, churches tended to continue keeping these records for their own purposes.

Local congregations took pride and competed with one another in the church buildings they erected which required substantial capital investment and associated record-keeping. Surviving accounts of the building committee show that the distinctively octagonal Speedside Congregational Church in Eramosa Township cost only 35 pounds to build with another seven pounds for the window arches (#1444). Most of the church structures which still dominate the skylines of cities, towns and villages in Wellington County date from the 1860s or later.[3] Metropolitan architects were commissioned to design new

---

[1] John Webster Grant, **A profusion of spires: religion in nineteenth-century Ontario** (Toronto: University of Toronto Press, 1988): 3.

[2] George Emery, 'Ontario's civil registration of vital statistics, 1869-1926: the evolution of an administrative system,' **Canadian Historical Review** 64, 4 (1983): 472-3.

[3] William Westfall and Malcolm Thurlby, 'The church in the town: the adaptation of sacred architecture to urban settings in Ontario,' **Etudes canadiennes/Canadian Studies** 20 (1986): 49-59.

churches in neo-Gothic and Romanesque styles, some illustrated in this volume[4], and church members gave generously to pay the bills. The Catholic Church of Our Lady, the most impressive church building in the region, was reported to have cost $200,000 when opened in 1888 (#1940). A very large mortgage on the church was held by the Mutual Life Assurance Company of Waterloo.

To understand and use church records for the region, one must know something of the larger patterns of Canadian church history which were often caught up with movements outside Canada itself. Institutionally, local congregations were usually related to larger systems of church government such as dioceses, conferences or synods which required regular returns, reports and memoranda. The complexities of schisms and unions in Canadian church history have also called for the keeping of careful records. The various strands of Methodism, for example -- the Wesleyan Methodist Church in Canada that united with Canada Conference of the Wesleyan Methodist New Connexion of Canada in 1874 to form the Methodist Church of Canada, which in turn joined with the Primitive Methodist Church, the Methodist Episcopal Church and the Bible Christian Church in 1884.[5]

For the Presbyterian Church, one needs to know of the union in 1840 between the Canadian branch of the United Secession Church of Scotland and Presbyterians in connection with the Church of Scotland to form the Presbyterian Church of Canada. This suffered a disruption in 1844, when a Free Church Synod was organized. The effect of the disruption in most communities is typified by the letter of protest of 1845, signed by the minister and 40 leaders and members of the St Andrew's Church, Fergus, as they broke away to form the Melville Church (#1634). Presbyterian congregations that remained in connection with the Church of Scotland are usually named St Andrew's while those with Free Church beginnings are often named Knox. The two main Presbyterian bodies joined in 1875. In 1925 about two-thirds of Canadian Presbyterian churches united with the Congregationalists and Methodists to form the United Church of Canada in 1925.

Most historical church records are held in centralized repositories outside Wellington County, usually in specialized church archives in the regional, provincial or national seat of church government. Church authorities have tended to resist most efforts by secular archives to acquire church records, maintaining that they are needed for administrative, fiscal, legal and historical reasons.[6] But denominations differ in their attitudes to record-

---

[4] See also the section of Architectural Drawings.

[5] For a useful diagram that summarizes the main events in the history of Canadian Methodism, see Frederick H. Armstrong, **Handbook of Upper Canadian chronology** (Toronto: Dundurn Press, 1985): 261.

[6] For this debate see, for example, James Lambert, 'But what is Caesar's and what is God's: towards a religious archives programme for the Public Archives of Canada,' **Archivaria** 3 (1976/7): 40-56; and Marion Beyea, 'Archives and religious records,' **Archivaria** 4 (1977).

keeping and their policies of permitting 'outsiders' including scholars to consult their records. On the whole, Presbyterian congregations have done best at retaining their records, Baptist and other evangelical churches least well.[7]

Large collections of church records relating to Guelph and Wellington County are held in the United Church Archives and the Presbyterian Church Archives in Toronto, both of which have usefully preserved the records of smaller and defunct congregations. The larger Presbyterian and United churches, notably St Andrew's Presbyterian in Guelph, have retained their own records. Baptist church records are now held by the Canadian Baptist Archives at McMaster University in Hamilton, where the University Library's Special Collections has also accepted responsibility for all Anglican church records from the diocese that includes Wellington County. A few Catholic church records are held in the Diocese of Hamilton Archives but the most valuable material for the history of the Church of Our Lady is in the Archives of the Jesuit Fathers of Upper Canada, the order that served the Guelph parish from 1852 to 1931.

This **Inventory** includes references to at least some official records of 90 church congregations that existed in Guelph or Wellington County before 1940. It is far from complete, however. Of the 35 Guelph church congregations that can be traced from directories before 1940, we have found official records for only fourteen. Churches for which we have no official records tend to be those of the smaller denominations that no longer exist such as the British Methodist Episcopal (the Black Methodist churches in Guelph and Peel Township) or congregations that came into existence only in the 1920s and 1930s. Records have survived for the distinctive Rockwood Meeting of the Society of Friends over the period 1856 to 1937 (#1917).

The entries that follow are grouped by major denomination, then by the name of local congregation which has been systematized and shortened in most cases. Thus Anglican records are first, then Baptist, Congregational, Disciples, Lutheran, Methodist, Presbyterian congregations that continued in the Presbyterian Church of Canada distinguished from Presbyterian congregations that joined Methodist and Congregational churches in the United Church of Canada in 1925, Catholic, and United Church congregations formed after 1925. Miscellaneous items associated with papers and records of particular clergymen or non-denominational bodies have been grouped in a final section.[8]

Names of congregations begin with the place name, followed by the denominational name(s) used during the date span of the records. Complex denominational names have had to be shortened for the order key of INMAGIC to work properly, using the abbreviations that follow. The full names of each

---

[7] See also Shelley Sweeney, 'Sheep that have gone astray? Church record keeping and the Canadian archival system,' **Archivaria** 23 (1986-7): 54-69.

[8] For a useful summary of the genealogical applications of church records, see Ryan Taylor, **Family research in Waterloo and Wellington Counties** (1986): 57-84.

congregation are indexed for each entry as corporate subject terms and provide alternative access to the records that way. Thus records on St Andrew's Presbyterian Church in Guelph may be reached either by the Corporate Author name of **Guelph (St Andrew's) Pres** or by the Corporate Subject Heading of **St Andrew's Presbyterian Church, Guelph**.

Abbreviations for church records

Ang Anglican
Cong Congregational
EUB Evangelical United Brethren
Meth Methodist
MEpi Methodist Episcopal
MNew Methodist New Connexion
MWes Wesleyan Methodist
MPri Primitive Methodist
Pres Presbyterian
UC   United Church

For records of churches that formed the United Church and span the date of union in 1925, a sequence of codes is used as in following examples:
Ballinafad Pres-UC
Barrie Hill Cong-UC
Belwood Meth-UC
Clifford MNew-Meth-UC
Morriston-Aberfoyle EUB-UC

ANGLICAN CHURCH RECORDS - CENTRAL

1322. Anglican Church of Canada. **Wellington Deanery Magazine, 1900-1901.** 2 volumes. Loc: GCM.

An Anglican publication for Wellington County within the Diocese of Niagara. It includes brief reports from twenty-three area churches. The Anglican national magazines, The Canadian Church Magazine and Mission News, is incorporated into the Wellington Deanery Magazine.

1323. Upper Canada Clergy Society. **Map of Upper Canada, specifying the various stations occupied by missionaries of the Church of England, 1839.** 2-3/4 x 3-1/2 inches. Loc: NAC. H3/400/1839.

Plan of the Grand River Tract, with stations occupied by the Rev. B.C. Hill. The scale is 8 miles to an inch. There is little detail on Wellington County.

ANGLICAN CHURCH RECORDS - LOCAL

1324. Alma (Holy Trinity) Ang. **Baptisms. Register, 1874-1880.** 1 ledger. Loc: WCA.

The records are held in the Wellington County Historical Research Society Collection.

1325. Alma (Holy Trinity) Ang. **Church service register, 1889-1910.** 1 ledger. Loc: WCA.

A record of date, liturgical title of Sunday, attendance, offertory, Bible readings, name of preacher, and weather. There is no church name on the ledger, however internal evidence suggests it belongs with the Alma Anglican Church records. The records are held in the Wellington County Historical Research Society Collection.

1326. Alma (Holy Trinity) Ang. **Sunday School. Attendance register, 1887-1888.** 1 ledger. Loc: WCA.

The record is held with the Wellington County Historical Research Society Collection.

1327. Alma (Holy Trinity) Ang. **Vestry. Minutes, 1879-1934; 1938-1947.** 2 volumes. Loc: WCA.

The records are held in the Wellington County Historical Research Society Collection.

1328. Arkell (St Michael and All Angels') Ang. **Account book, 1862-1878.** 1 ledger. Loc: MUL. List of contents and date spans. Written permission of depositing church.

The account book records are held in the same ledger as the vestry minutes covering the years 1862 to 1942. The account book includes a historical sketch of the church noting the arrival of the first settlers to the area in 1831, the founding of the church and information on the church cemetery.

1329. Arkell (St Michael and All Angels') Ang. **Baptisms, 1861-1924; marriages, 1853-1915; burials, 1862-1930.** 1 ledger. Loc: MUL. List of contents and date spans. Written permission of depositing church.

The ledger is inscribed, 'Farnham Church otherwise known as Puslinch Plains Church'.

1330. Arkell (St Michael and All Angels') Ang. **Miscellaneous letters, financial statements, receipts, n.d..** Loc: MUL. List of contents and date spans. Written permission of depositing church.
     Only held in manuscript form. No dates listed in finding aid.

1331. Arkell (St Michael and All Angels') Ang. **Service register, 1918-1941.** 1 ledger. Loc: MUL. List of contents and date spans. Written permission of depositing church.

1332. Arkell (St Michael and All Angels') Ang. **Vestry. Minutes, 1862-1942.** 1 volume. Loc: MUL. List of contents and date spans. Written permission of depositing church.
     The minutes are held in the same ledger as the account books of the church from 1862 to 1898.

1333. Arthur (Grace) Ang. **Baptisms, 1859-1882; confirmations, 1873-1877; marriages, 1861-1882; burials, 1861-1882.** 1 ledger. Loc: MUL. List of contents and date spans. Written permission of depositing church.
     Parish register A includes entries for Luther, Arthur, Alma and Garafraxa Township. The finding aid notes Luther Village was later called Grand Valley.

1334. Arthur (Grace) Ang. **Baptisms, 1877-1922; 1940; confirmations, 1886; 1889; 1897-1899; 1901-1902; 1906; 1909; marriages, 1877-1922; burials, 1878-1921.** 1 ledger. Loc: MUL. List of contents and date spans. Written permission of depositing church.
     Parish register B includes entries for Amaranth, Luther Village (later renamed Grand Valley), Arthur and Garafraxa and Peel Townships.

1335. Arthur (Grace) Ang. **Baptisms, 1921-1962; confirmations, 1922-1960; marriages, 1922-1962; burials 1922-1962.** 1 ledger. Loc: MUL. List of contents and date spans. Written permission of depositing church.
     Parish register E includes entries for Fergus, Alma, Damascus, Arthur and the Townships of West Luther and Garafraxa.

1336. Arthur (Grace) Ang. **Cash book, 1908-1942.** 1 ledger. Loc: MUL. List of contents and date spans. Written permission of depositing church.
     Parish register K contains the accounts.

1337. Arthur (Grace) Ang. **Church families register, 1905; 1913-1914.** 1 ledger. Loc: MUL. List of contents and date spans. Written permission of depositing church.
     Parish register D contains the record of church families.

1338. Arthur (Grace) Ang. **Confirmation register, 1906; 1909; 1911; 1913-1916; 1918; 1920.** 1 ledger. Loc: MUL. List of contents and date spans. Written permission of depositing church.
     Parish register D contains the record of confirmations.

1339. Arthur (Grace) Ang. **Donations, 1923-1926.** 1 ledger. Loc: MUL. List of contents and date spans. Written permission of depositing church.
     Parish register D contains the record of donations.

1340. Arthur (Grace) Ang. **Marriages. Register, 1896-1922.** 1 ledger. Loc: MUL. List of contents and date spans.
    Parish register C includes entries for Colbeck and Arthur, and Luther, Garafraxa and Peel Townships.

1341. Arthur (Grace) Ang. **Membership list, building fund account and donations, 1916; 1926.** 1 ledger. Loc: MUL. List of contents and date spans. Written permission of depositing church.
    Parish register J contains the membership list for 1916 and the account book for 1926.

1342. Arthur (Grace) Ang. **Receipts, 1923-1924.** 1 ledger. Loc: MUL. List of contents and date spans. Written permission of depositing church.
    Parish register D contains the receipts.

1343. Arthur (Grace) Ang. **Service register, 1886-1905.** 1 ledger. Loc: MUL. List of contents and date spans. Written permission of depositing church.
    Parish register F includes entries for services in Holy Trinity Church, Alma, Orange Hall, West Luther, St Alban's Church, Dracon, Proton, St Paul's Damascus, as well as Arthur.

1344. Arthur (Grace) Ang. **Service register, 1905-1914.** 1 ledger. Loc: MUL. List of contents and date spans. Written permission of depositing church.
    Parish register D contains the record of services for several churches including Holy Trinity in Alma, Grace Anglican in Arthur, St Alban's in Grand Valley, St Paul's in Damascus, as well as services in the West Luther Orange Hall.

1345. Arthur (Grace) Ang. **Service register, 1915-1954.** 1 ledger. Loc: MUL. List of contents and date spans. Written permission of depositing church.
    Parish register G contains the record of services and includes a church history.

1346. Arthur (Grace) Ang. **Vestry. Minutes, 1879-1975.** 1 volume. Loc: MUL. List of contents and date spans. Written permission of depositing church.
    Parish register I contains the minutes.

1347. Clifford (Ascension) Ang. **Accounts, 1922-1944.** 1 ledger. Loc: MUL. List of contents and date spans. Written permission of depositing church.
    A listing of collections and expenses and a list of communicants for 1925. Held in Financial Register #1.

1348. Clifford (Ascension) Ang. **Families, 1902-1909; baptisms, communicants, 1901-1915; confirmations, 1914; services, 1901-1913; finances, 1912-1923.** 1 ledger. Loc: MUL. List of contents and date spans. Written permission of depositing church.
    Parish register C records events of parishioners.

1349. Clifford (Ascension) Ang. **Service register, 1926.** 1 ledger. Loc: MUL. List of contents and date spans. Written permission of depositing church.
    Parish register D records services.

1350. Clifford (Ascension) Ang. **Vestry. Minutes, 1923-1945.** 1 volume. Loc: MUL. List of contents and date spans. Written permission of depositing church.
Parish register G records minutes.

1351. Damascus (St Paul's) Ang. **Account book, 1895-1901.** 1 ledger. Loc: MUL. List of contents and date spans. Written permission of depositing church.
Parish register N contains the account book of the envelope system. Held with the records for Grace Anglican Church, Arthur.

1352. Damascus (St Paul's) Ang. **Vestry. Minutes, 1897-1969.** 1 volume. Loc: MUL. List of contents and date spans. Written permission of depositing church.
Parish register M contains the minutes. Held with the records for Grace Anglican Church, Arthur.

1353. Elora (St John the Evangelist) Ang. **Baptisms, confirmation, confirmation and burials, 1846-1965.** 4 ledgers. Loc: MUL. List of contents and date spans. Written permission of depositing church.
Parish registers A, B and C record these events in the lives of parishioners. A separate unlisted register records marriages only from 1858 to 1871.

1354. Elora (St John the Evangelist) Ang. **Report, 1938.** 1 document. Loc: WCA.
Held in the Wellington County Historical Research Society Collection. A report that lists statistics for membership, services and Sunday School attendance.

1355. Elora (St John the Evangelist) Ang. **Vestry. Minutes and accounts, 1848-1950.** 1 volume. Loc: MUL. List of contents and date spans. Written permission of depositing church.
Parish register D records minutes. The volume begins with a 7-page history of the area and the church from 1820 to 1848 when the minutes began to be recorded. The handwritten note in the margin states that the author was Andrew Geddes. Early contributors to the church include Andrew Geddes, George Elmslie, Adam Fergusson, Jasper Gilkison and the Rev. Arthur Palmer. A financial statement is included with the minutes for each year.

1356. Erin (All Saints) Ang. **Account books, 1872-1886; 1892-1896; 1912-1930.** 4 ledgers; 1 envelope. Loc: MUL. List of contents and date spans. Written permission of depositing church.
The ledger of accounts for 1892 to 1896 exists only in manuscript form. The information is held in Financial Registers #s 1, 2, 3, 5 and Envelope #1.

1357. Erin (All Saints) Ang. **Baptisms, confirmations, marriages, and burials, 1869-1947.** 1 ledger. Loc: MUL. List of contents and date spans. Written permission of depositing church.
Parish Register A records events of parishioners of the Erin church as well as St John's Church, Hillsburgh and Anglican Christ Church, Reading.

1358. Erin (All Saints) Ang. **Communicants register, 1886-1890.** 1 ledger. Loc: MUL. List of contents and date spans.
The information is recorded in Parish Registers B and D (the latter contains no dates). Parishioners are listed as belonging to the Erin church, St John's Anglican Church in Hillsburgh, Christ Church in Reading, or from Forks of the Credit or Alton.

1359. Erin (All Saints) Ang. **Confirmation register, 1885-1886; 1927; 1934. 3** ledgers. Loc: MUL. List of contents and date spans. Written permission of depositing church.

Parish Registers B, D and E record confirmations of the Erin church, St Johns' Church in Hillsburgh, and Christ Church in Reading.

1360. Erin (All Saints) Ang. **Families register, 1921; 1934.** 1 ledger. Loc: MUL. List of contents and date span.

The information is recorded in Parish Register D for the Erin church, St John's Church, Hillsburgh, and Christ Church, Reading.

1361. Erin (All Saints) Ang. **Marriages. Register, 1900-1919; 1927-1947.** 1 ledger. Loc: MUL. List of contents and date spans. Written permission of depositing church.

Parish Register C records marriages of the Erin church, St John's Church in Hillsburgh, and Christ Church in Reading.

1362. Erin (All Saints) Ang. **Service registers, 1885-1897; 1910-1918; 1923-1954.** 3 ledgers. Loc: MUL. List of contents and date spans. Written permission of depositing church.

A record of services held at the Erin church, St John's Church in Reading, and Christ Church in Hillsburgh. Register D records services from 1910 to 1918 and Register E services from 1923 to 1954.

1363. Erin (All Saints) Ang. **Vestry. Minutes, 1883-1886; 1896; 1922-1929; 1938-1953.** 4 volumes. Loc: MUL. List of contents and date spans. Written permission of depositing church.

Minutes from 1883 to 1896 are in Financial Register #1, from 1922 to 1923 in Financial Register #2, 1923 to 1929 in Financial Register #4, and from 1938 to 1953 in Parish Register G.

1364. Erin (All Saints) Ang. **Women's Auxiliary accounts, 1926-1965.** Loc: MUL. List of contents and date spans. Written permission of depositing church.

The information is recorded in Financial Register #5.

1365. Farewell (St John's) Ang. **Baptism, confirmation, marriage and burial registers, 1904-1964.** 3 ledgers. Loc: MUL. List of contents and date spans. Written permission of depositing church.

Parish registers A to C contain a record of the events of parishioners. Until St John's Church was built at Farewell in 1892, its parishioners formed part of Trinity Anglican Church, North Arthur. Trinity joined Church of the Good Shepherd, Riverstown, when it opened in 1886.

1366. Farewell (St John's) Ang. **Cash books, 1913-1926.** 2 ledgers. Loc: MUL. List of contents and date spans. Written permission of depositing church.

Financial registers 1 and 2 contain a record of accounts.

1367. Farewell (St John's) Ang. **Service registers, 1903-1968.** 3 ledgers. Loc: MUL. List of contents and date spans. Written permission of depositing church.

Parish registers B, D and E contain a record of church services.

St John the Evangelist Anglican Church, Elora, c1885:
a photograph by John Connon. The church building was designed by Henry Langley in 1871-2 (#3393) with modifications by Langley and Burke in 1891-4 (#3389). (Wellington County Museum and Archives)

1368. Farewell (St John's) Ang. **Vestry. Minutes, 1920-1968.** 1 volume. Loc: MUL. List of contents and date spans. Written permission of depositing church.
Parish register F contains a record of minutes and a declaration register for 1925.

1369. Fergus (St James') Ang. **Baptism, confirmation, marriage and burial registers, 1867-1951.** 3 ledgers. Loc: MUL. List of contents and date spans. Written permission of depositing church.
Parish registers A to C contain a record of the events of parishioners.

1370. Fergus (St James') Ang. **Cash books, 1867-1894; c1900-1936.** 7 ledgers. Loc: MUL. List of contents and date spans. Written permission of depositing church.
Financial registers 1 to 7 contain a record of accounts including collections and pew rentals.

1371. Fergus (St James') Ang. **Service registers, 1894-1963.** 6 ledgers. Loc: MUL. List of contents and date spans. Written permission of depositing church.
Parish registers D to G contain a record of the church services. Register G also contains a list of communicants for 1901, 1911 and 1912.

1372. Fergus (St James) Ang. **Sunday School. Library circulation and catalogue, 1910-1934.** 1 ledger. Loc: MUL. Written permission of depositing church.
A record of titles, dates of circulation and names of borrowers. The information is recorded in Parish Register N.

1373. Fergus (St James') Ang. **Vestry. Minutes, 1867-c1880; 1891-1925; 1927-1942.** 4 volumes. Loc: MUL. List of contents and date spans. Written permission of depositing church.
Parish registers H to K contain a record of the minutes. Register K also contains a declaration register from 1909 to 1924.

1374. Guelph (St George's) Ang. **Anglican Young People's Association. Cash book, 1912-1919.** 1 ledger. Loc: MUL. List of contents and date spans. Written permission of depositing church.
Parish register UU contains the account records.

1375. Guelph (St George's) Ang. **Annual report, 1935.** 40 p. ill. Loc: GPL.
A summary of the births, marriages, and deaths of members of St George's Church in Guelph in 1935. A brief description is also given of church activities.

1376. Guelph (St George's) Ang. **Baptism, marriage and burial registers, 1833-1973.** 22 ledgers. Loc: MUL. List of contents and date spans. Written permission of depositing church.
Parish registers A to V record events of parishioners. Parish registers W to Z were returned to the church at their request, February 4, 1982.

1377. Guelph (St George's) Ang. **Cash books, 1874-1902; 1910-1912; 1927-1974.** 17 ledgers. Loc: MUL. List of contents and date spans. Written permission of depositing church.
Financial registers F1 to F17 contain a record of accounts including pew rentals, offerings, organ, carillon, clock and building accounts.

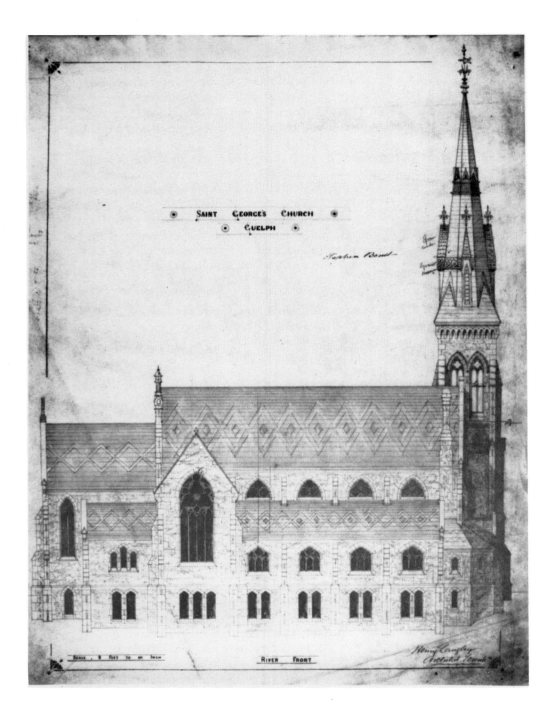

Henry Langley's design of St George's Anglican Church, c1870 (#3392).
(Langley Collection, Metropolitan Toronto Central Reference Library, and
Gilbert A. Stelter)

1378. Guelph (St George's) Ang. **Collection Notes. St George's Church, Guelph, 1843; 1845; 1865-1866.** 5 documents. Loc: WCA. MU50.

A series of individual collection notes of the church. The collection includes an 1845 circular lamenting the inability of members to pay church pew rental fees resulting in 'more than one third of the Clergymen's income . . . devoted toward defraying the expense of extensive improvements'.

1379. Guelph (St George's) Ang. **Land records, 1853-1939 (sporadic).** 1 box. Loc: MUL. Written permission of depositing church.

A collection of deeds and mortgages of land in Guelph purchased by individuals on behalf of the church. Transactions include Reverend Arthur Palmer and his wife, Catherine. Also included is a deed and plan of the church cemetery.

1380. Guelph (St George's) Ang. **Miscellaneous collection, 1920-1982.** 1 file. Loc: UGA. XR1 MS A071.

Articles, books and newspaper clippings regarding St George's Anglican Church, including an order of service for dedication of the War Memorial Tablet, c1920, a financial statement pamphlet, 1930 and the church histories, 1932 and 1982.

1381. Guelph (St George's) Ang. **Service registers, 1892-1905; 1918-1970.** 8 ledgers. Loc: MUL. List of contents and date spans. Written permission of depositing church.

Parish registers W to Z and AA to DD record services held. These registers were returned to the church in 1982.

1382. Guelph (St George's) Ang. **St George's Parochial Magazine, 1887-1888.** 4 brochures. Loc: GPL.

The parish magazines include sermons, services, poems, meditations, descriptions of parish events, and local business advertisments. Issues include January, September and October 1887, and May 1888. Part of the St James the Apostle Collection.

1383. Guelph (St George's) Ang. **Sunday School. Attendance registers, 1894-1906; 1913-1961.** 7 ledgers. Loc: MUL. List of contents and date spans. Written permission of depositing church.

Parish registers II, JJ and MM to OO contain attendance records. Register JJ also contains a record of receipts and expenditures from 1919 to 1942.

1384. Guelph (St George's) Ang. **Sunday School. Records, 1886-1893; 1924-1934.** 1 volume. Loc: MUL. List of contents and date spans. Written permission of depositing church.

Parish registers HH and LL contain the records.

1385. Guelph (St George's) Ang. **Sunday School Teachers. Minutes, 1924-1934.** 1 volume. Loc: MUL. List of contents and date spans. Written permission of depositing church.

Parish register LL contains the minutes.

1386. Guelph (St George's) Ang. **Vestry. Minutes, 1834-1918.** 2 volumes. Loc: MUL. List of contents and date spans. Written permission of depositing church.

Parish registers EE and FF record the minutes.

1387. Guelph (St James) Ang. **Anniversary service programs, 1910; 1920; 1938; 1940.** 4 documents. Loc: GPL.

Programs for the 20th anniversary in 1910, a consecration service in 1920, the dedication of three memorial windows in 1939, and the 50th anniversary in 1940.

1388. Guelph (St James') Ang. **Baptism, confirmations, marriage and burial registers, 1890-1972.** 9 ledgers. Loc: MUL. List of contents and date spans. Written permission of depositing church.

Parish registers A to I contain record of the events of parishoners.

1389. Guelph (St James) Ang. **Building Committee. Correspondence and land records, 1890-1942.** 21 documents. Loc: GPL.

Correspondence about the building, mortgages and deeds pertaining to the church property, a 1942 blueprint of the boiler room, and 1967 blueprints of minor alterations to sections of the building. Part of the St James the Apostle Collection.

1390. Guelph (St James) Ang. **Building Committee. Minutes, 1890-1892.** 1 volume. Loc: GPL.

Part of the St James the Apostle Collection.

1391. Guelph (St James') Ang. **Financial registers, 1890-1969.** 8 ledgers. Loc: MUL. List of contents and date spans. Written permission of depositing church.

Financial registers F1 to F8 contain a record of accounts.

1392. Guelph (St James) Ang. **Historical sketch, 1920. An historical sketch prepared and published on the occasion of the consecration of St James Church, Guelph on the 30th anniversary of the founding of the parish, 1920.** 16 pp. ill. Loc: GPL.

A description of the historical development of the parish including the building, leaders, rectors, Sunday School and choir. Part of the St James the Apostle Collection.

1393. Guelph (St James) Ang. **Historical sketch, 1940. St James Church, Guelph, Ontario: Golden Jubilee, 1890-1940.** 36 pp. ill. Loc: GPL.

A description of the development of the parish including the building, leaders, rectors, assistants, Sunday School, choir and memorials. Part of the St James the Apostle Collection.

1394. Guelph (St James) Ang. **Historical sketch, 1966. Church of St James the Apostle, Guelph, Ontario: seventy-fifth anniversary, 1890-1966.** 27 pp. ill. Loc: GPL.

A description of the historical development of the parish including rectors, leaders, activities, and memorials. Part of the St James the Apostle Collection.

1395. Guelph (St James) Ang. **Oral history tapes and transcripts, c1930-1987.** 13 tapes, 1 file folder. Loc: GPL.

A series of interviews with various parishoners who discuss the church's historical development, changes in leadership and liturgy, and their personal involvement in the church. The file also contains 26 tape release forms that list name of person interviewed, birthdate, occupation of family members and parents, and names of siblings. Part of the St James the Apostle Collection.

1396. Guelph (St James') Ang. **Parish Council. Minutes and financial statement, 1935.**
1 volume. Loc: MUL. List of contents and date spans. Written permission of
depositing church.
Parish register S contains a record of the meetings.

1397. Guelph (St James') Ang. **Service registers, 1890-1901; 1910-1969.** 7 ledgers.
Loc: MUL. List of contents and date spans. Written permission of depositing
church.
Parish registers J to P contain a record of church services.

1398. Guelph (St James) Ang. **St James' Church Parish Magazine, 1890-1900.** 53
brochures. Loc: GPL.
The parish magazines include sermons, services, poems, meditations,
descriptions of parish events, and local business advertisements. Part of the
St James the Apostle Collection.

1399. Guelph (St James) Ang. **St James the Apostle Collection, 1890-1987.** 4 boxes.
Loc: GPL.
A collection of records of the church that includes general correspondence,
newspaper clippings, historical sketches, membership lists, Young People's
Association minutes from 1907 to 1908, Building Committee minutes from 1890 to
1892, Alter Guild minutes from 1959 to 1962, Daughters of St James minutes from
1940 to 1985, Scouts minutes from 1969 to 1972, and sporadic Vestry minutes and
reports from 1940 to 1980. The records also contain tapes and transcripts of
oral interviews conducted in 1987 about personal impressions of the development
of the church. Comprises the St James the Apostle Collection.

1400. Guelph (St James') Ang. **Vestry. Minutes, 1890-1922.** 1 volume. Loc: MUL. List
of contents and date spans. Written permission of depositing church.
Parish register A contains a record of the minutes.

1401. Guelph (St James') Ang. **Women's Auxiliary. Cash books, 1912-1933.** 3 ledgers.
Loc: MUL. List of contents and date spans. Written permission of depositing
church.
Parish registers Z, AA and BB contain a record of accounts.

1402. Guelph (St James') Ang. **Women's Auxiliary. Minutes, 1906-1959.** 6 volumes. Loc:
MUL. List of contents and date spans. Written permission of depositing church.
Parish registers T to Y contain a record of the minutes.

1403. Guelph (St James) Ang. **Young People's Association. Minutes, 1907-1908.** 1
volume. Loc: GPL.
A record of weekly minutes that include newspaper clippings describing youth
activities. There are records of several debates, such as 'Immigration into
Canada is of benefit to the Country', and 'Protection versus Free Trade for
Canada at the present Time'. Free Trade lost. Part of the St James the Apostle
Collection.

1404. Harriston (St George's) Ang. **Baptism, confirmation, marriage and burial
registers, 1858-1969.** 7 ledgers. Loc: MUL. List of contents and date spans.

Written permission of depositing church.

Parish registers A to F contain a record of the events of parishoners. The charge also included Church of the Ascension in Clifford and Christ Church in Drew. Register B contains accounts for St George's from 1892 to 1893; a record of baptisms, confirmations, marriages and burials at the Church of the Ascension in Clifford, and an alphabetical index of parishioners at the back of the book.

1405. Harriston (St George's) Ang. **Baptism, confirmation, marriage and burial register, 1864-1945.** 1 ledger. Loc: MUL. List of contents and date spans. Written permission of depositing church.

Parish register B includes a record of baptisms, confirmations, marriages and burials at St George's and at the Church of the Ascension, Clifford. An alphabetical index of parishioners is included at the back of the book.

1406. Harriston (St George's) Ang. **Baptism, marriage and burial register, 1858-1886.** 1 ledger. Loc: MUL. List of contents and date spans. Written permission of depositing church.

Parish Register A includes entries for Clifford and Harriston.

1407. Hillsburgh (St John's) Ang. **Baptisms. Register, 1870-1904.** 1 ledger. Loc: WCA. A handwritten copy of the church register. Marriages from 1897 to 1916 and burials from 1878 to 1937 are also recorded in the ledger. Part of the Kortland Collection.

1408. Hillsburgh (St John's) Ang. **Burials. Register, 1878-1937.** 1 ledger. Loc: WCA. A handwritten copy of the church register. Baptisms from 1870 to 1904 and marriages from 1897 to 1916 are also recorded in the ledger. Part of the Kortland Collection.

1409. Hillsburgh (St John's) Ang. **Marriages. Register, 1897-1916.** 1 ledger. Loc: WCA. A handwritten copy of the church register. Burials from 1878 to 1937 and baptisms from 1870 to 1904 are also recorded in the ledger. Part of the Kortland Collection.

1410. Hillsburgh (St John's) Ang. **Service register, 1928.** 1 ledger. Loc: MUL. List of contents and date spans. Written permission of depositing church.

Parish register E records services. Held with the records of All Saints' Church, Erin.

1411. Hillsburgh (St John's) Ang. **Vestry. Minutes, 1913; 1921.** 1 volume. Loc: MUL. List of contents and date spans. Written permission of depositing church.

Held with the records of All Saints' Church, Erin.

1412. Moorefield (St John's) Ang. **Record of givings, 1931-1941.** 1 ledger. Loc: MUL. List of contents and date spans. Written permission of depositing church.

Held with records of St James Church, Rothsay.

1413. Mount Forest (St Paul's) Ang. **Baptism, confirmation, marriage and burial registers, 1859-1957.** 5 ledgers. Loc: MUL. List of contents and date spans. Written permission of depositing church.

The information is held in Parish registers A, B, C, D, and F.

1414. Mount Forest (St Paul's) Ang. **Service registers, 1887-1960.** 5 ledgers. Loc: MUL. List of contents and date spans. Written permission of depositing church.
Parish registers E to I record church services. Register E also records communicants for 1889-1890 and Register F also confirmations from 1896 to 1903.

1415. Mount Forest (St Paul's) Ang. **Sunday School. Account book, 1917-1960.** 1 ledger. Loc: MUL. List of contents and date spans. Written permission of depositing church.
Financial register #1 records the accounts.

1416. Mount Forest (St Paul's) Ang. **Vestry. Minutes, 1883-1961.** 2 volumes. Loc: MUL. List of contents and date spans. Written permission of depositing church.
Parish registers J and K record minutes. Register J also includes a declaration register from 1889 to 1934.

1417. Riverstown (Good Shepherd) Ang. **Church family register, 1904-1913.** 1 ledger. Loc: MUL. List of contents and date spans. Written permission of depositing church.
The information is recorded in Parish Register B.

1418. Riverstown (Good Shepherd) Ang. **Communicants register, 1904-1906.** 1 ledger. Loc: MUL. List of contents and date spans. Written permission of depositing church.
The information is recorded in Parish Register B.

1419. Riverstown (Good Shepherd) Ang. **Confirmations, 1904-1905; 1907; 1909.** 1 ledger. Loc: MUL. List of contents and date spans. Written permission of depositing church.
The information is recorded in Parish Register B.

1420. Riverstown (Good Shepherd) Ang. **Declaration register, 1877; 1879-1880; 1882-1889; 1924-1925.** 2 ledgers. Loc: MUL. List of contents and date spans. Written permission of depositing church.
Declaration registers to 1889 are in Parish Register A, and after 1924 in Parish Register C. The declaration is an oath of membership for the year and a declaration that the member has not voted as a member of any other congregation within the year.

1421. Riverstown (Good Shepherd) Ang. **Financial accounts, 1865; 1887-1894; 1896-1903.** 2 ledgers. Loc: MUL. List of contents and date spans. Written permission of depositing church.
Accounts for 1865 are held in Parish Register A and for all other years in Parish Register C.

1422. Riverstown (Good Shepherd) Ang. **Service register, 1936-1962.** 1 ledger. Loc: MUL. List of contents and date spans. Written permission of depositing church.
The record is contained in Parish Register D and records date, time, reader, preacher, number of present total amount of collection and an occasional comment about the weather.

1423. Riverstown (Good Shepherd) Ang. **Vestry. Minutes, 1865-1894; 1897-1904; 1907-1917; 1921-1933.** 2 volumes. Loc: MUL. List of contents and date spans. Written permission of depositing church.

   Minutes from 1865 to 1894 are in Parish Register A, and minutes from 1897 to 1904 are in Register C. From 1850 to 1886, parishioners from Riverstown and Farewell made up Trinity Church, North Arthur. In 1886, they began a new church in a new building named, Church of the Good Shepherd, Riverstown.

1424. Rockwood (St John's) Ang. **Baptism, confirmation, marriage and burial register, 1884-1973.** 1 ledger. Loc: MUL. List of contents and date spans. Written permission of depositing church.

   Parish register A records events of parishoners.

1425. Rockwood (St John's) Ang. **Cash books, 1893-1951.** 2 ledgers. Loc: MUL. List of contents and date spans. Written permission of depositing church.

   Parish registers E and F record church accounts.

1426. Rockwood (St John's) Ang. **Service registers, 1889-1950.** 2 ledgers. Loc: MUL. List of contents and date spans. Written permission of depositing church.

   Parish registers C and D record services held.

1427. Rockwood (St John's) Ang. **Vestry. Minutes, 1880-1912.** 1 volume. Loc: MUL. List of contents and date spans. Written permission of depositing church.

   Parish register B records the minutes.

1428. Rothsay (St James') Ang. **Baptism, confirmation, marriage and burial registers, 1883-1949.** 2 ledgers. Loc: MUL. List of contents and date spans. Written permission of depositing church.

   Parish register A and G record events of parishioners. The charge also included St John's in Moorefield and Christ Church in Drayton. Register A also includes a record of expenses from 1883 to 1907.

1429. Rothsay (St James') Ang. **Parish registers, 1893-1951.** 8 ledgers. Loc: MUL. List of contents and date spans. Written permission of depositing church.

   Parish registers B to J, excluding G, record services and members of the church. For some years, Rothsay, Moorefield and Drayton members are recorded separately. Registers D, E and F also record expenses.

BAPTIST CHURCH RECORDS

1430. Guelph (First) Baptist. **Marriages. Registers, 1896-1918.** Loc: CBA. Fee charged; written permission of depositing church.

1431. Guelph (First) Baptist. **Membership. Registers, 1859-1928; 1936-1974.** Loc: CBA. Fee charged; written permission of depositing church.

   Membership lists for the years 1868 to 1928 have been microfilmed.

1432. Guelph (First) Baptist. **Minutes, 1853-1936.** Loc: CBA. Fee charged; written permission of depositing church.

   The minute book for 1905-1908 includes a membership list for 1853-1931. The minute book for 1853-1879 has also been microfilmed.

1433. Guelph (Trinity) Baptist. **Membership. Register, 1890-1908.** Loc: CBA. Fee charged; written permission of depositing church.

1434. Guelph (Trinity) Baptist. **Minutes, 1907-1908.** Loc: CBA. Fee charged; written permission of depositing church.

1435. Hillsburgh Baptist. **Marriages. Register, 1896-1922.** Loc: CBA. Fee charged; written permission of depositing church.

1436. Hillsburgh Baptist. **Minutes, 1853-1953.** Loc: CBA. Fee charged; written permission of depositing church.
   Minutes from 1853 to 1910 available on microfilm, including membership list for 1884.

1437. Kenilworth Baptist. **Membership. List, 1859-1959.** Loc: CBA. Fee charged; written permission of depositing church.

1438. Kenilworth Baptist. **Minutes, 1905-1961.** Loc: CBA. Fee charged; written permission of depositing church.

1439. Monck Baptist. **Minutes, 1892-1973.** 2 volumes. Loc: CBA. Fee charged; written permission of depositing church.
   Membership lists are included with the minute books.

CONGREGATIONAL CHURCH RECORDS - CENTRAL

1440. Canadian Congregational Church. **Congregational yearbooks, 1873-1925.** 51 volumes. Loc: UCA.
   A series of published annual reports which lists members who made contributions to the church and provides details when specific churches were constructed, as well as noting the financial transactions of specific congregations. The reports include references to Congregational churches in Elora, Fergus, Guelph, Speedside and Garafraxa Township.

CONGREGATIONAL CHURCH RECORDS - LOCAL

1441. Ballinafad (Melville) Cong-UC. **Congregational Meetings. Minutes, 1881-1932.** Loc: UCA. Card index.

1442. Belwood Cong. **Congregational Meetings. Minutes, 1868-1925.** 2 volumes. Loc: UCA. Card index.

1443. Belwood Cong. **Membership. List, 1868-1908.** 1 volume. Loc: UCA. Card index.
   The annual congregational meeting minutes from 1890 to 1915 are recorded in the same ledger.

1444. Eramosa (Speedside) Cong. **Account of Building Committee, 1853.** 1 p. photostat. Loc: MTL.
   The account for the cost of constructing the distinctive octagonal chapel. The builders were James Wilson and William Armstrong. The cost is stated as thirty-five pounds 'as per contract', with an additional seven pounds for the window arches. The account is dated August, 1853 and receipted 25 October, 1853.

1445. Eramosa (Speedside) Cong. **Deeds, 1861; 1883.** 1 reel. mf. Loc: WCA.

1446. Eramosa (Speedside) Cong. **Sabbath School. Register, 1868-1875; 1877; 1879.** 1 reel. mf. Loc: WCA.

1447. Eramosa (Speedside) Cong-UC. **Baptisms. Registers, 1855-1892; 1902-1934.** 2 ledgers. Loc: UCA, WCA. UCA: Card index.
   The congregational meeting minutes from 1845 to 1963 and membership lists from 1864 to 1950 are also recorded in the ledgers. The church was renamed Speedside United in 1925 and from 1958 was associated with the Barrie Hill United in the Eramosa Pastoral Charge. The WCA has a microfilm copy of the registers for 1855-1875.

1448. Eramosa (Speedside) Cong-UC. **Congregational Meetings. Minutes, 1845-1963.** 2 volumes. Loc: UCA, WCA. UCA: Card index.
   The congregational meeting minutes from 1845 to 1963 and membership lists from 1864 to 1950 are also recorded in the volumes. The WCA has a microfilm copy of the minutes for 1845-1888 and 1898-1963.

1449. Eramosa (Speedside) Cong-UC. **Membership. Roll, 1864-1895; 1898-1950.** 2 ledgers. Loc: UCA, WCA. UCA: Card index.
   The congregational meeting minutes from 1845 to 1963 and baptism register from 1855 to 1934 are also recorded in the ledgers. The WCA has a microfilm copy of the roll for the years 1864-1895.

1450. Garafraxa W Cong. **Marriages. Registers, 1896-1922.** 1 mf. Loc: WCA.

1451. Garafraxa W Cong. **Minutes, 1856-1879.** 1 reel. mf. Loc: WCA.
   The record of several early entries including a subscription list for 1861, agreement to form a congregation and meetings convened by the church. The meetings were held frequently and include periodic financial statements.

1452. Guelph Cong. **Marriages. Register, 1889-1900.** 1 ledger. Loc: UCA. Card index.

1453. Guelph Cong. **Sunday School Teachers' Meetings. Minutes, 1891-1892.** 1 volume. Loc: UCA. Card index.
   The volume contains correspondence regarding the 1929 union of Trinity United Church and Chalmers United Church.

1454. Guelph Cong (Trinity) UC. **Congregational Meetings. Minutes, 1835-1929.** 4 volumes. Loc: UCA. Card index.
   The minutes record the inaugural service in Guelph of the United Church of Canada attended by members of Chalmers Presbyterian, Congregational, Dublin Street Methodist, Norfolk Street Methodist and Paisley Memorial Methodist. The service was held in the Norfolk Street Church on June 10, 1925 and was 'very largely attended'.

1455. Guelph Cong (Trinity) UC. **Correspondence, 1860-1929 (sporadic).** 11 file folders, 1 envelope. Loc: UCA. Card index.

1456. Guelph Cong (Trinity) UC. **Marriages. Registers, 1878-1929.** 1 ledger. Loc: UCA. Card index.

1457. Guelph Cong (Trinity) UC. **Membership. Roll, 1890-1927.** 1 ledger. Loc: UCA. Card index.

   The ledger includes a 1927 personal letter from J.W. Lyon requesting a transfer of membership to Norfolk Street United Church where his wife had attended since childhood.

1458. Guelph Cong. **Trustee Board. Minutes, 1867-1903.** 1 volume. Loc: UCA. Card index.

1459. Guelph (Trinity) UC. **Baptisms. Register, 1927-1929.** 1 ledger. Loc: UCA. Card index.

   The burials from 1927 to 1929 are also recorded in the same ledger.

1460. Guelph (Trinity) UC. **Burials. Register, 1927-1929.** 1 ledger. Loc: UCA. Card index.

   The baptisms from 1927 to 1929 are also recorded in the same ledger.

1461. North Erin Cong. **Membership. List, 1872-1878; 1894-1896.** 1 ledger. Loc: UCA. Card index.

   The membership list is held in the same ledger as the minutes of the church. The listing of members from 1894 to 1896 is held after the minutes. The record indicates the congregation was formed in 1872.

1462. North Erin Cong. **Session. Minutes, 1872-1881; 1890-1893; 1896.** 1 volume. Loc: UCA. Card index.

   A record of minutes of meetings which convened on an irregular basis. The records indicate the congregation was formed in 1872. The minutes were held in the same volume as the membership list of the church.

1463. Simpson's Corners Cong. **First Congregational Society of Christian Endeavor. Minutes, 1894-1899.** 1 volume. Loc: WCA. MU69.

   The minutes record activities and members of various committees including the Prayer, Social, Music, Flower and Lookout Committees.

1464. Simpson's Corners Cong. **Sunday School Convention. Minutes, 1918.** 1 file folder. Loc: WCA. MU69.

   James Grant from Mimosa gave an address entitled 'Democracy is dangerous without righteousness'. The minutes are held with the St John's Presbyterian Church, Belwood, records.

1465. Simpson's Corners Cong-UC. **Membership. Lists, 1887-1950.** 1 reel. mf. Loc: WCA.

   The document is not labelled but the microfilm box lists a membership list covering the period of Simpson's Corners Congregational Church.

1466. Simpson's Corners Cong-UC. **Session. Minutes, 1883-1952.** 1 reel. mf. Loc: WCA.

   The first page of the record indicates Simpson's Corners Congregational Church was united with Speedside in 1879. The end of the minutes includes a brief report highlighting the history of the church at Simpson's Corners. The report notes Simpson's Corners was united with St John's Presbyterian Church after church union in 1925.

EVANGELICAL UNITED BRETHREN CHURCH RECORDS

1467. Morriston EUB. **Annual Meetings. Minutes, 1893-1953**. 2 volumes. Loc: UCA. Card index.

A record of meetings which listed receipts and expenditures and motions carried at meetings. One entry from November 24, 1907 includes a pledge by several church members not to smoke or drink alcohol.

1468. Morriston EUB. **E.L.C.E. Minutes, 1934-1943**. 6 volumes. Loc: UCA. Card index.

A record of meetings held several times each month with references to the election of officers, attendance of members and collections made by the group. The organization was a women's society.

1469. Morriston EUB. **Finance Board. Minutes, 1917-1935**. 1 volume. Loc: UCA. Card index.

A record of plans to improve the finances of the church with reference to the finance budget of the Morriston Evangelical Church. The board only met periodically with brief references for each meeting.

1470. Morriston EUB. **Marriages. Register, 1862-1949**. 1 ledger. Loc: UCA. Card index.

A record of marriages with roughly 162 entries which is less than in most marriage registers covering long periods of time. The names listed include residents living in Morriston, Puslinch, Eden Mills, Guelph and Aberfoyle.

1471. Morriston EUB. **Quarterly Board. Minutes, 1858-1959**. 4 volumes. Loc: UCA. Card index.

A record of minutes with meetings from 1858 to 1897 being transcribed in German and in 1898 begin to be composed in English.

1472. Morriston EUB. **Sunday School. Attendance records, 1906-1941**. 1 ledger. Loc: UCA. Card index.

A record of weekly attendance which lists the collection figures, total attendance, and the number of teachers and students either present or absent. The weekly entries also describe the weather. The attendance records are held in the same ledger as the minutes of the Sunday School.

1473. Morriston EUB. **Sunday School. Minutes, 1905-1941**. 1 volume. Loc: UCA. Card index.

A record of election of officers and brief discussions of finances. The minutes are held in the same ledger as the attendance records of the Sunday School.

1474. Morriston EUB. **Young People's League. Minutes, 1930-1934**. 2 volumes. Loc: UCA. Card index.

A record of the meetings with the minutes indicating the league was formed in 1930. The meetings were held monthly and lists officials appointed and attendance of its members.

LUTHERAN CHURCH RECORDS

1475. Preston Evangelical Lutheran. **Baptismal, marriage and death registers, 1853-1860.** mf. Loc: NAC. FA: C-15758.
   The baptismal register covers 1853-1855 and 1860; the marriage register 1855 only, and the death register 1855 and 1860.

1476. Preston Evangelical Lutheran. **Baptisms. Registers, 1853-1855; 1860.** mf. Loc: NAC. FA: C-15758.
   The congregation included some members from Puslinch Township but was mainly drawn from Waterloo and Brant Counties.

1477. Preston Evangelical Lutheran. **Deaths. Register, 1855; 1860.** mf. Loc: NAC. FA: C-15758.
   The congregation included some members from Puslinch Township, but was mainly drawn from Waterloo and Brant Counties.

1478. Preston Evangelical Lutheran. **Marriages. Register, 1855.** mf. Loc: NAC. FA: C-15758.
   The congregation included some members from Puslinch Township, but was mainly drawn from Waterloo and Brant Counties.

METHODIST CHURCH RECORDS - CENTRAL

1479. Guelph District Methodist Church. **Correspondence with Prime Minister's Office regarding gambling, 1905.** Loc: NAC. FA #91.
   In Laurier Papers, pages 97813-97815.

1480. Methodist Church of Canada. **Conference. Minutes, 1883-1925.** 42 volumes. Loc: UCA.
   A series of published annual reports which includes references to the Guelph Conference which included Wellington County and other areas until 1895 when it became part of the Hamilton Conference. The reports include answers to questions pertaining to membership totals, local conference officials appointed, attendance figures of Sunday Schools and of financial expenditures. The reports refer to three circuits within Wellington County, including Guelph, Palmerston and Mount Forest.

1481. Methodist Church of Canada. **Minutes, 1884.** 80 p. Loc: UGL.
   A record of the minutes of the conference, held at Clinton in June 1884, that includes lists of Guelph District ministers, church membership and the amount of ministerial support given by each congregation. The minutes focus on general resolutions and committee reports of the Methodist Church in Ontario.

1482. Wesleyan Methodist Church of Canada. **Methodist Missionary Society. Reports, 1842-1921.** 60 volumes. Loc: UCA.
   Published reports of foreign, Indian and domestic missionary work that includes written assessments of particular congregations. The reports list individuals from each congregation and the amount of money each subscribed or donated to the work. In the 1858 report, the various missions are divided into districts, one of which is named 'Guelph District'. It included circuits centered in Guelph, Rockwood, Galt, Elora, Berlin, Blenheim, Peel, Georgetown,

Alma, Wallace and Howick. Branch missions of each circuit are also listed. By 1920, Guelph District included Norfolk Street, Dublin Street and Paisley Memorial Churches in Guelph, as well as churches in Elora, Fergus, Acton, Rockwood-Eramosa, Nassagaweya, Ponsonby, Belwood and Erin. Again all branches are noted if applicable. For example, three branches of Rockwood-Eramosa are noted as Bethel, Rockwood and Stone. Some volumes cover more than one year.

METHODIST CHURCH RECORDS - LOCAL

1483. Alma (Bethel) Meth-UC. **Women's Missionary Society. Minutes, 1920-1946.** 4 volumes. Loc: UCA. Card index.
Bethel Church was part of the Alma circuit.

1484. Alma (Bethel) UC. **Official Board. Minutes, 1925-1942.** 1 volume. Loc: UCA. Card index.
The minutes refer to the board as the board of the Alma and Bethel United Churches, which were both in the same circuit or pastoral charge. The annual congregational meetings are recorded in the volume in chronological sequence with the board meetings. The records suggest that a two-point charge was administered by one board.

1485. Alma Meth-UC Circuit. **Register, 1903-1935.** 1 ledger. Loc: UCA. Card index.
A record of members' names that occasionally notes when membership began and whether removed by change of boundary, letter, or death. The names are entered by geographical division of the circuit: Alma, Zion, Bethel, Creekbank, and Parker.

1486. Alma Meth-UC. **Deaths. Register, 1911-1912; 1930-1964.** 1 ledger. Loc: UCA. Card index.
A record of name, age, birthplace, cause of death, date, place of burial and name of minister. The records of baptisms, marriages, and deaths are held in the same ledger.

1487. Alma Meth-UC. **Marriages. Registers, 1911-1964.** 2 ledgers. Loc: UCA. Card index.
The marriage register is in the ledger with the birth and death registers. It records the full names of the bride and groom, age, station, residence, birthplace, religion, father's name, mother's maiden name, number and date of license, place and date of marriage and witnesses. The first register covers the years from 1911 to 1936, and the second register covers the years from 1913 to 1964. The second register records name, age, groom's occupation, usual residence, place of birth, previous marital status, religion, name of parents, witnesses and minister.

1488. Alma Meth-UC. **Quarterly Board. Minutes, 1884-1897; 1907-1926; 1931.** 2 volumes. Loc: UCA. Card index.
The minutes also include annual financial statements for the church. The Alma Church was the central point of a larger Methodist circuit that included small congregations at Creekbank, Bethel, Zion, and Parker. In 1925, the Alma Methodist Church became the Alma United Church.

1489. Alma Methodist Circuit. **Annual report, 1887-1888.** 1 document. Loc: WCA.
A printed record of receipts and expenditures which list the names and amount of donations by church members in the Alma, Zion, Bethel and Bloomsbury appointments. The report is for the year ending May 1888. The report is held with the Pollock Collection.

1490. Alma UC. **Annual financial statements, 1927; 1929; 1935-1944; 1946; 1953-1962; 1964; 1966-1971.** 35 brochures. Loc: UCA. Card index.

1491. Alma UC. **Baptisms. Register, 1930-1964.** 1 ledger. Loc: UCA. Card index.
A record of full name, residence, parents' names, date of birth, place of birth, date of baptism, place of baptism and officiating minister. The records of baptisms, marriage and deaths are held in the same ledger.

1492. Alma UC. **Historic roll, 1942-1966.** 1 ledger. Loc: UCA. Card index.
A record of members' names that occasionally notes when membership began and when removed by letter or death. The names are entered by geographical division of the circuit: Alma, Goldstone and Bethel.

1493. Alma UC. **Session. Minutes, 1925-1943.** Loc: UCA. Card index.
According to card index and record box, these records exist, but they could not be located by the GRP researchers.

1494. Amaranth MEpi. **Baptisms. Registers, 1849-1851; 1853-1858.** 1 ledger, 1 file folder. Loc: UCA. Card index.
A listing of the names of children, their date of birth and baptism and the names of their parents. The record of baptisms from 1853 to 1858 are held in the same ledger as the minutes of the quarterly board of the church for the period 1849 to 1884.

1495. Amaranth MEpi. **Church Building. Correspondence, 1849-1852.** 1 file folder. Loc: UCA. Card index.
A series of letters outlining plans to construct a church, including projections concerning the cost and structure of the building.

1496. Amaranth MEpi. **Quarterly Board. Minutes, 1849-1884; 1887.** 1 volume. Loc: UCA. Card index.
A record of minutes with the meetings convening in Orangeville Chapel. The minutes list board members attending meetings and provide financial statements for areas under the jurisdiction of the mission including Orangeville, Garafraxa Township and Melville. The minutes are held in the same ledger as the baptismal records from 1853 to 1858.

1497. Belwood Meth Circuit. **Marriages. Registers, 1890-1923.** 1 reel. mf. Loc: WCA.
A small number of entries with the religious affiliation of the circuit not being clearly labelled.

1498. Belwood Meth Circuit. **Register, 1914-1923.** 1 ledger. Loc: UCA. Card index.

1499. Clifford MNew-Meth. **Mortgage. Records, 1870; 1873-1879; 1889; 1901; 1909.** 2 file folders. Loc: UCA. Card index.
A record of the holding of land by the church including a total of twelve

original indenture and land declaration documents.

1500. Coningsby Meth. **Sunday School. Attendance, 1891**. 1 ledger. Loc: WCA. MU68.

1501. Damascus Meth. **Epworth League. Record books, 1895-1915**. 2 ledgers. Loc: UCA. Card index.

A record of active and associate members which lists the attendance of specific individuals and periodically outlines election of officers and the collections, contributions and expenditures of the organization.

1502. Damascus Meth. **Missionary Society. Subscription lists, 1907-1923**. 1 ledger. Loc: UCA. Card index.

An annual record of the amount of money donated by residents of Damascus and Mount View to the society with the two places listed as part of the Mount Forest District.

1503. Damascus Meth-UC. **Annual reports, 1904; 1908-1913; 1915-1932**. 1 file folder. Loc: UCA. Card index.

A record of the treasurer's reports of Mount View Methodist Church for the years 1904 and 1908 and of the annual financial statements of the Damascus Circuit Methodist Church from 1909 to 1913, and from 1915 to 1932. The records note the names of church subscribers and the amount given, collections, and overall receipts and expenditures each year.

1504. Damascus Meth-UC. **Congregational Meetings. Minutes, 1931-1958**. 3 volumes. Loc: UCA. Card index.

The congregational meetings usually convened only once annually. The individual minute entries contain references to the work of other church associations and are often quite brief. The congregational minutes for the years 1931-1951 are held in the same volume as the minutes of the official board and of the stewards and the subscription lists of the church.

1505. Damascus Meth-UC. **Quarterly Board. Minutes, 1904-1940**. 1 volume. Loc: UCA. Card index.

The records are labelled as minutes of the 'Damascus Circuit'. The minutes list members present, stewards, collection of funds for expenses, and the election of representatives for various areas in the circuit including Holstein, Mount View and Damascus. The meetings were usually convened at least once for a given two month period. In 1925 the meetings begin to be referred to as 'Damascus Pastoral Charge'. The minutes of the quarterly board are held in the same volume as the minutes of the congregational meetings, stewards meetings and subscription lists.

1506. Damascus Meth-UC. **Subscriptions. Lists, 1911-1937**. 1 ledger. Loc: UCA. Card index.

The record lists members of the Damascus Circuit which included Mount View and Damascus. The ledger notes the amount specific individuals pledged to the church in each quarter of a given year. The subscription lists are held in the same ledger as the minutes of the stewards, congregational meetings, and the minutes of the official quarterly board.

1507. Damascus Meth-UC. **Sunday School. Records, 1900-1941.** 3 ledgers. Loc: UCA. Card index.

A record of attendance of students, names of teachers, and the annual meetings of the Sunday School officers. The attendance records are divided into boys, girls, infants, and bible classes.

1508. Damascus Meth-UC. **Treasurer. Account book, 1909; 1911-1958.** 2 ledgers. Loc: UCA. Card index.

A record of monthly collections and of receipts and expenditures of the church.

1509. Damascus Meth-UC. **Women's Missionary Society. Minutes, 1923-1938; 1947-1948.** 1 volume. Loc: UCA. Card index.

A record of meetings which convened once each month. The minutes list the executive of the society elected each year and outline the topics discussed at each monthly meeting.

1510. Damascus UC. **Ladies Aid. Minutes, 1932-1945.** 1 volume. Loc: UCA. Card index.

A record of monthly meetings that lists membership dues, expenditures and at times the financial balance of the organization. The volume also lists members of the association in various years, indicating the dues paid by specific members.

1511. Damascus UC. **Stewards. Minutes, 1936-1940.** 1 volume. Loc: UCA. Card index.

The meetings usually convened only once annually with only brief entries each year. The stewards minutes are held in the same volume as the minutes of congregational meetings, subscription lists of the church and the minutes of the official quarterly board.

1512. Drayton Meth-UC. **Financial statements, 1902-1903; 1912-1947.** 36 volumes. Loc: UCA. Card index.

A record of the auditor's report for the years 1902 to 1903, and of annual financial statements in individually bound volumes for Drayton Methodist, and later Drayton United Church. The auditor's report lists church members, noting the amount donated by specific individuals. The annual financial statements list receipts and expenditures, contributions to church funds noting names of those granting funds, and the financial reports of various church associations. The volumes are labelled Drayton and Zion United Churches beginning in 1933 and also include financial statements and the church directory from 1933 to 1947.

1513. Elora Meth-UC. **Baptisms. Registers, 1893-1957.** 1 reel. mf. Loc: WCA.

1514. Elora Meth-UC. **Burials. Registers, 1906-1963.** 1 reel. mf. Loc: WCA.

1515. Elora Meth-UC Circuit. **Registers, 1883-1904; 1906-1925.** 1 reel. mf. Loc: WCA.

1516. Elora Meth-UC. **Marriages. Registers, 1896-1968.** 1 reel. mf. Loc: WCA.

1517. Elora Meth-UC. **Quarterly Board. Minutes and cash books, 1866-1911; 1933-1974.** 1 reel. mf. Loc: WCA.

1518. Eramosa Meth Circuit. **Financial report, 1898**. 1 report. Loc: WCA. MU13.
The statement lists contributors from individuals in the three circuit churches: Stone, Bethel and Everton.

1519. Eramosa Meth. **Quarterly Board. Minutes, 1917-1925**. 1 volume. Loc: UCA. Card index.
In 1920, the charge was called 'Rockwood-Eramosa Circuit'.

1520. Eramosa (Stone) UC. **Congregational Meetings. Minutes, 1926-1965**. 1 volume. Loc: UCA. Card index.
The membership roll from 1925 to 1958 is also recorded in the same ledger.

1521. Eramosa (Stone) UC. **Membership. Rolls, 1925-1958**. 1 ledger. Loc: UCA. Card index.
The congregational minutes from 1926 to 1965 are also recorded in the same ledger.

1522. Erin Meth. **Quarterly Board. Minutes, 1901-1925**. 1 file folder. Loc: UCA. Card index.
A record of meetings of the Erin Circuit which outlines activities, lists attendance of members and notes financial returns for areas in the circuit, including Erin, Ballinafad and Coningsby. The record is not identified as a Methodist Circuit but the minutes refer to Methodist church activities.

1523. Erin Meth-UC Circuit. **Register, 1904-1928**. 1 ledger. Loc: UCA. Card index.
A record of Erin Methodist Circuit which notes members living in Erin, Ballinafad and Coningsby.

1524. Erin Meth-UC. **Marriages. Register, 1896-1950**. 1 ledger. Loc: UCA. Card index.
A record of marriages in Erin, Coningsby and Ballinafad which does not regularly indicate the names of churches where ceremonies were held.

1525. Fergus Meth. **Marriages. Registers, 1849-1859; 1897-1947**. 2 ledgers. Loc: UCA. Card index.

1526. Fergus Meth. **Trustees' Meetings. Minutes, 1885-1926**. 1 volume. Loc: UCA. Card index.

1527. Glenallan Meth. **Official Board. Minutes, 1911-1920**. 1 volume. Loc: UCA. Card index.
The meetings usually convened once every two to three months. The minutes include brief financial statements and lists of members present.

1528. Glenallan Meth-UC. **Parsonage Trustee Board. Minutes, 1896-1902; 1933**. 1 volume. Loc: UCA. Card index.
A record of the meeting of the board of the Peel Methodist Circuit held in Glenallan which lists members of the board and brief financial statements and references to the formation of special committees. The minutes periodically include a listing of Glenallan parsonage subscriptions noting the amount specific individuals gave the church. The board minutes are held in the same ledger as the subscription lists of the circuit.

1529. Goldstone UC Circuit. **Financial statements, 1931; 1934-1935.** 2 reports. Loc: WCA. MU12.

Annual reports of the Goldstone circuit which includes Goldstone and Goshen. The reports list the names and amounts subscribed by specific members and the finances of various church clubs and associations.

1530. Goshen Meth. **Financial accounts, 1889-1912.** 1 ledger. Loc: WCA. MU12.

A record of receipts and expenditures tabulated in an inconsistent manner. The financial accounts are held in the same ledger as the trustee minutes of the church.

1531. Goshen Meth. **Financial records, 1900-1911.** Loc: WCA. MU12.

Financial statements of the church with number of references to receipts and expenditures for the construction of a shed.

1532. Goshen Meth-Pres. **Committee Reports. Minutes, 1882-1885.** 1 volume. Loc: UCA. Card index.

A record of a committee for construction of a new church and for general public meetings of the congregation. The volume contains only a few brief entries.

1533. Goshen Meth. **Trustee Board. Minutes, 1886-1922.** 1 volume. Loc: WCA. MU12.

A record of meetings held two to three times annually. The minutes indicate members present and motions passed by the board. The minutes are held in the same ledger as the financial accounts of the church.

1534. Goshen Sunday School. **Annual Meetings. Minutes, 1904-1916.** 2 volumes. Loc: WCA. MU12.

Minutes list individuals active on committees and report motions carried at each session. The ledger is not labelled as being part of a specific church but is held with records of the Goshen Methodist Church. The minutes covering the period 1904 to 1908 are in very poor condition. The minutes are held in the same ledger as the attendance registers of the Sunday School.

1535. Goshen Sunday School. **Attendance registers, 1908-1917.** 1 ledger. Loc: WCA. MU12.

A weekly listing of the number of students attending the school. The attendance registers are held in the same ledger as the minutes of the Sunday School and held with the records of the Goshen Methodist Church.

1536. Goshen UC. **Annual Meetings. Minutes, 1928-1938.** 1 volume. Loc: WCA. MU12.

A record of church administrators elected and of the activities of various church clubs and associations.

1537. Guelph (Dublin Street) Meth-UC. **Baptisms, burials and marriages, 1909-1983.** 3 volumes. Loc: GDU.

Each volume has sections for baptisms, marriages and burials. Baptismal records include details of place and date of birth, parents' names and place of residence. Burial records indicate birthplace, age at death and cause of death (until August 1970).

1538. Guelph (Dublin Street) Meth-UC. **Board of Trustees. Minutes, 1873-1985.** 1 volume. Loc: GDU.

Minutes of discussions held irregularly but approximately quarterly. The church was at first known as Second Wesleyan Church, Guelph.

1539. Guelph (Dublin Street) Meth-UC. **Marriages. Registers, 1888-1982.** 6 volumes. Loc: GDU.

Marriages for the period 1943 to 1965 are included in the general records for those years. The records include details of age, birthplace, religious denomination, previous marital status of both parties, and groom's occupation, as well as marriage license number and names of witnesses.

1540. Guelph (Dublin Street) Meth-UC. **Official Board/Session. Minutes, 1879-1928; 1950-1973.** 4 books. Loc: GDU.

Detailed records of the meetings including financial statements for some years.

1541. Guelph (Dublin Street) UC. **United Church Women. Minutes, 1958-1978.** 1 file. Loc: GDU.

Detailed reports of meetings and monthly and annual reports of the organization which was known as the Women's Missionary Society until 1962. Filed with the minute book are copies of a special order of service and a history of the Women's Missionary Society.

1542. Guelph (Dublin Street) UC. **Young People's Association Executive. Minutes, 1927-1938.** 1 book. Loc: GDU.

Detailed minutes of monthly meetings.

1543. Guelph MPri. **Account book, 1876-1884.** 1 ledger. Loc: UCA. Card index.

The accounts are divided by the localities of Guelph, Beech Grove and Paisley Block.

1544. Guelph MPri. **Baptisms. Register, 1857-1878.** 1 ledger. Loc: UCA. Card index.

The ledger also records deaths from 1857 to 1858, quarterly board minutes from 1856 to 1877, and membership from 1856 to 1877.

1545. Guelph MPri. **Cash books, 1871-1876.** 1 ledger. Loc: UCA. Card index.

The ledger also records trustees' meetings from 1876 to 1878.

1546. Guelph MPri. **Deaths. Register, 1857-1858.** 2 ledgers. Loc: UCA. Card index.

The ledger also records membership from 1858 to 1867, quarterly board minutes from 1856 to 1877, and baptisms from 1857 to 1878.

1547. Guelph MPri. **Marriages. Register, 1859-1879.** 1 ledger. Loc: UCA. Card index.

1548. Guelph MPri. **Membership. List, 1859-1867.** 1 ledger. Loc: UCA. Card index.

The ledger also records deaths from 1857 to 1858, quarterly board minutes from 1856 to 1877, and baptisms from 1857 to 1878.

1549. Guelph MPri. **Quarterly Board. Minutes, 1856-1884.** 2 volumes. Loc: UCA. Card index.

The first meeting in 1856 records the division of the Guelph Primitive

Methodist Mission from the Galt and Guelph Primitive Methodist Mission. The 1856 to 1877 volume also records members from 1859 to 1867, deaths from 1857 to 1858, and baptisms from 1857 to 1878.

1550. Guelph MPri. **Sabbath School Teachers' Meetings. Minutes, 1856-1859.** 1 volume. Loc: UCA. Card index.

The volume also records Sunday School attendance for the same years.

1551. Guelph MPri. **Sunday School. Attendance register, 1856-1859.** 1 ledger. Loc: UCA. Card index.

The ledger also records minutes of teachers' meetings for the same years.

1552. Guelph MPri. **Trustees' Meetings. Minutes, 1876-1878.** 1 volume. Loc: UCA. Card index.

The volume also records financial accounts from 1871 to 1876.

1553. Guelph (Norfolk Street) Meth. **Sunday School. Attendance register, 1844-1847.** 1 ledger. Loc: GCM.

The front page of the ledger indicates that the school was established in 1836. The ledger lists the weekly attendance of teachers and students. The record is held in a box entitled, Organizations.

1554. Guelph (Norfolk Street) Meth. **Sunday School. Fund ledger, 1849-1906.** 1 ledger. Loc: GNU.

1555. Guelph (Norfolk Street) Meth-UC. **Attendance. Register, 1917-1936.** 1 ledger. Loc: GNU.

Pages 2 to 40 are missing.

1556. Guelph (Norfolk Street) Meth-UC. **Board of Trustees. Minutes, 1855-1953.** 2 books. Loc: GNU.

Detailed accounts of proceedings of meetings which were held irregularly, but more often than monthly. The first volume, covering 1855 to 1886, has several newspaper clippings pasted in, describing the construction, improvements and reopening of the church building. Several handwritten bonds are included, as well as receipts from the Guelph Daily Mercury and Wagon Shop.

1557. Guelph (Norfolk Street) Meth-UC. **Cash receipts, 1906-1932.** 1 ledger. Loc: GNU.

Weekly entries summarizing receipts and disbursements with several financial statements held loosely in the book.

1558. Guelph (Norfolk Street) Meth-UC. **Church Register. Baptisms, 1920-1948; Burials, 1920-1948; Marriages, 1920-1921.** 1 book. Loc: GNU.

1559. Guelph (Norfolk Street) Meth-UC. **Marriages. Registers, 1857-1882; 1896-1957.** 5 ledgers. Loc: GNU.

Details include name, place of birth, residence, age, parents' names of both bride and groom, as well as witnesses' names and addresses and date of marriage. From 1936, the license number is also included.

1560. Guelph (Norfolk Street) Meth-UC. **Membership. Registers ?-1893; 1921-1928; 1936.** 3 ledgers. Loc: GNU.

1561. Guelph (Norfolk Street) Meth-UC. **Quarterly Board. Minutes, 1865-1899; 1931-1966.** 4 books. Loc: GNU.
Detailed proceedings reported by the recording steward to 1922, by the minister and secretary later. Loosely included are the financial statement for 1894, the treasurer's report for 1897 and annual reports for 1940 and 1941.

1562. Guelph (Norfolk Street) Meth-UC. **Sunday School Board. Minutes, 1883-1889; 1928-1960.** 3 books. Loc: GNU.
Minutes include attendance and reports of meeting discussions, as well as semi-quarterly, quarterly and annual reports.

1563. Guelph (Norfolk Street) Meth-UC. **Sunday School. Records, 1918-1924; 1928-1931.** 2 ledgers. Loc: GNU.
Records of attendance of officers and teachers, and details of attendance and offerings of each class. Names of secretaries and treasurers, cash accounts and weather on day of school are all included.

1564. Guelph (Norfolk Street) Meth-UC. **Sunday School. Roll book, 1898-1934.** 1 book. Loc: GNU.
Lists of members of the Sunday School classes in all years.

1565. Guelph (Norfolk Street) Meth-UC. **Weekly Offerings. Ledgers, 1896-1906; 1931-1936; 1944; 1953; 1955; 1957.** 3 ledgers. Loc: GNU.
The earliest ledger also contains loose copies of the annual reports for 1886, 1891, 1893, 1895, 1898 and 1899 that identify church officers and provide financial statements.

1566. Guelph (Norfolk Street) UC. **Building Fund. Treasurer's reports, 1926-1942.** 1 ledger. Loc: GNU.

1567. Guelph (Norfolk Street) UC. **Christian Education Committee. Minutes, 1962-1974.** 1 book. Loc: GNU.

1568. Guelph (Norfolk Street) UC. **Communion. Rolls, 1937-1941; 1943-1947; 1953-1972; 1975-1981.** 6 books. Loc: GNU.

1569. Guelph (Norfolk Street) UC. **Session. Minutes, 1945-1970.** 1 book. Loc: GNU.
Detailed minutes of monthly meetings.

1570. Guelph (Norfolk Street) UC. **Stewards' Meeting. Minutes, 1926-1936; 1944-1969.** 4 volumes. Loc: GNU.
Detailed minutes and records of accounts and receipts.

1571. Guelph (Norfolk Street) UC. **United Church Women. Minutes, 1962-1967.** 1 book. Loc: GNU.

1572. Guelph (Norfolk Street) UC. **Young Ladies Bible Class. Reports, 1936-1940.** 1 book. Loc: GNU.
Minutes of monthly meetings.

1573. Guelph (Paisley) Meth Circuit. **Register, 1888-1908.** 1 ledger. Loc: UCA. Card index.

1574. Guelph (Paisley) Meth. **Official Board. Minutes, 1901-1931.** 2 volumes. Loc: UCA. Card index.

1575. Guelph (Paisley) Meth. **Sunday School Teachers' Meetings. Minutes, 1905-1916.** 1 volume. Loc: UCA. Card index.

1576. Guelph (Paisley) Meth. **Trustee Board. Cash book, 1908-1912.** 1 ledger. Loc: UCA. Card index.

1577. Guelph (Paisley) Meth-UC. **Marriages. Register, 1897-1928.** 1 ledger. Loc: UCA. Card index.

1578. Guelph (Paisley) Meth-UC. **Trustee Board. Minutes, 1907-1936.** 1 volume. Loc: UCA. Card index.

1579. Guelph (Paisley) UC. **Congregational Meetings. Minutes, 1931-1937.** 1 volume. Loc: UCA. Card index.

1580. Nassagaweya MNew-Meth. **Quarterly Board. Minutes, 1853-1916.** 3 volumes. Loc: UCA. Card index.
    The records include references to Salem, Eramosa Township and Ebenezer until 1859, and after that date only to Ebenezer.

1581. Nichol (Zion) Meth. **Financial statements, 1868-1869.** Loc: AO. FA: MU 2956.
    Part of Templin Family Collection.

1582. Orangeville MPri. **Baptisms. Registers, 1852-1881.** 1 ledger. Loc: UCA. Card index.

1583. Orangeville MPri. **Class lists, 1855.** 1 ledger. Loc: UCA. Card index.
    A record of the names of members by area including references to Orangeville and Garafraxa Township. It is held in the same ledger as the baptismal register, quarterly board minutes and membership rolls of the church.

1584. Orangeville MPri. **Membership. Roll, 1877.** 1 ledger. Loc: UCA. Card index.
    A listing of the names of members in 1877 residing in Orangeville or Garafraxa Township. It is held in the same ledger as the quarterly board minutes, class lists and baptismal registers.

1585. Orangeville MPri. **Quarterly Board. Minutes, 1855-1886.** 2 volumes. Loc: UCA. Card index.
    A record of meetings which lists activities and present more detailed financial statements than most early church minute books. The minutes from 1855 to 1878 are held in the same volume as the baptismal register, class lists and membership roll of the church.

1586. Peel Meth Circuit. **Quarterly Official Board. Minutes, 1862-1911.** 4 volumes. Loc: UCA. Card index.
    A record of the minutes of the Peel Wesleyan Methodist Circuit which included

Drayton, Hays, Goshen, Glenallen, Spring Hill, Hollin and several other small centres. The board usually met at least once every two to three months.

1587. Peel Meth Circuit. **Register, 1884-1904.** 1 ledger. Loc: UCA. Card index.
    A record of membership in the Peel Methodist Circuit which included Glenallan, Hollin, Spring Hill and Olivet. The register notes the names of members, where they lived and when they entered or left the church. The details of entries for each individuals varies, but the address of each is usually stated.

1588. Peel Meth Circuit. **Subscriptions. Lists, 1873-1876.** 1 ledger. Loc: UCA. Card index.
    A listing of the names of subscribers and the amount to the Peel Methodist Circuit by specific individuals. For the year 1876 the ledger notes the local settlements promising funds 'for the liquidation of the parsonage debt'. The subscription lists are held in the same ledger as the minutes of the parsonage trustee board of the circuit.

1589. Peel MPri. **Baptisms. Registers, 1845-1858.** mf. Loc: NAC. FA: C-15758.
    The congregation was also drawn from Wellesley Township in Waterloo County.

1590. Peel MPri. **Deaths. Register, 1858.** mf. Loc: NAC. FA: C-15758.
    The congregation was also drawn from Wellesley Township in Waterloo County.

1591. Rockwood Meth. **Quarterly Board. Minutes, 1887-1924.** 1 volume. Loc: UCA. Card index.

1592. Rockwood MWes-Meth. **Baptisms. Register, 1863-1909.** 1 ledger. Loc: UCA. Card index.
    Marriages from 1861 to 1909, and burials from 1902 to 1909 are also recorded in the same ledger.

1593. Rockwood MWes-Meth. **Burials. Register, 1902-1909.** 1 ledger. Loc: UCA. Card index.
    Baptisms from 1863 to 1909, and marriages from 1861 to 1909 are also recorded in the same ledger.

1594. Rockwood MWes-Meth Circuit. **Registers, 1858-1882; 1884-1904.** 2 ledgers. Loc: UCA. Card index.
    The church accounts for the years 1858 to 1875 are also recorded in the same ledger.

1595. Rockwood MWes-Meth. **Financial statements, 1858-1875.** 1 ledger. Loc: UCA. Card index.
    The circuit register from 1858 to 1882 is also recorded in the same ledger. The record is entitled 'Statistical History of the Rockwood Mission' and lists for each year minister; amount of money raised in Rockwood, Eden Mills, Everton and Arkell; number of members; amount of money spent in various categories; and amount owing for minister's salary.

1596. Rockwood MWes-Meth. **Marriages. Registers, 1861-1961.** 3 ledgers. Loc: UCA. Card index.
    Baptisms from 1863 to 1909 and burials from 1902 to 1909 are also recorded in

the first ledger. The first ledger records marriages from 1861 to 1909, the second from 1896 to 1961, and the third from 1896 to 1953 which is inscribed, 'Methodist Church, Eramosa Circuit'.

1597. Rockwood MWes-Meth. **Trustee Board. Minutes, 1868-1925.** 1 volume. Loc: UCA. Card index.

1598. Stirton Meth Circuit. **Financial statements, 1903; 1906; 1910-1912; 1914-1928.** 20 reports. Loc: WCA. MU 12, 19.
    Reports of receipts and expenditures for charges in Stirton, Goldstone and Goshen which were part of the Stirton Methodist Circuit. The reports also list names and amounts of specific member subscriptions and the finances of various church clubs and associations. The 1903 report is held in MU19.

1599. Stirton Meth-UC Circuit. **Register, 1886-1930.** 1 ledger. Loc: UCA. Card index.

1600. Stirton Meth-UC. **Marriages. Registers, 1897-1938.** 1 ledger. Loc: UCA. Card index.
    A record of marriages in Wellington County, with references to ceremonies in Stirton, Goldstone, Winfield and Peel Township.

PRESBYTERIAN CHURCH RECORDS - CENTRAL

1601. Church Union Movement. **Correspondence, newspaper clippings and pamphlets, 1911-1925.** 6 boxes, 4 linear feet. Loc: PCA. Preliminary finding aid.
    Miscellaneous papers relating to the movement within the Presbyterian Church in favour of church union with the Methodist and Congregational churches. The origins of the collection are uncertain but the individuals mainly responsible are believed to have been Frank Yeigh, William H. Rochester and Austin L. Budge. The collection includes, in Box 1, materials reporting the church union debate of 1911-1915 and the Survey of Church Conditions made by the Joint Committee (1912, 54 pages). Box 6, Files 1-3 contain materials on the work of the Presbyterian Church Association which was dedicated to maintaining the separate identity of the Presbyterian Church in Canada.

1602. Guelph Presbyterial, W.M.S. **Account book, 1885-1914; Treasurer's book, 1907-1908.** 2 ledgers. Loc: PCA. FA-WMSSP.

1603. Guelph Presbyterial, W.M.S. **Annual Meetings and Rallies. Minutes, 1925-1962.** Loc: PCA. FA-WMSSP.

1604. Guelph Presbyterial, W.M.S. **Executive. Minutes, 1884-1888; 1900-1914; 1925-1955.** Loc: PCA. FA-WMSSP.

1605. Guelph Presbyterial, W.M.S. **Historical reports of auxiliaries, 1934-1951.** Loc: PCA. FA-WMSSP.
    Annual reports on activities of auxiliaries submitted by Presbyterial Historian.

1606. Guelph Presbytery. **Minutes of meeting, 16 May 1905.** 1 p. typescript. Loc: PCA. Card index.

1607. Guelph Presbytery. **Report on statistics, 1883-1884.** 1 brochure. Loc: GPL.
A report of attendance and income for all the churches in the Presbytery, which includes congregations in Fergus, Elora, Mimosa, Garafraxa and East Puslinch, Alma and Nichol, Hillsburgh, Erin and Ospringe, Eramosa, Glenallan, Rockwood and Eden Mills. The brochure is held in the Brimmell Collection.

1608. **A history of the Presbyterian churches in the Presbytery of Guelph, c1950.** 80 p. typescript. Loc: PCA. Card index.
An outline history of each of the churches in the Presbytery, including Acton (Knox), Alma, Ayr (Knox), Baden (Livingston), Campbellville (St David's), Doon, Elmira (Gale), Elora (Knox), Fergus (St Andrew's), Galt (St Andrew's), Galt (Knox) Galt (Central), Guelph (St Andrew's), Guelph (Knox), Hespeler, Kitchener, Nassagaweya, Puslinch (Knox), Puslinch (Duff's), Waterloo (Knox) and Winterbourne (Chalmers). Only those churches that continued in the Presbyterian Church after 1925 are included.

1609. Presbyterian Church Association. **Correspondence, account books, minute books, advertisements, newspaper clippings, 1914-1925.** 4 cases. Loc: PCA. Preliminary finding aid by Rev. N.K. Clifford, 1973.
Files of the Reverend J.W. MacNamara, secretary of the organization to preserve the separate identity of the Presbyterian Church in Canada. Correspondence is filed alphabetically by surname and by year. There are copies of the mailing list and of all advertisements and reports on the results of the 1925 vote on church union in every presbytery and congregation (File 51, Case 3).

1610. Presbyterian Church in Canada. **Acts and proceedings of General Assemblies, 1875-.** 114 vols. Loc: PCA.
Annual printed volumes summarizing the status of the church at all levels of organization and including systematic statistical and financial information about each congregation. Study of past volumes shows that the Presbyterian congregations of southern Wellington County were grouped in Guelph Presbytery (with those of Waterloo County) while northwestern Wellington County was part of the Saugeen Presbytery. The Guelph and Saugeen Presbyteries were joined in the late 1960s and are now called the Waterloo-Wellington Presbytery. In 1988, the following congregations are part of the Waterloo-Wellington Presbytery: Knox, Elora (including St Andrew's, Alma); St Andrew's, Arthur (including St Andrew's, Gordonville); Knox, Palmerston (including Knox, Drayton); St Andrew's, Fergus; St Andrew's, Mount Forest (including Knox, Conn); St Andrew's, Guelph; Knox, Guelph; Westminster-St Paul's, Guelph; Duff's, Puslinch (including Knox, Crieff); and Rockwood (including Eden Mills). Congregations in the northeastern part of Wellington County are part of the Brampton Presbytery: Burns, Erin (including Knox, Ospringe); St Andrew's, Hillsburgh (including Bethel, Price's Corners); Knox, Grand Valley; and Orangeville (Tweedsmuir Memorial).

PRESBYTERIAN (CONTINUING) CHURCH RECORDS - LOCAL

1611. Arthur (St Andrew's) Pres. **Baptisms. Register, 1883-1950.** Loc: PCA. Card index.

1612. Arthur (St Andrew's) Pres. **Communion. Rolls, 1878-1881; 1885-1887; 1899-1904.** 3 file folders. Loc: WCA. MU68.

Photocopies of the originals which are held at the church.

1613. Arthur (St Andrew's) Pres. **Marriages. Registers, 1899-1973.** 3 file folders. Loc: WCA. MU 68.
Photocopies of the originals which are held at the church.

1614. Arthur (St Andrew's) Pres. **Session. Minutes, 1883-1964.** mf. Loc: PCA. Card index.

1615. Elora (Knox) Pres. **Annual reports, 1910-1958 (sporadic).** 48 reports. Loc: WCA, PCA. MU 12.
A series of printed reports of the activities of church officials, clubs and associations and of receipts and expenditures of the congregation. WCA has 1910-1916; 1918-1953. PCA has 1901; 1925-1932; 1934-1949; 1951-1953; 1955-1958.

1616. Elora (Knox) Pres. **Baptisms. Registers, 1837-1948.** 1 reel. mf. Loc: WCA.
The church was first called United Associate Church of Nichol, then United Presbyterian Church of Elora and, from 1865, Knox Presbyterian Church of Elora.

1617. Elora (Knox) Pres. **Communion Roll. Registers, 1854-1860; 1877-1890.** mf. Loc: AO.

1618. Elora (Knox) Pres. **Concert programs, 1911; 1914; 1916.** 4 booklets. Loc: GPL.
Programs of banquets and musical concerts held at the church.

1619. Elora (Knox) Pres. **Congregational Meetings. Minutes, 1837-1850.** 1 reel. mf. Loc: WCA.

1620. Elora (Knox) Pres. **Constitution, 1865.** 1 document. Loc: WCA. MU 33.
A photocopy of the original constitution.

1621. Elora (Knox) Pres. **Constitution of the congregation, 1870.** 5 p. Loc: PCA.
Copy from a booklet.

1622. Elora (Knox) Pres. **Marriages. Registers, 1856-1970.** 1 reel. mf. Loc: WCA, AO.
The Archives of Ontario has registers for 1856-1900 while the Wellington County Archives has those for 1897-1970.

1623. Elora (Knox) Pres. **Open letter by Henry Wissler, October 10, 1898.** 1 broadside. Loc: WCA, UGA, PCA.
Text of open letter by Wissler explaining his criticisms of the 'arbitrary, overbearing and unconstitutional conduct' of the Reverend John McInnis who had condemned Wissler from the pulpit for his opposition. McInnis was criticized for introducing new practices into services of worship and for ignoring the opposition of the Session.

1624. Elora (Knox) Pres. **Session. Minutes, 1837-1850; 1856-1901.** mf. Loc: AO, PCA.

1625. Elora (Knox) Pres. **War Memorial Window Dedication. Program, 1921.** 1 brochure. Loc: WCA. MU 45A.

1626. Fergus (St Andrew's) Pres. **Annual report, 1871.** 1 document. Loc: WCA. MU 66.
A printed report of receipts and expenditures which is held in the Byerly

Collection at the Wellington County Archives.

1627. Fergus (St Andrew's) Pres. **Annual report, 1922.** Loc: GPL.
Financial statements and reports of the church's various committees, clubs and organizations.

1628. Fergus (St Andrew's) Pres. **Annual reports, 1894-1924.** 1 reel. mf. Loc: UCA, PCA. Card index.
The reel also contains the church's baptismal register from 1837 to 1868 and marriage register from 1837 to 1845.

1629. Fergus (St Andrew's) Pres. **Appeal for contribution to pay off church debt, 1883.** Loc: AO. FA: MU 455.
Part of Byerly Papers.

1630. Fergus (St Andrew's) Pres. **Baptisms. Registers, 1837-1868.** 1 reel. mf. Loc: UCA. Card index.
The reel also contains the church's annual reports from 1894 to 1924 and marriage register from 1837 to 1845.

1631. Fergus (St Andrew's) Pres. **Baptisms. Registers, 1845-1900.** 1 reel. mf. Loc: WCA, AO, PCA.
The Presbyterian Church Archives also holds the original registers for 1836-1868.

1632. Fergus (St Andrew's) Pres. **Edict for induction of Rev. George Smellie, 1843.** Loc: PCA. Card index.

1633. Fergus (St Andrew's) Pres. **Letter from A.D. Fordyce (Trustee) to M.Y. Stark re inability of congregation to pay basic stipend of 100 pounds, 1842.** 3 p. Loc: PCA. Card index.

1634. Fergus (St Andrew's) Pres. **Letter of protest, 1845.** 1 document. Loc: WCA, AO. AO: MU 1016; WCA: MU 13.
A copy of the original letter in which certain trustees, elders, deacons and 'vast majority' of the congregation protest recent doctrinal statements of the Church of Scotland. The letter concludes by stating 'while leaving for the present the Church and other property belonging to the congregation of St Andrew's Church, Fergus, we protest that we do not thereby compromise our right at any future period to assert an interest in these premises and that we are most unjustly and unwarrantably interfered with'. The letter is signed 'G. Smellie, Minister', and forty leaders and members of the church. Burr Collection at the Wellington County Archives has a handwritten copy of the original letter. Adam Fergusson Papers at the Archives of Ontario.

1635. Fergus (St Andrew's) Pres. **Marriages. Registers, 1837-1845.** 1 reel. mf. Loc: UCA, PCA. Card index.
The reel also contains the church's annual reports from 1894 to 1924 and baptismal register from 1837 to 1868.

1636. Fergus (St Andrew's) Pres. **Sabbath School. Report, 1882.** 2 p. Loc: PCA. Card index.

1637. Guelph (Knox) Pres. **Annual reports, 1874-1935 (sporadic).** Loc: PCA. Card index.
   The Presbyterian Archives holds reports for 1874, 1904, 1905, 1918-1923, 1926, 1927, 1934 and 1935.

1638. Guelph (Knox) Pres. **Baptisms. Registers, 1853-1900.** 1 reel. mf. Loc: WCA, PCA, AO.

1639. Guelph (Knox) Pres. **Bible Class. Annual reports, 1914; 1916.** Loc: PCA. Card index.

1640. Guelph (Knox) Pres. **Bible Class. Minutes and attendance book, 1908-1916.** Loc: PCA. Card index.

1641. Guelph (Knox) Pres. **Biography of Alexander J. MacGillivray, 1867-1938.** 3 p. typescript. Loc: PCA. Card index.

1642. Guelph (Knox) Pres. **Board of Managers. Annual financial statements, 1893-1946 (sporadic).** 13 reports. Loc: PCA. Card index.
   Statements are held for 1893, 1895, 1902, 1928, 1935-1941 and 1945-1946.

1643. Guelph (Knox) Pres. **Board of Managers. Circular concerning pew rentals, 1865.** 1 page. Loc: PCA. Card index.

1644. Guelph (Knox) Pres. **Board of Managers. Minutes, 1915-1934.** Loc: PCA. Card index.

1645. Guelph (Knox) Pres. **Board of Managers. Report, 1866.** 2 p. Loc: PCA. Card index.

1646. Guelph (Knox) Pres. **Building Fund. Subscription list and treasurer's report, 1868; 1870.** 2 p. Loc: PCA. Card index.

1647. Guelph (Knox) Pres. **Choir. Minutes and register, 1894-1949.** 1 volume. Loc: PCA. Card index.
   Includes financial records.

1648. Guelph (Knox) Pres. **Communion Roll. Registers, 1848-1864; 1885-1905; 1911-1913; 1919-1925.** Loc: PCA. Card index.

1649. Guelph (Knox) Pres. **Congregational Meetings. Minutes, 1915-1934.** Loc: PCA. Card index.
   Minutes of the annual meetings.

1650. Guelph (Knox) Pres. **Constitution, n.d..** 6 p. Loc: PCA. Card index.

1651. Guelph (Knox) Pres. **Copy of 'Memorial' found in cornerstone of Old Knox Church, c1847.** Loc: PCA. Card index.
   The Memorial includes a history of the congregation.

1652. Guelph (Knox) Pres. **Documents and letters on early history, 1851-1853.** 15 items. Loc: PCA. Card index.

Included are references to the Reverend John G. MacGregor, Mark Y. Stark, Samuel Young, Evan MacDonald and the Presbytery of Hamilton.

1653. Guelph (Knox) Pres. **Financial Committee. Minutes, 1890.** Loc: PCA. Card index.

1654. Guelph (Knox) Pres. **Financial records, 1870; 1895.** 1 reel. mf. Loc: WCA.

1655. Guelph (Knox) Pres. **Financial reports, 1915-1934.** Loc: PCA. Card index.

1656. Guelph (Knox) Pres. **Financial statement, 1909.** Loc: PCA. Card index.

1657. Guelph (Knox) Pres. **Historical sketch of congregation, 1899.** 3 p. Loc: PCA. Card index.

Copied from an unidentified newspaper after Robert Martin's death in 1899.

1658. Guelph (Knox) Pres. **Ladies Aid. Minutes and financial reports, 1886-1941.** 4 volumes. Loc: PCA. Card index.

The volume for 1912-1919 includes Home Mission minutes.

1659. Guelph (Knox) Pres. **List of records in Archives at Knox College, received 1946.** 2 p. Loc: PCA. Card index.

1660. Guelph (Knox) Pres. **Membership. Change of address book and new members, 1915-1937.** Loc: PCA. Card index.

1661. Guelph (Knox) Pres. **Membership. Rolls, 1884; 1925.** Loc: PCA. Card index.

1662. Guelph (Knox) Pres. **Miscellaneous, 1944-1983.** 1 file. Loc: UGA. XR1 MS A069.

A miscellaneous collection of articles, pamphlets, photographs and newspaper clippings, including 100th anniversary service program, c1944 and a photographic montage c1954 displaying all ministers and church buildings since 1847.

1663. Guelph (Knox) Pres. **Mission Band. Minutes, 1890-1899.** 1 volume. Loc: PCA. Card index.

1664. Guelph (Knox) Pres. **Missionary Committee. Minutes, 1906-1907.** 1 volume. Loc: PCA. Card index.

1665. Guelph (Knox) Pres. **Missions. Treasurer's book, 1906-1916.** Loc: PCA. Card index.

1666. Guelph (Knox) Pres. **One hundred years at Knox Church, 1844-1944.** 56 p. Loc: PCA. Card index.

1667. Guelph (Knox) Pres. **Program for Scotch-Irish concert, March 1, 1904.** 1 p. Loc: PCA. Card index.

1668. Guelph (Knox) Pres. **Property. Cancelled mortgages, 1868-1911.** Loc: PCA. Card index.

Includes documents relating to 1868, 1869, 1874, 1878, 1881, 1890, 1897, 1898,

1900, 1905, 1911.

1669. Guelph (Knox) Pres. **Property. Deed of church site from Canada Company, 1849; 1868.** Loc: PCA. Card index.
Photocopy and original of the 1868 deed as well as other deeds.

1670. Guelph (Knox) Pres. **Property. Registrations of Knox Church property, 1869-1900 (sporadic).** 3 items. Loc: PCA. Card index.
Records are held for 1869, 1874 and 1904.

1671. Guelph (Knox) Pres. **Sabbath Offerings. Register, 1875-1885.** Loc: PCA. Card index.

1672. Guelph (Knox) Pres. **Sabbath School. Attendance register, 1898-1899.** Loc: PCA. Card index.

1673. Guelph (Knox) Pres. **Sabbath School. Collections, 1880-1897.** Loc: PCA. Card index.

1674. Guelph (Knox) Pres. **Sabbath School. Minutes, 1872-1881.** Loc: PCA. Card index.

1675. Guelph (Knox) Pres. **Session Fund. Records, 1884-1913.** Loc: PCA. Card index.

1676. Guelph (Knox) Pres. **Session. Membership list, 1931.** 3 p. Loc: PCA. Card index.

1677. Guelph (Knox) Pres. **Session. Minutes, 1847-1928.** Loc: PCA. Card index.

1678. Guelph (Knox) Pres. **Sunday School. Statistical reports, 1907-1908; 1916.** Loc: PCA. Card index.

1679. Guelph (Knox) Pres. **Visitation book, 1847.** Loc: PCA. Card index.

1680. Guelph (Knox) Pres. **Young People's Association. Minutes and membership list, 1930-1938.** Loc: PCA. Card index.

1681. Guelph (St Andrew's) Pres. **Anniversary programs, 1908; 1932-1933; 1951; 1953-1954; 1959; 1975; 1978.** 1 box. Loc: GSA.

1682. Guelph (St Andrew's) Pres. **Annual financial statements, 1859; 1919-1954.** 1 box. Loc: GSA.

1683. Guelph (St Andrew's) Pres. **Annual reports, 1887; 1891-1895; 1899-1902; 1904-1906; 1908-1910; 1913-1914; 1917; 1946; 1955-1984.** 6 boxes. Loc: GSA, PCA.
The annual report for 1887 is held in the archival box with church correspondence from 1857 to 1940. A copy of the 1906 annual report, including a church directory, is also held by the Presbyterian Church Archives.

1684. Guelph (St Andrew's) Pres. **Baptisms. Registers, 1821-1852; 1856-1872; 1878-1960.** 4 ledgers. Loc: GSA.

1685. Guelph (St Andrew's) Pres. **Baptisms. Registers, 1858-1899.** 1 reel. mf. Loc: WCA, AO.

1686. Guelph (St Andrew's) Pres. **Board of Managers. Minutes, 1880-1889; 1897-1908; 1918-1943; 1946-1954; 1955-1961.** 5 volumes. Loc: GSA.

1687. Guelph (St Andrew's) Pres. **Board of Managers. Reports and correspondence, 1877-1972 (sporadic).** 3 boxes. Loc: GSA.
    A collection of reports and correspondence regarding the business of the board.

1688. Guelph (St Andrew's) Pres. **Call to Reverend James Smith, 1831.** 1 framed document. Loc: GSA.
    The framed document hangs in the gallery of the church archives.

1689. Guelph (St Andrew's) Pres. **Cash books, 1870-1892.** 2 ledgers. Loc: GSA.
    The 1876 ledger holds a few financial statement and is held in the same ledger as the membership list for the year 1894.

1690. Guelph (St Andrew's) Pres. **Choir. Correspondence, 1882-1909.** 1 file folder. Loc: GSA.
    Correspondence regarding choir matters.

1691. Guelph (St Andrew's) Pres. **Collection book, 1865-1875.** 1 ledger. Loc: GSA.

1692. Guelph (St Andrew's) Pres. **Communion. Rolls, 1871-1876; 1878-1958; 1966-1970.** 17 ledgers. Loc: GSA.

1693. Guelph (St Andrew's) Pres. **Congregational Meetings. Minutes, 1836-1900.** mf. Loc: AO.

1694. Guelph (St Andrew's) Pres. **Congregational Meetings. Minutes and cash books, 1856-1900.** 1 reel. mf. Loc: WCA, AO.

1695. Guelph (St Andrew's) Pres. **Constitution, 1877.** 1 brochure. Loc: GSA.
    The constitution is held in a file folder entitled, 'General file St Andrew's and its people'.

1696. Guelph (St Andrew's) Pres. **Correspondence, 1857-1950.** 2 boxes, 1 wooden box. Loc: GSA.
    A collection of letters about membership records, speakers and business matters. The wooden box has the letters arranged alphabetically by name of sender and deal with appointment or resignation of church officials.

1697. Guelph (St Andrew's) Pres. **Daughters of St Andrew's. Program, 1926.** 1 file folder. Loc: GSA.
    A program for a banquet. Also included in the file is a pin worn by the King's Daughters of the church in the early 1900s.

1698. Guelph (St Andrew's) Pres. **Diary, 1858.** 1 file folder. Loc: UGA. XR1 MS A046.
    A small diary apparently connected with St Andrew's Church.

1699. Guelph (St Andrew's) Pres. **Donation book, 1875; 1888-1894.** 2 ledgers. Loc: GSA.

A record of the amounts members gave to the church.

1700. Guelph (St Andrew's) Pres. **Election and call of James Smith, 11 October 1831.**
11 p., photo. Loc: PCA.

1701. Guelph (St Andrew's) Pres. **Election of elders, 1909.** 1 bundle. Loc: GSA.
A series of voting ballots with each document listing six candidates in order
of preference. Each ballot is signed by the person casting it. The records are
held in a black box.

1702. Guelph (St Andrew's) Pres. **Genealogies, 1830-1900 (sporadic).** 1 file folder.
Loc: GSA.
Correspondence regarding genealogical searches of family history including
Peter McLaren, Ann Aird, John McMillan, Margaret Barclay, Elizabeth Black and
James Black.

1703. Guelph (St Andrew's) Pres. **King's Helpers Circle of Daughters of St Andrew's.
Collection book, 1926-1947.** 1 ledger. Loc: GSA.

1704. Guelph (St Andrew's) Pres. **King's Helpers Circle of Daughters of St Andrew's.
Minutes, 1927-1961.** 4 volumes. Loc: GSA.

1705. Guelph (St Andrew's) Pres. **King's Helpers Circle of Daughters of St Andrew's.
Cash book, 1923-1948.** 1 ledger. Loc: GSA.
A record of monthly receipts and expenditures.

1706. Guelph (St Andrew's) Pres. **Ladies Aid Society. Minutes, 1900-1915.** 2 volumes.
Loc: GSA.
The first volume includes a copy of the constitution of the society dated
1899.

1707. Guelph (St Andrew's) Pres. **Land records, 1856; 1881.** 1 file folder. Loc: GSA.
A record of the decision to purchase Lots 932 and 933 of the Canada Company
Survey for the church and manse.

1708. Guelph (St Andrew's) Pres. **Land records for St Andrew's Church Glebe, 1874-1881
(sporadic).** 1 bundle. Loc: GSA.
A record of land transactions on property in St Andrew's Glebe. The bundle
includes a map of lots north and south of St Andrew Street between Kathleen and
Exhibition Streets. The records are held in a black box.

1709. Guelph (St Andrew's) Pres. **Marriages. Register, 1858-1900.** mf. Loc: AO.

1710. Guelph (St Andrew's) Pres. **Marriages. Registers, 1832-1852; 1858-1875;
1890-1940.** 5 ledgers. Loc: GSA, WCA.
The WCA holds the records from 1858 to 1876 and 1890 to 1900 on microfilm.

1711. Guelph (St Andrew's) Pres. **Membership. List, 1894.** 1 ledger. Loc: GSA.
A list of church members with their street addresses. The membership list is
held in the same ledger as the cash book for 1876.

1712. Guelph (St Andrew's) Pres. **Membership. Records, 1891.** 1 file folder. Loc: GSA.
A list of members of the church divided into districts for visitation by elders. The file is entitled, 'church districts'.

1713. Guelph (St Andrew's) Pres. **Missionary Association. Minutes, 1878-1903.** 2 volumes. Loc: GSA.
A record of meetings held only a few times each year. One volume, covering the period 1878 to 1887, outlines details of lectures given to the association.

1714. Guelph (St Andrew's) Pres. **Pew plan, 1938.** 2 plans. Loc: GSA.
The scale is 4 feet to an inch. One plan is marked '1938' and the other is marked 'prior to 1938'.

1715. Guelph (St Andrew's) Pres. **Pew rental financial statement, 1894.** 1 document. Loc: GSA.
A record of the names of members, where they sat in the church and the amount each person paid to the church. The record is held in the same box as the annual financial statements of the church.

1716. Guelph (St Andrew's) Pres. **Photographs, 1831-1955.** 29 framed photographs. Loc: GSA.
The photographs, in the gallery of the church archives, include images of members and the church building.

1717. Guelph (St Andrew's) Pres. **Receipts, 1880-1920.** 2 bundles, 1 envelope. Loc: GSA.
Receipts for various services to the church. The records are held in a black box.

1718. Guelph (St Andrew's) Pres. **Sabbath School. Attendance registers, 1881; 1884-1939.** 6 ledgers. Loc: GSA.

1719. Guelph (St Andrew's) Pres. **Sabbath School. Minutes, 1889-1918.** 1 volume. Loc: GSA.
A record of the annual meetings of the Sabbath School Association.

1720. Guelph (St Andrew's) Pres. **Scrapbooks, 1828-1985.** 2 scrapbooks. Loc: GSA.
A collection of newspaper clippings and memorabilia containing historical sketches of the development of the church.

1721. Guelph (St Andrew's) Pres. **Session. Minutes, 1832-1842; 1856-1978.** 6 volumes. Loc: GSA.
The date spans of ledgers overlap for some years. The first volume lists original members of the church.

1722. Guelph (St Andrew's) Pres. **Session. Minutes, 1832-1842; 1859-1899.** 1 reel. mf. Loc: WCA, AO.

1723. Guelph (St Andrew's) Pres. **Subscribers to Presbyterian church building, 1831.** 1 framed document. Loc: GSA.
List of thirty-two original subscribers to the cost of building the first Presbyterian church in Guelph in 1831. The amount of each donation is stated.

1724. Guelph (St Andrew's) Pres. **Sunday School. Reports, 1884-1900.** 1 bundle. Loc: GSA.

A series of quarterly reports of the Sunday School which includes aggregate attendance figures, notes those present at all classes and those absent once during the quarter. The records are held in a black box.

1725. Guelph (St Andrew's) Pres. **Sunshine Mission Band. Minutes, 1932-1937.** 1 volume. Loc: GSA.

1726. Guelph (St Andrew's) Pres. **Twentieth Century Fund. List of subscriptions and payments, 1900-1903.** 13 ledgers. Loc: GSA.

A list of contributions made by church members. The record lists the amount specific members gave to the church.

1727. Guelph (St Andrew's) Pres. **Women's Association. Annual report, 1926.** 1 report. Loc: GSA.

1728. Guelph (St Andrew's) Pres. **Women's Association. Minutes, 1936-1947.** 2 volumes. Loc: GSA.

1729. Guelph (St Andrew's) Pres. **Women's Foreign Missionary Society. Minutes, 1888-1893.** 1 volume. Loc: GSA.

A record of meetings usually held once each month.

1730. Guelph (St Andrew's) Pres. **Women's Missionary Society. Account books, 1903-1916.** 1 ledger. Loc: GSA.

1731. Guelph (St Andrew's) Pres. **Women's Missionary Society. Annual report, 1926.** 1 report. Loc: GSA.

1732. Guelph (St Andrew's) Pres. **Women's Missionary Society. Historical sketch, 1884-1923.** 1 file folder. Loc: GSA.

A brief historical sketch of the development of women's organizations in the church.

1733. Guelph (St Andrew's) Pres. **Women's Missionary Society. Minutes, 1893-1903; 1911-1920; 1925-1939.** 7 volumes. Loc: GSA.

A record of monthly meetings held by the society.

1734. Guelph (St Andrew's) Pres. **Young People's Association. Constitution and bylaws, 1881.** 1 brochure. Loc: GSA.

1735. Guelph (St Andrew's) Pres. **Young People's Society. Minutes, 1912-1915.** 1 volume. Loc: GSA.

1736. Guelph (St Paul's) Pres. **Communion Roll. Register, 1914-1917; 1928-1932; 1935-1959.** Loc: PCA. Card index.

1737. Guelph (St Paul's) Pres. **Congregational Meetings. Minutes, 1913-1959.** 2 volumes. Loc: PCA. Card index.

Includes news clippings on the history of the congregation in the 1936-1959 volume.

1738. Guelph (St Paul's) Pres. **Session. Minutes, 1913-1959.** 2 volumes. Loc: PCA. Card index.

1739. Guelph (St Paul's) Pres. **Sunday School. Weekly records, 1910-1927.** 1 volume. Loc: PCA. Card index.

1740. Moorefield (St Andrew's) Pres. **50th anniversary history, 1926.** 17 p. ill. Loc: PCA. Card index.

1741. Moorefield (St Andrew's) Pres. **Baptisms. Register, 1928-1974.** 1 volume. Loc: PCA. Card index.

1742. Moorefield (St Andrew's) Pres. **Board of Managers and Congregational Meetings. Minutes, 1926-1975.** 2 volumes. Loc: PCA. Card index.

1743. Moorefield (St Andrew's) Pres. **Communion Roll. Register, 1926-1975.** 1 volume. Loc: PCA. Card index.

1744. Moorefield (St Andrew's) Pres. **History, 1925-1953.** 3 p. typescript. Loc: PCA. Card index.

1745. Moorefield (St Andrew's) Pres. **Session. Minutes, 1925-1975.** 1 volume. Loc: PCA. Card index.

1746. Morriston (Duff's) Pres. **Baptisms. Register, 1840-1899.** 1 reel. mf. Loc: WCA, AO, PCA.

1747. Morriston (Duff's) Pres. **Congregational Meetings. Minutes, 1835-1864.** 1 reel. mf. Loc: WCA, AO, PCA.

1748. Morriston (Duff's) Pres. **Marriages. Register, 1840-1899.** mf. Loc: AO, PCA. Card index.

1749. Morriston (Duff's) Pres. **Session. Minutes, 1844-1899.** 1 reel. mf. Loc: WCA, AO, PCA.
   The minutes are filmed with communion rolls for the same years.

1750. Nassagaweya Pres. **Communicants and a call to Andrew James MacAuley, 1853.** 3 p. Loc: PCA. Card index.

1751. Nassagaweya Pres. **History, 1861-1961.** 15 p. ill. Loc: PCA. Card index.

1752. Nassagaweya Pres. **One hundred years at Nassagaweya Presbyterian Church, 1836-1936.** 24 p. ill. Loc: PCA. Card index.

1753. Palmerston (Knox) Pres. **Annual reports, 1918-1956; 1959-1976.** Loc: PCA. Card index.

1754. Palmerston (Knox) Pres. **Baptisms. Register, 1879-1958.** Loc: PCA. Card index.

1755. Palmerston (Knox) Pres. **Board of Managers. Minutes, 1891-1910; 1953-1969.** 2 volumes. Loc: PCA. Card index.

1756. Palmerston (Knox) Pres. **Communion Roll. Registers, 1932-1937; 1939-1943; 1946-1970.** 6 volumes. Loc: PCA. Card index.

1757. Palmerston (Knox) Pres. **Diamond Jubilee. Souvenir historical booklet, 1863-1923.** 11 p. Loc: PCA. Card index.

1758. Palmerston (Knox) Pres. **Eighty years of Presbyterianism in Palmerston, 1863-1943.** 32 p. ill. Loc: PCA. Card index.

1759. Palmerston (Knox) Pres. **Golden Jubilee. A history of the congregation, 1863-1913.** 28 p. ill. Loc: PCA. Card index.

1760. Palmerston (Knox) Pres. **Marriages. Registers, 1879-1920; 1943-1964.** 4 volumes, loose certificates. Loc: PCA. Card index.

1761. Palmerston (Knox) Pres. **Report on the condition of the church by Kyles and Kyles, Architects, 1958.** 1 volume. Loc: PCA. Card index.
Following this report, the church decided to replace its existing building. Records of the financing and building of the new structure are also held.

1762. Palmerston (Knox) Pres. **Session. Minutes, 1934-1964.** Loc: PCA. Card index.

1763. Palmerston (Knox) Pres. **W.M.S. Minutes and dues book, 1925-1931; 1936-1954.** 3 volumes. Loc: PCA. Card index.

1764. Puslinch (Knox) Pres. **Annual report, 1920.** 1 brochure. Loc: WCA. MU 25.
The record is held with the Wellington County Historical Research Society Collection.

1765. Puslinch (Knox) Pres. **Baptisms. Register, 1857-1901.** mf. Loc: AO, PCA.
The Presbyterian Church Archives have microfilms for the years 1855-1901.

1766. Puslinch (Knox) Pres. **Correspondence. Letter to Edinburgh, Scotland, 1856.** 1 letter. Loc: WCA. MU 12.
A letter offering the Rev. Andrew Maclean a post as minister in Puslinch Township and outlining conditions in Canada. The letter does not state the religious affiliation of the congregation, but indicates the congregation was Gaelic speaking.

1767. Puslinch (Knox) Pres. **An historical sketch, 1840-1920.** 13 p. typescript. Loc: PCA. Card index.

1768. Puslinch (Knox) Pres. **Marriages. Register, 1897-1900.** mf. Loc: AO, PCA.

1769. Puslinch (Knox) Pres/ Morriston (Duff's) Pres. **Membership. List, 1844.** 1 document. Loc: WCA. MU 25.
The report is held with the Wellington County Historical Research Society Collection.

1770. Salem Pres. **Baptisms. Register, 1848-1968**. 1 volume. Loc: PCA. Card index.

1771. Salem Pres. **Centennial historical booklet, 1859-1959**. 28 p. Loc: PCA. Card index.

1772. Salem Pres. **Communion Roll. Register, 1874-1967**. Loc: PCA. Card index.

1773. Salem Pres. **Session. Minutes, 1875-1968**. Loc: PCA. Card index.

PRESBYTERIAN CHURCHES (UNITING) RECORDS - LOCAL

1774. Ballinafad (Melville) Pres. **Accounts, 1900-1908**. Loc: UCA. Card index.

1775. Ballinafad (Melville) Pres-UC. **Baptisms. Register, 1859-1945**. 2 ledgers. Loc: UCA. Card index.
    The communion roll from 1874 to 1948, and the session minutes from 1871 to 1951 are also held in the ledger.

1776. Ballinafad (Melville) Pres-UC. **Communion. Roll, 1874-1942**. 2 ledgers. Loc: UCA. Card index.
    The communion roll from 1874 to 1928 is held in the same register as the baptismal register from 1859 to 1945, and the session minutes from 1871 to 1951. The second communion roll records members from 1914 to 1942.

1777. Ballinafad (Melville) Pres-UC. **Congregational Meetings. Minutes and accounts, 1881-1922; 1926-1930**. 1 volume. Loc: UCA. Card index.
    The financial accounts for the years 1906 to 1908 are held in the same ledger.

1778. Ballinafad (Melville) Pres-UC. **Marriages. Register, 1914-1944**. 1 ledger. Loc: UCA. Card index.

1779. Ballinafad (Melville) Pres-UC. **Session. Minutes, 1871-1951**. 1 volume. Loc: UCA. Card index.
    The communion roll from 1874 to 1948, and the baptismal record from 1859 to 1945 are also held in the ledger.

1780. Belwood (St John's) Pres. **Baptisms. Register, 1858-1890**. 1 volume. Loc: UCA. Card index.
    The session minutes from 1862 to 1900, and the register of elders, deacons, burials and marriages are also recorded in the ledger.

1781. Belwood (St John's) Pres. **Burials. Register, 1813-1891**. 1 volume. Loc: UCA. Card index.
    The Session minutes from 1862 to 1900, and the registers of elders, deacons, marriages and baptisms are also recorded in the ledger.

1782. Belwood (St John's) Pres. **Communion. Roll, 1894-1917**. 1 reel. mf. Loc: WCA.

1783. Belwood (St John's) Pres. **Deacons. Register, 1860-1863**. 1 volume. Loc: UCA. Card index.
    The Session minutes from 1862 to 1900, and the register of elders, burials, marriages and baptisms are also recorded in the ledger.

1784. Belwood (St John's) Pres. **Elders. Register, 1856-1911.** 1 volume. Loc: UCA. Card index.

The Session minutes from 1862 to 1900, and the register of deacons, burials, marriages and baptisms are also recorded in the ledger.

1785. Belwood (St John's) Pres. **Marriages. Register, 1842-1896.** 1 ledger. Loc: UCA, WCA. Card index.

The Session minutes from 1862 to 1900, and the register of elders, deacons, burials, and baptisms are also recorded in the ledger. The WCA holds a microfilm of the register from 1859 to 1896.

1786. Belwood (St John's) Pres. **Minutes, 1890-1899.** 2 volumes. Loc: WCA. MU 69.

1787. Belwood (St John's) Pres. **Receipts, 1885-1898 (sporadic).** 3 file folders, 1 envelope. Loc: WCA. MU 69.

1788. Belwood (St John's) Pres. **Session. Minutes, 1862-1900.** 1 volume. Loc: UCA. Card index.

The registers of elders, deacons, burials, marriages and baptisms are also recorded in the volume.

1789. Belwood (St John's) Pres. **Trustees' and Elders' Meetings. Minutes, 1886-1890.** Loc: UCA. Card index.

The minutes of the Board of Managers' meetings from 1891 to 1959, and the congregational meetings minutes from 1886 to 1959 are also recorded in the same ledger.

1790. Belwood (St John's) Pres-UC. **Baptisms. Registers, 1891-1966.** 1 reel. mf. Loc: WCA.

1791. Belwood (St John's) Pres-UC. **Board of Managers. Minutes, 1891-1959.** 1 volume. Loc: UCA. Card index.

The minutes of the annual congregational meetings from 1886 to 1959, and the trustees and elders meetings from 1886 to 1890 are also recorded in the volume.

1792. Belwood (St John's) Pres-UC. **Communion. Register, 1919-1924.** 1 reel. mf. Loc: WCA.

1793. Belwood (St John's) Pres-UC. **Congregational Meetings. Minutes, 1886-1959.** 2 volumes. Loc: UCA. Card index.

The minutes of the Board of Managers' meetings from 1891 to 1959, and the trustees and elders meetings from 1886 to 1890 are also recorded in the first volume.

1794. Belwood (St John's) Pres-UC. **Ladies Aid. Minutes, 1934-1945.** 4 volumes. Loc: UCA. Card index.

1795. Belwood (St John's) Pres-UC. **Session. Minutes, 1900-1961.** 1 reel. mf. Loc: WCA.

A record of meetings usually held at least once a month.

1796. Belwood (St John's) Pres-UC. **Women's Missionary Society. Minutes, 1917-1961.** 2 reels. mf. Loc: WCA.
A record of monthly meetings which outlines activities, motions passed and officers elected.

1797. Belwood (St John's) United. **Women's Association. Minutes, 1926-1953.** 2 reels. mf. Loc: WCA.
A record of monthly meetings.

1798. Dracon (6th Line) Cong-Pres. **Building Committee. Minutes and account book, 1886-1893.** 1 ledger. Loc: UCA. Card index.

1799. Dracon (6th Line) Cong-Pres. **Session. Minutes, 1878-1888.** 1 volume. Loc: UCA. Card index.
The 6th Line Presbyterian Mission Station of Knox Presbyterian Church, Dracon apparently evolved from the Douglas Congregational Church.

1800. Dracon (Knox) Pres. **Account book, 1884-1893.** 1 ledger. Loc: UCA. Card index.
The account book indicates that until approximately 1888, the church was called the 6th Line Presbyterian Church.

1801. Dracon (Knox) Pres. **Annual Meetings. Minutes, 1888-1918.** 1 volume. Loc: UCA. Card index.

1802. Dracon (Knox) Pres/ Metz (St Paul's) Pres. **Baptisms. Registers, 1906-1977.** 1 reel. mf. Loc: WCA.
The record is a list of baptisms in the united congregation of Dracon Knox and Metz St Paul's Presbyterian Churches.

1803. Dracon (Knox) Pres. **Cash book, 1894-1912.** 1 reel. mf. Loc: WCA.

1804. Dracon (Knox) Pres. **Membership. Roll, 1885-1887.** 1 ledger. Loc: UCA. Card index.

1805. Dracon (Knox) Pres. **Scrapbook, 1884-1920.** 1 envelope. Loc: WCA. MU 82.
A photocopy of a scrapbook of people and events and a brief history of the church. The original is held at St Paul's United Church, Metz.

1806. Dracon (Knox) Pres-UC. **Annual Meetings. Minutes, 1920-1966.** 1 reel. mf. Loc: WCA.

1807. Dracon (Knox) Pres-UC. **Baptisms. Register, 1885-1962.** 1 ledger. Loc: UCA. Card index.
The session minutes from 1920-1960 are also recorded in the ledger.

1808. Dracon (Knox) Pres-UC. **Communion. Roll, 1885-1929.** 1 reel. mf. Loc: WCA.

1809. Dracon (Knox) Pres-UC. **Marriages. Registers, 1900-1949.** 1 reel. mf. Loc: WCA.

1810. Dracon (Knox) Pres-UC. **Meetings. Minutes, 1920-1938.** 1 reel. mf. Loc: WCA.

1811. Dracon (Knox) Pres-UC. **Session. Minutes, 1885-1900; 1920-1960.** 2 volumes. Loc: UCA. Card index.
  The baptismal register from 1885 to 1962 is recorded in the 1920-1960 volume. The church also administered the Metz Mission Station.

1812. Dracon UC. **Official Board. Minutes, 1931-1940.** 1 volume. Loc: UCA. Card index.

1813. Dracon UC. **Re-arrangement Committee. Minutes, 1940.** 1 volume. Loc: UCA. Card index.

1814. Eden Mills Pres. **Baptisms. Register, 1862-1899.** mf. Loc: AO, PCA. Card index.

1815. Eden Mills Pres. **Communion Roll. Register, 1900.** mf. Loc: AO, PCA. Card index.

1816. Eden Mills Pres. **Session. Minutes, 1857-1900.** mf. Loc: AO, PCA. Card index.

1817. Elora (Chalmers) Pres. **Annual reports, 1900-1902; 1906-1908.** 7 reports. Loc: WCA, GPL. WCA: MU 12; MU 13 for years 1900-1901.
  Printed reports listing church officials, the activities of church clubs and societies and financial statements of the congregation. The 1906 report is held at the Guelph Public Library.

1818. Elora (Chalmers) Pres. **Baptisms. Registers, 1856-1916.** 1 reel. mf. Loc: WCA, AO, PCA.

1819. Elora (Chalmers) Pres. **Cash book, 1863-1889.** 1 ledger. Loc: WCA. MU 1.
  A record of monthly receipts and expenditures.

1820. Elora (Chalmers) Pres. **Communion Roll. Registers, 1856-1893.** mf. Loc: AO, PCA.
  The Presbyterian Church Archives holds records for 1859-1893 only.

1821. Elora (Chalmers) Pres. **Documents re early church history, 1856.** 4 items. Loc: PCA. Card index.
  Documents include: 1) Report of Committee of Presbytery of Hamilton, February 21, 1856 re formation of the church; 2) petition to Presbytery of Hamilton, April 1, 1856 (including subscription list); 3) letter from George Smellie to M.Y. Stark, May 1856 re election of James Middlemiss as pastor; and 4) extract of Presbytery minutes, June 3, 1856 re ordination of James Middlemiss.

1822. Elora (Chalmers) Pres. **Marriages. Registers, 1856-1896.** 1 reel. mf. Loc: WCA.

1823. Elora (Chalmers) Pres. **Sabbath School Teachers' Association. Rules, 1882.** 1 page. Loc: PCA. Card index.
  Also a scheme of lessons for sabbath schools dated 1884.

1824. Elora (Chalmers) Pres. **Session. Minutes, 1856-1899; 1901-1916.** mf. Loc: AO, PCA.
  Minutes for 1856-1899 are held on microfilm. Only the Presbyterian Archives has the original minutes for 1901-1916.

1825. Elora (United) Pres. **Financial report, 1858.** Loc: PCA. Card index.

1826. Elora (United) Pres. **Membership. Roll, 1854-1865.** 1 reel. mf. Loc: WCA.
The church later became Knox Presbyterian Church, Elora.

1827. Eramosa (Barrie Hill) Pres. **Deeds, 1836-1878.** 1 file folder. Loc: UCA. Card index.
A collection of original and photocopied debentures and deeds relating to church property.

1828. Eramosa (Barrie Hill) Pres. **Library. Subscriptions, 1884-1879.** 1 ledger. Loc: UCA. Card index.
A list of subscribers' name and amount paid (normally 50 cents per year). The ledger also records titles of volumes purchased for the library whose purpose was 'to promote the interests of religion and to diffuse useful knowledge'.

1829. Eramosa (Barrie Hill) Pres. **Seat rentals and stipend accounts, 1853-1889.** 1 reel. mf. Loc: WCA.

1830. Eramosa (Barrie Hill) Pres. **Stipend accounts, 1890-1906.** 1 reel. mf. Loc: WCA.

1831. Eramosa (Barrie Hill) Pres. **Subscription book, 1844-1879.** 1 reel. mf. Loc: WCA.
A record of amounts given by individuals to the church library.

1832. Eramosa (Barrie Hill) Pres-UC. **Account book, 1924-1956.** 1 ledger. Loc: UCA. Card index.
The church was named First Presbyterian Church until 1925 when it was renamed First United Church, Eramosa. In 1938 the name was changed to Barrie Hill United Church. From 1958, annual reports show that both Barrie Hill United and Speedside United (former Congregational) were grouped in the Eramosa Pastoral Charge.

1833. Eramosa (Barrie Hill) Pres-UC. **Annual reports, 1906-1907; 1909-1940; 1942-1951.** 85 brochures. Loc: UCA. Card index.
The church was named First Presbyterian Church until 1925 when it was renamed First United Church, Eramosa. In 1938 the name was changed to Barrie Hill United Church. From 1958, annual reports show that both Barrie Hill United and Speedside United (former Congregational) were grouped in the Eramosa Pastoral Charge.

1834. Eramosa (Barrie Hill) Pres-UC. **Baptisms. Register, 1882-1955.** 1 ledger. Loc: UCA, WCA. Card index.
The only reference to the church's name is the archival note on the front of the ledger, 'Eramosa Pastoral Charge'. The originals are in the United Church Archives while the Wellington County Archives holds a microfilm copy.

1835. Eramosa (Barrie Hill) Pres-UC. **Communion. Roll, 1916-1950.** 1 reel. mf. Loc: WCA.

1836. Eramosa (Barrie Hill) Pres-UC. **Congregational Meetings. Minutes, 1853-1953.** 1 volume. Loc: UCA, WCA. Card index.
The church was formerly First Presbyterian, Eramosa. The originals are held by the United Church Archives; the Wellington County Archives has a microfilm copy.

1837. Eramosa (Barrie Hill) Pres-UC. **Eramosa Bible Society. Minutes, 1892-1961.** 2 volumes. Loc: UCA, WCA. Card index.

    The original minutes are held by the United Church Archives while the Wellington County Archives has a microfilm copy.

1838. Eramosa (Barrie Hill) Pres-UC. **Marriages. Register, 1889-1952.** 1 ledger. Loc: UCA. Card index.

    A note in the front of the ledger states that in 1925 the Speedside Congregational Church became the Speedside United Church, and in 1942 joined the Barrie Hill United Church.

1839. Eramosa (Barrie Hill) Pres-UC. **Membership. Rolls, 1843-1962.** 3 ledgers. Loc: UCA, WCA. UCA: Card index.

    The first ledger is entitled 'membership roll of the United Secession Congregation Eramosa'. An archival note on the front of the ledgers labels them 'Barrie Hill'. The original rolls are held by the UCA while the WCA has a microfilm copy for the years 1843-1880, 1883, 1894, 1899 and 1905-1910.

1840. Eramosa (Barrie Hill) Pres-UC. **Session. Minutes, 1838-1983.** 2 volumes. Loc: UCA, WCA. Card index.

    The church was formerly First Presbyterian Church, Eramosa.

1841. Eramosa (Barrie Hill) UC. **Quarterly Board. Minutes, 1939-1956.** 1 reel. mf. Loc: WCA.

1842. Eramosa (First) Pres. **Day book, 1831-1832; 1860-1861.** 1 ledger. Loc: UCA. Card index.

    The front of the ledger is inscribed, 'Bookkeeping by Elizabeth Wood, Eramosa, 5th Oct 1857'. The 1831 to 1832 accounts are titled 'Dublin' and appear to be a store account for spices and liquors. The 1860 to 1861 accounts appear to be a church building account. The back of the ledger contains a list of women's names titled, 'Trained nurses of First Presbyterian Church, Eramosa'. The names are: Harriett Brydon, Helen Brydon and Harriett Harreth.

1843. Eramosa (First) Pres. **Register, 1868.** 1 ledger. Loc: UCA. Card index.

    First Presbyterian Church was renamed First United in 1925 and Barrie Hill United in 1938.

1844. Eramosa (First) Pres. **Seat rental accounts, 1853-1901.** 1 ledger. Loc: UCA. Card index.

    A record of name and amount paid, normally every 6 months. The amounts vary from 3 to 20 dollars per year. In 1889 the account title is changed from 'seat rentals' to 'stipend subscription'.

1845. Erin Pres-UC. **Baptisms. Register, 1896-1948.** 1 ledger. Loc: UCA. Card index.

    A record of baptisms which is labelled as the Erin Hillsburgh Charge. The records are labelled as part of Caledon West Township Church until 1931 and then there are few references to baptisms at North Erin United Church.

1846. Erin Pres-UC. **Communion. Registers, 1902-1955.** 1 ledger. Loc: UCA. Card index.

    A record of church members which indicates Erin Township residents were, prior to 1925, part of Knox Church Congregation in Caledon Township. The record refers to Erin Township Knox Church beginning in 1925.

1847. Erin Pres-UC. **Session. Minutes, 1895-1938.** 1 volume. Loc: UCA. Card index.
    The first entry in 1895 indicates that North Erin Knox Church, Erin Vanalter Presbyterian Church and Waldemar Presbyterian Church were being united into a single congregation. The meetings were convened at least four times annually.

1848. Fergus (Melville) Pres. **Annual reports, 1872; 1892-1907; 1909-1924.** 29 brochures, 1 photocopy. Loc: UCA, WCA. UCA:Card index; WCA:MU33.
    The Wellington County Archives holds only a photocopy of the 1872 report; all others are in the United Church Archives.

1849. Fergus (Melville) Pres. **Baptisms. Register, 1889-1926.** 1 ledger. Loc: UCA. Card index.

1850. Fergus (Melville) Pres. **Financial report, 1879.** 1 file folder. Loc: AO. FA: MU 2956.
    Details of receipts and disbursements for the church, its sabbath and missionary association. The file folder also contains programs for the opening of the new Melville church in 1899-1900, the Melville hall in 1930, the dedication of the chimes in 1942 and the 100th anniversary in 1945. Part of the Templin Family Collection.

1851. Fergus (Melville) Pres. **Historical sketch, 1845-1920.** 16 p. ill. Loc: PCA. Card index.

1852. Fergus (Melville) Pres. **Marriages. Register, 1896-1925.** 1 ledger. Loc: UCA. Card index.

1853. Fergus (Melville) Pres. **Subscribers to new church, 1844-1846.** 1 document. Loc: WCA. MU 52; Detailed list of contents.
    A handwritten copy of names of individual subscribers and amount of money each contributed. Part of the Isabel Cunningham Burr Collection.

1854. Fergus (Melville) Pres. **Subscribers to new church and manse, c1847.** Loc: AO. MU 1016.
    A printed list of all donors and subscribers to the building fund to establish a new church after most members broke away from St Andrew's Presbyterian Church. Among more than one hundred subscribers are the names of Adam Fergusson, Reverend George Smellie, Charles Allan, A.D. Fordyce and A.D. Ferrier. Held with Adam Fergusson Papers. A very similar list, dated 1843, is held with the Templin Family Collection.

1855. Fergus (Melville) Pres-UC. **Programs, 1920; 1931; 1942.** 1 envelope. Loc: WCA.
    Three service programs for the church. Part of the Templin-Dow Collection.

1856. Fergus (Melville) UC. **Melville Men's Club. Minutes, 1926-1927.** 1 volume. Loc: WCA.
    The club had four committees: membership and attendance, program, flower-relief-sick and visiting, and recreation. The records are held with the Templin-Dow Collection.

1857. Glenallan Pres. **Session. Minutes and correspondence, 1857-1864**. 1 file folder. Loc: UCA. Card index.

A record of the minutes and correspondence of the United Congregation of Peel and Maryborough Townships. The records indicate that in 1856 a Presbytery committee of Reverend Smellie of Fergus and R.D. McKay visited Allansville to determine the 'state of the district as to whether it was ripe for organization as a congregation'. A congregation was formed in 1857. The records outline early activities and list the names of church officials.

1858. Guelph (Chalmers) Pres. **Building Fund. Subscription book, 1869-1873**. 1 ledger. Loc: UCA. Card index.

1859. Guelph (Chalmers) Pres. **Congregational Meetings. Minutes, 1874-1919**. 2 volumes. Loc: UCA. Card index.

1860. Guelph (Chalmers) Pres. **Deaths. Register, 1918**. 1 ledger. Loc: UCA. Card index.

1861. Guelph (Chalmers) Pres. **Open Collection. Account, 1917-1918**. 1 ledger. Loc: UCA. Card index.

1862. Guelph (Chalmers) Pres. **Religious Education Council. Minutes, 1921**. 1 volume. Loc: UCA. Card index.

The volume contains the minutes for three meetings of Sunday schools.

1863. Guelph (Chalmers) Pres. **Session and Managers. Minutes, 1906-1910**. 1 volume. Loc: UCA. Card index.

1864. Guelph (Chalmers) Pres. **Sustentation fund, 1875-1882; 1903-1912**. 2 ledgers. Loc: UCA. Card index.

A record of names, amount of subscription and monthly payments. According to Presbytery minutes, the fund was generally used to support poorly paid ministers and missionaries.

1865. Guelph (Chalmers) Pres-UC. **Annual Congregational Meetings. Minutes, 1868-1957**. 6 volumes. Loc: UCA. Card index.

The volumes also include board of managers' meeting minutes for the same period.

1866. Guelph (Chalmers) Pres-UC. **Annual reports, 1879; 1897-1803; 1905-1921; 1923-1967; 1969-1972**. 77 volumes. Loc: UCA. Card index.

1867. Guelph (Chalmers) Pres-UC. **Baptisms. Register, 1868-1952**. 1 ledger. Loc: UCA. Card index.

1868. Guelph (Chalmers) Pres-UC. **Board of Managers. Minutes, 1868-1957**. 6 volumes. Loc: UCA. Card index.

The volumes also include annual congregational meeting minutes for the same period.

1869. Guelph (Chalmers) Pres-UC. **Cash books, 1894-1976; 1918-1926; 1932-1946.** 5 ledgers. Loc: UCA. Card index.

1870. Guelph (Chalmers) Pres-UC. **Communion. Rolls, 1894-1905; 1932-1951.** 5 ledgers. Loc: UCA. Card index.
The rolls record attendance at communion.

1871. Guelph (Chalmers) Pres-UC. **Correspondence and reports, 1890-1952 (sporadic).** 21 documents; 5 file folders. Loc: UCA. Card index.
Correspondence and reports of special meetings regarding new members, ministers or special events.

1872. Guelph (Chalmers) Pres-UC. **Marriages. Registers, 1896-1962.** 5 ledgers. Loc: UCA. Card index.

1873. Guelph (Chalmers) Pres-UC. **Membership. List, 1924; 1947; 1956.** 3 volumes. Loc: UCA. Card index.
A record of names and addresses of members.

1874. Guelph (Chalmers) Pres-UC. **Missionary Association. Minutes, 1886-1954; 1960-1963.** 4 volumes. Loc: UCA. Card index.
Both women and men attended meetings of this organization.

1875. Guelph (Chalmers) Pres-UC. **Missionary Association. Subscription list, 1878-1884.** 1 ledger. Loc: UCA. Card index.

1876. Guelph (Chalmers) Pres-UC. **Session. Minutes, 1868-1909; 1939-1964.** 3 volumes. Loc: UCA. Card index.

1877. Guelph (Chalmers) Pres-UC. **Sunday School. Treasurer's books, 1915-1927; 1946-1957.** 2 ledgers. Loc: UCA. Card index.

1878. Guelph (Chalmers) Pres-UC. **WFMS Wardrope Auxiliary. Minutes, 1890-1910; 1919-1961.** 10 volumes. Loc: UCA. Card index.
The foreign missions' auxiliary was named in honour of Reverend Thomas Wardrope who was minister of the church from 1869 to 1893.

1879. Guelph (Chalmers) Pres-UC. **WFMS Wardrope Auxiliary. Mission Band minutes, 1888-1890; 1933-1944; 1948-1955.** 5 volumes. Loc: UCA. Card index.
The 1937 minute book also records monthly attendance from 1938 to 1944. The foreign missions' auxiliary was named in honour of Reverend Thomas Wardrope who was minister of the church from 1869 to 1893.

1880. Guelph (Chalmers) Pres-UC. **WFMS Wardrope Auxiliary. Treasurer's book, 1908-1951.** 2 ledgers. Loc: UCA. Card index.
The foreign missions' auxiliary was named in honour of Reverend Thomas Wardrope who was minister of the church from 1869 to 1893.

1881. Guelph (Chalmers) Pres-UC. **WHMS Hart Auxiliary. Cash books, 1905-1935; 1937-1961.** 2 ledgers. Loc: UCA. Card index.
The home missions auxiliary was organized by Mrs Hart.

1882. Guelph (Chalmers) Pres-UC. **WHMS Hart Auxiliary. Minutes, 1905-1914; 1917-1961.** 9 ledgers. Loc: UCA. Card index.
The home missions auxiliary was organized by Mrs Hart.

1883. Guelph (Chalmers) Pres-UC. **WMS Mission Band. Cash books, 1938-1961.** 3 ledgers. Loc: UCA. Card index.

1884. Guelph (Chalmers) UC. **Annual report, 1937.** 1 document. Loc: GPL.
A printed report listing church officials, statements of the board of management, receipts and expenditures, and the activities of various clubs and societies of the church.

1885. Guelph (Chalmers) UC. **Ministers and administrators, 1929.** 2 p. Loc: GPL.
A pamphlet of Chalmers United Church which lists ministers and administrators of church organizations for the year 1929.

1886. Guelph (Chalmers) UC. **Women's Association. Cash book, 1924-1941.** 2 ledgers. Loc: UCA. Card index.

1887. Guelph (Chalmers) UC. **Women's Association. Minutes, 1941-1948; 1960-1961.** 5 volumes. Loc: UCA. Card index.

1888. Melville-Bethel Pres-UC. **Marriages. Register, 1899-1943.** 2 ledgers. Loc: UCA. Card index.
The documents are labelled as the property of 'Melville and Bethel Presbyterian Churches' and many of the marriages listed took place in Mount Forest. The record includes references to residents of Wellington County including individuals who lived in Mount Forest, Minto Township, Clifford, Arthur and Arthur Township.

1889. Metz (St Paul's) Pres-UC. **Annual reports, 1924-1931; 1934-1961.** Loc: WCA. MU 105.

1890. Metz (St Paul's) Pres-UC. **Congregational Meetings. Minutes, 1932-1987.** 2 file folders. Loc: WCA. MU 82.
Photocopies of the originals which are held at St Paul's United Church, Metz.

1891. Metz (St Paul's) Pres-UC. **Session. Minutes, 1900-1987.** 2 file folders. Loc: WCA. MU 82.
Photocopies of the originals which are held at St Paul's United Church, Metz.

1892. Metz (St Paul's) UC. **Dracon and Metz Young People's Union. Minutes, 1935-1942.** 1 file folder. Loc: WCA. MU 82.
Photocopies of the originals which are held at St Paul's United Church, Metz.

1893. Metz (St Paul's) UC. **Historic roll, 1933-1987.** 1 file folder. Loc: WCA. MU 82.
Photocopies of church membership. Originals are held at St Paul's Presbyterian Church, Metz.

1894. Mimosa Pres. **Account books, 1889-1908.** 2 ledgers. Loc: UCA. Card index.
A record of money paid to church officers, amounts of church collections and occasionally references to funds raised in church events. The record also lists

the expenditures of the church. The account books are held in the same ledgers as the minutes of the congregational meetings.

1895. Mimosa Pres. **Annual report, 1903.** 1 brochure. Loc: WCA. MU 86.
Includes a report of the session, a financial statement for the year and a list of members' contributions.

1896. Mimosa Pres. **Baptisms. Register, 1862-1911.** 1 ledger. Loc: UCA. Card index.
A listing of persons baptized, their date of birth and baptism, place of residence, name of parents and the attending minister. After 1890 the record lists the occupation of the father. The baptismal register is held in the same ledger as the session minutes of the congregation from 1875 to 1910.

1897. Mimosa Pres. **Collection. Account books, 1898-1901; 1911-1925.** 3 ledgers. Loc: UCA. Card index.
A record of the name of members of the church and the amount each person gave to the church in collection envelopes.

1898. Mimosa Pres. **Congregational Meetings. Minutes, 1889-1910.** 2 volumes. Loc: UCA. Card index.
A record of annual and special congregational meetings held each year. The entries for most meetings are brief. The minutes are held in the same ledgers as the account books of the church.

1899. Mimosa Pres. **Diary. Weather conditions, church union, 1924-1925.** 1 volume. Loc: UCA. Card index.
A brief record of weather conditions and church events with several entries each month during 1924. The diary includes a reference to the issue of the union of churches in 1925 noting that 114 people were entitled to vote but only 70 cast ballots with 53 favouring union and 17 rejecting it. The diary is held in the same volume as the collection accounts for the years 1918-1925.

1900. Mimosa Pres. **Session. Minutes, 1866-1873; 1875-1910.** 2 volumes. Loc: UCA. Card index.
The minutes of November 1866 indicate that Mimosa and Everton were united as a joint congregation. The meetings usually convened each month. The minutes are held in the same volume as the baptismal register from 1861 to 1911.

1901. Mimosa Pres-UC. **Presbyterian Missionary Auxiliary. Minutes, 1918-1926.** 1 ledger. Loc: UCA. Card index.
A record of monthly meetings with early meetings referring to the work of the group in donating supplies to hospitals.

1902. Mount Forest Pres. **Annual reports, 1899-1906.** 9 volumes. Loc: WCA. MU 2.
A record of printed volumes which lists church officials and the contributions of specific members and includes the reports of various groups and clubs of the church. In 1904 the name of the church was changed from Mount Forest Presbyterian Church to Westminster Church.

1903. Orangeville (Bethel) Pres. **Baptisms. Register, 1852-1885.** 1 ledger. Loc: UCA. Card index.

1904. Orangeville (Bethel) Pres. **Congregational Meetings. Minutes, 1867-1878.** 1 volume. Loc: UCA. Card index.

A series of brief entries with the meeting held October 30, 1867 outlining plans to construct a new church.

1905. Orangeville (Bethel) Pres. **Deaths. Registers, 1866-1873.** 1 ledger. Loc: UCA. Card index.

1906. Orangeville (Bethel) Pres. **Membership. Roll, 1869.** 1 ledger. Loc: UCA. Card index.

A listing of catechisms and families, including names of parents and children attending the church.

1907. Orangeville (Bethel) Pres. **Session. Minutes, 1859-1875.** 1 volume. Loc: UCA. Card index.

A record of minutes of meetings held on an irregular basis.

1908. Orangeville (St Andrew's) Pres. **Marriages. Register, 1859-1885.** 1 ledger. Loc: UCA. Card index.

A records of marriages which lists residents of Wellington County in areas including Orangeville, Garafraxa Township, Amaranth Township and Erin Village. The end of the ledger includes a lengthy message entitled 'Address to Young Persons'.

1909. Orangeville (Zion) Pres. **Communion. Roll, 1878-1885.** 1 ledger. Loc: UCA. Card index.

A record of members of Zion Presbyterian Church which includes a few references to residents of Orangeville. The record is very incomplete in listing the residence and occupation of church members.

1910. Rockwood Pres. **Cash books, 1871-1883.** 2 ledgers. Loc: UCA. Card index.

The congregational meeting minutes from 1871 to 1879 are also recorded in the same ledger.

1911. Rockwood Pres. **Congregational Meetings. Minutes, 1862-1879.** 2 volumes. Loc: UCA. Card index.

The cash books from 1872 to 1879 are also recorded in the second volume.

1912. Rockwood Pres-Meth-UC. **Young People's Society. Minutes, 1920-1931; 1934-1937.** 3 volumes. Loc: UCA. Card index.

A record of meetings which were held several times each month.

1913. Rockwood Pres-UC. **Baptisms. Registers, 1862-1958.** 2 ledgers. Loc: UCA. Card index.

1914. Rockwood Pres-UC. **Marriages. Register, 1896-1941; 1945-1959.** 1 ledger. Loc: UCA. Card index.

1915. Rockwood Pres-UC. **Session. Minutes, 1861-1952.** 2 volumes. Loc: UCA. Card index.

1916. Simpson's Corners Pres-UC. **Treasurer's book, 1906-1952 (sporadic).** 1 reel. mf. Loc: WCA.

A record of collections, subscription lists and receipts and expenditures.

SOCIETY OF FRIENDS RECORDS

1917. Society of Friends. **Rockwood Meeting. Minutes and other records, 1856-1937.** 3 files, 1 reel. mf. Loc: AO. MS 3403, B-2-43/44/45, Reel 20.

Minutes of the monthly meetings, including statements of belief and principles, correspondence and indentures. Until 1912 the Rockwood group was legally subordinate to the Pelham Congregation and was called the Rockwood Preparative Meeting. In 1903, it became a separate congregation, a status recognized legally in 1912 when the meeting house and burying ground property which had been deeded by John Harris in 1840 to Pelham was returned to the Rockwood Congregation. Prominent Rockwood Quakers were William Wetherald of the Rockwood Academy and members of the Harris family who operated local mills. By the 1930s, the Rockwood congregation dwindled to include some Harris descendants.

CATHOLIC CHURCH RECORDS - CENTRAL

1918. Foyster, Ken. **Anniversary reflections: 1856-1981, a history of the Hamilton Diocese.** 128 pp. Loc: DHA.

A history of the diocese, formed in 1856, that includes a section on Wellington County on pages 90 to 98. In 1830, St Patrick's Church was built. A resident pastor was appointed in 1837, Rev. Thomas Gibney, who directed the construction of St Bartholomew's Church in 1844, after St Patrick's was destroyed by fire. In 1852, the Society of Jesus took charge of the Guelph Parish, and directed missions throughout Wellington, Bruce and Grey Counties. The chapter gives a brief overview of the establishment of churches in Elora, Fergus, Kenilworth, Arthur, Mount Forest, Peel Township, Drayton, Rockwood and Oustic.

1919. Jesuit Fathers of Upper Canada. **Centenary of Father John Holzer's arrival in Guelph, 1952.** 1 file folder. Loc: JA.

Newspaper clippings commemorating the arrival of Holzer in Guelph in 1852, following the transfer of the Jesuit Mission from New Germany (now Maryhill). Held in Box 1 of Guelph records.

1920. Jesuit Fathers of Upper Canada. **Correspondence and newspaper reports concerning withdrawal from Guelph Parish, 1931.** 1 file folder. Loc: JA.

Correspondence between May 15 and September 25 between J.T. McNally, Bishop of Hamilton and W.H. Hingston, Provincial of the Jesuit Order. The Jesuit Fathers received $50,000 'in requital for services' to the Guelph parish during the previous eighty years. The Bishop and Provincial both made it clear that the decision to withdraw from Guelph was made by the Jesuit Fathers, who believed that their vocation was to Indian missions in Western Canada. Held in Box 2 of Guelph records.

1921. Jesuit Fathers of Upper Canada. **Letter read at High Mass, Church of Our Lady, September 5, 1931.** 9 p. Loc: JA.

Letter formally telling parishioners that the Jesuits were about to relinquish the care of the Guelph parish. The Guelph parish had been entrusted to the Jesuits in perpetuity by a Papal Act of 1866, in order to be a base for Indian missions and the site of a college for boys. As it no longer had either of these functions, the Guelph parish was being returned to the Diocese of Hamilton, while the Jesuits moved to Western Canada. Held in Box 2 of Guelph records.

1922. Jesuit Fathers of Upper Canada. **Universal catalogue, 1924-1987**. Loc: JA.
Printout of a database created by H. Logan, S.J., with details of every man who entered or was associated with the Order in Upper Canada. Sources included the annual catalogues (1924-1987) and records of all at the St Stanislaus Novitiate, Guelph. Details include name, province of origin (outside Upper Canada), dates of entry, ordination, final vows, death or leaving order, as well as age at death or departure. The data are organized (a) alphabetically; (b) those from out-of-province; (c) those from Upper Canada only; (d) those deceased who lived to at least eighty years; (e) the one hundred oldest living members; (f) calendar of the dead by date of birth; and (g) calendar of the living by date of birth.

1923. **The Jesuits in the making of Ontario: Toronto, Guelph and districts, c1934.** 10 p. photocopy. Loc: JA.
A brief outline of the establishment of the Jesuit Mission at Guelph that mentions that five hundred families of working people were employed on the three railway lines being built around Guelph in the 1850s.

1924. Loyola College, Montreal. **Jesuits who served in Upper Canada, especially at Guelph, 1852-1931.** 1 binder. Loc: JA.
Brief entries, in alphabetical order, of all members of the Jesuit order, with notes on the sources of biographical facts.

1925. Society of Jesus. **Agreement with Hamilton Diocese, 1861.** 1 file folder. Loc: JA.
Originals and copies of the formal letters concerning the administration of the Guelph Mission by the Jesuit Fathers. Held in Box 1 of Guelph records.

1926. Society of Jesus. **Catalogues, 1855-1987.** Bound volumes. Loc: JA.
Annual printed volumes under various detailed titles that list in Latin the places in which Jesuit missions and colleges were based and the names of all members of the order in each place. Until 1863, the relevant directory was entitled, Catalogus sociorum et officiorum Provinciae Franciae; in 1864 the Catalogus sociorum et officiorum Provinciae Campaniae; from 1870 to 1879, it was the Catalogus Missionis Neo-Eboracensis et Canadensis; from 1880 to 1907, the Catalogus Missionis Canadensis; from 1908 to 1924, Catalogus Provinciae Canadensis; and since 1925, Catalogus Vice-Provinciae Canadae Superioris. Each annual volume also includes a statistical summary of all Jesuit missions and residences and an alphabetical index of all priests, students and lay brothers with dates of birth and entry into the order. The 1855 catalogue notes that the Residentia Guelphensis was staffed by Fr John Holzer, Fr Gaspar Matoga and Fr Henry du Ranquet with lay brothers Andreas Tragsail and Jacob Mallen. By 1864, Holzer is listed as superior at the Collegium Inchoatum Guelphense. The Guelph Mission is referred to as St Bartholomew's Church for the first time in 1876 and as Church of Our Lady from 1879. Details of the St Stanislaus Novitiate are provided from 1914.

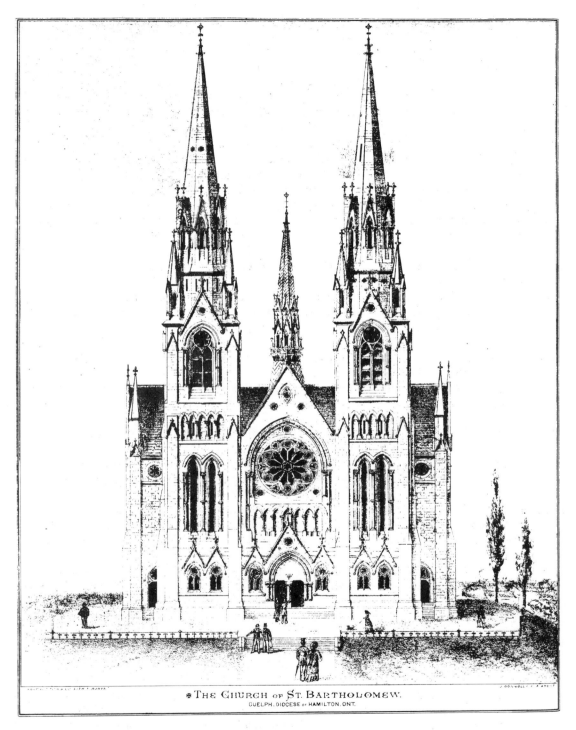

✠ THE CHURCH OF ST. BARTHOLOMEW.
GUELPH, DIOCESE OF HAMILTON. ONT.

Joseph Connolly's design for the Church of Our Lady, Guelph, c1876.
The church was opened in 1888 (#1940) without the twin spires that were a striking feature of Connolly's design; twin towers were completed instead in 1926. In this drawing from Walker & Miles's <u>Illustrated Atlas of the County of Wellington</u> (1877) the church is still named St Bartholomew's.

1927. Society of Jesus. **Memorials of visitations to Guelph, 1870-1900.** 1 bound vol. Loc: JA.

Reports, most in Latin and many in copperplate calligraphy, of visits by superiors of the Jesuit order to the Guelph Mission. The Jesuits were responsible for the administration of the Catholic church in Guelph and district between 1851 and 1931. Held in Box 1 of Guelph records.

1928. Woodstock College, Maryland. **Woodstock Letters, 1872-1987.** Bound volumes. Loc: JA.

Annual printed selections from letters of Jesuit priests throughout North America. The Index to Volumes 1-80 (1872-1951), compiled by George Zorn and published by the Woodstock College Press in 1960, has entries for John Holzer (vol. 17, p. 244; vol. 42, p. 303), Gaspar Matoga (vol. 38, p. 351), as well as references to the opening of the new St Stanislaus Novitiate (vol. 42, p. 302; vol. 43, p. 1222) and to the raid during World War I (vol. 47, p. 396-9; vol. 49, p. 249). The Jesuit Archives lack volumes 5-43, but there are copies in an adjoining building at Regis College, Toronto.

1929. Woodstock College, Maryland. **Woodstock Letters. Obituary of Father John E. Holzer, 1817-1888.** photocopy. Loc: JA.

The obituary quotes one of Holzer's letters describing the Catholic cause on his arrival in 1853 as 'sadly neglected and in deplorable condition'. Holzer is credited with having 'instructed the ignorant, pacified the rebellious' and built school, convent, hospital, home for the aged and rectory as well as caring for a dozen outlying missions. Photocopy held in Box 1 of Guelph records.

CATHOLIC CHURCH RECORDS - LOCAL

1930. Arthur (St John's) Catholic. **Correspondence, historical sketches and photographs, 1865-1956.** 1 file folder. Loc: DHA.

The file includes general correspondence to the bishop, names of pew holders for 1896 and 1897, names of contributors listed by marital status and amounts donated for 1896, 1902 and 1914, an auditor's report for 1893, a school inspector's report of Arthur Township RCSS #4 in 1927, and a photograph of the rectory.

1931. Collins, Thomas, Rev. **The Church of Our Lady: a chronology, 1988.** 8 p. typescript. Loc: JA.

A summary of the main events since June 1827. The author notes that the parish was part of the Diocese of Kingston to 1841, then part of the Diocese of Toronto to 1856, and thereafter part of the Diocese of Hamilton, and outlines the role of the pioneer priests in the establishment of education in Guelph and in starting mission stations at fifty-six points in the hinterland north and northwest of Guelph. Guelph was the base from which churches were built at Fergus (1854), Morriston (1856) and Mount Forest (1857) as well as many other places beyond Wellington County. Arthur was made a separate parish in 1861, Mount Forest in 1862 and Fergus and Elora in 1865. Part of Box 2 of Guelph records.

1932. Drayton (St Martin's) Catholic. **Correspondence, historical sketches and photographs, 1859-1942.** 1 file folder. Loc: DHA.

A collection of letters to the bishop about parish matters, several brief historical sketches of the church which was built in 1881, and several photographs of the building. The church evolved from St Anthony's, which was on Concession 12 of Peel Township.

1933. Elora (St Mary's) Catholic. **Correspondence, historical sketches and photographs, 1850-1954. 1 file folder. Loc: DHA.**
A collection of correspondence to the bishop about church matters from 1885 to 1929, photographs of the church and school, and newspaper clippings about the church's development. A brief historical sketch indicates Elora began to have services in 1850 and a resident priest arrived in 1854. The parish provided a mission in Fergus until 1978 when the Fergus church received its own resident priest. The file also contains two old undated petitions of Catholics in Fergus and Elora requesting the services of a resident priest, and listing amounts of money individuals agreed to pay to support the priest. The Fergus list has 49 names and the Elora list has 58 names. Both lists included the signatures of several women.

1934. Foyster, Ken. **Parish histories, 1827-1982. 1 file folder. Loc: DHA.**
Wellington County parish histories refer to early settlement patterns, priests, parish development, parish correspondence to the bishop, and important issues of dispute within each parish, such as support for separate schools. Churches include St John's in Arthur (1843); St Martin's in Drayton (1881); Church of Our Lady in Guelph (1885), which incorporates some history of St Patrick's (1827) and St Bartholomew's (1846); Sacred Heart in Guelph (1908); Sacred Heart in Kenilworth (1851); St Mary's in Mount Forest (1852); Sacred Heart in Rockwood (1852); and St Peter's in Oustic (1852). The dates refer to first services held in the area, rather than the official origin of the parish, which is dated from the arrival of a resident priest.

1935. Guelph Catholic Parish. **Marymount Cemetery. Rules and regulations, 1928. 14 p. Loc: JA.**
A small printed booklet produced at the time a new Catholic cemetery was opened on the Elora Road to replace St Joseph's Cemetery on what is now Westmount Road.

1936. Guelph (Church of Our Lady) Catholic. **A brief survey of the history of the Church of Our Lady, 1939. 15 p. typescript. Loc: JA.**
An outline history that includes a list of all the priests. Held in Box 2 of Guelph records.

1937. Guelph (Church of Our Lady) Catholic. **Building the Church of Our Lady, c1926. 4 p. typescript. Loc: JA.**
A much edited typescript apparently compiled about the time the church's square towers were erected. The unnamed author stresses the construction of the successive church buildings. Held in Box 2 of Guelph records.

1938. Guelph (Church of Our Lady) Catholic. **Controversy over Protestant Orangemen's church services, 1881. 1 file folder. Loc: JA.**
Newspaper reports of controversy excited by sermons preached by the Reverend Alexander Dixon of St George's Anglican Church and Reverend William Williams of Norfolk Street Methodist Church at a service attended by parading Orangemen. The

Catholic community was incensed by anti-Catholic sentiments in the sermons. Held in Box 1 of the Guelph records.

1939. Guelph (Church of Our Lady) Catholic. **Correspondence, historical sketches and photographs, 1853-1957.** 2 file folders. Loc: DHA.

A collection of correspondence to the bishop about parish matters, historical sketches of the development of the church and parish schools, photographs of the building and parishoners, and several newspaper clippings of special events.

1940. Guelph (Church of Our Lady) Catholic. **Dedication Ceremony. Newspaper reports, 1888.** 1 file folder. Loc: JA.

Detailed reports of the ceremony on October 11, 1888, at which the newly completed building was dedicated by Bishop Walsh of London. The church building is noted to have cost nearly $200,000 and its design by Toronto architect Joseph Connolly in the French Gothic style is praised for its 'magnificence and purity of architecture'. The church is described as constructed of Guelph limestone with columns of Bay of Fundy granite. Reports from the Evening Mercury, The Empire, the Catholic Register, the Catholic Weekly Review and the Daily Herald are included. Held in Box 1 of Guelph records.

1941. Guelph (Church of Our Lady) Catholic. **Foundation Stone Ceremony. Program and newspaper reports, 1877.** 2 file folders. Loc: JA.

Detailed reports of plans for the ceremony in July 1877, which was attended by the Papal Delegate, Dr Conroy. Local Catholics who were active supporters of the church building project are noted, including John Harris, J. Lambert, William Kelly, James Hazleton, T.J. Day, Edward O'Connor, J.M. MacMillan, E. O'Donnell, John Greene, J. Mays, Thomas Heffernan, John Murphy, P. Mahon, Brian Carroll, Patrick Molloy, James McNaughton, James Synott, Tim O'Connor and Alexander Kennedy. The records include newspaper reports of the censure by Protestant ministers of the decision by the Guelph Town Council to accept the church's invitation to attend the ceremony. Held in Box 1 of Guelph records.

1942. Guelph (Church of Our Lady) Catholic. **History of Our Lady's Parish, Guelph, 1827-1937.** 6 p. typescript. Loc: JA.

A brief outline of the church's history that stresses the first thirty years and quotes from John Holzer's diary as to the evidence of poverty in Guelph when he arrived in 1852. Held with Box 2 of Guelph records.

1943. Guelph (Sacred Heart) Catholic. **Historical sketches, 1908-1956.** 1 file folder. Loc: DHA.

Brief historical sketches of the parish.

1944. Hamel, Peter. **Letters exchanged with Patrick Boyle, 1878.** 1 file folder. Loc: JA.

Correspondence includes response by Boyle, editor of the Toronto weekly newspaper, The Irish Canadian, to Hamel's denunciation of the paper from his Guelph pulpit, Hamel's reply and Boyle's petition to the Bishop of Hamilton. Held in Box 1 of Guelph records.

1945. Heffernan, Thomas. **Letter to Bishop of Hamilton concerning financing construction of new church, 1875.** 1 file folder. Loc: JA.

An appeal to the Bishop against diverting proceeds of selling Catholic glebe lands in Guelph to Hamilton building projects. Heffernan cites local tradition and assurances of the late Bishop Farrell in arguing that any sales of glebe land should benefit the Guelph church building fund. He refers to the 'large sums of money subscribed [in Guelph] for the immense structure which has never been of any use to the Catholic community of Guelph. The Catholics here are unanimous in calling for a new Church and are prepared to subscribe liberally in accordance with their means in creating a Handsome Church, one worthy of the magnificent site we possess'. Heffernan claims that he represents nearly four-fifths of the church members of the Guelph parish. Held in Box 1 of the Guelph records.

1946. Jesuit Mission, Guelph. **Bishop of Toronto's letters of appointment, 1853-1855.** 1 file folder. Loc: JA.

Printed letters in the name of Bishop Charbonnel with the particular details entered by hand. The letter for John Holzer is dated 20 October 1853 and for Gaspar Matoga, 15 June 1855. The file, in Box 1 of Guelph records, also contains a Table of Fees for various Catholic services dating from 1843 but in effect in the 1850s, and an 1863 letter from Bishop Farrell of Hamilton appointing Father Archard to Guelph.

1947. Jesuit Mission, Guelph. **Correspondence, 1852-1866.** 1 file folder. originals. Loc: JA.

The earliest letter appears to be from Bishop Charbonnel of Toronto to the Catholics of New Germany (now Maryhill) explaining the decision to transfer the base of the Jesuit Mission to Guelph (13 March 1852). Charbonnel also writes to John Holzer at Guelph in December, 1852 discussing his task to liquidate the large debt of the Catholic parish in Guelph by, among other means, securing the payment of pew rents in advance. One letter, apparently written by Holzer on 17 September 1859, refers to his satisfaction with the success of the Guelph Mission and to assurances on three occasions by the Bishop of Hamilton that the Jesuits would never be disturbed in their care of the Guelph parish and that in fifty years Guelph would probably be the site of a bishopric. Holzer also mentions that the Bishop planned to build a church of 'huge dimensions with astonishing rapidity'. A letter by Bishop John Farrell on 20 May 1860 confirms that the care of the Church of St Bartholomew would be left to the Jesuit fathers for 'as long as they wish to retain it' and grants them the use of various parcels of church land in Guelph. There is also a letter by Bishop Farrell in 1865 appealing for the help of Guelph Catholics in the construction of St Joseph's Hospital in Hamilton. The file also includes a memorandum of several pages that outlines the history of the Guelph parish since 1827. The memorandum was dated 1866, but was written on Church of Our Lady notepaper. The Unknown author, possibly Father J. Archambault, notes the building of St Ignatius College in 1857 but its closing in 1865 for want of support and the laying of the cornerstone of the new church in 1863, the foundations alone costing five thousand dollars. The author concludes in 1866, '14 years have we toiled and now have $14,674 debt and no hope to pay. . . . Better leave, money wasted'.

1948. Jesuit Mission, Guelph. **Minutes and memoranda, 1862-1909.** 1 vol. Loc: JA.

Brief notes, recorded in Latin until 1886, of meetings of the Jesuit staff of the Guelph mission.

1949. Jesuit Mission, Guelph. **Newspaper clippings on the Scott Act, 1864.** 1 file folder. Loc: JA.

The file includes opinion and comment on the proposed legislation to regulate the sale and consumption of liquor as well as news of the poll results in which a 'fair majority' of Guelph voters were in favour of the new regulations. The clippings show that the Guelph Herald was editorially opposed to the new legislation. There is no evidence to show the Jesuit priests took any stand on the issue. Held in Box 1 of Guelph records.

1950. Jesuit Mission, New Germany. **Baptismal and burial registers, 1860.** mf. Loc: NAC. FA: C-15758.

The register includes entries for Guelph and Pilkington Townships.

1951. Kenilworth (Sacred Heart) Catholic. **Correspondence, historical sketches, 1843-1953.** 1 file folder. Loc: DHA.

A collection of correspondence to the bishop from 1902 to 1903, and historical sketches of the church. Services began in 1843, and in 1852 Jesuit missionaries served the church until 1870 when it was closed. In 1903 the church became an official parish when a resident priest was appointed.

1952. Mount Forest (St Mary's) Catholic. **Correspondence, historical sketches and photographs, 1856-1954.** 1 file folder. Loc: DHA.

A collection of correspondence to the bishop from 1863 to 1933, historical sketches, and a photograph of the rectory. The church first held services in 1856 as a mission of the Guelph Jesuits. It became an official parish in 1862 when a resident priest was appointed.

1953. Nunan, George. **History of the Catholic parish of Guelph, 1827-1927.** 7 p. typescript. Loc: JA.

A useful summary that names the first Catholic families of Guelph, including John Lynch (blacksmith), James McCartney, Bernard McTague, Thomas Kelly and the LaGuayran colonists Donald Gillies, James McQuillan, Joseph Mays, Thomas Daly and three families of Kennedys. Many of these Irish families settled in a block along the Waterloo Road known as Tinkertown. Held in Box 2 of Guelph records.

1954. O'Reilly, John A. and Sheady, W.J. **Church of Our Lady, Guelph, 1943.** 35 p. Loc: JA.

Following a brief historical outline that lacks any mention of the Jesuit Mission or the work of John Holzer, most of the booklet is devoted to a description of the structure and interior decoration of the church. Held with Box 2 of the Guelph records.

1955. Oustic (St Peter's) Catholic. **Dedication Ceremony. Newspaper reports, 1884.** 1 file folder. Loc: JA.

Guelph newspaper reports of the dedication of the church which was a mission of the Guelph Church of Our Lady. Held in Box 1 of Guelph records.

1956. Rockwood (Sacred Heart) Catholic. **Correspondence, historical sketches, photographs, 1936-1956.** 1 file folder. Loc: DHA.

A collection of 3 letters to the bishop from 1936 to 1939, 2 photographs of the building, and a brief historical sketch of the church. The church was a mission of the Guelph parish until it received its first resident priest in

1936. At that time St Peter's Church in Oustic became a mission of the Rockwood Church.

CHURCH OF LATTER DAY SAINTS RECORDS

1957. Arthur Latter Day Saints. **Marriage register, 1900-1959.** 3 p. Loc: GPL, WCA.
A list of entries taken from the marriage register for the Arthur branch of the Reorganized Church of Jesus Christ of Latter Day Saints. The photocopy is from the journal, Families, Volume 26, 1987. Fred McLean is listed as church elder. A printed copy of the register is also held at Wellington County Archives.

UNITED CHURCH (POST-1925) RECORDS

1958. Erin UC. **Congregational Meetings. Minutes, 1925-1936.** 1 volume. Loc: UCA. Card index.
A record of annual congregational meetings of the Erin Union Church with some

of the meetings being held in Hillsburgh. The minutes in 1926 include references to the activities of the board of management and trustees' meetings, and to the official board of the church.

1959. Erin UC. **Ladies Aid Society. Minutes, 1929-1961.** 6 volumes. Loc: UCA. Card index.
A record of annual and monthly meetings which notes fund raising activities, attendance of members and the financial returns of the group.

1960. Erin UC. **Official Board. Minutes, 1925-1932.** 1 volume. Loc: UCA. Card index.
A record of meetings held alternately in Erin United Church, Hillsburgh United Church and Coningsby United Church. The meetings usually convened roughly three times each year.

1961. Erin UC. **Women's Association. Cash books, 1928-1946.** 2 ledgers. Loc: UCA. Card index.
A record of financial statements with the ledger covering the years 1928 to 1938 being referred to as the treasurer's book and including outlines of the activities of the group at monthly meetings. The organization is labelled as the North Erin Church Ladies Aid Society initially and by 1939 includes the Women's Association and Women's Missionary Society.

1962. Erin UC. **Women's Association. Minutes, 1926-1936.** 1 volume. Loc: UCA. Card index.
A record of monthly meetings which indicates the home where meetings were convened as well as listing members of the group.

1963. Hillsburgh UC. **Ladies Aid. Minutes, 1927-1947.** 5 volumes. Loc: UCA. Card index.
A record of meetings which convened once each month. The minutes list members, outline activities, and include financial statements of the group.

1964. Hillsburgh UC. **Sunday School. Attendance register, 1933-1942; 1944.** 1 ledger. Loc: UCA. Card index.

A listing of the number of students attending various age levels of the school each month and the amount of money contributed. The attendance register is held in the same ledger as the minutes of the Sunday School.

1965. Hillsburgh UC. **Sunday School. Minutes, 1933-1937.** 1 volume. Loc: UCA. Card index.
   A record of annual meetings with brief entries noting officers elected and motions passed at meetings. The minutes are held in the same ledger as the attendance register of the Sunday School.

1966. Ponsonby UC. **Marriages. Registers, 1933-1953.** 1 reel. mf. Loc: WCA.

1967. Rockwood UC. **Account book, 1925-1961.** 2 ledgers. Loc: UCA. Card index.
   One ledger is not labelled but is boxed with the records of the Rockwood United Church.

1968. Rockwood UC. **Congregational Meetings. Minutes, 1925-1958.** 1 volume. Loc: UCA. Card index.

1969. Rockwood UC. **Sunday School Teachers' Meetings. Minutes, 1925-1970.** 1 volume. Loc: UCA. Card index.

1970. Rockwood UC. **Women's Missionary Society. Minutes, 1926-1954.** 4 volumes. Loc: UCA. Card index.

CHURCH AND CLERGY RECORDS - MISCELLANEOUS

1971. Barker, Enoch, Rev. **Baptisms. Register, 1872-1877.** 1 ledger. Loc: UCA.
   A record of the baptisms by Reverend Enoch Barker with a number of references to residents of Wellington County including Fergus, Elora, Drayton and the Townships of Nichol, Eramosa and West Garafraxa.

1972. Barker, Enoch, Rev. **Marriages. Register, 1874-1877.** 1 ledger. Loc: UCA.
   A record of roughly fifty marriages performed by Reverend Enoch Barker in Elora, Fergus, Clifford, Drayton and the Townships of West Garafraxa, Eramosa and Erin. The record lists marriage partners, their place of residence, when and where married, and the fee paid for the ceremony.

1973. Bindemann, Frederick W., Rev. **Marriage registers for Unorthodox Evangelical Lutheran Congregation, 1855.** mf. Loc: NAC. FA: C-15758.
   The register has entries for a very large area centered in Berlin, including Guelph, Nichol, Peel and Puslinch Townships in Wellington County.

1974. Black, James, Rev. **Eramosa Township. Marriage registers, 1828-1842; 1858-1882.** 1 file folder; 1 volume. Loc: WCA, GPL. MU 21.
   A record of marriage partners and their places of residence, date of marriage, list of witnesses and whether married 'by banns or licence'. The ledger is the record of marriages performed by Reverend James Black with most marriage partners residing in Erin and Eramosa Townships. The ledgers do not indicate the religious denomination which Reverend Black represented in the county. Part of the Pollock Collection. The register from 1858 to 1882 and a printed copy are held at GPL.

1975. Elora Branch Bible Society. **Annual reports, 1890-1892; 1907. 4 documents.** Loc: WCA.

A record of printed reports which lists subscriptions and general receipts and expenditures. The reports also list the officers of the society. Part of the Pollock Collection.

1976. Guelph Ministerial Association. **Jesuit Novitiate case: a statement and an editorial, 1918. 1 brochure.** Loc: GCM, JA.

A statement from the Ministerial Association in support of a raid by the military police on the Jesuit Novitiate in search of defaulters from military service who were eligible for service under the Military Service Act. The Protestant ministers state that their attitude 'is not that of religious intolerance, bigotry or prejudice, but a question of common fairness and equal rights to all, whether Catholic or Protestant'. The brochure reprints an editorial from the Toronto Evening Telegram, on June 25, 1918, which indicates that the federal government became involved in the case by demanding the military police withdraw from the Novitiate, offering an apology and instituting press censorship over the issue.

1977. Guelph Ministerial Association. **Queen's Jubilee Service. Program, 1897.** 1 brochure. Loc: GCM.

A record of the service held on June 20, 1897 in the Royal Opera House at which a special offering was taken for the Guelph General Hospital. Several clergy participated in the event including Rev. Wardrope, Rev. B.B. Williams, Rev. R.J.M. Glassford and Rev. S. Sellery.

1978. Jewitt, J.A., Rev. **Burials. Register, 1918-1921.** 1 ledger. Loc: UCA. Card index.

A number of burial records of Reverend J.A. Jewitt with only a minimal number of references to Wellington County residents. The areas mentioned include Erin, Ballinafad, Everton and Coningsby.

1979. Killean Sabbath School. **Library subscription list, 1883.** 1 document. Loc: WCA.

Held in the Wellington County Historical Research Society Collection. A list of donors and amount each gave.

1980. Marden Sunday School. **Receipt book, 1889-1908.** 1 ledger. Loc: WBE.

A Sunday School that apparently used the Marden School building. Held with Guelph Township school records.

1981. Nisbet, James, Rev. **Pocket diary recording tour of Canada West, 1848.** Loc: NAC. MG 24, J 25.

Nisbet was a Presbyterian clergyman whose tour, on behalf of the Canada Sabbath School Union, included Galt, Guelph and Fergus as well as most other towns in Canada West.

1982. Reid, Hugh, Rev. **Erin Township. Marriage register, 1858-1875.** 1 file folder. Loc: WCA.

A transcription of originals which lists brides, grooms, their ages, place of birth and residence, names of parents and witnesses, and the date of marriage. The Wellington County Archives has developed a much more readable copy of the registers. Part of the Pollock Collection.

1983. Slight, Benjamin, Rev. **Diary, 1839-1840**. 1 reel. mf. Loc: UCA.
A personal memoir about the spiritual impact of Slight's sermons held in various places in Upper Canada that includes references to several meetings in Guelph and Eramosa. Slight was a Wesleyan Methodist circuit preacher.

1984. Smitherman, George W., Rev. **Marriages. Register, 1903-1917**. 1 ledger. Loc: UCA.
A record of marriages including several references to ceremonies performed by Reverend George W. Smitherman in Drew Station and Rockwood. The ledger does not directly indicate the religious affiliation of Smitherman but most of the parties married are listed as Methodists.

On the rocks at Rockwood: an excursion of an unidentified group, possibly a scientific, literary or church society, c1880.
(Wellington County Museum and Archives)

VOLUNTARY ASSOCIATIONS

In no country in the world has the principle of association been more successfully applied to a greater multitude of objects; associations are established to promote the public safety, commerce, industry, morality and religion. There is no end that the human will despair of attaining through the combined power of individuals united into a society.[1]

Alexis de Tocqueville's generalization about the role of what he called the civil or 'intellectual and moral' associations in American society in the earlier nineteenth century might be equally applied to Canada a little later. He remarked on 'not only commercial and manufacturing companies ... but associations of a thousand other kinds -- religious, moral, serious, futile, extensive or restricted, enormous or diminutive ... associations to give entertainments, to found establishments for education, to build inns, to construct churches, to diffuse books, to send missionaries to the antipodes; [to] found hospitals, prisons and schools. If it be proposed to advance some truth, or to foster some feeling by the encouragement of a great example, they form a society.' De Tocqueville 'admired the extreme skill with which the inhabitants succeed in proposing a common object to the exertions of a great many men, and in getting them voluntarily to pursue it.'[2]

In his analysis of voluntary associations in the social organization of Cincinnati in 1840, Walter Glazer included 'any group, formal or informal, permanent or ephemeral, open or restricted, which was organized for the common benefit of its members and in which participation was voluntary.'[3] Voluntary associations served a wide variety of functions. In a social order otherwise dominated by individualism and unprotected from the vicissitudes of life, they had valuable purposes in providing a mix of social activities, insurance benefits, philanthropic work, character-building and personal development exercises and adult education.[4] Participation and leadership in voluntary associations were perceived by contemporaries to be meritorious contributions to community-building.

---

[1] Alexis de Tocqueville, **Democracy in America**, ed. Phillips Bradley (New York, 1945 ed.) I, 198-9; II, 110.

[2] Alexis de Tocqueville, **Democracy in America**, translated by Henry Reeve (New York: The Colonial Press, 1900), II, 114-118.

[3] Walter Glazer, 'Participation and power: voluntary associations and the functional organization of Cincinnati in 1840,' **Historical Methods Newsletter** 5 (1972): 151-168.

[4] This introduction has benefited from unpublished reports of intensive research on voluntary associations by Professor George Emery of the University of Western Ontario, for the Landon Project of the mid-1970s.

While these associations were voluntary in membership and participation, they varied in the extent of local autonomy and in the involvement with government. Some associations were purely local, existing in a single community; others were local branches of a regional, national or even international federation. In the latter case, notably in the case of fraternal associations, the autonomy of the local branch might be limited. Some may also have had some quasi-official status in being eligible for government grants because of the public service they performed or because their activities were deemed socially useful. This was true of the agricultural societies, the mechanics' institutes, some musical societies, the militia, women's institutes, children's aid societies, and the YMCA/YWCA. Records were more likely to be retained if there was some official link of this nature.

The associations represented in the following section of the **Inventory** are only a small proportion of those that must have existed in Guelph and Wellington County at any time between 1830 and 1940. In addition, there were numerous associations of which the only surviving evidence consists of listings in directories and some newspaper reports of activities. There were, for example, 27 voluntary associations listed in the Guelph directory for 1873 compared with only 12 churches for a population of about 7,000, 43 associations and 14 churches for about 10,000 people in 1886, and 47 societies and 18 churches for 11,500 people in 1901. But we have traced records for only 12 of the 64 different Guelph associations identified in directories for these three years. Other associations were too evanescent or informal to be listed in directories.

For some associations we have quite good records in the form of minute books, cash books, membership registers, constitutions and bylaws, and correspondence, but for other groups the only records we have traced are ephemeral fragments. Records in this section are grouped by type of association: agricultural, business, cultural, fraternal, jubilee and reunion, labour, musical, political, sports, temperance, militia and veterans', women's, and youth welfare.

Agricultural societies

Only a broadside has survived of the records of the Wellington District Agricultural Society in the 1840s (#2019). Agricultural societies were set up in some parts of the county by the 1860s, with records for the Guelph Township society spanning the period from the mid-1850s to 1905, and for the Puslinch Farmers' Club from 1874 to 1898. More typically, local agricultural associations were founded as farmers' institutes from the later 1870s, following the initiative of the OAC President, James Mills. One farmers' institute in each Ontario electoral district qualified for a provincial grant of $24. Farmers' institutes began to wane from 1910 and virtually ceased in the mid-1920s. There are also a few records of the quasi-official organization, the Ontario Provincial Winter Fair, based in Guelph from the late 1880s to 1939 (#2010-#2013).

Only a short-lived cash book from the 1890s survives to document the local activities of the Patrons of Industry, popularly known as the Grange (#2014). A militant offshoot of the earlier Patrons of Husbandry, the Grange developed from a secret society for farmers only into an active political party. The years of activity of the Arthur Association, one of a reported 2000 local clubs, coincide with the peak years of this movement in Ontario.[5]

Business associations

In Guelph, as in other Canadian towns and cities from the 1860s to about 1920, community businessmen identified strongly with the local board of trade. The powers of these bodies were then larger and their status higher than their name might suggest and than the image of their modern successors, the chambers of commerce.[6] In an era before the formation of social and service clubs, the board usually attracted most members of the local elite as members and tended to espouse community causes. The Guelph Board of Trade, incorporated by a provincial statute in 1868, listed 74 charter members and played an influential role in promoting business growth and boosting the city's image. During the period to 1940, Mount Forest (in 1893) was the only other centre in Wellington County known to have formed a board of trade, though chambers of commerce have since been created in several other towns. But formal records survive for neither Guelph nor Mount Forest, so that any analysis of the role of boards of trade must depend on newspaper reports.

Cultural and scientific societies

Several distinctive societies of this type have left records, notably the North Wellington Teachers' Association (1859-1862), the Elora School Museum of the 1870s and the Guelph Scientific Society (1886-1892). Most numerous are records of the mechanics' institutes which were the forerunners of the public library system of the twentieth century. Except for some subscription libraries begun before 1850, of which examples are known for Fergus and Lower Nichol, the first library in most communities was provided by a mechanics' institutes.[7] These depended primarily on members' dues, sometimes matched by grants from the provincial government. Of the 67 institutes had been incorporated and

---

[5] S.E. Shortt, 'Social change and political crisis in Ontario: the Patrons of Industry, 1889-1896,' in Donald Swainson, ed. **Oliver Mowat's Ontario** (Toronto: Macmillan, 1972): 211-235.

[6] Elizabeth Bloomfield, 'Boards of trade and Canadian urban development,' **Urban History Review** 12 (1983): 83.

[7] The most useful primary source on Ontario mechanics' institutes to 1880 is the 'Special report of the Minister of Education on the mechanics' institutes of Ontario,' **Ontario Sessional Papers** 46 (1881). The general history and philosophy of the township libraries or mechanics' institutes are discussed in Jim Blanchard, 'Predecessor to the public library: mechanics' institutes in Upper Canada and Ontario,' **Expression** (Fall 1981) 25-28, and 'Anatomy of failure: Ontario mechanics' institutes, 1835-1895,' **Canadian Library Journal** 38 (1981) 393-198; John A. Wiseman, 'Phoenix in flight: Ontario mechanics' institutes, 1880-1920,' **Canadian Library Journal** 38 (1981) 401-405. For an account of the township school libraries promoted in the 1840s and 1850s by Egerton Ryerson, see Bruce Curtis, '"Littery merrit", "useful knowledge" and the organization of township libraries in Canada West, 1840-1860,' **Ontario History** 78 (1986): 285-312.

receiving grants in Canada West by 1858, four were in Wellington County.

From the early 1870s, provincial legislation and grants again supported mechanics' institutes to provide library service as well as evening classes in technical and literary subjects. David Boyle's work for the Elora Mechanics' Institute in the 1870s fulfilled the spirit as well as the letter of the legislation.[8] Guelph, Elora and Mount Forest reported activity from 1871, Harriston from 1874, Arthur and Ennotville from 1879. Wellington County had three of the 41 Institutes in Ontario receiving aid in 1871, and seven of the 74 reporting in 1879.

In 1880, supervision of the institutes was transferred from the Department of Agriculture to the Department of Education and Dr S.P. May was appointed to survey the resources and services of the 121 institutes incorporated by 1880. His recommendations that library service should be a charge on the municipality rather than the legislature led to the Free Libraries Act of 1882 which was adopted by only a few of the larger towns and cities, including Guelph. But in rural areas, mechanics' institutes continued to 'constitute the public library system of the Province.'[9] In 1900, two-thirds of all the communities with library service of some kind had 'public association' libraries, as the mechanics' institutes were renamed from 1895. The public association libraries continued until the 1960s when library services were rationalized in various ways by sweeping independent library boards into county and district co-operative systems designed to encourage larger and more efficient units of service.

Excellent records survive of the Elora and Guelph institutes from the 1850s, but the Ennotville institute has both archival and artifactual interest. The North Wellington (later renamed Ennotville) Farmers' and Mechanics' Institute, which took over the earlier Lower Nichol Subscription Library in 1856, seems to have been a remarkable exception among Ontario rural libraries in having its own library building from the 1850s. The building has since been the community centre for most local voluntary associations, including a temperance lodge, a non-denominational sunday school, the farmers' institute and the women's institute, as well as for regular social events of all kinds. Like most rural libraries, Ennotville remained independent of municipal government and lasted as an association library until the mid-1960s; it was then incorporated as the Ennotville Historical Library. The library's records, recently transferred to the Wellington County Archives, provide valuable evidence of the social history of a rural community. The surviving book collection is a kind of time capsule of a mechanics' institute library in the late nineteenth century.

Records of the free public libaries that became the responsibility of the municipal councils from the 1880s are grouped in the earlier section of Public

---

[8] Gerald Killan, **David Boyle: from artisan to archaeologist** (Toronto: University of Toronto Press, 1983): 42-46.

[9] 'Annual report of Inspector of Public Libraries,' **Ontario Sessional Papers 1891, No. 4.**

Libraries under the major heading of Government Records.

Fraternal societies

Fraternal orders frequently combined fellowship and character-building activities with mutual benefit insurance schemes for the protection of families against sickness and death. The various orders of Odd Fellows, in which benefits were a subsidiary element, are well represented by the records of the Gordon Lodge of the Independent Order in Palmerston from 1885 to 1957. Insurance purposes were dominant in the various Orders of Foresters. Harriston's branch of the Canadian Order of Foresters, from 1871 to 1901, coincides with the heyday of this order. The Ancient Order of United Workmen, founded in Pennsylvania in 1868, is represented by some records of an Elora branch around 1900.[10] The Order of Chosen Friends, founded in Indiana in 1868, pioneered old age and disability insurance, and had a branch in Guelph in the 1890s. In the years around 1900, Erin had a 'tent' of the Knights of the Maccabees of the World (KOTM), which had been founded in London, Ontario, in 1878. Though there were as many as seven Masonic Lodges in Wellington County in the later nineteenth century, none of their records have come into the public domain.

Several fraternal lodges had a strong ethnocultural or denominational bias. The Loyal Orange Association combined militant Irish Protestantism and a ardent loyalty to the British monarchy with character-building activities and insurance benefit schemes. The Grand Lodge of British North America was formed in 1830, and was particularly strong in Ontario; records survive especially for the Harriston Lodge with a fragment also for Rockwood.[11] Roman Catholic orders, that notably included the Catholic Order of Foresters and the Knights of Columbus, are represented in the surviving records only by the Elora Catholic Benefit Association. Societies also flourished for citizens of Scottish, English or Irish extraction but only the minutes of the St Andrew's Society of Guelph have been traced (#2071).

Labour associations

Very little in the way of labour association records has been traced, apart from printed programmes of labour parades and conventions. Guelph had five Local Assemblies of the Knights of Labor in the mid-1880s, with a peak

---

[10] See also Helen Schmid, 'The Ancient Order of United Workmen,' **Families** 21, 2 (1982): 67; 'More AOUW assessment notices,' **Families** 26, 4 (1987): 234-5.

[11] For a geographical analysis of the Orange Order in Canada, see Cecil J. Houston and William J. Smyth, **The sash Canada wore: a historical geography of the Orange Order in Canada** (Toronto, 1980). G.C. Kealey has analyzed Orangeism in Toronto in terms of class in 'The Orange Order in Toronto: religious riot and the working class,' in G.S. Kealey and P. Warrian, eds. **Essays in Canadian working class history** (Toronto: McClelland and Stewart, 1976): 13-34.

total of 350 members in 1886.[12]   The Guelph Trades and Labor Council was established in 1898, but no formal records from before 1940 have come to light.   To make up for this deficiency to some extent, we may consult the monthly reports submitted by the Guelph correspondent to the **Labour Gazette** from 1900.

Musical societies

Long runs of records survive for the Presto Music Club of Guelph, spanning the period from 1908 to 1963. More ephemeral fragments show that Elora had an Amateur Brass Band in the 1850s and a Philharmonic Society in the 1880s.   Only a program survives of the first Guelph Music Festival organized in May 1929.

Political associations

Local elections -- municipal, provincial and federal -- usually generated a great deal of rhetoric and activity. It is disappointing that so little archival evidence has come to light so far on the activities of local political associations, but at least they usually received considerable newspaper coverage.

Sports associations

Records of athletic and sporting associations have survived surprisingly well.   There are ephemeral fragments only for such groups as the Wheelman's Asssocation, the Guelph Boxing Club, the Guelph Cricket Club, the Guelph Cross Country and Road Race Association, Guelph's Orange and Black Hockey Club and the Guelph Snowshoe and Toboggan Club, but enough to give an impression of the variety and vitality of such groups in the past.   Excellent records survive for the Fergus Curling Club from 1834 to 1938, the Elora Lawn Bowling Association (1906-1945) and quite good materials for the Maple Leaf Baseball Team owned by the brewer George Sleeman in the last quarter of the nineteenth century.

Social and service clubs

Incomplete records only, for the Guelph Rotary Club, have been traced before 1940.

Temperance associations

A special type of fraternal order was devoted overwhelmingly to temperance and the prohibition of alcohol.[13]   The first of these orders, the Sons of Temperance, was introduced into Ontario from New York in 1848. According to directory evidence, there was a Guelph branch in the 1870s; this group may also be represented in the short-lived minute books for Elora and Pilkington in the early 1850s (#2121-#2122). The Independent Order of Good Templars, also introduced from New York in the early 1850s, did not organize insurance benefits but allowed women an equal role with men in membership

---

[12] Gregory S. Kealey and Bryan D. Palmer, **Dreaming of what might be: the Knights of Labor in Ontario, 1880-1900** (Cambridge University Press, 1982).

[13] Ruth Elizabeth Spence, **Prohibition in Canada** (Toronto, 1919): section III, Organizations.

and office-holding; the Beaver Lodge of Guelph in the 1870s and 1880s was part of this order but has left no records. The Morning Star Lodge at Ennotville, of which good records survive from c1860, also seems to have belonged to this order, which in 1876 united with three other temperance societies to form the United Temperance Association, with its National Lodge based in London, Ontario. In 1878 the Order united with the Royal Templars of Temperance, an order founded in Buffalo that offered insurance benefits; local lodges in Guelph, Fergus and Mill Creek (Puslinch) have left some records.

Militia and veterans' associations

Militia organizations may not usually be grouped with voluntary associations but it can be argued that, prior to conscription, they have features in common with the fire companies which are usually included but for which we have found no primary records locally. After some earlier militia activity from the 1830s, the 30th Wellington Battalion of Rifles was founded in 1866 during the Fenian scare, with ten Rifle Companies distributed through the County. Guelph had the 11th and 16th Batteries, of which some records survive and there are some primary materials also for the Elora Volunteer Rifle Company from the 1860 to about 1900.

This section also includes the records of the Guelph War Memorial Association in the 1920s (#2145-#2146) and the Royal Canadian Legion as well as other materials relating to the Guelph Armouries and the founding of the Colonel John McCrae Birthplace Society.

Women's associations

Voluntary associations were mainly segregated by gender in the period before 1940. The most notable group of women's organization, apart from their church groups, was the womens' institutes that were formed by and for rural women in the early twentieth century. As agencies of adult education, particularly designed to promote domestic science and stabilize the rural social order, local institutes were officially supported by grants from the Ontario Government through the Department of Agriculture's Institutes Branch. They could also call upon the expertise of the Macdonald Institute established in association with the Ontario Agricultural College at Guelph in 1903.[14] From the 1930s, local institutes were encouraged by Lady Tweedsmuir to compile scrapbooks of local history about their communities that became known as the Tweedsmuir Histories. Very good primary records of the women's institutes of Wellington County have been preserved in the Wellington County Archives and copies of all the local Tweedsmuir histories survive, most of them also in microfilm copies.

Associations by urban women are represented only in the Guelph Business and Professional Women's Club that included teachers, nurses, business secretaries, social workers, librarians and book-keepers. The club was founded in 1928, had 34 members by 1934 and appears to have been active in relief work during the depression of the 1930s. Fairly complete records to 1975 have

---

[14] Terry Crowley, 'The origins of continuing education for women: the Ontario Women's Institutes,' **Canadian Woman Studies** 7, 3 (1986): 78-81.

been preserved in the Archives of Ontario (#2150).

Youth welfare associations

Philanthropic organizations for the welfare of young children were associated with a concern for animals in the formation of the Guelph Humane Society in the early 1890s. Later renamed the Children's Aid Society, it had quasi-official status and government funding to take responsibility for the placement and welfare of 'neglected' children. A full set of minutes and official correspondence for the whole period since 1893 are held by the organization (#2168-#2169).

Local branches of the Young Men's and Young Women's Christian Associations were established in Guelph as in other Ontario towns and cities.[15] Guelph had a YMCA with 40 members by 1886, but no primary records survive from before 1913 except for some land deeds. Minutes and other records have been preserved for the Guelph YWCA which was founded in 1913. All local YMCA and YWCA records that have been traced are held by the Guelph Public Library.

[15] For the YMCA, the official history is Murray G. Ross, **The Y.M.C.A. in Canada: the chronicle of a century** (Toronto: Ryerson, 1951); see also David MacLeod, 'A live vaccine: the YMCA and male adolescence in the United States and Canada, 1870-1920,' **Histoire sociale/Social History** 11 (1978): 5-25. For the general context of the YWCA, see Josephine Perfect Harshaw, **When women work together: a history of the Young Women's Christian Association in Canada** (Toronto: Ryerson, 1966); Wendy Mitchinson, 'The YWCA and reform in the nineteenth century,' **Histoire sociale/Social History** 12 (1979): 368-384; Diana Pedersen, '"Building today for the womanhood of tomorrow": boosters and the YWCA, 1890-1930,' **Urban History Review** 15 (1987): 225-242.

AGRICULTURAL AND FARMERS' ASSOCIATIONS

1985. Central Farmers' Institute of Ontario. **List of Farmers' Institutes with secretaries, 1886.** 1 file folder. Loc: AO. FA: MU 3773, File 2.
List is filed with records of the Canadian Mutual Aid Association. It shows that W.J. Cockburn was secretary of the South Wellington Institute, George Wright of the Centre Wellington Institute, James McEwing of the West Wellington Institute and Dr H.P. Yeomans of the North Wellington Institute (Mount Forest).

1986. Centre Wellington Agricultural Society/ Nichol Tp Agricultural Societies. **Report and prize list, September 1899.** 1 volume. Loc: WCA. MU 23; List of document contents.
A record of a union agricultural exhibition of the Centre Wellington and the Nichol Township Agricultural Society held in Fergus. The printed document lists the rules and regulations of the event, and individuals who won prizes in various agricultural competitions. The document also lists the officers and directors of the two societies which indicate William Beattie Senior was the president of the Nichol Township Agricultural Society. The report is held with the Beattie Collection.

1987. Centre Wellington Agricultural Society. **Union exhibition, Elora, 1873.** 1 volume. Loc: UGA. XR1 MS A115026.
A printed list of rules and regulations and the prize list for an agricultural show to be held in Elora in 1873. Held with the Connon Collection.

1988. Centre Wellington Farmers' Institute. **Minutes, 1896-1905.** 1 volume. Loc: WCA. MU 43.
A record of meetings held only periodically each year, with a list of total attendance at meetings and the names of speakers and the topics each addressed at the institute. The meetings were held in several localities, including Elora, Alma, Ennotville, Metz, Ospringe, Hillsburgh and Orton.

1989. Clifford Horticultural Society. **Minutes, 1919-1931.** 1 volume. Loc: WBE.
Filed with Clifford school records.

1990. Elora and Salem Horticultural Society. **Prize lists, 1876.** Loc: AO. FA: MU 455.
Part of Byerly Papers.

1991. Elora Horticultural Society. **Minutes, 1878-1912.** 145 p. Loc: WCA.
A record of meetings, annual reports, committee members, accounts, and list of directors. Inserted in the book are prize lists for the years 1903, 1907, 1910, and 1911. Filed with Elora municipal records.

1992. Elora-Pilkington Agricultural Society. **Minute book, 1896-1907.** 145 p. Loc: WCA.
A record of meetings, prize lists, accounts, and lists of members. Filed with Elora municipal records.

1993. Eramosa Agricultural Society. **Prize certificates, 1863-1864.** 2 documents. Loc: WCA. MU 42.
A record of Isaac Anderson winning first prize in the 'best spring wheat' and 'other oats' division.

1994. Guelph Fat Stock Club. **Member's ticket, 1889.** 1 document. Loc: GCM.
A record of membership of Joseph Fletcher. Thomas Waters is listed as President.

1995. Guelph Fat Stock Club. **Member's ticket, 1891.** 1 document. Loc: WCA. MU 12.
A member's ticket which cost one dollar and a note that James Miller was president of the club and that John McCorkindale was secretary.

1996. Guelph Fat Stock Club. **Minutes, 1881-1891.** 1 volume. Loc: WCA. MU 3.

1997. Guelph Horticultural Society. **Advertisements, 1915; 1917.** 2 brochures. Loc: WCA. MU 13.
The brochures announce officers, committee members and competitions.

1998. Guelph Horticultural Society. **Annual report, 1967.** 44 p. ill. Loc: GPL.
A brief description of the founding and subsequent activities of the Guelph Horticultural Society and a list of presidents who served the society.

1999. Guelph Horticultural Society. **Annual. The auster city, 1922.** 28 p. Loc: UGL.
A brochure of the Guelph Horticultural Society that outlines activities of the organization for the year 1922, lists prizes for competitions, and lists several prominent members of the society. The brochure also offers advice for the cultivation of various plants and vegetables and contains advertisements for several local industries.

2000. Guelph Horticultural Society. **Prize list, 1876.** 13 p. Loc: GPL.
A list of society members in 1875. The work also contains a list of prizes for plants and flowers entered in the competitions of the society to be held in 1876.

2001. Guelph Township Agricultural Society. **Membership and accounts, 1873-1905.** 1 ledger. Loc: WCA. MU 101.
The ledger includes the minutes of a meeting held January 15, 1873.

2002. Guelph Township Agricultural Society. **Minutes, 1857-1871; 1873-1906.** 3 volumes. Loc: WCA. MU 3, 101.

2003. Guelph Winter Fair. **Poster, December 1-8, 1916.** 1 item, oversize. Loc: UGA. XR2 MS A002.
A poster announcing the fair, with pictures of its officers, including William Smith, M.P., as well as a description of the program of judging in arena.

2004. Maryborough Agricultural Society. **Prize lists, 1895-1897; 1899; 1902; 1904; 1908-1909.** 29 volumes. Loc: WCA. MU 54.
A series of printed prize lists which list rules and regulations and prizes for various competitions. The collection includes several copies of prize lists for some years. The event was held annually in Moorefield.

2005. Mount Forest Agricultural Society. **Meetings. Minutes, 1906-1919; 1924-1978.** 4 volumes. Loc: WCA. MU 83.
A record of motions carried, members present and activities relating to upcoming agricultural exhibitions. The meetings were usually held at least once

each month.

2006. Mount Forest Horticultural Society. **Fall exhibitions, 1880.** 50 p. Loc: WCA.
A collection of advertisements of firms who supplied agricultural goods and services in the Mount Forest area. Printed by the Examiner Newspaper. Held in the Pamphlet Collection.

2007. Mount Forest Horticultural Society. **Prize list, 1876; advertisements, 1876.** 15 p. Loc: WCA.
A printed list of various commercial enterprises that placed advertisements in the society's printed list of prize winners. The brochure offers a good profile of the range of businesses that produced agricultural goods and services in the Mount Forest area. Held in the Pamphlet Collection.

2008. Ontario Board of Agriculture. **Wellington County Board of Agriculture. Members, 1917-1918.** 1 ledger. Loc: WCA. MU51.
A list of members, alphabetically by name, which also notes the place of residence of each member. It appears that the ledger lists Wellington County residents who paid a small fee to a local farmers' club to be linked to the Ontario Board of Agriculture.

2009. Ontario Department of Agriculture. **Farmers' Institute Branches. Reports and correspondence, 1886-1906.** 3 boxes. Loc: AO. FA: RG16, Series 16-85.
Farmers' Institutes were first set up in Ontario by James Mills, President of the Ontario Agricultural College from 1879 to 1904, along the lines already established in the United States. F.W. Hodson was the first administrative secretary and became the first superintendent in 1895, being succeeded by G.C. Creelman in 1899, then by G.A. Putnam (1904-1934). One institute in each Electoral District qualified for an annual grant of $25.00. Farmers' Institutes began to wane about 1910 and virtually ceased in 1924, while Women's Institutes gained in strength. These records include a list of Farmers' Institutes in 1886-1887, a list of those visited by speakers from the O.A.C. in 1886, annual reports from 1887 to 1890, lists of officers and directors in the years 1904-1906, and two bound letterbooks (each one thousand pages long) of the superintendent for 1894-1895 and 1895-1896. The records include reports from the South Wellington Institute (Aberfoyle) and the West Wellington Institute (Drayton) from 1887 and for the Centre Wellington (Elora) from 1888.

2010. Ontario Department of Agriculture. **Ontario Provincial Winter Fair. Guelph file, 1932-1961.** 1 file folder. Loc: AO. FA: RG 16, Series 16-09, Box 159. Restricted for 30 years; access possible only by application under Freedom of Information legislation.
The O.P.W.F. was a corporate association responsible for organizing annual winter fairs in Guelph between 1883 and 1939 when the fairs were suspended because of the outbreak of war. The association received substantial provincial grants to support its agricultural promotional activities. By the 1930s the president was Dr W.J.R. Fowler and the secretary-treasurer was an official of the Livestock Branch of the Department of Agriculture. The file contains a copy of the O.P.W.F. Review 1883-1919 with its history of the association's activities, details of the association's new constitution in 1937, as well as correspondence relating to the suspension of fairs in 1939, later attempts by rural interests in Wellington County to revive the fairs, and the final

dissolution of the association in 1949. The association's assets were invested in Hydro bonds which increased to a value of $16,000 by 1961.

2011. Ontario Provincial Winter Fair. **Catalogue, 1933**. 2 volumes. Loc: GCM.
A record of various competitions held in Guelph that list class, prizes and entries for livestock and crops. Many Wellington County farmers are listed.

2012. Ontario Provincial Winter Fair. **Prize list, 1925**. 1 volume. Loc: OAM.
A note of prizes available for various categories of competitions. The document also lists judges and administrators of the event.

2013. Ontario Provincial Winter Fair. **Souvenir catalogue, 1900**. 1 brochure. Loc: GCM.
A catalogue of categories of competitions, prize winners and advertisements that include several Guelph companies. The brochure is entitled, First Amalgamated Ontario Provincial Winter Fair, Guelph, December 11 to 14, 1900.

2014. Patrons of Industry, Arthur Association No. 678. **Cash book, 1891-1892**. 1 reel. mf. Loc: WCA.

2015. Peel, Maryborough and Drayton Agricultural Society. **Annual financial statements, 1930-1945**. 1 file folder. Loc: WCA.
Annual reports of receipts, expenditures, judges, awards and donations. Filed with Maryborough Township records.

2016. Puslinch Agricultural Society. **Prize list, 1923**. 23 p. Loc: UGL.
A list of prizes for various categories of entries in an agricultural fair held in Aberfoyle in 1923, as well as a list of individuals who donated money for prizes at the event. The brochure lists the rules and regulations and the administrators of the event.

2017. Puslinch Farmers' Club/ South Wellington Farmers' Institute. **Minutes and cash book, 1874-1896**. 2 volumes. Loc: AO. MU 2086.
The objects of the club are stated to be the mutual improvement of the members and the advancement of the agricultural interests of the county. From May 1887, the club was also known as the South Wellington Farmers' Institute, with meetings held in Guelph and Eramosa as well as Aberfoyle and Arkell. The club appeared to lapse c1890 but revived in 1895-1896. Membership averaged seventy-five in the earlier years but was forty by 1890. Presidents included Duncan Macfarlane, Robert Buchanan, Hugh Reid, William Black, Joseph Smith, John Smith, James Blair, Peter Mahon and James Laidlaw.

2018. Wellington County Agricultural Society. **Cash book, 1884-1894**. 1 ledger. Loc: WCA. MU 102.

2019. Wellington District Agricultural Society. **Broadside of cattle show, 1841**. 1 file folder. Loc: UGA. XR1 MS A166014.
John Harland's name is on the broadside as secretary of the society. Part of Goodwin-Haines Collection.

2020. Wellington South Agricultural Society. **Minutes, 1878-1895**. 1 volume. Loc: WCA. MU 101.

2021. West Wellington Farmers' Institute. **Minutes and annual reports, 1915-1929.** 1 volume. Loc: WCA. MU 34.

BUSINESS ASSOCIATIONS

2022. Guelph Board of Trade. **Announcement of monthly meeting, 1912.** 1 document. Loc: GCM.

A note sent to John McAteer informing him when a monthly meeting of the Board of Trade was to be held in Guelph. The note indicates T.G. McMaster was president of the Board of Trade and James Watt was the secretary.

2023. Guelph Board of Trade. **City of Guelph, 1927.** 3 p. Loc: GPL. Envelope 7.

A promotional article, published in Canadian Progress, on the development of Guelph, 'a city of opportunity', designed to attract branch plants of international manufacturing corporations. The article offers free factory sites and promises 'public utilities, cheap power, pure water, excellent transportation, provincial highways, accessible markets, contented labour, reasonable wages, wholesome environment, delightful climate, ideal location'. It includes photographs of St George's Square, lower Wyndham Street, Carnegie Library, G.C.V.I. and the O.A.C. Part of the Douglass Collection.

2024. Guelph Board of Trade. **Correspondence with Prime Minister's Office regarding tariffs, 1902 and Welland Canal, 1909.** Loc: NAC. FA #91.

In Laurier Papers, pages 62920-62921.

2025. Guelph Board of Trade. **Guelph, its industrial advantages, c1928.** Loc: GCM.

An undated booster document which lists the city's population at 21,000 and provides a brief description of the city as a suitable location for industries.

2026. Guelph Board of Trade. **Guelph, Ontario, 1919.** 1 brochure. Loc: GCM.

A brochure to induce American and British firms to 'investigate Guelph' as a place to develop their industrial interests.

2027. Guelph Board of Trade. **Guelph, the Royal City: the city beautiful, prosperous and progressive, c1910.** 1 brochure. Loc: GCM.

A brochure to attract industries to Guelph. It concludes that 'Canadian trade can only be retained by manufacturing in Canada. Why not locate your Canadian Branch Factory in Guelph?'

CULTURAL AND SCIENTIFIC ASSOCIATIONS

2028. Drayton Mechanics' Institute Library Association. **Record book, 1884-1905.** 1 ledger. Loc: WCA.

A record of individuals and amount paid, apparently for membership fees.

2029. Elora Mechanics' Institute. **Constitution and bylaws, 1858.** 1 item. Loc: UGA. XR1 MS A115.

A manuscript of the constitution, declaration and bylaws of the Elora Mechanics' Institute. Held with the Connon Collection.

Rally in St George's Square, c1885: the space in front of the Post Office building was used for outdoor election meetings and for gatherings such as the one shown here. Judging by the emblems on the banner, this may have been a labour parade. (Guelph Public Library)

2030. Elora Mechanics' Institute. **Constitution, bylaws and catalogue of books, 1881.** 1 printed booklet. Loc: AO. MU 2019.

The Elora Institute was incorporated in 1871, with Charles Allan, Charles Clarke and David Boyle among its prominent members. Part of Mechanics' Institutes of Ontario Collection.

2031. Elora Mechanics' Institute. **Insurance policy, 1879.** Loc: WCA.

An insurance policy of the Elora Mechanics' Institute with the Mutual Fire Insurance Company. The record indicates F.W. Stone was president of the insurance company and that Charles Davidson was the secretary.

2032. Elora Mechanics' Institute. **Minutes, 1857-1869; 1878-1886.** 2 volumes. Loc: WCA. MU 60.

A record of meetings held approximately once every two months. The first volume lists the bylaws, constitution and members of the institution. The minutes for the entire period include periodic financial statements.

2033. Elora Mechanics' Institute. **Subscription list, 1878-1893.** 2 ledgers. Loc: WCA. MU 60.

A record of members of the institute which indicates the subscription paid by specific individuals each year.

2034. Elora School Museum. **Circular letter from David Boyle, 1876.** Loc: AO. FA: MU 455.

Part of Byerly Papers.

2035. Ennotville Association Library. **Annual reports, 1914-1958 (sporadic).** Loc: WCA. MU 107.

A collection of the annual returns that were required under the Public Libraries Act to qualify for the provincial library grants. The Ennotville Library, originally established in 1847, qualified as a public library in the 'Association' category from 1895 until 1966. The returns contain information on receipts and disbursements, assets and liabilities, numbers of members and users, numbers of books, staff, hours of service, and names of board members and officers.

2036. Ennotville Association Library. **Circulation records, 1908-1934; 1950-1959.** 5 files. Loc: WCA. MU 106.

Records of books borrowed by members.

2037. Ennotville Farmers' and Mechanics' Institute/ Ennotville Association Library. **Board. Minutes, 1879-1985.** 4 volumes. Loc: WCA. MU 106.

The first volume, covering the period 1879 to 1937, is prefaced by a copy of the 1856 constitution of the institute. In 1857 what had been the Lower Nichol Subscription Library amalgamated with the Ennotville Farmers' and Mechanics' Institute. The library occupies a stone building dating from the 1850s, which was also used by a Sunday School until 1947 and by the Morning Star Temperance Lodge from c1860 to c1905. There is a reference in the minutes to the use of the building by the North Wellington Farmers' and Mechanics' Institute in the later nineteenth century. Large numbers of nineteenth and early twentieth century books are part of the present collection. The Institute qualified for a provincial grant as an Association Library in 1895, and was incorporated as the

Ennotville Historical Library in 1965.

2038. Ennotville Farmers' and Mechanics' Institute/ Ennotville Library. **Cashbooks, 1886-1966**. 2 files. Loc: WCA. MU 106.

2039. Ennotville Library. **Correspondence and financial records, 1931-1984**. 12 files. Loc: WCA. MU 107.
    The records also include details of book acquisitions for 1917, 1921, 1925-7, 1930-1, 1934-5, 1951-60 and 1964.

2040. Ennotville Library. **Membership. List, 1925-c1945**. 1 notebook. Loc: WCA.
    A list of members with telephone numbers. Local families that have supported the library throughout its history have been the Beatties, the Broadfoots, the Cunninghams, the Jamiesons and the Elmslies.

2041. Everton Library Society. **Minutes, 1910-1922**. 1 volume. Loc: WCA. MU 50.
    A record of attendance of members at weekly meetings, books used by the society, with only a few brief entries outlining activities of the organization. The first page of the volume notes the society was founded in 1902.

2042. Guelph Farmers' and Mechanics' Institute. **Annual reports, 1854; 1860; 1883**. 4 documents. Loc: GPL. List of archival box headings.
    The 1854 report is signed by David Allan, President of the Institute. The 1883 report records the motion to transfer ownership to the City of Guelph. It was moved by W. Stewart.

2043. Guelph Farmers' and Mechanics' Institute. **Catalogues, 1850-1851**. 2 volumes. Loc: GPL. List of archival box headings.
    A printed record of authors and titles organized by categories of biography, fiction, history, voyage and travel, general literature, poetry and drama, periodicals, theology and religion, science, industrial science and art, reference and illustrated.

2044. Guelph Farmers' and Mechanics' Institute. **Constitution, rules and regulations, 1850; 1855**. 1 brochure, 11 p. Loc: GPL.
    The 1855 brochure contains a list of the regulations of the institute whose purpose was to advance literature and diffuse useful knowledge. The constitution states that 'no subject connected with religious or political controversy shall be introduced at any meeting of the Institute, but all instruction delivered . . . shall be based on the distinct recognition of the authority of Divine Revelation'.

2045. Guelph Farmers' and Mechanics' Institute. **Financial records, 1852-1854; 1856-1857; 1868**. 38 documents. Loc: GPL. List of archival box headings.
    A record of receipts and expenditures.

2046. Guelph Farmers' and Mechanics' Institute. **Minutes, 1850-1883**. 2 volumes. Loc: GPL. List of archival box headings.
    A record of motions carried in meetings that were usually held once a month. The minutes of the 1850s include references to reports published in newspapers with several early entries outlining plans to deliver lectures. The end of the first volume, covering the years 1850 to 1872, includes the signatures of

individuals agreeing to form the institute in 1850. The minutes of March 1883 outline the intention to transfer ownership from the Guelph Farmers' and Mechanics' Institute to the City of Guelph. The records begin to list regular financial statements of the library in the 1880s.

2047. Guelph Farmers' and Mechanics' Institute. **Programs, 1856-1857**. 1 brochure, 2 sheets. Loc: GPL. List of archival box headings.

A catalogue of paintings displayed at the 'first Guelph art exhibition', and a list of 9 lectures held from February to April, 1856. Lectures were held at the Guelph Court House.

2048. Guelph Farmers' and Mechanics' Institute. **Subscription list, c1858**. 2 documents. Loc: GPL. List of archival box headings.

A list of subscribers who paid $1.50 or $2.50 per year to the reading room or library, which was located at the Town Hall. The subscribers include George Elliott, Thomas Sandilands, John Horsman and John Hogg.

2049. Guelph Scientific Society. **Minutes, 1886-1892**. 1 volume. Loc: GPL.

A record of meetings of the society that was first organized in 1886, in which both men and women participated. James Goldie was elected first president, and Reverend Robert Torrance was elected first secretary. The object of the society was to work for the 'advancement of scientific knowledge, special attention being given to our own neighbourhood'. William Tytler, Archdeacon Dixon and Professors James Mills and J.H. Panton were members of the council. The volume includes a list of members for 1888 and 1889.

2050. Guelph Scientific Society. **Proceedings, 1887**. 27 p. Loc: GPL.

A series of lectures given by the Guelph Scientific Society on the topics of songbirds and geological records of Wellington County.

2051. Guelph Scientific Society. **Report, 1886-1887**. 27 p. Loc: UGL.

A reprint of the society's constitution, secretary's report and abstracts of papers read at regular meetings. The papers include 'The Songbirds of Wellington County' by James Goldie, 'The Geological Records in the Vicinity of Guelph' by J. Hoyes Panton, 'Our Local Woods in May' by Miss Vail, 'Canadian Ferns in the Vicinity of Guelph' by A. Gilchrist, 'The Frontier Between Two Kingdoms - a Microscopical Study' by Robert Gausby, 'The Chemistry of Bread' by C. C. James, 'Dandelions' by W. Tytler, and 'Astronomical Wonders' by Ven. Archdeacon Dixon. The final paper relates the wonders of astronomy to the wonders of God, as seen in the Biblical book of Job. The secretary's report states that the total number of members for 1886-87 was 112.

2052. Morriston Library. **Library records, 1910**. 2 ledgers. Loc: UCA.

A record of books issued and what appears to be a list of members and fees paid to join the library. The records are in very poor condition.

2053. North Wellington Teachers' Association. **Minutes, 1859-1862**. 1 volume. Loc: AO. MU 973, Box 3, #7.

At the invitation of Mr A.M. Cosby of Fergus, the following teachers met at Fergus on 17 September 1859 to form a teachers' association: Alexander Smyth, James Tasker and John Anderson of Nichol; A.M. Cosby, G.H. Todd and T.A. Young of Fergus; William Crewson of Elora; P.C. Matthewson and Robert Godfrey of

Pilkington; John Burke, James Hector and John Leneten of Peel; John Fleming, William Elmslie and S.P. Buckland of Garafraxa; William Bryans of Arthur; John Delahunt of Minto; and Mr Reynolds of Mount Forest. The purpose of the association was defined as 'mutual improvement and friendly intercourse', and the group resolved to meet in Fergus and Elora alternately on the first Saturday of every month. Members took turns reading prepared papers and also organized competitions in various subjects and skills among their pupils.

2054. Wellington (1st Division) and Guelph Teachers' Association. **Program of semi-annual meeting, c1887**. 1 item. Loc: AO. FA: RG-2, G-4, Box 1, Envelope #7.
   A program of the meeting held 17 and 18 November in Fergus that addressed the question 'Does the work done in the public schools conduce to popular culture?' The president of the association was G.W. Field and the secretary, Hugh Roberts.

2055. Wellington County Historical Research Society. **Minutes, 1928-1938**. 1 volume. Loc: WCA.
   A record of the work of the Women's Institutes of Centre Wellington County District in documenting the early history of the county. The meetings were held monthly and outline plans to gather information beneficial to learning more of the history of the county. The records also contain brief financial statements of expenses of the society. Held with the Wellington County Historical Research Society Collection.

FRATERNAL ASSOCIATIONS

2056. Ancient Order of United Workmen. **Financial. Cash book, 1903-1906**. 96 p. Loc: WCA.
   A notice to members is attached to the front end paper that lists insurance rates. Members are urged to recruit new members so that the 'great order' will grow and prosper and 'your wife and children will have its protection when death overtakes you'. The notice is signed by a 'Grand Master Workman'. Filed with Elora municipal records.

2057. Boyle, Everett M. **Map showing Masonic Districts and locations and types of lodges in Ontario, 1886**. 1 sheet, 30 x 23. Loc: AO. R-O.
   The map accompanied a report on the redistribution of districts which was signed by John Ross Robertson.

2058. Canadian Order of Foresters #34, Harriston. **Membership. Records, 1871-1901**. 1 ledger volume. Loc: AO.
   The ledger includes names of three hundred members with dates of admission, age at initiation, amount of insurance carried with records of monthly premiums and membership dues. The detailed financial information is for 1899-1901. Part of Harriston Collection.

2059. Elora Catholic Mutual Benefit Association. **Collection book, 1903-1916**. 1 ledger. Loc: WCA.
   A record of donations which indicates when specific individuals gave funds and lists the amount granted for either initiation fees, monthly dues or the sick benefit fund. Held with the Fischer Collection.

281

A labour parade of Union Brewery Workers No. 300:
employees of George Sleeman's Silver Creek Brewery, 1890 (#3467).
(Archival Collections, University of Guelph Library)

2060. Knights of the Maccabees of the World. Erin Tent No. 122. **Cash book, 1893-1904.**
1 ledger. Loc: WCA. MU 102.

The ledger is entitled, Finance Keeper's Cash book, K.O.T.M. The ledger records individuals' names, amount donated to Endowment Fund and amount of tent dues.

2061. Independent Order of Odd Fellows. Gordon Lodge #247, Palmerston. **Records, 1885-1957.** 1 ledger, 2 boxes. Loc: AO. MU 2220-2222.

After a false early start, the Grand Lodge of Canada West was formed at Brockville in 1855 and by 1923 there were over four hundred lodges and nearly 65,000 members. The objectives of the I.O.O.F. were to substitute charity and harmony for selfishness and malice. Their banner portrayed a beaver crouched over a triple-link chain with the motto, Friendship, Love and Truth. Members pledged themselves to spread the principles of benevolence and fraternity. The order also provided insurance services with funeral aid and relief to widows and orphans. The records for the Palmerston lodge include: members' register, 1885-1953; officer's roll book, 1921-1956; cash books, 1906-1957; initiation question book, 1906-1948; character report book, 1913-1953; minute books (2 volumes), 1932-1957; financial secretary's cash book, 1941-1957; dues accounts book, 1947-1957; and miscellaneous papers, 1938-1957. The lodge had nineteen members in 1885. Part of the Independent Order of Odd Fellows Collection, Series B-V.

2062. Independent Order of Odd Fellows, Guelph. **Jubilee Celebration. Program, 1875-1925.** 1 volume. Loc: GCM.

A description of a planned celebration which also includes a brief listing of the administrators for the period from 1875 to 1925. The record is held in a box entitled, Organizations.

2063. Loyal Orange Association, Rockwood. **Membership Form. William Osborne, 1880.** 1 document. Loc: WCA. MU 62.

A record indicating Osborne was a member in good standing.

2064. Loyal Orange Lodge #1152, Harriston. **Membership. Certificates, 1873; 1885.** 1 file folder. Loc: AO. MU 3633.

Membership certificates issued by the Loyal Orange Association of British America, one to Samuel Lennox from the Toronto District of the Order, the other to Thomas Moncrieff by the Mount Forest District. Part of Harriston Collection.

2065. Loyal Orange Lodge #1152, Harriston. **Minutes, 1868-1888.** 2 bound volumes. Loc: AO. MU 3683.

Minutes of meetings held monthly that include plans for celebration July 12 each year, usually with a dinner in another town such as Palmerston, Mount Forest or Listowel. Part of Harriston Collection.

2066. Loyal Orange Lodge #1152, Harriston. **Miscellaneous papers, 1877-1890.** 1 file folder. Loc: AO. MU 3633.

Various receipts and notes including a handbill advertising a July 12 gathering to be held in Guelph in 1889. This was intended to be one of the 'Grandest Demonstrations ever held in Ontario' to which all 'Orange Lodges, True Blues, Orange Young Britons and Prentice Boys' were invited. The master of the Guelph Lodge was C.H. Marriott and the secretary was David Scroggie. Part of

Harriston Collection.

2067. Loyal Orange Lodge #1152, Harriston. **Roll book, 1879-1916.** 1 small bound book. Loc: AO. MU 3633.
The file also includes a bill for construction materials supplied to the Harriston Orange Hall by a Preston firm in 1874. Part of Harriston Collection.

2068. Order of Chosen Friends, Guelph. **Membership. List, 1896.** 1 ledger. Loc: GCM.
A monthly listing of officers of the society for 1896. The record is held in a box entitled, Organizations.

2069. Raymond Employees' Mutual Benefit Society. **Rules and regulations, 1890.** 1 volume. Loc: GCM.
Details of the society organized by the workers of the Raymond Sewing Machine Company 'in order to ensure some pecuniary aid in time of sickness or accident, and in some measure to protect ourselves from being recipients of charity'. The brochure indicates the society was founded in 1873 and outlines the provisions in terms of eligibility of members and the types of benefits employees would receive. The brochure notes workers had to earn at least five dollars a week to be a member of the society.

2070. Royal Antebilubian Order of Buffalos. **Correspondence, 1938.** 2 documents. Loc: GCM.
Correspondence with the Guelph chapter dealing with acceptance of a new member and the general activities of the society. The organization performed charitable work in several cities in Ontario. The records are held in a box entitled, Organizations.

2071. St Andrew's Society of Guelph. **Minutes, 1859-1940.** 1 volume. Loc: GPL.
A record of annual meetings. The volume also contains newspaper reports of annual meetings and samples of public events and concerts.

CENTENNIAL AND REUNION ORGANIZATIONS

2072. Guelph Centennial Committee. **Old Home Week. Official program, August 1-6, 1927.** 16 p. Loc: GPL.
The official program for Old Home Week in Guelph in 1927, which includes references to the historical pageant, sporting events and other attractions.

2073. Guelph Old Home Week Committee. **Minutes, correspondence, guest registers, 1908, 1913.** 16 volumes. Loc: WCA.
A record of preparations including correspondence inviting former Guelph residents to the events and guest registers for various cities in Canada and the United States such as London, Hamilton, Winnipeg, Stratford, New York, Cleveland, Rochester, Buffalo, Chicago, and Detroit. The records vary regarding the amount of detail presented. Filed with the Guelph Township records.

2074. Guelph Old Home Week Committee. **Program, August 1908.** 40 p. ill. Loc: GPL.
A program for Old Home Week in 1908 which includes many advertisements and photographs of public buildings and notables in Guelph. The work lists the town council members for the year 1908, and the events planned for Old Home Week.

LABOUR ORGANIZATIONS

2075. Guelph Trades and Labour Council. **Correspondence with Prime Minister's Office regarding Alien Labour Law, 1901; tapestry weaving, 1902; and Trades Union Bill, 1910.** Loc: NAC. FA #91.
In Laurier Papers, pages 60352, 150497, 169213-4.

2076. Guelph Trades and Labour Council. **Souvenir. 28th annual convention Trades and Labor Congress of Canada, 1912.** 100 p. ill. Loc: UGA.
A souvenir of the convention held in Guelph in September 1912, that includes national and local manufacturing advertising. The book prints the principles of the Trades and Labor Congress of Canada that included free compulsory education with minimum living wage, exclusion of all Orientals and abolition of child and female labour in all branches of industrial life. It also gives brief histories of the Guelph Trades and Labor Council established in 1898, the Guelph International Molders' Union No. 212 established in 1881, the Guelph Co-operative Association established in 1904, the Guelph Carpet Weaver's Union No. 277 established in 1911, and the Piano and Organ Workers Union No. 34 established in 1902.

MUSICAL ASSOCIATIONS

2077. Elora Amateur Brass Band. **Band Meetings. Minutes, 1858-1865.** 1 volume. Loc: WCA.
A record of meetings with only brief entries for each session. The ledger also includes the constitution, bylaws of the band and financial statements for the year 1858. The minutes are held in the Meyler Collection at the Wellington County Archives.

2078. Elora Philharmonic Society. **Program, May 1884.** Loc: AO. FA: MU 455.
Part of Byerly Papers

2079. Guelph Federation of Musicians. **Price list, c1910.** 1 brochure. Loc: GCM.
The Federation is listed as Local 92 of the A.F. of M. The undated brochure describes types of events and lists prescribed cost per musician. For example, section 10 states, 'Vaudeville Pictures, and Opera House engagements of Operas, Dramas, Farce Comedies, Stock Companies, etc., $2.00 per man'. The brochure includes a directory of Guelph musicians organized alphabetically by musical instrument.

2080. Guelph Musical Festival Association. **Program, 1929.** 1 brochure. Loc: GCM.
A program for the first Guelph Music Festival held May 7 to 8, 1929. Patrons of the festival are listed as Edward Johnson, Hugh Guthrie, Lincoln Goldie and Mayor R.B. Robson. Edward Johnson and the Toronto Symphony Orchestra performed at the concert held in the Collegiate auditorium.

2081. Guelph Musical Society Band. **Cash book, 1921-1922.** 11 loose pages. Loc: GCM.
Pages for these years appear to have been torn from a ledger.

2082. Guelph Musical Society. **Minutes, 1925-1926.** 1 volume. Loc: GCM.
A listing of the activities of the society, members present at meetings and an outline of plans for concerts. The society usually held meetings once every two

months.

2083. **Official program of the band tournament and firemen's demonstration, Guelph, 1887.** 20 p. Loc: GPL.

A promotional pamphlet for a special community event in Guelph that was to feature musical bands and a firemen's exhibition. The work also contains a series of advertisements by Guelph businesses. Printed by Jasper Hough Junior.

2084. Presto Music Club of Guelph. **Cash book, 1920-1946.** 1 ledger. Loc: GPL.

2085. Presto Music Club of Guelph. **Financial statements, 1934-1961.** 1 file folder. Loc: GPL.

2086. Presto Music Club of Guelph. **Minutes, 1920-1963.** 3 volumes, 1 file folder. Loc: GPL.

2087. Presto Music Club of Guelph. **Programs, 1908; 1910-1911; 1914-1918; 1921-1939.** 13 brochures, 1 file folder. Loc: GPL, GCM.

Programs from 1923 to 1939 are held at GPL.

2088. Royal Opera House. **Programs, 1912.** 3 brochures. Loc: GCM.

Two advertisements of a coming Broadway musical entitled, 'The Rose Maid', and a vocal concert held at the Royal Opera House.

POLITICAL ASSOCIATIONS

2089. Clarke, Charles. **Election Proclamations. Centre Wellington, 1875; 1879.** 2 documents. Loc: WCA.

Clarke outlines his position for upcoming provincial elections in a circular distributed to electors in Centre Wellington. Clarke describes himself as a reformer and defends the actions of the government in the province. In his 1875 circular, he criticized the early management of the O.A.C. by noting 'I could not close my eyes to the fact that in its early management there was of a very unsatisfying character'. Part of the Clarke Collection.

2090. Crowley, Terry. **Oral interview conducted with Jack Ritchie, member of Communist Party in Guelph, 1916-1936.** 1 typescript, 1 cassette tape. Loc: UGA. XR1 MS A313.

An oral interview with discussion of Jack Ritchie's experiences as a member of the Communist Party in Guelph. The interview includes references to political literature read by Ritchie, political rallies, World War I and its influences, as well as the work experiences of Ritchie. The interview was conducted in 1979.

2091. **Election poster, 1857.** Loc: AO. FA: MU 454.

Poster announces the support of Orangemen of North Wellington for James Webster against Charles Allan. Part of Byerly Papers.

2092. Guelph Communist Party. **Correspondence, 1920.** 2 documents. Loc: GCM.

Correspondence of Albert Farley who belonged to the Guelph Communist Party, and who worked as a stoker at the Guelph Board of Light and Heat. The first letter is a declaration written August 10, 1920, stating that 'At the present it looks as if we were fast approaching the climax of the capitalist system to be followed we hope by the cooperative Commonwealth'. The statement was signed by Albert Farley, Tom Marcroft, Frank Horn and 7 Farley family members. The second letter, dated March 31, 1920, is addressed to 'Dear Comrade', Albert Farley, about a planned speech on political parties, and is signed, 'Yours in Socialism'. The correspondence was part of a small cache deposited in Farley's barn behind 570 Metcalfe Street by the Guelph group to record its activities. Also included is a One Big Union Bulletin of 1920 published by the Winnipeg Central Council, and 7 copies of 1920 newspapers from Toronto and British Columbia about labour issues. Constitutes the Communist Party of Canada Collection.

2093. North Wellington Constitutional Reform Association. **Constitution, 1859.** 2 p. Loc: AO. MU 4757, #11.

    A printed circular declaring the objectives of the political party and inviting supporters to a meeting at the St Andrew's Hotel in Fergus on 15 March, 1859. Adam Argo was president and Charles Clarke corresponding secretary.

SERVICE AND SOCIAL ORGANIZATIONS

2094. Guelph Rotary Club. **Programs, history, newspaper clippings, 1935-1970.** 1 file folder. Loc: GPL. Envelope 14.

    A collection of several programs, newspaper clippings about club events, and three manuscripts on the history of the club, including Douglass' 1970 draft. Held with the Douglass Collection.

2095. Priory Club Limited, Guelph. **Bylaws, 1908.** 1 volume. Loc: GCM.

    A listing of the bylaws, procedures and directors of what appears to have been a social club.

SPORTS ASSOCIATIONS

2096. Canadian Wheelman's Association. **Provincial meet program, 1899.** 1 brochure. Loc: GCM.

    The cover of the program includes a sketch of Petrie Park between Gordon Street and the Speed River. The sketch includes a skating rink, bath, pool and gymnasium, grandstand and a 1/5 mile board bicycle track. The brochure includes floor plans for a building entitled, A.B. Petrie's Hockey Rink. The brochure notes conditions of the race and indicates that the winner will receive the Bell Piano Company Trophy.

2097. Connor, Harry. **Scrapbook, including clippings of season with Guelph's Orange and Black Hockey Team, 1925-1926.** 2.75 cm. Loc: NAC. MG 30, C84.

    Connor played for the Guelph team early in his hockey career.

2098. East Middlesex Farmers' Institute. **Poster advertising farmers' excursion to O.A.C., Guelph, 1909.** 36 x 20 inches. original. Loc: UWO.

    An item illustrating the demonstration roles of the Ontario Agricultural College and Macdonald Institute in rural Ontario. Farmers are urged to 'take a day off before...the harvest; it will do you good, besides you can learn something while strolling about the College Farm. The McDonald and Consolidated Schools are now completed and in running order.' The Ladies' Institute and local teachers and students of the Normal School were also invited. The return fare by

287

Grand Trunk Railway was quoted at $1.25 for an adult.

2099. Elora Lawn Bowling Association. **Minutes, 1906-1945.** 3 file folders. Loc: WCA.
A record of annual meetings that lists motions carried at the meetings. The entries are very brief for most meetings. The collection also contains financial accounts of the association for the years from 1909 to 1931. Held with the Fischer Collection.

2100. Fergus Arena. **Minutes, 1926-1947.** 1 reel. mf. Loc: WCA.
A record of plans to build a new arena for playing hockey and curling in Fergus which lists shareholders, financial statements and the general operation of the structure.

2101. Fergus Curling Club. **Banquet program, 1934.** 1 envelope. Loc: WCA.
A program of a banquet in honour of the centennial of the Fergus Curling Club. Part of the Templin-Dow Collection.

2102. Fergus Curling Club. **Minutes, 1834-1938.** 2 microfilms. Loc: WCA.
The minutes for the years 1834 to 1835 have been lost but are summarized briefly by Bill Templin who at one time possessed the records. The record includes the rules of the club in 1836, members for the same year and financial statements. The record lists the results of matches Fergus played with other clubs in a series of newspaper clippings held with the minutes.

2103. Fergus Swimming Pool. **Banquet program, 1938-1939; 1947; 1952.** 1 envelope. Loc: WCA.
Announcements and programs of the banquet. Part of the Templin-Dow Collection.

2104. Fergus Thistle Curling Club. **Bonspiel programs, 1906; centennial banquet records, 1934.** 1 file folder. Loc: AO. FA: MU 2956.
Includes program of 1906 Bonspiel, program of 1934 Centenary Banquet and twelve-page text of banquet speech by Dr G.A. McQuibban, M.L.A. The names of the ten charter members in 1834 and of ten others who joined by 1838 are given in the commemorative booklet. Part of the Templin Family Collection.

2105. Fergus Thistle Curling Club. **Centennial bonspiel, 1934.** 4 p. Loc: UGA.
An announcement for a curling competition to be held January 9-11, 1934. The brochure lists the competitions, prizes and regulations for the event and original members of the club in 1834 and 1838.

2106. Guelph Baseball Club. **Photograph, 1927.** 1 photograph. Loc: UGA. XR2 MS A066.
A team photograph which lists the names of individual players.

2107. Guelph Boxing Club. **Tournament program, 1936.** 1 brochure. Loc: GCM.
A record of the club's first tournament to be held October 13, 1936. The program announces seven matches that includes eight Guelph men, one Hespeler man, two Galt men and two Kitchener men.

2108. Guelph Cricket Club. **Theatre program, 1882.** 1 document. Loc: GCM.
An announcement of a theatrical farce to be performed in the Guelph City Hall, November 14, 1882.

Crieff Base Ball Team 1897

Back row from left: John McLean, Duncan McAllister, James Armstrong, Archd McGeachy. Center: John McMillan, Capt., Donald Stewart, Manager. Gilmour Wheeler, Duncan and Kenneth, McDonald. Seated: Gilbert Dixon and Murdoch McIntosh

Longing for a home run: the Crieff Baseball team, 1897.
(Wellington County Museum and Archives)

2109. Guelph Cross Country Run and Road Race Association. **Ribbons, 1894; 1903; 1905-1906; 1908-1913; 1924-1926.** 18 ribbons. Loc: GCM.
     Several ribbons for various officers and patrons of the annual meetings of the athletic club.

2110. Guelph Lawn Bowling Club. **Tournament program and advertisement, 1911.** 3 documents. Loc: GCM.
     A list of events and rules of the tournament, and a score card for a record of games. Dr. G.C. Creelman is listed as president of the tournament committee.

2111. Guelph Rifle Association. **Tournament program, 1886.** 1 document. Loc: GCM.
     A list of competitions, prizes and rules of the tournament. George Sleeman is listed as president and John Crowe as secretary-treasurer.

2112. Guelph Snowshoe and Toboggan Club. **Membership ticket, 1887.** 1 document. Loc: GCM.
     A blank membership form that indicates Thomas Goldie was president and David Allan Jr was secretary.

2113. Guelph Trotting and Running Association. **Ribbons, 1896-1898; 1903.** 6 ribbons. Loc: GCM.
     Several ribbons for the president and judge of the horse racing association.

2114. Guelph Turf Club. **Admission tickets and programs of meets, 1872-1891.** 1 envelope. Loc: AO. MU 2117, 1872 #2.
     Members' tickets and race cards for various events, which show that F.C. Grenside was secretary and George Sleeman president in the 1870s. The backs of the race cards and programs carry local advertisements, such as Sleeman's Lager and the Guelph Herald.

2115. Guelph Turf Club. **Summer Races. Programs and ribbons, 1879; 1881-1883; 1885; 1890; 1892-1894.** 1 document; 16 ribbons. Loc: GCM.
     The program lists races for the day's events, June 18, 1885. The ribbons are for various officers and patrons of the horse racing club.

2116. Irvine Park Association. **Correspondence, agreements and minutes, 1873; 1876; 1884.** 1 file folder. Loc: UGA. XR1 MS A115007.
     A record of the original deed of settlement to purchase land for the founding of Irvine Park in Elora in 1873, bylaws and regulations of the management of the park and a list of shareholders in 1884. The records include a few brief entries of minutes of the Park Committee held in 1876. Held with the Connon Collection.

2117. Maple Leaf Baseball Club. **Admittance ticket, 1886.** 1 document. Loc: GCM.
     The ticket is stamped, 'Paid. Silver Creek Brewery'.

2118. Maple Leaf Baseball Club. **Constitution, 1875.** 7 p. Loc: GPL.
     A brief outline (printed by the Herald Cheap Book and Job Printing Office) of the regulations regarding the management of the Maple Leaf Baseball Club and the rules for the playing of games.

2119. Maple Leaf Baseball Club. **Correspondence, 1875-1887.** 1 box, 1 ledger. Loc: UGA. XR1 MS A334014.

Letters, receipts and telegraphs relating to the club's games with other clubs. The collection includes letters from players offering their services to the Guelph Maple Leafs. The letters sent to the club arrived from several cities in Ontario and the United States. Several letters were sent to Sleeman from a coloured baseball team in St Louis asking him to play the team and to help arrange games in other Canadian cities. The collection includes a cash book of the Guelph Maple Leafs covering the years from 1874 to 1876, and is part of the Sleeman Family Collection.

2120. Tecumseh Baseball Club of London. **Poster advertising championship baseball match vs Maple Leafs of Guelph, September 24, 1878.** Loc: UWO. CA9ONTEC304.

TEMPERANCE ASSOCIATIONS

2121. Canadian Temperance League, Pilkington Branch. **Minutes, 1853.** 1 volume. Loc: UGA.

A record of minutes of the first two meetings of the society that was formed for the 'purpose of procuring a Prohibitory Liquor Law for Canada'. At the first meeting the following executive members were elected: Daniel Kirbs as President, George Hamilton as Vice-President, Charles Clarke as Secretary, and Alexander Smart as Treasurer.

2122. Elora Friendly Society for the Suppression of Intemperance. **Minutes, 1851.** 1 volume. Loc: UGA.

A record of the minutes of the first four meetings of the society that was formed on February 1, 1851. The minute book includes the society's constitution and a list of members. At the first meeting the following executive members were elected: Charles Allan as President, Edwin H. Kertland as Vice-President, and Charles Clarke as Secretary-Treasurer. At the third meeting Kertland's name was struck from the membership because he was found 'guilty of a breach of the solemn pledge'. The pledge states, 'I solemnly declare that I will not hereafter use, or traffic in, intoxicating liquors, and that I will, by all suitable means, discourage their use, unless when required for the preservation of health.'

2123. Royal Templars of Temperance. Mill Creek Council. **Minutes, 1896-1898.** 1 volume. Loc: PUS.

A record of twenty-six meetings in support of prohibition.

2124. Independent Order of Good Templars. Morning Star Temperance Lodge. **Records, c1860-1905.** 1 box. Loc: WCA. MU 107.

The lodge, which was #27 of the Independent Order of Good Templars, met in the Ennotville Library building from c1860 to c1905. The records include the Order's constitution and procedures, a membership dues book for 1863 to 1864, minutes for 1875-1879, a cashbook and miscellaneous receipts for 1875.

2125. Royal Templars of Temperance. **Fergus. Minutes, 1892-1897.** 1 bound volume. original. Loc: AO. FA: MU 2957.

Part of the Templin Family Collection.

2126. Royal Templars of Temperance. **Guelph. Correspondence, 1884-1885**. 1 file folder. Loc: UGA. XR1 MS A005073.

Correspondence regarding prohibition to Nathaniel Higinbotham from head offices of the organization in Buffalo and Hamilton. Part of Allan-Higinbotham Collection.

2127. Royal Templars of Temperance. **Guelph. Minutes, 1909-1921**. 1 volume. Loc: UGA. XR1 MS A005073.

A record of monthly meetings of the Guelph Council. Part of Allan-Higinbotham Collection.

VETERANS' AND MILITARY ORGANIZATIONS

2128. 11th Field Artillery Regiment. **16th Battery. Membership roll, 1878-1914**. 1 ledger. Loc: GAB.

A record of battery number, date of enrolment, name, address, nationality, date of birth, age, religion, promotions and whether married or single. The ledger includes remarks at times indicating the subsequent military activities and fate of specific members of the battery. The ledger is labelled 'Ontario Field Artillery Roll' but most of the entries refer to Guelph residents or soldiers serving in the Guelph regiment.

2129. 11th Field Artillery Regiment. **B Battery. Order book, 1890-1894**. 1 ledger. Loc: GAB.

A record of orders of the B Battery outlining military procedures, training and drills. The ledger indicates that Captain William Clark conducted a number of drills at the Ontario Agricultural College. The cover of the ledger lists Major John Davidson as the commanding officer. It is probable that B Battery was also known as 16th Battery.

2130. 11th Field Artillery Regiment. **Scrapbook, 1865-1960**. 1 volume. Loc: GAB.

A contemporary scrapbook of the militia in the 1950s and 1960s, with occasional reference to the historical development.

2131. 11th Field Brigade. **Historical record, 1837-1942**. 1 volume. Loc: GAB.

The volume contains historical notes and membership lists issued by the Department of Defence about local militia, including the 1st Wellington Battalion, Voluntary Reserve, Guelph Rifle Company, Guelph Artillery Company and Wellington Field Battery. The record includes excerpts from official reports of the local militia.

2132. 16th Battery. **War record, 1914-1918**. 1 ledger. Loc: GCM.

An outline of participation of the Guelph 16th Battery in World War I. The ledger lists members, their rank, when specific men joined and when they were wounded. The record is held in a box entitled, Militaria.

2133. 2nd Wellington Battalion. **Militia records, 1856-1870**. 1 file folder. Loc: WCA.

A record of the militia rolls of the 2nd Battalion of the Wellington County militia which notes officers, regular militiamen, whether married or single and the age category of specific members. The record also includes several government documents recognizing the contributions of Captain William Leslie who was an officer in the 2nd Battalion. The collection includes a single letter written to William Leslie in 1882 recognizing his contributions as a reeve in Puslinch Township. Held with the Pollock Collection.

2134. **30th Regiment, Wellington Rifles, Elora. Drill pay list, 1909.** 1 document. Loc: UGA. XR1 MS A115004.

A record of the rank, name, length of training period, pay of rank, efficiency pay and total amount due to each member; the document is labelled 'D Company'. Held with the Connon Collection.

2135. **30th Regiment, Wellington Rifles, Guelph. Regimental and Bridge orders, 1901-1906.** 1 volume. Loc: GPL.

A record of training procedures of the regiment which indicates that brigade camps were held in London.

2136. **30th Wellington Battalion of Rifles. Order book, 1889-1898.** 1 ledger. Loc: GAB.

A record of battalion orders which includes references to military training procedures and training camps that were held in London, Ontario.

2137. **Canada Department of Defence. The artillery of Guelph, 1866-1966: 11th Field Artillery Regiment, Royal Canadian Artillery.** 15 p. Loc: UGL. CA1 ND 66A63.

A brief history of the development of area militia, including dates of the many name changes. In 1866, the 30th Wellington Battalion of Rifles was formed with ten Rifle Companies throughout the county, including the Guelph Rifle Company. The regiment formally disbanded in 1936, after several name changes. The Guelph contingents included the 11th Battery and 16th Battery. The present official title of the regiment is, 11th Field Artillery Regiment, Royal Canadian Artillery. The brochure also lists types of guns used, and officers in World Wars I and II, including John McCrae and George Drew.

2138. **Canadian Expeditionary Force. Discharge certificate, 1918.** 1 document. Loc: GCM.

Details of the discharge from active service of Robert Donelan who lived in Guelph. The record is held in a box entitled, Militaria.

2139. **Colonel John McCrae Birth Place Society. Correspondence, minutes and receipts, 1966-1984.** 5 boxes. Loc: JMH.

The information concerns the establishment of McCrae House as a museum.

2140. **Elora Volunteer Rifle Company. Company ledger and defaulters' book, 1866.** 2 volumes. Loc: AO. MU 2014.

The company ledger contains a roll of all members of the company. The defaulters' book has been ruled up with a double page for each man, but there are very few entries, mainly reporting drunkenness on duty or absence from parade. The records relate to periods of duty at Chatham and Point Edward under the command of Lieutenant Charles Clarke. Part of the Marston Collection.

2141. **Elora Volunteer Rifle Company. Correspondence, 1861-1869; 1875; 1885.** 4 file folders. Loc: WCA. MU69.

A collection of letters of Colonel Charles Clarke. Part of the Steele Collection.

A festive gathering: the Elora Templars of Temperance, c1900.
An early predecessor of the group was the Elora Friendly Society
for the Suppression of Intemperance, begun in 1851 (#2122).
(Wellington County Museum and Archives)

2142. Elora Volunteer Rifle Company. **Papers, 1860-1898.** 1 box. Loc: UGA. XR1 MS A198001-20.
    A collection of military reports and some correspondence relating to the rifle company, which was later named the 30th Wellington Battalion of Rifles. Held with the Gilkison-Fraser Collection.

2143. Guelph Armouries. **Inventory of barracks furniture, 1915.** 1 item. Loc: GAB.
    A list of barrack furniture mounted on a wooden board. The inventory is signed by Lieutenant-Colonel A.B. Petrie.

2144. Guelph Patriotic Fund. **Advertisement, 1916.** 1 brochure. Loc: WCA. MU 13.
    An advertisement of the local branch of the Canadian Patriotic Fund to increase support for the fund to help support needy families of soldiers in active service during World War I. The first page is titled 'British freedom or Prussian militarism: which?' Several leaders of the campaign are listed: Lincoln Goldie, J.W. Lyon, Evan Macdonald and Robert Harcourt.

2145. Guelph War Memorial Association. **Cash books, 1923-1928.** 4 cash books, 1 ledger. Loc: GCH.
    Cash books and a ledger compiled by Lt. Col. W. Simpson, Secretary-Treasurer. This association, sponsored by City Council, also raised funds from the public. The records are held in the Clerk's office vault.

2146. Guelph War Memorial Association. **Order of Service. Unveiling of memorial, 1927.** 8 p. Loc: GPL.
    A program of the Memorial Day Service held to honour those who died during World War I.

2147. Royal Canadian Legion. **Correspondence, 1944-1946.** 1 file folder. Loc: JMH.
    Correspondence and information about the founding of John McCrae Memorial Garden in 1946.

WOMEN'S ASSOCIATIONS

2148. Bon Accord Community Club. **Autobiographies of members, 1954-1979.** 1 volume. Loc: WCA. MU 37.
    A history of the women's club that was begun in 1954. It includes brief historical sketches of members' families in the early twentieth century and mentions the women's education and early employment.

2149. Federated Women's Institutes of Ontario. **Records, 1901-1976.** 19 boxes. Loc: AO. FA: RG 16, Series 16-87.
    Minutes, membership lists, lists of officers, founding dates, correspondence, subject files, maps showing geographical boundaries and essays, articles and notes on local history. Most records date from the 1930s or later. Boundary details on the Wellington Institutes are in Box 19.22 while historical files for Centre Wellington (1932-1973) are in Box 16.8, North Wellington (1939-1972) in Box 16.9, and South Wellington (1939-1975) in Box 17.1. Held with Ontario Department of Agriculture records.

2150. Guelph Business and Professional Women's Club. **Records, 1928-1975.** 2 boxes. Loc: AO. FA: MU 6358.

Reports, minutes, membership lists, committee reports and cash books for most years. Members included teachers, nurses, business secretaries, social welfare workers, bookkeepers and librarians. They met bi-monthly in the supper hour. From the fifteen charter members, the club grew to sixty in 1934. The club seems to have been active in relief work during the 1930s and in war work. It also supported the YWCA and the General Hospital. Other items include a brief history of the club's early years (1928-1935) and a profile of Charles Raymond as businessman and philanthropist. Among the club's officers in its early years were Irene Carter, Jean Carter, Alice Cabeldu, Greta M. Shutt, Florence Partridge and Anne Sutherland.

2151. Wellington County Women's Institutes. **Centre Wellington. Cash books, 1912-1973.** 15 ledgers. Loc: WCA.
A record of monthly and annual financial statements. The cash books are held in the same ledgers as the minute books.

2152. Wellington County Women's Institutes. **Centre Wellington. Membership books, 1918-1933.** 2 ledgers. Loc: WCA. List of membership book date spans.
Lists of names and addresses of members and fees paid.

2153. Wellington County Women's Institutes. **Centre Wellington. Minutes, 1906; 1915-1983.** 18 volumes. Loc: WCA. List of minute books date span.
Minutes of meetings including notes of activities, motions carried and lectures given to the institute. The minutes are held in the same volumes as the cash books.

2154. Wellington County Women's Institutes. **Eramosa. Minutes, 1931-1974.** 9 volumes. Loc: WCA.
Minutes of monthly meetings including reports of election of officers and descriptions of activities.

2155. Wellington County Women's Institutes. **Everton. Minutes, 1908-1914; 1921-1953.** 8 volumes. Loc: WCA.
Minutes of monthly meetings, motions carried, the election of officers and general activities of the institute.

2156. Wellington County Women's Institutes. **Hillsburgh Senior. Programs, 1932-1936.** 3 documents. Loc: WCA.
Three programs outlining monthly activities of the institution and listing its officers.

2157. Wellington County Women's Institutes. **Marden. Minutes, 1924-1926.** 1 volume. Loc: WCA.
Minutes of monthly meetings that report the institute's activities. The volume includes periodic financial statements.

2158. Wellington County Women's Institutes. **Mimosa. Minutes, 1921-1983.** 2 reels. mf. Loc: WCA.
Minutes of the monthly and annual meetings of the Mimosa Women's Institute which was formed in 1918.

2159. Wellington County Women's Institutes. **Royal Women's Institute. Minutes, 1927-1972.** 15 volumes. Loc: WCA. List of records with date span.

Minutes of monthly meetings which includes references to activities and motions carried and brief financial statements. The Wellington County Archives has developed a finding aid indicating the date span of the minutes.

2160. Wellington County Women's Institutes. **South Wellington District. Minutes, 1905-1910; 1922-1974.** 15 volumes. Loc: WCA.

A record of annual district meetings with early minutes referring to women's institutes operating in the Paisley Block, Aberfoyle, Marden, Rockwood and Killean. The minutes outline district activities and each year lists officers elected for each local women's institute. The minutes include brief financial statements for specific women's institutes operating in South Wellington.

2161. Wellington County Women's Institutes. **West Wellington. Cash books, 1903-1920; 1924-1930.** 6 ledgers. Loc: WCA. List of date span of minute books.

A record of monthly and annual receipts and expenditures. The cash books are held in the same ledgers as the minutes of the institute.

2162. Wellington County Women's Institutes. **West Wellington. Membership books, 1903-1920; 1924-1930.** 5 ledgers. Loc: WCA. List of membership book date span.

Lists of names and addresses of members, and in later years notes of membership fees.

2163. Wellington County Women's Institutes. **West Wellington. Minutes, 1903-1921; 1924-1930.** 7 volumes. Loc: WCA. List of date span of minute books.

A record of monthly meetings with brief entries and list of speakers and nature of topic addressed by specific lectures.

WELFARE ASSOCIATIONS

2164. Canadian Council on Social Development. **Guelph, Ontario. Relief, 1937.** Loc: NAC. MG 28 I10, v.126.

2165. Guelph Children's Aid Society. **Annual reports, 1916; 1926; 1931.** 3 printed reports. Loc: NAC. MG 30, C 97, FA 368.
Filed with the J.J. Kelso Papers.

2166. Guelph Children's Aid Society. **Annual reports, 1926; 1934.** 2 volumes. Loc: WCA.

Held with the Wellington County Historical Research Society Collection. A record of officers, financial statements, inspector's report and the activities of the organization. The 1926 report includes a history of the society noting it was founded in 1893 and listing individuals who served as administrators. A shelter was constructed in 1911 at a cost of $10,000.00.

2167. Guelph Children's Aid Society. **Circular, 1929.** 1 document. Loc: GCM.

A note of the mottos of the society and lists of administrators of the organization. The circular notes 'by saving the girls and boys to better lives, you crush out crime', and, 'it is wiser and less expensive to save the children than to punish criminals'. The record is held in a box entitled, Organizations.

2168. Guelph Humane Society/ Guelph Humane and Children's Aid Society/ Guelph Children's Aid Society. **Board. Minutes, 1893-1940.** 6 volumes. Loc: CAS.

The society holds a complete set of minutes from its inception to the present. The minute books include the constitution, bylaws, and occasional newspaper clippings, annual reports, inspectors' reports, financial reports and superintendents' reports. The founding meeting was held on Friday, November 17, 1893 in which the following executive members were elected: President, Nathaniel Higinbotham; 1st Vice-President, James Goldie; 2nd Vice-President, Annie Keating; Secretary, F.W. Galbraith; Treasurer, William Tytler. Ontario Superintendent of Neglected Children, J.J. Kelso, was present and spoke at the meeting. The minutes record the objectives of the society: 'The prevention of all cruelty; the promotion and development of a humane public sentiment; the care and protection of neglected, abandoned or orphaned children; the providing of such children as are lawfully committed or entrusted to the Society with suitable homes in private families and to guard their interests and promote their happiness and well-being'. Five committees of the executive were organized: cruelty and prosecution, humane education and literature, finance and audit, temporary homes and foster homes. An archival note states that the 'shelter' was responsible for children in Guelph and Wellington County, and was started in a few rented rooms on Waterloo Avenue and later moved into a house on the same street. In 1911, the society built its own building on Clarke Street, moved into the Gummer Building in 1948, and moved into its present Delhi Street building in 1958.

2169. Guelph Humane Society/ Guelph Humane and Children's Aid Society/ Guelph Children's Aid Society. **Correspondence and miscellaneous items, 1894-1940.** 3 file folders. Loc: CAS.

A small collection of administrative correspondence, occasional minutes, a draft of the 1894 constitution, a 1901 printed annual report, a 1909 inspector's report, and occasional newspaper clippings.

2170. Guelph YM-YWCA. **Annual reports, c1920-1940.** 1 file folder. Loc: GPL.

A series of reports describing the goals, finances and activities of the YMCA and the YWCA in Guelph. A number of the documents are undated but one report of the YWCA is noted to be the fourteenth annual report of the society.

2171. Guelph YMCA. **Annual reports, 1913-1940.** 2 file folders. Loc: GPL.

A series of official reports sent to the central office of the YMCA each year. The form lists the details of the Guelph YMCA noting its organization, property and finance, and social activities.

2172. Guelph YMCA. **Bylaw, 1913.** 1 document. Loc: GPL.

A carbon copy of Bylaw No. 1 that authorizes a $15,000 mortgage received from the Guelph and Ontario Investment and Savings Society, dated August 13, 1913.

2173. Guelph YMCA. **Correspondence, 1911-1919.** 1 file folder. Loc: GPL.

A number of letters from YMCA groups to the Guelph association outlining procedures for initiating the society in the city and a request to the city for taxation exemption. The record also includes details of insurance policies for the Guelph YMCA.

2174. Guelph YMCA. **Financial reports, 1933-1937.** 1 file folder. Loc: GPL.
A record of monthly receipts and expenditures and of members and subscriptions paid by each to the society. The records include a note of the activities of the society presented in the general secretary's report.

2175. Guelph YMCA. **Financial statements, 1926-1919; 1939.** 1 file folder. Loc: GPL.
A number of monthly and annual financial statements. The monthly statements include references to special projects of the society.

2176. Guelph YMCA. **Land records, 1867-1913.** 1 file folder. Loc: GPL.
A collection of land deeds and mortgages that traces ownership of Lot 81 in the Canada Company Survey, Guelph on the corner of Quebec and Yarmouth Streets. The land was purchased by Charles Raymond in 1867, John McLagan in 1875, T.A. Keating in 1875, Charles Yeates in 1910, Walter Ellis Buckingham in 1911 and the YMCA in 1913.

2177. Guelph YMCA. **Memorandum of Agreement, 1913.** 1 document. Loc: GPL.
A carbon copy of the agreement to incorporate the YMCA. The agreement states that any young man of good moral character may become a member and any male member in good standing in evangelical churches may vote.

2178. Guelph YMCA. **Minutes, 1913-1922.** 1 file folder. Loc: GPL.
A list of the original directors, building project activities of 1911, and motions passed by the board in the period. The minutes include periodic references to the finances of the society. The collection includes a history of the YMCA in Canada.

2179. Guelph YWCA. **Blue Triangle Committee. Minutes, 1921-1923.** 1 volume. Loc: GPL.
The minutes suggest that the committee held special events to raise money and perhaps organized girls' clubs.

2180. Guelph YWCA. **Board. Minutes, 1913-1925.** 4 volumes. Loc: GPL.
A record of meetings beginning with the first planning meeting in 1913. Mrs John Goldie, Mrs Thomas Goldie and Mrs Zavitz were in attendance.

2181. Guelph YWCA. **Board. Reports, 1926-1929.** 1 file folder. Loc: GPL.
A record of board meetings and of the annual reports of the general secretary. The records outline the ideals of the society and note special projects implemented by the YWCA in Guelph.

2182. Guelph YWCA. **Correspondence, 1929-1933.** Loc: GPL.
Correspondence between Mrs Fowler and the Missionary Society of the United Church about national conferences and leadership training for the YWCA. Fowler was president of the local branch. Included in the YWCA Collection is a photograph of the YWCA house on the southwest corner of St George's Square.

2183. Guelph YWCA. **Girls' Work Committee. Minutes, 1937-1941.** 1 volume. Loc: GPL.

2184. Guelph YWCA. **Guest register, 1927-1931.** 1 ledger. Loc: GPL.
A record of individuals visiting the Guelph YWCA which lists their place of residence and the amount given to the society by specific visitors.

2185. Guelph YWCA. **Membership. List, 1913-1920.** 1 ledger. Loc: GPL.
A record of members and amount of fees paid by each.

2186. Guelph YWCA. **Record of special events, 1931-1937.** 1 volume. Loc: GPL.
The board minutes from 1917 to 1921 are in the same volume.

300

The Ontario Agricultural College and Experimental Farm in Guelph, 1889.
This lithograph of a panoramic view of the campus and farm (#2196) was presented to subscribers by the Canadian Livestock and Farm Journal in Hamilton, Ontario. (Macdonald Stewart Art Centre)

SPECIAL INSTITUTIONS

Many of the records described in this **Inventory** are generally representative of primary material that might be found in other counties and regions of southern Ontario. More distinctive are the special institutions that have been located in Wellington County since the 1870s and have left sets of records that are not easily subsumed under other headings. Most of these are administered by higher governments or outside bodies and operate under provincial rather than municipal legislation. The special institutions for which records have been found are grouped here as educational, medical, penal and religious.

Special educational institutions have operated in the region for well over a century. The three colleges that were to unite to form the University of Guelph in 1964 have long been special elements in Guelph and Wellington County, linking the region to all of rural Ontario. As the colleges were administered until the 1960s by the provincial Department of Agriculture, there are also relevant official government records in the Archives of Ontario.

The Ontario Agricultural College, started as an experimental farm in 1874 and named a college from 1880, has a particularly large group of records. Its **raison d'etre** was to apply science, reason and documentation to farming in Ontario; it was also the model for colleges established later in other Candian provinces.[1] In addition to teaching the students who came into residence to earn degrees and diplomas, the college functioned as a vital base for extension education. There are hundreds of boxes of routinely generated administrative records, even to cheque ledgers that record the amount of every minor payment, though without details of payees or goods or services purchased!

The Macdonald Institute was founded (and endowed by Montreal philanthropist William Macdonald) to be an equivalent agency for training the young women of rural Ontario. Its establishment alongside the OAC in 1903 owed much to the efforts of Adelaide Hunter Hoodless and the support of James Mills, President of the OAC from 1879 to 1904.[2] Like the OAC, the Macdonald

---

[1] For useful surveys of the founding and early history of the OAC, based on departmental and annual reports and contempory published materials, see Alexander M. Ross, **The college on the hill: A history of the Ontario Agricultural College, 1874-1974** (Toronto, 1974); Douglas Lawr, 'Agricultural education in nineteenth-century Ontario: An idea in search of an institution,' in Michael B. Katz and Paul H. Mattingly, eds. **Education and social change: Themes from Ontario's past** (New York, 1975): 169-192; and Tom Nesmith, '"Pen and plough" at Ontario Agricultural College, 1874-1910,' **Archivaria** 19 (Winter 1984-5): 94-109.

[2] For a critique of the ideas of Hoodless about the women's proper roles and value of home economics, see Terry Crowley, 'Madonnas before magdalenes: Adelaide Hoodless and the making of the Canadian Gibson Girl,' **Canadian**

Institute served as a base for extension education and liaison with the Women's Institutes founded in the early twentieth century. Other materials documenting this role may be found with the records of the provincial Department of Agriculture.

The Ontario Veterinary College, founded in Toronto in the 1860s, was transferred to Guelph in 1922, to join the other two colleges though it firmly resisted any attempts to merge its identity with the OAC. There are voluminous records of administration and accounts and of faculty and student activities.

In the words of Barbara Lazenby Craig, 'hospital records are rich and varied sources ...that document the emergence of an important and novel aspect of human experience ...[but] have been largely unexplored by historians and archivists.'[3] Records of several local hospitals are held in regional repositories. The Homewood Sanitarium and St Joseph's Hospital maintain their own records in archives which may be used by approved researchers while the records of the Royal Alexandra Hospital of Fergus (renamed the Groves Memorial in 1932) have been acquired by the Wellington County Archives. We have been able to trace only fragmentary records for the Guelph General Hospital.

The Homewood Retreat Association was established in 1883 by John W. Langmuir and others as a private asylum for the insane and for inebriates and drug addicts. In 1900, it was renamed the Homewood Sanitarium and its capacity had been increased to serve about 300 patients by 1940. Its records are organized primarily by the reigns of the four medical directors during the period from 1883 to 1940. Several scholarly articles have been based on analysis of the Homewood's patient records.[4]

St Joseph's Hospital was opened in Guelph in 1861 by three members of the Sisters of St Joseph. Beginning as a 16-bed hospital and House of Providence to care for the poor and elderly, there were additions in 1877 and a major new building in 1895 and a School of Nursing was opened in 1899. The only records for the period before 1890 are scrapbooks and historical sketches compiled later; most of the records documenting medical treatment of

---

Historical Review 67 (1986): 520-547. Crowley's article is based on the Hoodless Papers as well as the official records of the Macdonald Institute, both of which are held in the University of Guelph Library: Archival and Special Collections.

[3] Barbara Lazenby Craig, 'The Canadian hospital in history and archives,' **Archivaria** 21 (Winter 1985-6): 52-67.

[4] See Cheryl L. Krasnick, 'The aristocratic vice: The medical treatment of drug addiction at the Homewood Retreat, 1883-1900,' **Ontario History** 65 (1983): 403-427 and Cheryl Krasnick Warsh, 'The first Mrs Rochester: wrongful confinement, social redundancy and commitment to the private asylum,' **Historical Papers/Communications historiques, Windsor 1988** (Canadian Historical Association, 1989): 145-167.

patients date from after 1910.

The village of Fergus obtained a hospital rather earlier than most communities its size, mainly through the efforts of Dr Abraham Groves, pioneer of surgical techniques and advocate of improved standards for community hospitals. Groves presented his small private hospital (started in 1901) to the community in 1907, when it was named the Royal Alexandra. In 1932, the hospital was renamed the Groves Memorial in honour of its founder. The most substantial records are the minutes from 1908 to 1931 which were preserved with the Fergus municipal records but there is a good range of more fragmentary material.

Following the report of a Special Committee on Prison Labour, Guelph became the site of the Ontario Reformatory, the provincial prison farm designed to rehabilitate offenders through useful work training. An 800-acre site just east of the city was bought in 1909 and the first prisoners arrived in April 1910, but construction was not completed until 1916. In 1917 it was commandeered for four years as the military Speedwell Hospital. From the beginning there were training facilities for woodwork, broom making, tailoring and shoemaking, as well as a woolen mill and machine and paint shop. The institution was renamed the Guelph Correctional Centre in 1968. The most significant records of the reformatory -- the case files and registers -- are held at the Archives of Ontario with the records of the Ministry of Correctional Services. The only historical records in the institution's own library are a set of annual reports since 1932 that include information about all penal institutions in Ontario.

The Jesuit Fathers of Upper Canada who served the Guelph Mission from 1852 to 1931 and built the Church of Our Lady also chose Guelph as the site of a novitiate to serve their order in all of English Canada. The St Stanislaus Novitiate was founded in 1913 on a site on the northern edge of Guelph; it was renamed St Ignatius College in 1960. Records of the Novitiate, held in the Jesuit Archives at Regis College in Toronto, include devotional and instructional materials as well as materials relating to the notorious 'Guelph Raid' of June 1918. These include minutes of evidence and the report of a Royal Commission of Enquiry in 1919 and the script of a play based on the event.

2187. Macdonald Institute. **Accounts ledgers, 1906-1946.** 3 volumes. Loc: AO. FA: RG 16, Series 16-50.

   The college operations were suspended between 1941 and 1946 when it was turned over to the Royal Canadian Air Force.

2188. Macdonald Institute. **Administration. Correspondence and accounts, 1903-1969.** 126 boxes. Loc: UGA. Itemized inventory.

   A collection of correspondence and accounts regarding courses, applications, staff, supplies, student societies, graduates, equipment and extension education. Mary Urie Watson was director from 1903 to 1920 and Olive R. Cruikshank was director from 1920 to 1947. Part of the Macdonald Institute Collection.

2189. Macdonald Institute. **Entrance records and exams, 1905-1964.** 22 boxes. Loc: UGA. Itemized inventory.

   A collection of entrance records, class lists and exams. Part of Macdonald Institute Collection.

2190. Macdonald Institute. **Faculty records, 1904-1964.** 8 boxes. Loc: UGA. Itemized inventory.

   A collection of notes, assignments, research projects and photographs of various faculty members. Part of Macdonald Institute Collection.

2191. Macdonald Institute. **Principal's office. Correspondence, 1903-1953.** 7 boxes. Loc: AO. FA: RG 16, Series 16-51.

   The records are part of the major record group associated with the Ontario Department of Agriculture which administered the college until the 1960s. Under the first principal, Mary Watson (1903-1926), teacher training was begun when the Macdonald Consolidated School started to provide opportunities for practice teaching.

2192. Macdonald Institute. **Reference library, 1904-1964.** 10 boxes. Loc: UGA. Itemized inventory.

   A collection of articles, pamphlets, leaflets and publications for extension programs. One box contains anniversary programs and another contains historical sketches of the Institute. The history box also contains personal correspondence with Sir W. Macdonald from 1886 to 1910 regarding manual training schools, Ontario Agricultural College and Macdonald Consolidated School. Part of Macdonald Institute Collection.

2193. Macdonald Institute. **Student notebooks, 1910.** 2 items. Loc: OAM.

   The notebooks of Marjorie Lee for sewing and cooking.

2194. Macdonald Institute. **Student records, 1904-1964.** 22 boxes. Loc: UGA. Itemized inventory.

   A collection of student society records, notebooks, photographs and programs of various students. Part of Macdonald Institute Collection.

2195. Macdonald, J. **Bird's-eye view of Ontario Agricultural College and Experimental Farm, Guelph, Ontario, 1903.** 27.4 x 59.7 cm. Loc: UGA, MSC. UGA:RE2 OAC A198; MSC:UGB900.082.

A coloured lithograph of the College campus and farm that identifies the main OAC building, Macdonald Institute, Macdonald Hall, Massey Hall and Library, Biology-Physics building, Mechanical Department, Chemical Laboratory, Home Dairy, Poultry Building and Cold Storage. It was published by Grip Limited of Toronto as a premium to subscribers of the Weekly Mercury. Part of the University of Guelph Art Collection at the Macdonald Stewart Art Centre. Acquired, 1970. Another copy is held by the University Library's Archival and Special Collections.

2196. Manly, Charles M. **Panoramic View of Ontario Agricultural College, 1906.** 28.9 x 44.4 cm. Loc: MSC. UGB900.084.

A coloured lithograph showing the campus, farm fields, Macdonald Institute and Hall, OAC Main Building and the Dairy School. It was lithographed by the Toronto Engraving Company for the Farmer's Advocate, signed 'C.M. Manly', and inscribed on the reverse, 'The Farmer's Advocate, December 13, 1906, page 1967 and 1970'. Part of the University of Guelph Art Collection. Acquired by the Macdonald Institute, 1970.

2197. Ontario Agricultural College. **Accounts ledgers, 1885-1961.** 7 volumes. Loc: AO. FA: RG 16, Series 16-153.

2198. Ontario Agricultural College. **Administration. Correspondence and accounts, 1873-1970.** 124 boxes, 25 volumes. Loc: UGA. Itemized inventory.

A collection of records that includes an 1873 plan of the campus, annual reports from 1874, miscellaneous committee minutes, minutes from Massey Library, minutes of Building Committee for War Memorial Hall, correspondence, programs, bursars' accounts, photographs and records of Presidents, including James Mills, George Christie and George Creelman. Part of Ontario Agricultural College Collection.

2199. **The Ontario Agricultural College and Experimental Farm, Guelph, Canada: premium presented to subscribers of 1889 by the Canadian Livestock and Farm Journal, Hamilton, Ontario, 1889.** 2 copies; 28 x 59.7 cm. Loc: MSC. UGB900.019 and UGB900.020.

An anonymous lithograph depicting a panoramic view of the campus and farm including the following identified buildings: Residence of Professor of Agriculture, Residence of Bursar, College and Lecture Rooms, Chemical Laboratory, Mechanical Department, and Barn and Other Out Buildings. Part of the University of Guelph Art Collection. Copy 1 was a gift of Mr W.J. Rae of Toronto, 1977. Copy 2 was a gift of Maxwell Ricker of Dunnville, Ontario, 1978.

2200. Ontario Agricultural College. **Annual reports, 1875-1961.** 5 boxes. Loc: UGA. REI OAC A0090.

The reports were printed by order of the Legislative Assembly until 1894, when they began to be published by the Ontario Department of Agriculture. Each volume includes a president's report with an overview of students and programs; financial report; professors' reports that refer to courses, practical work and research; physician's report; a report of experiments; and a report of the Agricultural and Experimental Union.

2201. Ontario Agricultural College. **Bursar. Correspondence, 1922-1985.** 8 boxes. Loc: AO. FA: RG 16, Series 16-22.

Started as an experimental farm in 1874, and named a college from 1880, the institution was directly administered by the Ontario Department of Agriculture until 1964 as its major educational and research facility.

2202. Ontario Agricultural College. **Campus map, 1924.** 1 map. Loc: UGA. RE2 OAC A209.
A drawing of the campus streets, shrubbery and buildings, including Macdonald Institute, Mills Hall, War Memorial Hall and Massey Library. Drawn by Bernard Dangerfield.

2203. Ontario Agricultural College. **College grounds with an inset of farm buildings, 1906.** Loc: UGA. RE6 OAC A010.
A framed coloured map of the O.A.C. in 1906 that shows the Consolidated School, Macdonald Institute, Main College building, Massey Hall and Library, Biology-Physics building, Mechanical Department, Chemical Laboratory, gymnasium, grain Experimental Building and Bacteriological laboratory, livestock pavilion, home dairy, Poultry building, cold storage and the Farm Mechanics/Manual Training [Blackwood Hall] building. The map also includes an inset of the farm buildings.

2204. Ontario Agricultural College. **Commission of inquiry into certain misconduct, 1884.** mf. Loc: UGL.
A microfiche reproduction of a handwritten report describing the consistent harassment of a mathematics master at the O.A.C. by several students. The harassment included repeated smashing of his windows and door and forced entry into his rooms. The students stated their actions were due to his 'plucking' of students at the examinations, his youthful appearance, his 'sneaking' way of separating students, and his inability to teach them. The report offers no recommendations.

2205. Ontario Agricultural College. Dairy School. **Diary of Gilbert Tucker, 1894.** Loc: AO. MU 6797-8.
The file also contains a notebook and examination papers for 1895.

2206. Ontario Agricultural College. **Departments. Correspondence and accounts, 1896-1970.** 292 boxes. Loc: UGA. Itemized inventory.
A collection of department records that includes correspondence, minutes, programs, publications and accounts. Departments include Apiculture, Horticulture, Engineering, Poultry Husbandry, Dairying, Agricultural Economics, Soil Science, Physics, Field Husbandry, Chemistry and English. Also included are Faculty Association minutes, slides as teaching aids and several collections of papers by faculty such as James Hayes Panton. Part of the Ontario Agricultural College Collection.

2207. Ontario Agricultural College. **Experimental Farm. Ledgers, 1909-1929.** 3 volumes. Loc: AO. FA: RG 16, Series 16-154.

2208. Ontario Agricultural College. **O.A.C. student notebooks, 1912-1914.** 3 items. Loc: OAM.
The notebooks of Gordon D. Lee for several subjects including chemistry, apiculture, economics, field husbandry and botany.

2209. Ontario Agricultural College. **OAC 100, 1874-1974.** 1 film. 16 mm film. Loc: UGL.

A description of current education and facilities in 1974 that includes a brief historical sketch of the opening years of OAC, using old photographs. The film is 16 minutes in length.

2210. Ontario Agricultural College. **OAC centennial interview of Dr L.H. Newman, 1903-1974.** 1 tape. videotape. Loc: UGL.

A 60 minute interview of Newman, who graduated from OAC in 1903, in which he discusses his early days at the college and his career after graduation.

2211. Ontario Agricultural College. **OAC centennial interview of P.E. Angle, 1909-1974.** 1 tape. videotape. Loc: UGL.

A 60 minute interview of Angle, who graduated from OAC in 1909, in which he discusses his early days at the college and his career after graduation.

2212. Ontario Agricultural College. **The Ontario Agricultural College and Experimental Farm, Guelph, Canada, 1889.** Loc: UGA. RE6 OAC A024.

A drawing of the O.A.C. in 1889 by Rolph, Smith and Company showing the residence of the professor of agriculture, residence of the bursar, college and lecture rooms, the chemical laboratory, mechanical department, and the barn and other outbuildings.

2213. Ontario Agricultural College. **Plan of buildings and grounds by Charles Miller, 1882.** 1 file folder. Loc: UGA. RE1 OAC A0229.

A plan of the O.A.C. grounds in 1882 that makes reference to all buildings and to the various types of vegetation on the grounds and in the Arboretum. The plan was printed by Miller and Yates of Philadelphia. Held as part of a collection of eight modern plans of the campus dating from 1935 to 1958.

2214. Ontario Agricultural College. **Plan of the Agricultural College Farm in the Townships of Guelph and Puslinch, 1873.** 1 map. Loc: UGA. RE2 OAC A055.

A map of the campus north of the Guelph and Puslinch Township border. It notes Dundas Road, lot numbers, concession numbers and wooded areas, and is drawn with ink on linen with water colours. The scale is 4 chains to an inch.

2215. Ontario Agricultural College. **Report to Department of Education, c1885.** 1 item. Loc: AO. FA: RG-2, G-4, Box 1, Envelope #1.

A brief statistical report in which it is noted that the college had six professors, ninety-three students, eighty-eight graduates, and four thousand, three hundred volumes in its library. Held with Miscellaneous School Records of the Ontario Department of Education.

2216. Ontario Agricultural College. **Student records, 1892-1970.** 131 boxes. Loc: UGA. Itemized inventory.

A collection of student records that includes class notes, prizes, examinations, councils, societies, correspondence, convocations, yearbooks, calendars and the student publication, O.A.C. Review. Part of the Ontario Agricultural College Collection.

2217. Ontario Veterinary College. **Administration. Correspondence and accounts, 1908-1976.** 22 boxes, 3 volumes. Loc: UGA.

A collection of correspondence and accounts from the bursar, dean and principal's office, and scrapbooks that include historical sketches. Several boxes, labelled MacNabb Memorial Library, contain announcements, several annual reports and student examinations. Part of the Ontario Veterinary College Collection.

2218. Ontario Veterinary College. **Bibliography compiled by Harry E. Turner, 1962.** 1 p. Loc: AO. MU 2138, Misc. Coll. 1962 #1.
A short list of primary sources for a history of the college, mainly from the nineteenth century.

2219. Ontario Veterinary College. **Faculty records, 1899-1974.** 93 boxes. Loc: UGA. Itemized inventory.
A collection of faculty correspondence, diaries, meeting minutes, lecture notes, essays and photographs. The collection includes records of Wilfred Fowler, F.C. Grenside, Robert McIntosh and George Buckland. Part of the Ontario Veterinary College Collection.

2220. Ontario Veterinary College. **OVC interview of Trevor Lloyd Jones, 1930-1968.** 3 tapes. videotape. Loc: UGA. REI OVC A0172.
An interview with Jones who was principal of the Ontario Veterinary College from 1952 to 1968. Jones recalls his memories of his childhood in Wales, his impressions of his student days at OVC starting in 1930 and the years during which he administered the college.

2221. Ontario Veterinary College. **Student records, 1903-1965.** 28 boxes. Loc: UGA. Itemized inventory.
A collection of reports of student societies, work records, calendars and yearbooks. Part of the Ontario Veterinary College Collection.

MEDICAL INSTITUTIONS

2222. Elliott Home. **Property Committee. Minutes, 1905-1916.** 1 volume. Loc: GPL.
The minute book is held with the YMCA Collection.

2223. Groves Memorial Hospital, Women's Auxiliary. **Historical sketches, 1933-1958.** 1 reel. mf. Loc: WCA.
A brief sketch of the founding of the hospital and its growth which emphasizes the key role played by Doctor Abraham Groves.

2224. Guelph General Hospital. **Benefit concert, 1887.** 1 brochure. Loc: GCM.
A benefit concert entitled, 'Ye Old Folkes Concerte' held in the town hall.

2225. Guelph General Hospital. **Committee. Minutes, 1861-1863.** 1 volume. Loc: GCH.
A record of the committee's early attempt to found a hospital that lists provisional directors and the 17 original subscribers. Funds, less expenses, were returned to donors when it became apparent that there was not yet widespread support for the 'absolute necessity of such an establishment in Guelph'. The last board meeting was held on February 21, 1863. The record is held in the Clerk's office vault.

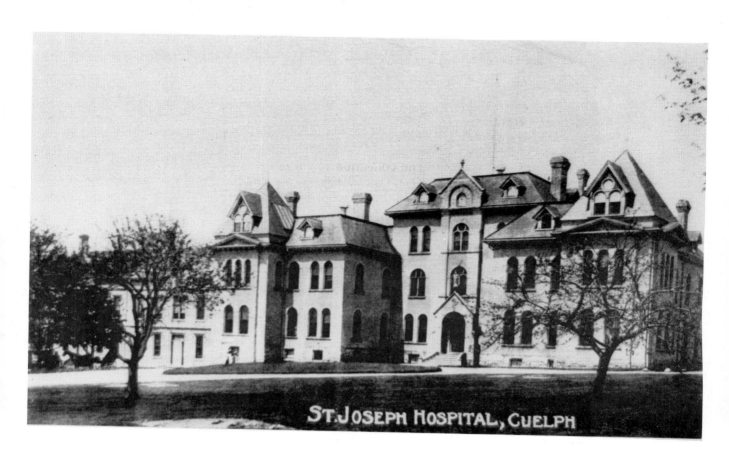

A view of the 1895 building of St Joseph's Hospital in Guelph, 1912.
The hospital and House of Providence opened in 1861 with sixteen 'inmates.'
(Archival Collections, University of Guelph)

2226. Guelph General Hospital. **Historical sketch, bylaws and rules, 1898**. 34 p. Loc: GCM.

A brief history of the hospital that was incorporated in 1861 and opened in 1874. The brochure describes rules of behaviour for the board, the Lady Superintendent, the Medical Dispenser, nurses, visitors, patients and medical staff. The rules state that patients admitted free of charge must, if able, assist in 'nursing the patients, making the beds, cleaning the wards, and doing such other work as the Lady Superintendent may direct'.

2227. Guelph General Hospital Ladies Committee. **Guelph Poster Show program, 1907**. 1 volume. Loc: GCM.

A program advertising a show to be held in the Guelph Winter Fair Building in June 1907. The event was sponsored by the Ladies Society of Guelph General Hospital. The program includes advertisements of Guelph businesses and lists of administrators of Guelph General Hospital and city officials.

2228. Homewood Sanitarium. **Administration records, 1883-1901**. 1 box. Loc: HSA. LET 100.001-LET 290.002.

Records generated during the administration of Medical Director, Dr. Stephen Lett. The collection includes articles written by Lett, advertisements for the Homewood, correspondence, transcripts of minutes of the the board of directors from 1883 to 1900, photographs, annual reports of the medical superintendent, annual reports of the president from 1883 to 1891, and a stock ledger from 1883 to 1939.

2229. Homewood Sanitarium. **Administration records, 1901-1923**. 1 box, 3 ledgers, 1 envelope. Loc: HSA. HOB 100.001-HOB 280.001.

Records generated during the administration of Medical Director, Dr A. T. Hobbs. The collection includes correspondence, photographs, postcards, newspaper clippings from 1905 to 1923, articles, excerpts from board minutes from 1902 to 1923, several annual reports, the 1914 will of J.W. Langmuir who founded the Homewood, patient accounts from 1918 to 1923, a 1922 report on the Homewood accounting system, auditors' statements from 1917 to 1920, laundry accounts, and statistical reports from 1909 to 1921.

2230. Homewood Sanitarium. **Administration records, 1923-1925**. 1 box, 1 ledger. Loc: HSA. FAR 110.001-FAR 290.008.

Records generated during the administration of Medical Director, Dr. C.B. Farrar. The collection includes correspondence, photographs, newspaper clippings, excerpts from minutes of directors' meetings from 1923 to 1925, financial reports and audits, transfer patients ledger from 1923 to 1938, and annual statistical returns from 1923 to 1924.

2231. Homewood Sanitarium. **Administration records, 1925-1942**. 6 boxes, 11 ledgers. Loc: HSA. CLA 100.001-CLA 300.063.

Records generated during the administration of Medical Director, Dr. H.C. Clare. The collection includes correspondence, photographs, a report on nurses graduating from 1928 to 1939, newspaper clippings, brochures on the Homewood, stock ledgers, accounting records from 1926 to 1939, tax records from 1926 to 1939, patient accounts from 1930 to 1942 and a transfer patients ledger from 1930 to 1960. Also included are legal records from 1935 to 1942 regarding a suit against the Homewood launched by Angus McIntosh while he was a patient in the institution.

2232. Royal Alexandra Hospital, Fergus. **Auditors' reports, 1931; 1932.** 2 volumes. Loc: WCA.

Two printed auditors' reports outlining receipts and disbursements of the hospital. Held with the Fergus municipal records.

2233. Royal Alexandra Hospital, Fergus. **Dinner in Honour of Dr Abraham Groves. Program, 1932.** 1 item. Loc: WCA. MU 77.

A commemorative program honouring Groves which lists nursing graduates of Royal Alexandra Hospital from 1905 to 1932. The brochure includes a photograph of Groves.

2234. Royal Alexandra Hospital, Fergus. **Graduation certificate, Augusta Rea, 1919.** 1 document. Loc: WCA. MU 77.

An acknowledgement that Rea had successfully completed a three-year nursing course at Royal Alexandra Hospital in Fergus.

2235. Royal Alexandra Hospital, Fergus. **Medical receipts, 1921; 1923-1924.** 4 documents. Loc: WCA.

Held in the Wellington County Historical Research Society Collection. A record of four receipts for medical care including two for care provided by Doctor Abraham Groves, and two payment forms for time spent at Royal Alexandra Hospital at a cost of $2.50 to $3.00 per day.

2236. Royal Alexandra Hospital, Fergus. **Minutes, 1908-1931.** 1 volume. Loc: WCA.

A record of minutes which indicates the first annual meeting was held in 1908. The volume includes a newspaper clipping from the Fergus News Record, dated March 12, 1914 which indicates the hospital was initiated as 'a private enterprise by one of our physicians', Doctor Abraham Groves. The minutes list administrators of the hospital, motions carried and brief entries regarding the operation of the hospital. One brief financial statement for the period 1922 to 1923 is included. Held with the Fergus municipal records.

2237. Royal Alexandra Hospital, Fergus/ Groves Memorial Hospital, Fergus. **Miscellaneous records, 1921-1955.** 1 file folder. Loc: AO. FA: MU 2956.

The collection includes the program of the jubilee banquet tendered to Dr A. Groves by his medical friends to mark his half-century in medical practice in 1921. There is a program of the complimentary dinner in 1932 that includes a list of all the graduates of the Royal Alexandra Hospital's training school, 1905-1931, and of the Groves Memorial Hospital in 1932. Other items include the constitution of the Women's Auxiliary of the Groves Hospital (c1932), the minutes of two meetings of the Groves Memorial Hospital Commission in December, 1954 and the program for opening of the new hospital building in 1955. Part of the Templin Family Collection.

2238. Royal Alexandra Hospital, Fergus. **Nursing examination records, 1926-1931.** 1 file folder. Loc: WCA.

Held in the Wellington County Historical Research Society Collection. A collection of the examination results of nurses with comments regarding the overall effectiveness of specific students.

2239. Royal Alexandra Hospital, Fergus. **Nursing graduates, 1905-1931.** 1 ledger. Loc: WCA.

> Held in the Wellington County Historical Research Society Collection. A list of the names of nursing graduates which indicates the year when specific nurses completed courses.

2240. Royal Alexandra Hospital, Fergus. **Recommendation letters, 1910; 1914.** 2 documents. Loc: WCA. MU 77.

> Two letters of reference for nurses who were graduates of the nursing school at the Royal Alexandra Hospital in Fergus.

2241. Royal Alexandra Hospital, Fergus. **School of Nursing. Commencement program, 1919.** 1 envelope. Loc: WCA. MU 19.

> A list of names of graduates.

2242. Royal Alexandra Hospital, Fergus. **School of Nursing. Notebooks, 1902-1905.** 2 volumes. Loc: WCA. MU 46.

> Student notebooks belonging to Kate McFadzean. Several lectures on anatomy and surgical techniques were given by Dr Abraham Groves.

2243. St Joseph's Hospital. **Accounts with city, 1915-1921.** 1 volume. Loc: SJA. Box 911.

> A record of indigent patients paid for by the City of Guelph that notes name, disease, doctor, total number of days in hospital, and total amount charged per person.

2244. St Joseph's Hospital. **Admission and discharge records, 1939-1940.** 1 volume. Loc: SJA. Box 961.

> A record of name, address, age, date of admission and discharge, and diagnosis of patients.

2245. St Joseph's Hospital/ St Joseph's House of Providence. **Annual report, 1908.** 1 document. Loc: DHA.

> An annual report and financial statement submitted to the Wellington County Council, January 29, 1908, that notes the installation of a new steam plant for the cost of $9,000. The report lists names of indigent patients sent by the county to the Hospital and House of Providence, and notes dates of admission and discharge, total days, and name of person who referred patient. In a private note to the Bishop, the Sister Superior refers to the Wellington County House of Industry and Refuge: 'As there is a County Refuge the Council will not recognize our House of Providence as they otherwise would. They instructed me to send anyone who wished to Fergus, but, My Lord, you know why we hesitate to send our poor there.'

2246. St Joseph's Hospital/ St Joseph's House of Providence. **Annual statistical reports, 1909-1927.** 1 ledger. Loc: SJA. Box 886.

> The annual reports list total number of inmates, discharges, deaths, beds and average length of stay. Total numbers are also classified by sex, religion, nationality, and numbers received from the city, county or province.

2247. St Joseph's Hospital. **Cash books, 1885-1898; 1905-1941.** 24 ledgers, 5 file folders. Loc: SJA. Box 886, 911, 936.

The records include a report of the 1895 building fund and expenditures.

2248. St Joseph's Hospital. **Correspondence, 1886; 1908**. 4 documents. Loc: DHA.
Correspondence in 1886 from the architect, John Day, and a member of the
Hospital Committee to the bishop regarding the cost of the proposed addition to
the hospital. When the bishop expressed displeasure about the cost and possible
debt that would result from the proposal, the Hospital Committee decided to
adhere to the bishop's wishes, and only build what it could afford.

2249. St Joseph's Hospital. **Historical sketches, 1861-1976**. 1 binder, 1 file folder.
Loc: SJA. Box 961, 936.
The binder includes several sketches of the development of the hospital,
including the brochure, 100 Years of Service, Sisters of St Joseph, Guelph:
1861-1961. The file folder, in Box 936, includes a 36 page typescript history
of the hospital entitled, And the Tree Grew. An archival note on the file
folder attributes authorship to Sister St Lawrence.

2250. St Joseph's Hospital. **Inmate daily records, 1907-1911; 1914-1917**. 2 volumes.
Loc: SJA. Box 886, 911.
A daily record of number of inmates in residence each morning and evening, and
the number admitted, discharged or died during each day.

2251. St Joseph's Hospital. **Inventory of hospital contents, 1935**. 1 binder. Loc:
SJA. Box 911.
The inventory lists contents and monetary value of each item.

2252. St Joseph's Hospital. **Legal records and correspondence, 1895-1934**. 10
folders; 23 documents. Loc: SJA. Box 886, 936.
A collection of 10 folders of agreements that include 1895 correspondence
regarding the stations of the cross added to the hospital chapel, an 1899
agreement for the city to supply water from the city's water works system, a
1904 agreement for the city to construct sewers, 1906 correspondence about the
construction of St James' and St Roch's Isolation Buildings, the 1907 will of
Maurice O'Connor in which he leaves some money to the hospital, and a 1911
agreement for the city to pay one dollar per day for indigent people admitted to
the hospital who were suffering from contagious diseases. The correspondence
from 1911 to 1934 is held in Box 936 and is regarding the administration of the
hospital.

2253. St Joseph's Hospital. **Record of operations, 1916-1923**. 2 volumes. Loc: SJA.
Box 936.
A record of patient's name, age, residence, disease, date of operation,
surgeon, assistant and anesthetist.

2254. St Joseph's Hospital. **Scrapbooks, 1861-1961**. 3 volumes. Loc: SJA. Box 886,
961.
The first scrapbook is a collection of newspaper clippings from the 1920s and
1930s about the hospital and its historical development. The second and third
volumes, in Box 961, were collected in the 1960s.

2255. St Joseph's Hospital. **Visitors' register, 1901-1942**. 1 ledger. Loc: SJA. Box
886.

A record of date, name and address of visitors. Only one quarter of the book is filled.

2256. St Joseph's House of Providence. **Accounts with city, 1917-1940.** 2 volumes. Loc: SJA. Box 911.

A record of patients paid for by the City of Guelph that lists name, number of weeks admitted, rate per week and total amount owing for 3 month periods.

2257. St Joseph's House of Providence. **Admission and discharge records, 1937-1940.** 1 box. Loc: SJA. Box 911.

A card index listing name, date of admission, birthplace, residence, occupation, marital status, names of parents, name of spouse, and record of discharges and re-admissions.

2258. St Joseph's House of Providence. **Cash books, 1920-1941.** 5 volumes. Loc: SJA. Box 911.

2259. St Joseph's House of Providence. **Financial and statistical reports, 1929-1935.** 7 documents. Loc: SJA.

Each year's report lists names of inmates, amount paid per week, age, date of admission and discharge, and total number of days in the institution. The report also includes a financial report for the year.

2260. St Joseph's House of Providence. **Index to patients, 1908-1937.** 1 volume. Loc: SJA. Box 911.

A record of date of admittance of inmate, residence, occupation, religion, time in Ontario, name of parents and spouse, and name of person who recommended admittance.

2261. St Joseph's House of Providence. **Inmate daily record, 1904-1917; 1921-1925; 1930-1954.** 10 volumes. Loc: SJA. Box 886, 911, 936.

A daily record of number of inmates in residence each morning and evening, and the number admitted, discharged or died each day. The 1934 to 1935 volume also contains salary lists of employees.

2262. St Joseph's House of Providence. **Inspector's reports, 1932; 1934-1936.** 1 envelope. Loc: SJA. Box 936.

A record of inspection and suggestions for improvement.

2263. St Joseph's House of Providence. **Pension register, 1933-1934.** 1 file folder. Loc: SJA. Box 911.

A record of name, amount of pension cheque, and amount refunded to pensioner. In all cases, the cheques were 20 dollars and the refunds were 2 dollars.

PENAL INSTITUTIONS

2264. Ontario Reformatory. **Case files, 1921-1970.** 62 reels. mf. Loc: AO. RG 20, Series D-8.

Originally planned to replace the Central Prison in Toronto. Construction was begun in 1909 and completed in 1916, but the facility was taken over by the military authorities as the Speedwell Military Hospital until the end of 1920. It reopened as a prison in January, 1921 and was renamed the Guelph Correctional

Centre in 1968. Part of the major record group for the Ontario Ministry of Correctional Services.

2265. Ontario Reformatory. **Registers, 1916-1976.** 15 volumes, 208 reels. Loc: AO. FA: RG 20, E-6, E-18.

Prison registers, 1916-1976; punishment registers, 1948-1969; and sampled case files. Prison registers before 1927 are in Series E-18, while the other records are in E-6. Part of the major record group for the Ontario Ministry of Correctional Services.

RELIGIOUS INSTITUTIONS

2266. Phelan, Horatio P. **The story of Ignatius College, September 6, 1963.** 128 p. typescript. Loc: JA.

An account of the founding of the St Stanislaus Novitiate in 1913 and of its subsequent history, including the raid by military police and the fire of 1954. The property, originally developed by Charles Mickle, was bought from Thomas Bedford in April, 1913 with subsequent purchases on the east side of the Elora Road in 1914 and 1917.

2267. St Ignatius College, Guelph. **Incorporation papers, 1862.** 1 file folder. Loc: JA.

Several copies of the 1862 private statute, 25 Victoria, cap. 83. The act was prompted by a petition by Bishop Farrell, the Reverend John Holzer and others, that noted that a college had been operating since 1855 'for the education of youth'. Held in Box 1, Guelph records.

2268. St Stanislaus Novitiate. **Annals of Loretto Convent, Guelph.** 6 p. typescript. Loc: JA. List of file folder contents.

A summary of the main events following the arrival of four members of the Loretto Community, invited to Guelph by Bishop Farrell and Father John Holzer. The author describes the establishment of two schools, St Agnes for girls and St Stanislaus for boys, and the subsequent role of the Loretto sisters in other Guelph separate schools, including the Loretto High School from 1926. Box 1 of Guelph records also contains another typescript document entitled, Loretto Convent, Guelph, 1856-1956 (6 p.), which has a similar, but not identical scope.

2269. St Stanislaus Novitiate. **Devotional and instructional texts, 1913-1958.** 2 boxes. Loc: JA.

A collection of texts used at the Novitiate. Includes texts brought from elsewhere when the Novitate was established and materials dating from after 1913. Examples of the first include Menology in English (3 volumes) and French (1 volume); the Consuetudinarium of rules and procedures in Latin (1911); rules and instructions and conference material in French (1906-1907); Instructions for the Novitiate (1909 - translated from French); a manuscript volume of Instructions for Novices derived from that compiled by Father Plowden of Hodder Place in Lancashire in the early nineteenth century. Examples of the second type include typed notes of instruction by Novice Masters for Long Retreats (including one set by Father A. McCaffrey, 1927-1928); the notebooks of novice Frank Byrne (1914-1916); a novice gardener's diary (1928-1932); and a diary of what was read at table in the refectory (1920-1954, incomplete).

2270. St Stanislaus Novitiate. **General specifications for villa addition, 1946.** 1 file folder. Loc: JA.

   Drawings by architect Lindsay A. Wardell of Toronto of a major addition to the Novitiate buildings to provide dormitories, a refectory, kitchen, chapel, recreation hall and sacristy.

2271. St Stanislaus Novitiate. **The Guelph Raid. Conscription and sectarian stress during the Great War.** 89 p. typescript. Loc: JA.

   A research paper written for the University of Toronto in 1978 by Fr Brian F. Hogan and also published in the Canadian Catholic Historical Association Study Session, 45 (1978): 57-80.

2272. St Stanislaus Novitiate. **The Guelph Raid. Correspondence and documents, 1918.** 1 file folder. Loc: JA.

   Includes initial letter of protest (June 8, 1918) by Fr Henri Bourque, Rector of the Novitiate, to Major-General Mewburn, as well as correspondence between the Rector and E.L. Newcombe (Deputy Minister of Justice), Fr W.H. Hingston and Colonel G. Godson Godson. The file also includes a list of all faculty, scholastics, novices and lay brothers at the Novitiate at the time of the raid. Some of the letters have been severely water-damaged but are now conserved in transparent sleeves.

2273. St Stanislaus Novitiate. **The Guelph Raid. Newspaper reports, 1918-1919.** 1 box with 13 file folders. Loc: JA.

   Collections of press reports of the raid by military police on June 7, 1918 and its consequences including a Royal Commission of Inquiry. Individual file folders contain mounted clippings from the Guelph Mercury, Guelph Herald, Toronto Star, Toronto Globe, Toronto Evening Telegram, Toronto World, Ottawa Journal, Ottawa Citizen, Montreal Gazette, Montreal Star, Catholic Record, Catholic Register and miscellaneous others including La Presse, The Sentinel and Orange and Protestant Advocate.

2274. St Stanislaus Novitiate. **The Guelph Raid. Pamphlets, 1918-1920.** 1 file folder. Loc: JA.

   Printed pamphlets, from various points of view, commenting on the raid and Royal Commission hearings. They include the Guelph Ministerial Association's pamphlet, Jesuit Novitiate Case: Statement and Editorial (1918); the Catholic Unity League's pamphlet, A Double Collapse of Bigotry; the Catholic War League Publicity Committee's pamphlet, Facts of the Raid upon the Jesuit Novitiate (reprinted by the Catholic Trust Society of Canada); and the Catholic Mind's pamphlet, Guelph Novitiate Inquiry (1920).

2275. St Stanislaus Novitiate. **The Guelph Raid. Recollections by Marcus Doherty and George Nunan, 1963.** 1 file folder. typescript. Loc: JA.

   Transcripts of the 1963 recollections of the 1918 raid by two of the men who were arrested as novices. Marcus Doherty was also son of the Federal Minister of Justice in 1918. George Nunan, who came of a Guelph family, was later associated with the Church of Our Lady in 1930-1 as a priest, and was Provincial of Jesuit Fathers of Upper Canada in the 1950s.

2276. St Stanislaus Novitiate. **The new Ignatius College, 1960.** 37 p. Loc: JA.

   Includes a brief history of the Jesuit Novitiate at Guelph, specifications of the new building and addresses at the opening ceremony.

2277. St Stanislaus Novitiate. **Newspaper clippings and articles, 1913-1970.** 1 box. Loc: JA.

The collection includes coverage of the 1954 fire that destroyed the main building, originally built as Langholm for the Charles Mickle family. There are also articles from The Globe magazine, one on the completion of the new 1960 buildings and the other, by William Johnson, on the changes caused by the Second Vatican Council in the 1960s.

2278. St Stanislaus Novitiate. **The Raid. Script of a play by L. Braceland, S.J., December 1950.** 1 file folder. Loc: JA.

Full script of a drama based on the raid of the Novitiate by military police in June 1918 and the consequences. Two scenes are set in the Novitiate, one in Guelph Protestant pulpits and two in the Supreme Court rooms of the Royal Commission in 1919. It would seem that the play was performed at the Novitiate.

2279. St Stanislaus Novitiate. **Royal Commission. Minutes of evidence, August-September, 1919.** 930 p., 1 bound volume. Loc: JA.

A transcript of all evidence presented at the Commission hearings and details of the witnesses called and the exhibits produced.

2280. St Stanislaus Novitiate. **Royal Commission. Report, October 6, 1919.** 10 p. Loc: JA.

Report by Commissioners W.E. Middleton and J.A. Chisholm on their official inquiry into the circumstances of the raid on the Novitiate on June 7, 1919. The report condemned the raid by the military police and the charges made by local Protestant ministers, notably Kennedy H. Palmer, that the Novitiate was sheltering young men from conscription for military service.

Suspended animation: a composition portrait of an unidentified family taken by the Mount Forest photographer, W. King, c1880. The technique involved creating a collage by adding separate photographs of physically absent members of the group to the main picture.
(Wellington County Museum and Archives)

FAMILY AND PERSONAL PAPERS

During the past twenty-five years, history as a discipline has been challenged by the 'new' social history, also called societal history or the history of societies. Among its hallmarks has been an insistence on analyzing the generality of human experience rather than the particularity of a few notables -- a view of 'history from the bottom up' rather than the 'top down.' The new approach has enriched history with techniques such as computer-assisted and statistical analysis and a new awareness of social categories such as women and children, ethnic minorities, the working class and of social units such as families, households and voluntary associations that had been previously left out.[1]

Personal and family papers can have great value in complementing the aggregate results of statistical analysis of large quantities of routinely-generated records. They can breathe life into the dry bones of statistical aggregates and means, from which we can however estimate their typicality. 'The family has been the setting of an enormously broad range of experiences over time and these have been recorded, considered and analyzed in the private correspondence of ordinary men and women.'[2] Personal and family papers can also illuminate more sentient qualities, the feelings and relationships between individuals and within families, as well as social rituals and behaviour.

What kind of people left personal and family papers relating to their time in Wellington County? Those who had the leisure and importance to commit their experiences and perceptions to writing and those whose families kept the papers so that they have survived to the late twentieth century tend to have been members of community elites and persisters or stayers.[3] Their

---

[1] There is a large literature on this subject; two reviews of the field in relation to archival materials are David Gagan and H.E. Turner, 'Social history in Canada: a report on the "state of the art",' **Archivaria** 14 (1982): 27-51; Tom Nesmith, 'Archives from the bottom up: social history and archival scholarship,' **Archivaria** 14 (1982): 5-25. For discussion of the scope and methods of social history in localities and regions, see the essays in two publications of the American Association for State and Local History: J.B. Gardner and G.R. Adams, eds. **Ordinary people and everyday life: perspectives on the new social history** (Nashville, 1980); D.E. Kyvig and M.A. Marty, **Nearby history: exploring the past around you** (Nashville, 1982).

[2] For a discussion of this approach to family history see W. Peter Ward, 'Family papers and the new social history,' **Archivaria** 14 (1982): 63-73.

[3] On the elite bias in archival collections of family and personal papers, see Dale C. Mayer, 'The new social history: implications for archivists,' **American Archivist** 48, 4 (1985): 388-399.

representativeness of the whole community should be questioned.

In this **Inventory** the papers of local 'great men' and elite families predominate. Some papers were left by each of the founders of directed settlements in the region: John Galt of Guelph, Adam Fergusson of Fergus and William Gilkison of Elora. Early settler families such as the Elmslies and Davidsons of Nichol Township and the Watson and Saunders families of Guelph Township each left some records that shed light on the process of farm making and the establishment of the first social and municipal institutions. So did members of the elite family led by the miller, David Allan of Guelph, and their relations by marriage, the Nathaniel Higinbothams. The Sleeman Papers left by the brewer, George Sleeman, illuminate his important roles in business, municipal government and organized sports. Some eminent representatives in provincial or federal politics such as Charles Allan of Elora left substantial sets of papers. There are records of some Wellington County residents who became famous outside the region such as the painter David Kennedy, the physician and war poet John McCrae and the opera singer Edward Johnson.

Various kinds of documents are included in this section. There are diaries, correspondence and also personal business records such as wills, title deeds, mortgages, passports and accounts. Such business papers are included here if they related more to general family business matters than to a specific business and if they were intermingled with other kinds of personal records. Papers relating to a person's or family's participation in local government and voluntary associations may also be included. Only in a very few cases do we have a full set of personal papers that spans a fair period of time.

The **Inventory** includes references to 56 diaries, those attempts 'how ever maudlin, to record one's feelings, perceptions and reflections,' whose authors 'vary greatly in their articulacy as well as in the amount of time they were prepared to devote to writing.'[4] Most diarists wrote rather sparse entries on such topics as the weather, family events, the annual round of farm tasks and sermons. Perhaps the most interesting diary was kept by a young articling lawyer who stayed only eight months in Guelph in 1858 and went on to an eminent career in Toronto that included compiling the **Canada Law Journal** for nearly sixty years. Henry O'Brien has given us a sparkling account of life and customs in Guelph, at least among the younger set of its elite families, as well as some more introspective insights (#2461).

Many local historical records strike a note of optimistic progress and relate to the mainstream course of social and economic development. The disillusioned tone of Dr Henry Orton's memoirs provides a rare and revealing contrast, as he dared to describe his life as 'a failure, an abortion, and I can't even say that I have had much enjoyment in it'(#1248). The memoirs of the Rev. George Nunan are exceptional in a different way, as they offer a glimpse of a Catholic childhood and upbringing in Guelph (#2460).

---

[4] John Stuart Bates, 'Seeking the Canadian Pepys: the Canadian Manuscript Diaries Project,' **Archivaria** 9 (1979/80): 126, 131.

Personal correspondence forms part of a good many entries in this section. Family relationships may be illuminated, as in the letter written by the 1837 rebel Samuel Peters, incarcerated in the Hamilton Gaol, to his wife Hannah as she struggled to maintain the farm in Eramosa Township (#2464). Or in the affection manifest in the letters exchanged between Charles Mickle and his wife and children from the 1850s to the 1870s (#2450-#2451). Or in the courtship letters between Lincoln Goldie and Estella Bricker in 1901-2 (#2372).

Correspondence inventoried here also documents the links between the first generation of settlers in Canada and the families they left behind in the old world. In quite a few cases the letters were exchanged with family members in Scotland.[5] Examples include the William Anderson family who came to Guelph Township in 1832 from Fifeshire, William and George Beattie of Nichol Township who left relatives in Strathdon Parish, Aberdeenshire in 1836, and John Alexander Davidson of Nichol Township who corresponded with William Robson of Grandholm Haugh near Aberdeen between 1838 and 1845. The Connons and the Alexander Watts of Elora and the Elmslies and Faskins of Nichol Township also wrote to relations in Aberdeenshire. These letters give some idea of the emotional impact of the separation of families by emigration and of the hardships of making a new life on the frontier.

As creators and subjects of these personal and family papers, women are in a small minority. The Mary Leslie Papers in the Archives of Ontario constitute an important exception (#2419-#2425). Leslie was born in 1842 into the family of J.T. Leslie, an emigrant from Surrey, England who settled in Guelph Township, and whose business papers are included. Mary Leslie travelled in Europe in 1867-8, but passed most of the rest of her life in the Wellington County communities of Rockwood and Belwood, attempting to live by her pen. Her business papers include evidence of her efforts to publish her literary works throughout her adult life and to start a ladies' college in Guelph around 1890. The object of the proposed college was 'to form perfect women, morally and physically as well as intellectually.' Leslie wrote a good many historical and literary texts for the young, mainly on Engish and Scottish subjects, but her most famous work, **The Cromaboo Mail Carrier** (1878) was published under a pseudonym. Another exception, Lillian Beattie's memoirs and correspondence are evidence of the greater professional success possible for a woman in the twentieth century (#2302).

It is interesting to consider how small a proportion of all the people and families of Guelph and Wellington County are represented in these personal and family papers. According to the census, the county's population reached about 25,000 in 1851, grew rapidly to a high of 65,000 in 1881, then actually declined to about 55,600 in 1901 and 54,160 in 1921, before growing again to just under 60,000 by 1941. A small and manageable total for social historical analysis, one might think. But how many different individuals lived in Wellington

[5] See also Michael B. Moir, 'Scottish manuscripts in Canadian repositories,' **Archivaria** 17 (1983/4): 146-161; Elizabeth Bloomfield, 'Sources for studying Scottish settlement and society in the Upper Grand Valley region,' Guelph Regional Project Working Paper #2 (July 1987).

County during the period from 1820 to 1940? Research into the phenomenon of mobility in nineteenth-century North America has shown that 'far more people lived within the city in the course of a year than the census taker could find present at any point in time.'[6] Boston, for example, had 363,000 people enumerated in the 1880 census and 448,000 in the 1890 census, but it has been estimated that about one and a half million different people actually lived in the city at some point in the decade between the two censuses.[7] In the relatively isolated Saguenay-Lac St Jean area of Quebec, 60 percent of the population moved between 1851 and 1871, half of the transients leaving the region altogether, half relocating within the region.[8] In nearby Peel County, Ontario, it has been estimated that less than 10 per cent of the 10,000 different families enumerated in the 1851, 1861 and 1871 census returns were permanent residents.[9] Even conservatively allowing for a lower rate of transiency and turnover in an inland agricultural region, and adjusting for such factors as mortality and the longer period, probably at least half a million people actually lived in Wellington County at some point between 1820 and 1940.

In compiling this section of the **Inventory**, we found personal papers created by only 180 familes or individuals, a tiny proportion of all that might have left some papers. Even our considerably larger list of personal subjects of all records in the **Inventory** has only 1,400 named individuals or families, or 2,700 different people or families in all if one adds the bibliographic records also in the Guelph Regional Project's database. When we calculate the largest of these figures in relation to the estimate of the total number of people who lived in Wellington County at any time between 1820 and 1940, we find that we have caught in our survey net only just over one-half of one per cent of all the people who ever lived here.

---

[6] Michael B. Katz, **The people of Hamilton, Canada West: family and class in a mid-nineteenth-century city** (Cambridge, MA: Harvard University Press, 1975), 19.

[7] Stephan Thernstrom and Peter Knights, 'Men in motion: some data and speculations about urban social mobility in nineteenth century America,' in Tamara K. Hareven, ed. **Anonymous Americans: explorations in nineteenth-century social history** (Englewood Cliffs, NJ: Prentice-Hall, 1971): 29.

[8] Cited by Gagan and Turner, 'Social history in Canada,' p. 37.

[9] David Gagan, **Hopeful travellers: families, land and social change in mid-Victorian Peel County, Canada West** (Toronto: University of Toronto Press, 1981), 95.

FAMILY AND PERSONAL PAPERS

2281. Allan, Charles. **Estate papers, 1841-1870.** 1 file folder. Loc: UGA. XR1 MS A115016.

Five indenture agreements and one indenture dated 1870 which is labelled 'Deed trustees Allan Estate'. Held with the Connon Collection.

2282. Allan, Christina. **Letterbooks, 1847-1885.** 3 volumes; 1 file folder. Loc: UGA. XR1 MS A005001/A005003.

Correspondence from and to Allan about family matters. Correspondents included William Allan and John and Mary Higinbotham. Part of Allan-Higinbotham Collection.

2283. Allan, Christina. **Miscellaneous books, 1856-1860.** 4 volumes. Loc: UGA. XR1 MS A005002.

Diaries of daily events, analysis of sermons and prayers. The ledgers contain only occasional entries. Part of Allan-Higinbotham Collection.

2284. Allan, David. **Business correspondence, 1859-1893.** 3 file folders. Loc: UGA. XR1 MS A005 013, 29.

Correspondence about financial transactions including purchase of a farm and several receipts from a trip to Edinburgh. One file folder also contains several financial statements of insolvent estates. Another contains a letter from David Kennedy in Philadelphia, 1886. Part of Allan-Higinbotham Collection.

2285. Allan, David. **Correspondence, 1856-1866; 1875-1895.** 3 file folders. Loc: UGA. XR1 MS A005 008-12, 26, 27.

Correspondence from grandchildren Andrew Fischer and John Idington in Toronto, David Allan Jr in Kingston Jamaica, William Higinbotham in Chile, Eddie Higinbotham in Regina and John Higinbotham in Regina. One file folder contains miscellaneous correspondence to Alice Higinbotham, William Allan and a will of Alison Worsley, sister of Christina Allan. Correspondence from 1856 to 1866 is from David's sister and brother-in-law, Helen and Andrew Cunningham in Allandale, Illinois. Part of Allan-Higinbotham Collection.

2286. Allan, David. **Correspondence, 1857-1887.** 1 volume. Loc: UGA. XR1 MS A005.

A book of carbon copies of letters to various family members. Part of Allan-Higinbotham Collection.

2287. Allan, David. **Diary, 1891-1892.** 1 volume. Loc: GCM.

A personal diary of daily events. An archival note suggests that the author is probably David Allan.

2288. Allan Family. **Family correspondence, 1915.** 1 envelope. Loc: WCA. MU 54.

A series of letters written from the son of Mr and Mrs A.S. Allan of Guelph describing activities as a soldier training in England during World War I.

2289. Allan Family and Blaney Family and Higinbotham Family and Torrance Family and Wallace Family. **Family reunion program, 1893.** 1 document. Loc: GCM.

A program announcing plans to hold a reunion of the Wallace, Blaney, Allan, Torrance and Higinbotham families at Riverview in Guelph. The program also notes the event would honour the 56th wedding anniversary of David and Christina Allan.

2290. Allan, William. **Business correspondence, 1815-1859; 1862; 1876.** 1 file folder. Loc: UGA. XR1 MS A005022.

The file folder also contains a copy of Allan's will in 1859. Part of Allan-Higinbotham Collection.

2291. Allan, William. **Correspondence, 1891-1892.** 1 file folder. Loc: UGA. XR1 MS A005008-10.

Correspondence to his parents, David and Christina Allan from Galt, Montreal and Toronto about family and business matters. Part of the Allan-Higinbotham Collection.

2292. Allan, William and Allan, David. **Historical sketch, 1832-1895.** 2 file folders. Loc: UGA. XR1 MS A005.

A brief sketch of the family history of William who came from Edinburgh in 1832 and purchased the Canada Company mill and ran it until 1859 when he died. David Allan, his son, took over the business until 1877 when he suffered a stroke. He married Christina Idington in 1837. Their children were William and Margaret. Margaret later married Nathaniel Higinbotham. The file folders also contain two town lot leases granted by the Canada Company in 1875 and a photograph of the letterhead of Allan's Mill. Part of the Allan-Higinbotham Collection.

2293. Anderson Family. **Correspondence, 1833-1870.** 1 file folder. Loc: UGA. XR1 MS A110.

Photocopies of original correspondence held at the Provincial Archives of Manitoba. The papers are letters to Thomas Anderson who came to Guelph Township in 1832 from Fifeshire, Scotland. The correspondence came primarily from family and friends in Kennoway and Edinburgh, Scotland. The Anderson family owned a farm at lot 16, concession 1 in Guelph Township. The papers contain a copy of a land instalment payment of Thomas Anderson to the Canada Company in 1833.

2294. Archibald Family. **Correspondence, 1893-1967.** 1 file folder. Loc: UGA. XR1 MS A193018.

Personal correspondence about family matters sent to Katherine Archibald Marston. Held with the Marston-Archibald Collection.

2295. Archibald, James. **Legal documents, 1883-1941.** 1 file folder. Loc: UGA. XR1 MS A193011.

A collection of legal papers including indentures and agreements between James Archibald and T.A. Gale regarding the Farmers' Banking House. Held with Marston-Archibald Collection.

2296. Archibald, James. **Miscellaneous announcements, 1836-1900.** 1 file folder. Loc: UGA. XR1 MS A193010.

A collection of birth and death notices, marriage licenses, wedding invitations concerning James Archibald, his wife Alice Snyder Archibald and their family. Held with Marston-Archibald Collection.

2297. Archibald, James. **Miscellaneous unidentified photographs, 1860.** 10 items. Loc: UGA. XR1 MS A193014.

The collection includes two photographs of James Archibald. Held with Marston-Archibald Collection.

2298. Archibald, Katherine. **Composition notebook, 1912-1929.** 1 file folder. Loc: UGA. XR1 MS A193019.

Several graded compositions on spring cleaning and the Grand River. Held with Marston-Archibald Collection.

2299. Balfour, D. **Correspondence, 1861.** 2 documents. Loc: WCA. MU 42.

Photocopies of family correspondence from D. Balfour in Dublin to his brother James Balfour who recently emigrated to Mount Forest.

2300. Beattie Family. **Correspondence, 1873-1927.** 1 box. Loc: WCA. List of document contents.

A record of business and municipal government correspondence of the Beattie family. The municipal government documents include financial records of the Beatties while family members functioned as Wellington County Clerk from 1873 to 1897. The business correspondence includes letters and receipts written between members of the Beattie family and other Wellington County residents for various financial transactions. Held with the Beattie Collection.

2301. Beattie Family. **Financial records, 1849-1942.** 1 box. Loc: WCA. List of document contents.

A record of indentures, promissory notes, securities, invoices, insurance policies, correspondence and financial statements of the Beattie family of Fergus. The Wellington County Archives has developed a detailed finding aid listing clients and individuals involved in specific financial transactions. The Beatties operated a bank in Fergus and had financial transactions with residents of Fergus, Elora, Arthur and Guelph and the Townships of West Garafraxa, Peel and Nichol. Held with the Beattie Collection.

2302. Beattie, Lillian A. **Correspondence and memoirs, 1911-1950.** 1 box. Loc: UGA. XR1 MS A004.

The collection contains a typed manuscript of the memoirs of Beattie who studied at Macdonald Institute from 1911-1913 and worked as a dietitian at Speedwell Hospital in Guelph, and later sold life insurance for Sun Life Assurance Company in the city from 1928 to 1934.

2303. Beattie, William and Beattie, George. **Correspondence. Letters from relatives, 1836-1842.** 2 file folders. Loc: WCA. List of document contents.

A series of photocopies of original letters to William and George Beattie of Nichol Township from relatives living in Strathdon Parish, Aberdeenshire, Scotland in the years 1836 to 1842. The letters outline social and economic conditions in Scotland and note the activities of relatives who were living in Scotland. Held with the Beattie Collection.

2304. Boyle, David. **Account book, scrapbooks and notebooks, 1859-c1902.** 9 volumes. Loc: MTL. Card index.

David Boyle (1842-1911) emigrated with his parents from Scotland in 1856. After apprenticing with a blacksmith in Eden Mills, he worked as a blacksmith in Elora, from 1860 to 1864, while attending the Elora Grammar School. Boyle taught at the Middlebrook Public School, Pilkington Township, from 1865 to 1871 and then served as principal of the Elora Public School from 1871 to 1881. He opened a book shop in Toronto but became an archaeologist and curator in the late 1880s. The scrapbooks of newspaper clippings (6 volumes, 1859-1870; 1873-1881) deal exclusively with schools and education in Wellington County and Guelph. A great deal of detail is included on school administration, inspection and teachers' organizations. The other three volumes relate to Boyle's activities after he moved to Toronto, but the account book includes details of books invoiced to the Harriston Mechanics' Institute and the Elora Mechanics' Institute in the early 1880s.

2305. Boyle, Frank. **Family history, 1834-1912.** 1 envelope. Loc: WCA. MU 13.
Includes a sketch of Boyle's farming life in Peel Township.

2306. Burnett, Arthur. **Property Assessment. Tax records, 1905; 1907; 1917-1927; 1929-1930; 1932-1966.** 1 envelope. Loc: WCA. MU 32.
A series of tax assessment notices of Arthur Burnett who was a farmer in Peel Township. The record includes the 1919 income tax return of Burnett.

2307. Burnett Family. **Family records, 1873-1917 (sporadic).** 4 documents. Loc: WCA. MU 62.
A series of documents of the Burnett family of Peel Township which includes a land deed, indenture, title search record and the school graduation certificate of a family member.

2308. Calder, John. **Family Correspondence. Letter, 1837.** 1 document. Loc: WCA.
Held in the Wellington County Historical Research Society Collection. A letter written from John Calder Senior in Scotland to his son who lived in Nichol Township. The letter discusses the health of Calder Senior, activities of relatives and friends in Scotland and asks questions about life in Upper Canada.

2309. Carder, Joseph. **Family history, 1833-1880.** 1 envelope. Loc: WCA. MU 19.
A photocopy of the history of Carder who was a British emigrant who settled in Nichol Township.

2310. Clarke, Charles. **Diary, 1866-1897.** 1 reel; 213 p. mf. Loc: WCA, AO. AO: MS 395.
The diary is prefaced by a short biography of Clarke who emigrated from England to Niagara and later moved to Elora in 1850. He edited the Elora Backwoodsman, became involved in Clear Grit and municipal politics and was active in the Elora Rifle Company and the Wellington Rifles. The diary recounts the events of daily life in Elora and surrounding area as well as larger political events in Ontario. In addition to the microfilmed diary, the Archives of Ontario has a transcribed typescript version for the years 1866-1871.

2311. Clarke, Charles Kirk. **Diary. Child's daily journal, 1865-1866.** 2 volumes. Loc: WCA. List of document contents.
A daily journal of the son of Charles Clarke of Elora. The daily entries describe the weather, social activities and school experiences. Charles Kirk Clarke was eight years old when he began making daily diary entries. Held with the Clarke Collection.

2312. Clarke, Charles. **Military Records. Promotion certificates, 1861; 1866-1867.** 1 file folder. Loc: WCA. List of document contents.

A record of the promotions of Charles Clarke during his time spent serving in the First Volunteer Militia of the Elora Rifle Company. Part of the Clarke Collection.

2313. Clarke, Charles. **Papers, 1841-1910.** 5 boxes, 3 reels. mf. Loc: AO. FA: MU 5825-5829; MS 76.

Charles Clarke (1826-1909) had a long and varied public career based in Elora. He was active in the Clear Grit/Reform party, served on the Elora Village Council from 1858 to 1868, represented Wellington Centre from 1871 to 1887 and Wellington North from 1887 to 1891, before becoming Clerk of the Legislative Assembly from 1891 to 1907. He is noted for having introduced the secret ballot bill in 1873-1874 and for the design of the mace used in the Ontario Legislative Assembly. The Clarke Papers held only by the Archives of Ontario are more concerned with his public political role, but they also have microfilm and typescript copies of the Clarke family correspondence from the Wellington County Archives.

2314. Clarke, Elizabeth. **Correspondence pertaining to the C.A. Clarke family, 1864-1917.** 1 box. Loc: AO. MU 1714.

These records have been preserved as part of the Mary Leslie Papers. Leslie's sister, Elizabeth, with whom she lived from the 1890s, was Mrs C.A. Clarke. Apparently, C.A. Clarke spent his last years at the Soldiers' Home in Washington and was a cousin of Admiral Byng.

2315. Clarke Family. **Correspondence, c1850-1890.** 1 box. Loc: WCA, AO. AO: MU 5825-5829; List of dates and contents of documents.

A series of letters between Charles Clarke and family and friends living in Lincoln, England. The collection also contains correspondence of Clarke's own family living in Canada and also Clarke's correspondence with political colleagues. The Wellington County Archives has developed a detailed finding aid indicating the date, content and individuals involved in specific correspondence; however, several letters are not dated. The Wellington County Archives has reproduced manuscript letters in microfilm and in typewritten form, copies of which are held by the Archives of Ontario together with other Clarke Papers. Part of the Clarke Collection.

2316. Clarke Family. **Photographs, 1840-1916.** 30 photographs. Loc: WCA. List of photograph contents.

A series of photographs of family members and one of the residence of Charles Clarke. The Wellington County Archives has developed a finding aid indicating the contents of photographs and the dates of some items. Part of the Clarke Collection.

2317. Clarke Family. **Scrapbook, 1865-1875.** 1 box. Loc: WCA. List of document contents.

A collection of newspaper clippings kept by Emma Kent wife of Charles Clarke who was a merchant and provincial member of parliament for Centre Wellington from 1871 to 1887. The scrapbook includes programs advertising Elora social events. Most of the newspaper clippings do not directly apply to the history of Wellington County. Part of the Clarke Collection.

2318. Cleghorn Family. **Papers, 1886-1892 (sporadic).** 1 envelope. Loc: WCA. MU 78; Detailed list of contents.

A letter appointing executors for the estate of Thomas Cleghorn and two receipts for the medical services of Dr D.L. Walmsley of Elmira for drugs and medical treatment. Part of the Laird Collection.

2319. Cleghorn Family. **Property Assessment. Notices, 1873-1883 (sporadic).** 1 envelope. Loc: WCA. MU 78; Detailed list of contents.

Seven assessment notices of the Cleghorn property in Guelph Township. Part of the Laird Collection.

2320. Cleghorn, James. **Receipts, invoices and insurance policy, 1858-1883 (sporadic).** 1 envelope. Loc: WCA. MU 78; Detailed list of contents.

A small collection of receipts and invoices from Day's Bookstore, Cossitt's Agricultural Implement Works and a policy from the Guelph Township Mutual Fire Insurance Company. Part of the Laird Collection.

2321. Cleghorn, John. **Papers, 1873-1934 (sporadic).** 1 file folder. Loc: WCA. MU 78; Detailed list of contents.

A collection of eighty-five documents that includes a deed and mortgage of land, a farm policy from several fire insurance companies and receipts and invoices from many different Guelph and area businesses and the Guelph Board of Light and Heat Commissioners. Part of the Laird Collection.

2322. Connon Family. **Photographs, correspondence and business records, 1850-1920.** 6 boxes. Loc: UGA. XR1 MS A115, Itemized list of contents.

A collection of photographs, slides, family correspondence, land records, business papers, genealogical records and newspaper clippings of the Connon family. Thomas Connon was an Elora photographer and inventor. His son, John, worked with him until Thomas's death in 1899 after which he devoted himself to historical research. He was the author of a history of Elora. Part of the Connon Collection.

2323. Connon, John. **Correspondence, newspaper clipping, c1931.** 1 envelope. Loc: WCA. MU 42.

A 1931 letter from John Connon to a friend about his heart condition and a newspaper article in memory of John Connon's recent death entitled 'Connons brought honour to Elora by photographic research'. The article gives brief biographies of Thomas and John Connon and described their inventions including the panoramic camera. Held with Byerly Papers.

2324. Connon, John. **Family letters, 1836-1878.** 2 boxes. Loc: AO. MU 752-753.

While most of the Connon Papers in the Archives of Ontario are concerned with Connon's photography business and efforts to gain recognition for his invention, there are also several file folders of family letters as well as later summaries of Connon family history that complement the collections at the University of Guelph and the Wellington County Archives.

2325. Connon, John. **Letter, 1929.** 4 p. Loc: NAC. MG 30, D 336.

Letter from John Connon possibly to his brother Thomas, 18 November 1929, regarding the publication of his book, Elora, with a list of proposed illustrations. There is also an invoice dated 1869.

2326. Connon, John. **Personal correspondence, 1883-1929.** 1 box. Loc: UGA. XR1 MS A115021-4.

The letters deal with the Connon photography business and with matters relating to John Connon's interest in the history of Elora. The record includes a few promissory notes of residents living in the Elora area dated 1857 to 1873. In the same box of the Connon Collection, there is an account book labelled 'Drugs and Miscellaneous Accounts', dated 1916, which may have belonged to John Connon. Held with the Connon Collection.

2327. Connon, Thomas. **Correspondence, 1852-1893.** 1 box. Loc: WCA. FA: MU 14.

A collection of the letters of Thomas Connon who emigrated from Elfhill, Scotland to Elora in 1853. Included are letters from his aunt Elizabeth Connon in Aberdeen, Scotland from 1852 to 1865 describing family and social conditions in Scotland and offering advice to Connon in beginning a new life in Canada. There are letters by Jean Keith Connon, wife of Thomas, to Elizabeth Connon between 1855 and 1857. The collection also contains letters from Thomas Connon to his aunt from 1860 to 1865 and his son John in the 1890s when John Connon was living in New York. The Wellington County Archives has developed a detailed finding aid which dates specific letters, notes who wrote and received letters, and briefly describes the contents of specific correspondence. Part of the Connon Collection.

2328. Connon, Thomas. **Daily weather observations, 1881; 1884.** 2 volumes. Loc: AO. MU 2014.

Quite detailed notes on daily weather in Elora, including readings of temperature, winds, rainfall and snowfall. The 1881 diary is more detailed. Part of the Marston Collection.

2329. Connon, Thomas. **Family correspondence, 1852-1859; 1867.** 1 file folder. Loc: UGA. XR1 MS A320.

A series of letters written by Connon to Elizabeth Connon who lived in Aberdeen, Scotland. The letters outline social and economic conditions in Canada and discuss family matters. The letters supplement a large collection of Connon correspondence held at the Wellington County Archives. Held with the Connon Collection.

2330. Connon, Thomas, Jr. **Family correspondence, 1894.** 1 file folder. Loc: UGA. XR1 MS A320.

A series of letters sent by Thomas Connon Junior in Brocton, New York to his father, Thomas Connon, in Elora. The letters outline activities and current issues in the United States and discuss family matters. Held with the Connon Collection.

2331. Corley Family. **Correspondence, 1900.** 1 envelope. Loc: WCA. MU 66.

Two letters from the Corley family in Mount Forest to their son who served in the Boer War. The letters outline family activities and the status of the war in Africa. The collection contains the military records of J.B. Corley including his discharge papers from the Boer War. Part of the Corley Collection.

2332. Cowan, William. **Correspondence, 1844.** 1 file folder. Loc: UGA. XR1 MS A117031.

A letter of thanks from William Cowan to the Reverend Thomas Christie for visiting the Paisley Block School to preach the gospel. A scarlet fever epidemic in 1844 is mentioned. Part of the Thompson-Christie Collection.

2333. Cromar Family. **Certificates, correspondence, photographs, 1870-1915.** 1 file folder. Loc: WCA. MU 78; Detailed list of contents.

A small collection of school graduation certificates for Margaret Cromar from the Fergus District High School in 1899, and the Wellington County Model School in 1905, and two letters of reference recommending Cromar as a teacher. The Collection contains postcards and photographs that include several scenes and people from the Elora, Fergus and Guelph area. Held with the Cromar Collection.

2334. Crowe Family. **Scrapbook, 1890-1935.** 2 volumes. Loc: GPL.

Scrapbooks of the Crowe family that contain newspaper clippings, photographs and correspondence about family activities. Part of the Shutt Collection.

2335. Cunningham, Robert. **Papers, 1860-1877.** 3 file folders. Loc: AO. FA: MU 762.

Robert and Annie Cunningham migrated from Stewarton, Scotland to Elora in 1868. Robert accompanied General Wolseley to the Red River in 1870 as a Globe correspondent, and remained there to found the weekly, The Manitoban. He was elected as a Liberal to the House of Commons and died suddenly in 1874. His wife returned to Elora where she taught school until 1877 and then moved back to Scotland. It would appear that some of her children continued to live in Canada. The letters include correspondence between Robert's father in Scotland and Barbara Cunningham, the young daughter of Robert and Annie. There is also a letter from David Boyle to Barbara Cunningham dated 28 February 1877 concerning the Elora school, the Elora Natural History Museum and other local news.

2336. Davidson, John Alexander. **Letters to William Robson of Aberdeen, 1838-1845.** 3 items. Loc: MTL. Card index.

Davidson emigrated from Scotland in 1835 and settled at 'Woodburn', Nichol Township, where he farmed and worked as carpenter and school teacher. He married Catherine Middleton, daughter of the Reverend James Middleton. The three letters to William Robson of Grandholm Haugh near Aberdeen, Scotland, discuss the progress of the Davidson garden and family, the organization of local common schools and the rift in the Presbyterian Church. Davidson reports the building of school houses in every township following the Common School Act in 1843 and explains how the schools were financed. He reports on the ministry of the Reverend William Barrie at Elora and Eramosa and comments on the conflict between the Church of Scotland and the Free Church over church property in Fergus. By 1845, Davidson claimed to have built the first stone house in Nichol west of the Grand River. He describes the beneficial changes in Elora caused by the building of new mills after 1842. Until then, in Davidson's opinion, Elora had been a 'despicable looking village'. In 1845, Davidson visited friends in Peel Township, then being opened for settlement, and reported a usual price of seven shillings per acre for quite superior land.

2337. Davidson, John. **Correspondence. Letter, May 6, 1839.** 1 document. Loc: WCA.

Held in the Wellington County Historical Research Society Collection. A photocopy of an original letter by Davidson who had recently arrived in Nichol Township from Scotland. The letter primarily focuses on discussing family and social matters and Davidson promises to give a few presents he had brought from Scotland.

2338. Davidson, John. **Photographs, scrapbooks, 1850-1926.** 1 box, 2 albums. Loc: UGA. XR1 MS A040001.

John Davidson's family scrapbook of letters, poems and miscellaneous newspaper clippings. Included in the scrapbook is a January 1855 letter from William Kennedy to his son David in Philadelphia in which he sketches two exterior views of his new stone house that was still in the process of being built. Floor plans for the first and second floors are drawn to the scale of 12 feet to the inch. John Davidson was son of the Guelph merchant Charles Davidson and grandson of William Kennedy, a Guelph stonemason. One photograph album is of the Wellington Rifles during World War I. Part of the Davidson-Kennedy Collection.

2339. Drew Family and Johnson Family. **Correspondence, clippings and photographs, 1912-1966.** 1 box. Loc: UGA. XR1 MS A199.

A few Christmas cards and photographs of George Drew and his family. The majority of the records are newspaper clippings describing the political activities of Drew in the 1950s and 1960s. The collection includes the wedding invitation of Drew and his wife, Fiorenza D'Arneiro.

2340. Duggan, Daniel. **Probate, 1920.** 1 document. Loc: GCM.

Records the will of Duggan who was a labourer in Guelph. Duggan died March 17, 1920.

2341. Duncan, Lavina. **Land records, 1886-1887.** 2 documents. Loc: WCA. MU74.

A record of a Quit Claim Deed of land held by Duncan in Elora.

2342. Ellis, G.C. **Chemistry notebook, c1907.** 1 volume. Loc: UGA.

A record of observations and conclusions of chemistry experiments that is inscribed, 'Chemistry Notes by G.C. Ellis, O.A.C.'

2343. Elmslie, George. **Correspondence. Elmslie family, 1840-1902 (sporadic).** 1 file folder. Loc: WCA. MU 32; List of date and contents of correspondence.

A photocopy of original correspondence between George Elmslie of Nichol Township and his family who lived in Aberdeen, Scotland. The letters outline family activities, the death of family members and friends and social activities. The Wellington County Archives has developed a finding aid indicating the date, contents and names of individuals involved in specific correspondence.

2344. Elmslie, George. **Journal, 1833-1834.** 1 volume. Loc: WCA. MU 59.

A transcript of Elmslie's diary that details his journey through the Niagara region and Perth and Waterloo Counties in search of a large block of land suitable for settlement. Alexander Watt and Mr Gibbons accompanied him. According to an archival note, Elmslie purchased 1,200 acres in Nichol Township in 1834 from William Gilkison. The archives also holds the original diary.

2345. Falkner, Theresa Goldie. **The Goldie saga, 1844-1884.** 15 pp. Loc: GPL.

An historical sketch of the John Goldie family, written in 1968. James and William Goldie emigrated to the United States in 1842. In 1844, their father, John and the rest of the family settled near Ayr in Dumfries Township. In 1860

James moved to Guelph to build and run Goldie Mill. The paper includes many references to early family correspondence.

2346. Faskin Family. **Correspondence, legal documents, family genealogies, 1839-1887.** 1 file folder. Loc: UGA. XR1 MS A180.

  Records of William Faskin and Margaret Mitchell who emigrated from Aberdeenshire, Scotland to Nichol Township in 1839. The finding aid contains a brief family history.

2347. Ferguson, Edra Sanders. **Family papers and records including some relating to G.C.V.I., 1938-1962.** Loc: NAC. MG 30, C 217, FA 1633.

  Edra Sanders was born in St Thomas where she practised law and was the first woman elected alderman. In 1940 she married and moved to Guelph where her husband, Donald H. Ferguson, taught history at G.C.V.I.

2348. Fergusson, Adam. **Narrative of Fergusson family history, 1775-1862.** 17 p. Loc: UGA.

  Photocopy of a manuscript outline of Fergusson family history. The first was written in 1775 by the Rev. Adam Fergusson of Mouline, Scotland and 'addressed to his sons for their information and amusement'. The second half consists of notes added by Adam Fergusson of Waterdown (and one of the founders of Fergus) between c1850 and 1856 and a few notes by Adam Johnston Fergusson-Blair in 1862. The copy was made possible by Mrs Ariel Dyer.

2349. Freure, Benjamin. **Diary, 1836-1842.** 124 p. Loc: MTL.

  Benjamin Freure emigrated from Suffolk, England, in 1836 with his wife and son Andrew, and settled in Eramosa Township where his sons Felix and Augustus were already farming. The family bought Lot 29, Concession 3, where they continued to farm for several generations. One-third of the diary records the journey from Suffolk to Eramosa. The rest describes the experiences of land clearance and farm making during the first six years. Some daily entries are very brief, with the words chopping, burning, logging, plowing and branding recurring frequently. There are some references to the Hindley family.

2350. Galt, John. **Correspondence to Blackwood Publishers in Edinburgh, 1819-1839.** 46 letters. Loc: NLS. No. 4004-4048.

  A collection of letters to William Blackwood, Galt's Edinburgh publisher of novels and magazine articles during the period when Blackwood published Galt's most important novels. Of particular interest are the letters Galt wrote while he was in the midst of his business activities with the Canada Company. These show the extent to which his business and literary pursuits competed for his attention. One example is the case of the publication of the work, The Last of the Lairds, in 1826. At Blackwood's insistence, Galt's literary friend, David Moir, revised the manuscript while Galt was totally occupied with his colonization venture. In later complaining to Blackwood, Galt claimed that the resulting novel had 'lost that assurance of truth and nature' that he had hoped to achieve. Part of the Blackwood Collection.

2351. Galt, John. **Correspondence to publishers, 1822-1831.** 54 letters. Loc: NLS. No. 10785.

  A collection of letters from Galt to Oliver and Boyd Publishers in London regarding the publication of his novels. During this time he was directly involved in organizing the Canada Company and colonizing places like Guelph. He specifically asked his publishers not to use his name on his novels, fearing that 'some folks are apt to think business may be neglected'.

2352. Galt, John. **Correspondence with Earl of Dalhousie, 1828-1835.** 5 letters. Loc: SRO. GD 45, Section 3.

   Letters from Galt in Guelph to the Earl of Dalhousie, the Governor General of the Canadas, who was headquartered in Quebec City. The collection includes two brief replies from Dalhousie. In the letters, Galt provides a candid analysis of his role as colonizer in the Guelph area and proposes a more comprehensive scheme in Lower Canada. He attributes his difficulties in Upper Canada, in part, to 'the evils of incompetent local legislators', a veiled reference to Lt Governor Colborne and Anglican Bishop John Strachan. Galt also mentions that a more serious liability was his limited power as superintendent of the Canada Company's operations. He confides to Dalhousie that the need to 'satisfy the wants and wishes of such a restless and needy race as emigrants usually consist of, is a task of more various cares than should rest on the shoulders of a mere mercantile agent'. Part of the Dalhousie Papers.

2353. Galt, John. **Family correspondence, 1827.** 1 document. Loc: UGA. XR1 MS A054.

   A letter written to Galt's cousin, Jeannie Spirling, in 1827 from Guelph, in which he discusses his success in founding 'the new city' of Guelph, 'which is prospering beyond all expectation'. It is part of a collection of six letters written by Galt between 1779 and 1839 to various family members. Part of the Lizars Collection.

2354. Galt, John. **Letter, November 20, 1827.** 1 document. Loc: WCA.

   A photocopy of an original letter by John Galt to a friend in Ireland which encourages him to emigrate to Canada. Galt also describes Guelph indicating 'it contains already well on to a thousand inhabitants'. Held in the Wellington County Historical Research Society Collection which also includes a letter written to the Wellington County Historical Research Society noting that the original Galt letter is held at the Archives of Ontario.

2355. Galt, John. **Manuscript of novel, The Last of the Lairds, 1826.** 1 document. Loc: NLS. No. 6522.

   A manuscript of the novel with David Moir's editorial changes and additions, published in 1826. In a note attached to the revised manuscript, Moir defends the changes he made: 'On the departure of the author some time ago from Upper Canada, the manuscript of The Last of the Lairds, on the change of editing it, were committed to me by him'. Moir suggests that the original task of editing would have been given to Galt had 'the opportunity been afforded the author himself of superintending the volume in its progress through its press'. Galt was preoccupied by his Canadian venture at the time, but was later unhappy with the changes made by Moir. Galt's original version of the novel did not appear until 1976 when Ian Gordon published it with the Scottish Academic Press.

2356. Galt, John. **Papers. Correspondence, poetry, plays, prose, notebooks, 1806-1839.** 2 reels. mf. Loc: AO. MS 861.

   John Galt (1779-1839) was a promoter of the Canada Company and secretary of its board of directors. Much of the collection relates to Galt's literary work. Series A, File 1, Correspondence, includes the typewritten copy of a letter from

Galt to Dr William Dunlop dated 19 March 1827 that instructs Dunlop to proceed with surveying and developing the townsites of Guelph and Goderich.

2357. Gay, James. **Biographical information and poetry by James Gay, 1880-1953.** 1 file folder. Loc: UGA. XR1 MS A187.

Photocopies of two books of Gay's poetry, Canada's Poet, and 'Master of All Poets This Day'. Also included is an article on Gay's poetry in the journal, Massey Messenger.

2358. Gibbon, William. **Obituary, 1835-1913.** 2 documents. Loc: WCA. MU 66.

An assessment of the life of Gibbon which indicates he came to Elora from Aberdeen, Scotland in 1835. The obituary notes he was a farmer and describes his community activities in Elora. The record includes a receipt for land bought in Nichol Township by Gibbon in 1847.

2359. Gilkison, Augusta. **Correspondence. Letters to John Connon, 1907-1910.** 25 envelopes. Loc: WCA. MU 43.

A series of letters from a friend who lived in Brantford. The letters discuss the activities of family members and express an interest in the history of Elora. Augusta Gilkison was the granddaughter of William Gilkison.

2360. Gilkison Family. **Correspondence and land records, 1840-1860.** 1 reel. mf. Loc: WCA.

Correspondence regarding family and business matters in Elora and land transfer documents in Elora and Nichol Township. Most of the correspondence is about family's interests in promoting railway construction in southern Ontario.

2361. Gilkison Family. **Family correspondence, 1832; 1854-1855; 1861.** 1 file folder. Loc: UGA. XR1 MS A115011.

A number of typescript reproductions of the letters of William Gilkison to family members. The record includes correspondence, several financial statements of the Wellington Foundry from 1855 to 1856 and a summons to appear in court for Archibald Gilkison and Joseph Rogers. Held with the Connon Collection.

2362. Gilkison Family. **Papers, 1808-1857.** 8 inches. Loc: NAC. MG 24, I 25.

The collection includes correspondence, will and estate of William Gilkison 1808 to 1842, will and estate of Alex Grant 1815 to 1831, diary of Robert Gilkison 1838 to 1839, correspondence and papers of Jasper Tough Gilkison 1842 to 1857, and a family scrapbook of newspaper clippings from 1842 to 1906.

2363. Gilkison, William. **Correspondence concerning settlement and land development, 1832-1833.** 5 letters. Loc: WCA. MU 19.

Photocopies of correspondence about early settlement and land development in Elora. The letters of Simon Fraser and William Reynolds are addressed to William Gilkison in Brantford.

2364. Gilkison, William and Fraser, Simon. **Correspondence concerning the development of store, school, church, bridge and property in Elora, 1832-1895.** 1 box. Loc: UGA. XR1 MS A116.

A collection of letters relating to the development of store, school, church, bridge and property in Elora. Most correspondence applicable to the region is between William Gilkison in Brantford and his agent, Simon Fraser, in Elora.

Held with the Gilkison-Fraser Collection.

2365. Gilkison, William and Gilkison, Jasper. **Diaries, letters and accounts, 1820-1895.** original, 5 cm. Loc: BCM.
     Part of a much larger collection of records presented to the museum by Miss Augusta Gilkison, this material contains some references to the founding and early development of Elora. Only a small part of the collection has been sorted and catalogued.

2366. Gilkison, William. **Diary, 1832-1833.** 93 p. Loc: UGA. XRI MS A277046.
     A photocopy of a typescript of Gilkison's diary in which he discusses his purchase of part of Nichol Township and the founding of Elora. Frequent mention is made of Jasper, Gilkison's son, who later promoted the Great Western Railway Company. Part of the H.B. Timothy Collection.

2367. Gilkison, William and Gilkison, Jasper. **Family and business correspondence, 1786-1910.** 5 inches, 1 reel. mf. Loc: AO. FA: MU 1143.
     William Gilkison (1777-1833) worked in the North American fur trade between 1796 and 1815, when he returned to Glasgow. In 1832, he migrated to Upper Canada, settled near Brantford, and negotiated with the Honourable Thomas Clark for the purchase of c14,000 acres in Nichol Township. Gilkison chose the area known as the Falls of the Grand River as the site of a village which he named Elora. His son, Jasper Tough Gilkison (1814-1906), settled in Hamilton in 1836 and was connected with the development of Nichol Township among many other business ventures. The Nichol-Elora settlement is mentioned in a letter from William to Jasper of November 24, 1832. On December 18, 1832, William refers to the first house built in 'that young and rising city of Elora'. William Gilkison also instructed his six surviving sons in a letter entitled 'The plan for settling Elora', dated March 3, 1833. The papers also include various indentures for land in Elora and miscellaneous Elora news in letters from members of the Andrew Geddes family to the Gilkisons. Items mentioned include a daily stage service between Guelph and Elora by 1848, a subscription of one hundred and ninety-seven pounds by Jasper Gilkison to the Elora and Fergus Road in November 1853, the erection of a foundry in Elora in 1854, and the granting of water privileges for a grist mill to E.H. Newman in 1856. These papers include the correspondence of William from 1818 to 1833 and of Jasper from 1829 to 1893, as well as family photographs, obituaries and other newspaper clippings.

2368. Gilkison, William. **Land records, 1851.** 2 documents. Loc: WCA. MU 19.
     Photocopies of a partition of Lots 2 and 3 in Nichol Township and a title search for several lots in the Village of Elora that had belonged to William Gilkison.

2369. Gilmour, Rev. **Copy of the Rev. Mr Gilmour's account of the last illness of Mr Galt, 1839.** 6 p. Loc: NLS. No. 6522.
     A copy of the document that describes John Galt's personality from 1834, when Gilmour first met him, until his death. Gilmour claims that Galt was orthodox in his religious beliefs. Other evidence suggests, however, that religion was not a central feature of Galt's life, although he considered churches as valuable assets in creating an orderly community. The original document is held in the Bodleian Library, Oxford.

336

A perspective on time: Larry Brohman of the Maryhill district, west of Guelph, 1910. (Wellington County Museum and Archives)

2370. Godfrey, Richard Johnston. **Officer's record of service, 1916-1918.** 1 booklet. Loc: WCA. MU 11.

The army service record of Godfrey who was a dental surgeon. The brief record lists innoculations, promotions and dates of service. His home address is listed as Elora.

2371. Goldie, James. **Letters addressed to J. Goldie from his father and brother, 1846-1850.** 1 file folder. Loc: UGA. XR1 MS A051.

The file includes letters to James Goldie in New York State from his father John and brother at Greenfield Mills, Ayr, North Dumfries as well as a manuscript account of John Goldie and his family, three photographs of Greenfield house and mill, and photocopies of letters. James Goldie later became an important businessman and community leader in Guelph.

2372. Goldie, Lincoln. **Courtship Letters. Lincoln Goldie, Guelph to Estelle A. Bricker, Waterloo, Ontario, 1901-1902.** 18 letters. Loc: GCM.

A series of courting letters of Goldie that stress his commitment to Bricker and include references to an engagement and planned marriage. Goldie outlines his business activities with the People's Mill in Guelph which included a good deal of travel to Montreal and Toronto. The collection includes a wedding invitation of Bricker and Goldie, noting they were to be married in 1902.

2373. Goldie, Roswell. **Family scrapbook, 1827-1960.** 1 volume. Loc: GPL. Card index.

A family scrapbook of Roswell Goldie that includes many newspaper clippings, personal memorabilia and correspondence. Most entries refer to James or William Goldie and their descendants.

2374. Gordon Family. **Family papers, 1895-1949.** 3 file folders. Loc: WCA. MU 46; List of document contents.

A collection of land and military records of the Gordon family of Minto Township. The records include some receipts of the family and most of the sources focus on World War II years. The Wellington County Archives has developed a detailed finding aid noting the contents, dates and individuals mentioned in specific sources. Part of the Gordon Collection.

2375. Gordon, Helen Dorothy. **Will, 1908.** 1 document. Loc: GCM.

A carbon copy of the will of Gordon who lived in Guelph and was the wife of William Gordon.

2376. Gordon, James Neil. **Land records and school certificates, 1883; 1895; 1921; 1938; 1940; 1944-1949.** 1 envelope. Loc: WCA. MU 46.

Deeds and mortgages for several land transactions in Minto Township of James Gordon Sr in 1883 and 1895, and school certificates of James Gordon in 1938 and 1940 from Minto Township S.S.#11 and Harriston High School. The collection includes nine letters to the family from the Royal Canadian Air Force Casualties Officer reporting Sergeant James Neil Gordon missing and presumed dead.

2377. Gordon, John. **Will, 1895.** 1 document. Loc: GCM.

A carbon copy of the will of Gordon who was a farmer in Guelph Township.

2378. Gorvett, John. **Land records, 1898; 1923.** 1 envelope. Loc: WCA. MU 69.

Two records recording a mortgage and farm lease given by Gorvett to Mary Ann

Stephenson and Arthur Gorvett for land in Arthur Township.

2379. Graham, John. **Certificates and correspondence, 1886-1897.** 2 envelopes. Loc:
WCA.
Held in the Wellington County Historical Research Society Collection. Nine
certificates that certify John Graham a public school teacher and a letter of
appreciation from school pupils.

2380. Grieve, S. **Account book of S. Grieve, baker and grocer, 1903.** 1 file folder.
Loc: UGA. XR1 MS A025.
A record of produce sold.

2381. Groves, Abraham, Dr. **Correspondence, 1848.** 1 envelope. Loc: WCA.
Held in the Wellington County Historical Research Society Collection. A
typewritten letter from William Gibson in Peterborough to Abraham and Margaret
Groves in Fergus discussing family matters.

2382. Groves, Abraham, Dr. **Land records, 1847-1901.** 1 file folder. Loc: WCA. MU 23;
Detailed list of contents.
A collection of land records related to the purchase of two tracts of land in
Fergus. Comprises the Groves Collection.

2383. Hadden Family and Worsfold Family. **Correspondence, indentures and receipts
concerning Lot 643 of Canada Company Survey, Guelph, 1878-1891.** 1 file. Loc:
UGA. XR1 MS A324020.
Part of the Guelph Historical Society Collection.

2384. Hadden Family. **Papers.** Loc: UGA. XR1 MS A265.
Papers of the family that owned Lot 643 of the Canada Company Survey in
Guelph. Their house at 83 Paisley Street has been researched for a LACAC report.

2385. Haines, Catharine. **Crown Land Grant, Upper Canada, 1832.** 1 file folder. Loc:
UGA. XR1 MS A122007.
A grant of 200 acres of land in Amaranth Township to Catharine Haines. Part of
the Goodwin-Haines Collection.

2386. Hales, Alfred Dryden. **The John Hales Family in Canada from 1859-1988.** 69 pp.
Loc: GPL.
A genealogy and historical sketch of the Hales family who settled in Guelph
around 1871 and developed a butcher business that was maintained by the family
for three generations.

2387. Harris Family. **Correspondence, 1875-1884.** 1 oversized box. Loc: UGA. XR1 MS
A258.
A large number of letters of Elizabeth Harris and family of Guelph which
includes correspondence with her brother, James Harris, who was a Methodist
minister in Brussels, Huron County. A number of letters are written in
cross-hatching style. The letters outline church, family and social activities.

2388. Hemsworth, George. **Correspondence. Teaching position, 1896.** 1 document. Loc:
WCA. MU 33.
A letter from George Hemsworth of Mount Forest, applying for a teaching

position in S.S.#2 West Garafraxa, outlining his qualifications and including two references.

2389. Hewat Family. **Photocopy of family crest and large genealogical charts, 1700-1900.** 2 p., 2 sheets. Loc: NAC. MG 25, #291.

The Hewat family was originally from Roxburghshire, Scotland. Andrew Hewat is reported to have settled in the Rockwood area; the family later moved to Guelph.

2390. Hewat, William. **Correspondence, 1834-1884.** 1 folder, oversized. Loc: UGA. XR1 MS A260.

Several letters by Hewat relating to his role as treasurer of the Wellington District. The collection also contains a few records acknowledging Hewat's activities in the local militia and his involvement in a deed agreement for land in Eramosa Township dated 1857. The file includes a manuscript copy of the Guelph Daily Herald dated March 18, 1884, which presents an obituary of William Hewat. The obituary notes Hewat came to Guelph Township in 1834, established Speedbank Farm there, and became treasurer of Wellington District in 1841, holding the position until 1868. Filed with the Hewat Family Collection.

2391. Hewat, William. **Receipts, 1843-1863.** 2 envelopes. Loc: WCA. MU 50.

A series of receipts for the business transactions of Colonel Hewat and family of Guelph.

2392. Higinbotham, Margaret Jane. **Cook book, 1877.** 1 volume. Loc: UGA. XR1 MS A005101.

A personal collection of recipes by the wife of Nathaniel Higinbotham. Part of Allan-Higinbotham Collection.

2393. Higinbotham, Nathaniel. **Correspondence, 1896-1899.** 1 file folder, 1 volume. Loc: UGA. XR1 MS A005.

Correspondence to individuals about family matters. Part of Allan-Higinbotham Collection.

2394. Higinbotham, Nathaniel. **Financial. Receipts, 1910-1911.** 2 file folders. Loc: UGA. XR1 MS A005.

A collection of receipts from local shops addressed to various family members. Part of Allan-Higinbotham Collection.

2395. Higinbotham, Nathaniel. **Poetry dedicated to Colonel N. Higinbotham, M.P., 1874.** 2 documents. Loc: GCM.

Two handwritten, anonymous, satirical political poems dedicated to Higinbotham who was elected as a Liberal M.P. for the North Wellington Riding. Higinbotham won the riding first in the 1872 election by a small majority. The poems make charges of corruption. One poem ends with the warning 'After the election/When there's time for reflection/Your Judas' conduct/You are sure for to rue'.

2396. Higinbotham, Nathaniel. **Scrapbooks of current events, 1887-1900.** 3 volumes. Loc: UGA. XR1 MS A005084-5/A005100.

A record of current events about westward expansion, railways, Humane Society activities and poetry. The scrapbooks are undated but an archival inventory notes the time period as 1887 to 1900. Part of Allan-Higinbotham Collection.

2397. Higinbotham, W.A. **Correspondence, 1885-1916.** 1 file folder. Loc: UGA. XR1 MS A005073.
    A small collection of letters from the Royal Templars of Temperance in Buffalo and the Canadian Patriotic Fund. Included in the folder is a scrapbook of newspaper clippings on unrestricted reciprocity with the United States. Part of Allan-Higinbotham Collection.

2398. Hogg, John. **Obituary for Dr John Hogg, 1877.** 1 file folder. Loc: GSA.
    An obituary and poem in memory of Dr Hogg who was minister of St Andrew's Presbyterian Church in Guelph from 1859 to 1877.

2399. Hoodless Family. **Correspondence, addresses, newspaper clippings, family scrapbooks and photographs, 1890-1966.** 4 boxes, 1 scrapbook. Loc: UGA. XR1 MS A001.
    A record of the Hoodless family with useful references to correspondence relating to the founding of the Macdonald Institute in Guelph in 1903. The correspondence includes discussions of education between Hoodless and O.A.C. faculty, including James Mills and George Creelman. The collection also contains reports by Hoodless and newspaper clippings outlining the founding of Women's Institutes. There are also a number of photographs and newspaper clippings describing the activities of Hoodless descendants.

2400. Howitt, James. **Correspondence, accounts, miscellaneous, 1885-1935.** 2 files. Loc: UGA. XR1 MS A324018.
    The files include certificate, receipts and passports and are part of the Guelph Historical Society Collection.

2401. Humphrey Family. **Photographs and obituary, 1870-1922.** 1 file folder. Loc: GSA.
    Memorabilia of the Humphrey family including photographs of Wilma and Rowena, an obituary of Wilma and a medal of P.C. Humphrey entitled, 'Red River 1870' for his service with the 30th Wellington Battalion. The family belonged to St Andrew's Presbyterian Church, Guelph and the collection is in the church archives.

2402. Hutchinson, Mary. **Reminiscences, c1940.** 1 file. Loc: WCA. MU 102.
    A handwritten account of recollections of growing up on a Nichol Township farm by Mrs Mary Orr of Arthur (1850-1947). The daughter of William Hutchinson who farmed Lot 12, Concession 3, Mary recalls the family house, school days, walking to Fergus, toll roads, making syrup, cheese and honey, weaving cloth, poverty and vagrants, treatment of animals, and lighting.

2403. Hutchinson, William. **Correspondence and family history, 1851-1873.** 1 box. Loc: UGA. XR1 MS A002.
    The papers include letters and a family history of William Hutchinson who emigrated from Yorkshire, England to Fergus in the 1850s. The family history reproduces the diary of Hutchinson from 1850 to 1868. The diary of Hutchinson describes his trip on the ship to Canada, his agricultural activities in Wellington County, including the prices of crops he sold in the 1860s, and regular descriptions of weather conditions. The collection also contains a number of letters written to the Hutchinsons from friends in England during the 1850s and 1860s, describing life in England.

2404. Jackson, Henry. **Correspondence. Letter from Eramosa Township settler, 1845.** 1 document. Loc: WCA. MU 33.

A typescript copy of a letter written by Henry Jackson to a friend in Grimsby. Jackson apologizes for some type of financial dispute between the two parties in the past and asks for forgiveness. The letter also briefly describes farming conditions in Eramosa Township.

2405. Johnson, Edward. **Biography, 1878-1959.** 2 file folders. Loc: UGA. XZI MS A725 020.

A two-page biography of Johnson, who received his early musical training in Guelph and later became a famous opera tenor and manager of the Metropolitan Opera Company of New York. Also included is a brief biography in a Toronto Star article of June 23, 1984.

2406. Johnson, Edward. **Concert programs, 1897-1946.** 3 file folders. Loc: UGA. XZI MS A725 020.

A collection of concerts held in various places in Canada and the United States including the Guelph Royal Opera House, Griffin's Opera House, Guelph Collegiate-Vocational Institute, St Andrew's Church, the Guelph Armoury, Dublin Street Methodist Church, St George's Church, St James Church, Chalmers Church and War Memorial Hall. Part of the Guelph Spring Festival Collection.

2407. Keating, T.A. and Keating, Eliza. **Wills, 1885; 1892.** 2 documents. Loc: GPL. Carbon copies of the Keating wills held with the YM/YWCA records.

2408. Kelso, John Joseph. **Correspondence with J.P. Downey, Guelph, 1909.** 1 file (#65) Loc: NAC. MG 30, C 99, FA 368. Letters regarding the welfare of children.

2409. Kennedy, David Johnston. **Business papers, 1885-1893.** 1 file folder. Loc: UGA. XR1 MS A005041.

A collection of Canada Life Assurance bonus certificates and a stock certificate for Guelph Agricultural and Exhibition Building and Curling Rink Company. Part of Allan-Higinbotham Collection.

2410. Kennedy, David Johnston. **Estate papers, 1880-1899.** 4 file folders. Loc: UGA. XR1 MS A005040/A005043-5.

Correspondence, wills, tax notices, statements of liabilities and legal documents concerning the settlement of David Kennedy's estate. Part of Allan-Higinbotham Collection.

2411. Kennedy, David Johnston. **Land records, 1869-1895.** 1 file folder. Loc: UGA. XR1 MS A005037-9.

Records of land transactions involving Kennedy. Part of Allan-Higinbotham Collection.

2412. Kennedy, David Johnston. **Receipts, 1893-1894.** 1 file folder. Loc: UGA. XR1 MS A005042.

A collection of receipts from Guelph stores, including Peter Anderson, General Grocer; R.H. Barber, House and Sign Painter; R. Campbell, Surgeon Dentist; Stewart's Planing Mill and Lumber Yard; and Jackson and Hallett, Grocers and Tea Dealers. Most receipts were directed to 'Estate of D. Kennedy'. Part of

Allan-Higinbotham Collection.

2413. Laidlaw, James. **Correspondence, 1899.** 1 envelope. Loc: WCA. MU 78; Detailed list of contents.
A brief letter to James Laidlaw from Wilfrid Laurier, thanking him for the 'receipt of your favour of the 28th of October'. Part of the Laird Collection.

2414. Laidlaw, Thomas. **Articles, essays, poems and addresses, 1872-1901.** 2 notebooks. Loc: AO. MU 454.
The first notebook (1872-1899) includes letters purporting to have been written by Janet Ogilvie describing migration to Canada, pioneer settlement in the Paisley Block and historical sketches of S.S.#5, Guelph Township. The second notebook (1893-1901) has An Old Guelph Fair and A Barn Raising among other literary sketches. It also includes notes of which items were published in the Guelph Mercury including an address by Laidlaw to the St Andrew's Society of Guelph and the first anniversary report of the Guelph Gaelic Society. Part of the A.E. Byerly Papers.

2415. Laidlaw, Thomas. **Poetic sketches or leaves gathered by the wayside, c1879-1907.** ms, 244 p. Loc: GPL. 211.00.
A series of brief writings on varied local themes including the cutting down of the first tree in Guelph, sleigh songs, the River Speed.

2416. Lamport, Carol and Lamport, Leslie. **The Lamport family: descendants of Henry and Elizabeth (Clarke) Lamport, pioneer families, 1828-1940.** 253 pp. Loc: GPL.
A genealogy and historical sketch of the Clarke, Carter and Lamport family. Jehu 'John' Clarke and his family moved from Woodstock to Guelph in 1828 where he farmed, and later operated a tannery.

2417. Landoni, Faustino. **Naturalization of alien's document, 1896.** 1 envelope. Loc: WCA.
Held in the Wellington County Historical Research Society Collection. A photocopy of original document of Faustino Landoni from Garafraxa East Township, formerly from Lombardy, Italy. Also included is a receipt for Landoni's purchase of a farm for $2,326.25 in 1903. Arthur is listed above the date.

2418. Larter Family and Wilson, John. **Property Assessment. Tax records, 1891; 1923-1925 (sporadic).** 4 documents. Loc: WCA.
Held with the Wellington County Historical Research Collection. Copies of tax assessments of the Larter family of Guelph Township for the years 1923 to 1925 and of John Wilson of Luther West Township for the year 1891.

2419. Leslie, J.T. **Papers, 1839-1869.** 1 volume, file folders. Loc: AO. MU 1717.
Mary Leslie's father settled in Guelph Township on the Eramosa Road in the 1830s. The records include his copybook of letters sent 1843-1851 and copies of letters received 1839-1869. The Mary Leslie Papers also include a plan commissioned by J.T. Leslie in the late 1850s to subdivided his property into five acre lots. The records suggest a connection with the Sockett family and that the Leslies and Socketts might have migrated from Surrey, England to the Guelph Block under the auspices of the Petworth Committee in 1833.

2420. Leslie, Mary. **Business correspondence, 1867-1916.** 1 file folder. Loc: AO. MU 1717.

Leslie, born in 1842 in Guelph Township, lived most of her life in Wellington County. Her business papers include evidence of her efforts to publish her literary works and to establish a ladies' college. The records include an invoice from F. Trollope Chapman for binding ninety-nine copies of Leslie's book, The Cromaboo Mail Carrier, in 1878 and an opinion from the Strand Magazine that the book was 'a little too outspoken.' The papers contain no reference to Leslie's pseudonym, James Thomas Jones, under which she sometimes published. Part of the Mary Leslie Papers.

2421. Leslie, Mary. **Correspondence regarding proposed ladies' college, 1890.** 1 envelope. Loc: GCM.

A letter to Joe Smith in Guelph by Leslie outlining plans to establish a ladies' college in Guelph. Leslie offers her friend a job as a photo engraver for a magazine she intends to publish for students of the college.

2422. Leslie, Mary. **Literary works, 1867-1917.** 3 boxes. Loc: AO. MU 1711-1713.

Works include The Power of Song, The Battle of Worcester, A Synopsis of English History for Young Students, and Historical Sketches of Scotland in Prose and Verse. Some works are held in typescript, galley proof and published formats. Part of Mary Leslie Papers.

2423. Leslie, Mary. **Personal correspondence, 1853-1919.** 2 boxes. Loc: AO. MU 1715-1716.

A large number of letters, including those written by Leslie to her parents while she visited Europe in 1867-1868. Leslie's correspondents included T. Williamson of Grosvenor Square, London, as well as various family members. Some letters concern her sister Elizabeth, wife of C.A. Clarke, with whom Leslie lived from the 1890s in Rockwood and Belwood. Leslie was apparently an active member of St John's Anglican Church, Rockwood. Part of Mary Leslie Papers.

2424. Leslie, Mary. **A plea for Rockwood, c1912.** 9 p. typescript, edited. Loc: AO. MU 1719.

An essay on Rockwood seen in terms of the contemporary 'Civic Movement in the United States'. Leslie deprecates the ruining of the original plan for Guelph by the railway and other developments which made it 'an undesirable place of residence, whatever its business prosperity'. Rockwood is described as 'a straggling town . . . greatly in need of police supervision and enforced sanitary laws'. Part of Mary Leslie Papers.

2425. Leslie, Mary. **Prospectus for proposed ladies' college, 1891.** Printed leaflet. Loc: AO. MU 1717.

The motto of the proposed college was 'Work like a beaver' and the object was 'to form perfect women, morally and physically, as well as intellectually'. Part of the Mary Leslie Papers.

2426. Macaulay, W.N. **Letter from Guelph, 1889.** 1 item. Loc: SRA. TD 1/958.

Letter to Mrs Susan Smith, wife of a professor at Trinity College, Cambridge, describing impressions of Guelph in September 1889. The writer approved of Guelph and the O.A.C., describing the surrounding country as 'pretty thickly populated' and Guelph as 'a finer town than we had expected'.

2427. Macdonald, Gordon A. **Entrance examination, 1910.** 1 document. Loc: WCA. MU 51.
A record of examination results entitling Gordon A. Macdonald to attend the Faculty of Education at Guelph.

2428. Macdonald, William. **Examination report, 1893.** 1 document. Loc: WCA. MU 51.
A matriculation certificate of William Macdonald of Elora indicating he was successful in an examination written for the Royal College of Dental Surgeons.

2429. Macdonell, Alexander, Rev. **Papers, 1801-1839.** 6 boxes. Loc: AO. FA: MS-709.
Original manuscripts or typescript copies of correspondence on personal, ecclesiastical, legal and political matters, often concerning the Scottish and Irish Catholics of Upper Canada and the priests under Bishop Macdonell's supervision. Several items refer to the foundation period of the Guelph settlement, including four letters to and one letter from John Galt in the period from 1827 to 1829.

2430. Marsh, Helen. **Land records, 1876.** 1 document. Loc: GCM.
A record of sale of land in Guelph Township.

2431. Marston, Katherine. **Personal writings, 1930-1970.** 1 file folder. Loc: UGA. XR1 MS A193022.
A collection of poems, anecdotes and editorials Marston wrote for the Elora Express in the 1940s. Held with the Katherine Marston Papers.

2432. Maude Family. **Property Assessment. Notices and tax papers, 1918-1947.** 1 file folder. Loc: UGA. XR1 MS A013.
Tax records on the Maude family property in Fergus. Held with the Maude Family Papers.

2433. Maude, Robert. **Receipts, 1924-1945.** 3 file folders. Loc: UGA. XR1 MS A013.
A collection of receipts to Robert Maude from the Superior Barn Equipment Company and the Fergus Garage. One folder includes Post Office Savings Bank deposit receipts addressed to Ethel Maude. Held with Maude Family Papers.

2434. McAteer, John. **Correspondence, 1908.** 1 document. Loc: GCM.
A letter to John McAteer, a Guelph alderman who was also proprietor of the American Hotel in Guelph, from John Hull asking for help in securing a post working for 'civic offices' in the city.

2435. McAteer, John and McAteer, Frank. **Family correspondence, 1918-1919.** 11 envelopes. Loc: GCM.
A series of letters from John McAteer to his family in Guelph outlining his experiences as a soldier in France during World War I. The letters include several letters from Frank McAteer who was training at Camp Petawawa. The letters are held in a box entitled, Militaria.

2436. McAteer, John. **Receipt for funeral, 1917.** 1 envelope. Loc: GCM.
A receipt for payment of thirty-eight dollars issued by the Guelph Catholic Rectory for the funeral of McAteer, proprietor of the American Hotel.

2437. McConnell, Donald. **Land records, 1856-1872 (sporadic).** 1 volume. Loc: WCA. MU 46.

A scrapbook of land and tax records of McConnell for land on concession 4, lot 33 in Minto Township.

2438. McCrae, David. **Journals, 1864-1866; 1869-1871.** 1 reel. mf. Loc: NAC. MG 30, D 29, #1239, Reel A-1103.

Journals of John McCrae's father discussing daily activities in Guelph and travels to other places. The later journal is more concerned with the business activities of McCrae and Company, Yarn Spinners. Weather and Sunday sermons are usually noted. Part of the John McCrae Papers.

2439. McCrae Family. **Scrapbooks, 1894-1984.** 5 volumes, 2 boxes. Loc: JMH.

One scrapbook is of undated inspirational newspaper clippings glued into a c1860 family account ledger of Thomas McCrae, John McCrae's grandfather. Two volumes include newspaper clippings about the Guelph contingent's activities in the Boer War; they contain information and portraits of many Guelph residents who were part of Guelph Battery D of the Royal Canadian Artillery. The articles are glued into two 1857 to 1866 account books of McCrae's Lumber Yard which was situated on Woolwich Street facing St George's Church and owned by Thomas McCrae. The accounts for 1862 are legible and not covered by clippings. Two scrapbooks, from 1916 to 1927, contain clippings about World War I, and obituaries and eulogies of John McCrae. The boxes contain copies of the poem, In Flanders Fields, answers to the poems by other poets and sheet music to set the words of the poem to music.

2440. McCrae, John. **Diary, letters and other papers, 1881-1918.** 13 p., 4 reels. mf. Loc: NAC. MG 30, D 29, #1239.

Correspondence of various McCrae family members while travelling or at school; McCrae's diary and letters in South African War and Great War.

2441. McCrae, John. **Miscellaneous, 1895-1986.** 1 box. Loc: UGA. XR1 MS A072.

An assorted collection of primary and secondary material, including one framed handwritten poem c1895, one copy of Punch, December 8, 1915 containing the first published version of 'In Flanders Fields', and a copy of McCrae's, 'Diary on Expedition to South Africa', c1900.

2442. McCrae, John. **Scrapbooks, 1882-1903.** 3 volumes. Loc: JMH.

A collection of personal memorabilia of McCrae that includes illustrations from the journal, Boy's Own Paper, his published essays and short stories while at the University of Toronto, newspaper clippings of honour lists and school examinations, photographs of Maryland, and items from Johannesburg. The first scrapbook was begun in 1882 when McCrae was ten years old. It includes illustrations of or information about the Ontario Agricultural College, Guelph Collegiate Institute and the Guelph Militia. The second scrapbook is about his time in the Boer War with Guelph Battery D of the Royal Canadian Artillery. It includes military telegrams and orders, photographs and newspaper clippings about the Boer War and clippings and photographs of an artillery train wreck in 1903 at the Bay of Quinte, Ontario. The third book contains photographs of the Guelph Battery D relaxing in army camps in South Africa.

2443. McCrae, John. **Sketch books, 1897; 1900.** 2 volumes. Loc: JMH.

A collection of landscapes of the Chesapeake Bay area, drawn in 1897 while McCrae was doing graduate work in Biology at John Hopkins University in Maryland. The second volume is a series of landscapes drawn in 1900 while he was in South Africa for the Boer War with Guelph Battery D of the Royal Canadian Artillery. Several sketches, loose and mounted, are held with the collection.

2444. McDermid, Jessie. **North Wellington entrance examination report, 1909.** 1 envelope. Loc: WCA. MU 13.

A notification of 'Honours' achievement. The name of school or college is not given. The notice was mailed to Farewell, Arthur Township, which is a few miles south of Mount Forest.

2445. McIntosh, James. **Correspondence, 1912-1918.** 1 box. Loc: UGA. XR1 MS A008.

The collection is primarily a group of letters from James McIntosh to his family in Guelph from Europe outlining his experiences as a soldier during World War I. The box includes bank passbooks and some photographs of the family, postcards of European scenes and the diary of Mary McIntosh describing the time she spent at Westdown School in Toronto in 1912. The bank passbooks refer to James Innes who sold his paper, The Guelph Mercury, to James Innes McIntosh who became chief editor in 1898.

2446. McKenzie, K.T. **Correspondence, August 17, 1864.** 1 file folder. Loc: UGA. XR1 MS A149.

A letter from McKenzie, a former resident of Guelph, to D. Kelleher describing his participation in the Civil War in the United States. McKenzie outlines the battle of Petersburg.

2447. McLean, J.K. **Papers, 1876-1881.** 1 box. Loc: AO. MU 3059.

James McLean (1851-1913) was a private surveyor whose papers include a field notebook describing surveys in Wellington and Grey Counties, though most of his commissions were in Western Canada. The papers also include letters from Lieutenant Donald H. McLean to his mother and one 1917 letter by Fred Jacob that contains Elora news.

2448. McQueen, James. **Land records, 1847; 1857; 1862.** 1 file folder. Loc: WCA. MU 69.

A record of the deed and mortgage McQueen held for land in Nichol Township purchased from Adam Fergusson.

2449. Mickle, Charles Julius. **Correspondence, 1833.** 1 file folder. Loc: UGA. XR1 MS A139009.

A letter from C. Mickle to his friend T. Fischer regarding church congregations in Canada. Held with the Goodwin-Haines Collection.

2450. Mickle Family. **Correspondence and financial records, 1823-1915.** 7 boxes. Loc: AO. MU 2024-2030.

Chronologically organized folders of mainly family correspondence, including letters by Ellen Mickle and the children that mention the family home, Langholm. After the death of Charles Mickle in 1879, the family seems to have moved to Toronto. Most of the letters from the 1890s are related to Sarah Mickle of Toronto. Part of Charles Mickle Papers.

2451. Mickle Family. **Correspondence, legal documents, accounts, photographs, clippings, publications and notebooks, 1832-1950.** 7 boxes. Loc: UGA. Itemized inventory.

A collection of material relating to six generations of the Mickle family. Charles Julius Mickle and his family emigrated from Scotland in 1832 to land now occupied by Ignatius College on the Elora Road. The collection includes Charles Mickle's estate records from 1856, and family correspondence. Part of Mickle Family Collection. Other collections of Mickle Family Papers are in the Archives of Ontario, the National Archives and the Metro Toronto Reference Library (Baldwin Room).

2452. Mickle Family. **Papers, 1813-1921.** 1 box. Loc: MTL. Card index.

Letters, receipts and legal papers, including the diary kept by Charles Julius Mickle on the journey from England to Elora in 1832, business papers concerning land purchases from the Canada Company, notes on the Congregational Church and other religious matters and family business correspondence. Family members with letters and papers in this collection include Alexander F. Mickle of Stratford; Henry W. Mickle, K.C.; Ellen Mickle, widow of Charles Mickle; and Miss Sarah Mickle. The family apparently moved from Guelph to Toronto after the death of Charles Mickle in 1879.

2453. Millar, James. **Architect's specifications for brick and stone farm dwelling, 1873.** 1 file folder. Loc: UGA. XRI MS A256.

The house was built for James Millar, July 18, 1873 and was situated on Edinburgh Road in Guelph. Also included is photocopied information relating to the Millar family in Hacking's 1873 Guelph Directory.

2454. Millog, Mary. **Letter, June 11, 1841.** 1 document. Loc: WCA.

A record of a brief letter to her mother lamenting the fact no one had written her lately. The letter does not indicate where the letter was written to but refers to a place called Dunuttach in comparing it to farming conditions in Erin Township. Part of the Pollock Collection.

2455. Mitchell, Fred. **Receipts, 1930-1941.** 3 file folders. Loc: WCA. MU 101.

A collection of receipts for family purchases in Fergus stores.

2456. Moir, David. **Biographical memoirs of John Galt, 1841.** 1 document. Loc: NLS. No. 6522.

A portion of Moir's memoirs of Galt published in 1841, only two years after Galt's death, that presents a balanced view of Galt's significance.

2457. Nelson, Jonathan Baxter. **The Benhams of Wellington County, Ontario, 1827-1966.** 1 volume. Loc: UGA. XR1 MS A310.

A thirty-seven page history of the family which indicates James Benham and his wife, Lucy Walton, came to Guelph in 1827 and moved to Eramosa Township in 1832. The work includes genealogical and biographical notes on the family and indicates James Benham was one of seven Eramosa Township farmers arrested as alleged rebels during the Rebellion of 1837.

2458. Nelson, Jonathan Baxter. **The Nelson family of Eramosa, 1824-1971.** 1 volume. Loc: UGA. XR1 MS A309.

A family history which indicates James Nelson came to Eramosa Township in 1824 and moved to Garafraxa Township in 1838. The work includes genealogical and biographical notes of the Nelson family.

2459. Nesbitt, Arthur and Nesbitt, Margaret. **Financial. Tax receipts, 1903-1912.** 1 envelope. Loc: WCA.

Photocopies of tax receipts from Peel Township for Margaret Nesbitt and Arthur Nesbitt. Held in the Wellington County Historical Research Society Collection.

2460. Nunan, George. **Papers, 1896-1983.** 1 box, 1 file drawer. Loc: JA.

A collection of lectures, teaching notes and drafts of Nunan's writings on ethics and some materials relating to his family and early life in Guelph. In several memoirs and recollections, apparently composed when he was in the Jesuit Infirmary at the end of his life in the early 1980s, Nunan recalls the influence of his father, Frank, as a devoted layman of the Church of Our Lady and a member of the Guelph Separate School Board for fifty years, and also the influence of Father Wafer Doyle. The memoirs describe Nunan's studies at the St Stanislaus Novitiate as well as at other Jesuit colleges. He was one of those arrested in the infamous raid of June, 1918. Nunan also recalls his efforts to persuade the Jesuit Fathers to retain their role in Guelph in 1931 when he was attached to the parish as priest. He later taught at Regis College in Toronto to 1950 and was Provincial of the Society of Jesus from 1951 to 1957.

2461. O'Brien, Henry. **Diary, 1858-1859.** 1 volume. original. Loc: MTL.

Part of a much larger collection of papers of O'Brien (1836-1931) who began to study law in 1855, worked in Guelph in the law office of John J. Kingsmill in 1858, and then practised law in Toronto for sixty years from 1859. He was editor of the Canada Law Journal from 1865 to 1922. His Guelph diary spans only four months, September to December 1858, but provides an excellent commentary on legal cases, social life, local politics and church matters. During his stay in Guelph, O'Brien boarded at the American Hotel, but dined out with various local families such as the Saunders, Hewats, Websters, Fergussons, Guthries and Kingsmills. He served as secretary of the Guelph Cricket Club and was a member of St George's Anglican Church, attending occasional services at St Andrew's Presbyterian Church. He reports 'indignation meetings' on September 18 and 20, 1858 during which George Brown, the Governor-General and Dr William Clarke were burned in effigy. Special days are described, such as St Andrew's Day, when all the Scots got drunk, and Gunpowder Treason Day (November 5) as celebrated by the Orangemen whom he describes as 'the Bulwark of Protestanism who never go to church and have as much Christian liberality as Ferdinand and Isabella'. There is also a reference to Andrew Geddes and Charles Allan of Elora winding up their land speculation business.

2462. Paget, Amy Kathleen. **Passport, 1917.** 1 envelope. Loc: WCA. MU 11.

A British passport for Paget for nursing duties with the U.S. Army. Paget was born in 1875 and baptized in St John's Anglican Church, Elora.

2463. Peacock, Thomas and Jacob, John. **Mortgage, 1868-1872.** 1 document. Loc: WCA. MU 13.

A mortgage given by Thomas Peacock to John Jacob of Elora for land purchased in Pilkington Township.

2464. Peters, James. **Letter to Hannah Peters from Hamilton Gaol, December 30-31, 1837.** 4 p. photostat. Loc: MTL.

James Peters was arrested with other 'rebels' of Eramosa Township in late 1837 and held in Hamilton for several months. His letter to his wife describes conditions of his imprisonment and discusses work that should be done on the family farm, the welfare and obedience of their children, and how she should cope financially through the winter.

2465. Pilkington, Robert. **Estate Papers. Correspondence, legal and business papers, 1834-1867.** 2 boxes. Loc: AO. MU 2319-2320.

Correspondence and legal documents relating to claims on the estate of General Robert W. Pilkington, mostly handled by his nephew Edward Tylee in London, England. Most of the material dates from the 1830s and 1840s. The item of most specific interest to the history of Wellington County is a large ledger page entitled, Statement of sales of land in Township of Woolwich, estate of the late General Pilkington, 1844. This list, by concession and lot number, states the number of acres and purchase price, names of those to whom the land was originally sold, the date of subsequent transfers and the names of occupants in 1844 with amounts of money paid and amounts still due. About seven thousand acres are accounted for and the original purchasers were nearly all still occupying their lots in 1844 and, on average, seventy-five percent of the purchase money was still due.

2466. Pritchard, R.T., Lieut-Col. **Military certificate, correspondence, 1916.** 1 envelope. Loc: WCA.

A record of Pritchard's qualification as Field Officer of the 30th Wellington Rifles, and a letter of support from 'Village Council' to Pritchard, officers and men of the 153rd Wellington Battalion before leaving to fight for 'the Great Empire we love so dearly'. The archival genealogical file lists his name as Lieutenant-Colonel Robert Thomas Pritchard, whose family farmed in Nichol Township.

2467. Rea Family. **Personal papers, 1854-1921.** 1 box. Loc: WCA. List of document contents.

Diaries, family correspondence, receipts and account books of the Rea family who farmed in Eramosa Township. The collection includes two ledgers of the farm diaries of William Rea for the years 1854 to 1857 and 1861 to 1868 outlining daily farm, travel and family activities. The record also contains one ledger listing the expenses of David Rea from 1865 to 1895, and his diary from 1857 to 1863. Part of the Rea-Armstrong Collection.

2468. Rea Family. **Personal papers, 1905; 1909.** 3 documents. Loc: WCA.

Held in the Wellington County Historical Research Society Collection. The papers include the marriage certificate of John Rea, a wedding invitation, and Rea's oath of allegiance in assuming the position of justice of the peace in Puslinch Township in 1909.

2469. Reynolds, William. **Correspondence, 1832; 1837; 1843.** 3 documents. Loc: WCA. MU 12.

Three brief letters sent to Reynolds that are difficult to read and do not provide any note as to the author of the documents. The letters are written in cross-hatching style.

2470. Reynolds, William. **Estate papers, 1878-1902.** 1 file folder. Loc: UGA. XR1 MS A115017.

A series of land sale agreements and announcements of public auctions of land in Elora. The records are held with the Connon Collection.

2471. Roadhouse, F.E. **Cormie ancestry, 1840-1984.** 1 file folder. Loc: UGA. XR1 MS A204.

A genealogical history of John Cormie and Ann Heggie Cormie who emigrated from Fifeshire, Scotland and settled in Nichol Township in 1840.

2472. Sandilands Family. **Estate papers, 1866-1903.** 3 file folders. Loc: UGA. XR1 MS A005052-4.

Correspondence, wills and land records of Thomas, Annie and George Sandilands. Nathaniel Higinbotham granted mortgages to the family. Part of Allan-Higinbotham Collection.

2473. Saunders, Thomas. **Letters, 1835-1840.** 1 file folder. photocopies. Loc: MTL. Card index.

Saunders (1795-1873) and his wife, Lucy Willcocks, emigrated from London, England in the early 1830s and settled near Guelph on land purchased from the Canada Company. In his letters to his uncles, Joshua and William, Saunders describes the difficulties of making a living in the new country: 'This is not the country for anyone above the rank of a mechanic or labourer except he has from one to ten thousand pounds or he has a family of three able-bodied sons. No land will pay to cultivate by hired labour during the first five years. . . . The Canada Company has much to answer for in inducing people out here and raising such false hopes in the minds of the emigrants.' Saunders himself survived the first few years only with the help of remittances from his uncles until, in 1840, he was appointed Clerk of the Peace for Wellington District, a post which brought fifty pounds a year in fees. Saunders' letters provide useful details of the expenses of farm making and the likely harvest values of various crops.

2474. Scarlett, Rolph. **Guelph Public Schools. Certificate of merit, 1900.** 1 document. Loc: MSC.

A certificate for 'First in drawing' awarded to Scarlett in Guelph on June 30, 1900, who was in the Second Senior Division. It was signed by S. Broadfoot, Chairman; W. Tytler, Inspector; D. Young Principal; and F. Billing, Teacher. Two of Scarlett's paintings, entitled Eramosa Silo and Gordon Street Bridge, are held at the Macdonald Stewart Art Centre. Held with the Art Centre files on the artist.

2475. Scott, Matthew and Skeritt, Minnie. **Newspaper report of marriage, 1908.** 1 envelope. Loc: WCA.

Held in the Wellington County Historical Research Society Collection. A typewritten copy of a newspaper clipping describing the marriage of Minnie Skeritt and Matthew Scott of Eramosa Township.

2476. Secord Family. **Estate records, 1899; 1926.** 1 file folder. Loc: UGA. XR1 MS A280.

A number of legal records which includes the will of Thomas Eugene MacNamara

Secord and an indenture of his wife, Ann Hadsworth.

2477. Shutt, Donald B. **Memoirs, c1960**. 1 file folder. typescript. Loc: AO. MU 2138, Misc. 1960 #3.

Shutt, one of the first dairy bacteriologists, recalls his early life in Toronto, his diploma and degree studies at the O.A.C., his experiences in both world wars, his teaching and research on the staffs of the Manitoba Agricultural College (1922-1924) and the Ontario Agricultural College (1925-1960). He refers to various Guelph institutions including St George's Anglican Church, the militia, and the Guelph School Board.

2478. Shutt, Greta M. **Scrapbooks, 1827-1973**. 12 volumes. Loc: GPL.

A collection of newspaper clippings of Shutt and Skinner correspondence about family activities and the historical development of Guelph. An oversized scrapbook contains early land records and family correspondence from 1864 to 1881 written from England to Guelph. Part of the Shutt Collection.

2479. Sinclair, Catherine. **Guardianship record, 1865**. 1 document. Loc: WCA. List of document contents.

A legal letter pertaining to the adoption of two children by Catherine Sinclair of Arthur Township. The document is described in a finding aid developed by the Wellington County Archives, where it is grouped with the Elora Land Records Collection.

2480. Sleeman Family. **Correspondence, 1859-1903 (sporadic)**. 6 file folders. Loc: UGA. XR1 MS A334045-50.

A large number of letters between Sleeman family members which often refer to business, travel and family matters. In one letter, written by George to his father John in 1876, Sleeman complains of the lack of business for the brewery, noting, 'I have never seen it so dull'. Part of the Sleeman Family Collection.

2481. Sleeman, George. **Account books, 1874-1888; 1902-1903**. 4 ledgers. Loc: UGA. XR1 MS A334.

A record of bills to be paid by George Sleeman to specific individuals and companies. One of the ledgers, covering the years 1902 to 1903, is labelled 'the building account'. Part of the Sleeman Family Collection.

2482. Sleeman, George. **Correspondence, 1910**. 1 file folder. Loc: UGA. XR1 MS A334051-2.

Several letters written by George Sleeman in 1910 concerning the work of the Board of Park Commissioners in Guelph. Part of the Sleeman Family Collection.

2483. Sleeman, George. **Municipal correspondence, 1880-1923**. 4 file folders. Loc: UGA. XR1 MS A334.

A record of candidates for municipal council in 1880, Sleeman's activities on council committees and his actions relating to efforts designed to ensure the preservation of the Priory Building in Guelph. Part of the Sleeman Family Collection.

2484. Sleeman, George. **Scrapbooks, 1860-1923**. 1 volume, 10 file folders, 2 oversize files. Loc: UGA. XR1 MS A334040-1.

A series of newspaper clippings primarily from 1870 to 1920 which highlight the social, economic and political activities of Sleeman in the city. The record indicates George Sleeman established the Spring Bank Brewery in the city in 1903. The collection includes an October 6, 1894 article in the Saturday Globe, which presents a brief history of the Guelph Maple Leaf Baseball Club. The record includes several copies of special Guelph newspaper editions which highlighted industrial and mercantile establishments in Guelph. Part of the Sleeman Family Collection.

2485. Smith Family. **Photographs and diaries, c1868-1889.** 1 envelope. Loc: UGA. XR1 MS A142.

Includes two diaries, one of an unidentified young male for the year 1869 and one of Suzie Smith for 1874. The diaries outline school, social and church experiences. The collection includes photographs of the family. The Smith family lived in Mount Forest.

2486. Smith, Samuel. **Diaries and field books, 1821-1854.** 1 box. Loc: AO. MU 2839.

The Canada Company contracted with Smith (1795-1857) to survey Guelph Township during the summer of 1828. The field books describe the vegetation cover of Guelph Township and adjoining areas while the diaries for 1828 contain a day-to-day narrative of events in the Guelph settlement. The Samuel Smith Papers also contain details of surveys in other townships of southwestern Ontario as well as Smith's business and personal papers.

2487. Sockett Family. **Land records, 1833-1849.** 2 file folders. Loc: AO. MU 1717.

Several indentures relating to land transactions by members of the Sockett Family, mainly in Eramosa Township. Parties included George Sockett and the Reverend Thomas Sockett, who may have come to the Guelph area from Surrey, England, under the auspices of the Petworth Committee in 1833. These records have been preserved as part of the Mary Leslie Papers; the Leslie and Sockett families seem to have been related by marriage.

2488. Somerville, Margaret. **Accounting notebooks, 1854.** 2 ledgers. Loc: WCA. MU 89.

Practice workbooks of Somerville who was the maternal grandmother of John Jeffrey, a Puslinch farmer. Part of Jeffrey Collection.

2489. Sunley, Ann Amelia Day. **Diary, 1878-1879.** 1 volume. Loc: WCA. MU 45A.

A typewritten copy of Sunley's diary which discusses her daily work and activities on the farm of her father, Thomas Day, and later on the farm of her husband, Noah Sunley, in Eramosa Township. An archival note states that she was born in 1853 and died in 1948.

2490. Sunter, William. **Diaries, 1893; 1895-1896; 1898; 1912-1914.** 5 volumes. Loc: UGA. XR1 MS A023.

The William Sunter Papers consist of farm diaries that note weather, chores, crops, family life, schools, and activities of Sunter's wife and children. An archival note states that Sunter was a farmer near Everton in Eramosa Township.

2491. Sutherland, Robert, Sr. **The Sutherland family: history and memories, 1875-1934.** 60 leaves (unpaged). ill. Loc: UGA. XR1 MS A364.

A printed collection of family reminiscences, letters, photographs and other records. One section describes the Saunders family from Kilkenny, Ireland who migrated to Beckwith Township, Lanark County and then to Greenock Township,

Bruce County in 1855. A second section describes the Sutherlands who migrated from Scotland in 1834 to the Galt area, where they were engaged in sawmilling. In 1870 John Sutherland (1853-1934) began to work for the Gore Fire Insurance of Galt, and in 1875 joined Robert Cunningham's Guelph insurance agency. This business was incorporated after Robert Cunningham's death as John Sutherland and Sons in 1912. There are biographies and obituaries of John Sutherland and Robert Sutherland Sr (1904-1978), which include accounts of Robert's encouragement of curling for schoolboys and his pioneering work for conservation in Puslinch Township and the Saugeen Bluffs. The Sutherlands belonged to St Andrew's Presbyterian Church. One of John's daughters, Anne Sutherland Brooks, wrote poetry and other literary works.

2492. Taylor, John. **Correspondence. Description of conditions in Guelph, 1837.** 1 document. Loc: GPL, UGA. UGA: XR1 MS A276.

A typed copy of a letter written by John and Jean Taylor of the Paisley Block near Guelph. The letter was sent to the children of Mr and Mrs John Taylor and discusses crop yields, the selling price of various goods, the wages carpenters could expect to earn in Guelph and the dances organized by Mrs Thomas Hood. The letter also indicates John Taylor had been experiencing poor health and that in Guelph there was a shortage of tools. The Taylors emigrated to Canada from Forfarshire, Scotland in 1834. John wrote the poem, The Paisley Block Ball.

2493. Templin, Hugh. **Assessment notice, 1925.** 1 envelope. Loc: WCA.

One assessment notice of Hugh Templin's property in Fergus. Part of the Templin-Dow Collection.

2494. Templin, Hugh. **Copyright certificate, 1933.** 1 envelope. Loc: WCA.

A framed copyright certificate for Templin's book, Fergus the Story of a Little Town. Part of the Templin-Dow Collection.

2495. Thornton, Major. **Excerpts from diary of Major Thornton of England, 1849.** 11 pp. Loc: GPL.

A typescript of the diary of Thornton's visit to Guelph between August 13 and 28. He recounts his impressions of the settlement, and his visits to Colonel and Mrs. Hewat, the Canada Company, the Court House, the Paisley Block, Dr. Clarke and Colonel Saunders.

2496. Ton, Ames. **Letter to Puslinch Township residence, 1844.** 1 document. Loc: GCM.

A letter written from 'Edin' which was likely Edinburgh, Scotland. Ames Ton describes the death of his wife to his brother Thomas who lived in Puslinch Township. The letter includes references to conditions in 'Edin' and the activities of friends there.

2497. Turner, Dick. **Impressions of a visit to Upper Canada, 1831.** 1 file folder. Loc: UGA. XR1 MS A312.

A series of brief notes with a few references to Guelph where he visited the farm of his brother. The references to Guelph include a short poem and a discussion of the author's dislike of mosquitoes and frogs in Guelph.

2498. Tytler, William. **Literature notebook, c1865.** 1 volume. Loc: GCM.

Notes and questions on works of classical authors, including Cicero. The first page of the volume is inscribed 'Wm. W. Tytler, University College, Toronto'.

2499. Tytler, William and Tytler, Martha Harrison. **Passport to Jamaica, 1919-1920.** 1 document. Loc: GCM.

The passport includes a physical description and photograph of Tytler and his wife.

2500. Wallace, Margaret Alice Higinbotham. **Financial. Receipts, 1919-1920.** 1 file folder. Loc: UGA. XR1 MS A005.

A collection of receipts from Yokohama, Japan and Seoul, Korea for household articles, material and clothing. Several receipts are addressed to Dr N. Wallace. Part of Allan-Higinbotham Collection.

2501. Wallace, Norman, Dr and Wallace, Margaret Alice Higinbotham. **Indentures, 1914.** 2 documents. Loc: UGA. XR1 MS A005.

A record of indentures arranged by the Wallaces for the estate of Margaret Jane Higinbotham. Part of Allan-Higinbotham Collection.

2502. Wardrope, David. **Wardrope family history, 1832-1839.** 1 document. Loc: UGA. XR1 MS A255.

A typescript historical sketch of David Wardrope, who emigrated with his parents and siblings in 1834 from Scotland to Puslinch and Guelph Townships where they farmed until 1839 when they moved to Flamboro Township. The anecdotal sketch describes the difficulties the family had as inexperienced farmers. David's brother Thomas, was possibly Rev. Thomas Wardrope, minister of Chalmers Presbyterian Church in Guelph from 1869 to 1892.

2503. Watson, Avice. **Diary, 1885-1891.** 1 envelope. Loc: WCA. MU 84.

A description by Watson of family, farm and social life, as well as notes regarding weather conditions. The record is a photocopy of the original diary. Part of the Watson Collection.

2504. Watson Family. **History, 1830-1905.** 2 envelopes. Loc: WCA. MU 84.

A 95-page report of the history of the Watson family who were farmers at Cottingham Cottage in Guelph Township. The report notes that Henry Watson came from London, England to Guelph Township where he purchased land from the Canada Company. The collection includes a few brief reports of the early history of S.S.#2 with Henry Watson being listed as one of the early school trustees in the township. Part of the Watson Collection.

2505. Watson Family. **Land records, 1833-1912 (sporadic).** 1 envelope. Loc: WCA. MU 33; List of contents and dates of documents.

A record of wills, land transfer records and claims for land of the Watson family of Guelph Township. The Wellington County Archives has developed a finding aid indicating the contents, dates and individuals involved in specific transactions. Part of the Watson Collection.

2506. Watson, Henry, Jr. **Diary, 1899-1908.** 3 envelopes. Loc: WCA. MU 84; List of contents and dates of documents.

A large number of entries which outline the farm, family, social and travel experiences of Watson. The record is a photocopy of original diaries. The Wellington County Archives has developed a finding aid indicating the date and contents of the diary. Part of the Watson Collection.

2507. Watson, John Richardson. **Diary, 1885-1899.** 1 envelope. Loc: WCA. MU 84.
A series of diary entries of John Richardson Watson which outline farm, family and social activities. The document is a photocopy of original diary entries. Part of the Watson Collection.

2508. Watt, Barbara Argo and Watt, Alexander. **Correspondence, 1837-1864.** 14 documents. Loc: UGA. XSI MS A054.
The Watt-Argo Collection of 14 letters written to Barbara Argo Watt and her husband Alexander, who were early settlers in the Bon Accord settlement near Elora. The letters are from relatives from the Parishes of Tarves and Foveran in Aberdeenshire. As well as offering a rich survey of rural life and problems in Scotland, the correspondence also shows the emotional impact of the loss of relatives through emigration.

2509. Webber, Maria. **Land deeds, 1892.** 1 envelope. Loc: WCA. MU 16.
Several deeds recording the purchase of land in Minto Township by Maria Webber from Alfred Webber.

2510. Wells, Gabriel. **Probate will, 1908.** 1 document. Loc: WCA. MU 13.
Gabriel Wells was a resident of Everton, Eramosa Township.

2511. Wheelihan, Nicholas. **Will, 1923-1927.** 6 documents. Loc: GCM.
A record of the will, estate and associated correspondence.

2512. White Family and Pentelow Family and MacIntyre Family and Stevenson Family. **Correspondence, cash books and legal documents, 1850-1960.** 2 boxes, 1 oversized box. Loc: UGA. XRI MS A 324001, XRI MS A263.
The collection concerns family and business matters. Howard Pentelow emigrated to Guelph from England c1890 to be chief accountant for the Bell Organ Company. William Stevenson was mayor of Guelph from 1885 to 1886. The collection includes family photographs; miscellaneous notebooks and diaries from Toronto, Galt, and unidentified places and people; land records of William Stevenson in Guelph; family correspondence to Colonel Morgan White, Margaret and Maude White; the will of Gilbert McIntyre in 1912 and revenue receipts in 1923; correspondence to William and Maude Pentelow; and accounting records for Bell Piano and Organ Company in 1929 to 1934. Part of the Guelph Historical Society Collection.

2513. White, William Wallace. **Certificates, 1894-1928.** 1 box. Loc: UGA. XR1 MS A263.
A collection of military items and certificates of Lieutenant-Colonel William Wallace White and his certificate of admission to the Hamilton Lodge of Free Masons. Held with the White Family Collection.

2514. Williams, Hawley. **Probate will, 1846.** 1 file folder, oversized. Loc: UGA. XR2 MS A059.

2515. Winstanley-Mackinnon Family. **Miscellaneous diaries, photographs, postcards, certificates, 1860-1960.** 2 boxes. Loc: UGA. XR1 MS A324002.
Elizabeth Winstanley was daughter of Israel Winstanley, law partner of George Palmer. Archibald Mackinnon was Master of the Chancery, Guelph. Part of the Guelph Historical Society Collection.

2516. Wissler, Sem. **Correspondence, 1874; 1894; 1921.** 6 documents. Loc: WCA. Detailed list of contents.

    A collection of five brief letters and one receipt, including a letter of condolence to Mrs John Mundell on the death of her husband from the Elora Irvine Lodge, signed by Sem Wissler, 'Worshipful Master'. Also included is a 1921 letter from the Sem Wissler Insurance Company regarding a renewal of policy. Part of the Wissler Collection.

2517. Wright Family. **Obituaries, 1832-1875.** 2 documents. Loc: GCM.

    The obituary of James Wright of Guelph Township notes that he held the positions of reeve and warden in Wellington County and was a key promoter of the building of Brock Road. The record also provides an obituary of Wright's wife, Maria, who died in 1875.

2518. Yeomans Family. **Papers, 1871-1955.** 5 file folders, 3 ledgers. Loc: WCA. List of document contents.

    Correspondence between family members, of membership in churches, clubs and societies. The collection includes a ledger pertaining to drug store transactions which appears to be related to the business of L.H. Yeomans of Mount Forest. The record also contains programs of Mount Forest school and church recitals. The Wellington County Archives has developed a detailed finding aid noting the content, date and names of individuals mentioned in specific sources. Also contains family photographs. Comprises the Rantoul Collection.

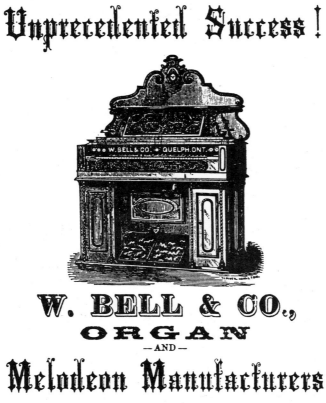

Unprecedented Success!

W. BELL & CO.,
ORGAN
— AND —
Melodeon Manufacturers
GUELPH, ONT

Received at Kingston Provincial Exhibition for 1871 A SILVER MEDAL
and ALL THE FIRST PRIZES. . . At London Western Fair, a DIPLOMA and
THE FIRST PRIZES. . . At the Central Exhibition, Guelph, three out of the
FIRST PRIZES, for the Best Melodeon and Best Cabinet Organ of any
kind. . . At the Great Central Fair, Hamilton, a DIPLOMA and ALL
four first for Music, viz: Both firsts for Organs, and first for best Melodeon
of any kind. Also, two Extra Prizes and the only Diploma awarded by the
Judges for general excellence.

☞ *All Instruments warranted for 5 Years.*
FOR ILLUSTRATED CATALOGUE ADDRESS   W. BELL & CO.

Unprecedented success! An advertisement for W. Bell and Company in Guelph,
which in 1887 became the Bell Organ Company.
Taken from Gazetteer and Directory of the County of Wellington for 1871-72,
(Hamilton: A.O. Loomis and Company, 1871), p. 8.

MISSES McLEAN & MITCHELL,
MILLINERS AND DRESSMAKERS
ELORA STREET, HARRISTON, ONT.

Dominion Fancy Store,
UPPER WYNDHAM STREET, GUELPH, ONT.
A full assortment always on hand. Agent for the celebrated Wanzer and other Sewing Machines. MRS. WM. WRIGHT, Proprietress.

MRS. KYLE,
(FORMERLY MRS. MOYES,)
Dealer in and manufacturer of
Ladies' Underclothing,
Childrens' Suits,
Chignons, Switches,
Brushes, Berlin Wools,
Baskets, Jewellery,
And other Fancy Goods.
A good stock always on hand. WEST MARKET SQUARE.

BERLIN WOOL & FANCY GOODS STORE.
MRS. HUNTER,
DEALER IN WOOLS OF ALL DESCRIPTION,
FANCY GOODS, TOYS, &c.
Market Square, Guelph.
Stamping done to order. A large and varied assortment always on hand.

MRS W. F. GALBRAITH,
GROCER AND PROVISION DEALER, PAISLEY STREET,
GUELPH, ONTARIO.

MRS. GEORGE SINCLAIR,
DEALER IN
Staple and Fancy Dry Goods, Millinery and Mantles,
CHOICE FAMILY GROCERIES.
ELORA, ONTARIO.

M. SHEPPARD,
WATCH - MAKER AND JEWELER,
A fine assortment of Watches, Clocks and Jewelery always on hand.
Agent for the celebrated American Watches.
GEDDES ST., ELORA, ONT.

MRS. C. IRVING,
Millinery and Dressmaking. I have a Select Stock of Millinery, comprising all the Latest Styles in Bonnets, Hats, Flowers, Feathers, Ribbons, Shapes, Dress Patterns, &c., at the very lowest figure. Dressmaking promptly attended to. Metcalf Street, Elora.

MISS A. SEVERIGHT,
Millinery and Berlin Wool Establishment,
Next door to the Post Office,
Metcalf Street, - - - - - Elora, Ontario.

Businesswomen in Wellington County c1870:
Business cards of women from Wellington County directories between 1869 and 1873.

GAZETTEERS AND DIRECTORIES

These printed materials can provide essential data for identifying and locating people and activities in the past. A **gazetteer** is a geographical dictionary that summarizes the salient details about localities in a region, province or country. A **directory** lists the names, addresses and occupations of the inhabitants of particular places. In addition, gazetteers and directories provide further contemporary evidence about the local organizations, key local officials, elected representatives and institutions which may be essential for understanding the fine detail presented in archival documents.

From early examples such as **Smith's Canadian gazetteer** (1846)[1] which provided bare details of the name, location and main economic activities and institutions of places, there was a rapid proliferation of such guides in the second half of the nineteenth century.[2] John Lovell of Montreal was specially active in the production of national and provincial directories that also combined features of gazetteers and set the pattern for other directory publishing businesses. Beginning with **Canada directory** (1851), Lovell's directories presented all places in a province in alphabetical order. Each place is first described in a short summary of its location and distance from other places, main economic activities, services and other distinctive features. Then follows an alphabetical list of the inhabitants (usually adult males) with their occupations and addresses.

Lovell's directories fed an appetite for useful knowledge. The publication of the **Canada directory for 1857-58** was greeted by Egerton Ryerson as 'without exception the most important and valuable book of the kind which has ever issued from the Canadian press. Though simply styled a "Directory", it is in truth a most valuable hand book, or guide to the Province of Canada, in its physical, social, educational, municipal and governmental aspects and relations.'[3] By 1871, Lovell's **Canadian Dominion directory** ran to more than 2500 closely printed pages and provided details for some 1300 places in Ontario and 550 in Quebec.

So rapid was the growth of population and the economy from the 1860s that there was a market for more regional and local directories. Special

---

[1] W.H. Smith, **Smith's Canadian gazetteer** (1846, Coles reprint 1970).

[2] Examples include **The Canadian almanac and repository of useful knowledge** published annually by Copp Clark of Toronto from c1848, followed by the **Canadian almanac & directory** 1890- . See also **The Canada guide**, and for more specialized users the Dun and Bradstreet reference books, law lists etc etc...

[3] Cited in D.E. Ryder, **Checklist of Canadian Directories 1790-1950** (Ottawa: National Library, 1979) vi.

directories, which were often called gazetteers as well, were compiled and published for counties or groups of counties, and for cities and towns. Five such guides were published for Wellington County between the first in 1867 and 1883. The Union Publishing Company of Ingersoll became particularly active from the 1880s in the production of Ontario county directories that listed all farmers by township, concession and lot number addresses and also all businesses in the local towns and villages.

Towns and cities of more than about 10,000 population were apparently large enough to warrant special directories of their own. These usually had three main sections in addition to general descriptive material and advertisements -- an alphabetical directory of residents (usually heads of households), a street directory with residents listed in street and street number order, and a classified business directory. At first local newspaper publishers may have produced directories as a sideline to their main business. But by the 1890s the compilation and publication of city directories had become a specialized line of business dominated in this region by Henry Vernon of Hamilton.

The directories found for Guelph and Wellington County are listed here in three groups. First are the national and provincial directories such as those of Lovell. Second, the county directories for Wellington County alone or for Wellington grouped with several adjoining counties. Third, there are directories for the city of Guelph. Only library and archival locations within this region are stated for each directory. For more distant locations the reader is referred to Dorothy Ryder's **Checklist** (1979).

Directories contain a wealth of interesting and useful information that can be used in conjunction with other primary sources.[4] However, users should be wary of assuming that any directory contains a complete and infallible guide. Several studies have compared the coverage of nineteenth-century directory with contemporary sources such as the manuscript census schedules or assessment rolls. Cross and Dudley found that only 60 per cent of the individuals in a 1871 census sample could be found in Lovell's 1871 directory for Montreal.[5] A comparison of the 1871 manuscript census evidence of industrial establishments in Guelph with details in Loomis's 1871 directory shows that only 10 per cent of the businesses listed in the census were not in the directory. However, the directory compilers seem to have had a gender bias, as hardly any of the female proprietors of industrial businesses recorded in the census source could be traced in the directory.[6]

---

[4] The value and limitations of directories for historical research are discussed in Gareth Shaw, 'Directories as sources in urban history: a review of British and Canadian material,' **Urban History Yearbook** (1984): 36-44 and Gareth Shaw, 'Nineteenth century directories as sources in Canadian social history,' **Archivaria** 14, (1982): 63-74.

[5] D.S. Cross and J.G. Dudley, 'Comparative study of street directories and census returns for 1871,' **Urban History Review** 3 (1972): 12-16.

[6] Research by Jane Turner for the 1871 Industrial Census Project, Guelph.

NATIONAL AND PROVINCIAL

2519. John Lovell. **Canada directory, 1851.** Montreal: John Lovell, 1851. 692 p. Loc: WCA, UGL.
The directory includes entries for Elora on page 79, Fergus on page 81, and Guelph on pages 92 and 586.

2520. John Lovell. **Canada directory, 1857.** Montreal: John Lovell, 1857. 1544 p. Loc: WCA, UGL.
Entries are listed alphabetically by name of village or town.

2521. John Lovell. **Lovell's 1871 Province of Ontario directory.** Montreal: John Lovell, 1871. 1122 p. Loc: WCA.
The directory has an index of place names.

2522. John Lovell. **Lovell's 1882 business and professional directory of the Province of Ontario.** Montreal: John Lovell, 1882. 1441 p. Loc: WCA.
The directory has an index of place names.

2523. Might Directories Ltd. **Business directory for Canada and Newfoundland, 1899.** Toronto: Might Directory Company, 1899. Pp. 507, 839, 881, 1185. Loc: WCA.
The directory lists types of businesses alphabetically by subject terms and has an index of advertisers by place of residence. The document lists six businesses operating in Guelph.

2524. Robertson and Cook. **Province of Ontario gazetteer and directory, 1869.** 718 p. mf. Loc: GPL, UGL.
The directory lists towns and villages in alphabetical order. It begins by describing each village and listing manufacturing establishments and numbers of 'hands' employed. The directory also lists names and occupations of individuals.

2525. Trade Publishing Company. **Canada's manufacturers, businesses and professional record and gazetteer, 1908.** Toronto: Trade Publishing Company, 1908. 896 p. Loc: GCM.
The directory lists name of individual or company alphabetically by province. There are several entries for Guelph and Wellington County in the Ontario section, from page 293 to 428. There is also a classified section arranged by business type.

2526. Union Publishing Company. **Business and professional directory of all cities in Ontario and includes Montreal, Quebec and Winnipeg, 1899-1900.** Ingersoll: Union Publishing Company, 1899. 527 p. Loc: UGL.
The directory is arranged alphabetically by business type. There are no separate entries arranged by geographical location.

2527. Union Publishing Company. **Province of Ontario gazetteer and directory, 1910-1911.** Ingersoll: Union Publishing Company, 1910. 1372 p. Loc: WCA.
A photocopy of Wellington County community entries.

COUNTY

2528. Armstrong and Delion. **Gazetteer and directory (1879-1880) of the County of Wellington**. Elmira: Armstrong and Delion, 1879. 186 p. mf. Loc: WCA.

2529. Evans, William W. **Wellington County (1883-1884) Gazetteer and directory**. 1883. 304 p. Loc: GPL, UGL.
 A listing of individuals or firms with a note of the occupation of county residents and their places of residence. The directory also lists individuals holding judicial and county government posts in 1883. The appendix of the directory includes a brief description of the townships, villages, and hamlets of the county. The directory also outlines the types of social institutions and businesses operating in the City of Guelph.

2530. Fisher and Taylor Publisher. **Gazetteer and directory (1875-1876) of the County of Wellington**. Toronto: Fisher and Taylor Publishers, 1875. 221 p. mf. Loc: WCA.

2531. Irwin and Burnham Publishers. **Gazetteer and directory (1867) of the County of Wellington**. Toronto: Henry Rounsell, 1867. Loc: WCA, GPL.

2532. A.O. Loomis and Company. **Gazetteer and directory (1871-1872) of the County of Wellington**. Hamilton: A.O. Loomis and Company, 1871. 238 p. Loc: WCA, GPL, UGL.
 The original directory was reprinted in 1971.

2533. Union Publishing Co. **Farmers' and business directory (1885-1886) for the Counties of Brant, Halton, Norfolk, Waterloo and Wellington**. Ingersoll: Union Publishing Company, 1885. 472 p. mf. Loc: WCA.
 The entries for Wellington County are on pages 117 to 193.

2534. Union Publishing Co. **Farmers' and business directory (1887) for the Counties of Waterloo and Wellington**. St Thomas: Union Publishing Company, 1887. Pp. 1-84. mf. Loc: WCA.

2535. Union Publishing Co. **Farmers' and business directory (1891) for the Counties of Halton, Peel, Waterloo and Wellington**. Ingersoll: Union Publishing Company, 1891. 408 p. mf. Loc: WCA.
 A photocopy of Wellington County community entries.

2536. Union Publishing Co. **Farmers' and business directory (1893) for the Counties of Peel, Waterloo and Wellington**. Ingersoll: Union Publishing Company, 1893. 364 p. mf. Loc: GPL.
 Wellington County entries begin on page 103 and are alphabetical by township and list name, post office, freeholder or tenant, and concession and lot number. The business directory is separate and lists towns and villages alphabetically, and notes name, occupation and establishments. The directory also contains a classified section that organizes businesses by type.

2537. Union Publishing Co. **Farmers' and business directory (1895) for the Counties of Grey, Waterloo and Wellington**. Ingersoll: Union Publishing Company, 1895. 153 p. Loc: GPL.
 Wellington County entries for cities, towns, villages and hamlets are

interspersed alphabetically with all other entries. The entries list name and occupation. There is a separate classified business directory that lists establishments by type.

2538. Union Publishing Co. **Farmers' and business directory (1896) for the Counties of Halton, Waterloo and Wellington.** Ingersoll: Union Publishing Company, 1896. 259 p. Loc: GPL, GCM.

The entries are alphabetical by township and list name, post office, freeholder or tenant, and concession and lot number. The directory includes a separate business directory, alphabetical by town or village, that lists the name of the proprietor and type of business. Entries for Wellington County are from pages 1 to 91.

2539. Union Publishing Co. **Farmers' and business directory (1899-1900) for the Counties of Halton, Waterloo and Wellington.** Ingersoll: Union Publishing Company, 1900. 529 p. mf. Loc: GPL.

Wellington County entries include name, post office, tenant or freeholder, and lot and concession number. The directory includes a separate business directory, alphabetical by town or village, that lists name of proprietor and type of business.

2540. Union Publishing Co. **Farmers' and business directory (1906) for the Counties of Halton, Waterloo and Wellington.** Ingersoll: Union Publishing Company, 1906. Pp. 113-216. Loc: GPL, WCA.

2541. Union Publishing Co. **Farmers' and business directory (1909) for the Counties of Dufferin, Halton, Peel, Waterloo and Wellington.** Ingersoll: Union Publishing Company, 1909. 467 p. Loc: GPL.

Wellington County entries begin on page 229 and include name, post office address, tenant or freeholder, and lot and concession number. The directory includes a separate business directory, alphabetical by town or village, that lists name or proprietor and type of business.

2542. Union Publishing Co. **Farmers' and business directory (1911) for the Counties of Dufferin, Halton, Peel, Waterloo and Wellington.** Ingersoll: Union Publishing Company, 1911. Pp. 227-319. mf. Loc: WCA.

2543. Vernon and Son Directories Limited. **Farmers' and business directories for Wellington County, 1915; 1918; 1924; 1931.** 1915. 4 volumes. Loc: GPL.

The microfilm is a copy of Wellington County entries which were part of a large directory of counties in Ontario. The directory lists the lot and concession number of residents and indicates whether individuals were freeholders or tenants. The directory also lists businessmen and their occupation, and indicates the names and locations of business firms in the county.

CITY

2544. Evans, William W. **Guelph directory, 1882-1883.** 1882. 242 p. Loc: GPL.

The directory includes a street directory and an alphabetical list of residents noting occupations. The directory also lists the location of business firms operating in the city.

2545. Evans, William W. **Guelph directory, 1885-1886.** Toronto: William W. Evans, 1884. 243 p. Loc: GPL.

A listing of social institutions, businesses and individuals living in the city. The directory includes a street and business directory of Guelph. The directory indicates the occupations of city residents.

2546. Hacking, J.H. **Directory of the Town of Guelph, 1873.** Guelph: Guelph Advertiser, 1873. 132 p. Loc: GPL, UGL.

A listing of residents which provides the 'name, business and place of residence of each adult male inhabitant'. The directory includes a brief historical sketch of the development of Guelph and a classified business directory.

2547. Henry Vernon. **City of Guelph directory (1894-1896), street, alphabetical, business and miscellaneous.** Hamilton: Henry Vernon Publisher, 1894. 152 p. mf. Loc: GPL.

A list of street name of residents, and of the occupation and name of the firm where specific individuals were employed in the city. The directory also notes the businesses operating in Guelph and the street name where each was located in the city, as well as listing social institutions and city and county municipal officials.

2548. Henry Vernon. **City of Guelph directory (1897-1899), street, alphabetical, business and miscellaneous.** Hamilton: Henry Vernon Publisher, 1897. 166 p. Loc: GPL.

2549. Henry Vernon. **City of Guelph directory (1901-1903), street, alphabetical, business and miscellaneous.** Hamilton: Henry Vernon Publisher, 1901. 190 p. Loc: GPL.

2550. Henry Vernon. **City of Guelph directory (1903-1905), street, alphabetical, business and miscellaneous.** Hamilton: Henry Vernon Publisher, 1903. 198 p. Loc: GPL.

2551. Henry Vernon. **City of Guelph directory (1905-1907), street, alphabetical, business and miscellaneous.** Hamilton: Henry Vernon Publisher, 1905. 210 p. Loc: GPL.

2552. Henry Vernon. **City of Guelph directory (1908-1909), street, alphabetical, business and miscellaneous.** Hamilton: Henry Vernon Publisher, 1908. 174 p. Loc: GPL.

2553. Henry Vernon. **City of Guelph directory (1910-), street, alphabetical, business and miscellaneous.** Hamilton: Henry Vernon and Son Publishers, Loc: GPL.

Beginning with the 10th edition in 1910, new editions were published annually except in 1919. The directories for the years from 1921 to 1927 are held only in hard copy.

2554. Taylor, William. **Charlton's gazetteer, business, street, and general directory of the Town of Guelph, 1875; 1876; 1877.** Toronto: R.M. Charlton Publisher, 1875. 122 p. mf. Loc: GPL, UGL.

An alphabetical listing of residents of the city which notes the street location of Guelph residents. The directory includes a listing of the occupation of residents and also presents an historical sketch of the city.

2555. Union Publishing Company. **Guelph city directory, 1889.** Ingersoll: Union Publishing Company, 1889. 120 p. mf. Loc: GPL.

A list of residents, alphabetical by name of businessmen, of private individuals, and of churches, city and county officers, and of various societies. The directory indicates the trade or profession of residents and their street number.

2556. Vernon Directories Limited. **City of Guelph directories (1930–1985), street, alphabetical, business and miscellaneous.** Hamilton: Vernon Directories Limited Publishers, Loc: GPL.

New editions were produced annually except in 1946 and 1948.

2557. W.H. Irwin and Company. **City of Guelph directory (1892–1894), street, alphabetical, general, miscellaneous and classified business.** Hamilton: Griffin and Kidner Printers, 1892. 128 p. mf. Loc: GPL, UGL.

A record of the trade or profession and the street name of residents of the city. The directory also lists businesses and social institutions functioning in Guelph. The directory is given the title years 1892 and 1894 but was published in 1892.

A collage of Guelph newspaper mastheads from 1847 to 1893,
reflecting the importance, variety and fragility of the newspaper
publishing industry in the nineteenth century.

NEWSPAPERS

Most Ontario communities have had at least one newspaper, usually a weekly[1]. Newspapers have had a powerful role in community development, both leading and reflecting public opinion and fostering local pride and loyalties. Susanna Moodie declared in 1853 that 'the Canadian cannot get along without his newspaper any more than an American could without his tobacco', though she also described a Canadian newspaper as 'a strange melange of politics, religion, abuse and general information'.[2] Pioneer weeklies boosted the community's sense of identity and prospects for growth, urging municipal incorporation and promoting innovations such as railways, new industrial enterprises and improved local services. From about 1850, local newspapers tended to be aligned with one political party or coalition, so that even quite small communities might have two or more rival papers. Though the grandiose names of the newspapers might suggest olympian detachment, most Ontario weeklies were in fact fiercely partisan.

Guelph and Wellington County produced their first local newspapers in the 1840s. Three Guelph weeklies, the **Herald** (1842, revived 1847-), **Advertiser** (1847-) and **Advocate** (1847-), began publication runs that lasted at least 25 years in each case. The **Guelph Herald** was started by Henry William Peterson who was first Registrar of the Wellington District and had previously published the first German-language newspaper in Canada, the **Canada Museum** in nearby Berlin.[3] The **Guelph Advertiser** was variously known as the **Guelph and Galt Advertiser and Wellington District Advocate**, the **Guelph Advertiser and General Intelligencer for the United Counties of Wellington and Grey**, and the **Guelph Advertiser and Elora and Fergus Examiner**. The **Guelph Mercury**, dates from 1854 as a weekly that was also known as the **Wellington Mercury and Guelph Chronicle** and the **Guelph Weekly Mercury and Advertiser**. From 1867 the **Mercury** ws also published as an evening daily; it took over the **Advertiser** in 1873 and the **Herald** in 1924 and has continued publication to the present. The **Guelph Herald** became a daily from 1871 until it was taken over

---

[1] The general patterns of newspaper development in communities across Ontario have been discussed in Elizabeth and Gerald Bloomfield, 'Local newspapers' in **Urban growth and local services: the development of Ontario municipalities to 1981** (University of Guelph: Occasional Papers in Geography 3, 1983).

[2] Susanna Moodie, Introduction to **Mark Hurdlestone** (1853), reprinted with first Canadian edition of her **Life in the clearings** (Toronto: Macmillan, 1959): 292-3.

[3] A.E. Byerly, 'Henry William Peterson' **Waterloo Historical Society** 19 (1931): 250-262. Articles about other newspaper publishers and editors are listed and indexed in **Guelph and Wellington County: a bibliography of settlement and development since 1900** (1988).

by the **Mercury** in 1924.[4] Twelve issues of an interesting weekly, the **Saturday Morning Sun**, were published in Guelph by James Hough Junior from October 1887.

The first weeklies of Elora and Fergus began in the 1850s and illustrate the distinctive names taken by Ontario newspapers and the way in which particular editors and publishers were linked through many different enterprises and mastheads. The **Elora Backwoodsman** lasted from 1852 to 1858 and the **Elora Satirist** from 1857 to 1859; in 1859 J.M. Shaw bought the **Backwoodsman** and proceeded to publish under the banner of the **Elora Observer**, sometimes lengthened with the addition of ...**and Guelph and Fergus Chronicle** or ...**and Salem and Fergus Chronicle**. In the late 1860s, the **Observer** took over the **Guelph Chronicle** and the **North Wellington Times** that had been published in Salem. By 1877 when it ceased publication the paper was known as the **Elora Observer and Centre Wellington Times**. The **Elora Express and County of Wellington Advertiser** was founded in 1869. J.M. Shaw became its publisher in late 1871 and the paper's name was changed to the **Lightning Express, Elora, Salem and Fergus News** when in 1874 it absorbed the **Elora News** (founded 1872). As the **Elora Express**, the paper was continuously published until 1972 when it amalgamated with the **Fergus News Record** to form the **Fergus-Elora News-Express**.[5]

In 1854 George Pirie founded the **Fergus Freeholder and General Advertiser for the Counties of Wellington and Grey**, which merged with a rival in 1857 to form the weekly with an even longer banner -- the **British Constitution, Fergus Freeholder and Nichol, Arthur, Guelph, Garafraxa, Amaranth and Orangeville Advertiser**. This newspaper was displaced in 1867 by the **Fergus News Record** which absorbed the **Canadian** in 1903 and continued to publish until its amalgamation with the **Elora Express** in 1972. Several short-lived weeklies were published in Elora and Fergus, sometimes connected with ventures in other Wellington County centres.

Various communities in Wellington County had their first local weeklies in the 1860s. In Arthur the **Advocate** began a short life and the **Enterprise** a much longer one that included amalgamation with a rival into the **Enterprise-News** in 1894.[6] The **Harriston Tribune** was published from 1869 after the demise of the earlier **Enterprise**. Three weeklies were established in Mount Forest in this decade, the **Confederate** (1867-) eventually prevailing and taking over rivals such as the **Examiner** and the **Representative**.

---

[4] An account of Guelph newspapers may be found in Hugh Douglass, 'A concise history of Guelph newspapers' **Publication of the Guelph Historical Society** 3, 3 (1963): 1-5.

[5] This account is based on 'Wellington County newspapers in the collection of the Wellington County Museum and Archives' (Wellington County Archives).

[6] The editorial content of the **Enterprise News** has been analyzed for booster attitudes in Patricia McGoldrick Goldberg, 'Editorial booster spirit in Arthur, 1900-1910' **Wellington County History** 1 (1987): 34-52.

Places that saw their first weeklies between 1870 and 1890 were Drayton (with two short-lived papers as well as the more enduring **Times** from 1885 and **Advocate** from 1889), Palmerston (the **Progress** and the **Telegraph**), Clifford (the **Express**) and Erin (the **Advocate**). Hillsburgh is unusual in Wellington County as an unincorporated centre that supported two weekly newspapers in the early 1880s (the short-lived **Wasp** and the more durable **Beaver**).

Our chronological summary and inventory are limited to those newspapers for which at least a few copies survive. It is hard enough to trace the connections between mastheads that might have been launched by the same editors and publishers who aspired to serve ever larger market areas. It is also a difficult task to specify the newspaper holdings of particular collections. We have depended on various compilations made by others -- the **Union list** of 1977[7], Gilchrist's **Inventory** of 1987[8] and local inventories made by the staff of the Wellington County Archives and Guelph Public Library[9], as well as our own enquiries.

But the transfer of surviving issues between collections can quickly date any compilation. For example, all the Wellington County newspapers listed by Gilchrist as held by the Regional History Collection at the University of Western Ontario were transferred to the University of Guelph Library's Archival and Special Collections and several newspaper issues were transferred from the Archives of Ontario to the Wellington County Archives in 1988. Similarly, our notations of the availability of newspapers on microfilm may be overtaken by new projects.

Newspapers can be an invaluable source of both factual and attitudinal evidence. Where other records have been lost, we may look to the newspapers for reports of all sorts of local events, from meetings of voluntary associations or municipal councils to details of new buildings. Local newspapers also produced occasional special issues including current and historical information not obtainable otherwise. From as early as the 1860s, Guelph and Elora papers ran series of historical articles about Wellington County that provide us with information about early settlement and development.[10] Most researchers in the

---

[7] National Library of Canada, **Union list of Canadian newspapers held by Canadian libraries** (Ottawa: 1977).

[8] J. Brian Gilchrist, comp. **Inventory of Ontario newspapers, 1793-1986** (Toronto: Micromedia, 1987).

[9] Linda J. Kearns, ed. **Guelph Public Library: list of microfilmed and manuscript newspapers** (Guelph: Guelph Public Library, 1984); **Wellington County newspapers in the collection of the Wellington County Museum and Archives**.

[10] The historical articles published in the **Mercury** have been listed and indexed in **Guelph and Wellington County: a bibliography of settlement and development since 1900** (1988). For a brief account of the articles in the **Observer**, see Steve Thorning, 'Historical writing on Wellington County'

history of communities have experienced the delightful distraction of straying into all the extraneous material surrounding whatever they were really searching for in local newspapers.

Only in the past decade has attention become concentrated on the issues of preserving newspapers and making their information more readily accessible[11]. Local historical research has been now greatly aided by recent projects of microfilming and indexing newspapers, in addition to inventorying them. The Guelph Mercury, in both its weekly and daily editions, has now been microfilmed by Intech for most of the period since 1870 (except when no originals have survived). Thanks largely to the efforts of genealogists, short runs of several local papers have been indexed. According to a recent National Library checklist,[12] there are indexes to the **Elora Backwoodsman** (April 1852-August 1853), the **Guelph Advertiser** (January 1847-c1850), the **Guelph Herald** (June 1850-June 1851) and to the Centennial Edition of the **Guelph Mercury** in 1927.

Wellington County History 1 (1987): 71-72.

[11]. The preface to Gilchrist's **Inventory** refers to the Decentralized Program for Canadian Newspapers developed by the National Library from 1979 and the Task Force on Ontario Newspapers that sponsored the production of the **Inventory**.

[12] Sandra Burrows and Franceen Gaudet, **Checklist of indexes to Canadian newspapers** (Ottawa: National Library of Canada, 1987).

2558. **Arthur Advocate, 1862.** Weekly. Loc: AO.
The Archives of Ontario holds three issues for March 22, 29 and June 27, 1862.

2559. **Arthur Enterprise, 1896; 1898-1899; 1902-present.** Weekly. Loc: AO, WCA.
The Archives of Ontario holds one issue for December 8, 1898. The Wellington
County Archives has incomplete holdings for the other years listed. The
newspaper began publication in 1863 and united with the Wellington News in 1894
to form the Arthur Enterprise-News.

2560. **Arthur Enterprise-News, 1896; 1899; 1902-1988.** Weekly. Loc: WCA.
The newspaper began publication in 1863 and is still in operation. The
Wellington County Archives has incomplete holdings for the years listed. In
1894, the Arthur-Enterprise joined with the Wellington News, to form the **Arthur
Enterprise-News.** The date of first publication for the Wellington News is c1892;
there are no known repositories.

2561. **Clifford Express, 1915; 1925-1927.** Weekly. Loc: WCA.
The newspaper was published from 1892 to 1933. Not all issues are held for the
years listed.

2562. **Drayton Advocate, 1892-1893; 1897-1963.** Weekly. Loc: WCA.
The newspaper was published from 1889 to 1966. Not all issues are held for the
years listed.

2563. **Drayton Enterprise, 1874.** Weekly. Loc: AO.
The only issue held for the newspaper is April 16, 1874. No information is
known about years of publication.

2564. **Drayton News Era, 1883.** Weekly. Loc: WCA.
One issue is held for April 26, 1883. The newspaper began publication c1883.

2565. **Drayton Times, 1888.** Weekly. Loc: WCA.
One issue is held for April 10, 1888. The newspaper was published from 1885 to
1902.

2566. **Elora Backwoodsman, 1852-1858.** Weekly. mf. Loc: WCA, UGL, AO, MUL, UTL.
The Wellington County Archives and the University of Guelph Library hold
sporadic issues from 1852 to 1858. Sporadic microfilmed issues are held by the
North York Public Library, the University of Guelph Library, the McMaster
University Library and the University of Toronto Library.

2567. **Elora Express, 1869-1972.** Weekly. Loc: GPL, UGL, WCA, UTL, AO.
The newspaper was published from 1869 to 1972. The Guelph Public Library holds
occasional issues for 1910, 1931 and 1933. The Wellington County Archives holds
sporadic issues from 1872 to 1887, a complete set from 1892 to 1972, as well as
occasional issues from 1869 to 1900 transferred from AO in 1988. The University
of Guelph Library holds sporadic issues from 1871 to 1887, 1891-2, 1897 to 1914,
and 1942, including issues formerly held by the University of Western Ontario
Library. The University of Toronto Library holds a complete set from 1869 to
1870. The Archives of Ontario holds occasional issues from 1909, 1931, 1940 and
1952. The title varies to c1880 as Elora Lightning Express and, after absorbing
the Elora News, as the Lightning Express, Elora, Salem and Fergus News.

2568. **Elora News, 1872-1874.** Weekly. Loc: WCA, AO, UGA.

The newspaper was published from 1872 to 1874. The Wellington County Archives holds sporadic issues from 1872 to 1874. Hard copies held by the Archives of Ontario were transferred to WCA during 1988. The University of Guelph Library holds sporadic issues from 1873 to 1874. At times the newspaper was also entitled Elora News: A Political, Commercial and Home-circle Journal.

2569. **Elora Observer, 1859-1877.** Weekly. Loc: WCA, AO, UGL.

The newspaper was published from 1859 to 1877. The Wellington County Archives holds complete issues for 1859, 1861 to 1867, and for January and February 1868. The Archives of Ontario and the University of Guelph Library hold complete sets on microfilm from 1859 to 1877. At times the newspaper was also entitled Elora Observer and Salem and Fergus Chronicle, and Elora Observer and Centre Wellington Times.

2570. **Erin Advocate, 1885; 1909-1929.** Weekly. Loc: AO, WCL, NLC.

The Wellington County Library holds a complete microfilmed set from 1909 to 1929. The Archives of Ontario holds sporadic issues from 1909 to 1929. The National Library of Canada holds an issue for June 11, 1885.

2571. **Fergus Advocate, 1885; 1889.** Weekly. Loc: AO.

The newspaper was published from 1885 to 1889. The Archives of Ontario holds two issues: September 16, 1885 and March 20, 1889.

2572. **Fergus Beaver, 1872.** Weekly. Loc: AO.

The newspaper began and ended c1872. The Archives of Ontario holds two issues: July 22, 1872 and August 1, 1872.

2573. **Fergus British Constitution, 1857-1866.** Weekly. Loc: UGA, WCA.

The Wellington County Archives holds issues from 1857 to 1866, any hard copies previously held by the Archives of Ontario having been transferred during 1988. The University of Guelph Library holds one issue for September 25, 1863. At times the newspaper was also entitled British Constitution and Fergus Freeholder; and British Constitution, Fergus Freeholder, Nichol, Arthur, Guelph, Garafraxa, Amaranth and Orangeville General Advertiser.

2574. **Fergus Canadian, 1899-1903.** Weekly. Loc: WCA, NLC, AO.

The newspaper was published from 1899 to 1903. It was absorbed by the Fergus News-Record in 1903. The Wellington County Archives holds sporadic issues from 1900 to 1903. The National Library holds one issue for March 2, 1899. The Archives of Ontario holds one issue for January 25, 1900, a complete set from May 1 to December 25, 1902, and a complete set from January 8 to October 22, 1903.

2575. **Fergus Express, 1871.** Weekly. Loc: AO.

The newspaper was published from 1871 to 1873. The Archives of Ontario holds occasional issues for 1871.

2576. **Fergus Freeholder, 1854-1857.** Weekly. Loc: WCA.

The newspaper was published from 1854 to c1857. It united with the Fergus British Constitution to form the British Constitution and Fergus Freeholder. At times the newspaper was also entitled Fergus Freeholder and General Advertiser for the Counties of Wellington and Grey. The Wellington County Archives holds sporadic issues from 1854 to 1857.

2577. **Fergus Lightning Express, 1872.** Weekly. Loc: AO.
The newspaper began and ended publication in 1872. At times it was entitled Lightning Express and Elora, Douglas and Arthur Chronicle. The Archives of Ontario holds a complete set from January 5, 1872 to October 31, 1872.

2578. **Fergus News-Record, 1867-1972.** Weekly. Loc: WCA.
The newspaper was published from 1867 to 1972. It absorbed the Fergus Canadian in 1903. The Wellington County Archives holds sporadic issues from 1867 to 1872 and a complete set from 1923 to 1972. The Archives of Ontario held occasional copies for 1869-71 and a complete set from January 5, 1872 to October 31, 1872, but all hard copies for 1869-1972 were transferred from AO to WCA in 1988.

2579. **Fergus Press, 1922-1923.** Weekly. Loc: WCA, AO.
The newspaper was published in 1922-1923. The Wellington County Archives holds issues for April 27, 1922 and May 1922. The Archives of Ontario holds two issues for April 27, 1923 and May 4, 1923.

2580. **Guelph Advertiser, 1847-1873.** Weekly. Loc: GPL, AO, UGL, UTL, NLC.
Not all issues are held for every year, and the paper has several name variations in its span of publication from 1844 to 1873. The Guelph Public Library has issues on microfilm from 1847 to 1857 and two original issues in 1864 and in 1865. The Archives of Ontario has a number of issues covering the period 1847 to 1873. The University of Guelph holds several issues on microfilm from 1847 to 1856 and one issue for 1860. The University of Toronto holds two issues in 1861.

2581. **Guelph Advocate, 1847-1900.** Daily. Loc: NLC, GPL, AO, UGA, WCA.
The Wellington County Archives holds issues from 1847 to 1861. The National Library of Canada holds only one issue for 1900. The Archives of Ontario holds one issue for 1897. The University of Guelph Library holds one issue for 1896.

2582. **Guelph Chronicle, 1867-1868.** Weekly. Loc: AO, UGL.
The Guelph Chronicle ran for only a few issues and was then absorbed by the Elora Observer in February 1868. The Archives of Ontario holds one issue in 1867 and several in January and February of 1868. The University of Guelph holds issues for January and February 1868.

2583. **Guelph Daily Herald, 1871-1923.** Daily. Loc: GPL, AO, NLC, UGA. UGA: XR2 MS A042.
The Guelph Herald was absorbed by the Guelph Mercury in 1924. The Guelph Public Library holds a number of issues from 1871 to 1910. The National Library of Canada holds one issue for 1878. The Archives of Ontario holds eight issues for the period 1876 to 1923. The University of Guelph Library has sporadic issues between 1872 and 1923.

2584. **Guelph Evening Mercury, 1867-present.** Daily. Loc: GPL, AO, NLC, MUL, UGL, UTL, WCA.
The Guelph Mercury newspaper was published as a daily from 1867 to 1873 when

it became known as the Guelph Evening Mercury. The Guelph Public Library holds a large number of issues dating from 1867 to the present with some gaps in the series. The McMaster University Library holds a series of issues from 1901 to 1920. The National Library of Canada holds sporadic issues from 1869 to 1980. The Archives of Ontario holds sporadic issues from 1867 to 1981. The University of Guelph Library holds sporadic issues dating from 1877 with more frequent holdings from 1901 to the present. The University of Toronto Library holds one issue from 1870. The Wellington County Archives holds sporadic issues from 1867 to 1978. The Guelph Herald was absorbed by the Guelph Mercury in 1924. Intech has produced a microfilm copy of most issues that have been traced.

2585. **Guelph Herald, 1842; 1847-1899.** Weekly. Loc: AO, UTL, GPL, UGL, WCA.
The Guelph Herald operated for only nine months in 1842, and began again in 1847. The Archives of Ontario holds a number of issues from 1842 to 1892. The University of Toronto holds two issues for 1842 and one for 1848. The Guelph Public Library holds issues for 1847, 1848 and 1850 to 1851, and single issues for 1887 and 1899. The University of Guelph holds sporadic issues from 1850 to 1899. The Wellington County Archives holds single issues in 1842, 1886, 1892, 1895 and 1889.

2586. **Guelph Mercury, 1854-1927.** Weekly. Loc: GPL, NLC, AO, MUL, UTL, UGA, WCA.
The Guelph Public Library holds a large number of issues from 1883 to 1928. The National Library of Canada holds a sporadic series of issues from 1854 to 1927. The Archives of Ontario holds several issues from 1862 to 1927. The McMaster University Library holds issues dating from 1902 to 1917, and the University of Toronto Library holds one issue for 1867. The University of Guelph Library holds a sporadic series of issues from 1866 to 1913. The Wellington County Archives holds a number of original issues dating from 1877 to 1927.

2587. **Guelph Weekly Pioneer, August 1, 1927.** Weekly. Loc: AO.
A single issue paper was published by the Guelph Mercury which is held at the Archives of Ontario.

2588. **Harriston Review, 1935.** Weekly. Loc: AO.
The newspaper commenced publication in 1896. The Archives of Ontario holds five issues for 1935.

2589. **Harriston Tribune, 1891.** Weekly. Loc: WCA.
The newspaper commenced publication in 1869. The Wellington County Archives holds one issue for 1891.

2590. **Hillsburgh Beaver, 1881-1911.** Weekly. Loc: WCA, AO.
The newspaper was published c1880 to 1911. It began as an election campaign paper for Dr George T. Orton. The Wellington County Archives and the Archives of Ontario hold occasional issues fron 1881 to 1911.

2591. **Hillsburgh Wasp, 1881.** Weekly. Loc: WCA.
The newspaper was published from c1880 to c1881. The Wellington County Archives holds one issue for October 8, 1881.

2592. **Mount Forest Confederate, 1867-1967.** Weekly. Loc: GPL, NLC, AO, WCA.
The newspaper began operations in 1862 and functioned as a weekly, absorbing

the Mount Forest Examiner in 1880 and the Mount Forest Representative in 1918. The Wellington County Archives holds sporadic issues from 1870 to the present. The National Library of Canada holds one issue for 1878 and two for 1967. The Archives of Ontario holds issues from 1870 to 1936. The Guelph Public Library holds two issues for 1933.

2593. **Mount Forest Examiner, 1862-1865.** Weekly. Loc: NLC, AO.
   The paper commenced publication in 1862 and was united with the Mount Forest Confederate in 1880. The National Library of Canada holds one issue from 1862 and one from 1864. The Archives of Ontario holds two issues from 1862 and one from 1863.

2594. **Mount Forest Express, 1861-1862.** Weekly. Loc: AO.
   The Archives of Ontario holds five issues for 1861 and one for 1862.

2595. **Mount Forest Representative, 1885-1918 (sporadic).** Weekly. Loc: AO, UGA, WCA.
   The newspaper commenced publication in 1885 and was united with the Mount Forest Confederate in 1918 to form the Mount Forest Confederate and Representative. The Archives of Ontario holds sporadic issues from 1885 to 1918. The Wellington County Archives holds four issues between 1885 and 1914.

2596. **Orangeville Sun, 1862-1933.** Weekly. Loc: AO, GPL, UTL.
   The newspaper commenced publication in 1861 and was absorbed by the Orangeville Banner in 1933. The Orangeville Banner office holds a complete set of the Orangeville Sun in hard copy and in microfilm, and HUD Associates of Orangeville have prepared a good part of a machine-readable index to the newspaper. The other repositories hold only sporadic issues.

2597. **Palmerston Observer, 1936 (sporadic).** Weekly. Loc: WCA.
   The newspaper commenced publication in 1933. The Wellington County Archives holds several issues for the year 1936.

2598. **Palmerston Progress, 1874-1875 (sporadic).** Weekly. Loc: AO.
   The Archives of Ontario holds a few issues for the years 1874 and 1875.

2599. **Palmerston Telegraph, 1879-1892.** Weekly. Loc: AO, WCA.
   The Wellington County Archives holds one issue in 1892. The Archives of Ontario holds two issues, one in 1879 and one in 1883.

2600. **Saturday Morning Sun, October 1887 to January 1888.** Guelph: James Hough Jr, 8 file folders. Loc: GPL.
   A weekly journal published by James Hough Junior with the files containing seven issues: numbers 1, 2, 4 to 6, 10, and 12. The journal includes editorials discussing labour issues, the temperance movement, and the national question of protectionism versus commercial union with the United States. The paper also presented reports of the activities of the city's police court, city council and board of education and of social and sporting events. The November 12 issues includes a brief discussion of the question of city industries being entitled to tax exemptions. The Saturday Morning Sun was sometimes critical of the journalism of the Guelph Mercury and referred to it as 'a disloyal journal'.

Canada Company town: Guelph in 1830, with the Priory store building in the centre. The forest cover, though which the road from Waterloo has been cut, is very evident, in contrast to the cleared landscape of the next plate. The earliest view of the town, published in <u>Fraser's Magazine</u>, November 1830. (National Archives of Canada)

LAND RECORDS

Land records have great potential research value. From the first surveyors' descriptions through the evidence of subsequent transactions that were filed in local registry offices we may trace the processes of surveying and subdividing the land for private ownership and development. Land records can be very useful in documenting family history and the wealth of individual property-owners[1]. The land records inventoried here are of four general types:

1. In the period of first settlement, the land of southern Ontario was surveyed into a **basic survey fabric** of townships, concessions and lots. **Surveyors' notebooks** and other papers describe the nature of the land surface -- its relief, drainage, vegetation cover, and potential for settlement and development. The largest collection of such records, spanning the period 1819-1855 for parts of Wellington County, has been microfilmed by the Ontario Ministry of Natural Resources.[2] The papers of various individual surveyors have also been preserved in several repositories. There is a large collection of the papers of Charles Rankin, who surveyed Minto Township and other areas in North Wellington, in the Metro Toronto Central Reference Library (#2738). The survey journal of Robert Wells for 1847, held in the University of Guelph Library's Special Collections, includes pen sketches of features of the landscape of South Wellington (#2782). Maps and plans of Wellington County drawn by surveyors are listed in the next section.

2. Original title to land was passed by **Crown patents**. Records of the first grantholders of land in Wellington County survive in various forms. The Canada Company's registers of sales and leases identify grantees, lessees and patentees who received land from the Company. The records of the Crown Lands Department and the Surveyor-General contain official details of grants and leases of land, including those of the Canada Company. The Wellington County Crown Land Agency, based at Elora from 1842 to 1879 to administer the local disposition of public land, has left unusually rich records (#2769). Details of those settlers who received original Crown land grants by deed or patent have been compiled into the Archives of Ontario's computerized Land

---

[1] An excellent example is the thesis of Marilyn Armstrong, 'Growth strategy and land ownership in the development of a community, Guelph, Canada West, 1852-1861' (M.A. thesis, University of Guelph, 1984). See also: Randy W. Widdis, 'Tracing property ownership in nineteenth-century Ontario: a guide to the archival sources,' in **Canadian Papers in Rural History** II (Gananoque: Langdale Press, 1980): 83-102.

[2] See also Louis Gentilcore and Kate Donkin, 'Land surveys of southern Ontario: an introduction and index to the field notebooks of the Ontario land surveyors, 1784-1859,' supplement to **Cartographica** 10, 1973, 116 p.

Records Index.[3]

3.   Miscellaneous items or small collections of land records have survived for particular localities.   One is the set of letters by John Arkell describing the survey and settlement of part of Puslinch Township in the early 1830s (#2604). Another is the series of petitions by black settlers in the Queen's Bush in the 1840s for exemption from a new requirement that settlers should buy land with a full cash payment (#2739-#2742).[4]   A third example is the Elora Land Records Collection, comprising records spanning the period 1826-1903 and arranged alphabetically by street name or concession and lot numbers for Elora and surrounding townships.

4.   Most of the land records inventoried here were accumulated in the two land **Registry Offices** of Wellington County.   In the period of district government of Upper Canada, Registry Offices were opened for each southern Ontario district (or county after 1850), and later for each electoral district if there was more than one in a county.   The first Registrar of Deeds for the District of Wellington was appointed in 1837, but a Registry Office was not erected in Guelph until 1847.   The Arthur Registry Office has served northern Wellington County since 1862.

The registry system of recording the ownership and transfer of land is one of the oldest continuous forms of government service in Ontario, having been first established in 1795.   The essential function of a registry office has been to receive, store and permit the retrieval of documents relating to land ownership and encumbrances.   The registry system does not verify the legality of these documents or guarantee title to land; solicitors acting for the parties in land transactions are responsible for these functions.   A 40-year rule was introduced in 1929, making it necessary to search back no further than forty years to establish ownership.[5]

The land records of the registry offices reflect several successive systems of land definition and registration:

*   Under the original 1795 legislation, the registrar had to copy details into a **Copy Book of Deeds** and witness the **memorial** of each land transaction after the initial patenting.   A memorial was an abstract or shortened form of the document, containing some details of the complete description of the land and parties to the transaction but often omitting price.   The memorials were numbered and the registrar had to keep an alphabetical calendar of all townships and parishes within the county and an index to the names of the

[3] Brenda Dougall Merriman, 'An interpretation of the Ontario Land Records Index,' **Families** 25, 2 (1986): 77-83.

[4] We are indebted to Ian Easterbrook for finding these records.

[5] The account given here is based in part on useful material compiled by Ken McCrea, the present Guelph Registrar, and by Susan Bellingham of the University of Waterloo Library in a 'Finding Aid to the Waterloo County Land Registration Copy Books.'

parties including both grantors and grantees. At first there was a single registry series for each district. The indexes were usually small separate volumes and not all have survived.

* For the period prior to 1846, searching titles can be done either backwards or forwards in time, using names as links between successive transfers of land. The search forward will be hampered if the original survey has not survived. A title search within the original boundaries of Guelph is made relatively easy by the existence of a carefully delineated plan and numbering system of lots made by the Canada Company from 1827.

* From 1846, separate registers had to be kept for each township, city, town or village and each registry had to have a fireproof vault. The 1846 Act also provided that all surveys and subdivisions of land into town and village lots could be registered, while an 1849 Act required that all such survey and subdivision plans had to be certified by a Provincial Land Surveyor and registered in a local Registry Office (this requirement was endorsed in an 1859 Act). The 1849 Act led to some confusion as it appeared to be retroactive only and not to apply to subsequent subdivisions. Mandatory registration of all survey plans was not enacted until 1859.

* In 1865, when the basic survey of southern Ontario was complete, the registration system was changed again. All documents or instruments were required to be registered at full length, no longer as a memorial. Each registrar was to create in a new volume an **Abstract Index to Deeds** register by entering under a separate heading each individual lot or part lot as originally patented by the Crown and every instrument concerning such lots identified by registration number, date, names of grantors and grantees, consideration of mortgage money paid, etc. The 1865 Act also required that any instrument to be registered should conform to the corresponding survey plan, and that all subdivision plans were to be registered within three months of the actual date of survey. The Abstract Indexes thus provide a capsule history by lot and concession with all documents indexed on a geographical basis. This is essentially the system used today. A page was set up for each township lot in the abstract book, and documents were registered and recorded on these pages in order of receipt. Separate books were opened for newly incorporated municipalities such as towns and villages. Whenever a register became unfit for use through age or continuous use, the registrar had to have a copy made and also keep the original.

* From 1865, **General Registers** were also started for the whole county to record wills, devises, powers of attorney affecting land, taking these out of the individual township registers. In the 1860s, instrument numbers became consecutive instead of distinct for each volume, and in the 1890s, individual volume indexes were discontinued.

* Other records held by registry offices are various types of maps and plans. These include the original county cadastral surveys of the 1850s showing the basic survey fabric of concessions and lots; registered subdivision plans; and compiled plans that fit together several interlocking plans and surveys to provide the total cadaster of a village, township or larger unit. All subdivision and compiled maps and plans are listed separately in the next section of this volume.

The Ontario Ministry of Consumer and Commercial Relations is now pursuing a policy of rationalizing the province's land records by microfilming and then purging most instruments relating to particular land transactions. All pre-1867 instruments have been microfilmed and the originals deposited in the Archives of Ontario. Instruments dating from between 1867 and 1948 have been purged after microfilming; the originals are to be destroyed, as are all records of discharged mortgages since 1948. The destruction of most of such records for Wellington County makes the surviving indexes and copy books held by record repositories all the more valuable. Wellington County's current land records are to be computerized, as part of the POLARIS (Province of Ontario Land Registry Information System) Project begun in 1972 and based on the model of Oxford County. In this system, each property is given a 19-digit property identification or PIN number.

As part of a records dispersal policy, **land registration copy books** and indexes for particular areas have been deposited in appropriate local collections. Thus the University of Guelph Library (Archival and Special Collections) has obtained the copy books and indexes for both North and South Wellington; microfilm copies are available for use by researchers. The Archives of Ontario also holds microfilm copies of most copy books. The **abstract indexes of deeds** are still in active use in the registry offices but microfilm copies of some, made by the Genealogical Society of Salt Lake City, are held in the Archives of Ontario.

LAND RECORDS

2601. Amaranth Tp. **Abstract index of deeds, 1823-1965.** 1 reel. mf. Loc: AO. GS 3538-3529.

Microfilmed by the Genealogical Society of Salt Lake City. The original volumes are held in the Orangeville Land Registry Office.

2602. Amaranth Tp. **Land registration copy books, 1847-1876.** 5 reels. mf. Loc: AO. GS 3530-3534.

Microfilmed by the Genealogical Society of Salt Lake City.

2603. Archives of Ontario. **Computerized land records index, 1780-1914.** 2 binders. Loc: AO, UGL, GPL. UGL: CA2ON RA 79C541-2.

A microfiche index to initial land grants in Ontario held at the Ontario Archives. It contains an alphabetical list by personal name of grantee and a separate alphabetical list by township. The information is derived from the Crown Land Records, Canada Company Papers and the Peter Robinson Papers, and refers only to the original alienation of land resulting in a deed or patent. The indexes list name of individual, township-town-city, lot number, concession number, issue date and archival reference number. All townships in the county are listed except Nichol and Pilkington. Guelph is the only urban centre listed.

2604. Arkell, John. **Letters to Honourable Peter Robinson, 1831-1833.** 7 letters. Loc: AO. FA: MU 1143.

Letters written to Peter Robinson in his capacity as Commissioner of Crown Lands regarding the survey and settlement of Puslinch Township and the need for roads to Hamilton and York. The Farnham Plains section of the township was being re-surveyed and John Arkell expresses his eagerness to settle that section with 'intelligent English people'. He reports on his plans and the progress of selling the two thousand acres of the Farnham Plains, including his own three hundred acres. The letter, dated 6 July 1831, includes a sketch plan identifying the owners of lots in NE Puslinch; most were said to be English with only one Irishman. A letter dated 10 September 1833 was once apparently part of the collection, but was reported missing in 1980 when the other letters were microfilmed. Part of the Peter Robinson Papers.

2605. Arthur Tp. **Abstract index of deeds, c1853-1987.** 10 volumes. Loc: ALR, AO. Volumes 45-54.

The index records land ownership of Concessions 1 to 12 and Lots 1 to 35 west and east of the Owen Sound Road, and roads and streets for the township. The index for the years 1846-1958 was microfilmed by the Genealogical Society of Salt Lake City, with copies in the Archives of Ontario (GS 3083-3084).

2606. Arthur Tp. **Index to land record registers, 1933-1959; 1972-1976.** 3 volumes. Loc: UGA.

2607. Arthur Tp. **Index to land records and location book, 1858-1954.** 1 volume. Loc: UGA.

2608. Arthur Tp: Kenilworth. **Abstract index of deeds, c1854-1986.** 1 volume. Loc: ALR. Volume 55.

The index records land ownership of Lots 1 to 227, park lots and Cushing's Surveys.

2609. Arthur Tp. **Land registration copy books, 1858-1954.** 32 volumes. Loc: UGA, AO. List of individual volumes.
     The microfilm copy made by the Genealogical Society of Salt Lake City covers the years 1847-1876 and is held by the Archives of Ontario (GS 3085-3092). Each reel has an alphabetical index of persons.

2610. Arthur V. **Abstract index of deeds, c1846-1988.** 9 volumes. Loc: ALR, AO. Volumes 78-86.
     The index records land ownership of the Crown Survey of Lots 1 to 109, and specific surveys including Chadwick's, Anderson's McCord's, Caroll's, Hollinger's, A.H. Macdonald's, Small's, Mitchell's and Clark's. The index for the years 1866-1952 was microfilmed by the Genealogical Society of Salt Lake City with copies in the Archives of Ontario (GS 3093).

2611. Arthur V. **Land registration copy books, 1872-1954.** 14 volumes. Loc: UGA, AO. List of individual volumes.
     The microfilm copy by the Genealogical Society of Salt Lake City covers the years 1872-1876 and is held by the Archives of Ontario (GS 3094). Each reel has an alphabetical index of persons.

2612. Brandon, Franklin. **Land records, Peel and Maryborough Townships, c1850-1950.** 7 boxes. Loc: WCA. MU 90-99.
     A collection of roughly 2,400 records kept by Franklin Brandon who was a land conveyance and insurance agent and Clerk-Treasurer of Drayton. Brandon lived from 1914 to 1986 but collected many earlier land records for Peel and Maryborough Townships. The collection includes deeds, insurance records, mortgages, patents, probate papers, and crown land sales.

2613. Burwell, Lewis. **Survey Diary. Luther Township, 1831.** 1 volume. Loc: AO. FA: RG-1, CB-1.
     Survey diaries and field notes describe the land surface and natural environment just prior to clearance and settlement. Held with records of the Surveyor-General.

2614. Burwell, Mahlon. **Survey Diary. Puslinch Township, 1827.** 1 volume. Loc: AO. FA: RG-1, CB-1.
     Survey diaries and field notes describe the land surface and natural environment just prior to clearance and settlement. Held with records of the Surveyor-General.

2615. Callaghan, P. **Survey Diary. Maryborough Township, 1848.** 1 volume. Loc: AO. FA: RG-1, CB-1, #8.
     Survey diaries and field notes describe the land surface and natural environment just prior to clearance and settlement. Held with records of the Surveyor-General.

2616. Canada Company. **Correspondence, land transfers and land grants, 1832-1862.** 35 items. Loc: MTL. Card index.
     Memorials of registration for land bought from the Canada Company. The only memorial for the Wellington County area is dated 1832 and refers to the purchase, by Andrew Fisher from Edinburgh, of one hundred acres of Lot 6, Concession 1, Division E in Guelph Township.

2617. Canada Company. **Indentures of lease for land, 1842-1850.** 1 oversize box with 327 items. Loc: MTL. Card index.

The collection includes indentures from all parts of Upper Canada (mainly for 1843) with twelve for Garafraxa Township in that year. The indentures, consisting of large printed forms, have specific details of each lessee (including name, current address and occupation) and a description of the lot. All twelve cases in Garafraxa Township were lessees of one hundred acre lots and all were due to pay three pounds, seven shillings and sixpence per annum. Added to each indenture was a caution that the lessee should consider very carefully the obligations set out in the text of the indenture, as rents had to be paid by the due dates or the lessee would forfeit all rights to the land.

2618. Canada Company. **Land business records, 1827-1951.** 45.5 m. Loc: AO. FA.

These records comprise grants, patents, releases and bonds, 1847-1859; surveys and field notes; registers and deed books, 1827-1949; natural resources records, 1863-1951; and miscellaneous land records. Registers and deed books include, as Volume 8, Register of Lands, Town Lots, Guelph, Goderich, Stratford, 1827-1880. Volume 23 includes a register of sales in various townships, including Guelph Township, 1827-1829; and Volume 28 is a register of contracts for Guelph, 1827-1910. Volumes 19-41 are indexed in the Computer Land Index and also available on microfilm. In the registers, each page is titled with the town/township name and has columns from left to right for running number (cumulative numbering of all lots in town), description (number and street), sale number, deed number, date of sale, and name of purchaser. Details for the Town of Guelph to the 1850s are on pages 74 to 136 of Volume 8.

2619. Canada Company. **Land Deeds. Guelph Township, 1834.** 2 documents. Loc: GPL. List of document contents; Envelope 4.

A deed of land granted to John Mitchell in 1834. Held with the Byerly Collection.

2620. Canada Company. **Land records, 1834-1836; 1843; 1845.** 15 documents. Loc: GCM.

A series of land deeds and leases for land in Guelph and Guelph Township to individuals including Richard Fowler Budd, Silas Edwards and Adam Fergusson.

2621. Canada Company. **List of lands for sale or lease, 24th October, 1859.** 1 item, oversize. Loc: UGA. XR6 MS A003.

A large broadside offering of lands, with a complete description of lots offered across Canada West including the County of Wellington (Townships of Garafraxa, Amaranth, Puslinch, Erin, Eramosa and one Guelph farm lot), as well as a description of terms of lease or sale and an invitation to deposit funds with company-sponsored savings and deposit banks.

2622. Clifford V. **Abstract index of deeds, c1854-1988.** 4 volumes. Loc: ALR, AO. Volumes 75-78.

The index records land ownership of Lots 1 to 358, park lots, a sawmill site, chair factory lot, cemetery lots and roads and streets in Clifford. The index for 1866-1958 was microfilmed by the Genealogical Society of Salt Lake City, with copies in the Archives of Ontario (GS 3288).

2623. Clifford V. **Land registration copy books, 1874-1954**. 7 volumes. Loc: UGA, AO.
List of individual volumes.
   The microfilm copy made by the Genealogical Society of Salt Lake City covers
the years 1874-1881 and is held in the Archives of Ontario (GS 3095). Each reel
has an alphabetical index of persons.

2624. Crown Lands Department. **Gore District. Inspection and valuation reports,
1829-1872**. 22 volumes. Loc: AO. FA: RG-1, A-VI-10.
   Volumes relevant to Wellington County are Volumes 1-2, clergy reserves,
1829-1837; Volume 3, certain lands in Puslinch, 1838; Volume 6, clergy reserves
in Peel Township, 1844; Volume 7, clergy reserves in Wellington District,
1844-1845; Volumes 12-14, Maryborough, 1849, 1858; Volume 16, certain lands in
Maryborough, Peel, 1858; Volume 17, certain lands in Peel Township, 1858; Volume
18, vacant lands in Minto, 1861; and Volume 22, certain lands in Wellington
County, 1872.

2625. Crown Lands Department. **Sales of clergy reserves, 1829-1924**. 12 volumes. Loc:
AO. FA: RG-1, C-III.
   Volume 9 specifically records sales in Puslinch Township, 1832-1834.

2626. Crown Lands Department. **Sales of Crown and Clergy Lands, 1827-1905**. 39
volumes. Loc: AO. FA: RG-1, C-III-5.
   In addition to various registers and index books, Volume 29 specifically
records sales of public lands in 1864 in Wellington County, and Volume 37 is an
index to Canada Company descriptions.

2627. Crown Lands Department. **Schedules and land rolls, 1784-1922**. 81 volumes. Loc:
AO. FA: RG 1, A-IV, MS 400.
   Volumes relevant to Wellington County are Volume 32, crown and clergy reserves
returned to Canada Company, 1824 (Reel 11); Volume 33, schedules for Canada
Company, 1825 (Reel 11); Volume 39, Canada Company land schedules, c1828 (Reel
12); Volume 65, squatters in Erin Township, 1850 (Reel 13); Volume 66, crown and
school lands in Township and Village of Arthur, 1851-1864 (Reel 13); and Volume
67, school lands in Huron, Bruce and Wellington Counties, 1857 (Reel 13).

2628. Drayton V. **Abstract index of deeds, c1866-1988**. 4 volumes. Loc: ALR, AO.
Volumes 71-74.
   A record of ownership of land on Lots 1 to 548 and the roads and streets of
the village. The index for 1862-1958 was microfilmed by the Genealogical Society
of Salt Lake City, with copies in the Archives of Ontario (GS 3098).

2629. Drayton V. **Land registration copy books, 1874-1954**. 9 volumes. Loc: UGA, AO.
List of individual volumes.
   The microfilm copy made by the Genealogical Society of Salt Lake City covers
the years 1875-1882 and is held by the Archives of Ontario (GS 3099). Each index
has an alphabetical index of persons.

2630. Elora Land Records Collection. **Elora, 1864-1903**. 6 file folders. Loc: WCA.
List of document contents by street name.
   A collection of land deeds, sale agreements and mortgages of specific
individuals living in Elora. The Wellington County Archives has developed a
detailed finding aid noting land transactions by street names and indicating the

dates of agreements and individuals involved in transactions.

2631. Elora Land Records Collection. **Garafraxa Township, 1831-1880.** 1 file folder. Loc: WCA. List of document contents.

A collection of correspondence, mortgages and land title searches conducted in Garafraxa Township. The Wellington County Archives has developed a detailed finding aid indicating contents, dates and individuals involved in specific land transactions.

2632. Elora Land Records Collection. **Luther Township, 1863-1878.** 1 file folder. Loc: WCA. List of document contents.

A record of two Crown land agreements of land transactions between two residents of Luther Township, and also between two residents of Elora.

2633. Elora Land Records Collection. **Maryborough Township, 1867.** 2 file folders. Loc: WCA. List of document contents.

A record of one land indenture agreement and two land conveyance documents.

2634. Elora Land Records Collection. **Minto Township, 1841-1872.** 1 file folder. Loc: WCA. List of document contents.

A record of receipts for payment of property taxes, indentures and land agreements. The Wellington County Archives has developed a detailed finding aid noting the date, contents and individuals involved in specific land agreements.

2635. Elora Land Records Collection. **Nichol Township, 1891-1904.** 1 file folder. Loc: WCA. List of document contents.

A collection of farm leases, one auction sale notice and correspondence regarding a land dispute written in 1904. The Wellington County Archives has developed a finding aid listing contents, dates and individuals involved in specific transactions.

2636. Elora Land Records Collection. **Peel Township, 1869-1877.** 1 file folder. Loc: WCA. List of document contents.

A registry office abstract of land transactions of a specific lot of land in Peel Township.

2637. Elora Land Records Collection. **Pilkington Township, 1861-1868.** 1 file folder. Loc: WCA. List of document contents.

A collection of various land agreements including mortgages, valuations, abstracts and indentures. The Wellington County Archives has developed a finding aid listing contents, dates and names of individuals involved in specific land transactions.

2638. Elora V. **Abstract index of deeds, 1854-1979.** 7 volumes. Loc: GLR, AO.

An index of land transactions in the village that notes date of registry, grantor, grantee, quantity of land, and consideration or amount of mortgage. The entries are entered in numerical order by lot, division and concession number. The index for 1850-1958 was microfilmed by the Genealogical Society of Salt Lake City, with copies in the Archives of Ontario (GS 3104-3105).

2639. Elora V. **Land agreements, 1859; 1864; 1874; 1876.** 6 documents. Loc: UGA. XR1 MS A115015.

A collection of six land records including a promissory note, three indentures, statement of lands in tax arrears in 1864 and a letter dealing with the construction of a fence at the Elora Cemetery in 1864. Held with the Connon Collection.

2640. Elora V. **Land registration copy books, 1860-1958.** 14 volumes. Loc: UGA, AO. List of individual volumes.

The microfilm held by the University of Guelph Archives begins in 1870. Each volume contains an index in alphabetical order by name of person. The microfilm copy made by the Genealogical Society of Salt Lake City covers the years 1860-1877 and is held by the Archives of Ontario (GS 3106-3108).

2641. Eramosa Tp. **Abstract index of deeds, 1823-1979.** 7 volumes. Loc: GLR, AO.

An index of land transactions in the township that notes date of registry, grantor, grantee, quantity of land, and consideration or amount of mortgage. The entries are entered in numerical order by lot, division and concession number. The index for 1809-1958 was microfilmed by the Genealogical Society of Salt Lake City, with copies in the Archives of Ontario (GS 3113-3114).

2642. Eramosa Tp. **Deeds, 1875; 1891; 1909; 1913; 1931; 1935.** 11 documents. Loc: ETO.

A record of land transactions including several for the Eramosa Agricultural Society.

2643. Eramosa Tp. **Land records, 1845; 1854.** 2 envelopes. Loc: WCA. MU75.

A record of two land purchase transactions in Eramosa Township.

2644. Eramosa Tp. **Land registration copy books, 1854-1958.** 24 volumes. Loc: UGA, AO. List of individual volumes.

The microfilm held in the University of Guelph Archives begins in 1868. Each volume contains an index in alphabetical order by name of person. The microfilm made by the Genealogical Society of Salt Lake City covers the years 1847-1876 and is held in the Archives of Ontario (GS 3115-3121).

2645. Eramosa Tp. **Register of memorial abstracts, 1819-1854.** 3 volumes. Loc: UGA. List of individual volumes.

A record of land transactions of Bargain and Sale Lands.

2646. Erin Tp. **Abstract index of deeds, 1801-1988.** Loc: GLR, AO.

The index for 1801-1948 was microfilmed by the Genealogical Society of Salt Lake City, with copies in the Archives of Ontario (GS 3122-3123).

2647. Erin Tp. **Land records, 1854.** 1 document. Loc: WCA. MU51.

A document labelled as a 'clergy sale grant' of land being granted to Johnston Speirs.

2648. Erin Tp. **Land records, 1874-1899 (sporadic).** 14 documents. Loc: WCA. MU 4.

A record of indenture agreements for Lot Dd in Erin Township. The record includes a copy of a land title search conducted in 1893 to trace the ownership of the lot.

2649. Erin Tp. **Land records, 1929.** 1 document. Loc: WCA. MU 51.

A record of land purchased in Erin Township in 1929.

2650. Erin Tp. **Land registration copy books, 1853-1958**. 38 volumes. Loc: UGA, AO. List of individual volumes.

The microfilm held in the University of Guelph Archives is from 1868 to 1957. Each volume contains an index in alphabetical order by name of person. The microfilm copy made by the Genealogical Society of Salt Lake City covers the years 1847-1876 and is held by the Archives of Ontario (GS 3124-3135).

2651. Erin Tp. **Register of memorial abstracts, 1822-1859**. 3 volumes. Loc: UGA. List of individual volumes.

The register from 1853 to 1859 is microfilmed with the land registration copy books of Erin Village, Reel 37. A record of land transactions of Bargain and Sale Lands.

2652. Erin V. **Land registration copy books, 1882-1959**. 6 volumes. Loc: UGA. List of individual volumes.

The microfilm is from 1893 to 1959. Each volume contains an index in alphabetical order by name of person.

2653. Erin V. **Register of memorial abstracts, 1822-1850**. 1 volume. Loc: UGA. List of individual volumes.

A record of land transactions of Bargain and Sale Lands.

2654. Fergus V. **Abstract index of deeds, 1841-1988**. 16 volumes. Loc: GLR, AO.

The index for 1841-1958 was microfilmed by the Genealogical Society of Salt Lake City, with copies in the Archives of Ontario (GS 3139-3140).

2655. Fergus V. **Land registration copy books, 1860-1958**. 19 volumes. Loc: UGA, AO. List of individual volumes.

Each volume contains an index in alphabetical order by name of person. The microfilm made by the Genealogical Society of Sale Lake City covers the years 1860-1876 and is held by the Archives of Ontario (GS 3141-3143).

2656. Garafraxa E Tp. **Abstract index of deeds, 1822-1933**. 1 reel. mf. Loc: AO. GS 3539.

Microfilmed by the Genealogical Society of Salt Lake City. The original volumes are held in the Orangeville Land Registry Office.

2657. Garafraxa E Tp. **Land registration copy books, 1823-1877**. 5 reels. mf. Loc: AO. GS 3540-3544.

Microfilmed by the Genealogical Society of Salt Lake City.

2658. Garafraxa Tp. **Index to land records and location book, n.d.**. 1 volume. Loc: UGA. List of individual volumes.

2659. Garafraxa Tp. **Land records, 1859**. 1 document. Loc: WCA.

A photocopy of an original agreement for the sale of land by Patrick Cassidy to S.S.#10 in Garafraxa Township. The document is part of the Wellington County Historical Research Society Collection.

2660. Garafraxa W Tp. **Abstract index of deeds, c1825-1988**. 8 volumes. Loc: ALR, AO. Volumes 58-65.

A record of ownership of land on Concessions 1 to 8, roads and streets for the township, and river bed. The index for 1821-1958 was microfilmed by the Genealogical Society of Salt Lake City, with copies in the Archives of Ontario (GS 3145-3146).

2661. Garafraxa W Tp. **Land register copy books, 1854-1954.** 28 volumes. Loc: UGA, AO. List of individual volumes.

The microfilm copy made by the Genealogical Society of Salt Lake City covers the years 1847-1877 and is held by the Archives of Ontario (GS 3147-3156). Each reel has an alphabetical index of persons.

2662. Garafraxa W Tp. **Register of memorials, 1822-1842; 1847-1854.** 3 volumes. Loc: UGA. List of individual volumes.

2663. Gibson, D. **Survey Diary. Puslinch Township, 1828.** 1 volume. Loc: AO. FA: RG-1, CB-1.

Survey diaries and field notes describe the land surface and natural environment just prior to clearance and settlement. This diary also has additions and revisions dating from 1831-1832. Held with records of the Surveyor-General.

2664. Guelph. **Abstract index of deeds, 1829-1979.** 35 volumes. Loc: GLR, AO.

An index of land transactions in the town and village that notes date of registry, grantor, grantee, quantity of land, and consideration or amount of mortgage. The entries are entered in numerical order by lot, division and concession number. The first volume, covering land transactions in the Village and Town of Guelph for the period from 1829 to 1865, is held separately from other volumes. The index for 1830-1958 was microfilmed by the Genealogical Society of Salt Lake City, with copies in the Archives of Ontario (GS 3181-3185).

2665. Guelph. **Land deed, Guelph, John Ford to Mary Passmore Card, 1896.** 1 document. Loc: UGA. XR1 MS A281.

2666. Guelph. **Land records, 1836; 1849; 1868; 1876; 1878; 1904.** 7 documents. Loc: GPL.

A record of several miscellaneous land transactions in various parts of Guelph.

2667. Guelph. **Land records, 1841; 1849; 1854; 1859-1860; 1863; 1892-1893.** 9 documents. Loc: GCM.

A record of mortgages and deeds for land sales in Guelph.

2668. Guelph. **Land Records. List of lots and farms, 1858.** 1 reel. mf. Loc: WCA.

List of owners and lot numbers in various surveys and farms in the town.

2669. Guelph. **Land registration copy books, 1830-1958.** 153 volumes. Loc: UGA, AO. List of individual volumes.

Each volume contains an index in alphabetical order by name of person. The microfilm copy made by the Genealogical Society of Salt Lake City covers the years 1830-1938 and is held in the Archives of Ontario (GS 3181-3185).

Rural tranquillity: an oil painting entitled 'Landscape' of sheep grazing in an Ontario Agricultural College farm field, 1939 (#3503). The artist was Daniel Herbert Jones who was Professor of Bacteriology at the college from 1914 to 1936. (Macdonald Stewart Art Centre)

2670. Guelph. **Register of memorial abstracts, 1829-1856**. 1 volume. Loc: UGA. List of individual volumes.
    A record of land transactions of Bargain and Sale Lands.

2671. Guelph Tp. **Abstract index of deeds, 1837-1953**. 7 volumes. Loc: GLR, AO.
    An index of land transactions in the township that notes date of registry, grantor, grantee, quantity of land, and consideration or amount of mortgage. The entries are entered in numerical order by lot, division and concession number. The index for 1829-1954 was microfilmed by the Genealogical Society of Salt Lake City, with copies in the Archives of Ontario (GS 3207-3208).

2672. Guelph Tp. **Land records, 1857-1905 (sporadic)**. 21 documents. Loc: GPL.
    A collection of land deeds and mortgages for lot 13 in the Thompson Survey in Guelph Township. The land was first purchased by John Thompson.

2673. Guelph Tp. **Land registration copy books, 1874-1958**. 25 volumes. Loc: UGA, AO. List of individual volumes.
    The microfilm held in the University of Guelph Archives is from 1872 to 1957. Each volume contains an index in alphabetical order by name of person. The microfilm copy made by the Genealogical Society of Salt Lake City covers the years 1862-1877 and is held in the Archives of Ontario (GS 3209-3212).

2674. Harriston T. **Abstract index of deeds, c1854-1988**. 7 volumes. Loc: ALR, AO. Volumes 99-103.
    The index records ownership of land on streets in Harriston. The index for 1866-1958 was microfilmed by the Genealogical Society of Salt Lake City, with copies in the Archives of Ontario (GS 3238).

2675. Harriston T. **Land records, 1938**. 1 envelope. Loc: WCA. MU 50.
    Several legal documents including a summons for the plaintiff to appear before the Supreme Court of Ontario to deal with funds due on a mortgage for a parcel of land in Harriston.

2676. Harriston T. **Land registration copy books, 1873-1954**. 13 volumes. Loc: UGA, AO. List of individual volumes.
    The microfilm copy made by the Genealogical Society of Salt Lake City covers the years 1866-1958 and is held in the Archives of Ontario (GS 3238).

2677. Kerr, Francis. **Survey Diary. Mount Forest, 1853**. 1 volume. Loc: AO. FA: RG-1, CB-1.
    Survey diaries and field notes describe the land surface and natural environment just prior to urban settlement. Held with records of the Surveyor-General.

2678. Kerr, Robert W. **Survey Diary. Peel Township, 1843**. 1 volume. Loc: AO. FA: RG-1, CB-1, #2.
    Survey diaries and field notes describe the land surface and natural environment just prior to clearance and settlement. Held with records of the Surveyor-General.

2679. Luther E Tp. **Abstract index of deeds, 1836-1939**. 1 reel. mf. Loc: AO. GS 3547.
    Microfilmed by the Genealogical Society of Salt Lake City. The original

volumes are held in the Orangeville Land Registry Office.

2680. Luther E Tp. **Land registration copy books, 1841-1877.** 1 reel. mf. Loc: AO. GS 3548.
    Microfilmed by the Genealogical Society of Salt Lake City.

2681. Luther Tp. **Index to land records and location book, n.d..** 1 volume. Loc: UGA. List of individual volumes.

2682. Luther W Tp. **Abstract index of deeds, c1857-1988.** 6 volumes. Loc: ALR, AO. Volumes 39-44.
    A record of land ownership of lots in Concessions 1 to 14 and roads and streets for the township. The index for 1836-1958 was microfilmed by the Genealogical Society of Salt Lake City, with copies in the Archives of Ontario (GS 3215-3216).

2683. Luther W Tp. **Index to land record registers, n.d..** 1 volume. Loc: UGA. List of individual volumes.

2684. Luther W Tp. **Land registration copy books, 1867-1954.** 25 volumes. Loc: UGA, AO. List of individual volumes.
    The microfilm copy made by the Genealogical Society of Salt Lake City covers the years 1847-1876 and is held in the Archives of Ontario (GS 3217-3220). Each reel has an alphabetical index of persons.

2685. Maryborough Tp. **Abstract index of deeds, c1860-1988.** 6 volumes. Loc: ALR, AO. Volumes 19-24.
    A record of land ownership in Concessions 1 to 17, and the roads and streets of the township. The index for 1856-1958 was microfilmed by the Genealogical Society of Salt Lake City, with copies in the Archives of Ontario (GS 3223-3225).

2686. Maryborough Tp. **Copy book of land survey affidavits, 1880-1884.** 1 volume. Loc: MBH.
    A record of oaths taken by landowners verifying the authenticity of land surveys. Each oath is signed by the landowner and the Provincial Land Surveyor, C.J. Wheelock.

2687. Maryborough Tp: Hollin. **Abstract index of deeds, c1849-1988.** 2 volumes. Loc: ALR. Volumes 14-15.
    A record of ownership for land in W.F. Mendell's Survey, Thomas Henderson's Survey, Ira Edmund's Survey, George Henderson's Survey, and roads and streets in the village.

2688. Maryborough Tp: Houstonville. **Abstract index of deeds, c1854-1986.** 3 volumes. Loc: ALR. Volumes 11-13.
    A record of ownership of land in Lots 1 to 233, Market Square, school lot and letter lots.

2689. Maryborough Tp. **Index to land record registers, n.d..** 1 volume. Loc: UGA. List of individual volumes.

2690. Maryborough Tp. **Index to land records and location book, 1865-1954**. 1 volume. Loc: UGA. List of individual volumes.

2691. Maryborough Tp. **Land records, 1871; 1880; 1881**. 3 documents. Loc: WCA. MU 33.
A record of a deed, indenture and land title search document for a specific plot of land near Hollin in Maryborough Township.

2692. Maryborough Tp. **Land registration copy books, 1853-1954**. 32 volumes. Loc: UGA, AO. List of individual volumes.
The microfilm copy made by the Genealogical Society of Salt Lake City covers the years 1853-1875 and is held in the Archives of Ontario (GS 3226-3231). Each reel has an alphabetical index of persons.

2693. Maryborough Tp: Moorefield. **Abstract index of deeds, c1870-1988**. 2 volumes. Loc: ALR. Volumes 25-26.
A record of ownership of land in Moore's Survey, Reserve and Gore Lots and Maple Grove, Loughran's Survey, Metcalf's Survey and King's Survey.

2694. Maryborough Tp: Stirton. **Abstract index of deeds, c1864-1988**. 1 volume. Loc: ALR. Volume 57.
A record of land ownership in the Village of Stirton which is located on the boundary with Peel Township.

2695. McNab, A. **Survey Diary. Arthur Township, 1846**. 1 volume. Loc: AO. FA: RG-1, CB-1, #10.
Survey diaries and field notes describe the land surface and natural environment just prior to clearance and settlement. Held with the records of the Surveyor-General.

2696. Minto Tp. **Abstract index of deeds, c1859-1988**. 10 volumes. Loc: ALR, AO. Volumes 27-36.
The index records land ownership in Concessions 1 to 18, and roads and streets for the township. The index for 1859-1958 was microfilmed by the Genealogical Society of Salt Lake City with copies in the Archives of Ontario (GS 3238-3239).

2697. Minto Tp. **Index to land record registers, 1916-1957**. 2 volumes. Loc: UGA. List of individual volumes.

2698. Minto Tp. **Index to land records and location book, 1866-1954**. 1 volume. Loc: UGA.

2699. Minto Tp. **Land records, 1874**. Loc: WCA.
A record of the sale of 100 acres of crown land to James Best in Minto Township. The records are part of the Wellington County Historical Research Society Collection.

2700. Minto Tp. **Land registration copy books, 1866-1954**. 32 volumes. Loc: UGA, AO. List of individual volumes.
The microfilm copy made by the Genealogical Society of Salt Lake City covers the years 1856-1876 and is held by the Archives of Ontario (GS 3239-3245). Each reel has an alphabetical index of persons.

2701. Minto Tp: Rothsay. **Abstract index of deeds, c1854–1988**. 3 volumes. Loc: ALR. Volumes 16–18.
A record of ownership of land in Lots 1 to 361 and park lots.

2702. A. Moore Land Records. **East Luther Township, 1866–1902**. 24 documents. Loc: WCA. MU 32A.
A total of twenty-four records of land transactions in East Luther Township including indentures, mortgages and deeds. The Wellington County Archives has developed a detailed finding aid listing the lot, type of transaction, date and names of individuals involved in specific land transfers.

2703. A. Moore Land Records. **Mortgage agreement, 1880**. 1 document. Loc: WCA. MU 32A.
An indenture agreement between John Rea and William Sunley for land in Eramosa Township.

2704. A. Moore Land Records. **Pilkington Township, 1862–1912**. 7 documents. Loc: WCA. MU 32A.
A total of seven land records for land agreement transactions in Pilkington Township including indentures, deeds, mortgages and land abstracts. The Wellington County Archives has developed a detailed finding aid listing the lot, type of transaction, date and names of individuals involved in specific land transfers.

2705. Mount Forest T. **Abstract index of deeds, c1856–1988**. 11 volumes. Loc: ALR, AO. Volumes 107–116.
A record of land ownership on streets in Mount Forest. The index for 1856–1958 was microfilmed by the Genealogical Society of Salt Lake City, with copies in the Archives of Ontario (GS 3253).

2706. Mount Forest T. **Indentures, 1865–1935 (sporadic)**. 7 bundles. Loc: MFH.
A record of land transactions in Mount Forest.

2707. Mount Forest T. **Index to land record registers, n.d.**. 1 volume. Loc: UGA.
List of individual volumes.

2708. Mount Forest T. **Land registration copy books, 1859–1954**. 21 volumes. Loc: UGA, AO. List of individual volumes.
The microfilm copy made by the Genealogical Society of Salt Lake City covers the years 1858–1877 and is held by the Archives of Ontario (GS 3254–3256). Each reel has an alphabetical index of persons.

2709. Mount Forest T. **Register of land patents, 1857–1858**. 1 volume. Loc: UGA.

2710. Nichol Tp. **Abstract index of deeds, 1807–1988**. 15 ledgers. Loc: GLR, AO.
The index for 1807–1958 was microfilmed by the Genealogical Society of Salt Lake City, with copies in the Archives of Ontario (GS 3260–3261).

2711. Nichol Tp. **Land registration copy books, 1847–1958**. 18 volumes. Loc: UGA, AO. List of individual volumes.
The microfilm held in the University of Guelph Archives begins in 1856. Each volume contains an index in alphabetical order by name of person. The microfilm copy made by the Genealogical Society of Salt Lake City covers the years

1847-1898 and is held in the Archives of Ontario (GS 3262-3269). Each reel has an alphabetical index of persons.

2712. Nichol Tp. **Register of memorial abstracts, 1822-1844**. 1 volume. Loc: UGA. List of individual volumes.

A record of land transactions of Bargain and Sale Lands.

2713. Ontario Ministry of Natural Resources. **Ontario Land Surveyors. Field notebooks, 1784-1859**. 20 reels. mf. Loc: MNR.

Field notebooks from before 1859 survive as original Field Books or as transcribed Written Volumes. Surveys of 277 townships are in the 867 Field Books (20 reels), while 34 township surveys are in the 21 Written Volumes (6 reels). For Arthur Township, there are surveys by McDonald in 1841 (Volume 18, page 189), and McNab in 1846 (Volume 18, page 642), Kerr in 1854 (FB 288), and Walker in 1843 (FB 803). For Eramosa Township, there are surveys by Ryckman in 1819 (FB 203), and by Sterrett in 1821 (FB 243). For Erin Township, Ryckman in 1821 (FB 203) and Ryckman in 1821 (FB 242) have left records. For Garafraxa East there ia an 1821 survey by Ryckman (FB 815), and for Garafraxa West an 1843 survey by Walker (FB 803). For Luther East, there is an 1831 survey by Burwell (FB 500), and for Luther West, an 1854 survey by Philips (FB 368). For Nichol there is an 1843 survey by Walker (FB 803). For Peel, Jones made a survey in 1855 (Volume 18, page 449), and for Puslinch, McDonald made a survey in 1835 (FB 452).

2714. Orangeville T. **Abstract index of deeds, 1872-1958**. 2 reels. mf. Loc: AO. GS 3577-3578.

Microfilmed by the Genealogical Society of Salt Lake City. The original volumes are held in the Orangeville Land Registry Office.

2715. Orangeville T. **Land registration copy books, 1825-1877**. 5 reels. mf. Loc: AO. GS 3579-3583.

Microfilmed by the Genealogical Society of Salt Lake City.

2716. Palmerston T. **Land registration copy books, 1875-1946**. 17 volumes. Loc: UGA, AO. List of individual volumes.

The microfilm copy made by the Genealogical Society of Salt Lake City covers the years 1875-1877 and is held by the Archives of Ontario (GS 3270). Each reel has an alphabetical index of persons.

2717. Palmerston V. **Abstract index of deeds, c1873-1988**. 10 volumes. Loc: ALR, AO. Volumes 87-96.

A record of land ownership on streets in Palmerston. The index for 1866-1950 was microfilmed by the Genealogical Society of Salt Lake City, with copies in the Archives of Ontario (GS 3237).

2718. Peel Tp. **Abstract index of deeds, c1848-1988**. 11 volumes. Loc: ALR, AO. Volumes 1-10; 57.

A record of ownership of land on Concessions 1 to 19, roads and streets for the township, Concessions A and B, Ellen and Daniels Survey and the Village of Stirton which is located on the boundary with Maryborough Township. The index for 1851-1958 was microfilmed by the Genealogical Society of Salt Lake City, with copies in the Archives of Ontario (GS 3272-3273).

2719. Peel Tp: Glenallan. **Abstract index of deeds, c1859-1988.** 2 volumes. Loc: ALR. Volumes 56-57.

A record of ownership of lands in Ghent's Survey, John Vernon's Survey, Allan and Sutherland's Survey and Donald Sutherland's Survey.

2720. Peel Tp. **Index to land registers and location book, n.d..** 1 volume. Loc: UGA.

2721. Peel Tp. **Land records, 1856.** 2 documents. Loc: WCA. MU 75.

A record of Crown land purchased by a farmer in Peel Township.

2722. Peel Tp. **Land records, 1869.** 1 file folder. Loc: WCA. MU 54.

A record of the correspondence of Sheriff Peter Gow's office of the county which outlines a dispute regarding a parcel of land in Peel Township.

2723. Peel Tp. **Land registration copy books, 1863-1954.** 40 volumes. Loc: UGA, AO. List of individual volumes.

The microfilm copy made by the Genealogical Society of Salt Lake City covers the years 1855-1876 and is held by the Archives of Ontario (GS 3274-3280). Each index has an alphabetical index of persons.

2724. Pilkington Tp. **Abstract index of deeds, 1799-1988.** 7 ledgers. Loc: GLR, AO.

The index for 1798-1958 was microfilmed by the Genealogical Society of Salt Lake City, with copies in the Archives of Ontario (GS 3282).

2725. Pilkington Tp. **Indentures, 1861.** 1 file folder. Loc: WCA. MU 23.

An agreement to sell the land of General Pilkington to Donald Cameron in Pilkington Township.

2726. Pilkington Tp. **Land records, 1855.** 1 document. Loc: PKH.

A record of purchase of the west half of Lot 3, Concession 1, south of the Grand River by George Greer from the estate of General Robert Pilkington.

2727. Pilkington Tp. **Land records, 1867-1911.** 1 box. Loc: PKH.

A record of land transactions of John Bosomworth.

2728. Pilkington Tp. **Land records, 1882; 1886-1887; 1903; 1920.** 7 documents. Loc: PKH.

Seven land records of Pilkington Township residents which include five deeds, a mortgage, one bill of complaint and one letter of administration. A number of the documents are relating to the property of Alexander McIntosh, a Pilkington Township farmer. The documents are on loan from a family descendent and are on display at the Pilkington Township office.

2729. Pilkington Tp. **Land records, 1890; 1903; 1914; 1919.** 4 documents. Loc: WCA. MU 74.

A record of deeds for lot 13 on concession 5 in Pilkington Township purchased by Samuel Reitzel, William Pilkinghorn and Edward Dobberthien.

2730. Pilkington Tp. **Land registration copy books, 1852-1958.** 14 volumes. Loc: UGA, AO. List of individual volumes.

The microfilm held in the University of Guelph Archives begins in 1866. Each volume contains an index in alphabetical order by name of person. The microfilm copy made by the Genealogical Society of Salt Lake City covers the years 1852-1878 and is held by the Archives of Ontario (GS 3283-3287). Each reel has an alphabetical index of persons.

2731. Pilkington Tp. **Land search, 1886.** 1 envelope. Loc: WCA. MU 14.
A record of a title search by the Wellington County Registry Office for lot 16, concession 3 in Pilkington Township.

2732. Puslinch Tp. **Abstract index of deeds, 1843-1977.** 6 volumes. Loc: GLR, AO.
An index of land transactions in the township that notes date of registry, grantor, grantee, quantity of land, and consideration or amount of mortgage. The entries are entered in numerical order by lot, division and concession number. The index for 1833-1958 was microfilmed by the Genealogical Society of Salt Lake City, with copies in the Archives of Ontario (GS 3292-3294).

2733. Puslinch Tp. **Clergy reserve sales, 1834-1856.** 1 file folder. Loc: WCA. MU 88.
Part of the Wellington South Land Registry Office Record Collection.

2734. Puslinch Tp. **Land records, 1854.** 1 document. Loc: WCA. MU 66.
A receipt for Clergy Reserve land purchased by Andrew Geddes in 1854 in Puslinch Township.

2735. Puslinch Tp. **Land registration copy books, 1858-1958.** 25 volumes. Loc: UGA, AO. List of individual volumes.
The microfilm held in the University of Guelph Archives begins in 1866. The microfilm copy made by the Genealogical Society of Salt Lake City covers the years 1847-1877 and is held by the Archives of Ontario (GS 3295-3298). Each index has an alphabetical index of persons.

2736. Puslinch Tp. **Register of memorial abstracts, 1833-1844; 1847-1858; 1860-1865.** 3 volumes. Loc: UGA. List of individual volumes.
The abstracts from 1860 to 1865 are on Reel 166 with the land registration copy books.

2737. Rankin, Charles. **Survey Diary. Mill sites on the Owen Sound Road, 1845-1846.** 1 volume. Loc: AO. FA: RG-1, CB-1, #10.
Survey diaries and field notes describe the land surface and natural environment just prior to clearance and settlement. Held with records of the Surveyor-General.

2738. Rankin, Charles. **Survey papers, 1820-1874.** 63 file folders. Loc: MTL. S16.
Licensed as a surveyor in 1820, Rankin (1797-1886) was based first in Malden Township, then in Toronto (1840-1850) and finally in Owen Sound. Among the many surveying contracts he undertook, two were in Wellington County. In 1837 he surveyed Garafraxa Road, then defined as the route from Oakville to Owen Sound, particularly the part north of Arthur. In 1852, he surveyed Minto Township. These are the private papers of a surveyor and complement the records of the Crown Lands Department. They include official instructions, the survey report (which presented a general picture of topography, climate, geology, possibilities for settlement, mill sites, draining and habitation), the survey diary (an outline of day-to-day movements of the survey party), survey or field

notes (official measurements and bearings), and the vouchers, accounts and pay lists. The records for Minto Township include a 30 by 36 inch map of the projected plan.

2739. Settlers of Queen's Bush. **Petition, 1842, to James Durand, MP for Dundas.** 4 pp. Loc: AO. RG 1, C-I-1, Box 42.

An appeal for special consideration by refugees from slavery who had squatted in Peel and Wellesley Townships. The petitioners explain that they had previously worked as day labourers for the older settlers of Waterloo and Woolwich Townships, but for the sake of their families had moved into the unsurveyed woods of Peel and Wellesley Townships. They mention their concern about a report that wild land could only be bought with cash, and they could only pay in instalments. They also request that lots be surveyed no more than 200 acres in size. The petition was referred to the Surveyor-General and is now held with the records of the Ministry of Natural Resources.

2740. Settlers of Queen's Bush. **Petition, 1843, to Governor-General of British North America.** 4 pp. Loc: AO. RG 1, C-I-1, Box 42.

An appeal for special consideration in land grants. The petitioners declare that they are 'labouring under many disadvantages, land not being surveyed and no regular road, and a distance of fifteen miles to the nearest mill, and being extremely poor having lately emigrated from England and the Southern States where we have suffered all the horrors of slavery'. The names of 143 settlers are attached to the petition, which is held with the records of the Ministry of Natural Resources.

2741. Settlers of Queen's Bush. **Petition, 1847, to Governor-General of British North America.** 4 pp. Loc: AO. RG 1, C-I-1, Box 42.

An appeal by 91 'Coloured Inhabitants' of the Queen's Bush to be allowed to pay by instalments for the land on which they had settled. The petitioners, whose spokesperson was Henry Miller, describe the improvements made to their land and predict great distress if they are forced to leave their lands with their large families.

2742. Settlers of Queen's Bush. **Petition, 1850, to Governor-General of British North America.** 2 pp. Loc: AO. RG 1, C-I-1, Box 42.

The petition, signed by ten black settlers, refers to a proclamation issued in 1840 that every 'man of colour assisting in putting down the Rebellions of 1837 and 1838' could claim a grant of 50 acres of land in the Queen's Bush and purchase a further 50 acres if he could afford it. The petitioners report 'that after nine years privation and hard labour . . . (they) have succeeded in clearing on an average 20 acres of land with corresponding improvements'. They also note that they have been informed by Mr Gayters (Andrew Geddes), Crown Land Agent in Elora, that 'their farms and improvements are in the market'.

2743. Surveyor-General. **Correspondence. Subject files, 1790-1890.** 21 volumes. Loc: AO. FA: RG-1, A-I-7.

Relevant volumes are Volume 2, Canada Company, 1827-1859 (4 envelopes) and Volume 21, Surveys of Wellington District, 1821-1841 (1 envelope).

2744. Surveyor-General. **Land Grants. Descriptions, 1794-1982.** 197 feet. Loc: AO. FA: RG-1, C-I-7.

The official description recorded all details of the land grant or lease and was the provincial secretary's authorization to prepare the patent. Indexes to these documents were arranged alphabetically by the grantee's names. This series includes fifteen volumes of Canada Company description books, 1829-1859.

2745. Surveyor-General. **Township papers, 1783-1870.** 561 boxes. Loc: AO. FA: RG-1, C-IV, MS-658.

Township papers are arranged by township, concession and lot and contain copies of Orders-in-Council, location certificates and location tickets, assignments, certificates of settlement duties, copies of receipts, inquiries, copies of Surveyor-General's descriptions, and a few patents. There are separate entries for each township in Wellington County.

2746. Surveyor-General. **Township Papers. Arthur Township, c1830-c1870.** 1628 p. Loc: AO. FA: RG-1, C-IV, MS 658, Reels 18-19.

2747. Surveyor-General. **Township Papers. Arthur Village, c1835-c1870.** 139 p. Loc: AO. FA: RG-1, C-IV, MS-658, Reel 18.

2748. Surveyor-General. **Township Papers. Elora Village, c1830-c1870.** 8 p. Loc: AO. FA: RG-1, C-IV, MS 658, Reel 129.

2749. Surveyor-General. **Township Papers. Eramosa Township, c1825-c1870.** 1285 p. Loc: AO. FA: RG-1, C-IV, MS 658, Reels 133-134.

2750. Surveyor-General. **Township Papers. Erin Township, c1825-c1870.** 2204 p. Loc: AO. FA: RG-1, C-IV, MS 658, Reels 134-136.

2751. Surveyor-General. **Township Papers. Fergus Village, c1830-c1870.** 7 p. Loc: AO. FA: RG-1, C-IV, MS 658, Reel 145.

2752. Surveyor-General. **Township Papers. Garafraxa Township, c1830-c1870.** 2564 p. Loc: AO. FA: RG-1, C-IV, MS 658, Reels 153-155.

2753. Surveyor-General. **Township Papers. Guelph Township, c1827-c1870.** 3 p. Loc: AO. FA: RG-1, C-IV, MS 658, Reel 170.

2754. Surveyor-General. **Township Papers. Luther Township, c1830-c1870.** 2362 p. Loc: AO. FA: RG-1, C-IV, MS 658, Reels 256-259.

2755. Surveyor-General. **Township Papers. Maryborough Township, c1835-c1870.** 1948 p. Loc: AO. FA: RG-1, C-IV, MS 658, Reels 288-290.

2756. Surveyor-General. **Township Papers. Minto Township, c1835-c1870.** 3586 p. Loc: AO. FA: RG-1, C-IV, MS 658, Reels 303-307.

2757. Surveyor-General. **Township Papers. Mount Forest, c1835-c1870.** 424 p. Loc: AO. FA: RG-1, C-IV, MS 658, Reel 325.

2758. Surveyor-General. **Township Papers. Nichol Township, c1824-c1870.** 14 p. Loc: AO. FA: RG-1, C-IV, MS 658, Reel 341.

2759. Surveyor-General. **Township Papers. Palmerston, c1850-c1870.** 436 p. Loc: AO. FA: RG-1, C-IV, MS 658, Reel 383.

2760. Surveyor-General. **Township Papers. Peel Township, c1830-c1870.** 2815 p. Loc: AO. FA: RG-1, C-IV, MS 658, Reels 383-388.

2761. Surveyor-General. **Township Papers. Pilkington Township, c1825-c1870.** 34 p. Loc: AO. FA: RG-1, C-IV, MS 658, Reel 395.

2762. Surveyor-General. **Township Papers. Puslinch Township, c1825-c1870.** 3565 p. Loc: AO. FA: RG-1, C-IV, MS 658, Reels 406-409.

2763. Wellington Co. **Deeds, 1807-1952.** 4 file folders. Loc: WCA. MU 88.
A small collection of deeds to land in Nichol Township 1807 to 1839, Eramosa Township 1914 to 1941, Pilkington Township 1863 to 1943, and Puslinch Township in 1952. Part of the Wellington South Land Registry Office Record Collection.

2764. Wellington Co. **Index of land patents, 1820-1876.** 1 volume. Loc: UGA. List of individual volumes.
The volume includes a tracing of Lots 3, 4, 5 and 6 in Concession 9 and Lots 7, 8 and 9 in Concession 10 of Puslinch Township. The plan includes property of Thomas Arkell and F.W. Stone.

2765. Wellington Co. **Land patents, 1846-1867.** 22 file folders. Loc: WCA. MU 88.
A record of land patents in Wellington County. Part of the Wellington South Land Registry Office Record Collection.

2766. Wellington Co. **Land records, 1829-1959 (sporadic).** 1 envelope. Loc: WCA. MU 51; List of contents and dates of documents.
A series of deeds and mortgage agreements of land transfers in Guelph and the Townships of West Garafraxa and Eramosa. The Wellington County Archives has developed a finding aid indicating the date, nature of agreements and individuals involved in specific transactions.

2767. Wellington Co. **Register of memorial abstracts, 1809-1873.** 6 volumes. Loc: UGA. List of individual volumes.
A record of land transactions of Bargain and Sale Lands.

2768. Wellington Co. **Register of wills, 1840-1901.** 14 reels. mf. Loc: WCA.

2769. Wellington County Crown Land Agency, Elora. **Records, 1842-1879.** 31 volumes. Loc: AO. FA: RG-1, D-7.
Crown land agencies were established from 1838 to administer locally the disposition of public land, under the general responsibility of the Commissioner of Crown Lands. There were twenty agencies by 1843 and twenty-five by 1851. Most agents left very incomplete records, but the most detailed surviving records are those of Wellington District/County based in Elora. The agents were J. Durand (1842-1845), Andrew Geddes (1845-1865), J. Ross (1865-1869) and A.S. Cadenhead (1870-1879). This richly detailed source includes the following kinds of records for the Townships of Arthur, Eramosa, Erin, Garafraxa, Luther, Maryborough, Minto, Peel and Puslinch: account books and monthly returns for sales of school, crown and clergy reserves; land rolls; journals; letterbooks and registers of

patents. Volume 11 contains details of applicants for land in Peel Township in 1845 and Volume 21 has schedules of occupants and land improvements in Arthur and Minto Township in 1861–1862. Held with records of the Commissioner of Crown Lands.

2770. Wellington North Registry Office. **General registers of wills, 1862–1954.** 20 volumes. Loc: UGA. List of individual volumes.

2771. Wellington North Registry Office. **Partnership registration records, 1871–1971.** Loc: AO. RG 55: FA.

Business partnership registration was first made mandatory in Ontario under the Registration of Company Partnership Act of 1869. Forms had to be filed with the county Registrar who had to maintain two sets of index books, the Firm Index and the Individual Index, as well as Declarations and Dissolutions of Partnership. These records were transferred to the Archives of Ontario where they are grouped with the records of the Ministry of Consumer and Commercial Relations. These also include microfiche indexes by name of Expired Partnerships, Proprietorships and Name Style Registrations for Ontario in 5-year ranges.

2772. Wellington North Registry Office. **Register of wills, 1903–1988.** 4 volumes. Loc: ALR. Vol. 117–120.

A record of wills in North Wellington County involving land transfers which lists the instrument, grantee and grantor and number of entry. The entries are listed alphabetically by name of deceased.

2773. Wellington South Registry Office. **General register, probates, administration, power of attorney, 1824–1988.** 3 volumes. Loc: GLR.

An index that includes name, reference number of document and date of entry. The index is organized alphabetically by name. Volume 1 includes all records prior to July 1, 1956.

2774. Wellington South Registry Office. **General registers of wills, 1866–1958.** 25 volumes. Loc: UGA. List of individual volumes.

2775. Wellington South Registry Office. **Land patents, deeds and Clergy Reserve sale agreements, 1846–1953.** 2 boxes. Loc: WCA. MU 87–88.

Most records are from 1846 to 1867. The patents record names of grantees, location, number of acres, description and dates, and are organized alphabetically by place name for each year. The early records list land transactions for the entire county.

2776. Wellington South Registry Office. **Partnership registration records, 1870–1974.** Loc: AO. RG 55: FA.

Firm and Individual Indexes survive only for the period 1953–1974, together with Declarations for 1870–1967 and indexed Copybooks for 1870–1872 and Limited Partnerships for 1861–1941. Transferred to Archives of Ontario, with records of Ministry for Consumer and Commercial Relations.

2777. Wellington South Registry Office. **Register of Bankruptcy Act, 1920–1950.** 1 volume. Loc: UGA.

2778. Wellington South Registry Office. **Register of bylaws and debentures, 1858-1870.** 1 volume. Loc: UGA. List of individual volumes.

2779. Wellington South Registry Office. **Register of land records judgements, 1859-1861.** 2 volumes. Loc: UGA. List of individual volumes.
A record of legal judgements regarding land disputes.

2780. Wellington South Registry Office. **Registration of titles, 1824-1915.** 1 box. Loc: WCA. MU 87.
A record of name of patentee, lot, concession, number of acres and date of patent in Eramosa, Puslinch and Erin Townships, and for Wellington South region. Part of the Wellington South Land Registry Office Record Collection.

2781. Wellington South Registry Office. **Subdivision plan book, 1831-1940.** 1 volume. Loc: GLR.
An index of plan number and geographical location of surveys and plans.

2782. Wells, Robert. **Survey journal, 1847.** 1 volume. Loc: UGA. XR1 MS A275.
A survey notebook kept by Wells with descriptions and pen sketch drawings of the physical landscape in Guelph, Fergus, Nichol Township and Eramosa Township. The work includes sketches marking Allan's Mill, Clark's Mill and the Irvine River.

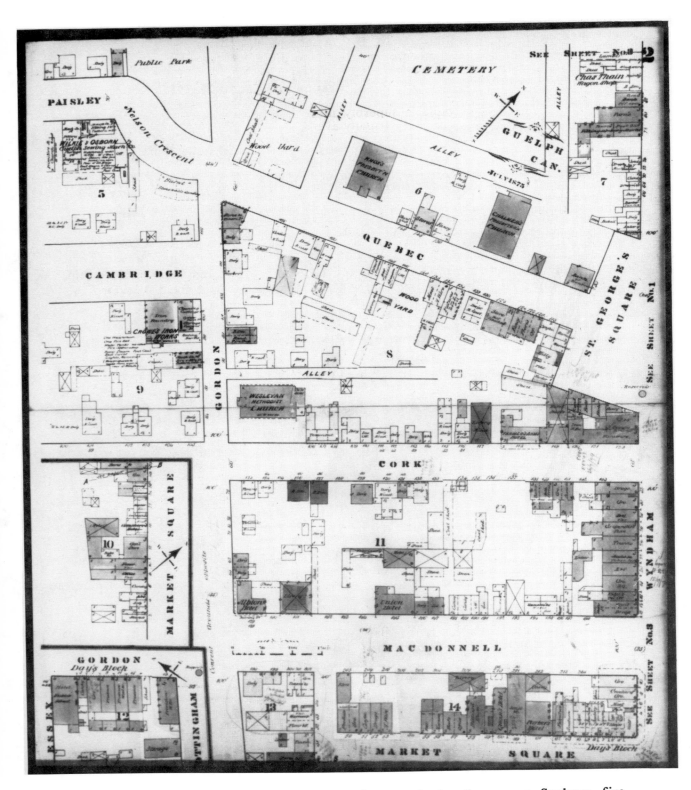

Central Guelph in 1875: Section of one of the three rare Sanborn fire insurance plans of Guelph, 1875 (#2841). (John Sutherland and Sons Insurance in Guelph).

MAPS AND PLANS

Old cartographic materials are important documents in their own right and also provide the essential link between other data sources and the landscape. Their value is superbly illustrated in **Ontario's History in Maps**, which includes examples of virtually every type of map.[1] As Joan Winearls has remarked in a cartobibliographical essay for that volume, 'impressive numbers of maps of Ontario survive... [but] are often neglected'.[2] Maps and plans are difficult to store and to retrieve and there have been too few bibliographies and guides devoted to these resources.

Over 600 maps and plans of Wellington County are included in this Inventory and more will doubtless come to light. It has been said that maps, like words, have uses rather than meanings. Researchers interested in maps should understand the original purposes for which they were produced. Three main groups of maps and plans are distinguished here:

1. General maps of Wellington County at relatively small scales;

2. Fire insurance plans;

3. Subdivision plans and compiled plans of townships and urban centres.

General Maps of Wellington County

Most maps in this group that date from before 1850 were drawn to assist in the organization of land survey and settlement. Some, such as the Canada Company's **Diagrams of Upper Canada**, define the boundaries of townships and districts and show land available for sale (#2784). Others illustrate the routes of actual or projected roads and railways, early examples being the planned survey of a route between Guelph and York in 1827 (#2807) and John McDonald's 1829 map of the the 'Communication Road' through the Huron Tract from Guelph to Goderich (#2802).

In the second half of the nineteenth century, we have a series of maps of the whole county that show township boundaries, numbered concessions, rivers, roads, railways, town and village sites, and often the locations of such

---

[1] R.L. Gentilcore and C.G. Head, **Ontario's history in maps** (Toronto: University of Toronto Press, 1984). Other major map guides include: C.F.J. Whebell, 'Printed maps of Upper Canada 1800-1864', **Ontario History** 59 (1957): 139-144; N.L. Nicholson & L.M. Sebert, **The maps of Canada: a guide to official Canadian maps, charts, atlases and gazetteers** (Hamden, CT: Archon Books, 1982).

[2] Joan Winearls, 'Sources for the early maps of Ontario,' in **Ontario's history in maps**, 276.

rural services as post offices, schools and churches. These were drafted by private surveyors and published commercially; some are attractively decorated with marginal drawings of buildings and local scenes. We have traced such maps by Kertland (1855), Leslie and Wheelock (1861), Cotterell (1877), Evans (1895), Hutcheon (1897) and Lloyd (1906, with later reprints).

Cotterell's and Lloyd's county maps were associated with more detailed township maps showing also lot boundaries and the names of rural landowners that were published together in county atlases. Like most Ontario counties, Wellington County was the subject of an illustrated historical atlas published in the 1870s, but Wellington is unusual among Ontario counties in being described in a second and more detailed atlas of 1906.[3] County atlases can provide a remarkably accurate guide to features of the time but, as with other documents prepared for subscription sales, the user should be aware of bias and omissions.[4] For Wellington County, we have also a third atlas, identifying rural landowners and showing other details for most townships, in the **Guidal commercial directory atlas** of 1917 (#2799).

From the period of World War I, there are the first topographic and highway maps of Wellington County produced by government agencies -- the federal Department of the Interior (1916) and Department of National Defence (1935), and the provincial Department of Public Highways (1928).

Fire Insurance Plans

A special class of plan was produced from the 1870s to the 1940s to serve the needs of the fire insurance companies by recording the detailed characteristics of buildings. Fire was a very real hazard in nineteenth-century cities, with their crowded frame buildings and inadequate water supply systems.[5] In keeping with their purpose, fire insurance plans were drawn at very large scales and used colour, symbol and detailed annotation to describe

---

[3] **Illustrated atlas of the County of Wellington** (Toronto: Walker and Miles, 1877); **Historical atlas of the County of Wellington** (Toronto: Historical Atlas Publishing Co, 1906). Both atlases were reprinted in 1972 by Mark Cumming of Port Elgin and the 1906 atlas also by Mika of Belleville. Individual township maps from both atlases were cited in the Guelph Regional Project's **Bibliography** and are not repeated here. Wentworth County (1903) was the only other Ontario county to have a second atlas published.

[4] L.R. Benson, 'Historical atlases of Ontario: a preliminary checklist,' **Ontario Library Review** 28 (1944): 45-53; 'The Illustrated Historical Atlases of Ontario with special reference to H. Belden & Co,' in **Aspects of nineteenth-century Ontario**, edited by F.H. Armstrong et al. (Toronto: University of Toronto Press, 1974): 267-277; Heather Maddick, **County maps: land ownership maps of Canada in the nineteenth century** (Ottawa: Public Archives of Canada, 1976).

[5] John C. Weaver and Peter de Lottinville, 'The conflagration and the city: disaster and progress in British North America during the nineteenth century,' **Histoire sociale/Social History** 13 (1980): 417-449.

the inside and outside construction of buildings including materials, height and fire walls. All the plans were produced by accurate survey but also with great rapidity, Goad plans being surveyed, drawn, printed and coloured within four months of the original field work.[6] As they name the owners and occupants of buildings and clearly show their locations, the plans can be used for various kinds of historical research.

The first fire insurance plans for some fifteen Canadian cities were produced in the mid-1870s by the Sanborn Map Company of the United States. Then a Canadian plan business was started and vigorously promoted by Charles Goad. By 1885 some 340 places had been surveyed, and by the time of Goad's death in 1910 there were detailed standardized plans for about 1300 urban centres. The Goad company promoted other mapping products such as general land use atlases for the larger cities and industrial surveys and extended its operations to the British Isles and numerous other countries in Europe, Africa and Latin America.

In 1917, the Canadian Fire Underwriters' Association formed its own plan-making business, the Underwriters' Survey Bureau Ltd, which in 1931 purchased the remaining assets of Goad's Canadian plan business. From 1918 to 1960, the U.S.B. produced plans of cities and towns in Ontario, Quebec and the Maritimes. In 1960, it amalgamated with the Western Canada Underwriters' Association and the British Columbia Underwriters' Association to form the Canadian Underwriters' Association. Plan-making ceased in 1975 in response to changes in the recording of information for insurance purposes and the reduction of large-scale fire hazards.

Only a small proportion survives of all the insurance plans produced. Insurance agents were supposed to return old plans on receipt of revised editions and sometimes new editions were printed on the reverse side of earlier returned plans. Hardly any Canadian plans by Sanborn have come to light, a notable exception being a set of three plans for Guelph (1875) which have survived in the offices of John Sutherland and Sons, an insurance agency which began in Guelph in the early 1870s (#2841). This set is interesting as it bears some correction slips pasted on by Goad and is accompanied by a Goad key plan of 1878 (#2832). Plans have also been traced for most other urban centres in Wellington County, at intervals from 1900 to the 1940s.

Subdivision Plans

The greatest number of plans we have inventoried are those drawn by registered surveyors to accompany formal applications for the subdivision of urban or suburban land. Such plans were usually filed in registry offices from 1849 and became mandatory from 1859. Most of these plans are for urban places. When the dates of these plans are analyzed, we see that most coincided with periodic land booms. In Guelph, for example, there was a rush

[6] G.T. Bloomfield, 'Canadian fire insurance maps and industrial archeology,' **IA: The Journal of the Society for Industrial Archeology** 8 (1982): 67-80. See also Robert J. Hayward, 'Sources for urban historical research: insurance plans and land use atlases,' **Urban History Review** 1 (1973): 2-9.

of subdivision plans in the 1850s, in a fever of development associated with the promotion of the Toronto-Guelph railway that became part of the Grand Trunk Railway in 1856. Nearly one quarter of all the maps and plans we have found for Guelph before 1940 are subdivision plans of the 1850s. Similarly, twelve of the eighteen plans traced for Palmerston date from the years 1872-1878, coinciding with the arrival of the railway and the town's incorporation. Some of these subdivision plans were embellished with colour and marginal information for use as sale plans.

Some subdivision plans were registered for 'paper towns' where the promoters' high hopes were never realized. Examples include Ballinard, Hartfield, Sweaborg and Trafalgar, all in Guelph Township and registered in 1855-6. Plans for Aboyne, Ennotville, Gluyasville, Irvinedale, Kinnettles, Ryckmantown, Strathallan and Thorpville had similar fates in Nichol Township. Subdivision plans made for parts of larger centres could also be so premature or ill-considered that their promoters lost their investment. The most famous land investor to fail in Wellington County was the Hon. John A. Macdonald who tried in vain to capitalize on the arrival of the Grand Trunk Railway with a subdivision southeast of the Guelph town centre in 1855 (#3168).

The subdivision plans are grouped in this **Inventory** by township or other municipal unit, together with any compiled plans showing the complete cadaster of the area. Other maps and plans of whole cities, towns and villages are also placed in this section, including the local example of a bird's eye view of a city (2974).[7]

In this **Inventory** our main purpose has been to describe the informational content of the maps and plans. Where possible, we have also noted the status of the map as original print or manuscript rather than a transcription, photostat or photocopy. For more definitive details of this kind, the user is referred to Joan Winearls' forthcoming bibliography.[8]

---

[7] J.W. Reps, **Views and viewmakers of urban America: lithographs of towns and cities in the United States and Canada 1825-1925** (Columbia, Mo.: University of Missouri Press, 1984).

[8] Joan Winearls, whose 900-page annotated bibliography of manuscript and printed maps of Upper Canada to 1867 will be published in 1990, generously shared the results of her researches with us.

DISTRICT AND COUNTY MAPS

2783. Burwell, Mahlon. **Map of tract of land purchased by government from Chippewa Indians in London and Western Districts, 1828.** col ms, 64 x 98 cm. Loc: AO. C-59; SR 6943.

Full title continues 'upon which is drawn from actual survey the northern boundary of the Purchase . . . a line for a road from Guelph towards Burlington Bay and rivers, brooks, rills and swamps as found on an exploring expedition for the Canada Company'.

2784. Canada Company. **Diagrams of Upper Canada, c1823-1826.** printed volume. Loc: UGA, MTL, AO.

Plans of townships including those of the Home and Gore Districts, on which Crown and Clergy Reserves are specified and lots purchased by the Canada Company are shaded green. The University of Guelph has a copy only of the second volume (in map drawer 7), which apparently belonged to Lt. Col. F.A. Mackenzie Fraser, Assistant Quarter Master General, some time after Upper Canada had become part of the Province of Canada. He annotated his copy with such details as boundary lines in degrees and minutes. Volume 2 contains an index map. The Archives of Ontario and the Metro Toronto Central Reference Library (Baldwin Room) each hold both volumes.

2785. Canada Company. **Map of townships of Upper Canada with Great Northern and Great Western Railways and plank roads, 1843.** Loc: NAC. #2872/400/1843.

The railways, details of which were probably added later than 1843, are noted as being 'pushed' by Toronto and Hamilton respectively. The scale is 50 miles to an inch.

2786. Canada Department of Interior. **Ontario, Guelph sheet, 1916.** 1 sheet, 88 x 71 cm. Loc: KPL. Card index.

A sheet of the Standard Topographical series at the scale of 3.93 miles to an inch that shows Wellington, Grey, Bruce and Dufferin Counties, as well as part of Halton, Peel, Perth, Huron, Waterloo and Simcoe Counties. County boundaries, lot and concession lines and numbers, villages, railways and roads are all indicated.

2787. Canada Department of National Defence. **Topographic map of Guelph area showing portions of Wellington, Waterloo and Halton Counties, 1935.** scale 1 inch to 1 mile. Loc: AO. C-17.

Predecessor of the National Topographic Series of one-inch maps.

2788. Cotterell, A.T. **Map of the County of Wellington, 1877.** 1 sheet, 15-3/4 x 23-3/4. Loc: NAC. 420/Wellington/1877.

Published in Walker and Miles, Topographical and Historical Atlas of the County of Wellington, pages 6-7 at a scale of 3 miles to an inch, and also in Miles & Co, The New Topographical Atlas of the Province of Ontario, page 32. Shows townships and concessions, railways, roads and major buildings.

2789. Devine, T. **Plan of townships in Wellington and parts of Huron and Simcoe Districts, 1848.** col ms, 80 x 102 cm, scale 1 inch to 200 chains. Loc: AO. SR 5970.

A compiled map showing the state of the various township surveys and roads projected and built, including the Durham Road, the Toronto and Hurontario Road and Saugeen Road. A note has been added on surveys and roads to 1851.

2790. Evans, William W. **Map of Wellington County, Province of Ontario, 1885.** 1 sheet, 32-3/4 x 32. Loc: UGL, GCH, NAC, AO, WCA, UGA. NAC: 420/Wellington/1885/#16782; AO: A-11.

Map of Wellington County in its pre-1882 extent, that marks property owners of lots, concession roads and railway lines. There is a detailed inset map of Guelph showing street and ward names, as well as inset maps of Elora, Fergus and the O.A.C. The map includes a table of distances between villages within the county, acreage and population of each township, electoral districts and advertising by various Guelph and county merchants and industrialists. The scale is 60 chains to the inch.

2791. Good, Joel. **Plan of road leading from Village of Waterloo to Village of Arthur, 1842.** col ms, 40 x 287 cm, scale one inch to 20 chains. Loc: AO. R-W.

The plans shows the territory from Jacob Snider's mill in Waterloo north through Woolwich Township and the Crown and Clergy Reserves to Arthur. It includes details of the survey grid, mills, other roads and relief.

2792. Hutcheon, James. **Map of the County of Wellington corrected to date, 1897.** Loc: UGL.

A map of the County of Wellington that shows concession and lot numbers, railway lines, towns, villages and rural school houses and churches. The map is 'corrected to date' in that the Townships of Luther, Garafraxa East and Amaranth are not included as they had become part of Dufferin County in 1882. No scale is given.

2793. Kerr, Robert. **Plan and profile of the road recently surveyed through the Wellington District from Puslinch in the District of Gore to the Village of Arthur, 1842.** col ms, 71 x 269 cm. Loc: GCI, NAC. NAC: 78510.

The map includes a description entitled, 'Clergy Reserves for the Six Nations Lands'. The road goes from Arthur Village in the northwest, to Fergus, to Guelph, along Woolwich Road, to the corner of Mr Sandilands' property in Guelph Township, to Puslinch, to the division between Wellington District and Gore District. The scale is 20 chains to the inch. The copy in the National Map Collection was made in 1845 by the Office of the Board of Works; and a photographic reproduction was made of this for the GCVI archives.

2794. Kerr, Robert W. **Plan of proposed improvements in the road allowance between Orangeville and Arthur, c1860.** Loc: AO. C-16.

The line of the road, through Garafraxa, Mono, Amaranth and Luther Townships, was later followed by Highway 9.

2795. Kertland, Edwin H. **Map of County of Wellington compiled from various surveys, 1855.** 3 sections. Loc: NAC. 420/Wellington/1855/#48666.

A more detailed compilation of the other Kertland map of 1855, giving details of landowners of all rural lots with lists of subscribers in margins.

2796. Kertland, Edwin H. **Map of the County of Wellington, Province of Canada West, 1855.** print, hand col, 95 x 96 cm. Loc: UGL, NAC, AO. NAC: 420/Wellington/1855/#19781; AO: A-11/sr 2639.

A map of Wellington County in 1855, mounted on linen, that provides county boundaries, surveys grid, numbered concessions, roads, rivers, railway lines, town and village sites, divisional court boundaries and taverns. No scale is given. One copy at the Archives of Ontario show the telegraph lines of the Toronto, Grey and Bruce Railway.

2797. Leslie, Guy and Wheelock, C.J. **Map of the County of Wellington, Canada West, 1861.** print, hand col, 160 x 160 cm, scale 1 inch to 60 chains. Loc: NAC, AO, GCM, KPL. AO:A-12; NAC:420/Wellington/1861/#13205; UGA:XR2 MS A047.
A map of Wellington County stored in six large sections that marks property owners of lots, concession roads and railway lines. The map includes a list of subscribers from each township and from the villages of Salem, Mount Forest, Erin, Elora, Glenallan, and the town of Guelph. It includes insert maps of Fergus, Guelph, Kinnettles, Aboyne, Elora, Salem and Orangeville. The map is decorated with small etchings of ten residential, industrial and church buildings, and has an inch wide border of maple leaves. The map at the University of Guelph Archives is only a photocopy.

2798. Lloyd's Map Publishers. **Wellington County, c1920.** 1 map. Loc: GCH.
Internal evidence suggests that this map of the county was published in the post World War I era. The map marks county roads, county suburban roads, provincial highways and some schools, and is stamped 'Lloyd's Map Publishers of Toronto'. The scale is 1-3/4 miles to an inch. It is held in the Clerk's office vault.

2799. Map and Advertising Co. Ltd. **Guidal commercial directory atlas of Wellington County, 1917.** 12 sheets bound as atlas. Loc: UWO. CA80NWE 71CE.
Detailed maps of most townships of Wellington County showing landowners' names, roads, railways, towns, lakes and streams. The maps of Puslinch, Guelph, Nichol, Pilkington, Erin and Arthur also show rural mail routes. There are also maps of Minto, Eramosa, Peel, Maryborough and West Garafraxa as well as a large coloured key map of Wellington County and another showing the region in relation to all of western Ontario.

2800. **Map of proposed Grand River-Saugeen Road, 1848.** ms. Loc: AO. RG-1, Petitions.
Map accompanies petition from inhabitants of Nichol and Woolwich Townships.

2801. Map Specialty Co. **Map of Wellington County including Nassagaweya, Waterloo and Woolwich Townships, 1910.** 1 sheet, 50-1/4 x 31-1/2. Loc: NAC. 420/Wellington/1910/#48685.
A coloured map, drafted by F.P. Lloyd and including current statistics.

2802. McDonald, John. **Map of Huron Tract belonging to Canada Company, showing the Communication Road from Guelph to Goderich Harbour, 1829.** col ms, 44 x 63 cm. Loc: AO. B-38; SR 4750.
Drawn at the scale of one inch to four miles.

2803. McDonald, John. **Plan of Owen Sound Road and tier of lots from Sydenham Township to Arthur Township, 1842.** col ms, 220 x 37 cm, scale 1 inch to 40 chains. Loc: NAC. #78510.

2804. Ontario Department of Public Highways. **Road map of the County of Wellington, 1928.** 1 sheet, 37 x 34 cm. Loc: UGL, NAC, AO. AO:B-55; NAC:420/Wellington/1928.
A map of Wellington County in 1928 illustrating all major provincial highways

and county roads, and how they connect with parts of Halton and Waterloo Counties. All concession roads and lots numbers are given, as well as all place names and railway lines.

2805. Parke, Thomas. **Proposed line of road between Wellington District and the mouth of the River Saugeen, 1842**. col ms, 67 x 103 cm, scale 1 inch to 4 miles. Loc: AO. SR 5964.
Plan shows the Owen South Road and Arthur and Luther Townships and the proposed road from Woolwich Township running northwest between Wellesley and Peel, Maryborough and Mornington Townships to Saugeen.

2806. **Plan of routes of Wellington, Grey and Bruce and Toronto, Grey and Bruce Railways, 1870**. 1 sheet, 62 x 32 cm, part coloured. linen. Loc: AO. A-4.
The scale of map is 1:316,800.

2807. **Plan of survey of route for a road between Guelph and York, 1827**. ms. 15 x 45 inches. Loc: MTL. #209.
A map at a scale of approximately one-half an inch to a mile showing the territory between Guelph and York (renamed Toronto in 1834). A table of distances over several possible routes shows that a road built through Streetsville and Dundas Street would be the shortest. Previously with the Canada Company Papers.

2808. Rankin, Charles. **Niagara, Gore and Western Districts, 1845**. original print. Loc: AO. A-16.

2809. Rankin, Charles. **Plan of line for a road from Owen Sound to Garafraxa and thence to Oakville, 1837**. 3 ms maps each 74 x 53 cm, scale 1 inch to 20 chains. Loc: AO. SR 7219/7220/7221.
Shows details of the road line including mill sites. A related map (SR 6557) contains the same informaion at a smaller scale of 1 inch to 2 miles on one sheet.

2810. Rankin, Charles. **Plan of mill-sites on Owen's Sound Road, 1846**. col ms, 7 sheets. Loc: MNR. SR 2709.
Sheet 7 shows the crown reserves on both sides of the Garafraxa Road through Arthur Township and notes that there were 'no good mill sites'.

2811. **Road from Beverly to Guelph copied from M. Burwell's Plan of Survey, 1827**. ms, 70 x 37 cm, scale 1 inch to 40 chains. Loc: AO. SR 5815.

2812. **Sketch of the proposed District of Wellington, 1837**. ms. Loc: NAC, AO. AO:C.O.42, Vol.432, p.149a; NAC:409/Wellington/1837/#59325.
A plan that marks township boundaries and the Grand River system. Townships include Proton, Melancthon, Luther, Amaranth, Garafraxa, Erin, Eramosa, Guelph, Nichol, Woolwich, Waterloo and Wilmot. Crown land and Six Nations land are also included. Guelph is marked as 'proposed district town'.

2813. **Wellington County, c1923**. 1 sheet. Loc: AO. C-79.
Shows roads, railways and location of schools at a scale of 1:95,040.

FIRE INSURANCE PLANS

2814. Goad, Charles E. **Arthur. Fire insurance plan, 1884; revised 1899**. 1 sheet. Loc: NAC. NAC: 440/Arthur/1899/#13905.
     Plan, at scale of 1:600, showing in detail by means of colour and symbol, the character of inside and outside construction of buildings, fire walls, height and occupancy or use.

2815. Goad, Charles E. **Arthur. Fire insurance plan, 1904**. 2 sheets. Loc: NAC, GPL, UWO. NAC: 440/Arthur/1904/#9285.
     Plan, at scale of 1:600, showing in detail by means of colour and symbol, the character of inside and outside construction of buildings, fire walls, height and occupancy or use. Population stated to be 1500, with no fire protection. GPL copy is monochrome microfiche.

2816. Goad, Charles E. **Clifford. Fire insurance plan, 1885**. 1 sheet. Loc: NAC, UWO. NAC: 440/Clifford/1885/#10621.
     Plan, at scale of 1:600, showing in detail by means of colour and symbol, the character of inside and outside construction of buildings, fire walls, height and occupancy or use. Population given as 605, with no fire proection. Copy at University of Western Ontario printed on reverse of 1885 plan of Drayton.

2817. Goad, Charles E. **Clifford. Fire insurance plan, 1885; revised 1904**. 1 sheet. Loc: NAC, UWO. NAC: 440/Clifford/1904/#13925.
     Plan, at scale of 1:600, showing in detail by means of colour and symbol, the character of inside and outside construction of buildings, fire walls, height and occupancy or use.

2818. Goad, Charles E. **Drayton. Fire insurance plan, 1885**. 1 sheet. Loc: NAC, UWO, DVO. NAC: 440/Drayton/1885/#13931.
     Plan, at scale of 1:600, showing in detail by means of colour and symbol, the character of inside and outside construction of buildings, fire walls, height and occupancy or use. The map extends to the Conestoga River in the west and north, Edward Street in the east and Spring Street in the south. The map lists the population as 790, with no fire appliances.

2819. Goad, Charles E. **Drayton. Fire insurance plan, 1894**. 1 sheet. Loc: NAC, DVO, UWO. NAC: 440/Drayton/1894/#9403.
     Plan, at scale of 1:600, showing in detail by means of colour and symbol, the character of inside and outside construction of buildings, fire walls, height and occupancy or use. Population is given as 970.

2820. Goad, Charles E. **Drayton, Ontario, population 970, no fire appliances, 1894; revised 1899 and 1904**. 2 maps. Loc: DVO.
     A plan bordered by the Conestoga River in the west and north, Edward Street in the east and Spring Street in the south. The scale is 50 feet to an inch. The map lists the population for 1904 as 804. The maps are stamped as showing revisions of the 1894 original in the years 1899 and 1904.

2821. Goad, Charles E. **Elora. Fire insurance plan, 1890**. 2 sheets. Loc: NAC, UWO, GPL. NAC: 440/Elora/1890/#16288.
     Plan, at scale of 1:600, showing in detail by means of colour and symbol, the

character of inside and outside construction of buildings, fire walls, height and occupancy or use. GPL copy is monochrome microfiche.

2822. Goad, Charles E. **Elora. Fire insurance plan, 1890; revised 1894**. 2 sheets. Loc: NAC, UWO, GPL. NAC: 440/Elora/1894/#9414.
    Plan, at scale of 1:600, showing in detail by means of colour and symbol, the character of inside and outside construction of buildings, fire walls, height and occupancy or use. GPL copy is monochrome microfiche.

2823. Goad, Charles E. **Elora. Fire insurance plan, 1890; revised 1904**. 2 sheets. Loc: NAC, UWO. NAC: 440/Elora/1904/#13942.
    Plan, at scale of 1:600, showing in detail by means of colour and symbol, the character of inside and outside construction of buildings, fire walls, height and occupancy or use.

2824. Goad, Charles E. **Erin. Fire insurance plan, 1891; revised 1896**. 1 sheet. Loc: NAC. 440/Erin/1896/#13944.
    Plan, at scale of 1:600, showing in detail by means of colour and symbol, the character of inside and outside construction of buildings, fire walls, height and occupancy or use.

2825. Goad, Charles E. **Erin. Fire insurance plan, 1907**. 2 sheets. Loc: NAC, UWO, UGL, GPL. NAC: 440/Erin/1907/#9420.
    Plan, at scale of 1:600, showing in detail by means of colour and symbol, the character of inside and outside construction of buildings, fire walls, height and occupancy or use. GPL copy is monochrome microfiche.

2826. Goad, Charles E. **Fergus. Fire insurance plan, 1890**. 2 sheets. Loc: NAC. 440/Fergus/1890/#13947.
    Plan, at scale of 1:600, showing in detail by means of colour and symbol, the character of inside and outside construction of buildings, fire walls, height and occupancy or use.

2827. Goad, Charles E. **Guelph. Fire insurance plans, 1897**. 25 sheets. Loc: NAC, UWO, GPL. NAC: 440/Guelph/1897/#9462.
    Plan, at scale of 1:600, showing in detail by means of colour and symbol, the character of inside and outside construction of buildings, fire walls, height and occupancy or use. The set at the National Archives consists partly of 1897 sheets reprinted during the following decade. The original sheet 5 of 1897 shows buildings along Farquhar, Garden (sic), Quebec and Wyndham Streets; GPL has a monochrome microfiche copy of this sheet.

2828. Goad, Charles E. **Guelph. Fire insurance plans, 1897; revised 1911**. 34 sheets. Loc: NAC, GPL. NAC: 440/Guelph/1911/#9463.
    Plan, at scale of 1:600, showing in detail by means of colour and symbol, the character of inside and outside construction of buildings, fire walls, height and occupancy or use. GPL copy is monochrome microfiche.

2829. Goad, Charles E. **Guelph. Fire insurance plans, 1897, revised 1916**. 38 sheets bound as atlas. Loc: UWO.
    Plans, at scales of 1:600 and 1:1200, showing in detail by means of colour and symbol, the character of inside and outside construction of buildings, fire

walls, height and occupancy or use.

2830. Goad, Charles E. **Harriston. Fire insurance plan, 1894, revised 1904.** 2 sheets. Loc: UWO.
Plan, at scale of 1:600, showing in detail by means of colour and symbol, the character of inside and outside construction of buildings, fire walls, height and occupancy or use.

2831. Goad, Charles E. **Hillsburgh. Fire insurance plan, 1907.** 2 sheets. Loc: NAC, UWO, GPL. NAC: 440/Hillsburgh/1907/#9480.
Plan, at scale of 1:600, showing in detail by means of colour and symbol, the character of inside and outside construction of buildings, fire walls, height and occupancy or use. GPL copy is monochrome microfiche.

2832. Goad, Charles E. **Key plan of Guelph, 1878.** 1 sheet. Loc: UGA.
A plan of the whole area of the town of Guelph drawn to accompany Goad's revisions to the three Sanborn plans of Guelph (1875).

2833. Goad, Charles E. **Key plan of Guelph, 1897.** 2 sections. Loc: NAC, UWO. NAC: Map 0009463.
A fire insurance plan that extends to Silver Creek Road in the west Speedvale Road in the north, Metcalfe Street in the east and Forest Street in the south. Section 2 includes small plans of several properties: Silver Creek Brewery, the Guelph electric street railway, Corinthian Stone Company and the Ontario Agricultural College and Experimental Farm. The scale is 100 feet to an inch.

2834. Goad, Charles E. **Palmerston. Fire insurance plan, 1890.** 1 sheet. Loc: NAC, UWO, GPL. NAC: 440/Palmerston/1890/#9616.
Plan, at scale of 1:600, showing in detail by means of colour and symbol, the character of inside and outside construction of buildings, fire walls, height and occupancy or use. GPL copy is monochrome microfiche.

2835. Goad, Charles E. **Palmerston. Fire insurance plan, 1914.** 2 sheets. Loc: NAC, UWO, AO. NAC: 440/Palmerston/1914/#9617.
Plan, at scale of 1:600, showing in detail by means of colour and symbol, the character of inside and outside construction of buildings, fire walls, height and occupancy or use.

2836. Goad, Charles E. **Rockwood. Fire insurance plan, 1904.** 2 sheets. Loc: NAC, UWO, AO, GPL. NAC: 440/Rockwood/1904/#9672.
Plan, at scale of 1:600, showing in detail by means of colour and symbol, the character of inside and outside construction of buildings, fire walls, height and occupancy or use. GPL copy is monochrome microfiche.

2837. Provincial Insurance Surveys. **Arthur. Fire insurance plans, 1936.** 4 sheets. Loc: UWO.
Key plan and three sheets at scale of 1:500. showing in detail by means of colour and symbol, the character of inside and outside construction of buildings, fire walls, height and occupancy or use.

2838. Provincial Insurance Surveys. **Elora. Fire insurance plans, 1936.** 5 sheets. Loc: UWO.

Plans showing by means of colour and symbol the character of inside and outside construction of buildings, fire walls, height and occupancy or use.

2839. Provincial Insurance Surveys. **Fergus. Fire insurance plans, 1936.** 7 sheets. Loc: UWO.

Plans, at scales of 1:600 and 1:1200, showing by means of colour and symbol, the character of inside and outside construction of buildings, fire walls, height and occupancy or use.

2840. Provincial Insurance Surveys. **Mount Forest. Fire insurance plans, 1937.** 9 sheets. Loc: UWO.

Plans showing by means of colour and symbol the character of inside and outside construction of buildings, fire walls, height and occupancy or use.

2841. Sanborn, D.A. **Guelph. Fire insurance plans, 1875; revised 1878.** 3 sheets. Loc: UGA.

A set of three sheets showing the exact location of all buildings in the central business district with details of their dimensions and building materials. The area shown extends as far north as Robertson's Foundry at the corner of Eramosa and Mitchell, includes the various mills along the Speed River and then follows the line of Dublin Street to London Road in the northwest. The original plans have been revised by Charles Goad. A marginal note states that Guelph had a population of 9,000 in 1875, and that its water facilities were 'not good'. These remarkably early plans survived in the care of John Sutherland and Sons Insurance Limited and have been donated to the University of Guelph Archival and Special Collections.

2842. Underwriters' Survey Bureau. **Fergus. Fire insurance plans, 1921.** 6 sheets. Loc: NAC, UGL, GPL, UWO. NAC: 440/Fergus/1921/#9427.

Plan, at scale of 1:600, showing in detail by means of colour and symbol, the character of inside and outside construction of buildings, fire walls, height and occupancy or use. GPL copy is monochrome microfiche.

2843. Underwriters' Survey Bureau. **Fergus. Fire insurance plans, 1921; revised 1935.** 6 sheets. Loc: NAC, AO, GPL, UWO. NAC: 440/Fergus/1935/#9428.

Plan, at scale of 1:600, showing in detail by means of colour and symbol, the character of inside and outside construction of buildings, fire walls, height and occupancy or use. GPL copy is monochrome microfiche.

2844. Underwriters' Survey Bureau. **Guelph. Fire insurance plans, 1922, revised 1946.** 54 sheets bound as atlas. Loc: UWO.

Plans showing in detail by means of colour and symbol the character of inside and outside construction of buildings, fire walls, height and occupancy or use.

2845. Underwriters' Survey Bureau. **Guelph. Fire insurance plans, 1922; revised 1929.** 42 sheets. Loc: AO, UWO.

Detailed plans, using colour and symbol, showing the character of inside and outside construction of buildings. Most plans are at the scale of 1:600 and some of the peripheral parts of the town are at 1:1200. The set at the University of Western Ontario is bound together as an atlas.

2846. Underwriters' Survey Bureau. **Guelph. Fire insurance plans, 1960.** 93 sheets.
Loc: NAC, UGL, AO, GPL. NAC: 440/Guelph/1960/#23296.
Plan showing in detail by means of colour and symbol, the character of inside
and outside construction of buildings, fire walls, height and occupancy or use.
Scales range from 1:1200 to 1:7200. GPL copy is microfilm microfiche.

2847. Underwriters' Survey Bureau. **Harriston. Fire insurance plans, 1894; revised
1920.** 2 sheets. Loc: NAC, UGL, AO, GPL, UWO. NAC: 440/Harriston/1920/#9467.
Plan, at scale of 1:600, showing in detail by means of colour and symbol, the
character of inside and outside construction of buildings, fire walls, height
and occupancy or use. GPL copy is monochrome microfiche.

2848. Underwriters' Survey Bureau. **Mount Forest. Fire insurance plans, 1904; revised
1926.** 5 sheets. Loc: NAC, AO, UWO. NAC: 440/Mount Forest/1926/#9569.
Plan, at scale of 1:600, showing in detail by means of colour and symbol, the
character of inside and outside construction of buildings, fire walls, height
and occupancy or use.

MAPS AND SUBDIVISION PLANS OF MUNICIPAL UNITS

AMARANTH

2849. Black, Hugh. **Map of the Township of Amaranth, 1823.** Loc: NAC, AO. NAC:
430/Amaranth/1823.
Map of original survey in 1823 at scale of 40 chains to an inch. From original
in Ontario Department of Lands and Forests, Surveys Branch, Reel M.308, page
469.

2850. Parke, Thomas. **Amaranth Township, c1843.** Loc: AO. C-3.

ARTHUR TOWNSHIP

2851. Davis, John. **Plan of lots laid out for Geo. Cushing, Esq., being a subdivision
of the 4th subdivision of Lot 20, east of the Owen Sound Road, Arthur Township,
1905.** 1 map. Loc: ALR.
Plan of George Cushing's Survey bounded by the Owen Sound Road in the west,
Roman Catholic Church property in the north, the Canadian Pacific Railway line
in the east and a road allowance between Lots 20 and 21 in the east. The scale
is 60 feet to an inch.

2852. Map and Advertising Co. Ltd. **Guidal landowners' map of Township of Arthur, 1917.**
1 sheet, 19-3/4 x 11-1/2. Loc: NAC, AO. NAC: 430/Arthur/1917/#48691.
A detailed map showing lot owners' names at a scale of 1 inch to a mile.
Marginal advertisements.

2853. McDonald, John. **Arthur, County of Wellington, 1842.** 1 map. Loc: ALR.
Crown Survey of the township drawn to the scale of 40 chains to an inch.

2854. McDonald, John. **Map of Arthur Township west of Luther and north of Purchase
Line surveyed in 1828; 1841.** Loc: NAC. 430/Arthur/1841.
Map of original surveys, showing lots along the Owen Sound Road. From original
in Department of Lands and Forests, Surveys Branch, Reel M.308, p. 493.

2855. McDonald, John. **Township of Arthur, 1841.** Loc: NAC, AO. AO:C-5; NAC:430/Arthur/1841.

Map of original survey at scale of 40 chains to an inch. From original in Ontario Department of Lands and Forests, Surveys Branch, Reel M.305, page 492.

2856. **Plan of part of Arthur Township, 1844.** Loc: AO. C-5.

2857. Wilson, Hugh. **Plan of the subdivision of Divisions 1 and 2, Lot 2, Range 1, west of the Owen Sound Road, Township of Arthur, 1875.** 1 map. Loc: ALR.

Plan of McDonald's (sic) Survey that extends to the west and east of Martin and South Water Streets. The scale is 3 chains to an inch. The owner is listed as A.H. MacDonald.

ARTHUR VILLAGE

2858. Boultbee, William. **Plan of lots in the Village of Arthur of the property of Timothy Carroll, Esq., 1857.** 1 map. Loc: ALR.

Plan of Timothy Carroll's Survey showing lots north of Frederick Street and west of Smith Street. The scale is 1 chain to an inch.

2859. Boultbee, William. **Plan of lots in the Village of Arthur, the property of Andrew Mitchell, 1857.** print, ms add, 56 x 70 cm, scale 1 inch to 2 chains. Loc: ALR, AO. AO: D-1.

Plan of Mitchell's Survey that extends to Frederick Street in the west, Frances Street in the north, Eliza Street in the east and Catharine Street in the south. A slip attached to the copy in the Archives of Ontario announces a sale of land on 15 September.

2860. Crown Lands Department. **Arthur, Ontario, 1846.** ms. Loc: AO. D-1.

2861. Henry, James. **Plan of building and park lots adjoining the Village of Arthur being a subdivision of the north half of Lot 1, Concession 1, Township of Luther, c1870.** 1 map. Loc: ALR.

Plan of MacDonald's Survey that extends east of the road between the Townships of Arthur and Luther.

2862. McDonald, John. **Plan of reserve in the southern extremity of the Township of Arthur as laid into town and park lots, 1842.** col ms, 63 x 75 cm, scale 1 inch to 5 chains. Loc: MNR, AO. SR 6497.

A plan of the triangular area that became the Village of Arthur bounded by Catharine, Wells and Eliza Streets, showing the dimensions of town and park lots, the mill pond and dam, and the recommended reserves for market and burial ground. A related map that was the office copy of the Surveyor General and adds the names of some patentees is held by the Archives of Ontario, which also has a printed map dated 1846 that contains the same information.

2863. **Plan of part of the Town of Arthur surveyed for Andrew Mitchell, 1855.** print, 51 x 43 cm, scale 1 inch to 4 chains. Loc: KPL.

The map has a note regarding a sale of lots on 1 June 1855.

2864. West, Robert. **Plan of D.T. Small's subdivision of portions of Park Lots 1 and 2, south of Domville Street in the Crown Survey of the Village of Arthur, 1907.** 1 map. Loc: ALR.

Plan of Small's Survey showing lots that extend south of Domville, Adelaide and Walton Streets. The scale is 2 chains to an inch.

2865. Wheelock, C.J. **Plan of building and park lots in the Village of Arthur laid out for Messrs Chadwick and Anderson on a subdivision of the north half of Lot 1, Concession 1 in the Township of Luther, 1878.** 1 map. Loc: ALR.

Plan of Chadwick and Anderson Survey that extends to Eliza Street in the west, Draper Avenue in the north, Lorne Avenue in the east and Carrill Street in the south. The scale is 2 chains to an inch.

2866. Wheelock, C.J. **Plan of building lots in the Village of Artur (sic), laid out for Ellen M. Daniels on a portion of Lot 23, Concession B in the Township of Peel, 1877.** 1 map. Loc: ALR.

Plan of Ellen Daniel's Survey that extends west of Owen Sound Road and north of the Burwell line.

2867. Wheelock, C.J. **Plan of building lots laid out for Mr William Clarke on a portion of Park Lot 2, Ranges 1 and 2, Village of Arthur, 1876.** 1 map. Loc: ALR.

Plan of William Clarke's Survey bounded by Clarke Street in the west, Domville in the north, Tucker in the east and Smith Street in the south. The scale is 2 chains to an inch.

2868. Wheelock, C.J. **Plan of subdivision of Lots 4 and 5 of Carroll's Survey and subdivision of Lots 33, 34 and 35 on Isabella and Frederick Streets in the Village of Arthur, laid out for Mr J.F. Hollinger, 1876.** 1 map. Loc: ALR.

Plan of Hollinger's Survey showing lots that extend west of Isabella Street and south of Frederick Street and west of Frederick Street and south of Smith Street. The scale is 1 chain to an inch.

2869. Wheelock, C.J. **Plan of subdivision of Park Lot A on the south side of Domville Street and Park Lot A on the north side of Frederick Street, Village of Arthur, 1876.** 1 map. Loc: ALR.

Plan of 'McCord's first survey'. The scale is 100 feet to an inch.

2870. Wheelock, C.J. **Plan of subdivision of Park Lots 2 and 3 in Range 3, Village of Arthur, the property of A.J. McCord, Esq., 1875.** 1 map. Loc: ALR.

Plan bounded by Andrew Street in the west, the Toronto, Grey and Bruce Railway line in the north, McCord Street in the east and Domville Street in the south. The plan is labelled as 'McCord's 2nd survey north of Domville Street'. The scale is 200 feet to an inch.

2871. Wheelock, C.J. **Plan of the Village of Arthur in the County of Wellington, 1873.** 1 map. Loc: ALR.

Plan that extends from Catharine Street in the west, Wells Street in the north, Macauley Street in the east and the junction of Elizabeth and Catharine Streets in the south. The scale is 4 chains to an inch.

2872. Wheelock, C.J. **Subdivisions of Lots 4 and 5, Carroll's Survey, Village of Arthur, 1876.** 1 map. Loc: ALR.
   Plan of T. Carroll's Survey showing subdivisions of Lots 33, 34 and 35 on Isabella and Frederick Streets. The scale is 1 chain to an inch.

CLIFFORD

2873. Carroll, C. **Plan of survey, subdivision of Park Lot 16 in the Village of Clifford, 1875.** 1 map. Loc: ALR.
   Plan of Clifford Park Lot 16 showing land north of Allan Street and west of Cecilia Street. The scale is 2 chains to an inch.

2874. Kertland, E.H. **Plan of the Village of Minto comprising lots 59 and 60 in Concessions C and D surveyed for Charles Allan and James Geddes.** print, col, 89 x 63 cm, scale 1 inch to 3 chains. Loc: ALR, WCA.
   A plan, registered 26 January 1857, showing lot numbers and sizes in a subdivision from Main Street to James Street and Brown Street to Howick Street and road connections to Hamilton, Southampton and Elora. Minto was renamed Clifford.

2875. LaPenotiere, W.H. **Plan of the Village of Clifford, being composed of the southwest half of Lots 58, 59, 60 and 61 in Concession C and Lots 58, 59 and 60 and 80 acres of Lot 61 in Concession D, Township of Minto, County of Wellington, 1874.** 1 map. Loc: ALR.
   Plan of Clifford bounded by Concession 15 of Minto Township in the west, the road allowance between Clifford and Howick Township in the north, Brown Street in the east and Main Street in the south. The scale is 4 chains to an inch.

DRAYTON

2876. Bolton, Lewis. **Plan of the Village of Drayton, 1893.** 1 map. Loc: ALR.
   Plan showing lots east and west of Wellington Street and north and south of Main Street. The scale is 4 chains to an inch.

ELORA

2877. Bowman, E.P. **Plan of subdivision of Lots 9 and 10 north of Peel Street and east of Metcalfe Street in the Village of Elora as laid out on Plan 56 dated July 12, 1851 said lots being the property of Ann Webster's estate, 1910.** 1 map. Loc: GLR. Map 331.
   Plan drawn to the scale of 30 feet to an inch.

2878. Burke, J.W. **Plan of Park Lot 21 on the west side of Geddes Street in the Village of Elora, 1858.** 1 map. Loc: GLR. Map 101.
   Plan showing River and Geddes Street, the Elora and Salem Road, and the Irvine River bordering the park lot. The lot was surveyed for W.P. Newman. The scale is 1 chain to an inch.

2879. Burke, J.W. **Plan of part of the Village of Elora and of Lot 18, Concession 11, Nichol Township, 1859.** 1 map. Loc: GLR. Map 112.
   Plan that extends from the Elora and Saugeen Road to the west, Emily Street to the north, Irvine Street t the east and Colborne Street to the south. The

property was owned by Charles Allan and James Mathieson. The scale is 4 chains to an inch.

2880. Burwell, Lewis. **Plan of the village of Elora, c1832.** print, ms add. Loc: WCA.
An early plan showing the village laid out for William Gilkison on the south side of the Grand River. Manuscript additions include signed names of Gilkison's sons on particular lots as they divided these among themselves in the later 1830s after their father's death.

2881. Gilkison, W.S. **Town of Elora, compiled from the Surveys of Burwell, Kertland, Percival and MacIntosh, c1855.** print, col, 95 x 62 cm. Loc: NAC, AO, KPL, WCA. AO:D-3: NAC:440/Elora/n.d./#21072.
A printed and coloured map showing the streets and lot lines and identifying many buildings. Lots coloured red were offered for sale on 4 October. The copy at the Archives of Ontario has manuscript additions.

2882. Kertland, Edwin H. **Plan of Elora (title missing), 1856.** print, c 50 x 45 cm, scale 1 inch to 3 chains, top half missing. Loc: GLR. Map 111.
Plan of part of Elora from the Guelph Road east to Waterloo Street and beyond Queen street to Fergus Road, showing Victoria Circus, several other crescents and a few buildings. Names of various owners and surveys have been added by hand. Survey registered 20 May 1859 as plan 111 in the Guelph Land Registry.

2883. Kertland, Edwin H. **Plan of the village ground of Elora in Nichol as divided into village and park lots, proposed to be annexed to the Pilkington Tract, Woolwich, according to application made to Parliament in the session of 1850, containing 976-1/2 acres excluding water.** col ms, 52 x 32 cm. Loc: MNR. SR 90.
A plan of unnumbered village and park lots that extend north and south of the Grand River.

2884. Kertland, Edwin H. **Plan of the Village of Elora comprising Lots 1, 2, and 3, broken front on the north side of the Grand River and Lots 1, 2, 3, broken front on the south side of the Grand River in the Township of Nichol, 1851.** print, ms adds, 78 x 49 cm. Loc: MNR, GLR. MNR: SR 91; GLR: Map 56.
Plan of Elora between the Guelph road allowance, Colborne Street, a sideline between Lots 3 and 4 and a road allowance in front of Concession 1. The plan shows churches, schools, and mills and 'also the number of Professional men, Tradesmen, and Mechanics at present residing there'. The population of Elora is given as 400 in 1850. The scale is 4 chains to an inch. The Registry Office copy is a transcript of the original.

2885. LaPenotiere, W.H. **Plan of part of Elora showing Binkley and Hamilton Streets, 1882.** 1 map. Loc: GLR. Map 286.
Plan bordered by the Elora Guelph Road in the west, York Street in the north, Park Road in the east and Binkley Street in the south. The scale is 3 chains to an inch.

2886. LaPenotiere, W.H. **Plan of subdivision of Lots 1, 2 and 3 east side of Metcalfe Street and Lot 4 west side of Geddes Street, Elora, County of Wellington, 1869.** 1 map. Loc: GLR. Map 191.
Plan of J. Godfrey's Survey drawn to the scale of 33 feet to an inch.

2887. LaPenotiere, W.H. **Plan of subdivision of plan 58 northwest of David Street in the Village of Elora, surveyed for E. Evans, Esq., 1876.** 1 map. Loc: GLR. Map 247.
Plan bordering on Geddes Street in the west, Tupper Street in the east and David Street in the south. The scale is 1 chain to an inch.

2888. LaPenotiere, W.H. **Plan of the Village of Elora, 1868.** 1 map. Loc: GLR. Map 181.
Plan bordered by Elora and Guelph Road in the west, David Street in the north, Bridge Street in the west, and Fergus Road in the south.

2889. Macintosh, James. **Plan of part of the Town of Elora, 1853.** print, 59 x 47 cm, ms adds, scale one inch to 4 chains. Loc: NAC, AO. AO:D-3; NAC:440/Elora/1853/#21084.
A plan based on E.H. Kertland's Survey north of the river and Percival's Survey west of Arthur Road. South of the river, Waterloo Street and Arthur Road are shown. Sale by auction is announced for 29 July and 9 September and there are later manuscript notes on the sales.

2890. Macintosh, James. **Plan of part of the Town of Elora being composed of Lot 18, Concession 11, Nichol Township, 1854.** 1 map. Loc: GLR. Map 76.
Plan that includes Erb, Geddes and South Streets. The scale is 4 chains to an inch. James Mathieson, from Hamilton, is listed as owner of the land.

2891. McLean, J.H. **Plan of Lot 1 and part of Lot 2 east of Geddes Street, Elora, 1893.** 1 map. Loc: GLR. Map 304.
Plan bordered by Geddes Street in the west and Colborne Street in the east. The scale is 20 feet to an inch.

2892. McLean, J.H. **Plan shewing subdivision of Lot 82 east of Geddes Street and Lot 83 west of Princess Street in Elora, 1893.** 1 map. Loc: GLR. Map 303.
Plan drawn to the scale of 40 feet to an inch.

2893. Newman, R.M. **Plan of subdivisions of part of broken Lot 4 in the Village of Elora and broken Lot 5 in the Township of Nichol north of the Grand River, 1876.** 1 map. Loc: GLR. Map 246.
Plan of lots to the north and south of David Street. The scale is 4 chains to an inch.

2894. Smith, Henry. **Plan of subdivision of Lots 1, 2, and 3 west of Metcalf (sic) Street in the Village of Elora, County of Wellington, 1870.** 1 map. Loc: GLR. Map 211.
Plan showing lots bordering on Margaret, James and Metcalfe Streets. The scale is 33 feet to an inch.

2895. Smith, Henry. **Plan of subdivisions of part of broken front Lot 1, south side of the Grand River in the Village of Elora, County of Wellington, 1870.** 1 map. Loc: GLR. Map 194.
Plan that extends to Guelph Road in the west and Owen Sound Street in the north. The scale is 3 chains to an inch.

ERAMOSA

2896. Dyer, H.L. **Village of Rockwood, 1938**. 1 sheet, 35.5 x 27.7. Loc: NAC. 440/Rockwood/1938/#19888.
   The plan shows streets, lots and some names of landowners.

2897. Haskins, William. **Map of building lots in the Village of Eden Mills being subdivision of township Lot 1 in Concession 2 of Eramosa, the property of Henry Hortop and John A. Davidson, 1855**. ms. Loc: GLR. Map 69.
   Map showing the boundaries to be Main Street, Elm Street and the Eramosa Township border to the south. The scale is 1 chain to an inch.

2898. Horne, William. **Plan of building lots in the Village of Rockwood, 1857**. 1 map. Loc: GLR. Map 66.
   Plan showing a concession road, Mill Street, a mill pond, a grist mill and Private Road.

2899. Kerr, Francis. **Plan of building lots in the Village of Eden Mills, property of Mr H. Hortop, 1854**. 1 map. Loc: GLR. Map 68.
   Plan that extends from Concession 1 in the west, Main Street in the north, mill property in the east and the Eramosa Township line in the south. The scale is 4 chains to an inch.

2900. **Map of the Village of Everton being parts of Lots 11 and 12, Concession 7, Eramosa Township, property of Messrs Everts and Stewart, c1854**. ms. Loc: GLR. Map 70.
   Plan that extends from Market Street in the west, Albert Street in the north, Evert Street in the east, and Wellington Street in the south.

2901. Niven, D.A. **Plan of the lands and premises of the Harris Woollen Mills being part of Lot 4, Concession 4, Eramosa and Lots 149 to 157 in Block F, Rockwood, Ontario, 1919**. 1 map. Loc: GLR. Map 282.
   Plan that extends south of Rock Street and east of Fall Street. The scale is 100 feet to an inch.

2902. Parke, Thomas. **Eramosa Township, 1843**. Loc: AO. C-14.

2903. **Plan of building lots in the Village of Eden Mills in the Township of Eramosa, the property of Adam Lind Argo, 1852**. 1 map. Loc: GLR. Map 67.
   Plan of Eden Mills which originally formed part of Lot 1 in Concession 2 of the Township of Eramosa. The plan includes the lots north and south of Main Street and the south branch of the Speed River. The scale is 2 chains to an inch.

2904. Strange, Henry. **Henry Strange's Survey of part of Lot 5, Concession 5 in the Township of Eramosa and Block C in the Western Division as shown in Plan 260 of the Village of Rockwood, 1885**. 1 map. Loc: GLR. Map 291.
   Plan of lots to the north and south of Dowlen Street.

2905. Strange, Henry. **Plan of the Village of Rockwood in the Township of Eramosa, County of Wellington on the property of H. Strange, 1856**. 1 map. Loc: GLR, AO. AO:D-8; GLR:Map 150.

Plan which is bordered by Red Street in the west, Fall Street in the north, Main Street in the east and the Eramosa Branch of the Grand River in the south. The scale is 4 chains to an inch. The document shows the property of H. Strange indicating it was to be sold in December 1856.

2906. Strange, Henry. **Plan of the Village of Rockwood in the Township of Eramosa, County of Wellington, on the property of H. Strange, 1876**. 1 map. Loc: GLR. Map 280.
Plan that extends to Fall Street in the west, Queen Street in the north, Eramosa River in the east and Frederick Street in the south. The scale is 4 chains to an inch.

ERIN TOWNSHIP

2907. Bouthillier, T. **Erin Township, 1846**. 1 sheet, 84 x 64 cm. Loc: AO. C-14.
Crown land survey at a scale of 1:31,860.

2908. Cooper, T.W. **Plan of building lots in Village of Hillsburg (sic) being a subdivision of part of the east half of Lot 25, Concession 7, Township of Erin, 1869**. 1 map. Loc: GLR. Map 187.
Plan showing lots south of Main Street. The scale is 50 feet to an inch.

2909. Cooper, T.W. **Plan of part of the Village of Hillsburg (sic) being a subdivision of part of Lot 25, Concession 8, Township of Erin, 1869**. 1 map. Loc: GLR. Map 188.
Plan of lots between Main Street in the west and Barker Street in the east. The scale is 66 feet to an inch.

2910. Kerr, Francis. **Plan of building lots in the Village of Hillsburg (sic), composed of part of the west half of Lot 23, Concession 8, Township of Erin, Canada West, 1857**. 1 map. Loc: GLR. Map 95.
Plan that includes Guelph, Market and Wellington Streets. The property was owned by George Henshaw. The scale is 2 chains to an inch.

2911. Kerr, Robert W. **Plan of proposed improvements in road between Concessions 7 and 8 of Erin Township, 1842**. 1 sheet, 48 x 66 cm. Loc: AO. C-14.

2912. Map and Advertising Co. Ltd. **Guidal landowners' map of Township of Erin, 1917**. 1 sheet, 20 x 12. Loc: NAC, AO. AO:C-53; NAC:430/Erin/1917/#48695.
A detailed map showing lot owners' names at a scale of 1 inch to 0.875 miles.

2913. Moore, John. **Plan of the Village of Bristol in the Township of Erin, 1854**. 1 map. Loc: GLR. Map 63.
Plan of the east half of Lot 13 in Concession 7, and the west half of Lot 13 in Concession 8 that includes King, Queen, Nelson and James Streets. Thomas Bush is noted as owner. The index notes that Bristol was also known as Brisbane.

2914. Parke, Thomas. **Erin Township, 1843**. Loc: AO. C-14.

2915. Strange, Henry. **Plan of part of the Village of Hillsburg (sic) comprising parts of Lots XXV and XXVI of Concession 8 and of Lot XXV on Concession 7 in the Township of Erin as surveyed for Nazareth Hill, Esq., c1856**. 1 map. Loc: GLR.

Map 62.
　　Plan which borders on lots in Concessions 7 and 8, and the boundary line between Lots 24 and 25. The index book of plans notes this survey of Hillsburgh was never registered.

2916. Wheelock, C.J. **Plan of building lots in the Village of Hillsburg (sic) the property of George Gooderham laid out and portion of the east half of Lots 24 and 25 in Concession 7 of the Township of Erin, 1880.** 1 map. Loc: GLR. Map 280.
　　Plan that extends from the C.N.R. Station grounds in the north, George Street in the east and Main Street in the south. The scale is 2 chains to an inch.

2917. Wheelock, C.J. **Plan of building lots in the Village of Hillsburg (sic) laid out for Mr Donald McMillan, 1876.** 1 map. Loc: GLR. Map 240.
　　Plan located in the west half of Lot 25 in Concession 8 of Erin Township. The plan shows lots bordering on Main, Queen, Barber and Ann Streets. The scale is 2 chains to an inch.

2918. Wheelock, C.J. **Plan of building lots in the Village of Hillsburg (sic) being part of Lot 23, Concession 7, of the Township of Erin, the property of William How, 1862.** 1 map. Loc: GLR. Map 155.
　　A map showing numbered lots that extend between Main and William Streets.

2919. Wheelock, C.J. **Plan of building lots in the Village of Hillsburg (sic) the property of George Gooderham, Esq. laid out on part of Lots 24 and 25, Concession 7, Erin Township, 1877.** 1 map. Loc: GLR. Map 276.
　　Plan showing lots on Station, Bungy, Worts and Main Streets and immediately north of the C.N.R. Station grounds. The scale is 2 chains to an inch.

2920. Wheelock, C.J. **Plan of park lots as laid out on part of easterly half of Lot 15, Concession 9 in the Township of Erin, 1868.** 1 map. Loc: GLR. Map 193.
　　Plan drawn to the scale of 2 chains to an inch.

2921. Wheelock, C.J. **Plan of park lots laid out by William Clark comprising a portion of Lot 12, Concession 10, Erin, 1865.** 1 map. Loc: GLR. Map 164.

2922. Winter, Mr and Abrey, Mr. **Plan of part of the Village of Ballinafad, Township of Erin, 1860.** 1 map. Loc: GLR. Map 129.
　　Plan showing a subdivision of part of the southwest half of Lot 1 in Concession 8 of Erin Township. The document shows the property of John Smith's Appelbe's Farm. The scale is 1 chain to an inch.

ERIN VILLAGE

2923. Kennedy, Charles. **Erin Village, 1852.** print. scale 1 inch to 1 chain. Loc: GLR. Map 61.
　　Plan of the east half of Lots 13, 14 and 15 in Concession 9, and the west half of Lots 14 and 15, Concession 10. The plan extends from the Guelph Road in the west, Mill Pond in the north, and Church Street in the east. The index notes the plan was never registered.

2924. Schofield, M.C. **Map of Erin Village, County of Wellington, Ontario, 1893.** 1 map. Loc: GLR. Map 282.

Plan that extends to the Credit Valley Railway Station to the west, the village limits to the north, Guelph Road to the east and the village limits to the south. The scale is 2 chains to an inch.

2925. Wheelock, C.J. **Plan of building and park lots in the Village of Erin, laid out on a portion of the east half of Lot 14, Concession 9, Erin Township, 1868.** 1 map. Loc: GLR. Map 179.
Plan that marks location of a homestead and sawmill. The scale is 2 chains to an inch.

2926. Wheelock, C.J. **Plan of building lots in Erin Village as laid out on a portion of Lot 15, Concession 10 of the Township of Erin, County of Wellington, the estate of the late Daniel McMillan, 1858.** 1 map. Loc: GLR. Map 102.
A plan showing numbered lots along Main, Daniel and Wheelock Streets. The scale is 2 chains to an inch.

2927. Wheelock, C.J. **Plan of building lots in the Village of Erin as laid out in a portion of Lot 13, Concession 10, Township of Erin in the County of Wellington, 1858.** 1 map. Loc: GLR. Map 107.
Plan drawn to the scale of 1 chain to an inch. John Shingler was the owner.

2928. Wheelock, C.J. **Plan of building lots in the Village of Erin, composed of the easterly half of Lot 15 in Concession 9 of Erin Township, 1861.** 1 map. Loc: GLR. Map 157.
Plan drawn of the property of Thomas Brown. The plan shows George, James, Ann, Margaret, Henry and Antrim Streets. The plan also marks road allowances between Concessions 9 and 10 and between 15 and 16. The scale is 2 chains to an inch.

2929. Wheelock, C.J. **Plan of building lots in the Village of Erin laid out for Duncan McMillan on a part of the west half of Lot 16, Concession 10, Township of Erin, County of Wellington, 1884.** 1 map. Loc: GLR. Map 290.
Plan showing lots bordering on Pine and Daniel Streets and a road allowance between Concessions 9 and 10. The scale is 2 chains to an inch.

2930. Wheelock, C.J. **Plan of building lots in the Village of Erin laid out for Duncan McMillan on a part of the west half of Lot 16, Concession 10, Township of Erin, County of Wellington, 1879.** 1 map. Loc: GLR. Map 278.
Plan bordered by the 'Credit Valley Railway Station Grounds' in the west, May Street in the north, Pine Street in the west and Main Street in the south. The scale is 1 chain to an inch.

2931. Wheelock, C.J. **Plan of lots in the Village of Erin surveyed for William and John Carnock on part of the southwest half of Lot 14, Concession 10 of Erin, 1884.** 1 map. Loc: GLR. Map 287.
Plan that extends north of Main Street and west of Mill Street. The scale is 2 chains to an inch.

2932. Wheelock, C.J. **Plan of park and building lots in the Village of Erin as laid out for Messrs Moffatt, Murray and Beattie upon a portion of Lot 14 in Concession 10 of the Township of Erin, 1860.** 1 map. Loc: GLR. Map 174.
Plan showing Main, John and Mill Streets and the lots bordering these streets.

The scale is 2 chains to an inch.

2933. Wheelock, C.J. **Plan of the Village of Erin situate on Lots 13, 14 and 15, Concessions 9 and 10 of the Township of Erin, County of Wellington, 1861.** 1 map. Loc: GLR. Map 203.

Plan that extends north and south along Main Street. The scale is 2 chains to an inch.

2934. Wheelock, C.J. **Plan of village and park lots in the Village of Erin as laid out on part of the easterly half of Lot 15, Concession 9 of the Township of Erin, the property of Charles McMillan, 1865.** 1 map. Loc: GLR. Map 167.

Plan of lots along the Mill Privilege Pond.

FERGUS

2935. Armstrong, W. **Plan of part of Town of Fergus, 1853.** print, 73 x 56.5. Loc: NAC, MNR. NAC: 440/Fergus/1853/#26373; MNR: SR 101.

A plan at a scale of 1:2,400 of the eastern end of the town between Tower, Herrick, Hill and Wellington streets, indicating 'shaded lots for sale by George D. Fergusson without building obligation'. The 'Valuable property' was to be sold by auction on July 6.

2936. Barker, W.H. **Plan of part of Fergus, 1854.** print, 70 x 53 cm. Loc: NAC. 440/Fergus/n.d./#22333.

A map of a subdivision extending east from Herrick to Baker and Lamond Streets and from Hill Street south to Union Street that also shows mill property and the Glenlivet distillery. The lots were to be sold by public auction on 12 October 1854. The plan was lithographed at the office of the Hamilton Spectator.

2937. Bowman, Herbert. **Plan of part of Lot 13, Concession 1, Township of Nichol now in the Village of Fergus, 1912.** 1 map. Loc: GLR. Map 350.

Plan that extends east of Grand River and west of Union Street. The scale is 2 chains to an inch.

2938. Grain, William. **Belsyde Survey, plan of part of the Village of Fergus as laid out for A.D. Ferrier, Esq., 1863.** 1 map. Loc: GLR, AO. AO:B-66; GLR:Map 154.

Plan showing Belsyde, Union, Thistle, Princess and Scotland Streets. The scale is 3 chains to an inch.

2939. Grain, William. **Plan of part of the Village of Fergus known as part of the Mill Lot, 1873.** 1 map. Loc: GLR. Map 239.

Plan of the lot that is surrounded by St Andrew Street, St David Street and Queen Street. The scale is 1 chain to an inch.

2940. Grain, William. **Woodside Survey, plan of part of the Village of Fergus, being part of Lot 21, Concession 15, Nichol, 1860.** 1 map. Loc: GLR. Map 111.

Plan done for John Perry drawn to a scale of 2 chains to an inch. The document includes lots surrounding Perry and Woodside Streets and the plan borders are Garafraxa Street and the Owen Sound Road.

2941. Hagedorn, G.C. **Plan of subdivision of part of Block 1 of the Westwood farm, Fergusson Survey, Lot 2 and parts of Lots 1, 3, 10 and 11, plan 225, in the**

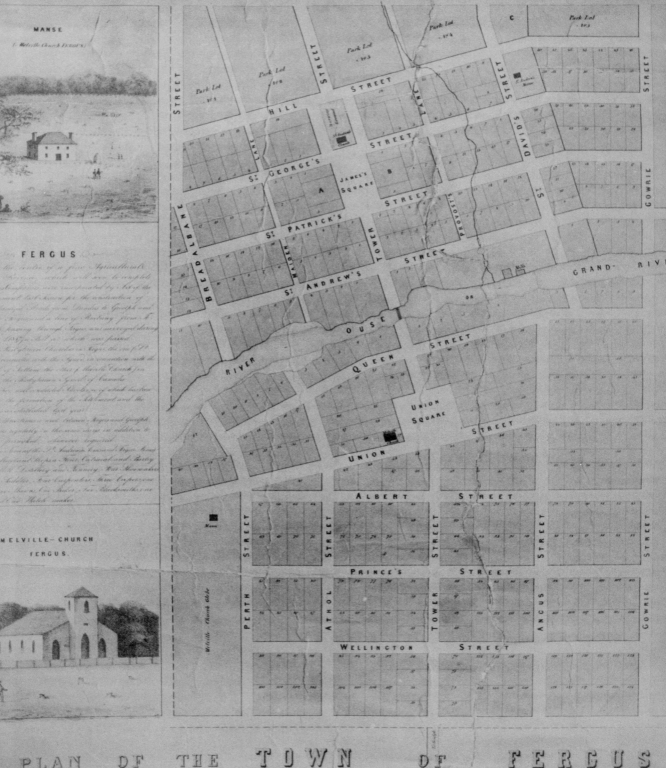

Plan of the Town of Fergus, 1847 (#2953). The original plan, only part of which is reproduced here, is bordered by illustrations of Fergus viewed from the south and the east and views of local churches.
(Wellington County Museum and Archives)

Village of Fergus, 1926. 1 map. Loc: GLR. Map 390.
Plan bordered by a road between Concessions 14 and 15 in the west, St Andrew Street in the north, Johnston Street in the east and the Grand River in the south. The scale is 60 feet to an inch.

2942. Haskins, William. **Map of the subdivision of Park Lot 12 on the northwest side of the Grand River in the Town of Fergus, 1855.** 1 map. Loc: GLR. Map 60.
Plan showing Forfar, James and St John Streets. The scale is 50 feet to an inch. John Platt of Guelph is listed as owner of the land.

2943. Howitt, Alfred. **Plan of subdivision of Park Lot 2, northwest of Garafraxa Street in the Village of Fergus, County of Wellington, 1882.** 1 map. Loc: GLR. Map 284.
Plan showing Owen Sound Road to the west, Forfar Street to the north, James Street in the east and Garafraxa Street in the south. The scale is 1 chain to an inch.

2944. Hutcheon, James. **Plan of subdivision of part of Block 2, the Westwood farm of Fergusson Survey in the Village of Fergus, 1913.** 1 map. Loc: GLR. Map 360.
Plan that extends to Johnston Street in the west, St George Street in the north, Breadalbane Street in the east and St Andrew Street in the south. The scale is 100 feet to an inch.

2945. Kerr, Francis. **Plan of part of Fergus, Canada West, 1856.** print, 55 x 82 cm. scale 1 inch to 200 feet. Loc: AO, WCA. AO:D-3.
The plan shows land ownership and mills in the area as far as Gowrie Street and St George Street and includes the houses of Adam Fergusson and A.D. Ferrier. Lots coloured green are noted to be the property of Mr Gartshore.

2946. Kertland, Edwin H. **Plan of lands at Fergus as surveyed for James Mathieson and Charles Allan, 1858.** 1 map. Loc: ALR.
Plan that extends to River Street in the west, Hill Street in the north, the town line in the east and Union Street in the south. The scale is 4 chains to an inch.

2947. Kertland, Edwin H. **Plan of lots in Fergus as sold by James Perry being part of Lot 21, Concession 15 in the Township of Nichol on the north side of Grand River, 1857.** 1 map. Loc: GLR. Map 104.
Plan drawn to the scale of 2 chains to an inch.

2948. Niven, D.A. **Plan of subdivision of part of Block 2, being part of the Westwood farm, Fergusson Survey, in the Village of Fergus, 1916.** 1 map. Loc: GLR. Map 374.
Plan that extends north and south of Kitchener Avenue, west of Johnston Street. The scale is 50 feet to an inch.

2949. Niven, D.A. **Plan of subdivision of part of Block 2, being part of the Westwood farm, Fergusson Survey, in the Village of Fergus, 1916.** 1 map. Loc: GLR. Map 376.
Plan that extends to Kitchener Avenue in the north, Johnston Street in the west and St Andrew Street in the south. The scale is 50 feet to an inch.

2950. Pollock, James. **Map of Watt Terrace adjoining the Village of Fergus, property of James McMillan, 1868.** 1 map. Loc: GLR. Map 178.

Plan of part of broken Lot 8, Concession 14 in Nichol Township. The scale is 1-1/3 chains to an inch.

2951. Schofield, M.C. **Map of a part of the Town of Fergus as laid out for James Webster, 1854.** 1 map. Loc: GLR. Map 55.
   A copy of the plan of part of Lots 12 and 13 in Concession 1, part of Lot 10 in Concession 16, and part of Lot 9 in Concession 15. The map extends from Tower Street in the west, Garafraxa Street in the north, Nichol Township boundary to the east and Eramosa Road in the south. The scale is 200 feet to an inch.

2952. Schofield, M.C. **Plan of subdivision of part of the Woodside Survey in the Village of Fergus for John Perry, 1871.** 1 map. Loc: GLR. Map 198.
   Plan of Lots 10 to 16 and 19 to 23 that extend along Perry and Woodside Streets.

2953. Schofield, M.C. **Plan of the Town of Fergus, Canada West, as laid out for sale, 1847.** litho, 66 x 47 cm, scale one inch to 300 feet. Loc: MNR, AO, UGA, WCA. MNR:SR 102; AO:D-3; UGA:XR2 MS A007.
   The plan shows the town layout from Hill Street south to Wellington Street and from Breadalbane to Gowrie as well as the location of mill buildings, churches and park lots. The plan is bordered by illustrations of Fergus viewed from the south and from the east, St Andrew's Church, Melville Church and the manse of each, Fergus' position on the road from Guelph to Owen Sound and a description of the town with a listing of establishments in 1847. The plan was lithographed in Edinburgh. The UGA has a copy of the 1982 reproduction made in connection with the publication of the Fergus History Book.

2954. Scobie and Balfour, Lithographers. **Plan of the Village of Fergus, 1847.** printed, 59 x 39 cm. Loc: NAC. 440/Fergus/1847/#3796.
   The plan appears to have been made from the Schofield survey of 1847, having the same street layout, squares and buildings.

2955. Scobie, Hugh. **Plan of part of Fergus, c1853.** print, 29.5 x 21.5, scale 1 inch to 200 feet. Loc: NAC, AO, WCA. NAC:440/Fergus/n.d./#22331.
   From the same plate as Armstrong's plan but showing more subdivided lots, so may be a little later than 1853. New town lots are shown north of Hill Street and east of Cameron Street, and there are some manuscript additions indicating buildings and some lot owners and an inset plan of park lots in A.D. Ferrier's Survey.

2956. Smith, Henry. **Plan of subdivisions of the Village of Fergus, County of Wellington, 1871.** 1 map. Loc: GLR. Map 199.
   Plan bordered by a road allowance between Concessions 14 and 15 in the west, Garafraxa Street to the north, Maiden Lane to the east, and St George's Street to the south. The scale is 2 chains to an inch.

2957. Strange, Henry. **Plan of part of the Village of Fergus and South Kinettles (sic), surveyed for Honourable Adam Fergusson, G.D. Fergusson and John Watt Esq., 1856.** print, scale 1 inch to 4 chains. Loc: GLR, WCA. GLR:Map 77.
   Plan with borders extending from Garafraxa Street to Concession Road between Concessions 14 and 15 to South Kinnettles. The plan marks some property owners and St Andrew's Church in Fergus.

2958. Wadsworth, Mr. **Plan of the resubdivision of Lots 5, 6, 10, 11, 12, 13, 14, and 17 in the subdivision of Lots 19 and 20, Concession 16 of the Township of Nichol, County of Wellington, 1871.** 1 map. Loc: GLR. Map 207.
Plan that extends to the north and south of Gordon Street. A note on the map states that the land was annexed to the Town of Fergus. The scale is 3 chains to an inch.

2959. Wellington South Registry Office. **Plan of Fergus showing all registered plans to 1888.** 1 sheet, 99 x 90 cm. Loc: AO. D-3.
A 1923 copy of the original, drawn at a scale of 1:2376.

GARAFRAXA

2960. Carbert, J.A. **Plan of building lots in the Village of Douglas, Township of Garafraxa, laid out upon a portion of Lot 11, Concession 8, for Mr Paul Couse, 1880.** 1 map. Loc: ALR, AO. Map 279.
Plan that extends east of Frederick Street and north of North Broadway Drive.

2961. Grain, William. **Plan of subdivision of Lots 62, 63, 64 and 65 in Dobbin Street in the Village of Douglas, Garafraxa Township, 1860.** 1 map. Loc: GLR. Map 125.
Plan which shows Skene, McGill, Dobbin, North and St David Streets. The plan was drawn for George Douglass Fergusson and John Watt.

2962. Kerr, Robert W. **Plan of proposed road through Township of Garrafraxa (sic), surveyed by order of the District Council, 1842.** col ms, 42 x 119 cm, scale one inch to 40 chains. Loc: AO. C-16.
A plan of the new road from Guelph to Fergus, showing all abutting townships and details of the survey grid.

2963. Parke, Thomas. **Garafraxa Township, 1843.** Loc: AO. C-16.

2964. Ryckman, Samuel. **Garafraxa West, 1821.** ms. Loc: MNR, ALR.
The Crown Survey of the township.

2965. Strange, Henry. **Plan of part of the Village of Douglas, Township of Garafraxa, surveyed for G.D. Fergusson and John Watt, 1856.** 1 map. Loc: ALR.
Plan of Belwood (formerly Douglas) that extends to Patrick Street in the west, North Broadway in the north and east of St David Street.

GUELPH

2966. Bowman, E.P. **Plan of Stull Survey a subdivision of Lots 10 to 17 inclusive, registered plan 215, City of Guelph, 1925.** 1 map. Loc: GLR. Map 389.
Plan bordered by Woolwich Street in the west, Stull Avenue in the north, Dufferin Street in the west and Earl Street in the south. The scale is 40 feet to an inch.

2967. Bowman, E.P. **Plan of subdivision of part of Lot 28 and part of Lot 40, registered plan 215, City of Guelph, 1926.** 1 map. Loc: GLR. Map 392.
Plan showing lots north and south of Mac Avenue and bordered by Woolwich Street in the west and the Guelph and Goderich Railway lands in the east. The

scale is 40 feet to an inch.

2968. Bowman, E.P. **Plan of subdivision of part of Lots 1, 2 and 3 in Range III, Division A in the Township of Guelph, now in the City of Guelph, 1927.** 1 map. Loc: GLR. Map 393.

    Plan that extends to both sides of Barber Avenue, north of London Road. The owner is listed as Charles Barber. The scale is 40 feet to an inch.

2969. Bowman, E.P. **Plan of subdivision of parts of Lots 29, 30 and 31, registered plan 128 in the City of Guelph, 1925.** 1 map. Loc: GLR. Map 391.

    Plan that extends to Metcalfe Street in the west, Hepburn Avenue in the north, Jackson Street in the east and Grange Street in the south. The scale is 50 feet to an inch.

2970. Bowman, E.P. **Plan of subdivision of parts of Lots 3 and 4, Range III, Division F, in the City of Guelph, 1924.** 1 map. Loc: GLR. Map 388.

    Plan that extends to Stevenson Street in the west, Grand Trunk Railway in the north, Garibaldi Street in the east and the Malleable Iron Company in the south. J.W. Lyon is listed as owner. The scale is 60 feet to an inch.

2971. Bowman, E.P. **Plan of subdivision of parts of Park Lots 75, 76 and 77, Canada Company's Survey in the City of Guelph, 1929.** 1 map. Loc: GLR. Map 394.

    Map showing lots immediately south of Bedford and Bristol Streets. The scale is 40 feet to an inch.

2972. Bowman, E.P. **Plan of the Dodds Survey a subdivision of part of Lot 5, broken front, Division F, formerly in the township now in the City of Guelph, 1932.** 1 map. Loc: GLR. Map 397.

    Plan that extends west of Armstrong Avenue. The scale is 60 feet to an inch.

2973. Bowman, E.P. **Sketch of survey of part of Lot 6, Range I, Division F, City of Guelph, property of H.B. Higinbotham, 1924.** 1 plan. Loc: UGA. XR1 MS A005.

    A plan of the Ker Cavan lot that extends south of Palmer Street, west of Tyrcathleen Street and north of Grange Street. Part of Allan-Higinbotham Collection.

2974. Brosius, H. **Bird's eye view of Guelph, 1873.** 1 sheet, 45.7 x 59.5. Loc: UGA, NAC, AO. AO:D-3; NAC:440/Guelph/1873/#3844; UGA:XR2 MS A009.

    A view of Guelph from Alma Street in the west to Delhi Street in the east and from just north of London Road to the Speed River in the south. The map notes street names and notes all the churches in the town as well as the Court House, county jail, Town Hall, fairgrounds, schools, drill shed, Grand Trunk Railway stations and St Joseph's Hospital. Also included in the margins are sketches of the Court House and the Town Hall. A typed list of 'references' is taped to the reverse of the copy in the National Archives. The map was reprinted in 1982 courtesy of Hammond Manufacturing Company.

2975. Canada Company. **Town plan of Guelph, 1853.** ms. Loc: AO. Row 61, Package 5, #141.

    Plan includes a note of 1 May 1830 and was probably originally made in the 1830s with later additions; lots and streets are similar to the 1847 plan.

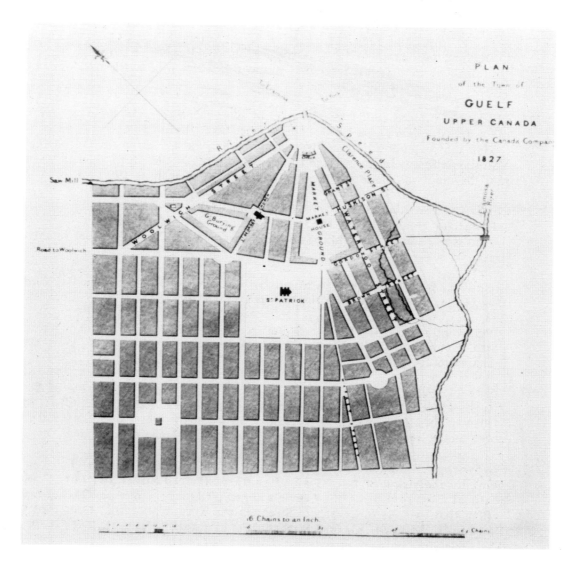

Plan of Guelph, 1827. F. Cattlin's plan (#2976) that was engraved by
J. & C. Walker and printed in Joseph Bouchette, <u>British Dominions in North
America</u> (1831).

2976. Cattlin, F. **Plan of the Town of Guelf, Upper Canada founded by the Canada Company, 1827.** 21 x 27.3 cm. Loc: MSC, MTL. MS984.042.

Cattlin's plan was engraved by J. & C. Walker in England and included in Joseph Bouchette's 1831 monograph, The British Dominions in North America, Volume I, opposite page 118. Part of the Macdonald Stewart Art Centre Collection; purchased in 1984. A copy is also held by the Metro Toronto Central Library. The plan notes street names and the location of market ground, burying ground and St Patrick's Church.

2977. Chadwick, F.J. **Amended map of part of Grange's Survey in the Town of Guelph made for the executors, 1877.** 1 map. Loc: GLR. Map 258.

Plan that extends to Alma Street in the west, Paisley Street in the north, Edinburgh Street in the east and Inkerman Street in the south. The index notes that the map was made for the Grange estate. The scale is 198 feet to an inch.

2978. Chadwick, F.J. **Amended map of subdivision of Park Lot 25 in the Town of Guelph laid out for Henry Hatch, 1863.** 1 map. Loc: GLR. Map 156.

Plan that extends to Dublin Street in the north and Suffolk Street in the east. The scale is 1 chain to an inch.

2979. Chadwick, F.J. **Amended plan of subdivision of Lots 9 to 22 inclusive, Range I, Division A, Town of Guelph, as shewn by plan 205, 1872.** 1 map. Loc: GLR. Map 253.

Plan that extends to Division Street in the west, Woolwich Street in the north, Extra Street in the east and Exhibition Street in the south. The scale is 2 chains to an inch.

2980. Chadwick, F.J. **Chadwick's Survey, London Road being a subdivision of Lots 1 and 2 in Kirkland's Survey in the Town of Guelph, 1877.** 1 map. Loc: GLR. Map 257.

Plan of lots that extends to Yorkshire Street in the west, London Road in the north and Kirkland Street in the east. The scale is 1 chain to an inch.

2981. Chadwick, F.J. **Map of Chadwick survey on Liverpool Street in the Town of Guelph being a subdivision of Lots G and 1 south of Oxford Street and Lots F and 1 south of Liverpool Street in Arnold's survey, 1876.** 1 map. Loc: GLR. Map 241.

Plan that extends to Liverpool Street in the west, Wellington, Grey and Bruce Railway in the north, Oxford Street in the east and Edinburgh Road in the south. The scale is 1 chain to an inch.

2982. Chadwick, F.J. **Map of City of Guelph, 1891; revised 1906.** 1 document. Loc: GPL.

A 1906 copy of an 1891 map drawn to a scale of four chains to an inch. The map shows Guelph from Water Street in the south, to Silvercreek in the west, to Speedvale Avenue in the north and Victoria Road in the east. The map includes the name and location of several surveys conducted in the city.

2983. Chadwick, F.J. and Clawson, E.E. **Map of City of Guelph, 1891; revised 1913.** Blueline print, 113.5 x 136, 4 sections. Loc: NAC, UGL. NAC: 440/Guelph/1913(1891)/#19592.

Cadastral map, at scale of 1:3168, that shows streets, waterways, railways, lots (with dimensions) and lot numbers in the area from Silvercreek Street in west to Willow Road and Speedvale Road in the north, Victoria Road to the east and the Eramosa and Speed Rivers to the south.

2984. Chadwick, F.J. **Map of Grange Street Survey being part of Lot 5, Range II, Division F, Guelph, 1891.** 1 map. Loc: GLR. Map 298.
Plan of lots south of Grange Street and west of Stevenson Street. The scale is 2 chains to an inch.

2985. Chadwick, F.J. **Map of subdivision of Lots 9 to 22 inclusive in Range I, Division A, Town of Guelph, 1872.** 1 map. Loc: GLR. Map 205.
St Andrew's Glebe Survey extends to Exhibition Street in the west, Division Street in the north, Woolwich Street in the east and Tiffany Street in the south. The scale is 2 chains to an inch.

2986. Chadwick, F.J. **Map of subdivision of Lots 978, 979, 983 and 984 in the Canada Company Survey, Guelph, made for J.C. Chadwick, 1877.** 1 map. Loc: GLR. Map 261.
Plan bordered by Cork Street in the west, Durham Street in the east and Glasgow Street in the south. The scale is 30 feet to an inch.

2987. Chadwick, F.J. **Map of survey for A.R. McDonald in the Town of Guelph, 1855.** 1 map. Loc: GLR. Map 20.
Plan of part of Lot 22, Division A in Guelph that includes Paisley Road to the north, Glengarry Street to the east and Breadalbane Street to the south.

2988. Chadwick, F.J. **Map of survey made for the trustees of St Andrew's Church being a subdivision of Park Lots 12, 13 and 14, Range II, Division A, Town of Guelph as shown on Plan 148, 1877.** 1 map. Loc: GLR. Map 264.
Plan that extends to Kathleen Street in the west, Exhibition Street to the west and Division Street to the south. The scale is 2 chains to an inch.

2989. Chadwick, F.J. **Map of the City of Guelph, 1891.** 4 parts. Loc: UGA. XR2 MS A003.
Part of the Guelph Historical Society Collection.

2990. Chadwick, F.J. **Map of the Morris Survey in the Town of Guelph being a subdivision of Park Lots 15, 16 and part of 17 as shown on a plan made for St Andrew's Glebe trustees, 1875.** 1 map. Loc: GLR. Map 242.
Plan bordered by Kathleen Street in the north, Division Street in the east and Hospital Street in the south. The document is a subdivision of a plan done originally in 1862 by F. Kerr. The plan marks the properties of M. Smith, F.J. Chadwick and R. Thompson.

2991. Chadwick, F.J. **Map of the Town of Guelph from recent surveys and original maps, 1855.** print, 76 x 103 cm, scale 1 inch to 6 chains. Loc: UGL, NAC, AO, MTL. AO:D-3; NAC:440/Guelph/1855/#26374.
A map of Guelph from Alma Street in the west to Metcalfe Street on the east, and from just south of York Road to just north of London Road. The map includes street names, lot numbers and railway lines. The copy in the National Archives has been endorsed by John Smith and shows the proposed division into wards and the population of each ward. The University of Guelph has only a copy.

2992. Chadwick, F.J. **Plan of Lots 1, 2 and 3, east side of Eramosa Road and Lots 6, 7 and 8 in the Range II, Division F formerly in the township, now in the Town of**

Guelph shewing the portions of the same laid out into park lots, 1860. 1 map.
Loc: GLR. Map 128.
  Plan that extends from Metcalfe Street to the west, Eramosa Road to the north
and Grange Street to the south. The scale is 4 chains to an inch. The index
notes the property belonged to John Macdonald.

2993. Chadwick, F.J. **Plan of lots laid out in the Town of Guelph for George M.
  Stewart, 1860. 1 map. Loc: GPL, GLR. GLR: Map 133; GPL: Envelope 4.**
  Plan of part of Lots 9 and 10, Range 1, Division F, at the scale of 2 chains
to an inch. The lots include an area bordering Eramosa Road from King Street to
Havelock to Delhi Street and running northwest to Derry and Spring Street. A
copy at a smaller scale in the Guelph Public Library's the Byerly Collection
shows that the lots were to be sold at a public auction in Guelph in 1860.

2994. Chadwick, F.J. **Plan of lots of George M. Stewart in the Town of Guelph, 1862.**
  1 map. Loc: GLR. Map 146.
  Map showing Spring, Delhi, Derry, King and Havelock Streets.

2995. Chadwick, F.J. **Plan of northeast halves of Lots 38 and 39 in the original St
  Andrew's Glebe Survey in the Town of Guelph, made for the trustees, 1876. 1
  map. Loc: GLR. Map 245.**
  Plans showing lots bordering the town boundary line in the north and Woolwich
Road in the west. The scale is 1 chain to an inch.

2996. Chadwick, F.J. **Plan of proposed alteration of part of Queen Street, 1861.** Loc:
  GCH.
  A plan showing the proposed alterations of Queen Street in the area bounded by
Neeve Street, Queen Street and the Speed River, land which belonged to the Hon.
John A. Macdonald. The survey includes the course of a stream tributary to the
Speed as well as bridges over water courses. The scale of the plan is 1 chain to
an inch and it is attached to Bylaw No. 110, 15 July, 1861.

2997. Chadwick, F.J. **Plan of resubdivision of Lots 12 and 13 in Range III of Division
  A in the Town of Guelph, made for David Allan, 1876. 1 map. Loc: GLR. Map 254.**
  Plan of lots along Hospital, Jessie and Kathleen Streets north of Division
Street. The scale is 2 chains to an inch.

2998. Chadwick, F.J. **Plan of subdivision of Lots 7 and 8 in the first range and west
  part of Lot 6 in broken front Division F, otherwise known as Albert Place as per
  survey of A.W. Simpson, formerly in the township now in the Town of Guelph, the
  property of John Macdonald, Esq., 1860. 1 map. Loc: GLR. Map 127.**
  Plan with the borders being Metcalfe and Palmer Streets and Eramosa Road and
the Speed River. The scale is 3 chains to an inch.

2999. Chadwick, F.J. **Plan of subdivision of Park Lot 51 of the Canada Company's
  Survey in Guelph made for the trustees of the late J.C. Chadwick, 1890. 1 map.
  Loc: GLR. Map 296.**
  Plan bordered by Yorkshire Street in the west, Cork Street in the north,
Glasgow Street in the east and Durham Street in the south. The scale is 1 chain
to an inch.

3000. Chadwick, F.J. **Plan of survey for John Macdonald of part of the Town of Guelph, 1864.** 1 map. Loc: GLR. Map 161.

Plan that extends to Queen Street in the west, Grange Street in the north, Metcalfe Street in the east and Lane Street in the south. A note on the map states that Macdonald is from Goderich. The scale is 3 chains to an inch.

3001. Chadwick, F.J. **Plan of survey made for A.M. Clark being subdivision of parts of Lots 2, 3 and 4 in Range II, Division F, City of Guelph, 1888.** 1 map. Loc: GLR. Map 293.

Plan that extends to Sackville Street in the west, Elizabeth Street in the north, Stevenson Street in the east and Alice Street in the south.

3002. Chadwick, F.J. **Plan of the subdivision of Park Lot 25 in the Town of Guelph laid out for Henry Hatch, 1862.** 1 map. Loc: GLR. Map 153.

Plan that extends to Dublin Street in the north and Suffolk Street in the east. A note on the map states that Lot 25 is in the Canada Company Survey. The scale is 1 chain to an inch.

3003. Chadwick, F.J. **St George's Glebe being a subdivision into lots of Lot C with reserve in the Town of Guelph, 1872.** 1 map. Loc: GLR. Map 215.

Plan which is bordered by the town boundary to the west, the Speed River to the north, Clarence Street to the east and Woolwich Street to the south. The scale is 2 chains to an inch.

3004. Clark, Alister M. **Plan of subdivision of Lots 2, 3 and part of 4 in Range II, and parts of Lots 3 and 4 in Range I, Division F, formerly in the township now in the Town of Guelph, 1875.** 1 map. Loc: GLR. Map 231.

Plan bordered by Duke Street in the west, Elizabeth Street in the north, Morris Street in the east and Lane and Alice Streets in the south. The plan shows the route of the Grand Trunk Railway, Allan's Mill and the property of Thomas Smith. The scale is 4 chains to an inch. The index book of plans indicates that the surveyor was Alister M. Clark.

3005. Coleman, R.H. **Plan of part of the City of Guelph shewing new streets dedicated by the Canada Company, 1889.** 1 map. Loc: GLR. Map 294.

Plan showing the northeasterly sixty-six feet of Park Lots 1, 2 and 3 in the Canada Company Survey. The plan is bordered by Edinburgh Road in the west, London Road in the north, Yorkshire Road in the east and Liverpool Street in the south. The scale is 264 feet to an inch.

3006. Cooper, T.W. **Map of survey in the Town of Guelph for George J. Grange, Esq., 1869.** 1 map. Loc: GLR. Map 190.

Plan showing Lots 172, 173, 174 and 175 in Block C in Guelph. The plan shows lots immediately north and south of Inkerman Street and marks land owned by David Allan and J.T. Cunningham bordering on Edinburgh and Waterloo Roads. The plan also shows Alma Street and the Grand Trunk Railway and Galt and Guelph Railway lines. The scale is 200 feet to an inch.

3007. Cooper, T.W. **Map of the Town of Guelph in the County of Wellington, Canada West, 1862.** print. Loc: GCM.

The original map that was later reproduced c1890. The map has illustrations of the Town Hall, Court House, panorama of the town, residence of Nathaniel

Higinbotham and the Horsman Brothers Hardware store. The map extends to Silver Creek Road in the west, Speedvale Road in the north, Victoria Road in the east and the Speed River in the south. The scale is 4 chains to an inch.

3008. Cooper, T.W. **Map of the Town of Guelph in the County of Wellington, Province of Ontario, from actual surveys and original plans, c1875-1879.** Loc: UGL, GCH.

A map of the Town of Guelph that shows street names, lot numbers, churches, schools and gives the names of prominent land owners. The map has illustrations of the Town Hall and market area, court house and jail, and a panorama view of the town. The map's boundaries are Silvercreek to the west, Victoria to the east, Speedvale to the north, and Water Street, York Road, River Street and Charles Street to the south. The scale of the map is four chains to an inch. Internal evidence seems to suggest that the map depicts Guelph in the period between 1875 and 1879. The date of publication is not given; however, there is an indication that it might possibly be 1890.

3009. Cooper, T.W. **Plan of a lane laid out on Lots 7, 8, 9, 10, 11 and 16 in A.H. Macdonald's Survey of Park Lots 20, 22 and 22 in the Town of Guelph, 1877.** 1 map. Loc: GLR. Map 228.

Plan of the land that runs south from Garth Street and west to Yorkshire Street. The scale is 60 feet to an inch.

3010. Cooper, T.W. **Plan of building and park lots being a subdivision of Lots 1 and 2 west of Eramosa Road and Lots 13 and 14 in Range II in Division F, formerly in the township now in the Town of Guelph, 1877.** 1 map. Loc: GLR. Map 265.

Plan of William Hood's property that extends from Emma Street in the west, to Eramosa Road in the east and Metcalfe Street in the south. The scale is 2 chains to an inch.

3011. Cooper, T.W. **Plan of building lots being a subdivision of Block B in G.J. Grange's Survey, amended plan of part of Lot 4, Division A formerly in the township now in the Town of Guelph, 1877.** 1 map. Loc: GLR. Map 267.

Plan bordered by Paisley Street in the north, Edinburgh Road in the east and Omar and Raglan Streets in the south. The scale is 60 feet to an inch.

3012. Cooper, T.W. **Plan of building lots being a subdivision of part of Lot 2 in Range I, Division F, formerly of the township now in the Town of Guelph, property of Henry H. Oliver, 1876.** 1 map. Loc: GLR. Map 244.

Plan that extends to Queen Street in the west, Alice Street in the north, Metcalfe Street in the east and Manitoba Street in the south. The scale is 1 chain to an inch.

3013. Cooper, T.W. **Plan of building lots being a subdivision of parts of Park Lots 2, 3, 4, 5 and 6 in Range III, Division A formerly in the township now in the Town of Guelph, 1876.** 1 map. Loc: GLR. Map 277.

Plan of lots to the west of London Road and south of Kathleen Street. The scale is 1 chain to an inch.

3014. Cooper, T.W. **Plan of building lots in the Town of Guelph being a subdivision of a portion of Park Lots 78, 79, 80, 81 and 82 in the Canada Company's survey, 1876.** 1 map. Loc: GLR. Map 248.

Plan of lots south of Bedford Street and west of Wellington Street. The scale is 1 chain to an inch.

3015. Cooper. T.W. **Plan of lots owned by John Mitchell, 1874.** 1 document. Loc: GPL. Envelope 4.

A map of the lots owned by John Mitchell that were to be sold at a public auction in 1874. The map was surveyed by T.W. Cooper and was published by Copp, Clark and Company. The boundaries of the map run north along the Guelph, Eramosa, Erin and Gravel Road from Perth Street to Metcalfe Street, and west to the original road. The southern portion of the map begins at the Guelph, Elora and Fergus Gravel Road and runs north to Metcalfe Street. A number of lots include the names of owners, including Doctor William Clarke, Donald Guthrie and John Hogg. The scale is three chains to an inch. Held with the Byerly Collection.

3016. Cooper, T.W. **Plan of part of Lot 950 in the Canada Company Survey, Town of Guelph, 1868.** 1 map. Loc: GLR. Map 176.

Plan showing part of a lot between Cardigan and Woolwich Streets. The scale is 1 chain to an inch.

3017. Cooper, T.W. **Plan of part of the London Block, 1866.** Loc: GCH.

A survey of lots bordering the Speed River between Norfolk and Woolwich Streets and King Street and Eramosa Road, showing a portion of London Road between Cardigan Street and the river proposed for closure. The plan delineates millpond and millraces, road and lot dimensions and is held in a Schedule of Guelph Bylaw No. 159, 7 January, 1867. The scale is 4 feet to an inch.

3018. Cooper, T.W. **Plan of property situate on Lot 49 and part of Lot 48 and part of Lot 19, Prior's Block, Town of Guelph, estate of the late Thomas Heffernan, 1876.** 1 map. Loc: GLR. Map 250.

Plan of lots to the east of St George's Square and to the south of Douglas Street. The scale is 20 feet to an inch.

3019. Cooper, T.W. **Plan of subdivision of part of Park Lot 46, Canada Company's Survey, Town of Guelph, 1877.** 1 map. Loc: GLR. Map 259.

Plan bordered by Suffolk Street in the west, Lane Street in the north, Liverpool Street in the east and Yorkshire Street in the south. The scale is 20 feet to an inch.

3020. Cooper, T.W. **Plan of subdivision of portions of Lots 5 and 6, Division A, formerly in the township now in the Town of Guelph, 1875.** 1 map. Loc: GLR. Map 229.

Plan showing lots bordering on Guelph and Alma Streets and on Paisley Road. The scale is 2 chains to an inch.

3021. Cooper, T.W. **Plan of the resubdivision of Lots 2, 3, 4, 5, 6 and 7 in Andrew Lemon's Survey of Lots 56, 57, 58 and 59 in Albert Place in the Town of Guelph, 1877.** 1 map. Loc: GLR. Map 270.

Plan bordered by Eramosa Road in the north, Lemon Street in the east and Edward Street in the south. The plan marks the property of Frederick Biscoe. The scale is 30 feet to an inch.

3022. Cooper, T.W. **Plan of the subdivision of a portion of St Andrew's Church Glebe in the Town of Guelph, 1865.** 1 map. Loc: GLR. Map 172.

Plan of Lots 23, 24 and 25 in Range 1, Division A. The map is signed by church trustees John McCrae, Robert Patterson, David Allan and Andrew Quarrie. The scale is 2 chains to an inch.

3023. Cooper, T.W. **Plan of the subdivision of Lot 5 and part of Lot 4 in Range III, Division F now in the Town of Guelph, property of William Hearn, 1875.** 1 map. Loc: GLR. Map 230.

Plan of lots to the east of William and Hardy Streets, south of Grange Street and north of the Grand Trunk Railway. The scale is 2 chains to an inch.

3024. Cooper, T.W. **Plan of the subdivision of Lot 9 and part of Lot 8 in the Priory grounds in the Town of Guelph, William Meldrum proprietor, 1878.** 1 map. Loc: GLR. Map 273.

Plan showing Priory Street to the north, a 'street opened by Bylaw No. 69' in the west and Woolwich Street in the south. The scale is 20 feet to an inch.

3025. Cooper, T.W. **Plan of the subdivision of Lot 950 in the Canada Company Survey of the Town of Guelph, 1868.** 1 map. Loc: GLR. Map 175.

Plan of land between the junction of Woolwich and Cardigan Streets. The plan marks the location of a house and stable. The scale is 1 chain to an inch.

3026. Cooper, T.W. **Plan of the subdivision of Lots 28 and 29 in St Andrew's Church Glebe Survey, Town of Guelph, property of Messrs George Neville and John Verney, 1876.** 1 map. Loc: GLR. Map 251.

Plan bordered by Woolwich Road in the north, a road allowance between Lots 22 and 23, Division A in the east and a road allowance between Ranges I and II, Division A in the south. The scale is 66 feet to an inch.

3027. Cooper, T.W. **Plan of the subdivision of Lots 3 and 4 in Dyson's Survey of part of Park Lot B in the Town of Guelph, 1878.** 1 map. Loc: GLR. Map 272.

Plan showing lots bordering on Donnington and Wellington Streets. The plan also shows Gordon Street. The scale is 30 feet to an inch.

3028. Cooper, T.W. **Plan of the subdivision of Lots 32 and 33 and part of 31 in the John Macdonald Survey of part of Lot 6, Range II, Division F, Town of Guelph, property of John Jackson, Esq., 1875.** 1 map. Loc: GLR. Map 236.

Plan bordered by Metcalfe Street in the west, Palmer Street in the north, Jane Street in the east and Grange Street in the south. The scale is 1 chain to an inch.

3029. Cooper, T.W. **Plan of the subdivision of Lots 78 to 83 and Lots 84 to 89 inclusive in Allister M. Clark's Survey of parts of Lots 2 and 3 and part of Lot 4, Range II, Division F, formerly in the township now in the Town of Guelph, 1877.** 1 map. Loc: GLR. Map 263.

Plan bordered by Metcalfe Street in the west, Elizabeth Street and the Grand Trunk Railway in the north, a road allowance between Ranges 2 and 3 in the east and Alice Street in the south. The scale is 2 chains to an inch.

3030. Cooper, T.W. **Plan of the subdivision of Park Lot B in the Town of Guelph, property of William and Joseph Dyson, 1861.** 1 map. Loc: GLR. Map 136.

Plan that extends from Dundas Street in the west, Speed River in the north and east and Wellington Street in the south. The scale is 1 chain to an inch.

3031. Cooper, T.W. **Plan of the subdivision of Park Lots 14, 15 and 16 in the Town of Guelph, 1862.** 1 map. Loc: GLR. Map 152.
Plan that extends to Yorkshire Street in the west, London Road in the north and Glasgow Street in the east. The scale is 1 chain to an inch.

3032. Cooper, T.W. **Plan of the subdivision of Park Lots 23 and 24 in the Town of Guelph, 1861.** 1 map. Loc: GLR. Map 145.
Plan that extends to Glasgow Street in the west, Division Street in the north, Chambers Street in the west and Suffolk Street in the south. The scale is 1 chain to an inch.

3033. Cooper, T.W. **Plan of the subdivision of part of Lot 6, Range I, Division F, formerly in the township now in the Town of Guelph, property of the Venerable Archdeacon Palmer, 1874.** 1 map. Loc: GLR. Map 235.
Plan of lots along Metcalfe Street, St Catharine Street and Tyrcathlen Terrace that run between Palmer Street and Grange Street. The scale is 66 feet to an inch.

3034. Cooper, T.W. **Plan of the subdivision of part of Park Lot 47 in the Town of Guelph, 1872.** 1 map. Loc: GLR. Map 204.
Plan showing lots bordering on Oxford, Yorkshire and Liverpool Streets. The plan also shows Glasgow Street. The scale is 1 chain to an inch.

3035. Cooper, T.W. **Plan of the subdivision of parts of Lots 1, 2 and 3 in Division A, formerly in the township now in the Town of Guelph, 1878.** 1 map. Loc: GLR. Map 274.
Plan that extends from the Grand Trunk Railway in the west, St Arnaud Street in the north, Waterloo Avenue in the east and Beechwood Avenue in the south. The scale is 60 feet to an inch.

3036. Cooper, T.W. **Plan of the subdivision of parts of Lots 1, 2 and 3, Division A, formerly in the township now in the Town of Guelph, 1877.** 1 map. Loc: GLR. Map 262.
Plan that extends to Hearn Avenue in the west, Grand Trunk Railway in the north, St Arnaud in the east and Waterloo Avenue in the south. The scale is 60 feet to an inch.

3037. Cooper, T.W. **Plan of the subdivision of parts of Lots 6, 7 and 8, Division A on the northeast side of Woolwich Road formerly in the township now in the Town of Guelph, 1875.** 1 map. Loc: GLR. Map 234.
Plan bordered by Woolwich Road in the west, Marcon Street in the north and Cardigan Street in the east. The scale is 1 chain to an inch.

3038. Cooper, T.W. **Plan of the subdivision of the reserve lot in the Canada Company's Survey and Lots 5, 6, 7, 8 and 9 in the Neeve Survey in the Town of Guelph, 1877.** 1 map. Loc: GLR. Map 269.
Plan of lots that extend north of Neeve Street and to the east and west of Surrey Street. The scale is 66 feet to an inch.

3039. Cooper, T.W. **Plan shewing the subdivision of part of Lot 9, Range I, Division F, formerly in the township now in the Town of Guelph, estate of the late John Mitchell, Esq., 1876.** 1 map. Loc: GLR. Map 243.

Plan bordered by Derry Street in the west, Delhi Street in the north, Eramosa Road in the east and King Street in the south. The plan indicates each 'regular lot contains 1/7 of an acre'. The scale is 1 chain to an inch.

3040. Cooper, T.W. **Plan showing the subdivision of part of Park Lot 53 in the Canada Company's survey of the Town of Guelph, property of Henry Hatch, Esq., 1870.** 1 map. Loc: GLR. Map 196.

Plan showing land bordering on Oxford, Glasgow and Liverpool Streets. The plan also shows Dublin Street. The scale is 66 feet to an inch.

3041. Cooper, T.W. **Plans of the subdivision of Lot 15 and portions of Lots 9, 10, 11, 12, 13 and 14, Range I, and part of Lot 2 in the broken front of Division F formerly in the township now in the Town of Guelph, 1874.** 1 map. Loc: GLR. Map 221.

Plan that extends to Speedvale Road in the west, Metcalfe Street in the north, Eramosa Road in the east and Guelph and Elora Road in the south. The scale is 3 chains to an inch.

3042. Cooper, T.W. **Sketch of lots on northwest side of Cork Street, Guelph, n.d..** 1 document. Loc: UGA. XR1 MS A334070.

An undated sketch by J.W. Cooper of lots in the Town of Guelph stretching from Quebec Street to Cork Street. The scale is 1 chain to an inch. Part of the Sleeman Family Collection.

3043. Davis, John. **Plan of a subdivision of Lot 1, Range II, Division F, formerly in the township but now in the City of Guelph, 1906.** 1 map. Loc: GLR. Map 321.

Plan prepared for James Walter Lyon that includes a marking for a proposed factory site. The plan is bordered by Metcalfe Street in the west, the Canadian Pacific Railway line in the east and York Road in the south. The scale is 60 feet to an inch.

3044. Davis, John. **Plan of a subdivision of Lot 27 in St George's Glebe Survey, plan 215, Guelph, 1906.** 1 map. Loc: GLR. Map 319.

Plan bordered by Woolwich Street in the west, the northwest limit of the city in the north, the 'Guelph and Goderich Railway lands in the east' and Victoria Street in the south. The scale is 60 feet to an inch.

3045. Davis, John. **Plan of a subdivision of Lots 1, 2 and 3, plan 18, Tiffany's Survey, City of Guelph, 1906.** 1 map. Loc: GLR. Map 323.

Plan bordered by Woolwich Street in the west, Clarence Street in the north and Lane Street in the east. The scale is 30 feet to an inch. The plan lists John Stockford as the owner of the land.

3046. Davis, John. **Plan of a subdivision of Lots 20 and 21 north of Paisley Street, and Lot 20 south of Oxford Street, Arnold's Survey of the City of Guelph, property of Marion Webster, 1886.** 1 map. Loc: GLR. Map 292.

Plan showing lots bordering on Oxford, Glasgow and Paisley Streets. The scale is 40 feet to an inch.

3047. Davis, John. **Plan of a subdivision of Park Lot 8 in the Canada Company Survey, City of Guelph, County of Wellington, 1906.** 1 map. Loc: GLR. Map 318.
Plan of lots along Home Street south of London Road and east of North Street. The scale is 50 feet to an inch. The property belonged to J.W. Lyon.

3048. Davis, John. **Plan of a subdivision of parts of Lots 1 and 2, Range II, Division F, formerly in the township but now in the City of Guelph, the subdivision on Lot 2 being a subdivision of part of A.H. Clark's Survey Plan 293, City of Guelph, County of Wellington, Ontario, 1906.** 1 map. Loc: GLR. Map 322.
Plan that extends to Morris Street in the west, Alice Street in the north, Stevenson Street in the east and York Road in the south. The scale is 100 feet to an inch.

3049. Davis, John. **Plan of subdivision of part of Lot 6, Range I, Division F, formerly in the township, now in the City of Guelph, 1889.** 1 map. Loc: GLR. Map 295.
Plan that extends to the east of Palmer Street and north of Queen Street. The scale is 50 feet to an inch.

3050. Davis, W.M. **Plan of subdivision of Park Lot R, Plan 293, Clark's Survey, east of Morris Street and north of C.P.R. in the City of Guelph prepared for Hugh Ferguson, 1909.** 1 map. Loc: GLR. Map 329.
Plan drawn to the scale of 40 feet to an inch.

3051. Evans, William W. **Map of Guelph, 1882.** Loc: GPL. Detailed description of contents.
A map of Guelph to accompany Evans' City Directory of 1882 that extends from Silvercreek Road to the west to Speedvale Road to the north, Metcalfe Street to the east, and the Speed River to the south. Part of the Douglass Collection.

3052. Grand Trunk Railway. **Plan of siding at Guelph station, 1859.** Loc: GCH.
Construction details for a siding proposed to run from the Grand Trunk Railway main line at a point east of the passenger station, immediately abutting the Speed River viaduct, to lot 15. Douglas J. Sutherland, GTR Engineer, gave assurances that the siding would not disrupt activities at the Market Square. The scale is 100 feet to an inch and is attached as Schedule A to Guelph Bylaw No. 85, 5 September, 1859.

3053. Grand Trunk Railway. **Proposed Guelph passenger station and alterations to track, 1910.** 1 map. Loc: GCH.
A plan and profile of proposed alterations to the Grand Trunk Railway between the Speed River Bridge and Glasgow Street. The scale is 40 feet to an inch. The plan identifies buildings along Kent, Wyndham and Carden Streets. The plan is labelled 'Schedule to Bylaw 815'.

3054. Guelph. **Plan of public burying ground and properties in the vicinity, 1892.** Loc: AO. D-3.
Accompanies Petition #159 to Ontario Legislative Assembly by Guelph City Council.

3055. Haskins, William. **Lots in Range III, Division A in the Town of Guelph belonging to Messrs Jarvis and Scott, 1856.** print. Loc: GLR, AO. AO:B-66; GLR:Map 36.

Plan showing Emilia and Augusta Streets and two proposed road allowances. The scale is 1 chain to an inch. The copy in the Archives of Ontario was part of the Jarvis-Powell Papers.

3056. Haskins, William. **Map showing part of Tyrcathlen the property of Rev. Arthur Palmer in the Town of Guelph, 1855.** print, scale 1 inch to 66 feet. Loc: GCM, GLR. Map 32.

Plan of the front portion of Lot 6 in Range VI of Division F that extends to Palmer Street in the west, to Queen Street in the north, to Grange Street in the east and the Speed River in the south, laid out into building lots.

3057. Haskins, William. **Map showing the subdivision of broken Lot 1 and the southeast part of broken front Lot 2, Range I, Division F, formerly in the township but now in the Town of Guelph, property of John Thorp, 1860.** print. Loc: GLR. Map 120.

Plan that notes the property of the Wellington Place Reserve, Hon. John A. Macdonald, and the Upper Canada Building Society. The scale is 1 chain to an inch.

3058. Haskins, William. **Plan of park and town lots being a subdivision of the southwesterly halves of Lots 1, 2 and 5 in Concession 5, Division G, formerly of the township but now in the Town and of Guelph being part of the estate of the late Mr Charles McTague, 1857.** 1 map. Loc: GLR. Map 39.

Plan of Forest, Bellevue, Cedar and Maple Streets.

3059. Haskins, William. **Plan of the estate of Robert Thompson formerly in the township but now in the Town of Guelph, c1854.** print, 43 x 27 cm, scale 1 inch to 2 chains. Loc: GLR. Map 37.

Plan of the east halves of Lots 1 and 2 in Concession 3 of Division G that extends southeast from the River Speed, bounded by Water Street, the Guelph-Dundas road, Forbes Street and Mary Street. According to Johnson, the lots were laid out and sold in July 1854.

3060. Hobson, J. **Amended copy of C.J. Buckland's Survey, Guelph, Ontario, 1868.** 1 map. Loc: GLR. Map 182.

Plan of Range III, Division A that extends west of London Road. The scale is 2 chains to an inch.

3061. Hobson, J. **Map of Guelph, 1868.** Loc: GCH.

A map detailing limits of the Town of Guelph with individual surveys and subdivisions, and original Canada Company lots and boundaries marked. Scale approximately 5 chains to 1 inch. The record is held in the Clerk's office vault.

3062. Hobson, J. **Map of town lots in Guelph surveyed for Adam J. Fergusson, Esq., 1855.** 1 map. Loc: GLR. Map 27.

Plan bordered by Market, Edinburgh, Paisley and Yorkshire Streets. The scale is 152 feet to an inch.

3063. Hobson, J. **Plan of subdivision by J.J. Kingsmill of Lots 989, 990, 991 and 992, Canada Company's Survey in the Town of Guelph, 1869.** 1 map. Loc: GLR. Map 185.

Plan that extends south of Durham Street and west of Dublin Street. The scale is 40 feet to an inch.

3064. Hobson, J. **Plan of survey for James McCartney, Esq., northeast of Woolwich Road, Town of Guelph, 1855.** 1 map. Loc: GLR. Map 21.

Plan of McCartney's land which includes Woolwich and London Roads, Mill and Cardigan Streets. The document notes the plan is part of Lots 1, 2, 3, 4 and 5 in Division A of the Town of Guelph.

3065. Howitt, Alfred. **Plan and judge's order filed by Jane Howitt cancelling plan 297, being a subdivision of J.A. MacDonald's Survey, Lot 3, Division F, Guelph, 1895.** 1 map. Loc: GLR. Map 306.

Plan bordered by Crawford Street in the west, Surrey Street in the north, Neeve Street in the east and York Road in the south. The scale is 2 chains to an inch.

3066. Howitt, Alfred. **Plan made for Charles E. Howitt shewing the subdivision into building lots of John Macdonald's Survey of the City of Guelph, 1891.** 1 map. Loc: GLR. Map 297.

Plan bordered by Crawford Street in the west, Waterloo in the north, Neeve in the east and York Road in the south. The scale is 2 chains to an inch.

3067. Howitt, Alfred. **Plan made for Christian Kloepfer being a subdivision of a portion of Lot 1, Concession 2, Division G, formerly in the township and now in the City of Guelph, 1892.** 1 map. Loc: GLR. Map 302.

Plan that extends to the Guelph and Dundas Road to the west and the Eramosa River to the east.

3068. Howitt, Alfred. **Plan of a portion of the estate of Peter Gow into a subdivision into park lots of broken lot in Concession 3, Division G, Guelph, otherwise known as Riverside Park, 1892.** 1 map. Loc: GLR. Map 301.

Plan bordered by Edinburgh Road in the west, the Speed River in the north, Wellington Street in the east and Water Street in the south. The scale is 2 chains to an inch.

3069. Howitt, Alfred. **Plan of George Elliott's Survey being a subdivision of Park Lots 17, 18 and 19 as shown on the Canada Company's registered plan of the Town (now the City) of Guelph, 1891.** 1 plan. Loc: GLR. Map 299.

A plan of numbered lots that extend south of London Road, east of Glasgow Street and west of Dublin Street. The scale is 66 feet to an inch.

3070. Howitt, Alfred. **Plan of Maxwelton the property of Hugh Walker being a subdivision of a portion of Park Lot 42 in the Canada Company's survey of the Town (now the City) of Guelph and also a subdivision of Lots 11, 12, 13, 14 and 15 on the southeast side of Gladwin Street as shown on the plan of Arnold's survey in the said City of Guelph, 1894.** 1 map. Loc: GLR. Map 305.

Plan that extends to Clinton Street in the west, Gladwin Street in the north, Yorkshire Street in the east and Elora Street in the south. The scale is 66 feet to an inch.

3071. Hutcheon, James. **Laurine Survey, plan of subdivision of part of Lot 7, Range II in Division F, Guelph Township, now in the City of Guelph, 1912.** 1 map. Loc: GLR. Map 342.

Plan showing lots east and west of Laurine Street, west of Lane Street and north of Palmer Street. The scale is 80 feet to an inch.

3072. Hutcheon, James. **Parkholm subdivision of parts of Lots 29, 30, 31 in John McDonald's Survey, registered plan 128, in the City of Guelph, 1913. 1 map. Loc: GLR. Map 357.**
Plan bordered by Metcalfe Street in the west, Palmer Street in the north, John Street in the east and Hepburn Avenue in the south. The scale is 60 feet to an inch.

3073. Hutcheon, James. **Plan of a resubdivision of Lot 20 on the south side of Paisley Street and Lots 20 and 21 on the north side of Cambridge Street in Arnold's Survey registered plan 29, Guelph, 1906. 1 map. Loc: GLR. Map 326.**
Plan bordered by Paisley Street in the north, Glasgow Street in the east and Cambridge Street in the south. The scale is 60 feet to an inch.

3074. Hutcheon, James. **Plan of a resubdivision of Lots 632, 633, 634 and part of Lot 635 and part of Lot 54 in the Canada Company's survey, City of Guelph, 1906. 1 map. Loc: GLR. Map 324.**
Plan that extends along Glasgow Street to the west, Oxford Street to the north, Dublin Street to the east and Paisley Street to the south. The scale is 80 feet to an inch.

3075. Hutcheon, James. **Plan of a resubdivision of Lots 92, 93, 94, 95, 96, 102, 103, 104, 105, 106 and 107 of registered plan 243 in the City of Guelph, 1912. 1 map. Loc: GLR. Map 341.**
Plan that extends south of Queen Street and north of King Street. The scale is 50 feet to an inch.

3076. Hutcheon, James. **Plan of a subdivision of part of Lot 1 of Division A in the survey of Guelph Township now in the City of Guelph and also a resubdivision of Lots 14, 15, 16 and 17 of registered plan 317, 1907. 1 map. Loc: GLR. Map 327.**
Plan that extends to St Arnaud Street in the west and Waterloo Street in the south. The scale is 100 feet to an inch.

3077. Hutcheon, James. **Plan of Holliday's subdivision of the tannery lot in the Canada Company Survey, City of Guelph, 1903. 1 map. Loc: GLR. Map 314.**
Plan that extends to Yorkshire Street in the west, Grand Trunk Railway in the north and Waterloo Avenue in the south. The scale is 50 feet to an inch. The property belonged to the estate of Thomas Holliday.

3078. Hutcheon, James. **Plan of lots in part of Guelph, 1906. 1 document. Loc: UGA. XR1 MS A002.**
A plan which shows lots stretching north from Bellevue Street to Cedar and Water Streets. The scale is 2 chains to an inch. Part of Sleeman Family Collection.

3079. Hutcheon, James. **Plan of Parkview being a subdivision of Lot 170 and part of Lot 171 in John McDonald's Survey, plan 113 in the City of Guelph, 1912. 1 map. Loc: GLR. Map 344.**
Plan bordered by the Speed River in the west, Crawford Street in the east and Bridge Street in the south. The plan marks the location of the Canadian Textile

Company. The scale is 60 feet to an inch.

3080. Hutcheon, James. **Plan of resubdivision of Lots 31, 32, 33, 34, 35 and 36 in Kingsmill's Survey, registered plan 23 in the City of Guelph, 1913.** 1 map. Loc: GLR. Map 355.
   Plan showing lots west of Edinburgh Road and bordered by Merion Street in the north and Paisley Street in the south. The scale is 60 feet to an inch.

3081. Hutcheon, James. **Plan of resubdivision of Lots 7 and 8 and part of Lot 24, Division A of the survey of Guelph Township now in the City of Guelph, 1911.** 1 map. Loc: GLR. Map 334.
   Plan that extends to Vera Street in the west, North Boundary Road in the north, Edinburgh Road in the east and Cannon Street in the south. The scale is 200 feet to an inch.

3082. Hutcheon, James. **Plan of resubdivision of Lots 8, 9, 10, 11, 12 and 13 in G.M. Stewart's Survey as laid down on registered plan 433, Guelph, 1902.** 1 map. Loc: GLR. Map 312.
   Plan bordered by King Street in the west, Spring Street in the north and Havelock Street in the east. The scale is 50 feet to an inch.

3083. Hutcheon, James. **Plan of subdivision of Cathcart Place and of part of the unnumbered block in Grange's Survey Plan 28 the said lands being originally parts of Lots 2 and 3, Division A of the survey of Guelph Township now in the City of Guelph, 1905.** 1 map. Loc: GLR. Map 325.
   Plan that extends east along Crimea and Canrobert Streets to the Grand Trunk Railway. The scale is 100 feet to an inch.

3084. Hutcheon, James. **Plan of subdivision of Lot 89, registered plan 243, Guelph, 1910.** 1 map. Loc: GLR. Map 332.
   Plan showing lots at the corner of Derry and Queen Streets. The scale is 30 feet to an inch.

3085. Hutcheon, James. **Plan of subdivision of Lots 53 and 54 of the Roman Catholic Glebe Survey as laid down on registered plan 205, Guelph, 1911.** 1 map. Loc: GLR. Map 333.
   Plan showing lots at the corner of Central and Clarke Streets. The scale is 50 feet to an inch.

3086. Hutcheon, James. **Plan of subdivision of Park Lot 50 in the Canada Company's Survey, Guelph, 1896.** 1 map. Loc: GLR. Map 307.
   Plan that extends to Yorkshire Street in the west, Cambridge Street in the north, Glasgow Street in the east and Cork Street in the south. The scale is 80 feet to an inch.

3087. Hutcheon, James. **Plan of subdivision of Park Lot K in A.M. Clark's Survey registered plan 293 and Lots 9 and 10 in Ferguson's Survey in the City of Guelph the property of T.J. Hannigan, 1911.** 1 map. Loc: GLR. Map 337.
   Plan that extends along Wheeler Avenue south of Elizabeth Street and north of Ferguson Street. The scale is 60 feet to an inch.

3088. Hutcheon, James. **Plan of subdivision of Park Lots 44 and 45 in the Canada Company's Survey, City of Guelph, property of the late Thomas Robinson, 1904.** 1 map. Loc: GLR. Map 315.
Plan bordered by Fergus Street in the west, Elora Street in the north, Yorkshire Street in the east and Robinson Avenue in the south. The scale is 60 feet to an inch.

3089. Hutcheon, James. **Plan of subdivision of part of broken front Lot 5 in Division F of Guelph Township now in the City of Guelph, property of Mr J.W. Lyon, 1913.** 1 map. Loc: GLR. Map 354.
Plan that extends from Menzie Avenue in the west, York Road in the north, Audrey Avenue in the east and Eramosa River in the south. The scale is 100 feet to an inch.

3090. Hutcheon, James. **Plan of subdivision of part of broken front Lot 5 in Division F of Guelph Township now in the City of Guelph, property of Mr J.W. Lyon, 1912.** 1 map. Loc: GLR. Map 352.
Plan of area from Menzie Avenue in the west, York Road in the north, Audrey Avenue in the east and the Eramosa River in the south. The scale is 100 feet to an inch.

3091. Hutcheon, James. **Plan of subdivision of part of broken Lot 5 in Division F of Guelph Township, now in the City of Guelph, property of Mr W.T. Tanner, 1913.** 1 map. Loc: GLR. Map 353.
Plan showing lots east and west of Kingsmill Avenue and bordered by York Road to the north and the Eramosa River to the south. The scale is 100 feet to an inch.

3092. Hutcheon, James. **Plan of subdivision of part of broken Lot 5, Division F, Guelph Township now in the City of Guelph, property of J.W. Lyon, 1912.** 1 map. Loc: GLR. Map 351.
Plan showing lots east and west of Hays Avenue and bordered by York Road in the north and the Eramosa River in the south. The scale is 100 feet to an inch.

3093. Hutcheon, James. **Plan of subdivision of part of Lot 1, Division A of the survey of Guelph Township now in the City of Guelph, 1905.** 1 map. Loc: GLR. Map 317.
Plan showing lots located along St Arnaud Street in the west and along Waterloo Avenue in the south. The scale is 100 feet to an inch.

3094. Hutcheon, James. **Plan of subdivision of part of Lot 6 of Range III, Division F in the survey of Guelph Township, now in the City of Guelph, 1911.** 1 map. Loc: GLR. Map 336.
Map showing lots immediately north of Stevenson Street, running from Palmer Street in the west to Grange Street in the east. The scale is 50 feet to an inch.

3095. Hutcheon, James. **Plan of subdivision of part of township Lot 1, Division A in the survey of Guelph Township now in the City of Guelph and also a resubdivision of registered plans 317 and 327, 1912.** 1 map. Loc: GLR. Map 348.
Plan that extends to St Arnaud Street in the west, Allan Avenue in the north, Meadowview Avenue in the east and Waterloo Avenue. The land was owned by A.S. Allan. The scale is 100 feet to an inch.

3096. Hutcheon, James. **Plan of subdivision of parts of Lots 1 and 2, Concession 3, Division F, Guelph Township now in the City of Guelph, 1912.** 1 map. Loc: GLR. Map 343.

Plan that extends to Stevenson Street in the west, Beverly Street in the north, Audrey Avenue in the east and York Road in the south. The land was owned by J.W. Lyon. The scale is 100 feet to an inch.

3097. Hutcheon, James. **Plan of subdivision of parts of Lots 2, 3, 4 and 5, Range III, Division A of the Canada Company Survey being part of J.D. Williamson estate, 1905.** 1 map. Loc: GLR. Map 316.

Plan of lots along Yorkshire Street north of London Road and west of Kathleen Street. The scale is 100 feet to an inch.

3098. Hutcheon, James. **Plan of subdivision of the northeast half of Lot N of registered plan 161 and of Lot 20 of registered plan 227 in the City of Guelph, property of T.J. Hannigan, 1911.** 1 map. Loc: GLR. Map 338.

Plan bordered by Grange Street in the north, Stevenson Street in the east and Grove Street in the south. The scale is 60 feet to an inch.

3099. Hutcheon, James. **Plan of subdivision of the northerly part of broken front Lot 5 in Division F of Guelph Township now in the City of Guelph, the property of Mr J. W. Lyon, 1911.** 1 map. Loc: GLR. Map 340.

Plan that extends south of York Road and west of the northeast boundary road. The scale is 100 feet to an inch.

3100. Hutcheon, James. **Plan of subdivision of Victoria Place of Thompson Survey plan 37, property of Peter Martin, Guelph, 1909.** 1 map. Loc: GLR. Map 328.

Plan bordered by Mary Street in the west, James Street in the north, the Victoria School grounds in the east and Charles Street in the south. The scale is 60 feet to an inch.

3101. Hutcheon, James. **Plan of the Cunningham Survey being the subdivision of part of township Lot 1, Division A in the survey of Guelph Township, now in the City of Guelph, 1909.** 1 map. Loc: GLR. Map 330.

Plan showing lots north of Waterloo Avenue and west of Edinburgh Street. The scale is 80 feet to an inch.

3102. Kerr, Francis. **Guelph, plan of town lots, 1855.** print, 45 x 41 cm, scale 1 inch to 3 chains. Loc: NAC, UGL. NAC: 440/Guelph/n.d./#3843.

A plan of the area south of Guelph's central core and the Speed River. The line of the 'Toronto and Guelph Grand Trunk' is shown, the site of the 'Railroad Depot' and the 'Market Place'. Near Victoria Mills a proposed bridge is marked across the Speed River to link Huskisson Street and Crawford Street. Prospective buyers are advised to contact James Webster, A.E. Logie or J.E. Thomson. The original plan is part of the Sir John A. Macdonald Papers and resembles registered plan # 113 of 1856 in the Guelph Registry Office, differing slightly in the orientation of Huskisson and Crawford Streets and the layout of lots around Bridge and Neeve Streets. Lots owned by the Hon. John A. Macdonald were being sold in November 1855.

3103. Kerr, Francis. **Map of survey in the Town of Guelph shewing an alteration made in Blocks A, B and C for George J. Grange, 1859.** 1 map. Loc: GLR. Map 115.

Plan with the borders being Paisley Road, Edinburgh Street, Waterloo Road and Alma Street. The plan also labels the Grand Trunk Railway and the Galt and Guelph Railway. The scale is 200 feet to an inch.

3104. Kerr, Francis. **Plan of alterations, St George's Church ground, 1857.** Loc: GCH.

A plan of St George's Square with dimensions of the original English (Anglican) Church structure and lot, including portions proposed to be cut from the lot corners and purchased by the town. Few structural details are visible. The plan is held in Schedule A of Guelph Bylaw No. 68, 20 July, 1857. The scale is 20 feet to an inch.

3105. Kerr, Francis. **Plan of building lots in the Town of Guelph, property of A.J. Fergusson, 1858.** 1 map. Loc: GLR. Map 99.

A plan extending to London Street in the west, Mitchell Street in the north, Eramosa Road in the east and Woolwich Street in the south. The scale is 2 chains to an inch.

3106. Kerr, Francis. **Plan of building lots laid out in the Town of Guelph for Edwin Hubbard, Esq., 1855.** 1 map. Loc: GLR. Map 35.

Plan which borders on London Road, the Speed River and Liverpool and Dublin Streets. The scale is 2 chains to an inch.

3107. Kerr, Francis. **Plan of building lots laid out in the Town of Guelph for John Mitchell, 1855.** print. Loc: GCM.

The plan extends from Mary Street in the west, King Street in the north, Eramosa River in the east and Norfolk Street in the south. The map marks the location of taverns, distilleries, mills and foundries. The scale is 2 chains to an inch. Related to registered plan of the same year.

3108. Kerr, Francis. **Plan of building lots laid out in the Town of Guelph for John Mitchell, Esq., 1856.** 1 map. Loc: GLR. Map 40.

Plan which includes King and Perth Streets, Eramosa Road and the Speed River. The plan notes the location of George's Mill and indicates proposed locations for bridges over the Speed River. The scale is 2 chains to an inch.

3109. Kerr, Francis. **Plan of building lots laid out on a portion of Lot B, Division A, Guelph, otherwise known as the Pipe Lot, 1855.** 1 map. Loc: GLR. Map 31.

Plan which borders on Clarke and Woolwich Streets, London Road and the Speed River. The plan also marks a distillery, mill, tavern and the residences of F. George and John C. Wilson. The scale is 2 chains to an inch.

3110. Kerr, Francis. **Plan of lots in the Town of Guelph for sale by G.S. Tiffany, 1854.** print. Loc: GLR. Map 18.

Plan and notice of auction on 21 October for lots on Kerr, Tiffany, Powell, Clarke, George and Clarence Streets between Woolwich Street in the west and the Speed River in the east. The scale is 2 chains to an inch. Copy in Land Registry Office is a transcript.

3111. Kerr, Francis. **Plan of Park Lots being part of the subdivision of Scotch Glebe, Guelph, 1858.** 1 map. Loc: GLR. Map 98.

A plan that shows numbered lots extending to Woolwich Road in the east and Edinburgh Road in the west. The scale is 3 chains to an inch.

3112. Kerr, Francis. **Plan of park lots in Guelph, property of James Webster, c1858.** Loc: GCH.

A survey of lands including the northerly portion of King Street which was scheduled to be closed, including details of saw and grist mills, mill races and a millpond on the Speed River. The scale is 3 chains to an inch and the plan is attached as Schedule A to Guelph Bylaw No. 74, 12 July, 1858.

3113. Kerr, Francis. **Plan of Priory lots showing alteration in streets, 1860.** Loc: GCH.

A survey of lots and of Priory Street, part of which was to be closed in favour of another street nearby, in the area bounded by Market Street, Woolwich Street and the Speed River. The scale of the plan is 1 chain to an inch and it is attached to Bylaw No. 96, 16 July, 1860, as Schedule C.

3114. Kerr, Francis. **Plan of St Andrew's Church, Glebe Lot, Ranges I to IV, Guelph, 1862.** 1 map. Loc: GLR. Map 148.

Plan that extends to Edinburgh Road in the west, Guelph Township border in the north, Woolwich Street in the east and Division Street in the south. The map includes a note from John McCrae stating that the land belonged to St Andrew's Church congregation.

3115. Kerr, Francis. **Plan of subdivision of Lots 5, 6, 7 and 8, Woolwich Street in the Town of Guelph, 1857.** 1 map. Loc: GLR. Map 38.

Plan which borders on Glebe, Woolwich and Strange Streets and on London Road. The scale is 132 feet to an inch. The plan notes the lots were in Range I of Division A which was part of the southern portion of Woolwich Street.

3116. Kerr, Francis. **Plan of subdivision of Lots 63 and 64 in the Town of Guelph, Canada West, 1856.** print, scale 1 inch to 80 feet. Loc: GCM.

The plan extends from Market Square, Macdonell Street, Quebec Street, Woolwich Street to the Speed River. The map notes the location of the Post Office, a church in St George's Square, Registry Office, Court House and Jail, Court House Inn and Stable, International Hotel, British Hotel, Gore Bank, Town Hall and Market House and the 'New Stone Block' extending along Wyndham and Macdonell Streets. Based on Alex Simpson's plan of 1856.

3117. Kerr, Francis. **Plan shewing part of the Priory grounds in the Town of Guelph, 1856.** 1 map. Loc: GLR. Map 94.

Plan of the Priory grounds north of the Speed River that was property of the estate of George Tiffany. The scale is 2 chains to an inch.

3118. Kerr, Francis. **Plan shewing subdivision of Park Lots 4, 5, 6, 11, 12, 15, 26, 27, 28, 29, 36, 48, 49 and 57 in the Town of Guelph, 1855.** print, 44 x 54 cm, scale 1 inch to 2 chains. Loc: GLR, KPL. Map 29.

Plan which shows Edinburgh, Suffolk West, Liverpool, Paisley, Gladwin and Cambridge Streets. The copy at the Kitchener Public Library has an added manuscript note of the location of the intended Galt and Guelph Railway Station between Raglan and Sultan Streets.

3119. Kerr, Francis. **Plan shewing subdivision of Park Lots 87, 91, 93 and 94 in the Town of Guelph, surveyed for G. Palmer, Esq., 1861**. 1 map. Loc: GLR. Map 144.
Plan showing Norfolk, Cardigan and Norwich Streets and London Road and the Speed River. The scale is 2 chains to an inch.

3120. Kerr, Francis. **Plan shewing the subdivision of Lots 27, 28, 33 and 34 in the Town of Guelph for Mr William Nicholson, 1855**. 1 map. Loc: GLR. Map 41.
Plan that extends from Gordon Street in the west, Market Place in the north, Grant Street in the east and the Speed River in the south. The scale is 2 chains to an inch.

3121. Kerr, Francis. **Sketch of building lots in the Town of Guelph, property of G.S. Tiffany, 1847**. 1 map. Loc: GLR. Map 17.
Plan that includes Clarke, Powell, Tiffany and Kerr Streets between Strange Street in the east and Woolwich Street in the west.

3122. Kerr, Francis. **Subdivision of Lots 59 and 60 as laid out for Mr John Thorp, 1855**. 1 map. Loc: GLR. Map 26.
Plan of lots along Thorp Street that runs between Woolwich Street and the Speed River.

3123. Lloyd, Frank P. **Map of the City of Guelph, 1908**. Loc: UGL, AO. D-3.
A map of Guelph from Silver Creek Street in the west to Speedvale Road in the north, to Stevenson Street in the east, and the Ontario Agricultural College in the south. The map, at the scale of 1:10,800 marks all streets and 42 places of interest, including post office, banks, stores, industries, churches, schools and library.

3124. Malcolm, L. **Maple Leaf Subdivision, being a subdivision of Block A of Grange Executor's Survey, registered plan 258 in the City of Guelph, 1912**. 1 map. Loc: GLR. Map 347.
Plan bordered by Alma Street in the west, Paisley Street in the north and Omar Street in the south. The scale is 60 feet to an inch.

3125. Malcolm, L. **Plan of Royalview Heights being a subdivision of Lots 21 and 22. John Macdonald's Survey registered plan 161 and part of Lot 5, Concession 1, Division F, formerly in the Township of Guelph now in the City of Guelph, 1913**. 1 map. Loc: GLR. Map 358.
Plan that extends south of Metcalfe Street and west of Grove Street. The scale is 80 feet to an inch.

3126. Malcolm, L. **Plan of subdivision 'Industrial Row', part of Lot 2, Range III, Division F in the survey of Guelph Township now in the City of Guelph, 1912**. 1 map. Loc: GLR. Map 345.
Plan that extends to the north and south of Simcoe Street and west of Simmers Avenue. The scale is 50 feet to an inch.

3127. Malcolm, L. **Plan of subdivision of Lot L and Park Lot K of J. MacDonald's Survey, registered plan 161 in the City of Guelph, 1913**. 1 map. Loc: GLR. Map 362.
Plan showing lots east of Grange Street and south of Metcalfe Street. The scale is 80 feet to an inch.

3128. Malcolm, L. **Plan of subdivision of Lots 18, 19, 20 and part Lot 17, St Andrew's Glebe Survey, Range II, registered plan 148, City of Guelph, 1913.** 1 map. Loc: GLR. Map 361.

Plan that extends to Kathleen Street in the west, Berlin Road in the north, Exhibition Street in the east and Barton Street in the south. The scale is 80 feet to an inch.

3129. Malcolm, L. **Plan of subdivision of Lots 3, 4, 26 and 27 in McTague Survey according to registered plan 105 in the City of Guelph, 1914.** 1 map. Loc: GLR. Map 364.

Plan that extends to McTague Street in the north, Stace Street in the east and London Road in the south. The scale is 40 feet to an inch.

3130. Malcolm, L. **Plan of subdivision of part Lot 1 registered plan 218 and part Lot 2, registered plan 281 in the City of Guelph, 1912.** 1 map. Loc: GLR. Map 346.

Plan that extends south of Eramosa Road and east of Queen Street. The property was owned by Donald Guthrie. The scale is 50 feet to an inch.

3131. Malcolm, L. **Plan of subdivision of part of Lot 23, Division A of Guelph Township now in the City of Guelph, 1912.** 1 map. Loc: GLR. Map 349.

Plan bordered by Ridgewood Avenue in the west, Cannon Street in the north and Paisley Street in the south. The scale is 100 feet to an inch.

3132. **Map of Town of Guelph, 1856.** print. Loc: UGA. XR3 MS A005.

A map of Frederick George's Surveys of lots and hydraulic privileges, drawn to the scale of 1 chain an inch. The map stretches north from Cardigan Street, includes the Speed River and then Perth Street. The map includes references to specific surveys done in the town. This map is part of the Shutt Collection.

3133. McDonald, Donald. **Plan of the Town of Guelph according to the surveys thereof under the directions of the Canada Company, 1847.** col ms on tracing paper, 67 x 64 cm, no scale. Loc: MNR, UGA, GPL, MTL, AO, GCM. MNR: SR 117; UGA: XR2 MS A003.

A plan for the town of Guelph in 1847 that shows street names, 1058 town between Fleet Street and Yorkshire Road and 99 park lots. The map's boundaries are London Road in the north, Edinburgh Road in the west, Metcalfe Street in the east, and the Speed River in the south. The plan notes the location of the Market House, St Andrew's Church in the Market Square, St Patrick's Church, St George's Church in the Square, the Methodist Church on Norfolk Street and the Burying Ground. The original map is part of the survey records of the Ministry of Natural Resources. A printed version of the original was lithographed by Scobie and Balfour at a scale of one inch to 8 chains and measuring 34 x 44 cm; it lists the population, number of houses, occupations of the residents, and number of business and service establishments (including the cricket clubs) in the town. The map contains a note that the land between Eramosa Road and Palmer Street, Grange Street and Budd Street belonged to John McDonald. The copy at the Archives of Ontario was part of the Jarvis-Powell Papers. A photocopy of the printed version is in the Guelph Historical Society's collection of maps of Guelph in the University of Guelph Archives.

3134. **Plan of the Town of Guelph, 1855.** scale 1 inch to 4 chains. Loc: GPL.
A 1935 reproduction of a plan originally drawn in 1855, showing Guelph from Wellington Street in the south, to Edinburgh in the northwest, London Road in the north and the path of the Speed River in the town. Attributed to John McDonald but may be a copy of the Chadwick plan of 1855.

3135. McDonald, John. **Plan of the Town of Guelph copied from George Tiffany's plan, 1828.** ms. Loc: MTL.
Plan shows town lots 1-1058 and park lots 1-99 according to Tiffany's original plan which is referred to in Prior's Report but has not been located. It also shows the Burying Ground, Priory, Market Ground, St Patrick's Square and Clarence Place. An overlay dated 8 April 1829 changes the focal point of the plan and a later overlay of 6 December 1833 adds lots along the river (Stelter, John Galt, 31,38-9).

3136. Might Directories Ltd. **Map of Guelph, 1931.** 1 sheet, 26 x 23. Loc: NAC. 440/Guelph/1931/#22375.
A map, at the scale of 600 feet to an inch, with a street index.

3137. Nelles, C.L. **Map of City of Guelph, c1930.** 1 sheet, 45 x 60 cm. Loc: AO.
Shows the distribution of factories and other buildings at a scale of 1:660. C.L. Nelles published the map.

3138. Niven, D.A. **Map of Guelph, 1926, with additions by City Regional Planning consultants, 1945.** 1 map. Loc: GCH.
A survey and original plan by D.A. Niven of Guelph in 1926 with additions made by city planning consultants in June 1945 for the future changes in zoning to 1960. The scale is 200 feet to the inch. The map includes a chart indicating velocity and discharge in sewers 4 inches to 42 inches in diameter, velocity in feet per second, discharge in cubic feet per minute, and sewers flowing full. The 1940s plan suggests a ring road system linking roads including Edinburgh, Emma, Richard, Stevenson and York, and bridges, the Speed River to Gordon Street to Wellington at Gow's bridge. The map is held in the Clerk's office vault.

3139. Niven, D.A. **Parkside, a subdivision of part of broken Lot 5, Division F, formerly in the township now in the City of Guelph, 1919.** 1 map. Loc: GLR. Map 385.
Plan showing lots south of York Road and north of the Speed River. The document indicates J.W. Lyon held the 'owner's certificate' for the lots. The scale is 100 feet to an inch.

3140. Niven, D.A. **Plan of Arlington Place, a subdivision of Park Lots 4, 5 and 6, registered plan 37 in the City of Guelph, 1915.** 1 map. Loc: GLR. Map 367.
Plan showing lots south of Forbes Avenue, bordered by Ann Street and Fairview Boulevard. The scale is 50 feet to an inch.

3141. Niven, D.A. **Plan of Hillcrest, a subdivision of Lots 1 to 5, 14 and 15 of registered plan 36 in the City of Guelph, 1915.** 1 map. Loc: GLR. Map 370.
Plan that extends from Augusta Street in the west to Division Street in the north, Kathleen Street in the east and the Grand Trunk Railway in the south. The scale is 50 feet to an inch.

3142. Niven, D.A. **Plan of subdivision of Lot 3 and part of Lots 2 and 4, registered plan 263, in the City of Guelph, 1916.** 1 map. Loc: GLR. Map 371.
Plan bordered by Metcalfe Street in the west, the Grand Trunk Railway route in the north and Elizabeth Street in the south. The scale is 60 feet to an inch.

3143. Niven, D.A. **Plan of subdivision of Lots 57 and 58, plan 262, and Lots 101, 102 and 103, registered plan 274, in the City of Guelph, 1915.** 1 map. Loc: GLR. Map 369.
Plan bordered by Beechwood Avenue in the west, Alma Street in the east and Chadwick Avenue in the south. The scale is 60 feet to an inch.

3144. Niven, D.A. **Plan of Sunny Acres, a subdivision of Lots 81 to 86, 108 to 113, 120 to 122, part of Fergus Street and of an allowance for lane, registered plan 27, also of Lots M, K, part D and E, and of allowance for street, plan 214, City of Guelph, 1919.** 1 map. Loc: GLR. Plan 383.
Plan that extends to Edinburgh Road in the west, to Sydenham Street in the north, Clinton Street in the east and Argyle Street in the south. The scale is 60 feet to an inch.

3145. Niven, D.A. **Plan of the Fairfield Survey, a subdivision of Block K, registered plan 293, in the City of Guelph, 1916.** 1 map. Loc: GLR. Map 375.
Plan bordered by Morris Street in the west, the Guelph Junction Railway line in the north, Stevenson Street in the east and Alice Street in the south. The scale of the plan is 50 feet to an inch. The document indicates James Walter Lyon is the holder of the 'morgatee's certificate'.

3146. Niven, D.A. **Plan of the Grove Survey, a subdivision of part of Park Lots 78, 79, 80, 81 and 82 of the Canada Company's Survey in the City of Guelph, 1915.** 1 map. Loc: GLR. Map 368.
Plan that extends north and south of Raymond Street and west of Wellington Street. The scale is 80 feet to an inch.

3147. Niven, D.A. **Plan of the Johnston and Williams Survey, a subdivision of Lots 67 to 72, registered plans 205 and 253 in the City of Guelph, 1915.** 1 map. Loc: GLR. Map 372.
Plan that extends north and south of Cavell Avenue, east of Exhibition Street and west of Central Street.

3148. Niven, D.A. **Plan showing extension of Surrey Street from the southerly limit of the mill lands, as shown on registered plan 269 to Market Street in the City of Guelph, 1917.** 1 map. Loc: GLR. Map 379.
Plan that extends to Market Street in the west, Speed River to the north and east, and Neeve Street to the south. The scale is 50 feet to an inch.

3149. **Plan of Guelph lots, estate of Robert Thompson, c1880.** Loc: AO. D-3.
Plan of lots in the Thompson Survey east of the Speed River and south of the Dundas Road, fronting on Water, Albert, Ann, Mary, James and Charles Streets. The plan shows that the block between Charles, Mary and James Streets was designated as a reserve called Victoria Place. An earlier plan of this survey was drawn by William Haskins in 1856.

3150. **Plan of Red Mills, Guelph, 1870.** 1 document. Loc: UGA. XR1 MS A334065.
Several sketches, including one of Red Mills in Guelph which was owned by A. Robertson. The sketch is drawn to the scale of 2 chains to an inch and shows the area stretching north from Waterloo Road. Part of the Sleeman Family Collection.

3151. **Plan of the Town of Guelph, 1843.** printed, 30 x 36 cm. Loc: MTL.
A plan that extends to Edinburgh Road in the west, London Road in the north and the Speed River to the east and south. The plan also lists the population, employment and types of industries and institutions.

3152. **Plan of the Town of Guelph, c1830.** col ms, 65 x 89 cm. Loc: AO. Canada Company Maps, Pkg 5, #141.
A plan of Guelph that extends to Edinburgh Road in the west, London Road in the north, Speed River in the east and Wellington Street in the south and shows all original town lots and park lots, three churches, school house and grist mill. Exhibit 12 referred to in the deposition of Donald McDonald on 23 April 1853 in the case of Guelph vs the Canada Company.

3153. Pollock, James. **Dunbar's Survey in the Town of Guelph being composed of parts of Lots 4 and 5 in the 1st Range, and parts of Lots 4 and 5 in the 2nd Range, Division F, Township of Guelph, as laid out for the proprietor, Alex Dunbar, Esq., 1874.** 1 map. Loc: GLR. Map 227.
Plan with lots bordering on Duke, Metcalfe and Grove Streets and on the Grand Trunk Railway. The scale is 2 chains to an inch.

3154. Satterthwaite, J.H. **Plan of Guelph and neighbourhood, 1862.** 1 sheet, 14 x 15-3/4. Loc: NAC. 440/Guelph/1862/#26836.
An original coloured manuscript map at a scale of 4 miles to an inch, accompanying the Report of Commissioners Appointed to Consider the Defences of Canada, 1862, No. 7 (RG 8 II, vol. 8). The map identifies some buildings and shows sites of proposed fortified outwork and placement of arms.

3155. Schofield, M.C. **Amended plan of survey of parts of Lots 7 and 8, Range I, Division F now in the Town of Guelph, made for Owen Macdonald (sic), 1875.** 1 map. Loc: GLR. Map 232.
Plan of lots east of Eramosa Road including Metcalfe, Elizabeth, Stuart, Lemon and Palmer Streets. The scale is 2 chains to an inch.

3156. Schofield, M.C. and Hobson, J. **Map of Frederick George's survey and hydraulic privileges in the Town of Guelph, County of Wellington, c1872.** 1 map. Loc: GLR. Map 209.
A survey of lots on either side of the Speed River to Perth Street in the north and Cardigan Street in the south. The map includes the route of the hydraulic canal to John Harvey Tannery, and to unidentified flour mill, piggery and feeding sheds, distillery and moulding shed foundry. The map marks the location of George's residence. The scale is 1 chain to an inch. The index notes that the plan is not registered but is required for reference.

3157. Schofield, M.C. **Map of Lorne Place, Town of Guelph, surveyed for Donald Guthrie, 1872.** 1 map. Loc: GLR. Map 214.
Plan of Lots 106, 107, 123 to 126 along Sydenham, Clinton and Elora Street. The scale is 100 feet to an inch.

3158. Schofield, M.C. **Map of lots laid out for George J. Grange and Adam J. Fergusson, 1855**. print, 52 x 82 cm, scale 1 inch to 200 feet. Loc: GCM, GCH, AO. AO:B-66/SR 118.

A plan of lots surveyed in conjunction with the location of stations for the Grand Trunk Railway and the Galt and Guelph Railway and advertised for sale on January 6, 1855. The survey shows the GTR station as well as other buildings in the area bounded by Alma, Paisley, Yorkshire and Market Streets, and Waterloo Road. A smaller map places the area in the context of the rest of the municipality. The map notes that the lots to the west of Edinburgh Road belong to Grange and the lots to the east to Fergusson. The scale is 200 feet to an inch. The City Hall copy of the plan is attached to Guelph Bylaw No. 134, 1 August, 1864. Related to registered plans 27 and 28 at the Guelph Land Registry Office.

3159. Schofield, M.C. **Map of Park Lot 50, Town of Guelph, subdivided for Francis Shanly, Esq., 1855**. 1 map. Loc: GLR. Map 22.

Plan of land owned by Shanly which includes Yorkshire, Cork, Glasgow, Lane and Cambridge Streets.

3160. Schofield, M.C. **Map of Park Lots 7, 8, 9 and 10, and part of Lot 4, Division F of George Harvey's Survey in the Town of Guelph subdivided for John Thorp, Esq., 1855**. 1 map. Loc: GLR. Map 25.

Plan for Thorp which includes Hooper and Hood Streets, York Road to the Speed and Eramosa Rivers.

3161. Schofield, M.C. **Map of part of broken front Lot 5, Division F in the Town of Guelph, as laid out for John Thorp, 1855**. print, 47 x 67 cm. Loc: GLR. Map 24.

Plan that extends along Brockville Street from York Road in the west to the Eramosa River in the east. The scale is 50 feet to an inch.

3162. Schofield, M.C. **Map of part of Lot 4, Division F, Town of Guelph, 1855**. 1 map. Loc: GLR. Map 19.

Plan of George Harvey's land that extends along York Road to the north and the Eramosa River to the south.

3163. Schofield, M.C. **Map of survey for J.J. Kingsmill, Esq. in the Town of Guelph, 1855**. 1 map. Loc: GLR. Map 23.

Plan done for Kingsmill which includes Mount, Mercer, Melville, Merion, Alma and Edinburgh Streets and Paisley Road. The document notes the land to be a subdivision of Lots 5 and 6, Division F in Guelph.

3164. Schofield, M.C. **Map of survey in the Town of Guelph for George J. Grange, 1855**. 1 map. Loc: GLR. Map 28.

Plan of Lots 2, 3 and 4 of Division A that extends from Alma Street in the west, to Paisley Street in the north, to Edinburgh Street in the east to Inkerman Street in the south.

3165. Schofield, M.C. **Map of survey in the Town of Guelph for John Neeve, Esq., 1855**. 1 map. Loc: GLR. Map 33.

Plan which shows Grant, Waterloo, Surrey and Neeve Streets. The scale is 1 chain to an inch.

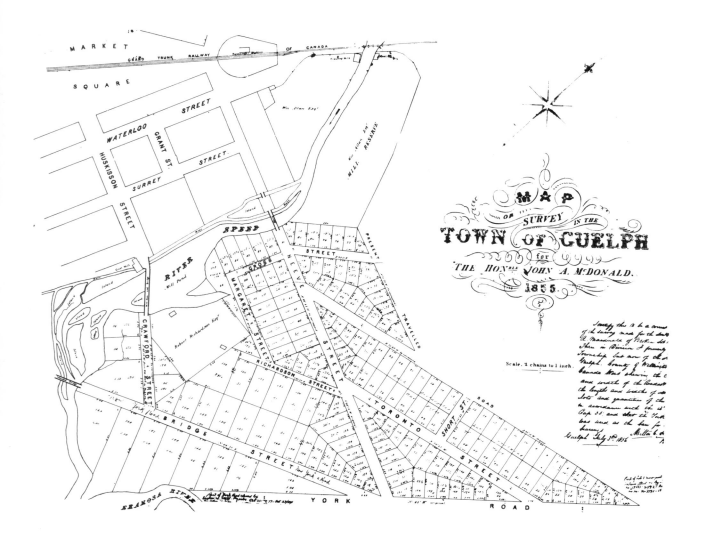

Land boom, 1855: Subdivision and sale plan (#3168) used by the Hon. John A. Macdonald, later Prime Minister of Canada, in an unsuccessful bid to realize a profit on his land investment on the southern edge of Guelph's central business district. (Marilyn Armstrong-Reynolds)

3166. Schofield, M.C. and Hobson, J. **Map of survey in the Township of Guelph for William Alexander, 1856.** 1 map. Loc: GCM.

The map includes Paisley Block Road, Alexander Street, Helen Street and Silver Creek Road. The plan shows the residence of William Alexander, a brewery and tannery, and a lot on Paisley Block Road. The plan also records the property of Thomas Sandilands. The scale is 2 chains to an inch.

3167. Schofield, M.C. **Map of survey of Lots 56, 57, 58, and 59 of Albert Place in the Town of Guelph, made for A. Lemon, Esq., 1873.** 1 map. Loc: GLR. Map 218.

Plan showing lots bordered by Queen, Eramosa, Lemon and Edward Streets. The scale is 1 chain to an inch.

3168. Schofield, M.C. **Map of the survey in the Town of Guelph for the Honourable John A. Macdonald, 1855.** 1 map. Loc: GLR. Map 113.

Plan of Lot 3 in Division F that extends from Crawford Street in the west, Market Square in the north, Toronto Street in the east and York Road in the south. The scale is 2 chains to an inch.

3169. Schofield, M.C. **Plan of Lots 9, 10, 11, 12, 13, 14 and 15, Range I, and part of Lot 2 in the broken front of Division F, Town of Guelph, County of Wellington as subdivided for James Webster, 1858.** 1 map. Loc: GLR. Map 121.

Plan of land between the junction of King Street to the west and Eramosa Road to the north. The scale is 3 chains to an inch.

3170. Schofield, M.C. **Plan of Park Lot 52, Canada Company's Survey, Town of Guelph, subdivided for Donald Guthrie, Esq., 1871.** 1 map. Loc: GLR. Map 208.

Plan bordered by Glasgow Street to the west, Suffolk to the north, Dublin to the east and Liverpool Street to the south.

3171. Schofield, M.C. **Plan of parts of Lots 7 and 8, Range I, Division F in the Town of Guelph made for Owen McDonald, 1874.** 1 map. Loc: GLR. Map 220.

Plan that extends south of Eramosa Road and includes Queen, Edward, Elizabeth and Metcalfe Streets. The scale is 2 chains to an inch.

3172. Schofield, M.C. **Plan of subdivision of southerly portions of Lots 6, 7 and 8, Woolwich Road, Division A, City of Guelph, 1891.** 1 map. Loc: GLR. Map 300.

Plan of lots to the east of Woolwich Street and south of Kerr Street. The scale is 50 links to an inch.

3173. Schofield, M.C. **Plan of subdivision part of Lot 51 of John Macdonald's survey of Lots 7, 8 and west part of Lot 6, Range I, broken front Division F now in the Town of Guelph, for John Hogg, Esq., 1872.** 1 map. Loc: GLR. Map 210.

Plan showing lots bordering on Queen Street, Private Lane and High Street. The plan also marks the properties of John Hogg and Lachlan Macdonald. The scale is 50 feet to an inch. The index book of plans indicates the plan was cancelled by a judge's order.

3174. Schofield, M.C. **Plan of survey made for Maria S. Harrison of subdivision of Park Lots 34 and 35 and of Lot 128 (Fergusson's survey) and a small triangular piece of Park Lot 42 situated at the northwest corner of said Park Lot, 1883.** 1 map. Loc: GLR. Map 285.

Plan of lots to the west and east of Harrison Avenue from Paisley Street in the north, to Sydenham Street in the south. The scale is 50 feet to an inch.

3175. Schofield, M.C. **Plan shewing alteration of part of the survey of Honourable J.A. Macdonald in the Town of Guelph, c1855.** 1 map. Loc: GLR. Map 113.
An alteration of the 1855 plan drawn by M.C. Schofield that notes a slight alteration in an untitled road that runs perpendicular to Cross Street.

3176. Schofield, M.C. **Plan shewing subdivision of Lots 3, 4 and 5 in Division C, Township of Guelph, surveyed for George S. Tiffany, May 1855.** print. Loc: GCM.
The plan extends from York Road in the west, the township line between Guelph and Puslinch in the east and the Speed River in the south. The scale is 4 chains to an inch.

3177. Schofield, M.C. **Resurvey of plan 270 of the resubdivision of Lots 2, 3, 4, 5, 6 and 7 in Andrew Lemon's Survey of Lots 56, 57, 58 and 59 in Albert Place in the Town of Guelph, 1877.** 1 map. Loc: GLR. Map 281.
Plan showing lots between Eramosa Road in the west and Lemon Street in the east. The plan marks the property of Frederick Biscoe. The plan includes a note stating 'lots one and two of this plan are intruded and do actually embrace lots one to nine inclusive of plan 270'. The scale is 30 feet to an inch.

3178. Simpson, Alex. **Plan of subdivision Lots 63 and 64 in the Town of Guelph, Canada West, 1856.** 1 map. Loc: GCM.
The plan extends from Market Square, Macdonell Street, Quebec Street, Woolwich Street to the Speed River. It marks the Court House and Jail, Registry Office and a church in St George's Square. The scale is 80 feet to an inch.

3179. Strange, Henry. **Map of the Priory Block and adjoining lots, c1855.** 1 map. Loc: GLR. Map 16.
Plan that extends from the Speed River and Mill Pond in the north to the Market Street Bridge in the east, to Woolwich Street in the south. The plan marks Lots 1 to 16 surrounding Priory Street.

3180. Strange, Henry. **Part of Town of Guelph as divided into building lots, 1855.** 1 map. Loc: GLR. Map 30.
Plan of Lots 1, 2, 3, 4, 5, 6 and half of 7 in Range III of Division A that includes London Road and Badian, Sussex and Heathfield Streets. The scale is 1 chain to an inch.

3181. Strange, Henry. **Plan of Lot D, Division A, formerly in the township but now in the Town of Guelph as surveyed for executor of the later James Oliver, 1856.** 1 map. Loc: GLR. Map 34.
Plan that extends from the town limits in the west, Waterloo Road in the north, Edinburgh Road in the east and the Speed River in the south. The scale is 2 chains to an inch.

3182. Strange, Henry. **Plan of lots in the Town of Guelph showing the vicinity of both railway stations, and the principal roads to them, 1855.** print. Loc: UGL.
An 1855 plan of a portion of the Town of Guelph, illustrating the roads that led to the Galt and Guelph railway station and the Grand Trunk railway station. The map's boundaries are Norfolk and Woolwich Streets to the east, just west of

Edinburgh Road in the west, Elliot Street in the north, and approximately Preston Street in the south. The scale is three chains to an inch.

3183. Strange, Henry. **Plan of Park Lots in I, II, III, IV first range southwest of Woolwich Road, Division A, new survey formerly in the Township but now in the Town of Guelph as surveyed for trustees of the estate of the late Mr Charles McTague, 1856**. 1 map. Loc: GLR. Map 105.
   Plan which shows Glebe, McTague and Stage Streets as well as London and Woolwich Roads. The scale is 1 chain to an inch.

3184. Strange, Henry. **Plan of part of Guelph, divided into building lots by C.I. Buckland, 1855**. Loc: GCH.
   Plan of an area in the Buckland survey bounded by London Road, including Heathfield and Elliott Streets which were scheduled to be closed, a watercourse running through the area and the location of Mr Buckland's residence. The plan has a scale is 4 chains to an inch and is a schedule appended to Bylaw No. 90, 6 January, 1860. The plan appears to be a more detailed section of Strange's 'Plan of lots in the Town of Guelph showing the vicinity of both railway stations and the principal roads to them. Guelph Advertiser, 1855'.

3185. Strange, Henry. **Plan of part of Town of Guelph comprising Park Lots LXVI, LXVII, LXVIII, LXIX and LXX as survey for Messrs John Elmslie and Company, 1856**. 1 map. Loc: GLR. Map 42.
   Plan showing Edinburgh, Market, Fleet and Bristol Streets. The scale is 2 chains to an inch.

GUELPH TOWNSHIP

3186. Bowman, E.P. **Plan of subdivision of parts of Lots 1 and 2, Concession 3, Division C, Park Lots 37 and 38, registered plan 53, in the Township of Guelph, 1929**. 1 map. Loc: GLR. Map 396.
   Plan bordered by Wells Street in the west, the Canadian National Railway line in the north, Galt Avenue in the east and a road allowance between Concessions 2 and 3, Division C in the south. The scale is 100 feet to an inch.

3187. Canada Company. **Map of Guelph Township, 1832**. 82 x 98 cm. original. Loc: MTL. Card index.
   The map shows the cadastral survey of the township and names the purchasers of each lot sold. Most land in Divisions A, E and F had been purchased, while in Divisions B, C and D only lots along the main roads to Waterloo, Woolwich and Eramosa had been taken up.

3188. Chadwick, F.J. **Amended map of Lot B, Division E, Township of Guelph, 1869**. 1 map. Loc: GLR. Map 192.
   Plan which is bordered by Chadwick Road in the west and Waterloo Road in the east. The index book of plans indicates it cancelled an earlier plan to establish Balinard Village. The scale is 4 chains to an inch.

3189. Chadwick, F.J. **Map of Chipchase farm, Guelph, 1865**. 1 map. Loc: GLR. Map 169.
   Plan of Lots 1 and 2, Concession 3, Division D in Guelph Township that belonged to the Chipchase family.

3190. Chadwick, F.J. **Plan shewing alteration in survey of the property known as 'Rocks' for James Webster, Esq., 1861.** 1 map. Loc: GLR. Map 168.
Plan drawn for David Allan and James Webster showing Lots 3, 4 and 5, Concession 1 and Lot 3, Concession 2, Division C in Guelph Township. The plan is bordered by a road allowance between Lots 5 and 6, the Eramosa River and a road allowance between Guelph and Puslinch Townships. The scale is 4 chains to an inch.

3191. Cooper, T.W. **Plan of the subdivision of parts of Lots 2, 3 and 4, Concession 2, Division G in the Town and Township of Guelph, the property of Evan Macdonald, Esq., 1876.** 1 map. Loc: GLR. Map 255.
Plan bordered by Bay Street in the west, Evan Street in the north, Inverness Street in the east and the Guelph Dundas and Hamilton Gravel Road in the south. The scale is 2 chains to an inch.

3192. Cooper, T.W. **Plan of the subdivision of the west south half of Lot 5, Concession 3, Division G, Township of Guelph, 1876.** 1 map. Loc: GLR. Map 249.
Plan showing land immediately north of the Ontario Agricultural College. The scale is 2 chains to an inch.

3193. Davis, John. **Plan of subdivision of Lots 3 and 4, Plan 139, Hubbard's survey of part of Lot 34 in Division A, Guelph Township, County of Wellington, Ontario, 1906.** 1 map. Loc: GLR. Map 320.
Plan that extends east of Woolwich Street to the Speed River. The property belonged to J.W. Lyon. The scale is 100 feet to an inch.

3194. **Guelph Township showing lots sold to 1832.** 1 sheet, 15 x 10 inches. Loc: AO. C-17.

3195. Haskins, William. **Map showing the subdivision of property belonging to George Fetherston Haugh, Esq. adjoining the Town of Guelph being part of Lot numbers 1 and 2 in Division E, Guelph Township, 1872.** 1 map. Loc: GLR. Map 206.
Plan showing lots on Silver Creek Street stretching from Napoleon Street in the north to Waterloo Road in the south. The plan marks the property of George Sleeman, Mr Carter, Mr Steel and Sheriff Grange. The plan also indicates the location of Mr Keating's survey between Victoria Street and Waterloo Road.

3196. Haskins, William. **Plan of park lots being a subdivision of Lot 11, Concession 3, Division D in the Township of Guelph, the property of Mr William Griffiths, 1857.** 1 map. Loc: GLR. Map 45.
Plan of park lots drawn to the scale of 4 chains to an inch.

3197. Hobson, J. and Chadwick, F.J. **Map of the Township of Guelph in the County of Wellington, 1858.** print, col, 83 x 116 cm, scale 1 inch to 20 chains. Loc: GCM, GPL, AO. AO: C-17.
A map of the township, printed by Maclear and Company of Toronto, that includes the survey grid, names of lot owners, roads, schools, school sections, wards of Guelph, streets and buildings.

3198. Howitt, Alfred. **Map of Guelph Grant, property of William Howitt situated near the City of Guelph, 1884.** 1 map. Loc: GLR. Map 289.
Plan of Lot 1, Concession 1 in Division E, Lot D in Concession 1 in Division

E, Lots 1, 2, 3, 4 and 5 in Concession 5 in Division G and part of Lot 1 in Concession 4 in Division G. The scale is 4 chains to an inch.

3199. Howitt, Alfred. **Map of James Howitt's farm comprising part of township Lots 1, 2, 3, 4 and 5 in Concession 4 and parts of Lots 1, 2, 3, 4 and 5 in Concession 5, Division G, Township of Guelph, 1882.** 1 map. Loc: GLR. Map 288.
Plan bordered by the Speed River in the west and north and a road allowance between Lots 5 and 6 in the south, one mile west of the Ontario Agricultural College. The scale is 4 chains to an inch.

3200. Howitt, Alfred. **Plans. Drainage ditch at Wingfield Farm, Puslinch, 1894.** 1 plan; 1 file folder. Loc: WCA.
Specifications for the ditch are held with the plan.

3201. Hutcheon, James. **Plan of Guelph Gardens being a subdivision of parts of northwest halves of Lots 1 and 2, Concession 5, Division C, Guelph Township, 1913.** 1 map. Loc: GLR. Map 359.
A copy of a plan bordered by Eramosa Road in the northwest, a concession road in the north, and the city boundary road in the west. The scale is 4 chains to an inch.

3202. Hutcheon, James. **Plan of subdivision of Lots 14 and 15, Division A, Township of Guelph, property of Jones and Johnston, 1911.** 1 map. Loc: GLR. Map 339.
Plan showing lots east and west of the Grand Trunk Railway line. The scale is 200 feet to an inch.

3203. Hutcheon, James. **Plan of subdivision of part of Lot 4, Concession 3, Division G, Township of Guelph, 1899.** 1 map. Loc: GLR. Map 308.
Plan bordered by a 'private lane' in the west, Dundas Road in the north and Lane Street in the south. The scale is 60 feet to an inch.

3204. Kerr, Francis. **Map of survey in the Township of Guelph and County of Wellington for John Galt, 1855.** 1 map. Loc: GLR. Map 53.
Plan of Lots 1, 2 and 3, Concession 3, Division C, including the Grand Trunk Railway line that extends south of the Paisley Block Road.

3205. Kerr, Francis. **Plan of park lots laid out on Concession 7, Township of Guelph for Mr J.T. Leslie, 1857.** 1 map. Loc: GLR, AO. AO:C-17; GLR:Map 48.
Map showing Eramosa Road, a side road between Lots 5 and 6, and the Speed River, in Division C of the Township. The scale is 1 chain to an inch.

3206. Kerr, Francis. **Plan of park lots near the Town of Guelph, March 1852.** 1 plan. Loc: WCA.
A plan of proposed park lots as part of Crawford's Survey showing areas around the Eramosa River including southeast Crawford Street and northeast York Road. The scale is three chains to the inch.

3207. Kerr, Francis. **Plan of part of Union Village composed of part of Lots 9 and 10 in Concession 10, Division C, Township of Guelph, for Mr Silas Edwards, 1858.** 1 map. Loc: GLR. Map 97.
A plan showing numbered lots along Edward, Silas and Nathaniel Streets. The scale is 2 chains to an inch.

3208. Kerr, Francis. **Plan of the Village of Marden, Township of Guelph, the property of E. Murton, Esq., 1852.** ms. Loc: GLR. Map 44.

Plan showing several streets with no names given, and Woolwich Road. The scale is 1 chain to an inch.

3209. Kerr, Francis. **Plan shewing the subdivision of part of Lot 34 in the Township of Guelph, 1861.** 1 map. Loc: GLR. Map 139.

Plan which indicates the lot was in Division A of Guelph Township. The plan is bordered by the Speed River, Woolwich Road and an unnamed side road. The scale is 1 chain to an inch.

3210. Kerr, Francis. **Plans. Hills, 1855.** ms. Loc: WCA.

Plans of a hill near Robert Oliver's and Shortreed's hill; the finding aid states that the plans were drawn in 1855.

3211. Malcolm, L. **College Heights, being a subdivision of Park Lot 4, Concession 3, Division G and of Lots 7, 8, 9, 10 Parker Survey according to the registered plan 308 in the Township of Guelph, 1914.** 1 map. Loc: GLR. Map 363.

Plan bordered by Talbot Street in the west, Dean Avenue in the north, Dundas Road in the east and University Avenue in the south. The scale is 100 feet to an inch.

3212. Malcolm, L. **Plan of Wellington Place being a subdivision of parts of broken front Lot 1, Range A and B, Division F of the Township of Guelph, 1912.** 1 map. Loc: GLR. Map 356.

Plan that extends to Wellington Boulevard in the west and north, Clive Avenue in the east and Berlin Road in the south. The land was owned by the Guelph Realty Company of which J.W. Lyon was president. The scale is 100 feet to an inch.

3213. Map and Advertising Co. Ltd. **Guidal landowners' map of Township of Guelph, 1917.** Loc: UGL, NAC, AO. AO:C-53; NAC:430/Guelph/1917/#48828.

A map of the Township of Guelph that includes concession and lot numbers as well as the names of the owners of each lot. The map is surrounded with advertisements of various Ontario businesses, including seven Guelph companies: Gowdy Brothers, Penfold Hardware and Carriage Company, and the Guelph Lumber Company.

3214. **Map of survey in the Township of Guelph for William Alexander, Esq. laid out in 1856.** 1 map. Loc: GLR. Map 54.

Map showing Silver Creek and Paisley Block Roads, Alexander Street and the route of the Grand Trunk Railway north of Paisley Block Road. The document indicates the survey area to be part of Lot 4, Concession 1, Division E in the Township of Guelph. The scale is 2 chains to an inch.

3215. **Map of the Township of Guelph, 1854.** Loc: UGL.

A plan of Guelph Township that marks lots, concession numbers, and Waterloo, Woolwich and Eramosa roads. The scale is 53 chains to the inch.

3216. McDonald, Donald. **Map of the Township of Guelph, c1843.** print, 30 x 36 cm, scale 1 inch to 53.6 chains. Loc: NAC, AO. NAC: #3464; AO: SR 1156.

The map shows Blocks A to E and G and Woolwich, Eramosa and Waterloo Roads as well as the streets and park lots of the Town of Guelph. A copy of the map was enclosed with the petition for the enlargement of the town boundaries.

3217. McDonald, John. **Map of the Township of Guelph, 1828.** 97 x 98 cm, scale 1 inch to 20 chains. Loc: AO.

A map of 42,338 acres, showing the roads from Waterloo, Woolwich, Eramosa and York and the town plot of Guelph with Quebec, McDonell, Market and Waterloo Streets. McDonald refers to 'the former map of 1827' believed to have been begun by George Tiffany which he was completing.

3218. Niven, D.A. **Plan of extension of MacDonald Avenue, part of Lot 4, Concession 2, Division G in the Township of Guelph, 1920.** 1 map. Loc: GLR. Map 387.

Plan of lots north of Dundas Road along MacDonald Avenue. The scale is 80 feet to an inch.

3219. Niven, D.A. **Plan of Guelph Township, November, 1915.** 1 plan. Blueprint. Loc: WCA.

A map of Guelph Township by D.A. Niven drawn to the scale of 2500 feet to one inch.

3220. Niven, D.A. **Plan of Lakeview Gardens, a subdivision of parts of Lots 7 and 8, Concession 2, Division D in the Township of Guelph, 1915.** 1 map. Loc: GLR. Map 365.

Plan that extends north and south of Bedford Road east of Elora Road. The scale is 200 feet to an inch.

3221. Niven, D.A. **Plan of subdivision of part of Lot 4, Concession 2, Division G in the Township of Guelph, 1917.** 1 map. Loc: GLR. Map 378.

Plan that extends west and east of MacDonald Avenue and north of Dundas Road. The scale is 40 feet to an inch.

3222. Niven, D.A. **Plan of subdivision of part of Lots 5, 6 and 7, plan 283, Township of Guelph, 1919.** 1 map. Loc: GLR. Map 384.

Plan showing lots bordering on College Avenue in the south and Moore Avenue in the north. The scale is 80 feet to an inch.

3223. Niven, D.A. **Plan of the Sloan Survey, a subdivision of Lot 36, registered plan 53, in the Township of Guelph, 1916.** 1 map. Loc: GLR. Map 377.

Plan bordered by Sloan Avenue in the west, the Grand Trunk Railway line in the north, Galt Avenue in the east and York Road in the south. The scale is 40 feet to an inch.

3224. Niven, D.A. **Plan of Wellington Place Annex, a subdivision of part of broken front Lot 1 in Division F, Township of Guelph, 1918.** 1 map. Loc: GLR. Map 382.

Plan showing lots south of Wellington Boulevard and north of Berlin Road. The document indicates J.W. Lyon was president of the company owning lots in the area. The scale is 150 feet to an inch.

3225. Ontario Department of Public Highways. **Blueprint plan of Guelph Township, 1917.** 1 plan. Loc: WCA.

Held with Guelph Township records.

3226. **Plan of park lots for sale near the Town of Guelph, c1843**. print, 28 x 24 cm, scale 1 inch to 8 chains. Loc: KPL.

Plan of lots on the north side of the Speed River east of Eramosa Road, showing the Court House and Gaol and names of some owners. The plan was lithographed by Hugh Scobie.

3227. **Plan of part of Division A in the Township of Guelph, c1855**. 1 map. Loc: GLR. Map 43.

Plan of Ranges I to IV in Division A that extends north of London Road between Edinburgh Road in the west and Cardigan Street in the east. The scale is 6 chains to an inch.

3228. **Plan of the subdivision of the northeast half of Lot 5 in Concession 3, Division G, Township of Guelph, 1882**. 1 map. Loc: GLR. Map 283.

Plan of lots north of the Ontario Agricultural College Farm.

3229. Schofield, M.C. **Plan of subdivision of lots for James Webster, 1855**. 1 map, oversize. Loc: UGA. XR2 MS A023.

A plan showing subdivision of lots 3, 4 and 5 in the Township of Guelph, surveyed for James Webster in May, 1855. The scale is 4 chains to an inch. The plan includes a description of terrain with watercourses, stands of timber, roads and a school on York Road. Much of the land described later became part of the Guelph Central Prison Farm. The map is attached to a deed given to D. Allan by the Township of Guelph in 1855. Part of the Allan-Higinbotham Collection.

3230. Strange, Henry. **Map of Hartfield Village, 1856**. print. Loc: GPL.

A plan of a survey of lots for sale in Guelph Township for the proposed village of Hartfield. The plan is divided into building and park lots and extends north of Guelph between Woolwich Street and the Owen Sound Road. The property was owned by Thomas Card. The scale is two chains to the inch.

3231. Strange, Henry. **Map of park lots laid out in Ballinard in the Township of Guelph, County of Wellington for John C. Chadwick, 1856**. print. Loc: UGA, GCM.

A map of what appears to be a planned community that never materialized. There is evidence to suggest that the land, just south of Guelph, was owned by John Chadwick and that it was to be sold to prospective landowners. Lots are marked out and numbered. The Galt and Guelph Railway line runs directly through 'Ballinard'. Instructions are given at the bottom of the map about the date of sales and terms of payment.

3232. Strange, Henry. **Plan of building lots in the Township of Guelph comprising part of Lots 1 and 2, Concession 1, Division E, surveyed for Thos. Keating, Esq., 1854**. 1 map. Loc: GLR. Map 52.

Plan showing Waterloo and Concession Roads and Napoleon and Victoria Streets. The plan also shows the route of the Galt and Guelph Railway. The scale is 1 chain to an inch.

3233. Strange, Henry. **Plan of the Village of Sweaborg in the Township of Guelph being part of Lot 4, Division B, southeast of Waterloo Road, as surveyed for Mr Edward C. Lowry, 1856**. 1 map. Loc: GLR. Map 46.

Plan showing Waterloo Road and McConnell, Lowry and Graham Streets. The scale is 1 chain to an inch.

3234. Strange, Henry. **Plan of the Village of Trafalgar being part of Lot 7, Concession 1, Division E of the Township of Guelph as surveyed for Robert Porter, 1856.** 1 map. Loc: GLR. Map 51.

Plan that extends from the Paisley Block Road in the west to Silver Creek Road in the north. The index notes that the plan is incomplete.

3235. Toronto and Guelph Railway. **Plans and sections of road crossing at station 145, 1853.** 1 plan. Loc: WCA.

A plan for the railway crossing at the corner of York Road and the side road between lots 5 and 6. Held with the Guelph Township records.

3236. **Township of Guelph, Gore District, c1830.** print, 41 x 29 cm. Loc: AO. Canada Company Records, A-4-3, vol. 4, Plate 52.

Shows the survey grid, town plot and town reserves, rivers and main roads.

HARRISTON

3237. Bolton and Johnston. **Plan of Town of Harriston showing lands to be detached, 1923.** 1 blueprint, 49 x 69 cm. Loc: AO. D-4.

3238. Bolton, E.D. **Plan of the Town of Harriston being composed of parts of Lots 84, 85, 86, 87, 88, Concession C, and Lots 83, 84, 85, 86, 87, 88, Concession D, in the Township of Minto, 1941.** 1 map. Loc: ALR.

Plan that extends to the Canadian National Railway tracks in the west, George Street in the north, Albert Street in the east and James Street in the south. The scale is 4 chains to an inch.

3239. Bolton, Lewis. **Plan shewing subdivision of Park Lots 3 and 13 in the subdivision of part of Farm Lot 87, Concession D, comprising part of the Town of Harriston, 1882.** 1 map. Loc: ALR.

Plan of Robertson's Survey, bounded by Young Street in the west, Margaret Street in the north and Pellissier in the east. The scale is 2 chains to an inch.

3240. Bolton, Lewis. **Plan shewing subdivision of part of Farm Lot 88, Concession C, formerly in the Township of Minto but now in the Town of Harriston, 1878.** 1 map. Loc: ALR.

Plan of lots that extend north and south of King and Queen Streets. The scale is 2 chains to an inch. The property owner is listed as Samuel Robertson.

3241. Bolton, Lewis. **Plan shewing subdivision of part of the north part of the south half of Lot 86, Concession D, formerly in the Township of Minto, now in the Town of Harriston, 1878.** 1 map. Loc: ALR.

'Wilson's Plan' bounded by Arthur Street in the west, Margaret Street in the north and Young Street in the east. The scale is 2 chains to an inch.

3242. Bolton, Lewis. **Plan shewing subdivision of sawmill property, Lots 1, 2, 3, 4, 5 and 6 and distillery site, all on the north side of Mill Street in the Village of Harriston, 1878.** 1 map. Loc: ALR.

Plan of Preston's Survey that extends to Arthur Street in the west, Elora

Street in the north, Elizabeth Street in the east and John Street in the south. The scale is 1 chain to an inch. George Preston is listed as owner.

3243. Davis, John. **Plan of a continuation of Young and King Streets in the Town of Harriston, c1880.** 1 map. Loc: ALR.

Plan of Young Street that extends north and south and King Street that extends west. The scale is 1 chain to an inch. James Moore is listed as proprietor.

3244. Davis, John. **Plan of building lots in the Town of Harriston, being a subdivision of part of the northeast half of Farm Lot 84, southwest of Elora Street, c1880.** 1 map. Loc: ALR.

Plan of Mary Wright's Survey that extends to the Stratford and Huron Railway in the south and west, Elora Street in the north and Louise Street in the east. The scale is 2 chains to an inch. The owner is listed as Mary Wright.

3245. Davis, John. **Plan of building lots in the Village of Harriston laid out for James Foster Wilson, Esq., being a portion of Lot 85, Concession D, Township of Minto, 1878.** 1 map. Loc: ALR.

Plan of Wilson's Survey bounded by a road allowance between Concessions D and 9 in the west, Livingstone Street in the east and Arthur Street in the south.

3246. Davis, John. **Plan of building lots laid out for Samuel Robertson, Esq. in the Town of Harriston and being a subdivision of a portion of Farm Lot 88, Concession C formerly comprising part of the Township of Minto, 1879.** 1 map. Loc: ALR.

Plan of Robertson's Survey bounded by Lorne Street in the west, George Street in the north, Anne Street in the east and Elora Street in the south. The scale is 1 chain to an inch.

3247. Davis, John. **Plan of the Town of Harriston in the County of Wellington, c1880.** 1 map. Loc: ALR.

Plan bounded by Wards 4 and 5 in the west, Concession C in the north, Wards 1 and 2 in the east and Ward 3 in the south.

3248. Davis, John. **Plan shewing subdivision of parts of Park Lots 1 and 2, Harriston, northeast of George Street, for James Moore, 1879.** 1 map. Loc: ALR.

Plan of Moore's Survey that extends to Maitland Street in the west, George Street in the east and George Street in the south. The scale is 1 chain to an inch.

3249. Kertland, Edwin H. **Harriston, Ontario, c1859.** print, 88 x 65 cm, 1 inch to 2 chains. Loc: AO, ALR. D-4.

Plan for subdivision of lots 85, 86 and 87 in Concessions C and D, between Pellisier and William, George and Margaret Streets, including sites for a tannery, brewery, chair factory and distillery. The plan itself has a manuscript date of 1859 but there is some evidence that some lots were first subdivided in 1855.

3250. LaPenotiere, W.H. **Plan of the Village of Harriston, being composed of the southwest half of Lots 84, 85, 86 and 87, Concession C and Lots 85 and 86 and northeast half of Lots 84 and 87, Concession D, Township of Minto, 1874.** 1 map. Loc: ALR.

Plan of LaPenotiere's Survey bounded by George Street in the north, William Street in the west, Pellissier Street in the east and Robinson Street in the south. The scale is 4 chains to an inch.

3251. Morison, W.G. **Plan of part of the Village of Harriston comprising portions of Lots 86 and 87, Concession D, Minto Township, 1873.** 1 map. Loc: ALR.
Plan of numbered lots that extend north of Arthur Street, east of Margaret Street, south of Younge Street and along both sides of Robertson Street. The scale is 2 chains to an inch. The property owner is listed as Samuel Robertson. The Wellington, Grey and Bruce Railway Station is marked at the corner of Margaret and Brock Street.

3252. West, R.F. **Plan of building and park lots laid out for Samuel Cowan on part of the southwest half of Lot 88, Concession C, Township of Minto, now in the Town of Harriston, 1881.** 1 map. Loc: ALR.
Plan of Cowan's Survey that extends to Elora Street in the west, Jessie Street in the north and King Street. The scale is 50 links to an inch.

LUTHER

3253. McLean, James. **Plan of the Village of Evansville part of Lot 1, Concession 14, Luther, the property of William Evans, 1876.** 1 map. Loc: ALR.
Plan of Conn (previously Evansville) showing twenty-eight subdivisions of the lot along unnamed streets. The village extends to the east of the Arthur Township line and south of the Proton Township line. The scale is 1 chain to an inch.

3254. Parke, Thomas. **Luther Township, County of Wellington, 1843.** 1 map. Loc: AO. C-25.
Plan of the Crown Survey drawn to the scale of 40 chains to an inch.

MARYBOROUGH

3255. Bolton, Lewis and Herman, Mr. **Plan of that part of the Village of Moorefield situated on the west half of Lot 10, Concession 9, Township of Maryboro (sic), County of Wellington, c1873.** 1 map. Loc: ALR.
Plan of Loughran's Survey showing land east of McGiveren Street, north of Booth Street and south of the Wellington, Grey and Bruce Railway line. The scale is 2 chains to an inch.

3256. Bolton, Lewis. **Plan of the subdivision of part of Farm Lot 9, Concession 8, Township of Maryborough, comprising part of the Village of Moorefield, 1902.** 1 map. Loc: ALR.
Plan of Metcalf Survey that extends south of Booth Street and west of McGiveren Street. The scale is 3 chains to an inch. Isaac Metcalf is listed as the owner.

3257. Burke, J.W. **Plan of Hustonville, Township of Maryboro (sic), being part of east half of Lot 11 and west half of Lot 12, Concession 8, 1861.** 1 map. Loc: ALR.
Plan showing lots east and west of the Conestoga River and bordered by Bridge Street in the south, Wallace Street in the east and Tromanhiser Street in the west. The scale is 2 chains to an inch.

3258. Burke, J.W. **Plan of part of the Village of Hustonville on west half of Lot 12, Concession 8, Township of Maryboro (sic), 1861.** 1 map. Loc: ALR.

Plan bounded by 'mill property' in the west, Main Street in the north, Mill Street in the east and Wallace Street in the south. The scale is not given for the plan.

3259. Kertland, Edwin H. **Map of the Village of Maryborough comprising part of Lots 10 and 13, Concession 14 of Maryborough surveyed for Messrs Allan and Geddes, 1855.** print. Loc: ALR.

Plan of Rothsay that extends to King Street in the west, Queen Street in the north, Paul Street in the east and Nelson Street in the south. The scale is 2 chains to an inch. Charles Adams and James Geddes are listed as owners.

3260. Kertland, Edwin H. **Plan of part of Hollin comprising Lots 18 and 19, Concession 5, Township of Maryboro (sic), the property of Wm. Mendell, Esq., 1861.** 1 map. Loc: ALR.

Plan of Mendell Survey, Hollin, bounded by Church Street in the west, High Street in the west, Elgin Street in the east and Jane Street in the south. The scale is 2 chains to an inch.

3261. LaPenotiere, W.H. **Plan of the Village of Stirton being composed of part of Lot 1, Concessions 8 and 9, Township of Peel and Lot 19, Concession 8, Township of Maryborough, 1872.** 1 map. Loc: ALR.

Plan showing lots east and west of Church and Queen Streets and north and south of King Street.

3262. LaPenotiere, W.H. **Plan of Village of Hollin, 1864.** 1 map. Loc: ALR.

Plan bounded by Wellington Street in the west, Elgin Street in the east and Raglan Street in the south. The scale is 3 chains to an inch.

3263. **Map of Maryborough Township, c1840.** 1 map. Loc: ALR.

Plan drawn to a scale of 40 chains to an inch.

3264. Schofield, M.C. **Plan of part of Lot 10, Concession 8, being part of the Village of Moorefield in the Township of Maryboro (sic), County of Wellington, laid out for J. King, Esq., 1875.** 1 map. Loc: ALR.

Plan of King's Survey showing lots north of Conestoga Creek and south of a road allowance between Concessions 8 and 9. The scale is 2 chains to an inch.

3265. Schofield, M.C. **Plan of part of the Village of Moorefield, Township of Maryboro (sic), County of Wellington, laid out for the Rev. George C. Moore, J.P., 1871.** 1 map. Loc: ALR.

Plan of Moore's Survey bounded by the 'supposed limit between the east and west halves of Lot 9' in the north, Reid Street in the west and McGiveren Street in the south. The scale is 200 feet to an inch.

3266. Schofield, M.C. **Plan of the Village plot of Moorefield, Township of Maryborough, 1872.** 1 map. Loc: ALR.

Plan of numbered lots that extend west of Booth Street and north of McGivern Street. Lots that have been sold are shaded. The parsonage of Reverend George Moore and the Wellington, Grey and Bruce Railway Station are noted.

MINTO

3267. Bolton, Lewis. **Plan shewing subdivision of west half of Lot 91, Concession 0, Township of Minto, the property of F.A. Carter, Esq., 1880.** 1 map. Loc: ALR.
Plan of Carter's Survey drawn to the scale of 3 chains to an inch.

3268. Kirk, Joseph. **Plan of subdivision of the north part of Lot 21, Concession 1 of Minto, County of Wellington, subdivided into park lots, 1876.** 1 map. Loc: ALR.
Plan of Kirk's Survey showing lots east and west of Brunswick Street and lots north and south of Lett Street. The plan is labelled as showing the property of 'Messrs Watson and Fuller'. The scale is 132 feet to an inch.

3269. Map and Advertising Co. Ltd. **Guidal landowners' map of Township of Minto, 1917.** 1 sheet, 19-3/4 x 11-1/2. Loc: NAC, AO. AO:C-53; NAC:430/Minto/1917/#48830.
A detailed map showing lot owners' names at a scale of 1 inch to a mile. Marginal advertisements.

3270. **Map of Minto Township, c1840.** 1 map. Loc: ALR, AO. C-29.
Map of the township drawn to a scale of 40 chains to an inch.

3271. Rankin, Charles. **Minto Township, 1852.** Loc: AO. C-29.

3272. Yarnold, W.E. **Plan of park lots on the northwest half of Lot 88, Concession D, Township of Minto, 1883.** 1 map. Loc: ALR.
Plan of Preston's Survey Part 88 Ghent, bounded by Margaret, John and Lorne Streets, and by the Wellington, Grey and Bruce Railway line.

MOUNT FOREST

3273. Kerr, Francis. **Plan exhibiting proposed subdivision of the town plot of Mount Forest, 1853.** col ms, 57 x 80 cm, scale 1 inch to 5 chains. Loc: AO. D-6; SR 204.
The Archives of Ontario also holds a related plan of Mount Forest dated 1854 and measuring 68 x 101 cm at a scale of 1 inch to 4 chains.

3274. Kertland, Edwin H. **Plan of a portion of Mount Forest in the Township of Arthur, the property of Messrs Allan and Geddes, Elora, 1855.** print, 58 x 98 cm, scale 1 inch to 2 chains. Loc: ALR, MNR. SR 204.
Plan of Allan and Geddes Survey in Divisions 3 and 4, Lot 2 on the west side of the Owen Sound Road. The map shows property for sale along Wellington, Mill and Bentley Streets, south of the Maitland River, and also the location of the mill pond, sawmill, flouring mill, chair factory, cloth factory and distillery. The plan was certified at the Land Registry in 1857.

3275. McLean, James. **Plan of Park Lot 6, south of Waterloo Street, Mount Forest, the property of C. Bodley, Esq., c1880.** 1 map. Loc: ALR.
Plan of Bodley's Survey, Munt Forest, that has no date listed but the surveyor did a number of plans in Wellington County during the 1880s. The plan is bounded by Waterloo, Lane, Dublin and Princess Streets. No scale is given.

3276. McLean, James. **Plan of Park Lot 6, south of Waterloo Street, Mount Forest, property of C. Bodley, c1860.** 1 map. Loc: ALR.
Plan of Bodley's Survey that is bounded by Princess Street, Dublin Street and Waterloo Street.

3277. McLean, James. **Plan of part of Lot 22 west of Main Street, Mount Forest, 1882.** 1 map. Loc: ALR.
Plan of McLean's Survey that extends south of Main Street and east of Queen Street. The scale is 1 chain to 2 inches.

3278. McLean, James. **Plan of subdivision of Lot 3, north of Durham Street, Mount Forest, the property of William Wyllie (sic), 1876.** 1 map. Loc: ALR.
Plan of Wylie's Survey that extends to the west and east of Henry Street. The scale is 1 chain to an inch.

3279. McLean, James. **Plan of subdivision of Park Lot 2, north of King and east of Church Streets, Mount Forest, the property of E.G. Hart, 1882.** 1 map. Loc: ALR.
Plan of Hart Survey drawn to the scale of 1 chain to 2 inches.

3280. McLean, James. **Plan of the subdivision of Park Lot 6 and the east half of Park Lot 7 south of Queen Street, Mount Forest, 1881.** 1 map. Loc: ALR.
Plan of Harris Survey bounded by Queen Street in the north, Dublin Street in the east and Waterloo Street in the south. The scale is 1 chain to an inch.

3281. McLean, James. **Plan of the subdivision of Park Lot 6, north of Birmingham Street, Mount Forest, 1880.** 1 map. Loc: ALR.
Plan of Watt's Survey that extends north of Birmingham Street and south of Durham Street. The scale is 1 chain to an inch. The owner is listed as James Watt.

3282. McLean, James. **Plan of the subdivision of the west half of Lot Q in Macdonald's Survey of Divisions 1 and 2, Lot 2, west of the Guelph and Owen Sound Road, Township of Arthur, 1878.** 1 map. Loc: ALR.
Plan of Joseph Harris Survey, Mount Forest, that extends north and south of Harris Street. The scale is 2 chains to an inch. The owner is listed as Joseph Harris.

3283. McLean, James. **Plan of the subdivision of the west part of Park Lot 6 between Wellington and Birmingham Streets, Mount Forest, 1898.** 1 map. Loc: ALR.
Plan of William Colcleugh's Survey bounded by Birmingham, Queen and Wellington Streets and by Colcleugh Avenue.

3284. McLean, James. **Plan of the subdivisions of Lot 6 between Birmingham and Wellington Streets, Mount Forest, 1860.** 1 map. Loc: ALR.
Plan of Flora Colcleugh's Survey drawn to the scale of 2 chains to an inch. The owner is listed as Flora Colcleugh.

3285. Murphy, F. **Plan shewing subdivision of Park Lot 2 on the east side of Main Street and west of Fergus Street, Mount Forest, County of Wellington, property of Thomas Easterbrook, 1873.** 1 map. Loc: ALR.
Plan of Easterbrook's Survey showing Fergus Street in the north, Durham Street in the east and Main Street in the south. The scale is 1 chain to an inch.

3286. **Plan of Mount Forest, 1860**. 1 map. Loc: ALR.
Plan showing Sligo Street, London Road and the Savey River in Mount Forest. The scale is 4 chains to an inch. The document is labelled as registered at the Crown Lands Department in Quebec.

3287. Wilson, Hugh. **Gardner Survey, plan of subdivision of Park Lots 2 and 3, west of Main Street, Mount Forest, 1885**. 1 map. Loc: ALR.
Plan of Gardner's Survey that extends to Foster Street in the west, Sligo Street in the north, Main Street in the east and Durham Street in the south. The scale is 1 chain to an inch. The owner is listed as Francis G. Gardner and is signed F.G. Gardiner.

3288. Wilson, Hugh. **Map shewing part of Lot 33, Concession 1 of Normanby laid out at the request of the proprietor, John Foster, Esq., 1864**. 1 map. Loc: ALR.
Plan of Foster's Survey, Mount Forest, bounded by Perth Street in the west, Duke Street in the north, Main Street in the east and Sligo Street in the south. The scale is 2 chains to an inch.

3289. Wilson, Hugh. **Mount Forest showing plan of town as proposed for incorporation, 1879**. Loc: AO. R-O.

3290. Wilson, Hugh. **Plan of Park Lot 1, east of Fergus Street, Mount Forest, the property of John Walker, 1875**. 1 map. Loc: ALR.
Plan of Walker's Survey that extends east of Fergus Street and south of Sligo Road.

3291. Wilson, Hugh. **Plan of part of Park Lot 1, east of Fergus Street, Mount Forest, property of John Walker, 1875**. 1 map. Loc: ALR.
Plan of Walker's Survey that extends east of Fergus Street and south of Sligo Road. The plan includes the names of several property owners. The scale is 1 chain to an inch.

3292. Wilson, Hugh. **Plan of that part of Park Lot 9 south of Queen Street, Mount Forest, the property of James Ellis, 1875**. 1 map. Loc: ALR.
Plan of Ellis Survey bounded by Queen Street in the north and Waterloo Street in the south. The scale is 1 chain to an inch.

3293. Wilson, Hugh and Black, S. **Plan of the Town of Mount Forest, 1883, revised to 1962**. 2 sections. Loc: ALR.
Plan of the entire Town of Mount Forest noting street names and lot numbers based on Hugh Wilson's 1883 plan and revised to 1962 by S. Black. The scale is 4 chains to an inch.

3294. Wilson, Hugh. **Plan shewing the north half of Lot 4 Gardiner's Survey, being composed of Park Lots 2 and 3 west of Main Street in the Town of Mount Forest, County of Wellington, sold by the late James Gardiner to James Doyle, 1868**. 1 map. Loc: ALR.
Plan of Doyle's Survey bounded by Sligo, Main, Durham and Foster Streets. The scale is 2 chains to an inch.

NICHOL

3295. Barker, W.H. **Plan of the property of William Moorhead, Village of Ryckmantown, Nichol Township, c1855.** 1 map. Loc: GLR. Map 71.

Plan of Lot 19, Concession 15 in Nichol Township. The index notes that the plan is for the Village of Ryckmantown. The scale is 3 chains to an inch.

3296. Blyth, Thomas A. **Plan of Township of Nichol showing names of landholders, 1845.** Loc: AO. C-32.

3297. Burwell, Lewis. **Plan of the Township of Nichol, 1832.** Loc: KPL. Card index.

An original map of the land survey pattern dated November 15, 1832, at the scale of 40 chains to an inch. Owners of about one-fifth of the lots are identified with some details of another one-fifth added later in pencil. The northwest quarter of the township is declared to have been surveyed in October 1832 by Lewis Burwell for William Gilkison. The northeast quarter was not yet surveyed.

3298. Fordyce, A.D. **Map of the Township of Nichol, 1845.** print, 46 x 64 cm, scale 2 inches to 1 mile. Loc: KPL, WCA, MNR. SR 1764.

An original map at the scale of 1 inch to a mile, showing the survey grid and cleared land and identifying the owners of about seventy-five percent of the lots. Inset are plans of Fergus and Elora and local views. Further details were apparently added later, perhaps by J.C. Templin, whose scrapbooks, held by the Archives of Ontario, include a facsimile copy of the Fordyce original. Another copy with annotations to 1852 is held by the Ministry of Natural Resources. May be related to Blyth's plan of 1845.

3299. Kertland, Edwin H. **Map of the Village of Ennotville, 1855.** 1 map. Loc: GLR. Map 109.

Plan showing lots in the village which includes Henry, Main, McLaren, Margarette and Mary Streets. The plan indicates Ennotville was situated in Lot 10, Concession 6 of Nichol Township.

3300. Kertland, Edwin H. **Plan of Strathallan Village, Nichol Township, 1860.** 1 map. Loc: GLR. Map 132.

Plan subdividing Lots 19 and 20, Concession 16 of Nichol Township. The plan was drawn for Charles Allan of Elora.

3301. Kertland, Edwin H. **Plan of the Village of Aboyne in the Township of Nichol, Wellington County, surveyed for Messrs Allan and Geddes, 1855.** print, col, 90 x 66 cm, 1 inch to 2 chains. Loc: GLR. Map 88.

Plan extends from Gilkison Street in the west, Union Street in the north and east, and Bartlett Street in the south and gives details of sizes and numbers of town and park lots. The property was owned by Charles Allan and James Geddes.

3302. Kertland, Edwin H. **Plan of the Village of Salem, 1856.** print, 26.25 x 32.25. Loc: NAC. 440/Wellington/1856/#19812.

Plan surveyed and drawn at scale of 2 chains to an inch for Messrs Wissler, Erb and Keith.

3303. **Map of the plan of the Village of Kinnettles in the Township of Nichol laid out for Alexander Harvey, 1855.** 1 map. Loc: GLR. Map 57.
Plan that extends from Canrobert Street in the west, Elora Street in the north, Sebastian Street in the east and the Grand River in the south. The scale is 2 chains to an inch.

3304. McLean, J.H. **Amended plan of Gluyasville now Cumnock on Lot 1, Concession 15, Township of Nichol, 1900.** 1 map. Loc: GLR. Map 311.
Plan that extends on either side of the Owen Sound Road. The scale is 4 chains to an inch.

3305. McLean, J.H. **Plan of Gluyasville being the southeast half of Lot 1, Concession 15, Township of Nichol, 1900.** 1 map. Loc: GLR. Map 310.
Plan showing lots north and south of Main Street and east and west of the Owen Sound Road. Gluyasville was later called Cumnock. The scale is 4 chains to an inch.

3306. Schofield, M.C. **Map of part of the Village of Kinnettles, Township of Nichol, 1855.** print, 21 x 28.5. Loc: NAC. 440/Kinnettles/1855/#22465.
Plan, at scale of 2 chains to an inch, of land surveyed for Alexander Harvey. Related to registered plan 57.

3307. Schofield, M.C. **Plan of Lot 18, Concession 15, Township of Nichol as subdivided for Robert Carver, 1855.** 1 map. Loc: GLR. Map 87.
Plan that extends from the concession road in the west to the Owen Sound Road in the east. The scale is 3 chains to an inch.

3308. Schofield, M.C. and Hobson, J. **Plan of the Village of Thorpville, composed of part of Lot 1 in Concession 9, Nichol, and part of Lot 15, Concession 1 of Pilkington County of Wellington, surveyed for John Thorp, Esq., 1856.** print. Loc: GLR. Map 93.
Plan showing lots along the 'Woolwich Gravelled Road', and also shows the road allowance between Concessions 8 and 9. The document marks the residences of Thomas Cummins and of Peter Gray and a church and school. The scale is 66 feet to an inch.

3309. Strange, Henry. **Plan of Village of Irvinedale, Lot 9, Concession 15, Nichol Township, 1861.** 1 map. Loc: GLR. Map 143.
Plan which was bordered by the Owen Sound Road and near the Irvine River.

3310. Wissler, Sem. **Plan of subdivisions of part of Lot 17, Concession 11 of the Township of Nichol, 1864.** 1 map. Loc: GLR. Map 164.
Plan showing South Street, Cemetery Avenue, the Irvine River and a road allowance between Nichol and Pilkington Townships. The plan indicates where Sem Wissler held land, and marks the location of the Elora Cemetery. The scale is 2 chains to an inch.

PALMERSTON

3311. Bolton, E.D. **Map of Town of Palmerston comprising parts of Lots 19, 20, 21, 22, 23 and east half of 24 in Concession 1, Township of Minto, County of Wellington and Lots 16, 17, 18, 19, 20 and 21, Concession 1 and parts of Lots 17, 18, 19,**

21, Concession 10 Wallace, County of Perth, 1941. 1 map. Loc: ALR.
A compiled plan which marks and describes details of twenty plans surveyed from 1871 to 1921, and corrected to 1941, which notes the lots covered and timing of specific surveys. The plan is bordered by King Street in the east, Nelson Street in the north and Toronto Street in the east. The scale is 3 chains to an inch.

3312. Bolton, Lewis. **Plan of part of the Village of Palmerston shewing the subdivision of part of the east half of Lot 22, Concession 1 of Minto, the property of Messrs J.D. Caswell and Clement, 1874.** 1 map. Loc: ALR.
Plan of Caswell and Clement's Survey bordered by Inkerman Street in the south, Mary Street in the north and the Wellington, Grey and Bruce Railway in the west. The scale is 1 chain to an inch.

3313. Bolton, Lewis and Herman, Mr. **Plan of part of the Village of Palmerston situate on part of Lot 19, Concession 11, Township of Wallace, County of Perth, 1874.** 1 map. Loc: ALR.
Plan (19-11 Wallace) that extends east of the Wellington, Grey and Bruce Railway station to the junction of Main and Queen Streets. The scale is 2 chains to an inch.

3314. Bolton, Lewis and Herman, Mr. **Plan of that part of Palmerston situate on Lot 18, Concession 11, Wallace, County of Perth, 1873.** 1 map. Loc: ALR.
Plan (18-11 Wallace) that extends to Queen Street in the west, Main Street in the north, York Street in the east and King Street in the south.

3315. Bolton, Lewis. **Plan shewing subdivision of Lot 21, formerly in Concession 11, Township of Wallace, now in the Town of Palmerston, Wellington County, property of R. Jamison, Esq., 1878.** 1 map. Loc: ALR.
Plan of P. Jamison's Survey showing lots north of King Street, south of Main Street and east and west of Jamison Street. The scale is 2 chains to an inch.

3316. Bolton, Lewis. **Plan shewing subdivision of part of Farm Lot 23, Concession 1, Minto, comprising part of the Town of Palmerston, the property of John McCombs, 1881.** 1 map. Loc: ALR.
Plan of lots north of Main and Clark Streets, east of the Stratford and Huron Railway line. The scale is 2 chains to an inch.

3317. Bolton, Lewis. **Plan shewing subdivision of part of the west half of Farm Lot 22 formerly in Concession 1 of the Township of Minto, now in the Town of Palmerston, property of Adam Borthwick, Esq., 1878.** 1 map. Loc: ALR.
Plan of Borthwick's Survey bounded by Mary Street in the north, the Wellington, Grey and Bruce Railway line in the east and Main Street in the south. The scale is 2 chains to an inch.

3318. Bolton, Lewis. **Plan shewing subdivision of south half of east half of Lot 22 formerly in Concession 1 of the Township of Minto, now in the Town of Palmerston, 1878.** 1 map. Loc: ALR.
Plan of Mary Caswell's Survey that extends west and east of Jane Street and north of Main Street. The scale is 2 chains to an inch.

3319. **Bolton, Lewis. Plan shewing the subdivision of Park Lots 12, 13 and 14 north side of Prospect Street in the subdivision of Farm Lots 16 and 17 formerly in Concession 11 of the Township of Wallace in the County of Perth, now of the Town of Palmerston, County of Wellington, 1895.** 1 map. Loc: ALR.

Plan of N. Prospect's Survey that extends north of Derby and Prospect Streets and west of Toronto Street. The scale is 2 chains to an inch.

3320. **Gilmour, Robert. Plan of the subdivision into park lots of portions of Lots 16 and 17, Concession 11, Township of Wallace, situated in Town of Palmerston, 1891.** 1 map. Loc: ALR.

Plan identified as Western Canada Loan and Savings (16-17, 11 Wall.) that extends to the west and east of Toronto Street, north of King Street and south of Main Street. The scale is 3 chains to an inch.

3321. **Gilmour, Robert. Plan of the subdivision into park lots of portions of Lots 16 and 17, Concession 11, Township of Wallace, situated in Town of Palmerston, 1891.** 1 map. Loc: ALR.

Plan of McComb's Survey that extends south of Main Street and north of King Street. The scale is 3 chains to an inch.

3322. **Grain, William. Map of part of the Village of Palmerston comprising parts of Lot 19, Concession 10 and Lots 19 and 20, Concession 11 of the Township of Wallace and County of Perth, 1874.** 1 map. Loc: ALR.

Plan of Grain's Survey that extends to the southern extension of the Wellington, Grey and Bruce Railway in the west, Main Street in the north, Queen Street in the east and Lane in the south. The scale is 2 chains to an inch.

3323. **Kirk, Joseph. Plan of subdivision of south half of Lot 21, Concession 1 of Minto, now in the Town of Palmerston, the property of Messrs Fuller and Watson, 1875.** 1 map. Loc: ALR.

Plan of Fuller and Watson Survey that extends to Norman Street in the west, Nelson Street in the north, Side Road in the east and Main Street in the south. The scale is 700 feet to 7/8 of an inch.

3324. **Miles, C.F. Proposed alterations of plan of subdivision of part of Lot 18, Concession 10, Township of Wallace, being a part of the Town of Palmerston, 1887.** 1 map. Loc: ALR.

Plan of Clark and Anderson Survey that extends east of Queen Street and south of King Street. The scale is 2 chains to an inch.

3325. **Morison, W.G. Map of part of Palmerston, comprising the southeast quarter of Lot 22, Concession 1, 1872.** 1 map. Loc: ALR.

Plan of Morrison's Survey bounded by Inkerman Street in the north, the Wellington Grey and Bruce Railway in the east and Main Street in the south. The scale is 2 chains to an inch.

3326. **Morison, W.G. Map of the Village of Palmerston comprising parts of Lots 17, 18, 19 and 20, Concession 11 and Lot 19, Concession 10 in the Township of Wallace, County of Perth, and part of Lot 22, Concession 1 in the Township of Minto and County of Wellington, 1872.** 1 map. Loc: ALR.

Plan of Morrison's Survey bounded by Henry Street in the west, Inkerman Street in the north, Queen Street in the east and King Street in the south. The scale is 2 chains to an inch.

3327. Walker, William. **Plan of part of the Town of Palmerston being a portion of Lot 19, Concession 10, Wallace, 1876.** 1 map. Loc: ALR.

Walker's plan (19-10 Wallace) that extends to Mill Land in the west, King Street in the north, Queen Street in the east and Lot 19 in the south. The scale is 1 chain to an inch.

3328. Walker, William. **Plan shewing subdivisions of Lots 9 and 10, southeast side of York Street, Palmerston, 1876.** 1 map. Loc: ALR.

Walker's plan that extends south of Main Street and east of York Street. The scale is 1 chain to an inch.

PEEL

3329. Burke, J.W. **Plan of the Village of Alma situated on part of Lot 1, Concession 1, Pilkington and Lot 22, Concession 14, Peel, County of Wellington, 1861.** 1 map. Loc: GLR. Map 134.

Plan with the borders of Alma being Simpson, Raglan, Hannah, Church and Pellisier Streets. The plan was drawn for Thomas McCrae, Thomas Graham and James Graham. The scale is 2 chains to an inch.

3330. Burke, J.W. **Plan of the Village of Alma situated on part of Lot 1, Concession 1, Pilkington and Lot 22, Concession 14, Peel, 1867.** 1 map. Loc: ALR.

Plan that extends to Church Street in the west, Simpson Street in the north, Raglan Street in the east and Hannah Street in the south. The scale is 2 chains to an inch.

3331. Kertland, Edwin H. **Plan of a portion of Allansville, laid out for Mr David Ghent, 1855.** print. Loc: ALR.

Plan of Ghent's Survey, Glenallan, that extends east of the Conistoga (sic) and south of Main Street.

3332. Kertland, Edwin H. **Plan of Glenallan, formerly Allansville, County of Wellington, 1857.** print, scale 1 inch to 3 chains. Loc: ALR.

Plan of MacDonald's Survey, bounded by Wellesley Street in the west, Maryborough Street in the north, Ghent Street in the east and George Street in the south. The plan also shows lots immediately north and south of the Conistoga (sic) River.

3333. LaPenotiere, W.H. **Plan of the Village of Glenallan, 1864.** 1 map. Loc: ALR.

Plan bounded by the Wellesley Road allowance in the west, Blind Lane in the north, Waterloo Street in the east and Wellesley Street in the south.

3334. McFadden, Moses. **Plan of John Vernon's Survey of the Village of Glenallen (sic) composed of north part of west half of Lot 6 in Concession 2, Township of Peel, County of Wellington, 1862.** 1 map. Loc: ALR.

Plan showing lots south of Main Street and north of George Street. The scale is 3 chains to an inch.

3335. Parke, Thomas. **Peel Township, 1844.** 1 map. Loc: AO.

Crown Survey of the township drawn to the scale of 40 chains to an inch.

PILKINGTON

3336. Kertland, Edwin H. **Plan of park lots, farm lots and mill sites being subdivisions of Lots 4 and 5, Concession 3 of Pilkington, property of Rev. Arthur Palmer, 1857.** print, ms adds, 59 x 84 cm, scale 1 inch to 3 chains. Loc: GLR. Map 140.
Plan of lots between the Grand River in the west and the road between Concessions 2 and 3 in the east. Plan was first certified 20 December 1860.

3337. Map and Advertising Co. Ltd. **Guidal landowners' map of Townships of Pilkington-Nichol, 1917.** 1 sheet, 19-3/4 x 11-1/2. Loc: NAC, AO. AO:C-53; NAC:430/Pilkington/1917/#48668.
A detailed map showing lot owners' names at a scale of 1 inch to 0.875 miles.

PUSLINCH

3338. Allan, David. **Diagram of part of Puslinch, 1831.** 1 map. Loc: GLR. Map 131.
Survey of property along Concession 11 that notes property owners including John Arkell, Thomas Arkell, James Orme and Peter Orme. The scale is 20 chains to an inch. The index notes the plan is a government survey of Farnham Village in Puslinch Township.

3339. Bowman, E.P. **Plan of Swastika Beach subdivision 1, a part of the north half of Lot 2, Concession 1 in the Township of Puslinch, 1929.** 1 map. Loc: GLR. Map 395.
Plan that extends north of Swastika Trail and Swastika Beach Boulevard. The owner is listed as Ross Barber. The scale is 60 feet to an inch.

3340. Bowman, E.P. **Plan of Swastika Beach subdivision 2, parts of the north halves of Lots 2 and 3, Concession 1 in the Township of Puslinch, 1937.** 1 map. Loc: GLR. Map 398.
Plan bordered by Swastika Trail in the north and Puslinch Lake in the south. The document indicates Ross Barber owned the property. The scale is 60 feet to an inch.

3341. Devine, Thomas. **Map of Puslinch Township, 1860.** 1 map. Loc: GLR. Map 130.
Map of crown lands in Puslinch Township drawn to a scale of 40 chains to an inch.

3342. Gibson, David. **Plan of road through southern block of clergy reserves in District of Gore, 1828.** 1 sheet, 59 x 32 cm. Loc: AO. C-36.
Plan is at scale of 1:31,860.

3343. Gibson, David. **Puslinch Township, 1828.** ms. Loc: AO. C-36.
This is a crown land survey. The Archives of Ontario also has J.G. Chewett's 1832 copy of Gibson's plan at a scale of 1:31,860.

3344. Kerr, Francis. **Plan of part of the Village of Aberfoyle forming a part of the northeast half of Lot 22, Concession 7 of the Township of Puslinch for the executors of the late G. Schatz, 1858.** 1 copy. Loc: GLR. Map 119.
Plan drawn to the scale of 2 chains to an inch.

3345. Kerr, Francis. **Plan of the subdivision of Park Lots 1, 2, 3, 4, 5, 6 and shewing some alterations in the town lots of the Village of Morriston, Township of Puslinch, 1859.** 1 map. Loc: GLR. Map 114.

    Plan showing Queen, Main, Ochs, Michael, John, William, James and Badenoch Streets. The document also shows alterations made in Lots 10, 18, 32 and 33 which was part of Lot 31 in Concession 8, Township of Puslinch.

3346. Kerr, Francis. **Plan showing the subdivision of Lot 8 in Concession 7, Township of Puslinch, late property of Mr James McCartney, 1856.** 1 map. Loc: GLR. Map 74.

    Plan showing a lot north of the 'macadamized road from Dundas'. The scale is 4 chains to an inch.

3347. Kerr, Robert W. **Plan of portion of Puslinch Township, 1843.** Loc: AO. C-36.

3348. Mackintosh, James. **Plan of part of the Village of Morriston, being part of A. Och's Survey, 1868.** 1 map. Loc: GLR. Map 183.

    Plan showing a side road and James, William, John, Michael and Ochs Streets. The scale is 2 chains to an inch.

3349. Mackintosh, James. **Plan of the Village of Morriston, 1860.** 1 map. Loc: GLR. Map 135.

    Plan of the northwest corner of Lot 31, Concession 7 and Lots 30 and 31, Concession 8. It extends to Queen Street in the west, North Street in the north, Gordon Street in the east and Fisher Street in the south. The scale is 2 chains to an inch.

3350. Map and Advertising Co. Ltd. **Guidal landowners' map of Township of Puslinch, 1917.** 1 sheet, 20 x 11-1/2. Loc: NAC, AO. AO:C-53; NAC:430/Puslinch/1917/#48670.

    A detailed map showing lot owners' names at a scale of 1 inch to 0.875 miles.

3351. Niven, D.A. **Plan of Eagle Park, a subdivision of part of Lot 6, Concession 1 in the Township of Puslinch, 1920.** 1 map. Loc: GLR. Map 386.

    Plan of lots that surround Lakeshore Drive. The scale is 50 feet to an inch.

3352. Niven, D.A. **Plan of Lakeside Park, a subdivision of part of Lot 3, Concession 1 in the Township of Puslinch, 1918.** 1 map. Loc: GLR. Map 380.

    Plan showing land bordering Puslinch Lake. The scale is 60 feet to an inch.

3353. Niven, D.A. **Plan of Puslinch Beach, a subdivision of part of Lot 5, Concession 1, Township of Puslinch, 1916.** 1 map. Loc: GLR. Map 373.

    Plan showing lots immediately north of Puslinch Lake. The scale is 120 feet to an inch.

3354. Parke, Thomas. **Puslinch Township, 1843.** Loc: AO. C-36.

3355. **Plan of Puslinch Lake area, c1888.** 1 document. Loc: UGA. XR1 MS A334068.

    An undated sketch of lots surrounding what appears to be Puslinch Lake. The scale is 40 chains to an inch. Part of the Sleeman Family Collection.

3356. Smith, D.W. **Plan for setting aside clergy reserves for Lincoln Township, 1795.**
ms watercolour, 27 x 44 cm, scale one inch to 10 miles. Loc: AO.

The sketch plan which accompanied Smyth's report on reserved lands is held with the Simcoe Papers in Envelope #43. The area was later defined as Puslinch Township.

Henry Langley's design for Chalmers Presbyterian Church, Guelph, 1869
Front and rear elevations (above) and sectional drawings (below). Langley's
firm also designed alterations to the church between 1895 and 1903 (#3390–
#3391) (Horwood Collection, Archives of Ontario, and Gilbert A. Stelter)

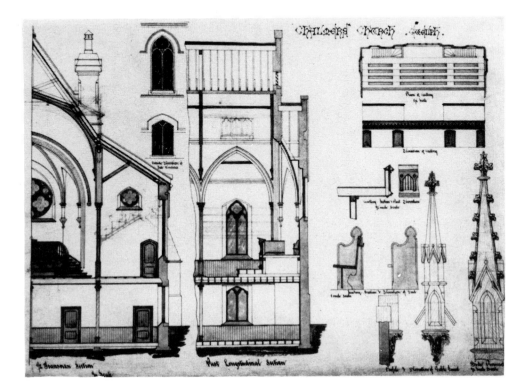

ARCHITECTURAL DRAWINGS

In addition to their aesthetic interest, architectural drawings can provide direct factual evidence of the location, dimensions, owner, architect and building contractors of particular structures. As Dorothy Ahlgren has remarked, such drawings can also convey a metaphoric message about the scale and style of buildings and the philosophy of their architects.[1] The hundreds of drawings and other records left by one architectural firm, Robinson, Tracy, Durand and Moore of London, Ontario, have been used for a distinguished study of Victorian architecture in London and southwestern Ontario.[2]

Relatively few architectural plans survive for Wellington County, mainly for churches, banks and government buildings. The notable Horwood Collection in the Archives of Ontario has plans by various partners of the Toronto firm that included architects Dick, Grant, Langley, Burke, Horwood and White over the period from the 1850s to the 1930s.[3] William Thomas's plans for St George's Anglican Church are at the Metropolitan Toronto Central Reference Library. Various plans by the Toronto architect G.M. Miller for the Ontario Agricultural College and Macdonald Institute are part of the Miller Collection in the Thomas Fisher Rare Books Room of the University of Toronto Library. The very large collection of architectural drawings in the National Archives includes some plans for government buildings such as the Guelph Post Office and Armouries.[4]

The National Archives, the Archives of Ontario and the University of Guelph Library also hold copies of measured drawings made by University of Toronto architectural students in 1967, of some seventeen houses and other small vernacular buildings dating from before 1860.

---

[1] Dorothy Ahlgren, 'Architectural drawings: sources for urban history,' **Urban History Review** 11 (1983): 67-72. See also James Knight, 'Architectural records and archives in Canada: toward a national programme,' **Archivaria** 3 (1976/7): 62-71 and, for a study exploring the metaphoric message of architectural records, Tom Brown, '" Architecture as therapy"', **Archivaria** 10 (1980): 99-123.

[2] Nancy Z. Tausky and Lynne DiStefano, **Victorian architecture in London and southwestern Ontario: symbols of aspiration** (Toronto: University of Toronto Press, 1986).

[3] See Gilbert A. Stelter, 'Henry Langley and the making of Gothic Guelph,' **Historic Guelph** (1989).

[4] Archibald, Margaret, **By federal design: the Chief Architect's Branch of the Department of Public Works** (Ottawa, 1984).

ARCHITECTURAL DRAWINGS

3357. Bayliss, D.J. **Lyon House, Queen Street. Architectural plan, 1967.** 2 sheets. Loc: AO. D1526-D1527.
Measured drawings of J.W. Lyon's Guelph residence, built c1880.

3358. Burke, Horwood and White, Architects. **Baptist Chapel, Woolwich Street, Guelph, 1909.** 3 items. Loc: AO. FA: #1011.
Includes plans, sections and elevations. Part of the Horwood Collection.

3359. Canada Department of National Defence. **Guelph Armouries. Floor plans, 1910-1967.** 7 plans. Loc: GPL.
Plans from 1966 and 1967 that record renovations to be made to the 1910 Armouries building. There are separate plans for the first, second, third and fourth floors, basement, site, roof, and exterior building from the front, rear, left side and right side elevation. According to the 1927 Mercury, the original building cost 140,000 dollars to construct. The scale is 1/8 inch to 1 foot.

3360. Canada Department of Public Works. **Guelph Military Building. Plans, 1904-c1910.** 33 sheets at various scales. Loc: NAC. RG 11, M, 79003/42.
Detailed plans for the original construction of the Guelph Military Buildings or Armouries. Held in the Cartographic and Architectural Archives Division.

3361. Canada Department of Public Works. **Guelph Post Office. Building plans, 1902.** 3 plans. Loc: NAC. Maps 0035874; 0035888; 0035889.
A plan showing the east, west and south elevation of the exterior of the three-storey building and a plan of the first floor, including renovations.

3362. Canada Department of Public Works. **Guelph Post Office. Building plans, pre 1902.** 2 plans. Loc: NAC, UGL. NAC: Maps 0035864; 0035868.
A plan showing the south elevation of the exterior of the two storey building and a plan of the unrenovated first floor.

3363. Canada Department of Public Works. **Guelph Public Building. Plans, 1876-1937.** 43 plans at various scales. Loc: NAC. RG 11, M, 79003/42.
Plans for the original structure and subsequent alterations of the Post Office and Inland Revenue and Customs Building. Held in the Cartographic and Architectural Archives Division.

3364. Coales, H.R. **Architectural sketches, 1928.** 3 documents. Loc: UGA. XR2 MS A045.
Sketches by the architect of the well cover, platform, flagstaff and bell tower for Ker Cavan. Part of Allan-Higinbotham Collection.

3365. Cowan, W.A. **The Priory, Guelph. Architectural plans, 1958.** 6 sheets. Loc: AO. D1716-D1721.
Measured drawings of the Priory built by the Canada Company in 1827 and demolished in 1921.

3366. Dick, D.S. **Bank of Commerce proposed, Guelph, 1883.** 3 items. Loc: AO. FA: #216.
Includes plans, elevations and sections. Part of the Horwood Collection.

3367. Dick, D.S. **Guelph Custom House proposed, 1884.** 1 item. Loc: AO. FA: #234.
Includes floor plans. Part of the Horwood Collection.

3368. Dick, D.S. **Henry Michie Residence proposed alterations, Fergus, 1885.** 2 items. Loc: AO. FA: #250.
Includes plans, elevations and sections. Part of the Horwood Collection.

3369. Dreisziger, K. **S.S.#11 Erin Schoolhouse. Architectural plan, 1967.** 2 large sheets. Loc: NAC. 450/Erin/1967/#133.
Measured drawings by students of School of Architecture, University of Toronto, of the typical one-room schoolhouse built in 1888 in brick with a timber and shingle roof.

3370. Drenters, Yosef. **Ontario Heritage Foundation. Easement agreement, 1978.** 1 envelope. Loc: WCA. MU 34.
A photocopy of the agreement between Drenters and the Foundation to preserve the Rockwood Academy. The report includes 47 pages of photographs of the exterior and interior of the building and two pages of floor plans.

3371. Fergus Carnegie Library. **Plans and specifications, 1910.** 1 envelope, 1 file folder, oversized. Loc: UGA. XR1 MS A057.
Building plans and written specifications for the library. W.A. Mahoney is listed as the architect.

3372. Forma, P.T. **McKay House, Guelph. Architectural plan, 1967.** 2 large sheets. Loc: NAC, AO. NAC: 450/Guelph/1967/#137; AO: D1484-D1485.
Measured drawings by students of School of Architecture, University of Toronto, of the house at 268 Woolwich Street, which was built c1855 and is a semi-detached example of the Guelph stone vernacular

3373. Geller, Mr and Yamashita, Mr. **Rockwood Academy. Architectural plan, 1967.** 7 large sheets. Loc: NAC. 450/Rockwood/1967/#150.
Measured drawings by students of School of Architecture, University of Toronto, of the boarding school established in 1854 by William Wetherald.

3374. Gemeiner, Y. **Old Hokin's House, Guelph. Architectural plan, 1967.** 2 large sheets. Loc: NAC, AO. NAC: 450/Guelph/1967/#134; AO: D1490-D1491.
Measured drawings by students of School of Architecture, University of Toronto, of the house built at 298 Edinburgh Road South for John Neeve in a late version of the Ontario Regency cottage style.

3375. Grant, James. **Central School House, Guelph, 1861-1863.** 1 item. Loc: AO. FA: #421.
Includes elevation. Part of the Horwood Collection.

3376. Guelph (Church of Our Lady) Catholic. **Plan for proposed completion of towers and spires, n.d..** G. Loc: JA.
Undated blueprint by architect Joseph Connolly at a scale of 1/8 inch to one foot. This design differed from the one which was eventually followed, in surmounting the twin towers with spires. Held in Box 1 of the Guelph records.

3377. Guelph Cutten Club. **Plans and specifications, 1930.** 1 file folder, oversized. Loc: UGA. XR2 MS A065.
A record of a written report of plans to build the club and detailed

specifications of the project. The record lists Douglas E. Kertland as the architect and the Jackson Lewis Company as the contracting engineers.

3378. Guelph. **St Patrick's Ward School. Addition and alteration plans, 1911.** 1 file folder, oversized. Loc: UGA. XR3 MS A009.
The architect is listed as W.A. Mahoney.

3379. Guelph Tp. **Plans. Bridge over River Speed at Armstrong's Mill, 1869.** 1 plan; 1 file folder. Loc: WCA.
A plan for the bridge that includes a written contract between William Pearson and the Township of Guelph that is signed and witnessed by both parties. Specifications and indentures for the bridge are held with the plan. The scale is 8 feet to an inch.

3380. Gundry and Langley. **St George's Church. Proposed new plans, 1867.** Loc: AO. D991.
Architectural plans for a new church building which were not carried out, being replaced by Langley's later design.

3381. Hall, J. **Drenters House, Rockwood. Architectural plan, 1967.** 2 sheets. Loc: NAC. 450/Rockwood/1967/#148.
Measured drawings by students of School of Architecture, University of Toronto, of the stone house built in 1840 in Classical style.

3382. Hartley, Ian. **Ellis Chapel, Puslinch Township. Architectural plans, 1967.** 2 large sheets. Loc: NAC. 450/Puslinch/1967/#147.
Measured drawings by students of School of Architecture, University of Toronto, of the chapel erected in 1861 for the Sterling Congregation of Wesleyan Methodists. Edward Ellis donated the land. The structure is a simply proportioned stone chapel with pointed windows, transitional in style between Classical and Gothic.

3383. Higinbotham, H.F. **Ker Cavan. Oversize plans, 1925-1928.** 1 file folder. Loc: UGA. XR2 MS A04516.
Plans and specifications of Ker Cavan, residence of H.F. Higinbotham, showing proposed alterations to the main building, ornamental ironwork specifications and a landscape design by H.R. Coales. Held with the Allan-Higinbotham Collection.

3384. Horwood and White, Architects. **Dublin Street United Church addition, Guelph, c1938.** 1 item. Loc: AO. FA: #1615.
Part of the Horwood Collection.

3385. Horwood and White, Architects. **Melville United Church Sunday School, Fergus, 1930.** 57 items. Loc: AO. FA: #1447.
Tracings of elevations, details, floor plans and blueprints. Part of the Horwood Collection.

3386. Horwood and White, Architects. **Norfolk Street United Church, Guelph, 1938.** 3 items. Loc: AO. FA: #1484.
Plans, elevations, sections and details of an addition to the church. Part of the Horwood Collection.

3387. Horwood and White, Architects. **Palmerston United Church proposed improvements, 1929.** 2 items. Loc: AO. FA: #1426.
  Plans, including notes. Part of the Horwood Collection.

3388. Kohn, H. **Williams House, Guelph. Architectural plan, 1967.** 2 large sheets. Loc: NAC, AO. NAC: 450/Guelph/1967/#135; AO: D1488-D1489.
  Measured drawings by students of School of Architecture, University of Toronto, of the Williams House, 8 Gledhill, which was built in 1850 for John Mitchell and is distinctive for its solid, load bearing, ashlar walls.

3389. Langley and Burke. **St John's Church, Elora. Alterations, 1891-4.** 4 items. Loc: AO. D446-D447.

3390. Langley and Langley. **Chalmers Church, Guelph. Alterations, 1895-1903.** 2 sheets. Loc: AO. D999-D1000.

3391. Langley, Henry. **Chalmers Church, Guelph, 1870-1873.** 7 sheets. Loc: AO. D992-D998.
  Front and rear elevations, interior plan and details.

3392. Langley, Henry. **Saint George's Church, Guelph, undated.** 2 large plans, 24 x 30 inches. Loc: MTL. #189-190.
  Drawings of c1870, at the scale of one inch to 8 feet, of the river front elevation and the basement floor plan. The plans also bear the signature of Stephen Boult as building contractor.

3393. Langley, Henry. **St John's Church, Elora, 1871-2.** 4 items. Loc: AO. D1012-D1015.

3394. Langley, Langley and Burke, Architects. **Baptist Chapel, Woolwich Street, Guelph, 1872.** 7 items. Loc: AO. FA: #619.
  Includes plans, elevations, sections and details. The church was known as the First Baptist Church from the 1890s. Part of the Horwood Collection.

3395. Langley, Langley and Burke, Architects. **Trinity Baptist Church, Woolwich Street, Guelph, 1892.** 3 items. Loc: AO. FA: #619.
  Includes plans, elevations, sections and details. Part of the Horwood Collection.

3396. Mahoney, W.A. **Bank of Montreal. Alterations, 1912.** 8 sheets. Loc: AO. D1666-D1673.

3397. Miller, G.M. **Homewood Sanitarium. Correspondence re specifications, 1907.** Loc: UTA. MS194.
  Specifications for improvements to the plumbing system.

3398. Miller, G.M. **Macdonald Institute and Hall. Photographs, 1979.** 2 photos. Loc: UTA. MS194.

3399. Miller, G.M. **Macdonald Institute. Plans, c1903.** 5 plans, c60 cm x c100 cm; 2 photos. Red, blue and black ink on linen. Loc: UTA. MS194.

Plan of ground floor at scale of 1/4 inch to one foot. More detailed plans at 1/2 inch to one foot of front entrance and boiler house, southeast elevation, southwest elevation and northwest elevation with sections.

3400. Miller, G.M. **Ontario Agricultural College. Plan of Massey Hall and Library, 1901.** 14 plans, 67.5 x 45 cm. Red, black and blue ink on linen. Loc: UTA. MS194.

Plans for the Library-Assembly Hall which was endowed with $41,000 from the Hart Massey estate, at scales of 1/8 inch to one inch for floor plans and 1/2 inch to one inch for details. There are plans of basement, ground floor, first floor, roof, side elevation, front elevation, rear and side elevations, two cross sections, two longitudinal sections, plans of reading room ceiling, windows, corbels and piers, elevation of tower, section through gable, section entrance steps and staircase.

3401. Miller, G.M. **Ontario Agricultural College. Sketch plan of Science Building, 1902.** 37 x 62 cm. Loc: UTA. MS194.

A sketch of the front elevation at a scale of 1/16 inch to an inch.

3402. Ordynec, Peter G. **The Manse, Guelph. Architectural plan, 1967.** 3 large sheets. Loc: NAC, AO. NAC: 450/Guelph/1967/#136; AO: D1479-D1481.

Measured drawings by students of School of Architecture, University of Toronto, of the house at 22-24 Oxford Street, built c1860 in the current Italianate style and somewhat altered in the twentieth century.

3403. Ottley, R.L. **Lyon House. Architectural plan, 1967.** Loc: AO. D1726.

Measured drawing of J.W. Lyon's residence, Wyoming, built c1880 on Queen Street, Guelph.

3404. Polsinelli, Ciro. **Lanthier House, Guelph. Architectural plan, 1967.** 2 large sheets. Loc: NAC, AO. NAC: 450/Guelph/1967/#139; AO: D1482-D1483.

Measured drawings by students of School of Architecture, University of Toronto, of the Lanthier House at 168 Waterloo Avenue. This is an example of Late Classical cottage (c1855) with string courses and window surrounds.

3405. Reed, Donald J. **Renovation plans of farmhouse, 1940.** 1 file folder, oversized. Loc: UGA. XR1 MS A061.

Site and building plans that are entitled, 'Renovation of and addition to farmhouse near Guelph, Ontario'. Donald J. Reed is listed as architect.

3406. Roman Stone Company. **Blueprints of erection diagram of Guelph Library, May 1903.** 9 prints. Loc: GPL.

Blueprints include southwest elevation, southeast elevation, northwest elevation, northeast elevation, radius of the front entrance from the centre dome, interior plan of fixtures, front elevation, steel gallery and stairs, and basement floor plans. The scale is 1/2 inch to a foot. The prints include dimensions of each exterior stone and each exterior column. The Roman Stone Company was a Toronto Company on Marlborough Avenue.

3407. Shanly, Francis. **Guelph station ground, 1855.** Loc: NAC. 450/Guelph/1855.

Original coloured manuscript plans at scale of 20 feet to an inch.

3408. Smith, Harold. **White House, Guelph. Architectural plan, 1967.** 2 large sheets. Loc: NAC, AO. NAC: 450/Guelph/1967/#140; AO: D1486-D1487.
Measured drawings by students of School of Architecture, University of Toronto, of the square log Regency cottage, built c1835, which has wings on either side and an attic dormer added later. It is located at the corner of Stevenson and Palmer streets.

3409. Stambler, Isaac. **Harcourt House, Guelph. Architectural plan, 1967.** 4 large sheets. Loc: NAC, AO. NAC: 450/Guelph/1967/#138; AO: D1471-D1474.
Measured drawings by students of School of Architecture, University of Toronto, of Harcourt House, also known as Summerhill House, at 25 Harcourt. The architect was Craig and the builders D. Kennedy and J. Dobbin; the house was built as a Classical villa and later altered with Italianate features.

3410. Stark, J.B. **Morriston Store. Architectural plan, 1967.** 3 large sheets. Loc: NAC, AO. NAC: 450/Morriston/1967/#141; AO: D1507-D1509.
Measured drawings by students of School of Architecture, University of Toronto, of the brick structure which was erected in 1887 by Mr R.B. Morriston for combined commercial and residential uses, and has Gothic and Italianate details.

3411. Stewart, P.D. **Claire House, Morriston. Architectural plan, 1967.** 3 large sheets. Loc: NAC, AO. NAC: 450/Morriston/1967/#142; AO: D1536-D1538.
Measured drawings by students of School of Architecture, University of Toronto, of the typical Victorian Gothic farmhouse built of stone in 1870.

3412. Stokes, Peter John. **Blueprints and building specifications for McCrae House, 1966.** 10 plans, 2 volumes. Loc: JMH.
Floor plans drawn by Stokes, a restoration architect from Niagara-on-the-Lake. The plans show original partitions of the 1858 building and its 1867 addition, as well as the 1966 restoration plans and building specifications.

3413. Temporale, Alex. **Hortop Mill, Rockwood. Architectural plan, 1967.** 3 large sheets. Loc: NAC. 450/Rockwood/1967/#149.
Measured drawings by students of School of Architecture, University of Toronto, of the stone feed mill built in 1820 and a well-preserved example of an original industrial building.

3414. Thomas, William. **St George's Church, Guelph, May 1856.** 6 items. Loc: MTL. FA: #s 191-195.
Designs for the proposed completion of the second St George's Church, including the west elevation and floor plans.

3415. University of Toronto School of Architecture. **Houses in Guelph. Architectural plans, 1967.** 17 items, oversize. Loc: UGA. XR2 MS A001.
A collection of architectural plans for seven Guelph houses dating from the first half of the nineteenth century. They include the Harcourt House (also known as Summerhill), the Lanthier House, the Manse, the McKay House, Old Hokin's House, the White House and the Williams House. A simple description of five of the seven structures is provided, with dates of construction, architects and builders. The plans were apparently drawn in 1967 by faculty or students of the University of Toronto School of Architecture. This Inventory also includes

488

entries for individual plans.

3416. Wellington Co. **Registry office. Architectural plans, 1917.** 4 blueprints. Loc: WCA.

A series of four blueprints of the Wellington County Registry Office in Arthur.

PHOTOGRAPHS

Visual evidence from paintings, picture postcards, photographs from the ground or from the air can provide a mirror of the past.[1] The technological revolution in means of communicating visual images during the past 150 years has coincided with the settlement and development of this region of southern Ontario.[2]

Official collections of visual material are still in the relatively early stages of cataloguing. In 1977 it was noted that ten million photographs were housed in Canadian archives.[3] But only a small proportion of these are documented, dated or indexed. In the National Photography Collection of the National Archives in Ottawa, for example, only three to five per cent of all the photographs have been indexed.

Wellington County lacks the heritage of a large photographic firm such as the Notmans of Montreal, Toronto and Ottawa.[4] But it has a small claim to photographic fame in the inventions of Thomas and John Connon of Elora, whose business records are distributed among the Archives of Ontario, the Wellington County Archives and University of Guelph Library. Between them the various regional repositories with materials on Wellington County have well over 20,000 photographs. The largest collection, at the Wellington County Archives, includes some of Connon's photographs. Wellington County has another photographic resource in the collection left by Professor Gordon Couling; though the photographs were taken after 1940 they are of historic subjects, mainly older buildings.

---

[1] For broader surveys of the historical interest of photographs, see Roger Hall and Gordon Dodds, **A picture history of Ontario** (Edmonton: Hurtig, 1978); Lilly Koltun, **Private realms of light: amateur photography in Canada 1839-1940** (Toronto: Fitzhenry & Whiteside, 1984). The value of postcards is illustrated in A. Anderson, **Greetings from Canada: an album of unique Canadian post cards from the Edwardian era 1900-1916** (Toronto: Macmillan, 1978).

[2] For a valuable survey of these technological developments in relation to archives, see Jim Burant, 'The visual world in the Victorian age,' **Archivaria** 19 (WInter 1984-5): 110-121.

[3] Richard J. Huyda, 'Photographs and archives in Canada,' **Archivaria** 5 (1977/8): 5-11. See also Christopher Seifried, ed. **Guide to Canadian Photographic Archives** (Ottawa: Public Archives of Canada, 1984).

[4] J.R. Harper & S. Triggs ed., **Portrait of a Period: a Collection of Notman Photographs 1856-1915** (Montreal: 1967).

Man's work: cutting seed potatoes, 1909. Photographed by the late R.R. Sallows, an early twentieth century artist photographer from Goderich, Ontario (#3459). (Ontario Ministry of Agriculture and Food)

Woman's work: peeling apples, 1912. Photographed by the late R.R. Sallows, an early twentieth century artist photographer from Goderich, Ontario (#3459). (Ontario Ministry of Agriculture and Food)

Photographs are a powerful medium for evoking images of the past. But how accurately do they depict past realities? As Lilly Koltun and Peter Robertson have argued, our perceptions of past realities through the medium of the photograph may be somewhat distorted. Though they claimed that their pictures faithfully represented their subjects, photographers staged and retouched their work to flatter their clients.[5] Moreover, whether their subjects are people or landscapes, photographers are selective. Historical photographs tend to feature the special and the spectacular -- the opening of grand new buildings that reflect credit on their owners or the citizenry, families in the best clothes and on their best behaviour -- rather than the humdrum scenes of everyday life.[6] How different would the scene have been if the camera has been pointed only twenty degrees to the left or right?

With these caveats in mind we could not however resist choosing some examples of the photographic heritage of Wellington County to illustrate this volume.

[5] Peter Robertson, 'More than meets the eye,' **Archivaria** 1 (1976): 34-36; Lilly Koltun, **City blocks, city spaces: historical photographs of Canada's urban growth, c1850-1900,** (Ottawa, 1980), 13.

[6] A remarkable exception was Reuben Sallows (1855-1937) who was a pioneer in leaving the artificiality of the studio to photograph people at their everyday tasks and in their natural surroundings. From his base at Goderich, he travelled about the northern hinterland of Wellington County as well as neighbouring counties. Two of his pictures are reproduced in this volume.

PHOTOGRAPHS

3417. **11th Field Artillery Regiment. Photographs of the regiment, 1885; 1914-1918; 1941.** 14 photographs, 1 painting. Loc: GAB.

A series of photographs including a view of officers of the First Brigade of Field Artillery of Guelph taken in 1885, pictures of seven Guelph Garrison officers who died in action during World War I and several photographs of the Guelph military regiment serving in World War I. The collection includes a photograph of Lieutenant-Colonel C.D. Crowe painted by Richard Mariantreu in 1941 and photographs of Captain B.B. McConkey, Flight Lieutenant Jack Simpson, Lieutenant J.S. McLachlan, Lieutenant-Colonel John McCrae, Flight Lieutenant G.B.G. Scott, Captain F.G. Bond and Major M.E. Wideman.

3418. **16th Battery. Photographs, 1915; 1935.** 2 framed photographs. Loc: GAB.

One photograph shows the 4th Brigade of the 16th Battery on April 7, 1915 in Guelph. The other shows various incidents during training at Petawawa Military Camp in 1935.

3419. Allan, David. **Photographs of Guelph, c1869.** 1 file folder. Loc: UGA. XR1 MS A088.

Three photographs of D. Allan's grist mill, carding mill and distillery and Grand Trunk Railway and station.

3420. Archives of Ontario. **Picture Collection. Photographs and sketches of Guelph, 1831-1933.** c50 items. Loc: AO. Card index with miniature photo inserts.

A varied collection of views of people, scenes, activities and buildings, including views of the O.A.C., Macdonald Institute, Macdonald Consolidated School, Homewood Sanitarium, the Priory, the Post Office, St George's Square and lower Wyndham Street, and St George's Church (1875). There are photographs of George Sleeman's first and second houses on Waterloo Avenue, the laying of street railway tracks, streetcars with cowcatchers and the first two employees of the Guelph Railway Company, a view of Holliday's Guelph Brewery and a group of three hotel keepers in 1895. Personal subjects include A.H. Macdonald, Mayor and Crown Attorney; Captain Clark, principal of the Guelph Collegiate Institute; and Colonel J.B. Armstrong of the Wellington Rifles. General scenes of Guelph include a sketch of the town in 1831, a Kennedy sketch of 1853, a view of the GTR bridge and market area c1862, pictorial booklets of 1889 and 1908, and an aerial view c1920. Miscellaneous other subjects include Janefield (home of Colonel John McCrae), the Royal Skating Rink (c1900) and the Guelph Township S.S.#1 schoolhouse.

3421. Archives of Ontario. **Picture Collection. Photographs of Elora, 1865-1914.** c20 items. Loc: AO. Card index with miniature photo inserts.

Photographers include Thomas and John Connon and J.W. Webster. There are views of buildings, including the Elora Methodist Church (1897), St John's Anglican Church, the J. Mundell Furniture Factory, the home of Colonel Charles Clarke (c1875), the dam and mill of Mr Watt on the Irvine River, Ellen Fitzpatrick's millinery shop (c1914) as well as street scenes from the 1860s and several views of the Elora Gorge. Other subjects include the Elora School Board (1898); Elora Model School classes in 1893, 1899 and 1906; the Elora Curling Team (1900); theatrical groups; officers of the Elora Volunteer Rifle Company (1866); and the first train (1870).

3422. Archives of Ontario. **Picture Collection. Photographs of Rockwood, 1856-1931.** c14 items. Loc: AO. Card index with miniature photo inserts.

The collection includes views of the falls, the Grand Trunk Railway bridge, various mill buildings, a ball team, the Rockwood Separate School (1909), the log house of the first settlers (John Harris and Jane Wetherald dating from the 1820s, the Rockwood Academy in 1856, 1926 and 1931 (the last by Eric Arthur) and a group of its students in 1872.

3423. Canadian Illustrated News Collection. **Lithographs, 1871-1874.** 9 illustrations. Loc: ROM. 978.359.730; 978.359.764; 978.359.778; 978.359.777; 978.359.747; 978.359.562; 978.359.788; 979.210.541; 979.210.671.

A collection of newspaper clippings of lithographs published in the Canadian Illustrated News including the following titles: Views of Guelph, Ontario, 1871; Guelph, Agricultural Machinery at the Central Exhibition, 1872; Guelph, Ontario, The Market House, 1873 by E. Haberer; Guelph, Ontario, Railway Viaduct, 1873 by E. Haberer; Guelph Mills, D. Allan Esq., 1873 by E. Haberer; La Ville de Guelph, Ontario, 1874 by W. Scheuer, published in L'Opinion Publique; Guelph, Ontario, The Central Exhibition General View of the Grounds, 1874 by P.W. Canning; The Court House, Guelph Ontario, and, Eramosa Bridge, Guelph, Ontario, 1874; Guelph, Ontario, The Central Exhibition Interior of the Rotunda, 1874. Catalogue numbers for these nine entries are listed in consecutive order. The newspaper clippings were a gift of Charles de Valpi, St Sauveur, Quebec. Part of the Sigmund Samuel Canadiana Collection.

3424. Connon, John. **Photographs of the Elora Gorge.** 5 items. Loc: MSC. UG 989.010-UG 989.014.

Five different views of the gorge in sepia tones. Several of the photographs were reproduced in Connon's book, The Early History of Elora and Vicinity, published in 1935.

3425. Connon, John. **Stereograph cards and photographs of Elora, c1880-c1930.** 2 file folders. Loc: UGA. XR1 MS A332.

A number of scenic views of landscapes and farm and residential buildings in the Elora area. The photographs of people in various settings are not identified. Held with the Connon Collection.

3426. Davidson-Kennedy Collection. **Photographs, c1890.** 3 photographs. Loc: UGA. XR2 MS A03516.

Selected from a larger collection, the items depict a view of the Grand River at water's edge looking downriver at Elora Gorge, and the interior of 'Sunnyside', the Davidson family home in Guelph.

3427. Douglass Collection. **Postcards of Guelph, 1900-1960.** 1 volume. Loc: GPL.

A number of postcards featuring views of downtown Guelph and numerous public and church buildings, and several views of the Guelph Old Home Week in 1908.

3428. Ferguson Collection. **Photographs. People and buildings of Elora and Fergus, 1875-1970.** 3 boxes. Loc: WCA. List of photographs.

A collection of approximately 200 photographs of residents of Elora and Fergus. Not all names of people and dates of photographs are listed. The records also include photographs of public, church, school and commercial buildings primarily in Fergus and Elora. The Wellington County Archives has developed a detailed finding aid specifying the location, subject and filing number of each photograph.

3429. Fischer Collection. **Photographs. Wellington County residents, 1890-1950.** 4 boxes. Loc: WCA. Detailed finding aid.

A collection of approximately 300 photographs primarily of unidentified people in a range of settings. The collection also has photographs of the Wellington County House of Industry, the Guelph Armouries, Massey Hall and Library at the Ontario Agricultural College, and St Joseph's Hospital in Guelph. The Wellington County Archives has developed a finding aid which describes each individual photograph and presents a file number for each one.

3430. Gilbank, Roberta. **Photographs. Guelph and Fergus, 1970.** 4 boxes. Loc: UGA. XR1 MS A016.

Photographs in the Roberta Gilbank Collection are primarily of houses and are arranged alphabetically by street names.

3431. Guelph (Church of Our Lady) Catholic. **Photographs, c1901-c1930.** Loc: JA.

The collection includes views of the church interior showing gaslight fixtures, the rectory c1901, the altar and nave, as well as sets of postcards and greeting cards. Held in Box 2 of Guelph records.

3432. Guelph Civic Museum. **Photographs, 1870-1950.** 19 boxes. Loc: GCM. Card index.

A large collection of photographs organized by date of occasion and subject heading.

3433. Guelph Co-operative Store. **Photograph, c1920.** 2 negatives. Loc: OAM.

Two photographic negatives of the store. The sign on the store front includes its motto, 'Each for all, all for each'.

3434. Guelph Cutten Club. **Photographs, c1930.** 8 photographs. Loc: UGA. XR1 MS A286.

Eight photographs of the Cutten Club Building taken in the 1930s.

3435. Guelph Free Public Library/ Guelph Public Library. **Photographs. Carnegie building, c1905-1960.** 1 file folder. Loc: GPL.

A series of photographs of the Guelph Public Library built in 1905. The pictures were primarily taken in the 1950s but include one early photograph of the building constructed with the aid of a Carnegie grant.

3436. **Guelph, Ontario, Canada: the Royal City, c1925.** 25 p. ill. Loc: GCM.

A printed collection of twenty-four photographs of various buildings in the city including Macdonald Hall, Macdonald Institute, Norfolk Street United Church, St Andrew's Presbyterian Church, Knox Presbyterian Church, St George's Anglican Church, Church of Our Lady, Central School, General Hospital, Elliott Home, the Goldie Dam and Mill, Guelph Armouries, Y.M.C.A., Court House, O.A.C., Ontario Reformatory, G.C.V.I. and Guelph Public Library.

3437. Guelph. **Portrait. Thomas James Moore, city clerk, 1920.** 1 photo, oversized. Loc: UGA. XR2 MS A052.

3438. Guelph Public Library. **Photographs. Buildings of Guelph and region, c1840-1960 (sporadic).** 2 file drawers containing over 500 photographs. Loc: GPL.

The photograph collection is well indexed and organized into categories of people, places and things.

3439. Guelph Public Library. **Photographs. People of Guelph and region, 1865-1960 (sporadic).** 2 file drawers. Loc: GPL.
A series of photographs of members of clubs and societies including the Guelph Volunteer Rifle Company, Daughters of the Regiment, and the Guelph Maple Leaf Baseball Club. There are also a number of photographs of prominent Guelph residents such as Charles Raymond, Thomas Goldie, William Tytler and James Watt. The photograph collection is well indexed and organized into categories of people, places and things.

3440. Guelph Railway Company/ Guelph Radial Railway. **Photograph, 1900.** 1 photograph. Loc: UGA. XR6 MS A005.
A photograph of eight conductors and motor men who worked for the street railway company.

3441. Guelph YMCA. **Photographs, c1914-1960.** 2 file folders. Loc: GPL.
A series of photographs of YMCA members including sports, social and outdoor activities. The majority of photographs appear to have been taken in the 1950s.

3442. Hillsburgh Baseball Team. **Photograph, 1888.** 1 photo. Loc: UGA. XRI MS A355.

3443. Howitt Family. **Photographs, 1870-1897.** 67 items. Loc: UGA. XRI MS A261.
Photographs of family and friends, a group photo of G.C.V.I. boys in 1894 and the Maple Leaf Baseball Club in 1897.

3444. Hydro Electric Power Commission. **Historical photograph collection, 1906-c1955.** 3 binders. Loc: OHA.
About 2500 photographs relating to the history of electrical power development in Ontario. The original photographs are held at the University Avenue offices of Ontario Hydro, but the Ontario Hydro Archives hold three large binders of captioned prints, arranged alphabetically by name of place. There are several views of Guelph and Mount Forest, including those used to illustrate Greta Shutt's history of the Board of Light and Heat Commissioners in 1966: street scene on Civic Holiday (HP-1030), old-style street lights (HP-1111), line gang c1900 (HP-1112), interior of transformer station (HP-1113), and Huskisson (now Wyndham) Street in 1930 (HP-1114).

3445. Ker Cavan. **Photographs, 1900-1980.** 1 file folder. Loc: UGA. XR1 MS A005090-1.
Part of Allan-Higinbotham Collection.

3446. Leslie Family. **Photograph albums, 1853-1919.** 5 albums, 1 file folder. Loc: AO. MU 1718.
Part of Mary Leslie Papers.

3447. Macdonald Consolidated School. **School photographs, c1904-1905.** 11 photographs. Loc: MSC. MS988.035-988.045.
A collection of silverprint photographs of school children, classrooms, gardens and exhibits arranged in the following order: 1. Unidentified classroom picture with the mat stamped, 'Jas. W. Rogers' 2. Cooking class with the mat stamped, 'Booth' 3. Girls in classroom 4. Girls in classroom 5. Children's

garden exhibit 6. Science display 7. Nature study laboratory 8. Sewing class with the mat stamped, 'Booth' 9. Cooking class with mat inscribed, 'Miss Margaret Park, Teacher, 1904-05' 10. Domestic Science classroom 11. School classroom with mat inscribed, 'Teacher Mr R. Painter/Miss Margaret Park about 1904-05'. Part of the Macdonald Stewart Art Centre Collection. Donated anonymously.

3448. McCrae, David. **Photograph album, 1867-1870.** 2 volumes, 1 box. Loc: JMH.
A collection of photographs of family and friends of McCrae and of several Guelph buildings. David was John McCrae's father. The albums include many identified area people, Scottish relatives and British monarchs. The box contains photographs of John McCrae's friends and colleagues.

3449. Mount Forest Town Council. **Photograph, 1865.** 1 photo. Loc: UGA. XRI MS A329.

3450. National Photographic Collection. **Photographs. Guelph buildings and scenes, c1855-c1945.** c100 photographs. Loc: NAC. Card index with small scale photographic prints.
At least one hundred photographs of Guelph buildings and scenes. Users of the National Photographic Collection are advised, however, that the index photographs constitute only three to five percent of all holdings. Photographers whose work is represented here include Thomas Connon, Charles Nelles and J. Woodruff and there are prints from the collections of M. Inch, H.J. Woodside, W.J. Topley, John Boyd, Ed McCann and the C.M.H.C. Scenes include St George's Square, Riverside Park, Lower Wyndham, Woolwich, Douglas, Glasgow and Carden Streets, the Speed River, the July 12th procession in 1906, several views of Guelph from an aeroplane (c1919), the 30th Regiment (1906), the Royal Tour of 1901, as well as public buildings including the C.N.R. Station (1924), the Post Office (1927), Court House (c1900), Carnegie Public Library, old C.P.R. Station, Armouries (1909), temporary prison (1911) and Reformatory (1925), Utoka School (built 1873), GTR Bridge and War Memorial (1927), as well as most structures of the Ontario Agricultural College, Macdonald Institute and the Macdonald Consolidated School. There are views of Allan's Mill (c1855), the Goldie Mill, Guelph Stove Company and a Sleeman delivery wagon. Church views include St George's (1931) and the Church of Our Lady. There are two scenes from the 1945 strike by employees of Federal Wire and Cable.

3451. Ontario Agricultural College. **Building photographs, 1887-1986.** 3 boxes. Loc: UGA. REI OAC A0207-A0229.
A collection of photographs of campus views and buildings, including Johnston Hall, Creelman Hall, Mills Hall, Blackwood Hall, Day Hall, Massey Library, War Memorial Hall and Zavitz Hall.

3452. Ontario Agricultural College. **Photographs, 1905-c1915.** 1 album. Loc: UGA. XR2 MS A038.
A photograph album of O.A.C. animals, buildings, residence life and M.H. Haley's barn. One photograph, taken by Kennedy, shows the inter-faculty assault-at-arms team, c1900, identifying ten members and the coach, Professor G.H. Unwin.

3453. Pat Mestern Collection. **Photographs. Fergus, 1892-1950.** 1 box. Loc: WCA. MU57. List of date and content of photographs.

A series of thirty-two photographs of Fergus churches and schools, and of Beatty Brothers displays and plants. The Wellington County Archives has developed a detailed finding aid indicating the contents and date of specific photographs.

3454. Pequegnat Family. **Photographs, c1920.** 1 file folder. Loc: UGA. XR1 MS A065.
A collection of undated photographs apparently from the early twentieth century.

3455. **Photograph. Rockwood Academy, 1866.** 7 x 14 in. Loc: KPL. Box 1.
A view of the building in the background with a group of people and a horse-drawn conveyance in the gateway. There is a good view of fence construction in the foreground.

3456. **Photographs, n.d..** 2 volumes, 1 file folder. Loc: UGA. XR1 MS A005.
A collection of unidentified people and buildings. Part of Allan-Higinbotham Collection.

3457. Rantoul Collection. **Photographs. Yeomans and Rantoul families of Mount Forest, c1875-1930.** 8 boxes. Loc: WCA. List of photograph contents.
A large collection of photographs of the Yeomans and Rantoul families who were related by marriage. The contents of photographs are described in a finding aid developed by the Wellington County Archives; however, a number of photographs are undated and many people in the pictures are unidentified.

3458. Rea-Armstrong Collection. **Photographs. Armstrong-Rea families, 1865-1920.** 1 box. Loc: WCA. List of photographs by subject and date.
The Wellington County Archives has developed a detailed finding aid noting the subjects and dates of specific pictures which are primarily of family members.

3459. Sallows Collection. **Photographs of Ontario agricultural history, 1900-1923.** 250 photographs. Loc: OMA.
A collection of approximately 250 photographs taken by Reuben Sallows, a portrait and landscape artist in the Goderich area. He opened his first studio about 1879 and became well known throughout North America for his innovative approach to photography. Instead of taking traditional formal portraits, he photographed men, women and children engaged in agricultural and domestic work settings on area farms. The collection, while not specifically of the Wellington County region, is a unique source documenting the agricultural history of southern Ontario. It includes examples of agricultural machinery, equipment and tools; planting and harvesting of crops such as corn, pumpkins, maple syrup, apples, mangels, flax, oats and wheat; and farm chores such as feeding animals, churning butter, baking bread, making soft soap, spinning, and washing clothes. The photographs also record types of work clothing worn by men, women and children, and show evidence of the type of agricultural work in which women and children participated.

3460. Shutt, Greta M. **Photographs. Guelph and region, 1890-1911.** 2 boxes. Loc: UGA. XR1 MS A014004.
A collection of eighty-six photographs and original slides of Guelph and area residents, local residential and public buildings, and of mills in the county. The collection includes photographs of buildings such as Goldie's Mill, Guelph

General Hospital and several Guelph churches. A large proportion of the photographs have been identified by University of Guelph archivists. Filed with Mrs D.B. Shutt Collection.

3461. Sleeman Family. **Photographs, c1890-1923.** 1 file folder, 1 oversize file folder. Loc: UGA. XR1 MS A334.

A series of photographs of Sleeman family members with several scenes at the Sleeman residence on Waterloo Avenue. The collection also contains several photographs of Springbank Brewery constructed by George Sleeman in 1903 on Edinburgh Road in Guelph. Part of the Sleeman Family Collection.

3462. St Joseph's Hospital School of Nursing. **Photographs of nurses' graduations, 1916-1918; 1920-1924; 1926-1935.** 18 photographs. Loc: SJA. Box 936.

3463. St Stanislaus Novitiate. **Photographs, 1913-1970.** 1 box. Loc: JA.

A collection of about one hundred photographs of people, buildings and scenery from all periods of the Novitiate's history. A 16-mm television film is included, showing the fire of 18 November 1954. There is also an aerial photograph of the whole property, showing the dates of construction of the various buildings.

3464. Stewart, Robert A.M. **Early history of Guelph. Photo album, 1969.** 59 p. mf. Loc: AO. FA: MS 206.

Photocopies of c470 illustrations (photographs, half-tones, drawings, engravings, maps, advertisements) with descriptions and sources of originals. Some of the illustrations are held in the Archives of Ontario Picture Collection: Acc. 6260: S8571-8400.

3465. Templin-Dow Collection. **Photographs, 1870-1960 (sporadic).** Loc: WCA. Detailed list of contents.

A collection of photographs that includes a small number of historic ones of Fergus institutions and residents.

3466. Templin Manufacturing Company. **Photographs of Templin family businesses, Fergus, c1880-1940.** 8 photographs. Loc: OAM.

A series of photographs of the Templin family business with two early photographs of the Templin Carriage and Wagon Works. There are also several photographs of Templin's Garage which began operations in the early 1920s.

3467. Union Brewery Workers No. 300, Guelph. **Photograph of parade, c1890.** 1 photo, oversized. Loc: UGA. XR2 MS A051.

3468. University of Guelph Archives. **Photograph. William Bell, n.d..** 1 photograph. Loc: UGA. XR2 MS A055.

William Bell owned the Bell Organ Company in Guelph.

3469. University of Guelph Archives. **Photographs. Guelph buildings, 1858-1920.** 1 file folder. Loc: UGA. XR1 MS A084.

The collection contains photographs, pamphlets and postcards of buildings in Guelph.

3470. University of Guelph Archives. **Postcards, 1900-1919; 1973**. 1 envelope. Loc: UGA. XR1 MS A290.
Fourteen cards that include scenes of Riverside Park and St George's Square in the early twentieth century.

3471. University of Guelph Archives. **Views of Guelph, 1900-1980**. 1 file folder, oversized. Loc: UGA. XR3 MS A007.
Four black and white photographs mounted on a display board: the University of Guelph buildings, Royal City Park, the floral clock at Riverside Park and the Church of Our Lady.

3472. Wellington County Archives. **Photographs of Wellington County**. 9100 photographs. Loc: WCA. Card index and 27 binders of prints.
A large collection of photographs of people, buildings and activities from all parts of the county.

3473. Wellington County Historical Research Society. **Photographs. History of Wellington County, c1840-1960**. 9 boxes. Loc: WCA. List of photograph contents.
A large collection of photographs of county residents, schools, churches, public buildings and landscapes in various areas through Wellington County. The Wellington County Archives has developed a detailed finding aid of the collection indicating the date and contents of specific photographs.

Guelph in 1882, its skyline dominated by smoking chimneys and church spires. By this date most of the churches that still stand in central Guelph had been built. These include Knox, St Andrew's and St George's to the right, Norfolk (and Central School) centre, and the Church of Our Lady still under construction to the left. From a pen and ink sketch by R.B. Schell (#3551). (Macdonald Stewart Art Centre)

Delicate sobriety: an oil painting of Mrs Sarah Gill, c1890, by her daughter Helen Raymond, who was the second wife of Charles Raymond (#3547). (Macdonald Stewart Art Centre)

ART WORKS

contributed by Judith Nasby

This section of the **Inventory** describes art works depicting the Wellington County area and created to 1940. Artists include internationally acclaimed individuals such as A.J. Casson and David Johnston Kennedy, as well as local residents such as Thomas Connon, John Connon, Daniel Jones and Effie Smith. Art works relating to Wellington County are held at the Royal Ontario Museum in Toronto, the Metropolitan Toronto Library, the Historical Society of Philadelphia and, primarily, at the Macdonald Stewart Art Centre in Guelph. Catlin's 1827 plan of Guelph, three plans of the Ontario Agricultural College and two collections of photographs are included in other sections of the book, although held in the art collection of the Macdonald Stewart Art Centre.

When the Macdonald Stewart Art Centre opened in 1980, an imaginative renovation gave new life to a turn of the century historic building. The building first opened in 1904 as the Macdonald Consolidated School through funding received from Sir William Macdonald, and served as a model for provincial education as the first consolidated school in Ontario. As a public art gallery, the Centre actively collects, researches and publishes on aspects of its art collection.

The primary resource of the Centre is the Permanent Collection that includes art owned by the Centre as well as the University of Guelph Art Collection, which has been placed on loan as a permanent resource. The collection consists of over 3,000 art works, covering three centuries of Canadian art, with specializations in contemporary Inuit drawings, outdoor sculpture and, to a lesser degree, regional subjects.

Although visual material about early county life is scant, the best known views are the watercolours and drawings that David Johnston Kennedy made of Guelph in the mid-nineteenth century. Another collection of Kennedy's art includes fourteen works held by the Historical Society of Philadelphia. Views were also produced to accompany travel accounts and to document towns and educational institutions, such as the Ontario Agricultural College.

Because of the time frame of the project, post-1940 works of artists such as Evan Macdonald, Gordon Couling and Yosef Drenters are not included. Macdonald's oil painting entitled, Wireless Air Gunner, 1942, deserves special mention for documenting the No.4 Wireless School of the Royal Canadian Air Force stationed by the Department of National Defence at the Macdonald Institute from 1941 to 1945. It is part of the University of Guelph Art Collection held at the Macdonald Stewart Art Centre.

The Art Centre staff has contributed cataloguing and research for 90 entries in the **Inventory** consisting of paintings, graphics and sculpture. Of these, 28 have been published previously in Judith Nasby's **University of Guelph Art Collection Catalogue** or **Visitors, Exiles and Residents: Guelph Artists Since 1827**.[1] Documentation for 62 works is published here for the first time and includes some portraits of University faculty and administrators and photographs of classroom activities at the Macdonald Consolidated School shortly after it opened.

In the following descriptions, measurements are in centimetres, height preceding width and depth. Inscriptions are recorded as they appear on the art works. The date given at the end of the title was not, however, formally part of the original title; it is included here for technical reasons and consistency with the other types of records in the **Inventory**.

---

[1] The following Art Centre publications on regional subjects may be purchased at the Art Centre Gallery Shop or ordered by mail:
C.A.V. Barker et al, **The Horse in Art and Science** (Guelph: Macdonald Stewart Art Centre, 1983); Ingrid Jenkner, **Evan Macdonald: A Retrospective** (Guelph: Macdonald Stewart Art Centre, 1986); Judith Nasby, 'David Johnston Kennedy, a Painter of Guelph,' **Canadian Collector** 11, 4 (1976): 26-31; Judith Nasby, 'The Macdonald Stewart Art Centre,' **Canadian Collector** 15, 5 (1980): 34-38; Judith Nasby, **The University of Guelph Art Collection: A Catalogue of Paintings, Drawings, Prints and Sculpture** (Guelph: University of Guelph, 1980); Judith Nasby, **Visitors, Exiles and Residents: Guelph Artists since 1827** (Guelph: University of Guelph, 1977).

ART WORKS

3474. Armstrong, William. **First home in Canada, from nature, in Palmerston, c1880.** 246 x 374 cm. Loc: ROM. 955.102.1.

A water colour with touches of gouache, pen and ink, showing family activities around a primitive log cabin in a clearing in the woods. Armstrong was born in Dublin, Ireland in 1822 and emigrated to Canada in 1851 where he worked as an engineer for railway companies. He turned to full time painting in the 1880s.

3475. Casson, A.J. **Elora and Salem: twenty sketches, 1927.** each reproduction 26.5 x 23.5 cm. Loc: UGA.

A limited edition reproduction of a portfolio of Casson's water colours depicting Elora and Salem village life on a cloudy day in autumn, bound in an oversized volume produced in 1979 entitled, Elora and Salem: Twenty Sketches. The titles of the plates are listed in consecutive order. 1. Autumn reflections: the outskirts of Elora 2. River's edge: the south side of the Grand River 3. Drying the wash: behind Mill Street looking across the Grand River 4. Early morning: the Metcalfe Street Mill Street junction 5. Quiet Street: Mill Street 6. Sunday best: Mill Street looking east 7. Rooftops: looking down Price Street 8. Sleepy afternoon: looking down Church Street 9. Church Street: looking across Metcalfe Street 10. Heading home: Metcalfe, the main street 11. Afternoon shadows: the west side of Metcalfe 12. The blacksmith shop: the Geddes and Metcalfe Street junction 13. John Connon's house: Elora 14. Backyards: Elora 15. Twilight: Union Street, Salem, Ontario 16. The edge of town: looking towards Elora 17. Village store: looking south at the Union Street junction 18. The Mill Pond, Salem: the mill pond between Water and Washington Streets 19. Sun showers: looking south on Water Street towards Salem 20. Autumn wind: the northern outskirts of Salem.

3476. Casson, A.J. **Old store at Salem, 1931.** 75.6 x 90.4 cm. Loc: AGO.

An oil painting of a Salem store in an autumn setting. It is based on his 1927 water colour, 'Village store: looking south at the Union Street junction', which is included as plate 17 in the limited edition book, Elora and Salem: Twenty Sketches.

3477. Chiles, G. **Guelph, 1830.** 21.5 x 26.9 cm. Loc: MSC, ROM. MSC: UG983.020 ROM: 957.253.7.

A lithograph showing the Priory in the new settlement of Guelph, which was published in Fraser's Magazine for Town and Country, Volume 2, November 1830, opposite p. 456. Part of the University of Guelph Art Collection. Presented in memory of Carol Page, FACS 1978, by her friends and classmates, 1980. The copy held at ROM is part of the Sigmund Samuel Canadiana Collection.

3478. Connon, Thomas. **Elora Gorge, c1853-1899.** 50 x 59.8 cm. Loc: MSC. UG986.014.

An oil painting on canvas of the Irvine River in the Elora Gorge. The painting is undated, but would have been done in Connon's Elora years, 1853 to 1899. Connon was a photographer, inventor of photographic equipment, and painter who was born in Scotland in 1832. He emigrated to Canada in 1852 and settled in Elora in 1853. Despite a lack of formal training, he painted landscapes and portraits and later opened a photography studio in the village. Part of the University of Guelph Art Collection. Presented on behalf of the late Géne Connon Meakins by J.A. Bamber, 1987.

3479. Connon, Thomas. **Elora Quarry, c1853-1899**. 39 x 31.5 cm. Loc: MSC. UG987.001.
An oil painting on slate showing the Irvine River and high rock formations of the Quarry. The painting is undated, but would have been done during Connon's Elora years, 1853 to 1899. Part of the University of Guelph Art Collection. Presented on behalf of the late Géne Connon Meakins by J.A. Bamber, 1987.

3480. Connon, Thomas. **John Keith, c1878-85**. 88.9 x 73.7 cm. Loc: MSC. UG974.046.
An oil portrait taken from an 1878 photograph taken by Connon. John Keith was one of the earliest settlers of the Bon Accord settlement near Elora. Part of the University of Guelph Art Collection. Presented on behalf of the late Géne Connon Meakins by J.A. Bamber, 1974.

3481. Connon, Thomas. **Mrs Robert Connon, c1867**. 25.2 x 20 cm. Loc: MSC. UG975.004.
A photograph on paper with watercolour and pastel. The negative of the photograph was made in Scotland in the 1860s and was probably taken by Thomas Connon of Elora when he visited his mother, Mrs Robert Connon, in 1867 at Elfhill Scotland. Part of the University of Guelph Art Collection. Presented on behalf of the late Géne Connon Meakins by J.A. Bamber, 1975.

3482. Connon, Thomas. **Robert Connon, c1867**. 25.2 x 20 cm. Loc: MSC. UG975.003.
A photograph on paper with watercolour and pastel. The negative of the photograph was made in Scotland in the 1860s, and was probably taken by Thomas Connon of Elora when he visited his father, Robert Connon, in 1867 at Elfhill, Scotland. Robert Connon died on December 7, 1873. Part of the University of Guelph Art Collection. Presented on behalf of the late Géne Connon Meakins by J.A. Bamber, 1975.

3483. **Edmund Morris and family, c1871**. 14.7 x 19.5 cm. Loc: MTL. 985-8-7.
An albumen print laid down on cardboard mount with printed border in light brown and gold. Inscribed in pencil, 'Aunt Lena Harman/ Aunt Hattie Spragge/ Great Uncle William Morris/ General Emma Morris/ (Aunt Minnie) Mrs Ogden Jones/ Grandfather James (ie: Edmund) Morris/ Grandmother, Percy Morris died in California (?) Robert S. Morris Dad James Morris/ Murney Morris. Taken in the family home at Guelph, about 1871'. Margaret Willina Harman (Lena), Harriet Elizabeth Spragge, William Morris and Edmund Morris were children of James Morris. Part of the John Ross Robertson Collection.

3484. **Fergus in 1837, c1912**. 16.5 x 28.8 cm. Loc: MTL. JRR 1053.
A water colour, gouache and pen and ink drawing on wove paper, possibly done by Owen Staples, c1912. The pen and ink drawing might have been done by Alexander Dingwall Fordyce (1816-1894), who made several drawings of Fergus around 1837. The view of the village is taken from Alexander David Ferrier's residence, 'Belsyde' that was built in 1836. Part of the John Ross Robertson Collection.

3485. Forbes, Kenneth K. **H.H. Dean, 1930**. 127 x 101.6 cm. Loc: MSC. UG900.198.
An oil on canvas of Henry H. Dean who was Professor of Dairying at the Ontario Agricultural College from 1891 to 1932. Forbes, the artist, was born in Toronto in 1892. Part of the University of Guelph Art Collection. Acquired in 1930.

3486. Forbes, Kenneth K. **W.R. Graham, 1940.** 111.8 x 87 cm. Loc: MSC. UG900.151.
An oil on canvas of Graham who was Head of the Poultry Department at the Ontario Agricultural College from 1899 to 1940. Part of the University of Guelph Art Collection. Presented by his friends in the poultry industry, 1940.

3487. Fordyce, Janet Dingwall. **Fergus, Upper Canada, c1835.** 8 x 12 7/8 " Loc: MTL, ROM. MTL: JRR 1051.
A hand coloured lithograph on wove paper depicting trees and stumps in foreground, and the town and church in background surrounded by forest. Printed by Forrester and Nichol in Edinburgh c1835. Part of the John Ross Robertson Collection at the Metro Toronto Library, and the Sigmund Samuel Canadiana Collection at ROM.

3488. Forster, John W.L. **Adelaide Hoodless, c1909.** 125.1 x 92.1 cm. Loc: MSC. UG900.154.
An oil painting on canvas. Forster was born in Norval, Ontario in 1850 and died in Toronto in 1938. Hoodless, who lived from 1857 to 1909, played an important role in the implementation of the teaching of domestic science in the Canadian educational system. In 1889 she became President of the first YWCA in Hamilton. Four years later she instigated the first class in Domestic Science and served as the Canadian delegate to the World Congress of Women that was held in Chicago. She is best known for her founding of the Women's Institutes in 1897. The Institutes received a Federal Charter in 1919 and eventually led to the formation of the Associated Countrywomen of the World in 1930. Hoodless convinced philanthropist Sir William Macdonald of the importance of teacher training in home economics. Macdonald soon after donated funds for the establishment in Guelph of Macdonald Institute in 1903, and Macdonald Hall and Macdonald Consolidated School in 1904. Part of the University of Guelph Art Collection. Presented by the Women's Institutes of Ontario, 1912.

3489. Forster, John W.L. **George Edward Day, 1918.** 137.4 x 106.4 cm. Loc: MSC. UG900.152.
An oil painting on canvas of Day who was Head of the Animal Husbandry Department from 1899 to 1917. Part of the University of Guelph Art Collection. Presented by Class of 1918 of the Ontario Agricultural College, 1918.

3490. Forster, John W.L. **The Honourable Adam Fergusson, c1920.** 102.3 x 76.8 cm. Loc: MSC. UG900.153.
An oil on canvas, taken from a previous portrait dated c1840, and painted in the early twentieth century. Fergusson was born in Perthshire, Scotland in 1783 and died at Woodhill, Upper Canada in 1862. He was co-founder of the town of Fergus, one of the founders of the first Agricultural Societies of Ontario, and chair of the 1862 committee appointed to elect the first principal of the Ontario Veterinary College. Fergusson departed from traditional farming methods of wheat monoculture to grow a variety of grains and practise crop rotation. He imported short-horned Durham cattle and soon built the first registered herd in Canada. He also helped start the Ontario Agricultural College and the Provincial Agricultural Association. Part of the University of Guelph Art Collection. Presented by G. Tower Fergusson and Robert G.B. Fergusson, c1920.

3491. Forster, John W.L. **James Mills, c1904.** 137.2 x 104.8 cm. Loc: MSC. UG900.157.
An oil painting on canvas of Mills. The plaque reads, 'James Mills, M.A.,

L.L.D. President 1879-1904. Presented by Class '04'. Mills was Principal of the Ontario Agricultural College from 1879 to 1880, and President from 1880 to 1904. Part of the University of Guelph Art Collection. Presented by the Class of 1904, Ontario Agricultural College, 1904.

3492. Forster, John W.L. **Mary Urie Watson, c1928.** 124.5 x 91.4 cm. Loc: MSC. UG900.158.
An oil painting on canvas of Watson who was Organizer and Director of Home Economics at Macdonald Institute from 1903 to 1920. Part of the University of Guelph Art Collection. Gift of the Alumni, Macdonald Institute, c1928.

3493. Forster, John W.L. **Sir William Macdonald, c1920.** 54 x 41" Loc: MSC. UG900.155.
An oil painting on canvas with a plaque that reads, 'William Christopher Macdonald, 1831-1917'. Macdonald was born in 1831 at Glenaladale, PEI, and died in Montreal in 1917. He was founder and president of the Macdonald Tobacco Company in Montreal, and donated funds for the building of Macdonald Institute, Macdonald Hall and the Macdonald Consolidated School in Guelph. Part of the University of Guelph Art Collection.

3494. Forster, John W.L. **W.E.H. Massey, c1902.** 134.6 x 101.6 cm. Loc: MSC. UG900.156.
An oil painting on canvas of Massey. The Massey Hall and Library at the Ontario Agricultural College was built with funds donated by the Hart Massey estate. W.E.H. Massey, son of Hart Massey, laid the corner-stone on August 14, 1901. Part of the University of Guelph Art Collection. Gift of the Massey family, 1902.

3495. **George Sleeman, c1885.** 72.5 x 57.8 cm. Loc: MSC. UG977.038.
An unsigned photograph on paper with chalk pastel and gouache. The photograph is mounted on canvas and the plaque reads, 'George Sleeman'. Sleeman was a Local brewer who was active in city affairs. He was Mayor of Guelph, 1880-1882 and 1905-1906, organized the Guelph Street Railway in 1894, and was owner of the Guelph Maple Leaf Baseball Club. Part of the University of Guelph Art Collection. An anonymous gift acquired in 1977.

3496. Grier, E. Wyly, Sir. **J. Hoyes Panton, 1904.** 134.9 x 85.7 cm. Loc: MSC. MS900.162.
An oil painting on canvas of Panton. Conservation treatment of the canvas, which was extensively damaged when found, resulted in the portrait being restored to a three quarter size portrait, instead of its original full length size. Grier was born in Melbourne, Australia in 1862, emigrated to Canada in 1891, and died in Toronto in 1957. Panton was Professor of Natural History at the Ontario Agricultural College from 1878 to 1897. He died in 1898. Part of the University of Guelph Art Collection. Gift of the Ontario Agricultural College Alumni, 1904.

3497. Grier, E. Wyly, Sir. **Joseph Benson Reynolds, 1929.** 137.5 x 91.8 cm. Loc: MSC. UG900.163.
An oil painting on canvas with the following inscription: 'OSA Annual Exhibition 1929/Title: J.B. Reynolds Esq. M.A., L.L.D., President Emeritus of OAC/Artist: E. Wyly Grier, RCA/Address: 771 George St., Toronto, April 1, 6 Crescent Road/ Canadian National Exhibition, 1929'. Reynolds was President of

the Ontario Agricultural College from 1920 to 1928. Part of the University of Guelph Art Collection. Presented by the Class of 1923, Ontario Agricultural College, 1929.

3498. Gross, P.A. **Fue-de-Joie (sic) on Dominion Day, 1875, at Brigade Camp, Guelph.** 39/4 x 56 cm. Loc: MSC. UGB900.059.

A coloured lithograph, produced by P.A. Gross of Toronto, depicting fields, tents and the main Exhibition Building. The location of the camp is probably the Guelph Exhibition Grounds on London Road. The printed title should read, 'Feu-de-Joie', which is French for a public bonfire or gun salute presented on a ceremonial occasion. Part of the University of Guelph Art Collection. University purchase, 1979.

3499. **Guelph, 1842.** 17.5 x 25.7 cm. Loc: MTL. JRR 4467.

A pencil and pale brown wash drawing inscribed, 'May 12, '42'. A key to the sketch of the town identifies the location of the 'Scots', 'Catholic' and 'Episcopalian' churches, and Galt's residence. Part of the John Ross Robertson Collection.

3500. Haberer, Eugene. **Guelph Mills, the property of D. Allan Esq., 1873.** 18.7 x 26.4 cm. Loc: MSC. UG987.031.

A hand-coloured lithograph of Allan's Mill from Canadian Illustrated News. Part of the University of Guelph Art Collection. Gift of John Goatley, 1987.

3501. Hornyansky, Nicholas. **Administration Building, Ontario Agricultural College, c1940.** 24.1 x 21.6 cm. Loc: MSC. UG900.223.

An aquatint and drypoint artist's proof inscribed, 'Administration Bldg. Ont. Agricultural College Hornyansky'. The work depicts the Administration Building, with a pond in the foreground. This proof was commissioned by the College for use as a card, but was never produced. Hornyansky was born in Budapest in 1896 and studied portraiture and aesthetics at the Academy of Fine Arts in Budapest, and later studied in Vienna and other cities. In 1919 he went to Belgium to study landscape painting in association with the school of Franz Hens, and emigrated to Toronto in 1929. He promoted printmaking in Canada through his work with the Society of Canadian Painter-Etchers and Engravers and as an instructor of printmaking at the Ontario College of Art from 1945 to 1965. Many of his works were reproduced in books and calendars and as Christmas cards. He died in Toronto in 1965. Part of the University of Guelph Art Collection. Gift of Ontario Agricultural College Students, 1974.

3502. Jones, Daniel Herbert. **The hedge garden, OAC, 1937.** 76.2 x 61 cm. Loc: MSC. UG900.071.

An oil painting on masonite of the grounds of the Ontario Agricultural College, signed 'November, 1937'. Part of the University of Guelph Art Collection. Gift of the artist, 1943.

3503. Jones, Daniel Herbert. **Landscape, 1939.** 90.8 x 122 cm. Loc: MSC. UG900.064.

An oil painting on masonite of sheep grazing under a tree on an Ontario Agricultural College farm field. Jones emigrated to Canada from England in 1901 and graduated from the Ontario Agricultural College in 1908. He joined the faculty of the College in 1914 and was Head of the Department of Bacteriology until he retired in 1936. His realistic views in bright colours depict the

Guelph area and scenes on the College campus. Part of the University of Guelph Art Collection. Gift of the artist, 1943.

3504. Jones, Daniel Herbert. **Oat harvest looking west from top of dairy hill, OAC, July scene, c1940.** 76 x 122 cm. Loc: MSC. UG981.012.
An oil painting on board of an oat field at Ontario Agricultural College. Part of the University of Guelph Art Collection. Gift of the artist, 1943.

3505. Jones, Daniel Herbert. **On a May morning, end of College Lane, West of OAC, 1940.** 61 x 91.4 cm. Loc: MSC. UG90.067.
An oil painting on masonite of College Lane, west of Ontario Agricultural College. Part of the University of Guelph Art Collection. Gift of the artist, 1943.

3506. Jones, Daniel Herbert. **Peaceful reflections (looking westward from bridge over River Speed on Edinburgh Road), 1938.** 76.2 x 61 cm. Loc: MSC. UG900.068.
An oil painting on masonite. Part of the University of Guelph Art Collection. Gift of the artist, 1943.

3507. Jones, Daniel Herbert. **Peony beds, OAC, 1938.** 44.5 x 59.7 cm. Loc: MSC. UG900.069.
An oil painting on board of peony flower beds at the Ontario Agricultural College. Part of the University of Guelph Art Collection. Gift of the artist, 1943.

3508. Jones, Daniel Herbert. **September morning on the Speed (looking east, from the Dundas Road Bridge), 1938.** 61 x 89.5 cm. Loc: MSC. UG900.070.
An oil painting on masonite. Part of the University of Guelph Art Collection. Gift of the artist, 1943.

3509. Jones, Daniel Herbert. **Wellington St Bridge and Dam, Guelph, September morning, 1939.** 61.3 x 91.4 cm. Loc: MSC. UG900.072.
An oil painting on masonite. Part of the University of Guelph Art Collection. Gift of the artist, 1943.

3510. Jones, Phyllis Jacobine. **Bessie Mark, Clydesdale Mare, 1935.** 48.3 x 60.9 x 15.2 cm. Loc: MSC. UG900.313.
A bronze sculpture of a mare owned by the Ontario Agricultural College. The sculpture is known as 'Year '31 Trophy' and is awarded annually to the OAC class obtaining the highest total number of points in the College Royal competition. Jacobine Jones first studied at the Regent Street Polytechnic in London and later in Denmark, Italy and France. She came to Canada in 1932 and the following year was invited to the Ontario Agricultural College where she did studies of various animals in the College herds. In 1938 two of her bronze animal sculptures were chosen for the exhibition, A Century of Canadian Art, held at the Tate Gallery in London, England. Jones's work was classical in approach, and based on accurate anatomical studies. She created simple and noble works through a style that emphasized lines, smooth planes and subtle surface textures. Part of the University of Guelph Art Collection. Presented in 1939 by the OAC Class of 1931.

3511. Jones, Phyllis Jacobine. **Highfield Dreaming Master, Jersey Bull, 1933**. 30.7 x 41.6 x 15.2 cm. Loc: MSC. UG900.314.

A bronze sculpture of the sire of the Ontario Agricultural College herd. The sculpture was presented to the College by Jacobine Jones in 1935 and has since been known as the 'Jacobine Jones Trophy'. Since then it has been awarded annually to the Grand Champion Showman in the livestock division of the College Royal competition. Part of the University of Guelph Art Collection. Gift of the artist, 1935.

3512. Keenan, Mary Ellen. **The original Johnston Hall, c1873**. 26.3 x 37.2 cm. Loc: MSC. UG900.241.

A pastel on paper, inscribed, 'The original Johnston Hall by Mary Ellen Keenan about 1873', and signed on an accompanying paper, 'Agricultural College/M.E. Keenan Loretto'. Keenan was born in 1857 on a Guelph Township farm on Brock Road, south of the OAC. She later attended Loretto Academy in Guelph where she painted this early piece. She married William Cassin in 1897 and spent most of her life in Guelph. She died in Tottenham in 1945. Part of the University of Guelph Art Collection. Gift of Mrs Agnes M. Keogh, Tottenham, 1970.

3513. Kennedy, David Johnston. **Allan's Mill on the River Speed, Guelph, Canada West, 1845**. 26.5 x 42.1 cm. Loc: MSC. UG973.030.

The watercolour and pencil sketch shows the mill built in 1830 by Horace Perry for the Canada Company. William Allan took over the mill in 1832, adding the distillery and carding mill seen on the opposite bank of the river. At right is the Priory, built in 1827 and used as the headquarters for the first settlers brought in by the Canada Company. The Delemere Tavern is on the far left. The painting is inscribed, 'Allans Mill, on the river Speed Guelph, Canada West, sketched from Strange's Hill in/November 1845 by D.J. KENNEDY of Philadelphia on a visit to W. Robert Allan/sketch taken from the brow of the hill opposite to the Court House and Jail - D.J.K.' The mat is inscribed, 'ALLANS MILL, GUELPH, ONTARIO . . . showing where the first tree was cut/in locating the city, the stump of which is shown in front of the horse and sled leaving the mill.' Kennedy was born in Scotland in 1816 and moved to Ireland with his family. In 1833 the family emigrated to Canada, first to Kingston, and then to Nichol Township. He later moved to Philadelphia where his sister lived, worked as a stone cutter and a railway agent, and painted in his precise watercolour style. His technique, noted for its clarity of detail and emphasis on line, is derived from his training in architectural drafting. Part of the University of Guelph Art Collection. Gift of the University of Guelph Alumni, Alma Mater Fund, 1973.

3514. Kennedy, David Johnston. **Grand Trunk Railway Bridge, Across the Speed at Guelph, Canada West, 1861**. 15.7 x 49.7 cm. Loc: MSC. UG973.032.

The watercolour and pencil sketch depicts the Toronto-Guelph line of the Grand Trunk Railway which began in 1854. The line opened the trade route to Toronto and Montreal for Guelph's various industries. The mat is inscribed, 'Grand Trunk Railway Bridge across the River Speed at Guelph Ontario. Sketched from Mothers front window 2nd story facing south on July 16, 1861./Mother died June 5th, 1861 at 20 minutes past 8 a.m. Father died Oct. 24th, 1874 at 30 minutes past 5 p.m.' Part of the University of Guelph Art Collection. Gift of the University of Guelph Alumni, Alma Mater Fund, 1973.

3515. Kennedy, David Johnston. **Guelph, 1845**. 19.3 x 34 cm. Loc: HSP. K: 11-104.
A watercolour that is similar to picture number UG973.030 in the University of Guelph Art Collection at Macdonald Stewart Art Centre.

3516. Kennedy, David Johnston. **Guelph, Canada West, 1853**. 18.1 x 47.2 cm. Loc: MSC. UG973.034.
The ink and pencil sketch is inscribed, 'Guelph Canada West/This pen and ink sketch was made on the east side of the River Speed, opposite to the 'Priory' in the summer of 1853 while on a visit to Father and Mother/and is taken from the front door of their cottage - The 'first tree' was cut on Mr Wm Allans hill by Mr Galt Mr Prior and Dr Dunlop on St Georges day, April 23, 1827. A large sugar maple tree which stood right in the centre of where the present road now is, the stump of which remained guarded by by (sic) a triangular fence as late as 1835, when it was removed, being considered a dangerous (sic) to strangers after dark. . . Mr Allans house (a log house) was the scene/of a grand festival with Indian chief and others.' Part of the University of Guelph Art Collection. Gift of the University of Guelph Alumni, Alma Mater Fund, 1973.

3517. Kennedy, David Johnston. **Guelph, Canada West, from top of Strange's Hill where Mr. Palmer's house now stands, January 19th, 1845**. 19.3 x 34 cm. Loc: HSP. K: 11-104.
A watercolour with pencil. This is the same view as painting number UG973.030 in the University of Guelph Art Collection at the Macdonald Stewart Art Centre.

3518. Kennedy, David Johnston. **Guelph, Ontario, April 5th, 1852, elevation of cut stone residence proposed to be erected opposite the Priory on the River Speed**. 16.2 x 24 cm. Loc: HSP. K: VII-58.
A watercolour with pencil and ink which depicts an elaborate plan for 'Sunnyside', the house that was later built in Guelph in 1854 for Kennedy's sister and brother-in-law, Charles Davidson.

3519. Kennedy, David Johnston. **Guelph Union Cemetery, Guelph, C.W., 1864**. 13.1 x 26.8 cm. Loc: HSP. K: 1-116.
A watercolour of a view of family plots in the cemetery, inscribed, 'Lots 27, 36, 37 Section F'.

3520. Kennedy, David Johnston. **The Kennedy Cottage, 1852**. 29.5 x 43.3 cm. Loc: MSC. UG973.033.
The watercolour, ink and pencil sketch records 'Yankee cottage', a brick house built in Guelph by the artist's father, William Kennedy, on the bank of the Speed River adjacent to Allan's Bridge. The free-standing temple on the porch roof was likely never constructed. Part of the University of Guelph Art Collection. Gift of the University of Guelph Alumni, Alma Mater Fund, 1973.

3521. Kennedy, David Johnston. **Log shanty on Elora Road, Township of Nichol, Canada West, 1835**. 9 x 18.4 cm. Loc: HSP. K: 1-103.
A watercolour and pencil drawing. Also entitled, In the Backwoods.

3522. Kennedy, David Johnston. **Mother's Grave and Monument, 17 feet high, erected in Guelph Union Cemetery, Guelph, C.W., c1861**. 18.2 x 12.2 cm. Loc: HSP. K: 1-115.
A watercolour, pencil and ink drawing of the limestone grave marker of Kennedy's mother who died in 1861.

3523. Kennedy, David Johnston. **Residence of A.M. Jackson, Esq. Guelph, Canada West, 1864.** 10.5 x 15.3 cm. Loc: HSP. K: 1-123.
A watercolour and pencil sketch.

3524. Kennedy, David Johnston. **Sketch of part of the Town of Guelph, Canada West, 1853.** 27.2 x 50.3 cm. Loc: MSC. UG973.031.
The watercolour is dated 1853 by the artist. The 1850 date which appears on the lower left was probably added by another hand. In addition to Allan's Mill (left) and the Priory (centre), this sketch shows the Court House and Jail, built in 1843 from a design by William Allan's son, David. The painting is inscribed, 'Sketch of part of the town of Guelph, Canada West/on the river Speed from Father's house in June 1853/Sketched from the front door of Father and Mothers cottage looking up to the town/Mr William Allans Mill on the left, and on the right the Court House and Jail.' Part of the University of Guelph Art Collection. Gift of the University of Guelph Alumni, Alma Mater Fund, 1973.

3525. Kennedy, David Johnston. **Spence Bank Township of Nichol, Canada West, c1835.** 13 x 17.6 cm. Loc: HSP. K: 7-21.
A watercolour with pencil and ink depicting the home of Kennedy's father, William Kennedy, who lived from 1783 to 1874. The house is the same as the one shown in picture number K: 11-107, but with stucco and two additions.

3526. Kennedy, David Johnston. **Spence Bank, Township of Nichol near Guelph, Canada West, 1835.** 17.7 x 32.5 cm. Loc: HSP. K: 11-107.
A watercolour and pencil sketch of the vertical log home built in 1835 for William Kennedy and demolished in 1875.

3527. Kennedy, David Johnston. **Tale of Kennedy's narrow escape from wolves in Canadian Backwoods, c1835.** 18.4 x 14.6 cm. Loc: HSP. K: 6-66.1.
A watercolour and pencil sketch on verso of picture number K: 6-66.

3528. Kennedy, David Johnston. **View on the River Speed, Guelph, C.W. from the R.R. bridge looking up on Oct 4, 1864.** 14 x 32.7 cm. Loc: MSC. UG973.035.
The painting is a watercolour with ink and pencil, and depicts the view north of Allan's Bridge showing the bath house of the Priory on the left. Part of the University of Guelph Art Collection. Gift of the University of Guelph Alumni, Alma Mater Fund, 1973.

3529. Kennedy, David Johnston. **Winter in the backwoods 'Canada' in 1835, Midnight, all alone, no house near, and a pack of wolves in full cry in my rear.** 18.4 x 14.6 cm. Loc: HSP. K: 6-66.
A watercolour and pencil sketch that illustrated an event in Kennedy's life while he lived in Nichol Township.

3530. Kennedy, David Johnston. **Worsfolds Corner, Eramosa, Canada West, 1848.** 8.3 x 14.9 cm. Loc: HSP. K: 1-103-1.
A watercolour.

3531. Kennedy, David Johnston. **Yankee Cottage, 1846.** 17 x 26.8 cm. Loc: HSP. K: 10-60.
A pencil and ink sketch of William Kennedy's residence in Guelph, which was

built in 1847.

3532. Kennedy, David Johnston. **Yankee Cottage, on the Speed, Guelph, Canada West, 1835.** 17 x 31.5 cm. Loc: HSP. K: 11-107a.

A watercolour with pencil and ink. The view is from the same location as picture number UG973.033 in the University of Guelph Art Collection at the Macdonald Stewart Art Centre. This view, however, shows a different portico without sculptural embellishments, which were planned but likely never built.

3533. Macdonald Stewart Art Centre. **William Wood Collection, 1861-1905.** 5 items. Loc: MSC. UG976.035.

The collection includes a book that Wood hand-bound in 1905. It contains ink sketches of English scenes by Wood and several British artists, and a group of eighteenth century lithograph etchings of English churches. As well, the collection includes a photograph of Wood, a brief biography by Hazel Mack, and a hand copied list of contributors to an art exhibition held in Guelph November 5 to 9, 1867 that was sponsored by the Mechanic's Institute. Local exhibitors included William Wood, Mr Higinbotham, Mr and Mrs Raymond, William Kennedy, William Allan and John McCrae. Wood was born in 1836 at Prestbury, Cheshire in England, emigrated to Arkell in 1861, and married Sarah Pemlott in 1863 at the Farnham Church. He worked for a short time in Mount Forest, and later moved to Rockwood where he did bookbinding, and worked as a weaver at the Harris Woolen Mills. He died in 1913 and is buried at the Farnham Cemetery in Arkell. Part of the University of Guelph Art Collection. Gift of Mrs Hazel Mack of Rockwood, 1976.

3534. MacGregor, Charles. **C.A. Zavitz, 1927.** 135.5 x 107.5 cm. Loc: MSC. UG900.189.

An oil painting on canvas of Zavitz who was Professor of Field Husbandry and Plant Breeding from 1904 to 1927 at the Ontario Agricultural College. Part of the University of Guelph Art Collection. Presented by the Class of 1927, Ontario Agricultural College, 1928.

3535. MacGregor, Charles. **Entrance to Johnston Hall, c1927.** 38.6 x 25.2 cm. Loc: MSC. UG900.087.

The oil painting depicts the original main building of the Ontario Agricultural College, which was replaced in 1930 by Johnston Hall. MacGregor was born in Scotland in 1893, emigrated to Toronto in 1924, and was elected a member of the Ontario Society of Artists in 1927. He was primarily a portrait artist and made this sketch while on campus to paint portraits of College administrators. Part of the University of Guelph Art Collection. Gift of Kay Beck, 1954.

3536. MacGregor, Charles. **Olive K. Cruikshank, 1931.** 94.3 x 68.6 cm. Loc: MSC. UG900.185.

An oil painting on canvas of Cruikshank who was Director of Macdonald Institute from 1920 to 1948. Part of the University of Guelph Art Collection. Presented by the Class of 1931, Macdonald Institute, 1931.

3537. MacGregor, Charles. **Wade Toole, 1930.** 120 x 97.3 cm. Loc: MSC. UG900.188.

An oil painting on canvas of Toole who was Professor of Animal Husbandry from 1918 to 1928 at the Ontario Agricultural College. Part of the University of Guelph Art Collection. Gift of the Class of 1924, Ontario Agricultural College,

1930.

3538. Mackie, Stella O. **Edward A.A. Grange, 1937**. 68.9 x 58.6 cm. Loc: MSC. UG900.192.

An oil painting on canvas of Grange who lived from 1848 to 1921, was a lecturer at the Ontario Agricultural College from 1874 to 1881, and was Principal of the Ontario Veterinary College from 1908 to 1918. The artist, Mackie, was born in England and was active in Ottawa c1935. Part of the University of Guelph Art Collection. Gift of the Ontario Veterinary College Alumni and Friends, 1927.

3539. March, Edward. **George C. Creelman, 1928**. 49.5 x 40" Loc: MSC. UG900.194.

An oil painting on canvas of Creelman, with the OAC crest on the top right. The plaque reads, 'G.C. Creelman/BSA, MS, LLD'/President 1904-1920/Presented by OAC Alumni 1928'. Creelman was born in 1869 in Collingwood, Ontario and entered OAC as a student in 1885. He later taught biology at the Agricultural and Mechanical College of Mississipi and became Superintendent of Farmer's Institutes in 1899. He was President of OAC from 1904 to 1920, and died in 1929. Part of the University of Guelph Art Collection. Presented by the OAC class of 1928 in 1928.

3540. March, Edward. **Katherine T. Fuller, 1928**. 37 x 27.25 ins. Loc: MSC. UG900.195.

An oil painting on canvas of Fuller with a plaque that reads, 'Katherine T. Fuller/Superintendent of/Macdonald Hall/1904-1931'. Fuller died August 16, 1938. Part of the University of Guelph Art Collection. Presented by the Macdonald Institute 1928 class, 1928.

3541. McConnell, M. Cary. **David W. Wardrope, c1870**. 34.5 x 44.5 inches. Loc: MSC. UG973.005.

An oil painting on canvas of Wardrope who who was born in Berwick Scotland in 1823 and emigrated with his family in 1834 to a farm in Puslinch Township . He died in Teeswater, Ontario in 1911. His brother, Thomas, was possibly Rev. Thomas Wardrope, minister of Chalmers Presbyterian Church in Guelph from 1869 to 1892. The artist, McConnell, was born in Blyth, Huron County of United Empire Loyalist heritage, and studied under M.E. Dignam and later in New York, Paris and Holland. In 1939 she was living in Bailey's Bay, Bermuda. Part of the University of Guelph Art Collection. Gift of Mr H.A. Dyde, 1973.

3542. Moncrieff, Alexander. **Rockwood, 1857**. 18 x 26.2 cm. Loc: ROM. 981.67.5.

A watercolour over pencil with touches of gouache inscribed, 'Rock Wood', and on a cut piece of leaf retained from album, 'Canada, 1857'. The picture depicts a river scene with a man on a wharf fishing in the foreground and a view of the bridge and town in the background. Part of the Sigmund Samuel Canadiana Collection. Purchased from John Howell Books, San Francisco, California.

3543. Napier, William H.E. **Woodlands, c1855**. 24.1 x 30 cm. Loc: MSC. UG980.003.

A watercolour with pencil of the stone residence and farmstead of Thomas Saunders in Puslinch Township, built in 1846. Napier grew up in Quebec where he trained as a civil engineer under Walter Shanly. He worked on various canal building projects in the United States, and was later employed on the Grand Trunk Railway. His precise watercolour style reflects his training in topographical drafting. Part of the University of Guelph Art Collection. Gift of the Florence G. Partridge Fund and Wintario, selected in consultation with the College of Arts, 1980.

3544. **Opening of the Wellington, Grey and Bruce Railway, c1870**. 22.9 x 34.3 cm. Loc: ROM. 957.186.5.

A coloured engraving incribed, 'Fergus, Ontario, 1870'. The scene depicts the train and station decked with boughs and flags, a red-coated band and a large crowd across the tracks. The engraving was reproduced in the Canadian Illustrated News, October 8, 1870. Part of the Sigmund Samuel Canadiana Collection.

3545. Pasfield, Donald Hessleton. **Back of old Johnston's Hall, c1933**. 14 x 20.6 cm. Loc: MSC. UG900.382.

A pen and ink sketch signed, 'D.H. Pasfield '35'. The sketch was reproduced in the OAC Review in 1933. Pasfield graduated with a Diploma in Agriculture from OAC in 1934, and lived for a time in Surrey, England. The 1935 date referred to in the inscription is possibly the intended date of his graduation from the college. Part of the University of Guelph Art Collection. Gift of the artist, 1933.

3546. Pasfield, Donald Hessleton. **The darkened forge, c1933**. 12.7 x 21.6 cm. Loc: MSC. UG900.382.

A pen and ink sketch of a blacksmith's forge that was identified by Gordon Couling as being located on the corner of Gordon and Wellington Streets in Guelph. Part of the University of Guelph Art Collection. Gift of the artist, 1933.

3547. Raymond, Helen Gill. **Mrs Sarah Gill, c1890**. 76.3 x 63.6 cm. Loc: MSC. UG980.009.

An oil painting on canvas of Gill who lived in Boston from 1787 to 1855. Raymond, the artist, was the daughter of Sarah Gill and the second wife of Charles Raymond. The painting is inscribed, 'from estate of Charles Raymond Sewing Machine Co., Guelph'. Part of the Macdonald Stewart Art Centre Collection. Gift of the Guelph Creative Arts Association, 1980. It was originally presented by Mrs. Greta Shutt, the grand-daughter of Charles Raymond.

3548. Revilo. **Mills Hall, c1933**. 9 x 10.27 cm. Loc: MSC. UGB900.094.

An etching of Mills Hall signed, 'Revilo Mills Hall'. Part of the University of Guelph Art Collection. Gift of Mr. R.S. Vair, 1974.

3549. Scarlett, Rolph. **Eramosa Silo, c1912**. 84 x 71.2 cm. Loc: MSC. UG977.091.

An oil painting on canvas which depicts a barn with a small silo in the foreground. Part of the University of Guelph Art Collection. Gift of the artist, 1977.

3550. Scarlett, Rolph. **Gordon Street Bridge, c1912**. 66.8 x 73.9 cm. Loc: MSC. UG977.090.

An oil painting on canvas that depicts the bridge crossing the Speed River at Gordon Street, with a house and barn on the right. Part of the University of Guelph Art Collection. Gift of the artist, 1977.

3551. Schell, R.B. **Guelph, 1882**. 17 x 16.4 cm. Loc: MSC. UGB900.097.
A wood engraving by W. Mollier with hand colouring applied taken from a pen and ink sketch by Schell. The city scene includes Knox, St Andrew's and St George's Churches on the right, Norfolk Church and Central School in the centre and the Church of Our Lady on the left. The print was cut from George Munro Grant's edited book, Picturesque Canada: The Country as it Was and Is, Volume 2, 1882, p. 469. Part of the University of Guelph Art Collection. Gift of Judith Nasby, 1974.

3552. Scheuer, W. **View of Guelph, 1874**. 23.1 x 35 cm. Loc: MSC. UG979.008.
A hand coloured lithograph of the town that was taken from the Canadian Illustrated News, January 24, 1874, p. 52. Scheuer was active as an artist from 1873 to 1883. Part of the University of Guelph Art Collection. Gift of Professor and Mrs Cameron Mann.

3553. Scroggie, Martha Ann. **Bridge and church, c1889-1905**. 30.5 x 45.5 cm. Loc: MSC. MS981.021.
An untitled oil painting on canvas done c1889-1905 depicting St George's Church on the right, and the foot bridge crossing the Speed River. 'Matt' Scroggie lived at 15 Oxford Street and was an art teacher, probably at Central School. She painted landscapes, still life subjects and portraits in both oils and watercolours. Part of the Macdonald Stewart Art Centre Collection. Bequest of Mr Innes M. Allen, 1981.

3554. Scroggie, Martha Ann. **Bridge, c1889-1905**. 17.75 x 30.25 cm. Loc: MSC. MS981.022.
An untitled oil painting on canvas of the stone bridge crossing the Speed River from McCrae Street to Wellington Street in Guelph. Part of the Macdonald Stewart Art Centre Collection. Bequest of Mr Innes M. Allen, 1981.

3555. Seavey, Julian R. **View of Elora**. 16 x 12 " Loc: ROM. 968.263.
A watercolour over pencil with touches of gouache on linen weave paper mounted on board. Inscribed, 'Elora' and signed 'J.R. Seavey'. The scene shows the Grand River and the backs of the houses along Mill Street. Part of the Sigmund Samuel Canadiana Collection. Purchased from Mr. Hugh Anson-Cartwright.

3556. Shaw, D.A. **Lime kiln, Rockwood, Ontario, 1896**. 5.25 x 8.5 " Loc: ROM. 969.120.4.
A watercolour over black pencil inscribed, 'D.A.Shaw '86'. On the back is inscribed,'Lime Kiln, Rockwood, Ontario'. The picture depicts a stone and board building on the side of a hill. Part of the Sigmund Samuel Canadiana Collection. Purchased from Sotheby and Co (Can) Ltd.

3557. Smith, Effie. **Riverside Park, Guelph, c1908**. 12 x 16.5 cm. Loc: MSC. UG988.022.
A watercolour inscribed, 'Riverside Park, Guelph about 1908/artist, Effie Smith. Guelph/from Mother and Dad's home. August 1959. (sale of our home that year)/Margaret Hales Starkey./Dick restored this/picture for me/Marg'. Smith was born in Cumberland, Ontario in 1867, came to Guelph in 1877, and later studied in Hamilton Ontario and at Dischoff-Auleck's in Chicago. She did china painting until 1935 and then began oil, watercolour and charcoal sketches, specializing in flowers. Part of the University of Guelph Art Collection. Gift

of Mrs. Margaret Hales Starkey, 1988.

3558. Staples, Owen. **St Georges Church, Guelph, Ontario, c1928**. 38.4 x 28.2 cm. Loc: ROM. 976.209.12.

An etching of the interior of the church inscribed, 'St George Church, Guelph, Ontario', and signed 'Owen Staples'. The etching was printed in the Journal of Royal Architectural Institute of Canada in 1928. Part of the Sigmund Samuel Canadiana Collection. Gift of Misses Dorothy and Madeline Staples, Toronto, Ontario.

3559. **View from Allan's Bridge up the River Speed, Guelph, c1873**. 58.1 x 70.8 cm. Loc: MSC. UG972.012.

An unsigned oil painting which includes a view of St George's Church and the Priory Bath House on the left side of the river. Part of the University of Guelph Art Collection. Gift of Phyllis Higinbotham, 1972.

3560. Whitefield, Edwin. **Michigan and Ontario sketchbook, 1863-1865**. 68 leaves. Loc: ROM. 955.215.2.

The sketch book contains a pen and ink sketch of Guelph City Hall and Market Square, stores at the end of Carden Street, and the Fire Hall and Jones Hotel south of City Hall. The sketches were done by Whitefield during a Michigan and Ontario tour from 1863 to 1865 and include two views of Fergus. Part of the Sigmund Samuel Canadiana Collection. Purchased from Mrs Flora Ramsay.

3561. Wyle, Florence. **Shepherd boy holding a lamb, 1928**. 86.7 x 24.8 x 26.2 cm. Loc: MSC. UG900.321.

A bronze sculpture of the son of Wade Toole, John Toole, who later died at an early age. It became known as the 'Wade Toole Memorial Trophy' and is presented to the winning exhibit at the annual College Royal competition held at the Ontario Agricultural College. Wade Toole was Professor of Animal Husbandry from 1918 to 1928. Florence Wyle originally studied science at the University of Illinois in prepartion for a career in medicine, but left to pursue a career as an artist. She emigrated to Canada in 1913, after studying at the Chicago Art Institute under C.J. Mulligan and Lorado Tuft. In 1928, she helped found the Sculptors' Society of Canada. Her early training for the medical profession influenced her style which emphasized structure, correct anatomy and classical form. She was appointed a Royal Canadian Academician in 1938. Part of the University of Guelph Art Collection. Presented by the staff and students of the Ontario Agricultural College in memory of Professor Wade Toole, founder of the College Royal, 1930.

Guelph Mills, the property of D. Allan. Esq., 1873:
lithograph by Eugene Haberer from the <u>Canadian Illustrated News</u>
(#3500). (Macdonald Stewart Art Centre)

INSTITUTE PICNIC AT THE WATSON FARM.

1900 near Clifford

A learned celebration: an Institute picnic held at the Watson farm near Clifford, 1900. The gathering was sponsored by a Women's Institute or Farmers' and Mechanics' Institute. Women's Institutes have been responsible for collecting historical information for Tweedsmuir histories of local regions. (Wellington County Museum and Archives)

COMPILATIONS AND COLLECTIONS

As Royce MacGillivray has remarked, 'what is popular in local history is the fun of the research, the writing and the publishing -- not the reading of the published material afterwards.'[1] Some local historians, indeed, are so reluctant to leave the research stage that they may die before writing up or publishing any of the work that has absorbed them for years. Other groups or individuals may have been more interested in collecting than in interpreting local historical records. Fortunately in some cases, collections of documents, photographs, photocopies or transcriptions of original materials, scrapbooks of newspaper clippings and other ephemera may be given to local historical societies, libraries and archives and thus become accessible to later researchers.

This section of the **Inventory** lists compilations, collections and surveys which either never reached publication or were the by-products of published works in local history. It also contains entries for most of the named collections of records in the Guelph Public Library, University of Guelph Library's Archival and Special Collections and Wellington County Archives. Many of these are 'artificial' collections in the sense that they were not generated routinely by a corporate body or by a person or family. Instead a person or agency gathered and arranged materials relating to their own time or an earlier period according to some interest or objective.

Individual items of these collections may have been separately recorded in the earlier sections dealing with the records of municipalities, businesses, families, churches or voluntary associations. Users should be aware of the selective bias of some of these collections and compilations, that items have been removed from their original context by the compilers, and that they may have been inaccurately or inadequately dated or explained. But on some topics it may well be necessary to consult these records as they are all that survive.

Wellington County has attracted the interest of a fair number of local historians from quite early times and some of these have left collections of their research materials as well as their publications. Notable among these are A.E. Byerly, John Connon and J.C. Templin, whose collections are dispersed among several repositories. Later writers of local history who have presented their preliminary compilations and notes include Pat Mestern on Fergus, Patricia Kortland on Hillsburgh, and Paul O'Donnel and Frank Coffee on Arthur, all of these to the Wellington County Archives.

A.E. Byerly was an osteopath from Iowa who came to Fergus in 1921, then to Guelph in 1924. He wrote articles on local and regional history for county newspapers and the **London Free Press** and published at least fourteen

---

[1] Royce MacGillivray, 'Local history as a form of popular culture in Ontario,' **New York History** (October 1984): 367-376.

works, notably his **History of Lower Nichol** (1930), **Fergus: or the Fergusson-Webster settlement** (1934), and **The beginnings of things in Waterloo and Wellington counties** (1935). He also left collections of materials on many topics that are now dispersed among in the Archives of Ontario, the Guelph Public Library, the University of Guelph Library Archives and the Wellington County Archives.

John Connon and his father Thomas were Elora photographers and inventors. After his father's death in 1899 John devoted himself to local history, eventually publishing **The early history of Elora and vicinity** (1930). There are Connon collections of local history materials in the University of Guelph Archives and the Wellington County Archives; another Connon collection in the Archives of Ontario is more concerned with the development and significance of the Connons' photography business.

Hugh Templin, whose father purchased the **Fergus News Record** in 1902 and remained proprietor and editor until his death in 1939, published **Fergus: the story of a little town** in 1933. The Templin Family Collection at the Archives of Ontario, that consists of four boxes of scrapbooks, correspondence, manuscript notes and ephemera, should be distinguished from the Templin family and business records in the Templin-Dow Collection at the Wellington County Archives.

The Guelph Public Library is particularly rich in collections of this kind. Hugh Douglass, a teacher of history, Verne McIlwraith, a journalist and Greta Shutt, a member of the Guelph Board of Education for many years, wrote articles, particularly about Guelph, for newspapers and journals. They also compiled and left large collections of local history materials on many topics.

The McIlwraith Collection comprises 36 boxes of copies of McIlwraith's historical columns in the **Guelph Mercury**, newspaper clippings, notes and other items. The Douglass Collection consists of an unpublished Annals of Guelph in five volumes and a large number of envelopes of articles, newspaper clippings, genealogies, obituaries, biographies, a bibliography, and transcriptions of original records relating to the history of Guelph and Elora. We are especially indebted to Douglass for transcribing many records of early school history, the originals of which have since been lost. The Shutt Collection includes correspondence, newspaper clippings and historical and genealogical sketches on various aspects of the history of Guelph, especially those with which Greta Shutt had some personal or family connection.

Professor Gordon Couling left two large collections of materials of all kinds of materials on the architectural history of the area. The Couling Collection at the Wellington County Archives includes 12,000 colour transparencies showing buildings in Guelph and Wellington County; there are further materials on local buildings among his more personal and professional records in the University of Guelph Archives.

Other local collections include the Hammill Collection of biographies and Guelph houses, the Higinbotham Collection on Guelph history, and the Brimmell Collection of Guelph school history at the Guelph Public Library; the Isabel Burr Cunningham scrapbooks at the Wellington County Archives; the H.B.

Timothy Collection of materials relating to John Galt in the University of Guelph Archives; and the Marston Collection of miscellaneous historical materials on Elora at the Archives of Ontario. In addition, the four main record repositories in the region have created collections of particular types of of records on specific topics; these are listed in this section except for photographs which have their own section.

Also included in this section are the inventories and indexes produced by the members of the Waterloo-Wellington chapter of the Ontario Genealogical Society, an organization which has been very active during the past decade.[2] These compilations consist mainly of transcribed cemetery records for most burial places in the county. But this members of this group have also indexed births, deaths and marriages reported in some church records and local newspapers. As part of a large provincial project, they have created machine-readable indexes to the manuscript household schedules of the 1871 Census of Canada for each township, town and village. Printed versions of these indexes are beginning to appear.

Historical societies and historical research projects have produced some compilations about the city or region. This section includes sets of material collected or sponsored by the Wellington County Historical Society (1925-1936), the Wellington County Historical Research Society (1928-   ) and the Guelph Historical Society (1961-   ). Two historical research projects, based at the University of Guelph, have deposited their records in the University of Guelph Archives. These are the Wellington County Project of the 1970s and the Guelph Regional Project, 1987-9, which has compiled this **Inventory** and the companion **Bibliography**.

---

[2] Ryan Taylor, **Family research in Waterloo and Wellington Counties** (Kitchener: Waterloo-Wellington Branch, Ontario Genealogical Society, 1986).

COMPILATIONS AND COLLECTIONS

3562. Allan-Higinbotham Collection. **Correspondence, business records, diaries and photographs, 1834-1955.** 21 boxes, 1 oversize file. Loc: UGA. XRI MS A005, Itemized list of contents.

A collection of correspondence, business records, land records, diaries, photographs, scrapbooks and estate papers of the Allan-Higinbotham family. William and David Allan operated Allan's Mill in Guelph. David's daughter, Margaret, married Nathaniel Higinbotham.

3563. Archives of Ontario. **Wellington County. Members elected to Ontario Legislature, 1792-1926.** 1 file folder. Loc: AO. MU 2099, Misc. Coll. 1792 #3.

A compilation by the Department of Public Records and Archives of all persons elected to represent Wellington County, in response to a request by Mr McIntosh of Guelph. The document also defines and explains the changing electoral areas in and around Wellington County. For the elections between 1902 and 1926, numbers of votes cast for all candidates are also specified.

3564. Arthur History Book Collection. **Source materials on Arthur and district, 1855-1971.** 2 boxes. Loc: WCA. List of document contents.

A collection of sources consulted by Paul O'Donnel and Frank Coffee in writing the book, Portrait: A History of the Arthur Area (1971). The Wellington County Archives has developed a detailed finding aid.

3565. Beattie Collection. **Correspondence, land records and financial records, 1836-1942.** 3 boxes. Loc: WCA. FA: MU 23,24,33.

A collection of correspondence, land and financial records generated by Beattie family members and Beattie's Banking House in Fergus.

3566. Beattie, David. **Mount Pleasant Methodist Church, Lower Nichol, 1967.** 7 p. typescript. Loc: AO. FA: MU 2956.

An account of the founding of the rural church from the early 1850s to the decision to disband in 1927. The church was located near S.S.#4 Nichol, on a lot given by Henry Metcalf and was part of a three-point charge with Bethany and Marden, and later of the Ponsonby-Nichol Circuit. The Metcalf and Flewelling families were longtime members of the church. The church minute book was reported to be in the care of Mrs E.H. Tolton of Guelph in 1967. Part of the Templin Family Collection.

3567. Blyth Collection. **Invoices from Guelph businesses, 1875-1895.** 20 file folders, 13 envelopes. Loc: WCA. MU62.

A collection of invoices from Guelph businesses to R. Forbes and Company in Hespeler. Guelph companies include Auld and Woodyatt Company, Guelph Soap Company, Guelph Carriage Goods Company, Guelph Carpet Works, Guelph and Ontario Investment and Savings Society, and J.B. Armstrong Manufacturing Company.

3568. Brimmell Collection. **Guelph's early school history: public schools, Collegiate Institute and Collegiate Vocational Institute, 1827-1927.** 1 binder. Loc: GPL.

A reprint of the school history article in the July 20, 1927 centennial edition of the Guelph Mercury. The article gives a detailed account of the development of Guelph schools, boards, teachers and administrators. The second part of the binder is a history of the Guelph Collegiate Institute written by Mrs C.R. Crowe.

3569. Broadfoot, Mary. **Ennotville articles, 1929-c1950.** 3 items. Loc: WCA. MU 107.
Two articles are on the Ennotville Library, one published in the Ontario Library Review in 1929, the other a longer manuscript marking the centennial of the library in 1947. The third article is Ennotville Sabbath School, a story of pioneer days in Nichol Township.

3570. Broadfoot, Mary. **History of area of S.S.#3, Nichol Township, c1937.** ms, 78 p. Loc: WCA. 978.30.
An account of early settlement in the Lower Nichol area that includes a list of settlers from an assessment roll and details of school teachers, students, trustees and superintendents.

3571. Burr, Isabel Cunningham. **Melville Presbyterian Church, Fergus. Programs, history, 1847-1945.** 1 file folder. Loc: WCA. Detailed list of contents.
A collection of four programs for anniversary services and several handwritten histories of the church. Part of the Isabel Cunningham Burr Collection.

3572. Burr, Isabel Cunningham. **Scrapbooks, 1895-1965.** 6 volumes. Loc: WCA. Detailed list of contents.
A collection of historical articles, poems and newspaper clippings of restored historical buildings. Burr was a researcher for the Wellington County Historical Research Society. Part of the Isabel Cunningham Burr Collection.

3573. Byerly, A.E. **Biographies and obituaries of prominent Guelph and Wellington County residents, 1832-1928.** 2 envelopes. Loc: GPL. Envelopes 1 and 1B.
A number of biographies and obituaries of prominent residents of Guelph, Elora, Drayton and the Townships of Eramosa and Pilkington. Part of the Byerly Collection.

3574. Byerly, A.E. **Historical sketches of Elora, 1931.** Loc: AO. FA; MU 455.
A collection of six articles published in the Elora Express between February and September, 1931. Part of Byerly Papers.

3575. Byerly, A.E. **History of Norfolk Street Methodist Church, Guelph, 1827-1840.** 1 document. Loc: GPL. Envelope 3.
A history of the church, handwritten by A.E. Byerly, highlighting the key role of Reverend James Evans and John Maclean in the congregation. The work notes the work of early Methodist missionaries important in the development of the church in Guelph and other areas. Part of the Byerly Collection.

3576. Byerly, A.E. **Miscellaneous papers on Fergus and Wellington County, 1819-1940.** 2 boxes. Loc: AO. FA; MU 454-455.
Dr Byerly, who came from the U.S. to Fergus in 1921 and Guelph in 1924, was 'indefatigable in searching out the historic past' of Wellington County and nearby areas. As well as writing histories himself, he collected historical materials of considerable volume and variety. The collection is organized chronologically. Items relevant to Wellington County are separately indexed in this inventory.

3577. Byerly Collection. **Correspondence, articles and manuscript notes, 1830-1937.** 1 box. Loc: UGA. XR1 MS A264.

Memorabilia from the A.E. Byerly estate and historical items relating to Odd Fellows Progress Lodge No. 156, Guelph Business College, Knox Presbyterian Church in Guelph, Guelph St Andrew's Society ribbons, several advertisements for local businesses and a 1934 election pamphlet.

3578. Byerly Collection. **Correspondence, articles, biographies and Guelph memorabilia, 1827-1940.** 21 envelopes. Loc: GPL. List of contents.
A collection of biographies, obituaries, correspondence, land deeds, newspaper clippings from Byerly's 'Our History' column, newspaper issues and notes about Guelph and area local history.

3579. Byerly Collection. **Guelph and Wellington County. Historical notes, pamphlets, 1827-1938.** 1 file folder, oversized. Loc: UGA. XR1 MS A264.
A series of clippings written in the 1930s outlining the early history of Guelph and Wellington County. The file also includes an election circular for the year 1934, two brochures of the Guelph Oddfellows dated 1932 and 1933, and a pamphlet commemorating the 100th anniversary of Knox Presbyterian Church in Guelph.

3580. Byerly Collection. **History of Wellington County, 1820-1940.** 17 envelopes. Loc: GPL. List of document contents; Envelopes 6A, 6B, 7, 7A, 7B, 7Ci, 7Cii, 7D, 7E, 7F, 7G, 8, 9, 9B, 9C, 10 and 11.
Notes, newspaper issues and clippings dealing with the settlement and subsequent history of the townships in the county. The finding aid provides specific dates and titles of documents held in a series of file folders. The documents outline the history of several areas including Salem, Guelph, Drayton, Stirton, Elora, Fergus, Peel Township and Eramosa Township. One report by Byerly discusses the settlement of Blacks in Peel Township in the 1840s.

3581. Byerly Collection. **Miscellaneous correspondence by Guelph residents, 1864-1925.** 2 envelopes. Loc: GPL. Envelopes 2 and 5.
Correspondence written by Guelph residents in which some of the writing is illegible. The file includes a letter written by Reverend W.F. Clarke in 1864 resigning his post as editor of The Canada Farmer and hoping to resume his position as a minister in Guelph in 1865.

3582. Byerly Collection. **Newspaper Clippings. Guelph and Toronto newspapers, 1870-1890.** 1 volume. Loc: WCA.
A collection of newspaper clippings of Guelph and Toronto newspapers describing political, economic and social events in Guelph. Subjects include the Raymond Employees Mutual Benefit Society. Unfortunately the clippings are undated in most instances.

3583. Byerly Papers. **Elora Merchants. Miscellaneous advertisements, 1868.** Loc: AO. FA: MU 455.

3584. Clarke Collection. **Correspondence, manuscripts and photographs, 1865-1916.** 2 boxes. Loc: WCA. FA.
A collection of family records of Charles Clarke who was active in local Elora politics, newspaper and militia.

3585. Cleghorn, Catharine. **Programs and certificates, 1906-1926 (sporadic).** 1 envelope. Loc: WCA. MU 78; Detailed list of contents.

A collection of concert programs of various Guelph clubs and institutions, including Griffin's Opera House, Guelph Operatic Club, St Andrew's Society Annual Concert, Guelph Burns Club Annual Dinner, Dublin Street Methodist Church Choir Concert, Chalmers Presbyterian Church Choir Concert, GCVI annual commencement and a high school entrance certificate. Part of the Laird Collection.

3586. Connon Collection. **Land records, Elora, 1851; 1871.** 2 documents. Loc: UGA. XR1 MS A115001.

One land petition document of Robert Gilkison dated 1851 and one indenture of land to be leased by W.H. LaPenotiere and Walter P. Newman dated 1871. The documents are held in the section of the Connon Collection entitled 'Miscellaneous history notes'.

3587. Connon, John. **Clippings of history of Elora, 1832-1930.** 3 boxes, 1 oversize file folder. Loc: UGA. XR1 MS A332.

The newspaper articles are dated from the 1870s to the early twentieth century and include historical sketches, biographies of prominent area residents and obituaries of Elora residents. The records include notes kept by John Connon that were later used in his book, History of Elora. Held with the Connon Collection.

3588. Connon, John. **Miscellaneous notes of the history of Elora and area, 1827-1930.** 2 boxes. Loc: UGA. XR1 MS A115001.

A large number of files of notes composed by John Connon which includes family histories, biographies of well-known Wellington County residents, notes of property assessments of early Elora residents, copies of various articles relating to the history of Wellington County and some notes regarding the history of Elora churches. The notes undoubtedly served as the basis for John Connon's history of Elora published in 1930. Held with the Connon Collection.

3589. Connon, John. Notes. **John Connon's history of Elora and vicinity, 1834-1934.** 1 envelope. Loc: WCA. MU 43.

A collection of photocopies of notes of John Connon utilized in the writing of his book, History of Elora and Vicinity.

3590. Couling Collection. **Photographs, newspaper clippings, commentary, 1820-1985.** 16 boxes, 10 slide containers. Loc: WCA. Detailed list of contents.

A collection of newspaper clippings, photographs, drawings, commentary and brochures relating to the architectural history of Wellington County. The collection is organized into binders by township and concession number of lots. There is a detailed study of Guelph, part of which is organized chronologically, part by street name or institution name, and biographical information of some area families. Also included are lecture notes on area architecture and an extensive slide collection that contains about 12,000 architectural views of Wellington County.

3591. Couling, Gordon. **Photographs, sketches, slides and biography, 1920-1985.** 19 boxes. Loc: UGA. Itemized inventory.

The collection includes biographical details, photographs, sketch books, resource files, slides and other memorabilia relating to Couling's work as a Guelph painter, stained glass artist and local art historian. Newly acquired material includes Couling's sketches of O.A.C. buildings, Guelph, his military career in Vancouver and abstracts. Six binders contain personal files for a book manuscript, and photographs of local architecture and Guelph sculptures. Two binders contain personal biographical details and family photographs. Also included are his research notes for an article he published on local stone masons. These records comprise the Couling Collection.

3592. Doon Heritage Crossroads. **Miscellaneous receipts, 1864-1868; 1885.** Loc: DHC. Computer printout of individual holdings.

A collection of receipts relating to Guelph businesses, mainly in the mid-1860s. Merchants or clients names include John L. Lewis and Brechbill and McFarlane. Some receipts mention the Guelph Commercial Market.

3593. Douglass Collection. **Articles, genealogies, biographies and correspondence, 1827-1965.** 25 envelopes. Loc: GPL. List of contents.

A collection of articles and newspaper clippings on Guelph and Elora history, genealogies, biographies, Guelph church histories, handcopied historical documents of schools and social events, several area maps, Douglass' extensive personal bibliography on local history and local history memorabilia.

3594. Douglass Collection. **Correspondence, 1827; 1836; 1838; 1922.** Loc: GPL. Envelope 2.

Copies of an 1838 letter to Fleming Hewitt from H.W. Peterson telling of the character and personal politics of John Howitt; an 1836 letter to Alexander Stewart from Daniel Stewart recounting his life in Eramosa; and an 1827 letter to Janet Dunlop Cathcart from Alexander Dunlop about his journey to Guelph with John Galt. Douglass has also copied several letters to John Connon about early settlers.

3595. Douglass Collection. **Elora Observer. Miscellaneous clippings, 1870-1872.** 1 envelope. Loc: GPL. Envelope 6.

Handwritten reproduction of clippings of poems, advertisements, Elora Baseball Club, auditor's report of Village of Elora, declaration of a public holiday, list of buildings erected in Elora in 'the present season' and other miscellaneous items.

3596. Douglass Collection. **Guelph and Wellington County Schools. Reports of administrators, 1849-1888.** 8 volumes. Loc: GPL. List of contents.

A copy of original reports of the administrators of Guelph schools which name teachers hired, discuss important issues confronting the school board, and in some years list students writing examinations. The reports also outline subjects to be taught in schools, and refer to schools operating in various parts of the county. The school records are held in the same volumes as reports by Douglass of the history of Wellington County.

3597. Douglass Collection. **Guelph Mercury Clippings. Handwritten copies, photographs, 1876-1877; 1882; 1884-1885; 1889-1891; 1902; 1907; 1958-1964.** 14 volumes. Loc: GPL.

A collection of newspaper clippings from the 'Thirty Years Ago' column in the Mercury. The photographs are clipped from the 'Pictorial Flashback' feature of the newspaper from 1958 to 1964.

3598. Douglass Collection. **Guelph Schools. History, correspondence, minutes, 1847-1957.** 1 envelope. Loc: GPL. Envelope 15.
The collection includes handwritten copies of articles in the 1906 and 1927 Mercury, the 1847 Toronto Globe, Guelph School Board minutes for 1857, a list of headmasters at the Guelph Grammar School from 1844 to 1855, which was later named Guelph Collegiate Institute, and head teachers for the Senior Girls' School from 1858 to 1869, which was later named Alexandra School.

3599. Douglass Collection. **Industry and Commerce. History, 1864-1954.** 1 envelope. Loc: GPL. Envelope 10.
The collection includes a brief historical sketch of the Bell Piano and Organ Company.

3600. Douglass Collection. **Laura Lemon Heath. Biography, correspondence, musical score, photographs, 1911-1973.** 1 envelope. Loc: GPL. Envelope 8.
The folder contains several biographies of Heath who lived from 1866 to 1924. The collection includes a list of her compositions, and several letters by Heath's daughters discussing their mother and her work.

3601. Douglass Collection. **Leone Hinds' Hotels and Taverns. Plans and correspondence, 1833-1965.** 1 envelope. Loc: GPL. Envelope 9.
The collection includes a list of the taxpayers of Guelph in 1852, and a hand-drawn copy of Donald McDonald's 1833 plan of Guelph that extends from St Andrew's Church in the Market Square in the west, Dublin Street in the north, Norwich Street in the east and the Speed River.

3602. Douglass Collection. **Miscellaneous. Genealogies, obituaries, newspaper clippings, correspondence, photographs, local histories, 1827-1965.** 4 envelopes. Loc: GPL. Envelopes 1, 2, 3 and 7.
A collection of various genealogies and obituaries of Guelph families, newspaper and journal articles on Guelph people and architecture. It includes mention of Charles Raymond, David Allan, Margaret Allan, Nathaniel Higinbotham, John Higinbotham, Anna Torrance, James Gay, Mary Leslie and Laura Lemon Heath.

3603. Douglass Collection. **Notes and handcopied historical documents, 1828-1961.** 1 envelope. Loc: GPL. Envelope 16.
A diverse collection of notes and newpaper clippings of historical interest, including an obituary of Rev. John Holzer, a history of the Scotch Block and a copy of a short article by George Sleeman entitled 'The Maple Leaf Baseball Club of Guelph, Ontario, Canada: Strictly Amateur'.

3604. Douglass Collection. **Receipts, 1925-1933.** 1 envelope. Loc: GPL. Envelope 13.
A collection of receipts issued to Day Brothers Contractors by various shops in Guelph, including the Guelph Lumber Company, the People's Cooperative, the Mercury and Crowe's Iron Works.

3605. Douglass Collection. **Scrapbooks. Guelph advertisements, 1888-1919.** 1 envelope. Loc: GPL. Envelope 17.
A collection of miscellaneous newspaper clipping advertisements filed in no apparent order. Many are undated.

3606. Douglass, Hugh. **Annals of Guelph, 1827-1967.** 5 3-ring binders. Loc: GPL. Chronologically by year.

An historical sketch of the history of Guelph and Wellington County which includes references to political, social, religious and economic aspects of the history of the county. The annals often indicate that the sources of information were from articles written in early Guelph newspapers and directories. Part of the Douglass Collection.

3607. Douglass, Hugh. **La Guayra immigrants.** ms, 9 p. Loc: GPL. 82.00.

An account of the arrival of the LaGuayran settlers in 1827 that includes details of their names and the concessions and lots they settled in Guelph Township.

3608. Douglass, Hugh. **Register of interments in Guelph Woodlawn Cemetery, 1854-1871.** 1 file folder. Loc: GPL.

A list of interments arranged chronologically listing date, name and cemetery lot and block number.

3609. Douglass, Hugh. **Reports of the history of Guelph, 1820-1890.** 4 volumes. Loc: GPL.

A series of reports copied from Guelph 19th century newspapers by Hugh Douglass that highlight building projects, the timing of the opening of schools, and include narratives of the early history of Wellington County. Dates of newspaper articles that were the basis of information in the reports are stated. The reports include several biographies of Guelph notables and list architects of public and residential buildings. The reports are held in the same volumes as the records of Guelph school administrators. Part of the Douglass Collection.

3610. Drayton Advocate. **Scrapbook. Historical sketches of Drayton, 1892-1903.** 1 volume. Loc: UGA. XR1 MS A140.

A series of undated newspaper clippings dealing with a narrative of key events which appear to have been written in the 1930s. The scrapbook is based upon information taken from articles in the Drayton Advocate. The series was entitled 'Dipping into the past' and includes references to prominent Drayton residents and the range of social, political and economic positions such individuals held.

3611. Durnford, Marjorie. **Historical sketch of Marden area, 1827-1987.** 1 file folder. Loc: WCA. MU 101.

An essay entitled, Looking At My Locality, about the historical development of the Marden area, Guelph and Guelph Township. The essay includes many photographs of local scenery and historical buildings.

3612. Elora Backwoodsman. **Elora. Births, deaths and marriages, 1852-1853.** 1 document. Loc: GPL.

A typescript of extracts taken from the newspaper, Elora Backwoodsman, of area births, deaths and marriages.

3613. Elora Land Records Collection. **Business and family papers, 1867-1905.** 25 file folders. Loc: WCA. List of document contents.

A collection of business, financial, legal and land records of residents of Elora that were stored and donated by the Village of Elora. The Wellington

County Archives has developed a detailed finding aid that notes the contents, date and names of individuals involved in specific transactions.

3614. Elora Land Records Collection. **Land records, 1826-1903.** 1 box. Loc: WCA. FA.
A collection of land records donated by the municipality of Elora. The records are arranged alphabetically by street name in Elora and by township. Townships include Arthur, Garafraxa, Luther, Maryborough, Minto, Nichol, Peel and Pilkington. The collection also includes records from several local families and businesses in Elora including the Elora Agricultural Machine Company, Elora Skating and Curling Rink Company, the Merchants Bank, Newman Brothers and the Reliance Loan and Savings Company.

3615. Ennotville Women's Institute. **Tweedsmuir history, 1914-1947.** 1 binder. Loc: EL, WCA, GPL.
The original is held by the Ennotville Library. Microfilm copies are held by Wellington County Archives and Guelph Public Library.

3616. Fergus Women's Institute. **Tweedsmuir history of Fergus, c1833-1952.** 1 reel. mf. Loc: UGA, AO. UGA: XRI MS A192095, Reel #44.
A history of Fergus that includes photographs, newspaper clippings and maps about the area's settlements, churches, schools, libraries, industries, newspapers, fraternal associations, sports and the region's war record.

3617. Ferguson Collection. **Photographs, insurance policies and receipts, 1910-1975.** 3 boxes. Loc: WCA. FA: MU 37.
A collection of commercial records generated by Burt Brothers Department Store in Elora from 1910 to 1925 and photographs of Fergus and Elora from 1875 to 1970.

3618. Fischer Collection. **Business records and photographs, 1870-1948.** 2 boxes. Loc: WCA. FA: MU 39.
A collection of burial registers and account ledgers of Christian Fischer's funeral business and dry goods and furniture store in Elora. Following Christian's death in 1919, his son Frank and his brother continued the business under the name Fischer Brothers until retirement in 1948. The collection also contains photographs of Wellington County.

3619. Gilkison-Fraser Collection. **Correspondence, 1832-1895.** 1 box. Loc: UGA. XRI MS A116, Itemized list of contents.
A collection of Gilkison family and business correspondence that includes the organization and management of settlement and business affairs in Brantford, Hamilton and Elora.

3620. Goldie Collection. **Scrapbooks, 1822-1965.** 5 volumes. Loc: GPL. Card index.
A collection of primarily modern, unidentified, newspaper and journal articles about the historical development of Guelph and Wellington County. Some scrapbooks contain a subject index and all have a separate card index arranged alphabetically by subject and name. The card index is entitled 'Goldie Scrapbooks Index'.

3621. Goodwin-Haines Collection. **Guelph Business Correspondence, 1832-1865.** 1 box. Loc: UGA. XRI MS A136001-31.

A collection of correspondence regarding business, property, religious and personal matters. It includes letters from Charles Julius Mickle, Thomas Fisher, Rev. Arthur Palmer, Dr Henry Orton, several to William Hewat from 1842 to 1853 while he was treasurer of Guelph, and a c1839 letter describing the opening of the Congregational Church on Quebec Street. An archival note suggests it was written by C.J. Mickle.

3622. Goodwin-Haines Collection. **Land records and legal records, 1774-1950.** 1 oversized box. Loc: UGA. XRI MS A166, Itemized list of contents.
A collection of crown land records, legal records, military records, historical sketches and correspondence throughout much of southern Ontario. The collection includes the extensive Guelph Business Correspondence file.

3623. Gordon Collection. **Land and military records, 1883-1949.** 4 file folders. Loc: WCA. FA: MU 46.
A collection of land and military records of the Gordon family of Minto Township.

3624. Goulding, William. **Architectural survey of Ontario, 1966-1969.** 25 boxes, 10 reels, 3 boxes photographs. Loc: AO. FA: MS 776.
Survey materials of a project led by Professor Goulding of the University of Toronto School of Architecture. The survey aimed at finding, recording and assessing every building erected before 1855 that was still useable. Another goal was to locate buildings in more isolated districts that had been erected by local craftsmen. Buildings identified in Wellington County were: five in Erin Township (folder 178), twenty-four in Guelph Township (folder 179), twelve in Nichol Township (folder 180) and one hundred and four in Puslinch Township (folders 181 and 182). Each building has been photographed, with details added on address, original and present owner, name of builder, and method of construction. Though the surveyors searched libraries, they were not able to find information on all points.

3625. Guelph C.V.I. Scrapbook. **Life of John McCrae, 1919-1987.** 1 box. Loc: GCI.
The John McCrae Collection consists of newspaper clippings and a letter written in 1919 describing the purpose of the John McCrae scholarship.

3626. Guelph Civic Museum. **Greeting cards, 1909-1916.** 1 box. Loc: GCM.
A collection of cards for various occasions including Christmas, Easter, Valentines, New Years, Mother's Day and calling cards for many Guelph women. The box is entitled, Greeting Cards, Calling Cards and Invitations.

3627. Guelph Civic Museum. **Guelph Genealogy. Vertical file, 1827-1950.** 1 file cabinet drawer. Loc: GCM.
A collection of brief family histories organized alphabetically by names. It includes approximately one hundred family names.

3628. Guelph Civic Museum. **Guelph History. Vertical file, 1827-1950.** 1 file cabinet drawer. Loc: GCM.
A collection of newspaper clippings and articles about the history of Guelph arranged alphabetically by subject, including agriculture, architecture, stores, education, hospitals, military, clubs and societies, churches, sports and special events.

3629. Guelph Civic Museum. **Guelph Industry and Trade. Vertical file, c1860-1970.** 1 file cabinet drawer. Loc: GCM.

A record of prominent industries and mercantile ventures with brief company histories and newspaper clippings. The collection includes photographs of organs manufactured by the Bell Organ Company of Guelph.

3630. Guelph Civic Museum. **Guelph Mercantile and Industrial Firms. Invoices, 1865-1931 (sporadic).** 5 file folders. Loc: GCM.

A large number of invoices of business transactions of Guelph business firms which offer details of the prices of goods sold by numerous companies in the city.

3631. Guelph Civic Museum. **Prescriptions, c1850-c1858.** 3 envelopes. Loc: GCM.

A recipe for colic that includes opium, spirit of turpentine, strong spirits, warm gruel and castor oil. Another prescription, from N. Higinbotham Wholesale and Retail Druggist, is for nitric acid in a glass of wine to be taken before meals. Another unidentified prescription is for reducing a fever.

3632. Guelph Civic Museum. **Souvenir programs, 1889; 1891; 1908; 1913; 1925; 1927.** 9 volumes. Loc: GCM.

A collection of programs for several city-sponsored events, including a band tournament and firemen's demonstration in 1889, Dominion Day celebration in 1891, Labour Day celebration in 1925 and Old Home Week and Summer Carnival celebrations in 1908, 1913 and 1927.

3633. Guelph Historical Society Collection. **Correspondence, legal records, financial records, local histories, scrapbooks and maps, 1832-1957.** 9 boxes, 1 oversize file. Loc: UGA. XRI MS A324, Itemized list of contents.

The collection includes novels written by Elinor Sutherland Glyn, medical accounts of Dr Will Kerr, Dr Trotter and Dr Langland, account books from several businesses and several maps of Guelph.

3634. Guelph Historical Society. **Guelph City Council Minutes. Scrapbook of clippings, 1895-1900.** 1 vol. Loc: UGA. XR1 MS A324016.

The clippings have been pasted into a volume of the Guardian for 1863. The scrapbook belonged to Mr James Hutcheon, a Guelph engineer and surveyor.

3635. Guelph Historical Society. **Guelph houses, 1830-1877.** 2 file folders. Loc: GPL. File folders #13 and #35.

File #35 contains handwritten notes on various Guelph buildings including William Bell's house, the Hewat house, House of Heads, Swan Hotel, McTague cottages and J.W. Lyon's house. The notes describe architecture, date built, building and sometimes the present owner. File #13 contains typed notes accompanied by photographs, notes on other houses and a brief history of Guelph City Hall. Part of the Hammill Collection.

3636. Guelph Historical Society. **Guelph land purchases, August 12, 1827.** 1 file folder. Loc: GPL. File folder #35.

Handcopied list of eighty-three lot purchases in Guelph from the Canada Company. The list was copied from Volume 8 of the Canada Company records held at the Ontario Archives. The record notes lot number, approximate present location and name of purchasee. Part of the Hammill Collection.

3637. Guelph Historical Society. **Miscellaneous postcards, photographs, newspaper clippings, reports, and programs, 1840-1974.** 1 box. Loc: GCI.
The collection includes the 71st annual report of the Guelph Bible Society, program of St George's Society annual banquet, and a newspaper reproduction of an article by Thomas Laidlaw describing the Guelph fair in 1840.

3638. Guelph Public Library. **Elworthy and Day family genealogy, 1832.** 1 file folder. Loc: GPL.
A genealogical file on the Elworthy family who emigrated in 1832 from England to Guelph, where William was an undertaker, casketmaker and carpenter. In 1838, his daughter Elizabeth married John Watson Day, who farmed in Guelph Township. The file contains photocopies of historical sketches, letters and information about the families.

3639. Guelph Public Library. **Ephemera. Programs, 1889-1965.** 4 boxes. Loc: GPL.
A collection of programs for various events and clubs including churches, schools, Presto Music Club, Guelph Choral Society, Royal Theatre, Guelph Burns Club, Guelph Rotary Club and Women's Literary Club.

3640. Guelph Public Library. **Guelph. Births, deaths and marriages, 1847-1852; 1854; 1901-1926.** 4 documents. typescript. Loc: GPL.
A typescript of extracts taken from Guelph newspapers of area birth, death and marriage notices.

3641. Guelph Regional Project. **Reports, memoranda and working papers, 1987-1989.** Loc: UGA.
The Guelph Regional Project, initiated by Professor Gilbert Stelter, was based in the Department of History for two years. A small research unit compiled a Bibliography of secondary and published sources and an Inventory of primary and archival sources, in order to support historical research on the local region. These research tools have been produced in both machine-readable and print formats. The project records, deposited in the University Archives, include working papers on substantive and methodological topics as well as administrative records of the project.

3642. H.B. Timothy Collection. **Pamphlets, articles, correspondence, 1820-1980.** 16 boxes. Loc: UGA. XRI MS A277, Itemized list of contents.
A collection of pamphlets, articles, research notes and newspaper clippings about John Galt, his wife Elizabeth Tilloch, and their son Alexander Tilloch Galt. The collection also includes family correspondence, literary works of Galt and a diary of Captain William Gilkison from 1832 to 1833.

3643. Hammill Collection. **Biographies, 1871-1924.** 1 file folder. Loc: GPL. File folder #5.
Several brief biographies, correspondence and genealogy of Laura Lemon Heath, a copy of an obituary of Charles Raymond dated January 4, 1904 and a genealogy of John Galt's family. Part of the Hammill Collection.

3644. Hammill Collection. **Biographies, land deeds, photographs, correspondence, pamphlets and clippings, 1827-1984.** 62 file folders. Loc: GPL. List of contents.

A collection of material that primarily concerns the 1970s and 1980s. It includes photographs and descriptions of old Guelph houses, 1827 Guelph land purchases and brief biographies of Guelph people.

3645. Higinbotham Collection. **History of Guelph, 1827-1958.** 14 envelopes, 4 scrapbooks. Loc: GPL. List of document contents.

Scrapbooks, newspaper clippings, historical sketches and correspondence highlighting the settlement and expansion of Guelph. The clippings outline the nature of pioneer life and the growth of social institutions, and offer biographies of prominent residents. The collection also includes correspondence from John Galt's grandson, Alexander Tilloch Galt, other correspondence about local history, and photographs of Guelph.

3646. Higinbotham Collection. **Reminiscences of the history of Guelph, 1850-1937.** Loc: GPL.

A series of discussions recorded in typed form outlining oral testimony about life in Guelph during the nineteenth century. The persons interviewed included Lenore Cutten, Harry Cutten, James Hurley and J.R. Hurley. The interviews and reminiscences were conducted in 1937.

3647. **Historical sketch of Everton, n.d..** 6 p. typescript. Loc: AO. MU 3566 #9.

An undated historical sketch of Everton. The author notes the stagnation of the settlement after it was bypassed by railways and highways. Businesses, schools, churches and associations are noted, including the Everton Literary Society formed in 1902. There is a sketch plan of the village in its prime. The document was apparently compiled while the mill was still being worked by William Hortop.

3648. **History of Arkell United Church, 1831-1963.** ms, 7 p. Loc: GPL. P47.00.

A brief outline of the church's history that includes a list of ministers.

3649. Kearns, L.J. **Biographical inventory of notable Guelph people, 1988.** mr. Loc: GPL.

A machine-readable collection of biographical summaries of Guelph people begun in 1988 by the local history archivist in response to reference enquiries. Each entry includes birth dates; salient features of education, career and community involvement; and notes on source materials. By December 1988, there were entries for the Alling family, John Armstrong, Robert Armstrong, the Murray family, the Ryan family, the Sharmon family, the Sleeman family, the Thorp family, Annie Thorp, Frederic Watt, James Watt, Mary Louise and Lila Watt, the Mitchell family, the Savage family, the Byerly family and the Duffy family. The inventory also includes a list of early physicians.

3650. Kortland Collection. **Directories, 1857; 1867; 1871; 1879; 1881; 1886; 1906.** 1 file folder. Loc: WCA. Detailed list of contents.

Photocopies of Erin Township and Hillsburgh entries in directories.

3651. Kortland Collection. **Scrapbooks, 1853-1978.** 3 volumes, 4 envelopes. Loc: WCA. Detailed list of contents.

A collection of newspaper clippings from the Erin Advocate on history, township events, obituaries, marriage announcements and family histories. The collection contains research material that Patricia Kortland used for her publication, Hillsburgh's Heyday.

3652. Laidlaw, Thomas. **Guelph Tp S.S.#5. Reminiscences, 1835-1899.** 20 p. Loc: GCM.
   A handwritten historical sketch of the development of the school that describes buildings, discipline, social events and a drill practise for the Rebellion of 1837. The author also describes several early teachers including William Hiscock, Hugh Barnet and William Cowan. The brochure is held in a box entitled, Diaries and Journals.

3653. Laird Collection. **Correspondence, land records, receipts and concert programs, 1858-1934.** 6 file folders. Loc: WCA. FA: MU 78.
   The collection includes programs for Guelph concerts, property assessment notices, insurance policies and land records for the Cleghorn family of Guelph. The collection also includes a letter to James Laidlaw from Wilfrid Laurier in 1899.

3654. Living Springs Women's Institute. **Tweedsmuir village history, 1925-1973.** 1 file folder. Loc: UGA, AO. AO: MS 8, Reel 50; UGA: XR1 MS A107.
   A photocopy of the history of the institute and area which is located northeast of Fergus in Garafraxa West Township. The history describes the geography of the region, early Indian occupation, development of the township, county roads, early pioneering families, schools and churches. The Archives of Ontario has a microfilm copy.

3655. Marston-Archibald Collection. **Correspondence, legal records, genealogies and business records, 1800-1961.** 4 boxes. Loc: UGA. XRI MS A193.
   A collection of correspondence, business records and family history of James Archibald and Katherine Marston who lived in Elora.

3656. Marston-Archibald Collection. **Miscellaneous correspondence and reviews about Elora, 1924-1958.** 1 file folder. Loc: UGA. XR1 MS A193032.
   A collection of announcements of special concert events in Elora.

3657. Marston Collection. **Miscellaneous records and papers, 1836-1925.** 1 large box. Loc: AO. MU 2014.
   Katherine Marston was editor of the Elora Express and most of the collection is connected with Elora and area. Several elements in the whole collection have been separately recorded, such as the Elora Observer correspondence and advertisements, Thomas Connon's weather diaries, the Elora Volunteer Rifle Company and various fragments of municipal records. The greater part of the collection dates from the 1860s.

3658. McIlwraith Collection. **Biographies of Wellington County residents, 1820-1980.** 5 boxes. Loc: GPL.
   A series of newspaper clippings providing biographies of Wellington County residents. The records are held in the vertical files of the McIlwraith Collection and are organized alphabetically by name.

3659. McIlwraith Collection. **Historical Sketches. Guelph, 1827-1980.** 7 boxes. Loc: GPL. List of column contents.
   A collection of McIlwraith's historical column in the Guelph Mercury entitled

'Current Comment' and 'As It Happened', which ran from 1952 to 1980. The aid lists the date and title of each column.

3660. McIlwraith Collection. **Historical Sketches. Guelph and Wellington County, 1820-1980.** 13 boxes. Loc: GPL.
    A collection of vertical files which contain clippings from twentieth century newspapers that relate to the history of Wellington County. The collection is filed alphabetically by subject headings and place names.

3661. McIlwraith Collection. **Historical Sketches. Wellington County, c1820-1960.** 11 volumes. Loc: GPL.
    A series of newspaper clippings highlighting various aspects of the history of the county. The collection includes historical columns by Findley Weaver written in the Guelph Mercury during the 1940s and 1950s.

3662. McIlwraith Collection. **Miscellaneous Collection. History of Guelph, 1827-1972.** 5 boxes. Loc: GPL. List of document contents.
    Notes by Verne McIlwraith on schools, churches, hospitals, politics and economic activities in Guelph and Wellington County. The collection also contains biographies of families and specific individuals. The Guelph Public Library has developed a detailed finding aid describing the contents and dates of specific documents.

3663. Mestern, Pat. **Historical notes used for writing of Looking Back: Fergus Through the Years, 1833-1980.** 1 box. Loc: WCA. MU57.
    A collection of historical notes and sources used in writing the book. Held with the Pat Mestern Collection.

3664. Metro Toronto Central Reference Library. **Archidont index, 1870-1940.** Card index file drawers. Loc: MTL.
    The Archidont Index is a collection of bibiographic references to to publications relating to architecture and the building industry. It is apparently kept up to date and organized primarily by major cities, though smaller centres and rural areas are also included occasionally. Index cards measuring 8" by 5" have been used, with space for a great many details on the dimensions and styles of buildings. Approximately 20 to 25 journals have been indexed. The Canadian Architect and Builder, Construction, and Contract Record seem to be cited most frequently for the Guelph area between the 1880s and 1930s, with Canadian Illustrated News and Dominion Illustrated occasionally cited in the earlier period. There are about 250 cards on Guelph, slightly fewer on Kitchener, and only a very few on any of the smaller centres in the Upper Grand area. Of the Guelph total, about one fifth refer to industrial and commercial buildings, nearly two-fifths to educational buildings including those of the colleges and University, over one quarter to public buildings such as post office, armoury, and correctional centre, and about one tenth each to religious and residential buildings. There are very few references to items published before the 1890s, the most cited period being from c1910 to the 1930s. The detail completed on the record cards is also quite fragmentary in almost all cases. However, the compilers of the index do seem to have searched the journals more closely than just scanning the journals's own index or table of contents. They appear to have selected local details from general summaries of building activity across Canada, such as 'Contracts Open' or 'Building in Canada

in ...(year)..', or 'Building Outlook for ..(year)..'. Only a handful of cards refer to whole articles on building and architectural subjects. In over half the cases the architect and/or contractor/carpenter/mason are named, and in about half the cases the dimensions and/or costs are specified. However, in some instances references are made to possible rather than actual building projects, so the index should be used with caution. Also, names of local people, streets etc are quite often mis-spelled. In many cases, the specific location of the building is not stated.

3665. Mickle Collection. **Correspondence, legal records and photographs, 1710-1950.** 7 boxes. Loc: UGA. XRI MS A279, Itemized list of contents.

A collection of correspondence, legal records, accounts, photographs, clippings, publications, notebooks and other miscellanea relating to six generations of the Mickle family. Charles Julius Mickle and his family emigrated to Canada from Scotland in 1832. They settled on land now occupied by Ignatius College on the Elora Road.

3666. Monaghan, Arthur P. **Notes on Guelph and Wellington County area, c1960.** 20 p. typescript. Loc: JA.

An extract from an unpublished History of the Diocese of Hamilton. The author quotes from the Macdonell Papers various letters relating to the early years of the Guelph Parish and lengthy quotations from Holzer's letter to Bishop Charbonnel in 1855 on the need to establish Catholic schools with trained teachers. Held in Box 1 of Guelph records.

3667. Mount Forest Public Library. **Historical file, 1821-1988.** 1 binder. Loc: MFL.

A series of historical materials divided in a number of sections entitled: Mount Forest and area, 1881 census, Mount Forest directories, Arthur Township, cemeteries, 1861 census, miscelleaneous, and a number of genealogical files on Mount Forest and area families. The census materials are typewritten notes of information available in the 1861 and 1882 censuses. The file also contains a photocopy of an 1865 director of Grey County with the pages referring to Mount Forest.

3668. Mount Forest Public Library. **Local interest items, 1864-1988.** 1 binder. Loc: MFL.

A brief description of a walking tour of various buildings and sites in the town. The binder also includes photographs of Mount Forest and area including the municipal building, Saugeen Bridge, Conn and Sacred Heart Catholic Church in Kenilworth.

3669. Mundell Collection. **Land records and business correspondence, 1849-1907.** 1 box. Loc: WCA. FA: MU 5.

A collection of land records of residential and commercial lots in Elora Village. It also contains miscellaneous correspondence from the office of John Mundell Manufacturing Company. Mundell founded the furniture factory in 1848, which was continued under the management of his son, John Cleghorn Mundell, until 1930.

3670. National Archives of Canada. **Checklist of trade catalogues held in other repositories, 1987.** c350 p. in binder. Loc: NAC, KPL.

Copies of record forms compiled for a project initiated by Dawn Monroe of the

National Archives of Canada. There are records for trade catalogues of businesses in the Waterloo-Wellington region. Wellington County businesses represented are J.B. Armstrong, Carriages and Sleighs (1908), Beatty Bros of Fergus (1925-1950), Canada Ingot Iron Culvert Company making Champion Crushing and Road Building Machinery (1910), Levi Cossitt making lawnmowers (nd), C. Kloepfer making carriages and blacksmith supplies (1906), Gilson-Moody Threshers (1920-), Partridge Rubber (1925), Louden Machinery (1928), Taylor Forbes (1910), Charles Thain making agricultural implements (1870), and Henry Wise Woodenware of Palmerston (1916).

3671. Ontario Genealogical Society. **Burial Records. Arthur Town123ship, 1845-1984.** 1 file folder. Loc: GPL.
A list of burial records of four cemeteries in Arthur Township.

3672. Ontario Genealogical Society. **Burial Records. Eramosa Township, 1850-1981.** 1 file folder. Loc: GPL.
A list of burial records of six cemeteries in Eramosa Township.

3673. Ontario Genealogical Society. **Burial Records. Erin Township, 1860-1984.** 1 file folder. Loc: GPL.
A list of burial records of twelve cemeteries in Erin Township.

3674. Ontario Genealogical Society. **Burial Records. Guelph Township, 1842-1875.** 1 file folder. Loc: GPL.

3675. Ontario Genealogical Society. **Burial Records. Guelph Township, 1842-1890.** 1 file folder. Loc: GPL.
A list of the burial records of the Jackson Cemetery in Guelph Township.

3676. Ontario Genealogical Society. **Burial Records. Maryborough Township, 1851-1886.** 1 file folder. Loc: GPL.
A list of the burial records of six cemeteries in Maryborough Township.

3677. Ontario Genealogical Society. **Burial Records. Minto Township, 1860-1930.** 1 file folder. Loc: GPL.
A list of the burial records of five cemeteries in Minto Township.

3678. Ontario Genealogical Society. **Burial Records. Nichol Township, 1837-1934.** 1 file folder. Loc: GPL.
A list of the burial records of six cemeteries in Nichol Township.

3679. Ontario Genealogical Society. **Burial Records. Peel Township, 1860-1910.** 1 file folder. Loc: GPL.
A list of the burial records of ten cemeteries in Peel Township.

3680. Ontario Genealogical Society. **Burial Records. Pilkington Township, 1840-1865.** 1 file folder. Loc: GPL.
A list of the burial records of three cemeteries in Pilkington Township.

3681. Ontario Genealogical Society. **Burial Records. Puslinch Township, 1824-1979.** Kitchener: Waterloo-Wellington Branch: Ontario Genealogical Society, 1 file folder. Loc: GPL.

A list of the burial records of two cemeteries in Puslinch Township.

3682. Ontario Genealogical Society. **Burial Records. St Joseph's Cemetery, 1847-1950.** 1 file folder. Loc: GPL, UGA. UGA: XR1 MS A316.

3683. Ontario Genealogical Society. **Burial records. St Mary's Cemetery, Hespeler, 1855-1951.** 1 file folder. Loc: GPL.
Because of the many links between Hespeler and Puslinch Township, some township residents were probably buried in the cemetery.

3684. Ontario Genealogical Society. **Burial Records. West Garafraxa Township, Bishop Private Cemetery, 1816-1979.** 2 file folders. Loc: GPL.

3685. Ontario Genealogical Society. **Burial Records. Woodlawn Cemetery, Block N, 1940-1985.** 1 file folder. Loc: GPL.

3686. Ontario Genealogical Society. **Burial Records. Woodlawn Cemetery, Block K Soldiers' Plot, 1897-1958.** 1 file folder. Loc: GPL.

3687. Ontario Genealogical Society. **Burial Records. Woodlawn Cemetery, Section Q, 1919-1984.** 1 file folder. Loc: GPL.

3688. Ontario Genealogical Society. **Burial Records. Woodlawn Cemetery, Section G and Cremation Gardens, 1860-1960.** 1 file folder. Loc: GPL.

3689. Ontario Genealogical Society. **Burial Records. Woodlawn Cemetery, Section I, 1925-1973.** 1 file folder. Loc: GPL.

3690. Ontario Genealogical Society. **Burial Records. Woodlawn Cemetery, Mausoleum, 1929-1984.** 1 file folder. Loc: GPL.

3691. Ontario Genealogical Society. **Burial Records. Woodlawn Cemetery, Block L, 1929-1985.** 1 file folder. Loc: GPL.

3692. Ontario Genealogical Society. **Burial Records. Woodlawn Cemetery, Block F, 1838-1978.** 1 file folder. Loc: GPL.

3693. Ontario Genealogical Society. **Burial Records. Woodlawn Cemetery, Block R, 1867-1950.** 1 file folder. Loc: GPL.

3694. Ontario Genealogical Society. **Burial Records. Woodlawn Cemetery, Block C, 1936-1984.** 1 file folder. Loc: GPL.

3695. Ontario Genealogical Society. **Burial Records. Woodlawn Cemetery, Block O, 1849-1979.** 1 file folder. Loc: GPL.

3696. Ontario Genealogical Society. **Burial Records. Woodlawn Cemetery, Block V, 'Black' and 'Jewish', 1960-1985.** 1 file folder. Loc: GPL.

3697. Ontario Genealogical Society. **Burial Records. Woodlawn Cemetery, Block D, 1900-1984.** 1 file folder. Loc: GPL.

3698. Ontario Genealogical Society. **Burial Records. Woodlawn Cemetery, Block J, 1919-1985**. 1 file folder. Loc: GPL.

3699. Ontario Genealogical Society. **Burial Records. Woodlawn Cemetery, Section G, 1854-1949**. 1 file folder. Loc: GPL.

3700. Ontario Genealogical Society. **Burial Records. Woodlawn Cemetery, Block M2, 1950-1986**. 1 file folder. Loc: GPL.

3701. Ontario Genealogical Society. **Burial Records. Woodlawn Cemetery, Block K, 1890-1959**. 1 file folder. Loc: GPL.

3702. Ontario Genealogical Society. **Burial Records. Woodlawn Cemetery, Section X, 1855-1957**. 1 file folder. Loc: GPL.

3703. Ontario Genealogical Society. **Burial Records. Woodlawn Cemetery, Block B, 1900-1986**. 1 file folder. Loc: GPL.

3704. Ontario Genealogical Society. **Harriston. Baptisms and burials, 1858-1875**. 1 document. Loc: GPL.
An extract of baptismal and burial information taken from records of St George's Anglican Church in Harriston.

3705. Ontario Genealogical Society. **Index for 1871 census, Eramosa Township**. 45 p. Loc: GPL, KPL, WCA.
A computer-generated index to all entries for Eramosa Township in the 1871 census manuscript schedules for households. The index is organized in alphabetical order by family name and includes columns for sex, age, church, ethnic origin, occupation and page and reel number in the original schedule.

3706. Ontario Genealogical Society. **Index to Guelph Advertiser (births, deaths, marriages), 1847-1849**. 1 printed index. Loc: KPL, GPL.

3707. Ontario Genealogical Society. **John and George Norris: from Chilham, Kent, England to Guelph Township, Wellington County Ontario, c1830-1885**. 10 pp. Loc: GPL.
A genealogy, written in 1986, about the Norris family who settled in Guelph Township about 1830. John was a tailor and George was a shoemaker.

3708. Ontario Genealogical Society. **Mount Forest and North Arthur. Baptisms, burials and marriages, 1858-1862**. 1 document. Loc: GPL.
An extract of baptismal, burial and marriage information taken from records at St Paul's Anglican Church in Mount Forest and Holy Trinity Anglican Church in North Arthur.

3709. Ontario Genealogical Society. **Pilkington Township. Assessment roll, 1858**. 1 brochure. Loc: GPL.
The assessment roll has been extracted and alphabetized from the original document.

3710. Ontario Genealogical Society. **St George's Anglican Church, Harriston. Burials and baptisms, 1858-1875**. 1 printed index. Loc: GPL, KPL, WCA.

3711. Ontario Genealogical Society. **Transcribed Cemetery Records. Arthur Township, 1840-1940.** 1 volume. Loc: WCA.

3712. Ontario Genealogical Society. **Transcribed Cemetery Records. Drayton, 1851-1889.** 1 volume. Loc: WCA.

3713. Ontario Genealogical Society. **Transcribed Cemetery Records. Elora, 1858-1951.** 1 volume. Loc: WCA.

3714. Ontario Genealogical Society. **Transcribed Cemetery Records. Erin Township, 1840-1977.** 1 volume. Loc: WCA.

3715. Ontario Genealogical Society. **Transcribed Cemetery Records. Eramosa Township, 1857-1965.** 1 volume. Loc: WCA.

3716. Ontario Genealogical Society. **Transcribed Cemetery Records. Fergus, 1838-1881.** 1 volume. Loc: WCA.

3717. Ontario Genealogical Society. **Transcribed Cemetery Records. Guelph Township, 1836-1874.** 1 volume. Loc: WCA.

3718. Ontario Genealogical Society. **Transcribed Cemetery Records. Maryborough Township, 1856-1950.** 1 volume. Loc: WCA.

3719. Ontario Genealogical Society. **Transcribed Cemetery Records. Mount Forest, 1884-1980.** 1 volume. Loc: WCA.

3720. Ontario Genealogical Society. **Transcribed Cemetery Records. Minto Township, 1850-1970.** 1 volume. Loc: WCA.

3721. Ontario Genealogical Society. **Transcribed Cemetery Records. Nichol Township, 1854-1973.** 1 volume. Loc: WCA.

3722. Ontario Genealogical Society. **Transcribed Cemetery Records. Pilkington Township, 1850-1983.** 1 volume. Loc: WCA.

3723. Ontario Genealogical Society. **Transcribed Cemetery Records. Peel Township, 1852-1969.** 1 volume. Loc: WCA.

3724. Ontario Genealogical Society. **Transcribed Cemetery Records. Puslinch Township, 1870-1976.** 1 volume. Loc: WCA.

3725. Ontario Genealogical Society. **Transcribed Cemetery Records. West Garafraxa Township, 1845-1977.** 1 volume. Loc: WCA.

3726. Pollock Collection. **Marriage Licenses. Wellington County, 1833-1862.** 6 documents. Loc: WCA.
A record of six marriage licenses which lists marriage partners and notes their places of residence prior to marriage.

3727. Potter Collection. **Correspondence, 1854-1894.** 7 file folders. Loc: WCA. FA: MU 8.

A collection of business correspondence to David Potter regarding payment for articles purchased from Potter's establishment, the Elora Foundry. The collection also contains correspondence from John McNaughton and from Galt Mills regarding price and purchase of wheat.

3728. Puslinch Pioneer. **Index. Volumes 1-11, 1977-1987.** Loc: UGA.

An index to topics and titles of all articles, compiled by

3729. Roberts, Janey. **Family history of George and Louisa (Brown) Wakefield, 1834-1986.** 100 pp. Loc: GPL.

A genealogy and historical sketch of the Wakefield family who emigrated from Gloucester in 1834 to Arkell in Puslinch Township where they farmed.

3730. Shaw, Stuart. **History of Rockwood Academy. Correspondence and notes, c1935.** 1 envelope. Loc: WCA. MU 101.

Materials apparently collected by Shaw in preparation for writing a history of the academy. They include a 4-page chronological note; a 4-page letter from Dugald McPherson of Orangeville who was a student at Rockwood from 1869 to 1872; a one-page letter from Miss E. Wetherald of Fenwick, Ontario, daughter of William Wetherald who founded the academy; and notes on an 1870s class picture. Miss Wetherald recalls that early records of the Rockwood Academy were destroyed when the old Wetherald house at Fenwick burned down in 1888. The file also include a promotional brochure for the Rockwood Academy dating from 1871.

3731. Shutt Collection. **Correspondence, articles, newspaper clippings and historical sketches, 1834-1965.** 2 boxes. Loc: GPL. List of document contents.

Materials on the history of Guelph which outline the growth of the Guelph Congregational Church, and include biographies and obituaries of notable Guelph residents. The collection has various references to the religious, educational and business activities of Charles Raymond and includes a letter from Reverend W.F. Clarke to the Guelph Congregational Church discussing his activities in the church and a photocopy of a brochure published in Guelph in 1891 celebrating Dominion Day with a description of the city and advertisements of local businesses. The collection also includes copies of the Shutt family newsletter that contain reports of genealogical research, correspondence of the Charles Raymond family, and a series of genealogical bibliographies and source books.

3732. Sleeman Family Collection. **Correspondence, business records and photographs, 1847-1926.** 6 boxes, 1 oversized box. Loc: UGA. XRI MS A334, Itemized list of contents.

Correspondence, photographs, business records, legal documents and newspaper clippings concerning George Sleeman and his family. Sleeman owned Silver Creek Brewery, was president of the Maple Leaf Baseball Club, owned and operated the Guelph Radial Railway and was involved in municipal politics.

3733. Sleeman Family Collection. **Sports in Guelph. Programs, 1872-1895.** 1 file folder. Loc: UGA. XR1 MS A334.

A series of programs of clubs and associations of which George Sleeman was a member, including the Guelph Rifle Association, Guelph Turf Club and Guelph Curling Club.

3734. Small, Marjorie. **History of S.S.#3, Guelph Township (Marden School), 1963.**
Loc: WCA. MU 104.

3735. Smithurst, John, Rev. **Photographs and newspaper clippings, 1855-1930.** 1
oversized box. Loc: UGA. XRI MS A330.
The collection contains material regarding Smithurst and his cousin and
reputed lover, Florence Nightingale. It contains a photograph of Smithurst, John
Connon's article about the pair, an 1853 balance sheet of Smithurst, and 1913 to
1924 newspaper clippings about Florence Nightingale.

3736. Templin-Dow Collection. **Family papers, business records and photographs,
1870-1960.** 1 box. Loc: WCA. FA: MU 53.
A collection of family and area commercial records for the Fergus region. John
Templin was founder of the Templin Carriage Works in Fergus and editor of the
Fergus News Record. Hugh Templin was editor of the Fergus News Record and was
the author of two books: Fergus, the Story of a Little Town, and, The Boy and
the River.

3737. Templin Family Collection. **Correspondence, manuscript notes and published
ephemera, 1843-1967.** 1 box. Loc: AO. FA: MU 2956.
John Charles Templin (1879-1939) purchased the Fergus News Record in 1902 and
remained proprietor and editor until his death. He was also President of the
Wellington District Press Association and Secretary of the Fergus Horticultural
Society. His son published Fergus, The Story of a Little Town (1933). The
collection includes a considerable variety of correspondence, manuscript notes
and ephemera relating to schools, churches and associations of Fergus, Elora and
Nichol Township. Some of these have individual entries in this inventory.

3738. Templin Family Collection. **Scrapbooks on Fergus, Elora and area history,
1918-1943.** 3 boxes. Loc: AO. FA: MU 2958-2960.
Scrapbooks in eight volumes, mainly comprising newspaper clippings of J.G.
Templin's own Historical Notes About Fergus and Vicinity, published in the News
Record in the 1920s, and similar articles by Byerly and Connon. The first
scrapbook includes copies of 1845 maps of Fergus and Elora which were said to
have been drawn by A.D. Fordyce and lithographed in Edinburgh.

3739. Thorning Collection. **Correspondence, 1829-1913.** 1 box. Loc: UGA. Card index.
A collection of approximately one hundred photocopied business and personal
letters sent to or by various Wellington County individuals, including A.D.
Ferrier, Robert Torrance, Charles Allan, Adam Fergusson, George J. Grange,
William Hewat, William Hiscock, C.J. Mickle, William Mickle, William Stevenson,
Andrew Geddes, Charles Clarke, A. Dingwall Fordyce, George Smellie and the Rev.
John Smithurst. The letters are arranged chronologically and are accompanied by
one card index arranged chronologically, and a second index arranged
alphabetically by addressor and addressee. Each record includes a copy of the
addressed envelope, postage stamp and cancelled post office stamp. Most of the
letters are from 1829 to 1859.

3740. U.S. National Archives. **Despatches from United States Consuls in Guelph,
Canada, 1883-1906.** 2 reels. mf. Loc: UGL. DOCFLM US1 GS90 61023.
A microfilmed collection of the manuscript reports sent by the consuls that

provide a useful account of the state of business in the city and county.
Detailed statistics are provided for specific businesses such as the Raymond
Sewing Machine and Bell Organ companies in April 1892. The report of February
1906 includes a 3-page description of the OAC.

3741. University of Guelph Archives. **Guelph industries, 1846-1980.** Loc: UGA. XR1 MS
A083.
    A collection of pamphlets, photographs and newspaper supplements about the
industries of Guelph. It includes an 1897 advertising newsletter from the
Raymond Manufacturing Company.

3742. University of Guelph Archives. **Guelph Schools. Report, 1874-1918.** 1 volume.
Loc: UGA. XR1 MS A076.
    A listing of the names of students and teachers, textbooks used and the types
of courses taught in specific schools. The volume does not have an author listed
but appears to be a twentieth century listing of materials copied from primary
records.

3743. University of Guelph Archives. **Miscellaneous collection on Guelph clubs and
associations, 1855-1982.** 2 boxes. Loc: UGA. XR1 MS A074.
    Pamphlets, articles and newspaper clippings about various local clubs,
including a report of proceedings of the Guelph Farmers' Club, c1855, Guelph
Lawn Bowling Club minutes, c1898-1946 and the Wellington Field Naturalists' Club
journal, c1908.

3744. University of Guelph Archives. **Scrapbooks, newspaper clippings and photographs
of Guelph's history, 1827-1986.** 5 boxes. Loc: UGA. XR1 MS A019.
    A collection of newspaper clippings primarily dating from the 1950s to the
1980s which outline the history of the city and includes several articles on the
historic houses, Wyoming, and the Fergusson house. The collection also contains
a number of undated photographs of Guelph bridges and rivers, the O.A.C. and the
interior of homes. A high proportion of newspaper clippings are related to
present-day events and activities in the city.

3745. University of Guelph Archives. **Scrapbooks of advertisements, 1843-1881.** 1
file folder. Loc: UGA.
    A number of miscellaneous newspaper advertisements, dating from the period
between 1843 and 1881, for Guelph and county businesses.

3746. University of Guelph Archives. **Trade cards, c1880-c1890.** 1 scrapbook. Loc:
UGA. XR1 MS A198.
    A collection of North American industrial trade cards that includes several
from W. Bell and Company and the Raymond Sewing Machine Company.

3747. Vigor, Frank. **An history of recreation in Guelph, 1972.** typescript, 4 p. Loc:
GPL.
    An historical sketch of sports and recreation that notes the periods in which
certain sports were popular. The formation of a cricket club in 1832 and the
popularity of tennis from 1892 are mentioned. The document is filed with
Churches, RC in the Vertical File.

3748. Watson Collection. **Diaries and family histories, 1856-1908.** Loc: WCA. FA: MU 84.

A collection of photocopied diaries of Henry Watson, John Watson and Avice Watson about family life in Guelph Township. The collection also includes four articles by John Nelles Watson: An historical sketch of education progress in the rural school section of No. 2, Guelph Township (15 p.); Watson's School (5 p.); Church and Sunday school in Watson's School (4 p.); and an untitled articles on the debating club that met in Watson's School (3 p.).

3749. Wellington County Archives. **Advertisements of Elora businesses, 1865-1867; 1894.** 1 file folder. Loc: WCA. MU13.

A series of advertisements for various Elora and area establishments and events including the Salem Monthly Fair, Aboyne Oatmeal Mills, Elora Flour Mill, a soiree at the Creekbank Wesleyan Methodist Church and John Mundell and Company Furniture Manufacturers.

3750. Wellington County Archives. **Elora Merchants. Miscellaneous receipts, 1884-1885.** 1 envelope. Loc: WCA. MU75.

Records of business transactions of several Elora merchants including Thomas Black, Joseph Stickney and Frank Clarke.

3751. Wellington County Archives. **Genealogy files, 1820-1980.** 6 file cabinet drawers. Loc: WCA. Detailed list of contents.

Newspaper clippings and family histories of approximately 800 families in the county. The files are arranged alphabetically by name.

3752. Wellington County Archives. **Miscellaneous receipts, 1857; 1873; 1913.** 5 documents. Loc: WCA. MU 42.

A collection of miscellaneous receipts including the American Hotel in Guelph in 1913, the North Wellington Teachers' Association in 1913, a tax receipt from Fergus in 1873 and a Wellington County debenture in 1857 purchased by A.D. Ferrier.

3753. Wellington County Archives. **Newspaper clippings, 1820-1980.** 4 file cabinet drawers. Loc: WCA.

A collection of newspaper clippings on a wide variety of topics on the history of the area. The collection is organized alphabetically by place.

3754. Wellington County Archives. **Scrapbooks. History of Wellington County, c1825-1960.** 8 envelopes. Loc: WCA. MU43.

A collection of twentieth century newspaper clippings highlighting the history of county churches, industries, century farms, schools and general overviews of community development. The files are subdivided into separate folders according to the subject of the articles.

3755. Wellington County Historical Research Society Collection. **Historical records, c1840-c1970.** Loc: WCA. FA.

A large and diverse collection of historical documents including receipts, correspondence, church records, government records, pamphlets, photographs, books, maps and newspapers pertaining to the Wellington County region.

3756. Wellington County Historical Research Society. **Historical essays, 1949-1986**. 3 boxes. Loc: WCA. List of essay topics by year.

A series of essays written between 1949 and 1986 for the Wellington County Historical Research Society. The essays cover a broad range of subjects including social, economic and religious aspects of the history of many areas in the county since c1820. The Wellington County Archives has developed a detailed finding aid noting the title, author and date of specific essays.

3757. Wellington County Historical Research Society. **Obituaries, 1834-1923 (sporadic)**. 1 envelope. Loc: WCA.

A handwritten collection of obituaries of Puslinch Township residents including Mary Reid McPhatter, Hugh McPherson, Archie McPherson, Donald Thomson, James Thomson, John McCormick, Grace McKinnon and Murdock Munro.

3758. Wellington County Project. **Research notes for book, On middle ground, 1973-1977**. 1 box, 5 tapes. Loc: UGA.

A collection of material from the 1973 to 1977 research project that studied the life and landscape of Wellington County from 1841 to 1891. Areas of study included geography, settlement, housing, roads, agriculture and works of art. The collection includes minutes and tapes of project meetings, grant applications, bibliographies, lists of local library resources, photocopies of a sample of local literature, a few photographs of buildings and scenery, and maps to be inserted in the project's publication, On Middle Ground. Members of the project included Gordon Couling, Douglas Hoffman, Kenneth Kelly, John Moldenhauer, Alexander Ross and Elizabeth Waterston.

3759. Wellington County Women's Institutes. **Tweedsmuir Histories**. 23 reels. mf. Loc: AO, WCA, GPL. AO:M58, Reel 34.

Lady Tweedsmuir, wife of John Buchan, Lord Tweedsmuir when he was Governor-General in the 1930s, encouraged the Women's Institutes of Canada to write up the histories of their localities. Six of the 122 Tweedsmuir Histories inventoried by the Archives of Ontario relate to Wellington County: Elora, also cited in the Guelph Regional Project's Bibliography, is on Reel 30, Erin on Reel 34, Fergus on Reel 44, Living Springs on Reel 50, Minto on Reel 1, Northgate on Reel 57. Various Tweedsmuir histories for Wellington County are held at the Guelph Public Library and have been cited in the Bibliography: Alma, Arkell, Badenoch, Brock Road, Eden Mills, Ennotville, Eramosa, Morriston, Mosborough, Riverside, Guelph, Speedside and West End. In addition, Wellington County Archives has copies of all these and several others: Farewell (Arthur Township), Hillsburgh, Mimosa, Cumnock, Little Ireland (Minto Township), Belwood, and Carry-On (Palmerston).

3760. Wellington South Land Registry Office Record Collection. **Land records, 1807-1952**. 2 boxes. Loc: WCA. MU 87-88.

A collection of Provincial Registrar's returns, land patents, deeds and clergy reserve sale agreements in Wellington County.

3761. Wissler, Lois. **History of Wisslers of Salem, c1950-c1975**. 1 large envelope containing scrapbook. Loc: WCA. MU 103.

Items collected and compiled relating to the founding of Salem by Sem Wissler in 1845, Wissler's varied business activities until his early death in 1865, and the subsequent decline of the village.

3762. Wright, Arthur W. **Fergus and vicinity scrapbook, 1902.** 39 p. Loc: AO. MU 2593.
A scrapbook of local historical sketches published in the Fergus News Record. In the first, Wright explains that the idea of such a series was prompted by the interest expressed in local history at the Fergus Old Boys' Celebration, c1901, and appealed for reminiscences and records relating to Fergus, Elora, Nichol, West Garafraxa and the upper half of Eramosa. The series mostly concerns Fergus and Nichol Township.

GUIDE TO ARCHIVES AND REPOSITORIES

GUIDE TO ARCHIVES AND REPOSITORIES

The following guide provides summary details for most of the repositories that contained primary and archival source materials on Guelph and Wellington County. Specific descriptions are not provided for repositories outside Ontario or for those libraries cited only for their holdings of microfilmed newspapers (as these may be obtained on inter-library or inter-archival loan) or for repositories not open to researchers.

ARCHIVES OF ONTARIO (AO)
77 Grenville Street, Toronto, M7A 2R9
Telephone: (416) 965-4030/965-6882

Hours: Monday to Friday, 8.15 a.m. to 4.30 p.m.; extended reading room hours to 10.30 p.m. on weekdays and 10 a.m. to 8 p.m. on Saturdays.

Contact: Ian E. Wilson, Archivist of Ontario

Cataloguing System and Services: Card catalogues, indexes, descriptive guides and file listings are available in the reading room, where Reference Archivists are on duty during business hours. Specialized enquiries, relating to particular departmental records for example, are referred to other Archives staff. An expanding proportion of records is on microfilm and accessible for self-service. Material may be retrieved during business hours and left in lockers for researchers' consultation during extended evening and weekend hours. Photocopying, microfilming and photo reproduction services are available at nominal cost.

Major Holdings: As the repository of the historic records of the government of Ontario, the Archives has very large holdings that are generally described in **A Guide to the Holdings of the Archives of Ontario** (1985, 9 microfiches). These include 120,000 cubic feet of provincial government records and the records of the Canada Company as well as the records of some municipal governments, businesses, churches and associations and the papers of individuals and families. There are also over 25,000 maps and plans, architectural drawings (notably the Horwood Collection) and photographs. The relevance to Guelph and Wellington County is reflected in the fact that the Archives of Ontario holds over 470 of the record series and items listed in this **Inventory**.

ARTHUR LAND REGISTRY OFFICE (ALR)
284 George Street, Arthur, Ontario N0G 1A0
Telephone: (519) 848-2300

Hours: Monday to Friday, 9 a.m. to 4:30 p.m.
Prior appointment is recommended.

Contact: Arvind Damley, Land Registrar

Cataloguing System:
    The abstract indexes of deeds are arranged alphabetically by place name

and the plans are stored alphabetically by name of property owner. Copies of all the plans have been deposited in the University of Guelph Library.

ARTHUR TOWNSHIP OFFICE (ATO)

Kenilworth, Ontario N0G 2E0
Telephone: (519) 848-3620

Major Holdings:

Records include council minutes, bylaws, cash books, assessment and collectors' rolls, and Board of Health minutes.

BRANT COUNTY MUSEUM (BCM)

57 Charlotte Street
Brantford, Ontario, N3T 2W6
Telephone: (519) 742-2483

Hours: Tuesday to Friday 9 a.m. to 5 p.m.; Saturday 1 p.m. to 5 p.m.

Major Holdings:

Records of Brant Historical Society and other material relating to Brant County and the Six Nations. Relevant to Wellington County is the large collection of Gilkison family papers presented by Miss Augusta Gilkison that includes some material on Elora to the 1860s.

CANADIAN BAPTIST ARCHIVES (CBA)

McMaster Divinity College
Hamilton, Ontario, L8S 4K1
Telephone: (416) 525-9140, ext. 3511

Contact: Judith Colwell, Librarian
Prior appointment essential. Researchers visiting the Archives are charged a fee of $10. per day; for those who cannot come in person, staff may undertake research at $10. per hour, as time permits.

Major Holdings: Records of the Canadian Baptist Federation, including basic records of individual congregations such as memberships rolls.
Primarily a closed collection that serves the churches of Canada from Quebec westward. The ownership of any records deposited in the Archives remains with the depositing church. Baptists do not keep birth and death records but marriage records (mainly since 1896), adult baptism records (no age cited), and subsequent church membership particulars. The church membership record may include notations of death or change of address. Genealogists and others interested in Wellington County may, at the discretion of the Archives staff, consult church records dating from 1819 to 1920. Records with a date span extending past 1920 may be researched only with the written permission of the church which continues to own the records.

CHILDREN'S AID SOCIETY, GUELPH (CAS)
Box 1088, 55 Delhi Street, Guelph, Ontario N1H 6N3
Telephone: (519) 824-2410

Hours: Monday to Friday, 9 a.m. to 5 p.m.

Contact: Jean Forsyth, Co-ordinator of Administration
Prior appointment and written permission are essential.

Cataloguing System:
The records are informally arranged. Researchers must provide a specific research proposal which will be assessed by a committee before permission is granted.

Major Holdings:
Holdings include a complete set of society minutes from 1893 to the present.

DIOCESE OF HAMILTON ARCHIVES (DHA)
700 King St West
Hamilton, Ontario L8P 1C7
Telephone: (416) 522-7263

Hours: Monday to Friday, 9:30 a.m. to 1 p.m.
Prior appointment and written permission are essential.

Archivist: Ken Foyster

Cataloguing System:
All items are described and arranged, but searches must be done through the archivist. Access is granted by written permission of the Chancellor of the Diocese, who responds to a written request to view records for a specific research proposal.

Major Holdings:
Holdings include individual parish histories, some parish correspondence to the bishop, newspaper clippings recording important events, and a small number of photographs of church buildings.

DOON HERITAGE CROSSROADS (DHC)
MacDonald-Cartier Freeway, Interchange 34
R.R. #2, Kitchener, Ontario N2G 3W5
Telephone: (519) 748-1914

Hours: Monday to Friday, 9 a.m. to 5 p.m.

Prior appointment is recommended.

Contact: Elizabeth McNaughton, Registrar-Researcher

Cataloguing System:
All items are arranged sequentially by catalogue number and each item is individually described in a computer print-out. There are no finding aids or indexes by subject or location, so extensive searches must be done to identify items required.

DRAYTON VILLAGE OFFICE (DVO)
Box 160, Wellington Street, Drayton, Ontario N0G 1P0
Telephone: (519) 638-3097

Major Holdings:
Records include council bylaws, minutes, cash books, auditors' reports, fire insurance plans, and voters' lists.

ELORA VILLAGE OFFICE (EMO)
Box 508, 136 Metcalfe Street, Elora, Ontario N0B 1S0
Telephone: (519) 846-9691

Major Holdings:
Records include council bylaws and minutes.

ERAMOSA TOWNSHIP OFFICE (ETO)
R.R. #1, Rockwood, Ontario N0B 2K0
Telephone: (519) 856-9951

Major Holdings:
Records include council minutes, bylaws, financial statements, cash books, jurors' books, and Rockwood Board of Health minutes.

ERIN VILLAGE OFFICE (EVO)
Box 149, 109 Main Street, Erin, Ontario N0B 1T0
Telephone: (519) 833-2604

Major Holdings:
Records include trustees' minutes and cemetery lot purchases.

GUELPH ARMOURIES (GAB)
7 Wyndham Street South, Guelph, Ontario N1H 4C4
Telephone: (519) 824-0351

Hours: Monday to Friday, 9 a.m. to 4 p.m.
By appointment only.

Contact: Lieutenant-Colonel Michael McKay, Commanding Officer

Cataloguing System:
   The records are informally held, with no finding aids or cataloguing system.

Major Holdings:
   Holdings include membership rolls, order books, historical records, scrapbooks and photographs for a variety of local militia groups.

GUELPH CITY HALL (GCH)
59 Carden Street, Guelph, Ontario N1H 3A1
Telephone: (519) 837-5603

Hours: Monday to Friday, 9 a.m. to 4:30 p.m.

Contact: Lois Giles, City Clerk

Cataloguing System:
   Records held in the clerk's office are stored in small labelled file drawers. Other records are informally arranged in the clerk's office vault and in the barrel vault. Researchers must be prepared for extensive searches to find required materials.

Major Holdings:
   Holdings include assessment rolls, collectors' rolls, bylaws, council minutes, and department and committee reports.

GUELPH CIVIC MUSEUM (GCM)
Dublin St.S., Guelph, Ontario N1H 4L5
Telephone: (519) 836-1221

Hours: Monday to Friday, 9 to 12 noon and 1 to 5 p.m.
Prior appointment essential to consult archival materials.

Contact: Wendy Hallman, Assistant Director of Museum

History of Collection:
   The Museum collects archival materials relevant to the history of Guelph,

with its main focus on material artifacts. The archival collection has been informally arranged since the mid-1970s.

Cataloguing System:
Except for the photographs, the collection is informally arranged, with no cataloging and no finding aids. Some of the material has been organized into boxes labelled by subject, such as industries, greeting cards and militia.

Major Holdings:
1. Photographs: The collection includes approximately 1,000 photographs, which are all catalogued. The description includes title and date, accession date, source, subject headings, physical attributes and content and significance of photograph. Often supplementary sources such as city directories have been used.
2. Maps: The collection includes several rare area maps.
3. Books and periodicals: A small collection of material relevant to the Guelph area.
4. Business records: The collection includes records of the American Hotel, owned and operated by John McAteer, the Guelph Railway Company, and several business catalogues.

GUELPH COLLEGIATE-VOCATIONAL INSTITUTE ARCHIVES (GCI)
155 Paisley Road, Guelph, Ontario N1H 2P3
Telephone: (519) 824-9800

Hours: Monday to Friday, 9 a.m. to 3:15 p.m.
Prior appointment is recommended.

Archivist: Bill McKinnie

Cataloguing System:
The records are all catalogued and are arranged by departments generating records.

Major Holdings:
Holdings include commencement programs, course calendars, departmental examination results, examination mark books, cash books, year books, and minutes for the Guelph Collegiate Institute Literary Society.

GUELPH LAND REGISTRY OFFICE (GLR)
21 Douglas Street, Guelph, Ontario N1H 2S7
Telephone: (519) 822-0251

Hours: Monday to Friday, 9 a.m. to 4:30 p.m.
Prior appointment is recommended.

Contact: Kenneth McCrea, Land Registrar

Cataloguing System:

The abstract indexes of deed are arranged alphabetically by place name. The plans are stored sequentially by catalogue number and are accompanied by an index book that relates title to plan numbers. Copies of all plans are being acquired for the University of Guelph Library.

GUELPH PUBLIC LIBRARY (GPL)
100 Norfolk Street, Guelph, Ontario N1H 4J6
Telephone: (519) 824-6220

Hours: Monday to Saturday, 10 a.m. to 8 p.m.
Prior appointment is required for retrieval of materials not on open access.

Archivist and Local History Librarian: Linda Kearns

History of Collection:

Guelph Public Library has a local history collection that has been used by academics, genealogists, students, amateur and professional historians, journalists and municipal officials. The Library has produced a 15-page summary of its holdings, **Genealogy and Local History** (1988 edition). The collection of 15,000 items of primary and secondary materials has been systematically catalogued and provided with finding aids. The process by which this was accomplished, using a VICTOR 9000 microcomputer and database management and word-processing software, is described in Linda J. Kearns, 'John Galt meets VICTOR 9000,' **Canadian Library Journal** 43, 2 (1986): 97-103.

Cataloguing System:

There are four distinct but interconnected indexes, one full record index for each of the major holdings in the collection, and the keyword index which is effectively an index to the whole collection. For public use, there are hard-copy versions of each index at the Reference Desk. There is also an index to all headings used in the Local History Vertical File. Inter-archival loan of microforms available.

Major Holdings:
1. Audio-visual: mainly photographs
2. Printed materials: such as books, manuscripts, minutes, typescripts, scrapbooks, legal documents, and ephemera.
3. Private collections: Each major collection has a separate finding aid held at the Reference Desk, that lists individual entries in each collection. Collections include the Brimmell Collection, Byerly Collection, Douglass Collection, Goldie Collection, Hammill Collection, Higinbotham Collection, McIlwraith Collection, and the Shutt Collection.

GUELPH ST ANDREW'S PRESBYTERIAN CHURCH ARCHIVES (GSA)
161 Norfolk Street, Guelph, Ontario
Telephone: (519) 822-4772

Hours: Tuesday to Friday, 9 a.m. to 3 p.m.
Prior appointment is essential.

Contact: Rev. Dr. Peter Darch, Minister

Cataloguing System:
    The records are all catalogued and are accompanied by a list that briefly describes and gives the shelf number for each item.

Major Holdings:
    Holdings include annual reports, financial statements, anniversary programs, baptismal registers, marriage registers, communion rolls, board of manager minutes, congregational meeting minutes, session minutes, land records and photographs.

GUELPH TOWNSHIP OFFICE (GTO)

R.R. #5, Guelph, Ontario   N1H 6J2
Telephone: (519) 822-4661

Major Holdings:
    Records include minutes, assessment rolls and collectors' rolls.

HARRISTON TOWN OFFICE (HTH)

Box 10, 68 Elora Street, Harriston, Ontario   N0G 1Z0
Telephone: (519) 338-3444

Major Holdings:
    Records include assessment rolls and a cash book for the 10th Judicial Divisional Court.

HISTORICAL SOCIETY OF PHILADELPHIA (HSP)

1300 Locust Street, Philadelphia, Pennsylvania, U.S. 19107

Major Holdings:
    The Society holds thirteen watercolours or sketches by David Johnston Kennedy about the Guelph region. Black and white photographs may be ordered at the above address.

HOMEWOOD SANITARIUM ARCHIVES (HSA)

150 Delhi Street, Guelph, Ontario   N1E 6K9
Telephone: (519) 824-1010

Hours: Monday to Friday, except Thursday morning, 9 to 11:30 a.m and 12 noon to 3:15 p.m.

Prior appointment essential.

Librarian: Joyce Pharoah

Cataloguing System:
The archival holdings are organized by the administration of each director of the Homewood: Dr. Stephen Lett from 1883 to 1901, Dr. A.T. Hobbs from 1901 to 1923, Dr. C.B. Farrar from 1923 to 1925, and Dr. H.C. Clare from 1925 to 1942. The card index has one descriptive entry for each item within each of these four major divisions. Permission from the Executive Director must be obtained, and researchers must sign a form consenting to the Homewood's policies for research.

Major Holdings:
The collection includes many photographs, some correspondence, a small number of legal records, and partial runs of accounting records, minutes and annual reports.

JESUIT FATHERS OF UPPER CANADA ARCHIVES (JA)
15 St Mary Street, Toronto, Ontario, M4Y 2R5
Telephone: (416) 968-7525 or 922-5474

Hours: Monday to Friday, 9 a.m. to 3 p.m.
Prior appointment essential.

Contact: Rev. Edward Dowling

Major Holdings:
Material relating to the work of the Jesuits in Ontario and Western Canada that has particular relevance to Guelph and Wellington County. The Jesuit Fathers served the Guelph Parish from 1852 to 1931 and were responsible for building the Church of Our Lady (opened 1888). Guelph was chosen in 1913 as the site of the St Stanislaus Novitiate to train priests for all of English Canada. There are separate collections of materials relating to Guelph and the Novitiate as well as general printed volumes that provide useful context on the organization of the Jesuit Order in North America.

JOHN McCRAE HOUSE (JMH)
108 Water Street, Guelph, Ontario N1G 1A6
Telephone: (519) 836-1482

Hours: Monday to Friday, 1 to 5 p.m.
Prior appointment recommended. Morning appointments can be arranged.

Curator: Mary Anne Neville

Major Holdings:
Records include family photograph albums, scrapbooks, a sketch book of McCrae's drawings, a diary about McCrae's service in the Boer War, and correspondence about the founding of John McCrae Memorial Garden and McCrae House.

KITCHENER PUBLIC LIBRARY (KPL):
GRACE SCHMIDT ROOM OF LOCAL HISTORY
85 Queen Street North, Kitchener, Ontario N2H 2H1
Telephone: (519) 743-0271

Hours: Monday to Thursday, 10 a.m. to 9 p.m.; Friday 10 a.m. to 5.30 p.m.: Saturday 9 a.m. to 5.30 p.m.

Contact: Susan Hoffman, Local History Librarian/Archivist

Major Holdings: Records of the Waterloo Historical Society and other materials relating to Kitchener-Waterloo include also some newspapers and maps and plans for parts of Wellington County, mainly Fergus, Elora and Nichol Township.

MACDONALD STEWART ART CENTRE (MSC)
358 Gordon Street at College, Guelph, Ontario N1G 1Y1
Telephone: (519) 837-0010

Hours: Tuesday to Friday, Noon to 5 p.m.
Prior appointment is necessary.

Contact: Judith Nasby, Director

Cataloguing System:
Each piece of art is catalogued and is accompanied by a file that includes accession information, occasional correspondence and a photograph of the work.

Major Holdings:
Records include approximately 90 sketches, paintings, graphics, photographs, maps and sculpture depicting the Wellington County area that were created during the period from 1830 to 1940. Artists include internationally acclaimed individuals such as A.J. Casson and David Johnston Kennedy, as well as local individuals such as Thomas Connon, John Connon, Daniel Jones and Effie Smith. Black and white photographs and coloured slides may be ordered. Some are available as reproductions, notes or postcards at the Gallery Shop.

MARYBOROUGH TOWNSHIP OFFICE (MBH)
Box 39, Adam Brown Street, Moorefield, Ontario N0G 2K0
Telephone: (519) 638-2831

Major Holdings:
Records include council bylaws, minutes, cash books, land records, Moorefield council minutes, and Maryborough Township S.S. #13 Board cash and minute books.

McMASTER UNIVERSITY LIBRARY: ARCHIVES AND RESEARCH COLLECTIONS (MUL)
1280 Main Street West, Hamilton, Ontario L8S 4L6
Telephone: (416) 525-9140 extension 2079

Hours: Monday to Friday, 9 a.m. to 5 p.m.
Prior appointment is recommended.

Archivist: Charlotte Stewart

Cataloguing System:
The archives hold Anglican church records for eighteen congregations in Wellington County which are accompanied by a card index arranged alphabetically by place name and name of church. There are detailed finding aids for the records of each church which give a brief history of the church, a general listing of the records, and a more detailed description of the parish registers and other documents. The records have been microfilmed, and researchers usually examine these rather than the originals. Researchers must have written permission from the rector of the particular church before being allowed to examine the records.

METROPOLITAN TORONTO REFERENCE LIBRARY (MTL)
2789 Yonge Street, Toronto, Ontario, M4W 2G8
Telephone: (416) 393-7155

Hours: Monday to Thursday, 10 a.m. to 9 p.m.; Friday and Saturday, 10 a.m. to 6 p.m.; Sunday, 1.30 p.m. to 5 p.m. Shorter summer hours.

Contact: Staff of Baldwin Room, 4th floor

Major Holdings:
Mainly material relating to the history of Metropolitan Toronto, but with some notable items relevant to Guelph and Wellington County. These include some Canada Company land records and maps and plans; family and personal papers; architectural drawings, art works and photographs. Materials are catalogued in a card index by place, person and corporate name.

MINTO TOWNSHIP OFFICE (MTH)
Box 160, Harriston, Ontario N0G 1Z0
Telephone: (519) 338-2511

Major Holdings:
   Records include council minutes, bylaws, cash books and Board of Health minutes.

MOUNT FOREST PUBLIC LIBRARY (MFL)
P.O. Box 307, Mount Forest, Ontario N0G 2L0
Telephone: (519) 323-4541

Hours: Monday to Friday, 1 to 5 p.m. and 6:30 to 9 p.m.

Librarian: Joan Moore

Major Holdings:
   Records include accession records, cash books and minutes of the board of the Mount Forest Public Library, which are informally held in the basement of the library.   The library also holds a small historical file on the Mount Forest area.

MOUNT FOREST TOWN OFFICE (MFH)
Box 188, 102 Main Street, Mount Forest, Ontario N0G 2L0
Telephone: (519) 323-2150

Major Holdings:
   Records include council bylaws, committee reports, cash books, assessment rolls and collectors' rolls.

MUTUAL LIFE OF CANADA ARCHIVES (MLA)
227 King Street South, Waterloo, Ontario, N2J 4C5
Telephone: (519) 888-2769

Hours: Monday to Friday, 8.30 a.m. to 4.30 p.m.
Prior appointment and approval of research essential.

Contact: Nancy Saunders-Maitland, Corporate Archivist

Major Holdings: Company records that have relevance include files on directors and officers, and evidence of agencies, persons insured, and mortgages and other investments in Guelph and Wellington County.

NATIONAL ARCHIVES OF CANADA/ARCHIVES NATIONALES DU CANADA (NAC)

395 Wellington Street, Ottawa, Ontario, K1A 0N3
Telephone: (613) 995-5138

National Archivist: Jean-Pierre Wallot

Hours: Monday to Friday, 8.30. a.m. to 4.45 p.m.; extended reading room hours.

Cataloguing System and Services: After registering in the main foyer, the researcher can consult inventories, finding aids, file listings, indexes and card catalogues relating to the large and varied holdings in the 3rd floor reference room. Specific material is requested and retrieved from the 3rd floor reading room, where it may be stored in lockers and consulted during extended hours. An expanding proportion of the material is on microfilm and can be consulted on a self-service basis. Photocopying, microfilming and photo reproduction services are available but will probably take several weeks.

Major Holdings:

As the national repository for records of the government of Canada and for materials relating to institutions and individuals of national significance, the Archives is not an obvious source for projects of local and regional history. Careful preparation is advisable to make the most of research visits. Materials that are relevant to Guelph and Wellington County include maps and plans, photographs and architectural drawings, the records of some government departments and the papers and records of various individuals and institutions. Guides to the holdings of the National Archives include:

Terry Cook and Glenn T. Wright, **Historical records of the Government of Canada** (Ottawa, 1981) that briefly describes all the record groups;
General Guide Series 1983: Federal Archives Division (Ottawa, 1983);
General Guide Series 1983: Manuscript Division (1984);
General Guide Series 1983: National Map Collection (Ottawa, 1985);
General Guide Series 1983: National Photography Collection (Ottawa, 1984);
Union List of Manuscripts in Canadian Repositories (Ottawa, 1975), and supplements to 1985.

ONTARIO AGRICULTURAL MUSEUM ARCHIVES (OAM)

Tremaine Road, P.O. Box 38, Milton, Ontario L9T 2Y3
Telephone: (416) 878-8151

Hours: Monday to Friday, 9 a.m. to 4 p.m.
Prior appointment is recommended.

Contact: Susan Bennett, Research-Reference Librarian

Major Holdings:

The collection includes several photographs and trade catalogues for area industries which can be identified by use of the card catalogue that is arranged alphabetically and by name of company and geographical location.

ONTARIO HYDRO ARCHIVES (OHA)
800 Kipling Avenue (KD 170), Toronto, Ontario M8Z 5S4
Telephone: (416) 231-4111 ext. 7102

Hours: Monday to Friday, 8 a.m. to 4 p.m.

Contact: Wendy Law, Corporate Archivist
Prior appointment necessary. Researchers wishing to visit the Archives should send a written statement of objectives to: Corporate Official Records Officer, Ontario Hydro, 700 University Avenue (H6 A17), Toronto, Ontario M5G 1X6.

Major Holdings:
The Archives was established to acquire, preserve and provide access to the historically valuable records of the corporation. Of particular relevance to Guelph are the records of the Guelph Radial Railway, the street railway system that was acquired and operated between 1920 and 1939 by the Hydro Electric Power Commission of Ontario (later Ontario Hydro). The Archives also has records of the electrification of Guelph and other Wellington County municipalities and historical photographs.

ONTARIO MINISTRY OF AGRICULTURE AND FOOD, PHOTOGRAPHIC SERVICES (OMA)
University of Guelph, Johnston Hall, Room 38
Telephone: (519) 824-4120 ext. 3323

Hours: Monday to Friday, 8:15 to 4:30
No appointment necessary.

Contact: Contact may be made with any office member.

Major Holding: Sallows Collection of photographs.

Cataloguing System:
The photographs are readily retrievable in small filing cabinets, and have a finding aid that lists each photograph by title and date. A brief biography of Sallows is included.

PEEL AND MARYBOROUGH FIRE INSURANCE COMPANY (PMF)
P.O. Box 190, Drayton, Ontario N0G 1P0
Telephone: (519) 638-3304

Hours: Monday to Friday, 9 a.m. to 4 p.m.

Contact: Jack Kidnie, Manager

Major Holdings:
Records include board minutes and a bank passbook of the company.

PEEL TOWNSHIP OFFICE (PTO)
Box 119, John Street, Drayton, Ontario N0G 1P0
Telephone: (519) 638-3314

Major Holdings:
Records include council bylaws, minutes, auditors' reports and a non-resident tax book.

PILKINGTON TOWNSHIP OFFICE (PKH)
Box 580, Elora, Ontario N0B 1S0
Telephone: (519) 846-9801

Major Holdings:
Records include cash books and land records.

PRESBYTERIAN CHURCH IN CANADA ARCHIVES (PCA)
59 St George Street, Toronto, Ontario, M5S 2E6
Telephone: (416) 595-1277

Hours: Monday to Friday, 8.30 a.m. to 12.15 p.m.; 1.15 to 4.30 p.m.

Contact: Rev. T.M. Bailey, Archivist; Kim Moir, Deputy Archivist
Prior appointment recommended.

Major Holdings:
Records of the General Assembly, synods, presbyteries and congregations. Materials on Guelph-Wellington relate mainly to the smaller congregations and are accessible through a card index catalogue.

PUSLINCH TOWNSHIP OFFICE (PUS)
R.R. #3, Guelph, Ontario N1H 6H9
Telephone: (519) 822-6499

Major Holdings:
Records include council bylaws, minutes, cash books, assessment rolls, Board of Health minutes, an Aberfoyle general store account book, and the Mill Creek Council of Royal Templars minute book.

REGISTRAR-GENERAL'S OFFICE (RGO)
Macdonald Block, 2nd Floor,
Queen's Park, Toronto, Ontario M7A 1Y5
Telephone: (416) 965-2280

Hours: Monday to Friday, 9 a.m. to 4 p.m.
By appointment only.

Contact: Barbara Holloway

Cataloguing System:
Statistics are arranged alphabetically by municipality. Details of arrangements for birth, death and marriage registers are extensively described in the inventory. Permission to use the vital statistics must be given by the Registrar-General, and an oath of secrecy must be taken.

ROYAL ONTARIO MUSEUM: SIGMUND SAMUEL CANADIANA LIBRARY (ROM)
14 Queen's Park, Toronto, Ontario
Telephone: (416) 586-5524

Hours: Monday to Friday, 10 a.m. to 4:30 p.m.
Appointment recommended

Contact: Reference librarian

Cataloguing System:
The card index is arranged by subject and geographical location and often includes a photograph of the work.

Major Holdings:
The collection includes a small number of regional paintings and lithographs reproduced in the Canadian Illustrated News, 1871 to 1874.

ST JOSEPH'S HOSPITAL ARCHIVES (SJA)
80 Westmount Street, Guelph, Ontario N1H 5H7
Telephone: (519) 824-2620

Hours: Monday to Friday, 9 a.m. to 4 p.m.
By appointment only.

Contact: Tim McClemont, Public Relations

Cataloguing System:
The records have recently been catalogued and organized by catalogue number into clearly labelled boxes. There is a card index that is arranged sequentially by catalogue number, and includes a brief description of each item.

Major Holdings:
Holdings include medical statistics on patients, administrative correspondence and cash books for both the hospital and the House of Providence.

UNITED CHURCH ARCHIVES (UCA)

73 Queen's Park Crescent, Victoria University
Toronto, Ontario   M5S 1K7
Telephone: (416) 585-4563

Hours: Monday to Friday, 8:30 a.m. to 4:30 p.m.

Archivist: Jean Dryden

Cataloguing System:

The records are well organized and carefully identified, and are accompanied by a card index that is arranged alphabetically by church name and geographical location.

Major Holdings:

Holdings include any surviving records from churches which in 1925 joined to form the United Church of Canada. Records include baptismal registers, death registers, marriage registers, communion rolls, minutes and cash books. Denominations of churches for which the archives holds records include Presbyterian, Methodist, Methodist New Connection, Wesleyan Methodist, Primitive Methodist, Congregational and Evangelical United Brethren. The archives also hold a complete set of the church newspaper, Christian Guardian, with an extensive subject index, and annual reports of missionary societies and general conferences.

UNIVERSITY OF GUELPH LIBRARY: ARCHIVAL AND SPECIAL COLLECTIONS (UGA)

Macdonald Stewart Room, University of Guelph Library
Guelph, Ontario N1G 2W1
Telephone: (519) 824-4120 extension 3413

Hours: Monday to Friday, 8:30 a.m. to 4:45 p.m.

Contact: Nancy Sadek, Librarian

Cataloguing System:

Access to archival material can be gained through use of the University of Guelph Library's CD-ROM online catalogue system to identify and locate materials. Examination of specific materials may be requested at Macdonald Stewart Room. Staff will retain acceptable identification of researchers while material is being examined. Inter-archival loan of microforms available.

Major Holdings:
1. University history and administration.
2. Rare books and early editions: including books on farming methods and veterinary practices.
3. Maps and plans: including early Guelph and Canada Company maps.

4. Newspapers: including the Canadian Farmer and the Canadian Agriculturist, spanning the period from the 1840s to the 1870s.
5. Private Collections: include the Allan-Highinbotham Collection, Byerly Collection, Connon Collection, Couling Collection, Gilkison-Fraser Collection, Goodwin-Haines Collection, Guelph Historical Society Collection, H.B. Timothy Collection and Marston-Archibald Collection, Mickle Collection, Sleeman Collection and the Thorning Collection.

Note: The location code UGL is used for rare books such as directories, fo newspapers and some maps and plans held in the University Library. The CD-ROM online catalogue will specify exact location and call number of each item.

UNIVERSITY OF TORONTO: THOMAS FISHER RARE BOOKS LIBRARY (UTA)
120 St George Street, Toronto, Ontario, M5S 1A5
Telephone: (416) 978-6107 or 978-5332

Hours: Monday to Friday, 9.00 a.m. to 5.00 p.m.

Contact: Richard Landry, Head; Katherine Martyn, Assistant Head

Major Holdings:
The only materials relevant to Guelph-Wellington are architectural drawings and other files of the Toronto architect, G.M. Miller, who designed the Macdonald Institute and Hall and the Massey Hall and Library.

UNIVERSITY OF WATERLOO RARE BOOKS COLLECTION (UWL)
DORIS LEWIS RARE BOOK ROOM
Waterloo, Ontario, N2L 3G1
Telephone: (519) 885-1211, ext. 3122

Hours: Monday to Friday, 9 to 12 a.m. and 1 to 4p.m; and by appointment.

Contact: Susan Bellingham, Head, Special Collections

Major Holdings: In the local history collection are a few items relevant to Wellington County.

UNIVERSITY OF WESTERN ONTARIO: REGIONAL HISTORY COLLECTION (UWO)
D.B. Weldon Library, University of Western Ontario,
London, Ontario, N6A 3K7
Telephone: (519) 661-3161 or 679-2111, ext. 4813

Hours: Monday to Friday, 9.00 a.m. to 5.00 p.m.

Contact: Edward Phelps, Librarian

Major Holdings:

Records and other material relating to southwestern Ontario, especially the City of London and Middlesex County. Many more materials for Guelph-Wellington were held in the past, but most of these have recently been transferred to the University of Guelph Library (Archival and Special Collections). The collection also includes a unique set of fire insurance plans. and the records of the Landon Project of the mid-1970s.

WELLINGTON COUNTY ARCHIVES (WCA)
Wellington Place, R.R. 1, Fergus, Ontario N1M 2W3
Telephone: (519) 846-0916

Hours: Monday to Friday, 8:30 a.m. to 12 noon and 1 p.m. to 4:30 p.m. Appointment recommended.

Archivist: Bonnie Callen

History of Collection:

The archives is a rapidly expanding repository for rare historical records relating to Wellington County, which has developed since the mid-1970s in association with the Wellington County Museum. Archives and Museum are located in the newly renovated Wellington Place, formerly the Wellington County House of Industry and Refuge.

Cataloguing System:

Access to the collections is provided by the card index and finding aids, located in the reading room. The card index is arranged alphabetically by municipality. Each municipal section is sub-divided into subjects, such as art, commercial, government, history, property, family, medical, military, religion and social. Throughout the entire index, individuals are cross-indexed alphabetically by family name. All microfilmed material are filed separately in the main office. The major collections all have separate finding aids, which list contents, dates and catalogue numbers.

Major Holdings:
1. Private Collections: include the Arthur History Book Collection, Isabel Cunningham Burr Collection, Byerly Collection, Connon Collecttion, Couling Collection, Kortland Collection, Mestern Collection, Superior Barn Collection, Templin-Dow Collection, and the Wellington County Society of Historical Research Collection.
2. Photograph Collection: over 8000 photos indexed by family name, location and subject.
3. Area Directories: dating from 1846-1911.
4. Newspaper Collection: Elora papers from 1852, Fergus from 1854, Drayton from 1892, Arthur from 1896, Guelph 1847-1856.
5. Pamphlets: on local, school and church history.
6. Census manuscripts: microfilms of 1851, 1861, 1871, 1881 and 1891 for Wellington County.

7. Municipal Records: Early assessment and collectors' rolls, minute books, bylaws, cash books for most municipalities in the County.
8. Land Records: microfilm copies of land abstracts and early deeds.
9. Genealogy Files: family histories indexed by family name.
10. Wills: Wellington County wills and probate papers, 1840-1901.

WELLINGTON COUNTY BOARD OF EDUCATION (WBE)
500 Victoria Road North, Guelph, Ontario N1E 6K2
Telephone: (519) 822-4420

Hours: Monday to Friday, 9 a.m. to 4:30 p.m.
Appointment is essential.

Contact: Rowena Lewis, Secretary to the Board

Cataloguing System:
The collection is informally organized alphabetically by school place name in filing cabinets and a separate storage room. Because there are no finding aids and everything is not in order, researchers must be prepared for extensive searches.

Major holdings:
The collection includes a large quantity of records for most township school sections, and many schools in Elora, Fergus and Guelph. The records include shcool and board minutes, cash books, attendance registers, and school census registers. Some school records are held by local municipalities and the Wellington County Archives.

WELLINGTON COUNTY SEPARATE SCHOOL BOARD (WSB)
P.O. Box 1298, 75 Woolwich Street, Guelph, Ontario N1H 6N6
Telephone: 821-4600

Hours: Monday to Friday, 9 a.m. to 4:30 p.m.
Prior appointment is required.

Contact: Patrick Murray, Director

Cataloguing System:
Records are informally arranged and have no finding aids or catalogue numbers.

Major Holdings:
The limited holdings include several cash books, board minutes and a small amount of correspondence.

INDEXES

CREATORS, CORPORATE

Morriston Spring Seed Fair: 1014.
Mount Forest (St Mary's) Catholic: 1952.
Mount Forest (St Paul's) Ang: 1413-16.
Mount Forest Agricultural Society: 2005.
Mount Forest Business College: 1091.
Mount Forest Horticultural Society: 2006-7.
Mount Forest Pres: 1902.
Mount Forest Public Library: 928-30, 3667-68.
Mount Forest T: 446, 447-62, 824-25, 2705-9.
Mount Forest Town Council: 3449.
Mundell Collection: 3669.
Munro, Fasken and Wilson: 1136.
Mutual Life Assurance Company: 1137-53.

Nassagaweya MNew-Meth: 1580.
Nassagaweya Pres: 1750-52.
National Archives of Canada: 3670.
National Photographic Collection: 3450.
Newman Collection: 1154.
Nichol (Zion) Meth: 1581.
Nichol Mutual Fire Insurance Company: 1156.
Nichol Tp Agricultural Societies: 1986.
Nichol Tp: 315-29, 732, 826-44, 864, 2710-12.
North Erin Cong: 1461-62.
North Wellington Constitutional Reform Association:
    2093.
North Wellington Teachers' Association: 2053.
Northern Assurance Company: 1157.

Ontario Agricultural College. Dairy School: 2205.
Ontario Agricultural College: 2197-98, 2200-2204,
    2206-16, 3451-52.
Ontario Board of Agriculture: 2008.
Ontario Board of Public Instruction: 950.
Ontario Department of Agriculture. Home Economics
    Branch: 939.
Ontario Department of Agriculture: 937-38, 2009-10.
Ontario Department of Education: 951-63.
Ontario Department of Public Highways: 2804, 3225.
Ontario Genealogical Society: 3671-3725.
Ontario Legislative Assembly: 965-68.
Ontario Ministry of Natural Resources: 2713.
Ontario Normal School of Domestic Science and Art:
    964.
Ontario Provincial Secretary: 972-75.
Ontario Provincial Winter Fair: 2011-13.
Ontario Reformatory: 2264-65.
Ontario Registrar-General: 969-71.
Ontario Veterinary College: 2217-21.
Orangeville (Bethel) Pres: 1903-7.
Orangeville (St Andrew's) Pres: 1908.
Orangeville (Zion) Pres: 1909.
Orangeville MPri: 1582-85.
Orangeville T: 463-65, 2714-15.
Order of Chosen Friends, Guelph: 2068.

Oustic (St Peter's) Catholic: 1955.

Palmerston (Knox) Pres: 1753-63.
Palmerston Public Library: 931.
Palmerston T: 2716.
Palmerston V: 466-72, 2717.
Pat Mestern Collection: 3453.
Patrons of Industry, Arthur Association No. 678: 2014.
Peel and Maryborough Mutual Fire Insurance
    Company: 1158-59.
Peel Meth Circuit: 1586-88.
Peel MPri: 1589-90.
Peel Tp: 330-41, 782, 845-66, 2718, 2720-23.
Peel Tp: Glenallan: 2719.
Peel, Maryborough and Drayton Agricultural Society:
    2015.
People's Railway Company: 1296.
Pilkington Tp: 342-54, 732, 842-44, 864, 867-76,
    2724-31.
Pollock Collection: 3726.
Ponsonby UC: 1966.
Potter Collection: 3727.
Presbyterian Church in Canada: 1610.
Presbyterian Church Association: 1609.
Presto Music Club of Guelph: 2084-87.
Preston Evangelical Lutheran: 1475-78.
Priory Club Limited, Guelph: 2095.
Provincial Insurance Surveys: 2837-40.
Provincial Mutual and General Insurance Company,
    Guelph: 1160.
Puslinch (Knox) Pres: 1764-69.
Puslinch Agricultural Society: 2016.
Puslinch Farmers' Club: 2017.
Puslinch Mutual Fire Insurance Company: 1161-64.
Puslinch Pioneer: 3728.
Puslinch Township, S.S.#1: 877.
Puslinch Tp: 56, 355-71, 878-83, 2732-36.

R.G. Dun and Company: 1100-1101.
Railway Committee of Privy Council: 994-95.
Rantoul Collection: 3457.
Raymond Employees' Mutual Benefit Society: 2069.
Raymond Manufacturing Company: 1206.
Raymond Sewing Machine Company: 1207.
Rea-Armstrong Collection: 3458.
Richard Boyle Contractor: 1297.
Riverbank Cheese and Butter Company: 1208.
Riverstown (Good Shepherd) Ang: 1417-23.
Robertson and Cook: 2524.
Rockwood (Sacred Heart) Catholic: 1956.
Rockwood (St John's) Ang: 1424-27.
Rockwood Academy: 1092-93.
Rockwood Meth: 1591.
Rockwood MWes-Meth Circuit: 1594.
Rockwood MWes-Meth: 1592-97.

30th Regiment, Wellington Rifles, Elora: 2134.
30th Regiment, Wellington Rifles, Guelph: 2135.
30th Wellington Battalion of Rifles: 2136.

CREATORS, PERSONAL

Abrey, Mr: 2922.
Allan Family: 2288-89.
Allan, Charles: 2281.
Allan, Christina: 2282-83.
Allan, David: 1094, 1170, 1231, 2284-87, 2292, 3338, 3419.
Allan, William: 1232, 2290-92.
Anderson Family: 2293.
Andrich, A.: 1030.
Archibald Family: 2294.
Archibald, James: 1095-96, 2295-97.
Archibald, Katherine: 2298.
Arkell, John: 2604.
Armstrong, Simon: 1031.
Armstrong, W.: 2935.
Armstrong, William: 3474.

Balfour, D.: 2299.
Barber, R.H.: 1033.
Barker, Enoch, Rev.: 1971-72.
Barker, W.H.: 2936, 3295.
Bayliss, D.J.: 3357.
Beattie Family: 2300-2301.
Beattie, David: 3566.
Beattie, George: 2303.
Beattie, Lillian A.: 2302.
Beattie, William: 2303.
Bindemann, Frederick W., Rev.: 1973.
Black, Hugh: 2849.
Black, James, Rev.: 1974.
Black, S.: 3293.
Blaney Family: 2289.
Blyth, Thomas A.: 3296.
Bolton, E.D.: 3238, 3311.
Bolton, Lewis: 2876, 3239-42, 3255-56, 3267, 3312-19.
Boultbee, William: 2858-59.
Bouthillier, T.: 2907.
Bowman, E.P.: 2877, 2966-73, 3186, 3339-40.
Bowman, Herbert: 2937.
Boyer, Peter: 1035.
Boyle, David: 2304.
Boyle, Everett M.: 2057.
Boyle, Frank: 2305.
Brandon, Franklin: 2612.
Broadfoot, Mary: 1262, 3569-70.
Brosius, H.: 2974.
Buchanan, Isaac: 1036, 1263.
Burke, J.W.: 2878-79, 3257-58, 3329-30.
Burnett Family: 2307.
Burnett, Arthur: 2306.
Burr, Isabel Cunningham: 3571-72.
Burwell, Lewis: 2613, 2880, 3297.
Burwell, Mahlon: 2614, 2783.

Byerly, A.E.: 3573-76.

Calder, John: 2308.
Callaghan, P.: 2615.
Campbell, Hugh: 1040.
Carbert, J.A.: 2960.
Carder, Joseph: 2309.
Carroll, C.: 2873.
Casson, A.J.: 3475-76.
Cattlin, F.: 2976.
Chadwick, F.J.: 2977-3003, 3188-90, 3197.
Chase, Caleb: 1176.
Chiles, G.: 3477.
Clark, Alister M.: 3004.
Clarke Family: 2315-2317.
Clarke, Charles Kirk: 2311.
Clarke, Charles: 1238, 2089, 2310, 2312-13.
Clarke, Elizabeth: 2314.
Clawson, E.E.: 2983.
Cleghorn Family: 2318-19.
Cleghorn, Catharine: 3585.
Cleghorn, James: 2320.
Cleghorn, John: 2321.
Coales, H.R.: 3364.
Coleman, R.H.: 3005.
Collins, Thomas, Rev.: 1931.
Connon Family: 2322.
Connon, John: 1041-42, 2323-26, 3424-25, 3587-89.
Connon, Thomas, Jr: 2330.
Connon, Thomas: 1043, 2327-29, 3478-82.
Connor, Harry: 2097.
Cooper, T.W.: 2908-9, 3006-42, 3191-92.
Corley Family: 2331.
Cotterell, A.T.: 2788.
Couling, Gordon: 3591.
Cowan, W.A.: 3365.
Cowan, William: 2332.
Croft, Nathaniel: 1044.
Cromar Family: 2333.
Cromar, Robert: 1000.
Crowe Family: 2334.
Crowley, Terry: 2090.
Cunningham, Robert: 2335.

Davidson, Alexander: 1045.
Davidson, James: 1046.
Davidson, John Alexander: 2336.
Davidson, John: 2337-38.
Davis, John: 2851, 3043-49, 3193, 3243-48.
Davis, W.M.: 3050.
Day, Thomas: 1001.
Devine, T.: 2789.
Devine, Thomas: 3341.
Dick, D.S.: 3366-68.
Dooley, J.M.: 1181.

PLACES

Eden Mills: 1101, 1470, 1594-95, 1607, 1610, 1750-52, 1814-16, 2160, 2524, 2897, 2899, 2903, 3473, 3754, 3759.

Edinburgh, Scotland: 1766, 2284, 2293, 2350, 2496.

Egerton: 1101.

Elfhill, Scotland: 2327, 3481-82.

Elora Gorge: 3421, 3424, 3426.

Elora: 16, 25-34, 37, 318, 397-414, 474-75, 479-80, 501-25, 906-15, 940, 943, 960-61, 968, 975, 980, 989-93, 1015-16, 1030, 1036-39, 1041-43, 1045, 1048, 1050-51, 1054, 1059, 1068, 1076, 1095-96, 1101-2, 1147, 1154-55, 1157, 1169, 1171, 1183, 1221-22, 1238, 1246, 1252-56, 1264, 1279, 1295, 1316-17, 1319, 1353-55, 1440, 1482, 1513-17, 1607-8, 1610, 1615-25, 1817-26, 1918, 1931, 1933, 1971-72, 1975, 1987-88, 1990-92, 2009, 2029-34, 2053, 2055-56, 2059, 2077-78, 2089, 2099, 2116, 2122, 2134, 2140-42, 2152, 2281, 2294-2298, 2301, 2304, 2310-13, 2315-17, 2322-30, 2333, 2335-36, 2341, 2358-68, 2370, 2428, 2431, 2447, 2461-62, 2470, 2516, 2519, 2524, 2566-69, 2630, 2632, 2638-40, 2748, 2790, 2797, 2821-23, 2838, 2877-95, 3389, 3393, 3421, 3425, 3428-29, 3475, 3478-80, 3555, 3573, 3574, 3576, 3580, 3583-84, 3586-90, 3593, 3595, 3612-14, 3617-19, 3633, 3655-57, 3662, 3664, 3669, 3713, 3727, 3735, 3737-38, 3749, 3750, 3753-54, 3759.

Ennotville: 1045, 1101, 1988, 2035-40, 2055, 2124, 3299, 3569, 3615, 3759.

Eramosa Township: 49, 50, 63, 67, 110, 189, 191-206, 208, 475, 478, 526-56, 932, 975, 988-92, 1001, 1005, 1011, 1074, 1098, 1101, 1147, 1184-85, 1190, 1301, 1309-10, 1444-49, 1482, 1518-21, 1580, 1591-97, 1607, 1751-52, 1814-16, 1827-44, 1896, 1910-15, 1917, 1955, 1967-68, 1969-72, 1974, 1983, 1993, 2017, 2041, 2055, 2063, 2154-55, 2336, 2349, 2390, 2404, 2452, 2457-58, 2461, 2464, 2467, 2475, 2487, 2489-90, 2510, 2603, 2621, 2641-45, 2703, 2713, 2749, 2763, 2766, 2769, 2780, 2782, 2799, 2897-2906, 3370, 3455, 3458, 3530, 3549, 3573, 3580, 3590, 3594, 3596, 3647, 3672, 3705, 3715, 3726, 3730, 3739, 3753, 3759.

Erasmus: 1101.

Erin Township: 51, 63, 67, 110, 209-28, 474, 478, 557-99, 975, 989-92, 1011, 1025, 1062, 1072, 1101, 1112, 1147, 1190, 1321, 1356, 1358, 1360, 1363-64, 1407-11, 1435-36, 1441, 1461-62, 1482, 1500, 1522-24, 1607, 1774-79, 1845-47, 1958-65, 1972, 1974, 1978, 1982, 1988, 2060, 2158, 2454, 2603, 2621, 2627, 2646-51, 2713, 2750, 2769, 2780, 2799, 2907-22, 2924-25, 2927-34, 3369, 3473, 3590, 3596, 3624, 3650-51, 3673, 3714, 3726, 3739, 3753, 3759.

Erin: 16, 37, 415-22, 479, 600, 975, 992, 1003, 1082, 1101, 1147, 1317, 1319, 1356-64, 1482, 1522-24, 1610, 1896, 1908, 1958, 1960-62, 1978, 2151-53, 2570, 2652-53, 2824-25, 2923-33, 3759.

Evansville: 3253.

Everton: 190, 1005, 1011, 1074, 1101, 1184-85, 1594-95, 1900, 1978, 2041, 2155, 2490, 2510, 2900, 3647.

Farewell: 1101, 1365-68, 2444.

Farmington: 1101.

Farnham: 1101, 1328-30, 1332, 2604, 3338.

Fergus: 5, 16, 37, 46, 69, 423-42, 474-75, 479, 601-9, 940, 943, 948, 960-61, 968, 975, 987, 989-93, 1008, 1012, 1018, 1036, 1042, 1048-49, 1065-67, 1069, 1081, 1097, 1101, 1136, 1147, 1155-56, 1168, 1172, 1186, 1189, 1203, 1220, 1226-28, 1244, 1256, 1260, 1264, 1278, 1295-96, 1316-17, 1319, 1335, 1369-73, 1440, 1482, 1525-26, 1607-8, 1610, 1626-36, 1848-57, 1918, 1931, 1933, 1971-72, 1981, 1986, 2053-55, 2100-2105, 2125, 2152, 2223, 2232-42, 2245, 2300-2301, 2304, 2315, 2329, 2333, 2336, 2343, 2348, 2379, 2381-82, 2395, 2402-3, 2432-33, 2455, 2467, 2493-94, 2519, 2521, 2524, 2569, 2571-79, 2654-55, 2751, 2782, 2790, 2793, 2797, 2826, 2839, 2842-43, 2935-59, 2962, 3368, 3371, 3385, 3428, 3430, 3453, 3465-66, 3484, 3487, 3490, 3544, 3560, 3565, 3571-72, 3576, 3580, 3590, 3616, 3662-64, 3670, 3716, 3736-39, 3752-54, 3759, 3762.

Fifeshire, Scotland: 2293, 2471.

Forfarshire, Scotland: 2492.

Forks of the Credit: 1358.

Freiburg: 948.

Fulton Mills: 1101.

Gallowflat, Scotland: 1205.

Galt: 1186, 1266-67, 1482, 1608, 1981.

Garafraxa East Township: 111, 229, 990-91, 2417, 2603, 2656-57, 2713.

Garafraxa Road: 2738.

Garafraxa Township: 63, 67, 230, 988-89, 1009, 1101, 1295, 1333, 1440, 1463-64, 1496, 1583-85, 1607, 1896, 1908, 2403, 2458, 2524, 2573, 2617, 2621, 2631, 2658-59, 2752, 2769, 2794, 2960-63, 2965, 3614, 3739, 3759.

Garafraxa West Township: 37, 52, 111, 231-47, 475, 478, 610-31, 745, 841, 866, 975, 990-92, 1008, 1010, 1012, 1019, 1147, 1155-56, 1201, 1296, 1334-35, 1340, 1442-43, 1450-51, 1465-66, 1497-98, 1525, 1780-1813, 1890-93, 1916, 1971-72, 1988, 2151-53, 2301, 2388, 2603, 2660-62, 2713, 2766, 2772, 2799, 2964, 3590, 3596, 3654, 3684, 3725, 3753-54, 3759.

Lebanon: 1101.

Leslie Station: 1101.

Living Springs: 1101.

Lombardy, Italy: 2417.

London, England: 1173, 2351.

London: 2120, 3739.

Luther East Township: 747-48, 1046, 2679, 2680, 2713.

Luther Township: 63, 111, 480, 981, 988-91, 1101, 1123, 1155, 1333-34, 2603, 2613, 2681, 2702, 2754, 2769, 2794, 2805, 2861, 2865, 3254, 3614, 3739.

Luther West Township: 274-83, 492, 733-49, 975, 992, 1132, 1147, 1335, 1340, 1343-44, 1439, 1501-11, 2418, 2632, 2682-84, 2713, 2772, 3253, 3596, 3753.

Macton: 948, 1101.

Marden: 1980, 2157, 2160, 3208, 3611, 3734.

Marsville: 1101.

Maryborough Township: 55, 63, 111, 284-304, 750-82, 865, 975, 988-92, 1031, 1035, 1101, 1147, 1155, 1208, 1256-27, 1529, 1588, 1598, 1857, 2004, 2008, 2015, 2162, 2603, 2612, 2615, 2624, 2633, 2685-94, 2755, 2769, 2772, 2799, 2805, 3255-65, 3596, 3614, 3676, 3718, 3739, 3753.

Maryhill: 1947.

Maryland: 2443.

Melgrund: 1101.

Metz: 1101, 1802, 1811-12, 1889-93, 1988.

Mimosa: 1101, 1156, 1482, 1607, 1894-1901, 2158, 3473.

Minto Township: 111, 305-14, 480, 783-823, 931, 975, 988-92, 1071, 1076, 1101, 1147, 1155, 1205, 1303, 1404, 1406, 1499, 1888, 1982, 2008, 2058, 2374, 2376, 2395, 2437, 2509, 2603, 2624, 2634, 2696-2701, 2738, 2756, 2769, 2772, 2799, 2874, 3267-72, 3317-18, 3323, 3590, 3596, 3614, 3623, 3677, 3720, 3739, 3753, 3759.

Monck: 1101, 1439.

Monticello: 1101.

Montreal: 1173, 3739.

Moorefield: 294, 297-98, 474, 780, 1031, 1035, 1101, 1317, 1412, 1428-29, 1740-45, 2004, 2008, 2162, 2693, 3255-56, 3264-66.

Morriston: 1014, 1040, 1101, 1161, 1467-74, 1746-49, 1769, 1931, 2052, 3345, 3348-49, 3410-11, 3759.

Mosborough: 1101, 3759.

Mount Forest: 16, 37, 446-62, 474, 480, 824-25, 928-30, 948, 968, 975, 987, 990-93, 1036, 1086, 1091, 1101, 1147, 1205, 1316-17, 1319, 1413-16, 1480, 1502, 1610, 1888, 1902, 1918, 1931, 1934, 1952, 2005-7, 2055, 2064, 2299, 2304, 2331, 2388, 2447, 2485, 2518, 2592-95, 2677, 2705-9, 2757, 2840, 2848, 2857, 3273-94, 3444, 3449, 3457, 3533, 3667-68, 3708, 3719.

Mount View: 1101, 1502, 1505.

Nassagaweya Township: 1482, 1608, 1751-52, 1814-16.

New Germany: 1947.

Nichol Township: 63, 67, 69, 111, 113, 154, 315-29, 478, 480, 732, 826-44, 864, 948, 961, 975, 988-92, 1013, 1018, 1059, 1078, 1097, 1101, 1147, 1155-56, 1166, 1205, 1241, 1256, 1295-96, 1525, 1581, 1607, 1770-73, 1848-49, 1852, 1971, 1973, 1988, 2035-40, 2055, 2124, 2148, 2300-2301, 2303, 2308-9, 2326, 2336-37, 2343-44, 2346, 2360, 2362, 2366-68, 2402-3, 2448, 2466, 2471, 2573, 2635, 2710-13, 2758, 2763, 2782, 2793, 2799-2800, 2879, 2890, 2895, 2950, 2957, 3295-3310, 3337, 3453, 3521, 3526-27, 3529, 3566, 3569-70, 3572, 3588-90, 3596, 3614-15, 3624, 3663, 3678, 3721, 3737-39, 3749, 3753, 3759, 3761-62.

Normanby Township: 3288.

Old Meldrum, Scotland: 2337.

Olivet: 1101, 1587.

Ontario: 3459.

Orangeville: 463-65, 990-91, 1101, 1495-96, 1582-85, 1610, 1903-9, 2573, 2596, 2714-15, 2794, 2797.

Orton: 1101, 1482, 1896, 1988, 2151-53.

Oshawa: 1205.

Ospringe: 1072, 1101, 1607, 1610, 1988, 2151-53.

Oustic: 1001, 1101, 1918, 1934, 1955-56.

Paisley Block: 1300, 1543, 2332, 2492, 3603.

Palmerston: 16, 466-72, 474, 480, 931, 968, 975, 987, 991-92, 1058, 1060, 1101, 1147, 1196, 1268, 1303, 1315-17, 1319, 1480, 1610, 1753-63, 2008, 2061, 2161-63, 2597-99, 2716-17, 2759, 2834-35, 3311-28, 3387, 3474, 3670, 3753.

Parker: 333, 1101, 1297, 1485.

Peel Township: 70, 111, 330-41, 480, 782, 845-66, 948, 975, 988-92, 1101, 1147, 1155-56, 1205, 1256, 1281, 1296-97, 1324-27, 1334, 1340, 1482-85, 1488, 1491-92, 1512, 1527-31, 1533-36, 1586-90, 1598, 1600, 1740-45, 1857, 1918, 1932, 1973, 1988, 2008, 2015, 2162, 2301, 2305-7, 2336, 2459, 2603, 2612, 2624, 2636, 2678, 2713, 2718-23, 2739-42, 2760, 2769, 2772, 2799, 2805, 2866, 3261, 3329-35, 3580, 3590, 3596, 3614, 3679, 3723, 3739, 3749, 3753, 3759.

Peepabun: 1101.

Pentland: 1101.

Petawawa: 3418.

Petherton: 1101.

Pilkington Block: 67.

SUBJECT HEADINGS

Accounting records: 1068, 2061, 2139, 2229-31, 2263.
Admission records: 91, 2244, 2246, 2250, 2257, 2260-61.
Adoption: 46, 2479.
Advertisements: 980, 986, 1014, 1017, 1028, 1032-33, 1046-47, 1052-55, 1073, 1080, 1087, 1173-74, 1176-77, 1181, 1188, 1200, 1203, 1207, 1221, 1226, 1229, 1238, 1241, 1255-57, 1261, 1297, 1305, 1382, 1398, 1609, 1997, 1999, 2006-7, 2013, 2019, 2074, 2076, 2083, 2088, 2110, 2117, 2144, 2227, 2317, 2470, 2523, 2621, 2790, 2852, 2912, 3110, 3213, 3269, 3337, 3350, 3464, 3577, 3583, 3595, 3605, 3656-57, 3670, 3731, 3741, 3745-46, 3749.
Aged: 2222.
Agreements: 426, 927, 1270.
Agricultural education: 962, 2195-96, 2198-2200, 2202-4, 2206, 2208-13, 2216, 2477, 3447, 3451-52, 3485-86, 3489-91, 3496-97, 3501-5, 3507, 3511-12, 3534-5, 3537-39, 3561.
Agricultural improvements: 938, 1989-97, 2001-3, 2006-7, 2010-11, 2013-15, 2018, 2020, 2200, 2215, 2477, 3511, 3743.
Agricultural land use: 3459.
Agricultural machinery: 3459.
Agricultural promotion: 1014, 2010, 2016, 2098.
Agricultural representatives: 937.
Agricultural research: 2477.
Agriculture: 988-90, 1002, 1023, 1308, 1986, 2004-5, 2008, 2016, 3758.
Annual reports: 124, 177, 213, 346, 643, 894, 911, 918, 932, 937, 941-43, 946-47, 972, 994-95, 1106, 1116, 1139, 1161, 1213, 1276, 1306, 1310, 1354, 1375, 1482, 1518, 1529, 1541, 1561, 1565, 1598, 1605, 1607, 1615, 1626, 1628, 1637, 1639, 1642, 1645, 1683, 1727, 1731, 1753, 1764, 1817, 1833, 1848, 1866, 1871, 1884, 1895, 1902, 1998, 2009, 2015, 2021, 2035, 2042, 2131, 2150, 2165-66, 2168-71, 2181, 2200, 2217, 2221, 2228-31, 2245, 2262, 2414, 3595.
Appenticeships: 1086.
Architects: 88, 3371, 3378, 3405, 3664.
Architectural conservation: 3412.
Architectural drawings: 3358, 3366-68, 3375, 3384-87, 3392, 3394-95, 3414.
Architectural plans: 1300, 3357, 3365, 3369, 3372-74, 3380-83, 3388-91, 3393, 3402-4, 3408-13.
Architecture, Gothic: 1940, 3376.
Architecture: 88, 1761, 2953, 3415, 3432, 3591, 3753.
Archives: 3641.
Art and artists: 1084, 2047, 2195-96, 2199, 2443, 2474, 3423, 3474-3561, 3591.

Assessment rolls: 78, 100, 104, 161-62, 166, 187, 191, 203-4, 206, 210, 219, 225, 229-30, 247, 250, 267-69, 271, 281, 300-301, 313, 315, 325-27, 340, 352-53, 357, 369-70, 375, 395-96, 413, 421, 436, 445, 459-61, 464, 471, 559, 2319, 3709.
Assessments: 697, 975, 1009, 3653.
Attendance records: 473, 478, 507-8, 518, 642, 948, 952, 1326, 1354, 1383, 1468, 1472-74, 1480, 1500-1501, 1507, 1522, 1534-35, 1550-51, 1553, 1555, 1562-63, 1607, 1640, 1672, 1718, 1724, 1856, 1870, 1879, 1959, 1964-65, 1988, 2041.
Auctions: 1002, 1032, 1046, 1084, 2470, 2635-36, 2989, 2993, 3015, 3110.
Auditors' reports: 141, 175, 214, 277, 319, 321, 335, 387, 404, 431, 438, 923, 1512, 2232, 3595.
Automobiles: 3630.

Bank passbooks: 239, 260, 452, 898, 1158, 1187, 2445.
Bank records: 79, 405, 1097, 1103, 1106, 1125, 2301, 3565.
Bankruptcy: 37.
Banks: 260, 1102, 1165, 2621, 3123, 3396.
Baptismal registers: 1324, 1329, 1333-35, 1348, 1353, 1357, 1365, 1369, 1376, 1388, 1404-7, 1413, 1424, 1428, 1447, 1459, 1475-76, 1491, 1494, 1513, 1537, 1544, 1546, 1558, 1582, 1589, 1592, 1611, 1616, 1630-31, 1638, 1684-85, 1746, 1754, 1765, 1770, 1775, 1780, 1783-84, 1790, 1802, 1807, 1814, 1818, 1834, 1845, 1849, 1867, 1896, 1903, 1913, 1950, 1971, 3704, 3708, 3710.
Bibliographies: 2218, 3641, 3758.
Biographies: 1032, 1641, 2369, 2405, 2441, 2456, 2484, 2491, 3533, 3573, 3578, 3587-88, 3593, 3606, 3609, 3642-45, 3649, 3658, 3662, 3731.
Birth registers: 969, 1375, 2296, 3612, 3640, 3706.
Boards of health: 115-17, 125, 179, 189, 207, 209, 231, 305, 330, 342, 356, 380, 415.
Boards of trade: 987, 2022.
Bonusing: 252, 968, 975, 1303, 2600.
Boosterism: 2023, 2025-27.
Boundaries: 67, 120, 351, 627, 2057, 2149, 2784-86, 2788, 2790, 2792, 2795-96, 2991, 3008, 3133, 3216, 3237.
Bridges: 70, 171, 266, 1295, 1297, 1302, 3379, 3438, 3509, 3550, 3553-54.
Building materials: 2814-19, 2821-31, 2834-39, 2841-48, 3664.
Building plans: 87-88, 108, 884, 977, 1302, 1714, 2270, 2276, 2338, 2453, 2840, 3361-62, 3364, 3370-71, 3378, 3399, 3400-3401, 3405, 3415, 3664.
Building societies: 1109.
Building specifications: 1298-99.

Financial statements: 74, 197, 213, 224, 274, 337, 407, 419, 911, 975, 1106, 1122, 1131, 1282, 1293, 1330, 1355, 1396, 1540, 1557, 1581, 1642, 1655-56, 1658, 1682, 1689, 1715, 1817, 1825, 1850, 1895, 1930, 2151, 2168, 2284, 2361, 2410.

Fines: 12, 363.

Fire protection: 146, 1159.

Fires: 2277, 3463.

Floods: 1219.

Flora and fauna: 2050-51, 3502, 3507.

Forests: 2486.

Fraternal associations: 2056-59, 2061, 2064-67, 2071, 2124-25, 2513.

Funerals: 1058, 1067.

Gaelic language: 1766.

Gazetteers: 2521-25, 2527-32, 2554.

Genealogy: 1702, 2305, 2309, 2322, 2345-46, 2386, 2389, 2416, 2471, 3590, 3593-94, 3600, 3602, 3627, 3638, 3643, 3655, 3667, 3707, 3729, 3751.

Geology: 2050.

Government documents: 2417, 2462.

Government, Federal: 977-78, 2413, 3360, 3363.

Government, Municipal: 59, 84-86, 130, 136, 145, 176, 197, 367-68, 933-34, 1278, 1308, 2243, 2256, 2390, 2434, 2996, 3017, 3052, 3104, 3112-13, 3158, 3184, 3437.

Government, United Canada: 978.

Government, Upper Canada: 935, 2464.

Health care: 117, 207, 209, 231, 249, 305, 330, 342, 380, 877, 1244, 1245, 1250, 1842, 2222, 2224, 2226, 2228-31, 2233-35, 2237, 2240, 2242, 2253.

Historical research: 3641.

Historical sketches: 425, 674, 1041, 1058, 1188, 1193, 1321, 1328, 1355, 1392-95, 1399, 1608, 1652, 1657, 1666, 1720, 1732, 1740, 1744, 1751-52, 1757, 1758-59, 1767, 1771, 1805, 1821, 1851, 1918, 1931-34, 1936, 1942-43, 1951-52, 1956, 2023, 2055, 2094, 2149, 2192, 2209, 2217, 2220, 2223, 2249, 2254, 2276, 2292, 2305, 2309, 2345, 2373, 2386, 2416, 2460, 2478, 2502, 3564, 3569-72, 3574, 3577-80, 3587-89, 3593, 3597-99, 3602, 3606, 3609-11, 3615-16, 3620, 3622, 3628, 3633, 3638, 3642, 3645, 3647, 3651-52, 3654, 3659-63, 3667-68, 3707, 3729, 3731, 3734-35, 3738, 3741, 3744, 3748, 3753-54, 3756, 3759, 3762.

Hospitals: 2223, 2225-26, 2228-33, 2235-64, 3465.

Hotels and inns: 273, 284, 324, 1027-29, 1032, 1218, 1243, 3560, 3601.

Households: 988-92.

Houses and housing: 129, 264, 1018, 3357, 3372, 3403, 3415, 3430.

Ice harvesting: 1081.

Incorporation charters: 973-74, 987, 998, 1263, 2267.

Indentures: 1212, 1499, 2281, 2292, 2487, 2501, 2617, 2639, 2659, 2702-4, 2706, 3586.

Indexes: 3728.

Indians, North American: 2783.

Industrial promotion: 968, 987, 2025-27.

Industries, Bakeries: 1181, 2380.

Industries, Barrel making: 1128.

Industries, Blacksmiths: 1201, 1225, 3546.

Industries, Breweries: 1210-17, 2480-81, 2484, 3461.

Industries, Bricks: 1182.

Industries, Carpentry: 1068.

Industries, Carpets: 2076.

Industries, Carriages and wagons: 1228, 3466.

Industries, Cheese: 1208.

Industries, Clothing: 1044.

Industries, Consumer goods: 1188, 1195.

Industries, Distilling: 3419, 3513.

Industries, Dress making: 1083.

Industries, Electrical goods: 1178.

Industries, Farm implements: 1172, 1177, 1220-22, 1226-27, 1229, 3453, 3630.

Industries, Flour mills: 1170, 1184-85, 1203, 3419, 3500, 3513, 3524, 3630.

Industries, Foundries: 1205, 3727.

Industries, Furniture: 1050, 1171, 3669.

Industries, Lumber Yards: 2439.

Industries, Meat packing: 207.

Industries, Metal products: 1200, 1223-24.

Industries, Millinery: 1083.

Industries, Moulding: 2076.

Industries, Musical instruments: 1173-75, 1204, 2076, 3468, 3599, 3629.

Industries, Oil refining: 1122.

Industries, Publishing: 1258, 1261.

Industries, Saw mills: 1191, 1202.

Industries, Sewing machines: 1194, 1204, 1206-7, 2069, 3629.

Industries, Shoemaking: 1045, 1082, 1190.

Industries, Textile: 1179-80.

Industries, Tobacco: 1197.

Industries, Veneers: 1128.

Industries, Woodworking: 1196.

Industries, Woollen mills: 2438.

Industries: 167, 169, 988-90, 1186, 1189, 2023, 3112, 3123, 3556, 3567, 3604, 3606, 3616, 3629, 3741, 3746, 3761.

Inheritance patterns: 6-7, 45, 1136, 2770, 2774.

Insurance agents: 1138.

Insurance companies: 1114, 1122, 1127, 1130, 1158-59, 1167, 1169, 2491.

Insurance records: 242, 506, 901, 932, 1038, 1099, 1112-13, 1137-43, 1146-53, 1156-57, 1159-64, 1166, 2031, 2056, 2173, 2320-21, 3617, 3653.

Inventions: 1041.

SUBJECTS, CORPORATE

Aberfoyle Mill: 3630.
Aboyne Oatmeal Mills: 3749.
Alexander Davidson Boots and Shoes: 1045.
Alexandra School, Guelph: 632-33, 3438, 3568, 3598.
All Saints Anglican Church, Erin: 1356-64.
Allan's Bridge: 3438.
Allan's Mill: 1170, 2292, 2782, 3419, 3423, 3432, 3438, 3450, 3500, 3513, 3524, 3629.
Allansville Presbyterian Church: 1857.
Alma Block, Guelph: 2797.
Alma Methodist Church: 1169.
Alma Methodist Circuit: 1485-89.
Alma United Church: 1484-93.
Alma Women's Institute: 3759.
Amalgamated Street and Electric Railway Employees Local 796: 114.
Amaranth Methodist Episcopal Mission: 1494-96.
American Express Company, Elora: 3613.
American Hotel: 1027-29, 1245, 2461, 3752.
Ancient Order of United Workmen: 2056.
Andrew Parker and Sons, Furniture Manufacturers: 1171.
Anglican Christ Church, Reading: 1357-62.
Anglican Church of the Ascension, Clifford: 1404-5.
Anglican Church of the Ascension, Harriston: 1406.
Anglican Church of the Good Shepherd, Riverstown: 1417-23.
Arch Thompson Boot and Shoemaker: 1082.
Argo Block, Fergus: 2797, 3428.
Arkell United Church: 3648.
Arkell Women's Institute: 3759.
Armstrong Manufacturing Company: 3629.
Armstrong's Mill: 3379.
Arthur Advocate: 2558.
Arthur Agricultural Society: 80.
Arthur Enterprise-News: 2559-60.
Arthur Enterprise: 1251, 2559-60.
Arthur High School Board: 493.
Arthur School Board: 494-95.
Arthur Separate School Board: 948.
Arthur Township S.S.#4: 486-88.
Arthur Township, R.C.S.S.#6: 961.
Arthur Township, R.C.S.S.#4: 1930.
Arthur Township, S.S.#1: 481.
Arthur Township, S.S.#2: 485.
Arthur Township, S.S.#5: 489.
Arthur Township, S.S.#6: 490.
Arthur Township, S.S.#7: 491.
Arthur Township, S.S.#10: 482.
Arthur Township, S.S.#11: 483.
Arthur Township, S.S.#15: 484.
Arthur Township, S.S.#16: 821.

Arthur Wellington News: 2560.
Arthur-Luther W, S.S.#12: 492.
Auld and Woodyatt Company: 3567.

B Battery, Guelph: 2129.
Badenoch Womem's Institute: 3759.
Bank of Commerce, Guelph: 1125, 3366.
Bank of Hamilton, Drayton: 1158.
Bank of Montreal, Elora: 405.
Barrie Hill Presbyterian Church, Eramosa: 1829-31, 1835, 1839, 3590.
Barrie Hill United Church, Eramosa: 1447-49, 1832-34, 1836-44.
Beattie's Banking House: 1008, 1097, 2301, 3565.
Beatty Brothers Limited: 1172, 3428, 3453, 3670.
Bell Organ Company: 1173-75, 1204, 2096, 2512, 3432, 3473, 3599, 3609, 3629, 3740, 3746.
Bell Telephone Company: 1316.
Belsyde Cemetery, Fergus: 424.
Belwood Congregational Church: 1442-43.
Belwood Methodist Circuit: 1497-98.
Belwood Women's Institute: 3759.
Bethel Methodist Church, Eramosa Township: 1518.
Bethel Methodist Church, Rockwood: 1519.
Bethel Methodist Circuit: 1483.
Bethel Presbyterian Church, Orangeville: 1903-7.
Bethel Presbyterian Church, Price's Corners: 1607.
Bethel United Church: 1483-84, 1491-92.
Blackwood Hall: 3451.
Blackwood Publishers: 2350.
Blyth's Tavern, Marden: 1278.
Bogardus and Barton Druggists: 1034.
Bogardus and Company: 1034.
Bon Accord Community Club: 2148.
Bond Hardware Company: 1064.
Boys' Separate School, Guelph: 884.
Brechbill and McFarlane: 3592.
Brewers' and Maltsters' Association of Ontario: 2484.
Brisbane Public School: 578.
British Constitution and Fergus Freeholder: 2573.
British Hotel, Guelph: 1278.
British Methodist Episcopal Church, Guelph: 3590.
Brooklyn Sunday School, Guelph: 3427.
Bullfrog Tavern: 3629.
Burns Presbyterian Church, Erin: 1610.
Burns' Presbyterian Church, Ospringe: 1607.
Burt Brothers Department Store, Elora: 1037-39, 3617.

Canada Company: 935, 999, 1098, 1233-40, 1310, 2293, 2352, 2354, 2356, 2452, 2473, 2486, 2616-21, 2624, 2626-27, 2743-44, 2783-85, 2802, 2975, 3135, 3152, 3187, 3236, 3365, 3636.
Canada Ingot Iron Culvert Company: 3670.
Canada Life Assurance: 2409.
Canada Sabbath School Union: 1981.

Goshen United Church: 1532, 1536.
Government of Canada: 933-34.
Gow Fergus Lime Kilns: 1189.
Gow's Bridge: 3438.
Gowdy Brothers, Guelph: 3213.
Grace Anglican Church, Arthur: 1333-46.
Grand Trunk Railway Station: 3419.
Grand Trunk Railway: 995, 1263, 1266, 1268-77, 1300, 1307, 1310-11, 1315, 2098, 3052-53, 3158, 3182, 3407, 3422, 3514.
Greenfield Cemetery: 1242.
Griffin's Opera House: 1087, 2406, 3585.
Groves Memorial Hospital, Fergus: 2223, 2237, 3465, 3473.
Guelph and Arthur Road Company: 69, 1262, 1278.
Guelph and Elora Road Commission: 1279.
Guelph and Galt Advertiser and Wellington District Advocate: 2580.
Guelph and Ontario Investment and Savings Society: 1076, 1104-11, 2172, 3567.
Guelph and Wellington Road Company: 1280.
Guelph Academy: 3645.
Guelph Advertiser and County of Waterloo Advocate: 2580.
Guelph Advertiser and Elora and Fergus Examiner: 2580.
Guelph Advertiser and Wellington District Advocate: 2580.
Guelph Advertiser: 3706.
Guelph Advocate: 2581.
Guelph Agricultural and Exhibition Building and Curling Rink Company; 2409.
Guelph Armouries: 977, 3359-60, 3429, 3432, 3436, 3450, 3664.
Guelph Artillery Company: 2131.
Guelph Axle Works: 3630.
Guelph Banking Company: 1011.
Guelph Baseball Club: 2106.
Guelph Battery D, Royal Canadian Artillery: 2439, 2442-43.
Guelph Bible Society: 3637.
Guelph Board of Common School Trustees: 644.
Guelph Board of Education: 36, 175, 637, 640-47, 649-51, 2600.
Guelph Board of Grammar School Trustees: 644.
Guelph Board of Health: 115-17.
Guelph Board of High and Public School Trustees: 637, 644-45.
Guelph Board of Light and Heat Commissioners: 151, 175, 1318, 2321, 3444.
Guelph Board of Parks Management: 118-19, 156, 2482.
Guelph Board of Trade: 2022, 2024, 3629.
Guelph Board of Water Commissioners: 120-23, 125-26.

Guelph Board of Works: 127-28.
Guelph Boxing Club: 2107.
Guelph Brigade Camp: 3498.
Guelph Burns Club: 3585, 3639.
Guelph Business and Professional Women's Club: 2150.
Guelph Business College: 1088-90, 2600, 3473, 3577.
Guelph Carnegie Library: 2023, 3406.
Guelph Carpet Mills Limited: 3567, 3629-30.
Guelph Carpet Weavers Union No. 277: 2076.
Guelph Carriage Goods Company: 1076, 3567.
Guelph Cartage and Oil Company: 1048.
Guelph Cartage Company: 127, 1285.
Guelph Catholic Parish: 3666.
Guelph Cemetery Commission: 175.
Guelph Centennial Committee: 2072.
Guelph Central Exhibition: 3423.
Guelph Central School: 643, 683, 3375, 3427, 3432, 3436, 3438, 3551, 3568, 3590, 3596, 3637, 3742.
Guelph Chamber of Commerce: 3629.
Guelph Children's Aid Society: 2165-69.
Guelph Choral Society: 3639.
Guelph Chronicle: 2582.
Guelph Cigar Company: 3630.
Guelph City Council: 74, 113, 131, 134, 143-44, 2483, 3634.
Guelph City Hall: 2108, 3427, 3432, 3438, 3473, 3560, 3635.
Guelph Co-operative Association: 2076, 3433.
Guelph Collegiate Institute: 175, 177, 642-43, 654-61, 671, 2442, 2600, 3420, 3596, 3598, 3645, 3742.
Guelph Collegiate Vocational Institute: 662-73, 676-82, 952, 953, 956, 2023, 2080, 2347, 3436, 3438, 3443, 3585.
Guelph Commercial Market: 3592.
Guelph Common School Trustees: 685.
Guelph Communist Party: 2092.
Guelph Congregational Church: 1452-58, 2334, 2452, 2478, 3427, 3438, 3731.
Guelph Corner Grocery Store: 1055.
Guelph Correctional Centre: 972, 2264.
Guelph Country Club: 3662.
Guelph Court of Revision: 164.
Guelph Court House and Jail: 3524.
Guelph Court House: 2047, 3008, 3423, 3438.
Guelph Cricket Club: 2108, 2461, 3606.
Guelph Cross Country Run and Road Race Association: 2109.
Guelph Curling Club: 3473, 3606, 3733.
Guelph Custom House: 3367.
Guelph Daily Herald: 2583.
Guelph District Methodist Church: 1479.
Guelph Drill Shed Committee: 156.
Guelph Elastic Hosiery Company: 3630.
Guelph Evening Mercury: 2584.

Puslinch Township, S.S.#1: 877-78.
Puslinch Township, S.S.#2: 879.
Puslinch Township, S.S.#3: 880.
Puslinch Township, S.S.#6: 881-83.

R. Campbell, Surgeon Dentist: 2412.
R.G. Dun and Company: 1100-1101.
R.H. Barber, House and Sign Painter: 2412.
Rainer and Company Pianos: 1204.
Raymond Employees Mutual Benefit Society: 2069, 3582.
Raymond Manufacturing Company: 1206, 3741.
Raymond Sewing Machine Company: 1204, 1207, 3547, 3629, 3740, 3746.
Rebellion of 1837: 2131, 2457, 2464, 3652.
Red Mill, Guelph: 3150.
Reform Association of North Wellington: 2313.
Reliance Loan and Savings Company: 3614.
Reorganized Church of Jesus Christ of Latter Day Saints, Arthur: 1957.
Richard Boyle Contractor: 1297.
Riverbank Cheese and Butter Company: 1208.
Riverside Park, Guelph: 3068, 3450, 3471, 3557.
Riverside School: 782.
Riverslea: 1084.
Rockwood Academy: 1092-93, 3370, 3373, 3422, 3438, 3455, 3473, 3596, 3645, 3730.
Rockwood Continuation School: 528.
Rockwood Fair: 3473.
Rockwood Methodist Church: 1591-97.
Rockwood Presbyterian Church: 1610, 1910-15.
Rockwood Public School: 529.
Rockwood Separate School: 3422.
Rockwood United Church Women's Missionary Society: 1970.
Rockwood United Church: 1912-15, 1968-70.
Roman Stone Company: 920, 3406.
Royal Alexandra Hospital School of Nursing, Fergus: 2237, 2241.
Royal Alexandra Hospital, Fergus: 2223, 2232-40, 2242, 3428.
Royal Antebilubian Order of Buffalos, Guelph: 2070.
Royal City Council, Order of Chosen Friends: 2068.
Royal City Park: 3471.
Royal Opera House, Guelph: 1977, 2088, 2406.
Royal Skating Rink: 3420.
Royal Templars of Temperance: 2125-27, 2397.
Royal Theatre: 3741.
Royal Women's Institute, Guelph: 2159.
Rust and Sandilands Dry Goods Merchants: 3630.

Sacred Heart Roman Catholic Church, Guelph: 1934, 1943.
Sacred Heart Roman Catholic Church, Kenilworth: 1934, 1951, 3668.

Sacred Heart Roman Catholic Church, Rockwood: 1934, 1956.
Salem Monthly Fair: 3749.
Salem Presbyterian Church: 1770-73.
Salem Public School: 838.
Saturday Morning Sun: 2600.
Scottish Imperial Insurance Company: 1130.
Second Presbyterian Church, Garafraxa: 1607.
Second Wesleyan Church, Guelph: 1538.
Sem Wissler Insurance Company: 2516.
Silver Creek Brewery: 1210-11, 1214-17, 2117, 2480, 2484, 2833, 3629, 3732.
Simpson's Corners Congregational Church, Garafraxa Tp: 1463-66.
Sixth Line Presbyterian Mission Station: 3654.
Sleeman and Sons: 1029, 1212.
Sleeman Brewing and Malting Company: 1213, 1215-16, 1285, 3450.
Society of Friends: 1917.
Society of Jesus: 1925.
South Wellington Farmers' Institute: 1985, 2009, 2017.
South Wellington Women's Institute: 2149, 2160.
Speed River Dam: 149.
Speedbank Farm: 2390.
Speedside Congregational Church, Eramosa: 1444-49, 1838.
Speedside Public Library: 932.
Speedside United Church, Eramosa: 1447-49, 1832-34.
Speedside Women's Institute: 3759.
Speedwell Military Hospital, Guelph: 2264, 2302, 3432.
Spring Bank Brewery: 2484, 3461.
St Agnes Separate School, Guelph: 2268.
St Alban's Church, Grand Valley: 1344.
St Andrew's Benevolent Society, Elora: 2317.
St Andrew's Presbyterian Church, Alma: 1608, 1610.
St Andrew's Presbyterian Church, Arthur: 1610-14.
St Andrew's Presbyterian Church, Bethel: 1610.
St Andrew's Presbyterian Church, Fergus: 1607-8, 1610, 1627-36, 1854, 2336, 2953, 3428.
St Andrew's Presbyterian Church, Galt: 1608.
St Andrew's Presbyterian Church, Gordonville: 1610.
St Andrew's Presbyterian Church, Guelph: 1607-8, 1610, 1681-1735, 2398, 2401, 2461, 2491, 2600, 2985, 2988, 2990, 2995, 3022, 3026, 3114, 3133, 3427, 3436, 3438, 3551.
St Andrew's Presbyterian Church, Hillsburgh: 1607, 1610.
St Andrew's Presbyterian Church, Moorefield: 1740-45.
St Andrew's Presbyterian Church, Mount Forest: 1610.
St Andrew's Presbyterian Church, Orangeville: 1908.
St Andrew's Presbyterian Church, Price's Corners: 1610.

Tyrcathlen: 3056.
Tytler School, Guelph: 694.

Union Brewery Workers No. 300, Guelph: 3467.
Union Curling Club: 3747.
United Associate Church, Nichol Tp: 1616.
United Presbyterian Church, Elora: 1616-19, 1622, 1624, 1826.
United Secession Congregation, Eramosa: 1839.
Unity Fire Insurance Company: 1130.
University of Guelph: 3471.
Upper Canada Building Society: 3057.

Victoria Cemetery, Drayton: 388.
Victoria Inn: 3438.
Victoria School, Guelph: 695, 3568.
Victory School, Guelph: 696, 3568.

W. and A. Roberts Butchers: 3630.
W. Bell and Company: 1204.
W.J. Brown and Co., Guelph: 2797.
Waldemar Presbyterian Church: 1847.
War Memorial Hall: 2202, 3451.
Waterloo Mutual Fire Insurance Company: 1169.
Waterloo Wellington Railway: 966-67.
Webster and Fordyce: 1049.
Wellington and Guelph Teachers' Association: 2054.
Wellington County Agricultural Society: 2018.
Wellington County Board of Education: 474, 477-80.
Wellington County Board of Public Instruction: 3596.
Wellington County Council: 84-86, 113.
Wellington County Court House and Jail: 17, 19, 88, 2797.
Wellington County Court House: 8, 87, 2974, 3427, 3450, 3606.
Wellington County Grammar School: 473, 670-71.
Wellington County Historical Research Society: 2055.
Wellington County Home for the Aged: 93.
Wellington County House of Industry: 66, 77, 91-96, 2245, 3429.
Wellington County Jail: 18.
Wellington County Model School: 475, 2333.
Wellington County Mutual Fire Insurance Company: 1112.
Wellington County Old Age Pension Board: 99.
Wellington County Registry Office, Arthur: 3416.
Wellington County School Board: 476.
Wellington County Suburban Roads Commission: 112.
Wellington County Surrogate Court: 6-7, 45-46, 2479.
Wellington County 10th Divisional Court: 24.
Wellington County 6th Divisional Court: 25-34.
Wellington County: 89-90.
Wellington Deanery Magazine: 1322.
Wellington District Advertiser: 2585.

Wellington District Agricultural Society: 2019.
Wellington District Council: 84.
Wellington District Court House and Jail: 59.
Wellington District Grammar School: 678, 3438.
Wellington District Mutual Fire Insurance Company: 1166-67.
Wellington District Press Association: 3737.
Wellington District Surrogate Court: 2.
Wellington Field Battery: 2131, 2137.
Wellington Field Naturalists' Club: 3743.
Wellington Foundry: 2361, 3438.
Wellington Hotel, Maryborough Tp: 2797.
Wellington Hotel: 3432, 3438, 3629.
Wellington Mercury and Guelph Chronicle: 2586.
Wellington Mutual Fire Insurance Company: 1130, 1215, 2484.
Wellington Oil Refinery: 1122.
Wellington Regiment: 2137.
Wellington Rifles: 2137, 2338, 3420.
Wellington South Agricultural Society: 2020.
Wellington Street Bridge and Dam: 3509.
Wellington Street United Church, Mount Forest: 2518.
Wellington, Grey and Bruce Railway Station: 3266.
Wellington, Grey and Bruce Railway: 966-67, 995, 1263, 1299, 1315, 2806, 3544.
Wesleyan Methodist Church, Drayton: 2797.
West End Women's Institute: 3759.
West Luther Orange Hall: 1344.
West Puslinch Presbyterian Church: 1769, 3473.
West Wellington Farmers' Institute: 1985, 2009, 2021.
West Wellington Women's Institute: 2161-63.
Westminster Church, Mount Forest: 1902.
Westminster-St Paul's Presbyterian Church, Guelph: 1610.
Wilson, Jack and Grant Law Firm: 1168.
Wingfield Farm: 3200.
Women's Missionary Society, Damascus: 1509.
Woodlands: 3543.
Woodlawn Cemetery: 3608.
Woodyatt and Company: 1224, 3629, 3630.
World Publishing Company: 1258, 1261, 3629.
Wyoming House: 3744.

Yankee Cottage: 3520.
Yeomans Drug Store, Mount Forest: 1086.
Young Ladies' School, Guelph: 3596.
Young People's Society, Rockwood United Church: 1912.

Zavitz Hall: 3451.
Zion Methodist Church, Nichol Tp: 1581.
Zion Presbyterian Church, Alma: 1607.
Zion Presbyterian Church, Nichol Tp: 1607.
Zion Presbyterian Church, Orangeville: 1909.
Zion United Church, Alma: 1512.

SUBJECTS, PERSONAL

Adams, Ezra: 3473.
Alexander, William: 3166, 3214.
Allan, A.S., Mrs: 2288.
Allan, A.S.: 2166, 2288, 3095.
Allan, Alexander: 3596.
Allan, Charles: 1166, 1253, 1634, 1854, 2030, 2091, 2105, 2116, 2122, 2281, 2461, 2874, 2879, 2946, 3259, 3274, 3300-3301, 3428, 3613, 3739.
Allan, Christina Idington: 2282-83, 2289, 2291-92, 3562.
Allan, David, Jr: 2112.
Allan, David: 37, 271, 1036, 1057, 1076, 1094, 1170, 1176, 1231, 2042, 2046, 2225, 2284-87, 2289, 2291-92, 2996-97, 3006, 3022, 3190, 3229, 3419, 3423, 3500, 3562, 3602, 3609, 3630.
Allan, Grace: 2281.
Allan, Margaret: 3562, 3602.
Allan, Robert, Dr: 2505.
Allan, William: 1232, 2282, 2284-85, 2290-91, 2292, 3513, 3516, 3524, 3533, 3562.
Alling Family: 3649.
Alling, Robert, Dr: 1166-67, 1248, 1312.
Alling, Susannah: 1160.
Anderson, Isaac: 1993.
Anderson, John: 2053.
Anderson, Margaret: 2293.
Anderson, Mr: 2865.
Anderson, Thomas: 2293.
Andrich, A.: 1030, 3613.
Angle, P.E.: 2211.
Archibald, Alice Snyder: 2296.
Archibald, E.T.: 1096.
Archibald, H.: 1096.
Archibald, James: 1095-96, 2295-97, 3655.
Archibald, Katherine: 317, 523, 2294, 2298, 2431.
Argo, Adam: 2093, 2327, 2329, 2903.
Argo, James: 1440, 2301, 2897.
Argo, Mr: 1169.
Arkell, John: 2604, 3338.
Arkell, Thomas: 1164, 2764, 3338, 3577.
Armstrong, Agnes: 3458.
Armstrong, Charles: 1234.
Armstrong, J.B.: 3420.
Armstrong, James: 157, 1044.
Armstrong, John: 1117, 3458, 3649, 3731.
Armstrong, Robert: 3649.
Armstrong, Simon: 1031.
Armstrong, William: 1444.
Arthur, Eric: 3422.

Bailey, E.E.: 655.
Bain, Mr: 1169.
Baker, A.A.: 1036, 1312.

Balfour, D.: 2299.
Balfour, James: 2299.
Barber, Charles W.: 2968, 3573, 3630.
Barber, R.H.: 1033, 2412.
Barber, Ross: 3339-40.
Barber, W.F.: 143.
Barker, Enoch, Rev.: 1971-72.
Barnet, Hugh: 3652.
Barrie, William, Rev.: 2336, 3458.
Barron, George: 3662.
Bathurst, Lord: 999.
Beattie Family: 2040.
Beattie, George: 2301, 2303.
Beattie, J.: 2225.
Beattie, Jack: 2300.
Beattie, James: 2301, 3565.
Beattie, John: 113, 1156, 2300-2301, 3565, 3662.
Beattie, Lillian A.: 2302.
Beattie, Mr: 1169, 2932.
Beattie, W.H.: 2167.
Beattie, William, Sr: 1986.
Beattie, William: 2301, 2303, 3565.
Beck, Adam, Sir: 1290.
Bedford, Thomas: 2266.
Bell, Matthew: 1021, 3438.
Bell, Robert: 1173, 2046.
Bell, William: 157, 1044, 1107, 1173, 1175, 2131, 3468, 3606, 3609.
Benham, James: 2457.
Best, James: 2699.
Bindemann, Frederick W., Rev.: 1973.
Biscoe, Frederick: 3021, 3177.
Bissell, T.E.: 3613.
Black, J.: 146.
Black, James, Rev.: 1974, 2957.
Black, John: 2102, 3750.
Black, Robert: 2068.
Black, Thomas: 3750.
Black, William: 2017.
Blair, James: 2017.
Blaney Family: 2289.
Bodley, C.: 3275-76.
Bollert, E.R.: 1204, 2166, 3744.
Bollert, Robert: 3606.
Bolls, Agnes: 45.
Bond, F.G.: 3417.
Borthwick, Adam: 3317.
Bosomworth, John: 2727.
Bough, Annie: 148.
Boult, Stephen: 87, 3392.
Bourque, Henri, Rev.: 2271-72, 2275, 2460.
Bowes, John G.: 1309-10.
Bowley, William H.: 1046.
Bowman, James: 1114.
Boyd, John: 3450.